Human Communication: Principles, Processes, and Contexts 3/e.

© Daniel O. Awodiya 2009, 2012, 2015

ISBN-13:   978-0-9887581-4-8
ISBN- 10: 0-9887581-4-8

Project development, Executive editing, and Marketing
By:

Springboard Communications

618 Nesting Lane
Middletown, DE 19709

For more information please visit us at:
www.springboardcommunications.net
Or email us at:
dan@springboardcommunications.net
Or call us at 302-897-1659

**Springboard communications is represented
in Africa by:
Clehez Communication Associates
1, Ajetumobi-Osho Street
Oluyole Estate,
Ibadan,
Nigeria
West Africa**

Cover Fractal Credit: Phoenix Triangular Multiswirl by "Weed."
www.wussu.com

Middletown * New York * Lagos * Ibadan

Human Communication

Third Edition
2015

Principles, Processes, and Contexts

DANIEL O. AWODIYA
Suffolk County Community College
Grant Campus,
Brentwood, New York

Springboard Communications

618, Nesting Lane
Middletown, DE 19709

Dedication and Acknowledgment

This book is first and foremost dedicated to the unseen hand and spirit that is always nudging me forward to greater heights, and that is always a voice of comfort when the light is dim and the desire is low. This is to the God of light, love and of my life, without whom the journey to write this book would never have started, let alone completed.

This book is specially dedicated to my family- my wife and four children. The task of writing a book like this could never have been accomplished without your dedication, encouragement, understanding, and love. This is to you, Oluyemi, my wife, and the children: Olamide, Olatomiwa, Olasubomi, and Pipelola.

The business of writing a book is never an individual task; it is actually a journey in which numerous people encourage, read, re-read, edit, suggest, add, subtract, and finally approve. This work, therefore, is the culmination of the efforts of several people too numerous to name here. I appreciate all of your effort and support. However, there are individuals who contributed immeasurably to publishing this book that their names must be mentioned here.

I say a big thank you to my reader and chief encourager, Dr. Yvon Joseph of Suffolk County Community College, whose second pair of eyes and incisive commentary proved indispensable to finishing this book. A big thank you also goes to Dr. Aida Pavese, whose support and willingness to listen to me ranting about my writing, was deeply cathartic. I also appreciate the comments and ideas of my colleague, Professor Alyssa Kauffman, who was always willing to review my ideas and added many of hers that are now incorporated into the book. To Professor Bill O'Connell, I say a big thank you for being so ever supportive of my work and always willing to review the contents of the book. Professor Virginia Horan was quick to volunteer to review my book and, as such, deserves my deepest appreciation. To Professor Bernadette Garcia, I say thank you for being there always to encourage me, especially when I appeared to be at my wits' end. Bern, I express my deepest appreciation to you for reading every page of this book!

I must also mention my other colleagues, who have been instrumental in one way or another in getting me to where I am now both as a person and a teacher. I thank Dr. Steven Epstein, Prof. Chris Holfester, Dr. Denise Sariego, Prof. Dawn Tracy-Hanley, Prof. Ralph Williams, Prof. Carol Mauro, Prof. Desario, Prof. Laolu Akande, Prof. Norman Daniels, Prof. Fraser and Liz Foley. My gratitude also goes to Christine Sinnott, Susan Connolly, and Jennifer Colagioia.

To all of my students over the decades, I acknowledge that I would not be the professor that I am today without the benefit of your invaluable experiences and contributions to my classes. I especially thank those whose works are included in this book as examples and illustrations.

I wish you well.

Dr. Daniel O. Awodiya

PREFACE

This book, *Human Communication: Principles, Processes, and contexts*, *3/e* is written by a seasoned communication scholar who has devoted his professional and academic life to the practice, study, and teaching of communication. Dr. Awodiya explores the principles, processes, contexts, and theories of communication in the introductory text and situates every idea in practical, skills-based contexts with witty examples and intercultural anecdotes. The real-life narratives contained in each of the eighteen chapters of the book will help the students apply the theories and principles of communication to their lives.

Aware of the wide latitude of topics of the different types and levels of communication usually covered in the communication introductory course, this book is a compendium of sort that can suffice as the basic text for four Introductory communication courses such as Introduction to Human communication, Interpersonal Communication, Small Group Communication, and Public speaking. With a comprehensive chapter on Mass Communication, it can also be used as a basic text for an introductory Mass Media Course. The academic utility value of this text is matched with its low cost, which makes it extremely attractive to students and instructors alike.

This new edition of the book has five sections. The first is titled Fundamentals of Human Communication and contains four chapters. Defining Communication, Communication Principles, Levels of Communication, and Basic Communication Models are covered in chapter one. In chapter two, Perception and Listening are fused because of their interrelatedness, followed by Verbal and Nonverbal Communication in chapters three and four respectively.
The next section of the book is titled: Interpersonal Communication in which there are five chapters. These chapters are titled The Self in Interpersonal Communication, Human Emotions, Interpersonal Relationships, Managing Interpersonal Conflicts, and Interviewing: A Specialized Interpersonal Communication.

In the next section of the book, which is titled Public communication, there are four different chapters on the basics of public speaking. The chapters are: Fundamentals of Public Speaking, including Managing Performance Anxiety; Relating With the Audience, Identifying and Researching the Speech Topic; Organizing the Speech; and Delivering the Speech.
Section four of this third edition of *Human Communication: Principles, Processes, and Contexts* contains two full-fledged chapters on The Informative Speech and The Persuasive Speech.

The last section of the book contains two chapters; one is Group Processes and the last, Mass Communication.

For the instructor, this new edition boasts of an Instructor's Manual, Chapter PowerPoint Slides and a Test Bank. Very useful for both the instructor and the students are the review questions at the end of each of the chapters in the book. An added advantage of the book is that most of the sample papers and speeches are student examples. This should serve as a motivating factor to other students of Communication.

Reviewers and Users Praise *Human communication: Principles, Processes, and Contexts.*

"After previously using several notable communication textbooks, there was something missing. Professor, Dr. Daniel Awodiya's scholarly work is designed to enhance our students' drive to understand how critical it is to possess core, leadership, and professional competency skills necessary to compete in the global village. Dr. Awodiya provides the tools desperately needed to communicate in a world filled with new challenges and global conflict. Further, students will learn how important it is to earn the competitive edge they need in the "new America" while keeping up to speed in a rapidly changing work environment internationally. Now more than ever students need to sharpen and test their communication skills. Therefore, I enthusiastically endorse Dr. Awodiya's work without a shadow of a doubt as his unique ability to communicate is rooted in deep intercultural perspective. More important, his extensive professional and business experience in the world of communication covers the full scope of persuasion and theory like no other. Adopt this textbook for your beginner communicators to the most experienced."
-----Professor William O'Connell, Suffolk County Community College.

"Awodiya's text, "Human Communication: Principles, Processes & Contexts", 3rd edition, presents the material in a fresh and innovative style, very easy for students to grasp concepts. Highly recommended for communication as well as Speech communication courses. My preferred text for the com 101 and Speech 105 courses."
-----Trevor Fraser, Adjunct Professor, New York Institute of Technology, Adelphi University, & Suffolk County Community College.

"Using this book--has been a tremendous help in my classes like very few books have.
From my observation, students find it very simple to follow, especially aspects of the chapters on certain class assignments. As a teacher I find Prof Daniel Awodiya's book very informative, comprehensive and sufficiently broad to cover the major topics for an introductory and basic course in Communication. My teaching the course Introduction to Communication has become so much a joyful experience significantly partly because of how this book has been written: with a notable demonstration of scholarship in a very elegant, profound and straightforward manner.
-----O. James Akande, Adjunct Professor, Suffolk County Community College.

"The Awodiya Human Communication book presents a comprehensive coverage of the basic skills, principles, and theories that are important for students of Communication to learn. That the book is written in an easy to understand language and is structured in a student-friendly manner is a great advantage. I recommend it for use in the introductory course."
-----Professor Chuka Onwumechili, School of Communication, Howard University.

TABLE OF CONTENTS

TABLE OF CONTENTS

TABLE OF CONTENTS

SECTION THREE: *Public Communication*

TABLE OF CONTENTS

TABLE OF CONTENTS

SECTION FIVE: *Group Processes & Mass Communication*

SECTION ONE

Fundamentals of Communication

1. *Communication Defined*

2. *Perception and Listening*

3. *Verbal Communication*

4. *Nonverbal Communication*

Photo by Bill O'Connell

Chapter One

Communication Defined

Communication is a commonly used concept by almost everyone who has some level of awareness. People see communication as being central to their lives in many ways. Many do acknowledge that developing their communication skills is central to their succeeding in school, in the world of work, and in their social relations. Correctly they claim that without communication, we 'humans' would lose our humanity! This is because communication defines who we are and who we are not; it limits or accelerates our success and; it reveals our competence or hides our idiocy. It assimilates us into human society or ostracizes us as belonging to the likes of the 'Wild Boy of Aveyron,' who was found in the South of France communing with animals and walking with four hinds. He ate just as fellow 'animals' did, and imitated their grunts in an attempt to communicate his feelings and desires in this animal kingdom, lacking in the social skills that humanize us all.

Communication is real as it has real consequences. Either for instrumental or personal satisfaction purposes, we all are communicative beings, and if we understand the nature of communication and apply its tenets to our lives, then we would improve our view on life and make the world a better place not only for ourselves, but for our loved ones and others we come in contact with.

Whenever many people think of their interpersonal relationships, they think of the adequacy and effectiveness of their communication- ascribing marriage and relational problems to failure of or the lack of communication. Often, they prescribe more communication rather than effective communication as a panacea to their marital and relational woes. When there are international and regional political conflicts, these multidimensional phenomena are blamed on lack of communication among the acrimonious partners or groups.

Humans have a need for communication, just as we desire food, water, air, and life's other necessities. Communication is the engine that drives and directs human life; it is the element that qualifies humans as social animals. However, communication, while it is so important to human life and survival, is not always the solution to all of human problems. To understand what communication is and what it is not, we have to define it, examine its various principles and contexts, and identify its different purposes and the possible consequences of its effective and ineffective usage.

What is Human Communication?

Scholars over the ages have attempted to define the term communication.
A writer once claimed that scholars have identified as many as 126 different published definitions of the term (Beebe and Beebe, 2001). That there are myriads of definitions available to students and scholars alike is underscored by the claim that there are as many definitions of the term as there are people trying to define it! Communication contains several fields of study,

which look at the concept from a variety of perspectives; therefore, having several definitions of the term is not farfetched, it is indeed expected.

Here an attempt is made to define the term by examining some of these available definitions. This exercise is certainly not an attempt to arrive at a comprehensive definition of the term or to assemble many of these definitions, but a random identification and analyses of five of these definitions taken from popular introductory texts in the field. Ultimately, these analyses will provide you, the reader, with the common concepts used in defining the term and present you with a general foundation of the perspectives influencing them.

Communication is viewed as what someone does to another, a one-way flow of information or message from a sender to a receiver.

Communication, therefore, is what a sender does to a receiver who, in turn does the bidding of the sender. It is believed that the receiver changes because of the information received and that when this happens, the sender has communicated. This does not represent human communication, as we now understand it. The receiver is not a static receptacle of information; neither is the sender always a commander, who bellows information to a receiver. The sender and receiver are sharing messages in a dynamic process of communication. Consequently, we can see both, interchanging their roles and prompting each other to action.

Communication, therefore, is a process, a dynamic phenomenon that impacts all of the people involved one way or another and serves as the basis for future behavior. We can claim that communication does not have a beginning or an end- the stream of communication is always rolling along. It does not start with anyone per se because any communication must have been prompted by some previous or series of prior messages. In addition, it does not end when someone has received a message, because, as the trite expression goes: "there is no action without reaction."

Communication is viewed as an interaction between a sender and a receiver.

This is an improvement over the previous linear perspective because it suggests that the communicators do interact in the process of exchanging messages. However, interaction suggests terminal action and reaction between the interacting elements. This suggests that when one person talks, for instance, the other listens until it's his or her turn to speak. In a true sense, this is the action-reaction understanding of how communication works. But does it actually work this way? Just by being there in the presence of another, say the receiver, are you not constantly sending messages that can be classified as verbal or non-verbal or vocal or non-vocal. The fact that you're not speaking does not mean that you're not sending messages to the receiver! Reality is that we are constantly sending messages instantaneously and simultaneously. If we send and receive messages all at the same time, then communication can be viewed as involving more than two people interacting.

Communication is a transaction between two or more people. **A transaction is an exchange that occurs simultaneously and in which the participants influence and are influenced by each other's experiences.**

We can liken this to a business transaction in which one person exchanges a thing of value for another thing of value, albeit at the same time. Communication always results in some type of effect, which in turn influences the subsequent exchanges of the players. This is a more illuminating perspective of communication in that it captures more parsimoniously the phenomenon of communication. We can consider communication to be **actional, interactional and transactional**.

Communication is defined as the simultaneous sharing and creating of meaning through human symbolic action (Seiler and Beal, 2007).

This is to suggest that humans jointly create understanding through symbolic interaction. This is an exchange facilitated using words, signs and gestures that can be directly interpreted by the receiver. Understanding is coming to a common agreement about what something or situation represents as presented by the sender to the receiver. Understanding therefore occurs in the minds of people through the evaluation of received messages. This is because words in and of themselves do not contain meaning and as such can reveal only the meanings imposed on them by their users. By implication, this definition underscores understanding as the joint goal of communicating- coming to a negotiated agreement of sort as to what something or some idea may mean to the communicators. However, understanding is not always possible in the process of communication because there are many unintended messages that may lead to unintended interpretations and outcomes.

Communication is a transactional process involving participants who occupy different, but overlapping environments and create relationships through the exchange of messages, many of which are affected by external, physiological, and psychological noise (Adler and Proctor, 2007).

This definition introduces the concepts transaction, environment and noise to the explanation of the term communication. A transaction is a simultaneously occurring exchange of values such as a business transaction in which the participants exchange one value for another. As such, both the sender and the receiver are both sending and receiving messages all at once. If this is so, then both communicators are senders and receivers since they are interchanging roles constantly. These participants occupy different environments that may sometimes overlap, that is, their interests, backgrounds, orientations, expectations, cultures, gender, etc., may be different yet be similar in some cases. The divergence of environments may lead to misunderstanding of messages, if the messages get across at all. Anything that may interfere with the communication process and renders it less effective is referred to as noise. There are different types of noise recognizable in the communication process. (Read more about noise in the communication process in the latter part of this chapter).

These definitions draw largely from the fundamental truths that scholars and practitioners alike have come to agree upon as basic principles of the nature of communication.

The Five Basic Principles of Communication

Principles are a basic generalization that is accepted as true and that can be used as a basis for reasoning or conduct (Miller, 2009). The five basic principles discussed here serve as the foundational truths about the nature of communication, which guide our explanation and understanding of all and varied cases of our communication experience and scholarship. The entire book is full of basic principles of the different forms of communication, summarizing the theoretical explorations and affirmations of scholars in the field and the syntheses of direct experience of practitioners.

In our daily lives we live these principles without paying much attention to them, but the critical awareness of them would help you to understand your relationships better, become a better person, and a more responsive and sophisticated human being.

Communication is a process

The word *process* as it is used here has two connected interpretations: one is that it represents a series of events, occurring one after the other or simultaneously, and two; it is a constantly changing series of actions that never cease.

Communication involves a series of activities that people engage in, knowingly or otherwise, that results in a form of meaning in the mind of one or more people. However, it is not something you can see or touch because it takes place inside of the communicators. In addition, it is a set of activities that is dynamic and does not have a beginning or an end; therefore, it cannot be considered as starting with somebody and ending with another. In the words of Berlo (1960), a process is something that is constantly moving and in which the elements interact with one another. Engleberg and Wynn (2011) define *process* as a set of constantly changing actions, elements, and functions that bring about a result.

Drawing from the explanation above, communication is a series of actions that have no beginning or an end, but that are constantly changing and influencing the participants one way or another. Imagine that you met someone for the first time and you decided to express your home training of polite exchange of greetings with the person; this you do to acknowledge that person and because it is the right thing to do. The receiver of your greetings, reciprocated by saying: "hello" or "how are you?"

The effects are partly that you both feel valued because you greeted someone and the person responded in kind, thus affirming both of you. The many other impacts we can only imagine, but many are the results of such a single act of communication, not to mention a complex form of exchange such as a conversation. The nature of the greeting and the reason for the greeting and, of course, the cultural training to greet people, did not start with either of you and did not even start with the parents or guardians who taught you this simple polite etiquette. We can go back as far as we can and we will still not get to the very beginning of this human activity.

The interacting elements, in the process of communication are as varied as there are different and collective impacts they have one on another. Yet these elements, their nature and their impacts on the participants are unique and, as such cannot be duplicated. Seiler and Beal (2011) clarify this by claiming that the interrelationships among people, environments, skills, attitudes, status, experiences, and feelings all determine communication at any given point.

We cannot pretend to capture the essence of communication, a multidimensional activity on paper, which is a two dimensional medium. Therefore, when models are used to represent communication activities, there is an assumption that we are freezing the process in time and space just as we do when we take the photographs of rivers or of the atmosphere. We are only taking a snapshot of a process that cannot be adequately represented by such drawing. Communication is likened to a river sometimes swiftly flowing and some other time hardly moving at all. But whether we participate or not in this process, the communication river continues to roll along (Insight Media, 2001).

Communication is a system

A system has been described as a set of interrelating elements operating within a boundary and the functioning of all of the constituent elements is dependent, to the extent that when any of the elements changes, the change is systemic, affecting every element individually and the system as a whole. Such is the nature of communication with all of its operating and interdependent elements of sender, receiver, encoding, decoding, context, noise, feedback, channel, and background. Any change in any of these elements will influence the meaning being shared among the communicators and; any imperfection in the system would be as a result of imperfection in one or more of the interdependent variables. Communication effectiveness depends on the members of the system working and cooperating in tandem; consequently ineffective or miscommunication would be a result of malfunction in any of the constituent elements.

The communication system can be likened to the functioning of the automobile or the human body; when one part is defective, it affects all other parts as well. Therefore, in your effort to communicate effectively, you have to understand all of the functioning parts of the communication system and to put them into view, when explaining yourself to another person and, when you are trying to assign meaning to the messages of others. A good understanding of the communication system would make you a diagnostic expert that can bring remedy to dysfunctional communication systems.

Communication is both interactional and transactional

While we understand that you constantly communicate with yourself, you also engage others in the process of communication. When you speak, another person listens and when you listen, another person speaks. This is the give-and-take exchange of meaning that is described as interactional. It suggests that we take turns in exchanging messages with one another when we engage them in the communication process. The interactional model still viewed speaking and listening as separate acts that did not overlap and that were not performed at the same time by the same person (DeVito, 2011). As scholars have now realized, the interactional model does not explain or adequately represent the nature of communication as it really occurs among the interacting people.

The transactional view of communication takes a different look at the communication process and as (Watzlawick, Beavin, & Jackson, 1987; Barlund, 1970; Wilmot, 1987) note, in the transactional view each person is seen as both speaker and listener, as simultaneously communicating and receiving messages. This perspective also underscores the dynamic nature of communication in which all of the interacting elements change because of change in one or more of these elements. Consequently, when one person's experience changes, it influences the meaning assigned to the communication episode in which the individual is interacting and thus leads to changes in the messages exchanged with receiver and the interpretations of the receiver. This creates a bandwagon effect whereby any little change in any of the elements in the system creates a domino effect that influences and changes the entire system. See "communication models" section to view how these different ideas are presented in diagrams in the following pages.

Communication can be intentional or unintentional

Communication is an activity that we may deliberately or unintentionally engage in. Often you say or do something for a specific purpose, but others may perceive such differently and attribute a different purpose to it than intended by you, the speaker. Yes, communication has purpose, but not all of the intentions are calculated well in advance, just as the consequences cannot be foretold. There are messages you intentionally send that are so received; however, there are messages you intentionally send, but are not received as intended. This means that there are unintentional receivers of your message. Again, you may unintentionally send a message to an intentional receiver or to an unintentional receiver.

When you write an e-mail to your colleagues about the "lack of managerial skills of your immediate boss" (this is an intentional message) and, instead of sending it to just your colleagues, you hit the "reply to all" button on your computer and the e-mail is sent to all of your colleagues and your boss (an unintended receiver). What do you imagine would be the consequence of this unintentional act and how can you deal with the situation? Or, you sent a gift of toiletry, including mouthwash to your boss for the holiday season (intentional gesture of appreciation). Instead of the "thank you" response you expected, he instead sent you a nasty e-mail stating that the reason you bought him the gifts was because you thought of him as an unkempt person who equally suffers from halitosis (unexpected response).

As you can see, intentionality is an important issue to bear in mind when communicating with people. Because of different mindsets, people misinterpret messages and sometimes send out unintended messages. However, unintended messages, either sent or received, are usually nonverbal, that is without the use of words. It may be your eyes that communicate something you are not aware of, or your mode of dressing that suggests a different meaning than you are aware of, you cannot control totally the meanings that others impose on the messages you send intentionally or unintentionally.

Communication is inevitable, unrepeatable, and irreversible.

Communication is inevitable. When something is described as inevitable, it means that its occurrence is not controllable by the action or inaction, in our case, of those who engage in the act of communication. The act of sending and receiving messages is often not controlled by the actors. When you show up for an appointment, you're communicating; when you show up late for the appointment, you're sending another message; when you don't show up for the appointment at all, you are yet sending another message. When you speak, you communicate; when you don't speak, you communicate. Your nonverbal, messages are not discrete, they are continuous, and as such, you're always communicating. Now, you can see why Watzlawick (1978) claims that we **cannot not communicate,** or that we cannot not influence the person with whom we communicate.

The elements in the communication system are always changing and, as such, we cannot repeat our communication with the exact choices of symbols and with the exact impact on the receiver, because time, situation, mindsets of the communicators would have influenced the nature of the exchange, that the meaning of the exchange would have changed. The same goes with the experience of drawing a glass of water from a running river. Certainly, you can physically dip your glass in the water twice, but each time you draw from a different pool of water. The pool of water you draw from the first time would be down the stream by the time you dip in your cup the second time. Though the water in the two different glasses may look the same, but they are also different—such is the nature of communication as an unrepeatable phenomenon. It is amazing how the contexts of communication influence communicative meaning sometimes with delicate subtlety and sometimes dramatically. As it is often stated, "you can't go home again." This expression also explains the dynamic nature of communication because, yet you can go home physically, but with the passage of time, you will change and your perceptions of home would not be the same as before. As DeVito (2011) explains, you can never repeat meeting someone for the first time, comforting a grieving friend, leading a small group for the first time, or giving a public speech.

When something is described as irreversible, it suggests that that thing cannot be taken back or erased or recalled. Communication is irreversible because of its nature of being received and interpreted by the receiver. Once your message is sent, the impact is inevitable. One way or the other the receiver will have a reaction of sort to the message. What is done, therefore, cannot be undone. Though there may be attempts to reduce the impact or change the meaning in order to influence the interpretation of the message, but the choice is no longer that of the sender, but of the receiver. Imagine that in a conversation with a friend he tells you that you're an arrogant person, but you don't believe you are. Seeing the frown on your face, your friend may try to recall his message to you by trying to say he did not mean it. Now the name-calling is out there and it has started a chain reaction in you, both physically and mentally, and there is no amount of retraction and mending that can be done because the effect is ongoing and cannot be erased. So what is said cannot be unsaid and *you cannot, not influence another person, even when you profusely apologize*. There is no preventing you from being self-conscious about the label that your friend has given you even when time has progressed and should have removed the impact of that message.

The Five Misconceptions about Communication

Using the principles identified above as the foundation for generalization about the nature of communication, it is possible, therefore, to identify conclusions and or claims that are at variance with the stated principles. Consequently, these general misunderstandings about communication, we can reason, are common claims that go against the established truths about the nature of communication. The insights that they reveal will open the eyes of the student to in-depth theoretical thinking that is necessary to grasp what a people perceive to be a rather easy to understand phenomenon.

Communication will solve all problems

Understanding the communication principles outlined and discussed earlier should give us an insight into the world of communication as a rather complex and nebulous thing that can aid us in many ways and that can be a source of problems to us. But many people attribute magical powers to communication and they see and act as if it were the panacea to all human problems. Often you hear people say that: "if you communicate and understand each other's points of view, you will resolve your conflict or problem." Yes, I may understand your point of view and, it is exactly that understanding that is the source of conflict that I have with you! If I didn't understand your point of view, I may still think that we should continue to be friends. As aptly put by Seiler and Beall (2011)," the act of communicating with others does not carry any guarantees. Obviously, without communication, we cannot solve our problems, but sometimes communication can create more problems than it solves. This fact leads us to the next misconceived idea about communication.

The more the communication the better

Does more communication mean better communication? Better still, does practice make perfect? The fact that you do something repeatedly does not mean it is right. If you repeat the mistakes of the past over, that, certainly, would cause more harm than good. Effective and competent communication is a result of doing more of the right thing at the right time, to the right person, and possibly with the right effect or outcome. "But if you practice bad habits, you're likely to grow less rather than be more effective," (DeVito, 2011). Again, Seiler and Beall (2011) conclude, "it isn't the act or the amount of communication, but the content of communication that makes the difference."

Words contain meaning

We have defined a symbol as anything that represents something else. Words are a representation of reality; they are not the things being represented, but are the codes we use for representation. The symbolic nature of words, therefore, indicates that they are labels we use to identify ideas and things for ease of reference, understanding and the sharing of meaning. Therefore, words are not inherently imbued with meaning. Thus, we can claim that meanings are not in words, but that they reside in people who created them for their own use.

Meaning is a personal experience though, and that is why we should further claim that no two individuals interpret the same experience the same way nor use words exactly the same way to mean the same thing. There are two general meanings of words: **denotative** and **connotative**. What a word denotes is not necessarily, what it connotes. The denotative meaning of a word is its general, common, public meaning that you can find in a dictionary. But the real meanings of words are in their usage to convey the private, emotional, and unique, meanings of an individual. Therefore, the real meanings of words reside in the individual as expressed through its unique contextual reference.

Take the word "husband" for instance. The dictionary meaning would reference a biological male who is married to a woman. Consider the case of two females who are married to male spouses, who have different connotations of the word husband. One has a good husband and describes him as "a great lover, provider, dependable, and rock of my life;" but the other woman does not share the sentiment of the first because of her different experience with her husband and, by extension, with the word "husband." To her, the word husband connotes "lazy, bum, irresponsible, son of a ..." Meanings are in our heads and not in inanimate, abstract words.

The impact of communication is reversible

Let us view the communication act as an egg, and the impact of communication on the actors as a broken egg. Once the egg is broken, its content cannot be scooped up into a shell to form an egg in its unbroken form. Furthermore, there two parts to the content of an egg: the yolk and the albumen. Consider the core yolk as the irretrievable, irreversible core impact of the messages of an act of communication, while the white albumen shield can be considered as the often forgiven, but not forgotten impact of the message. With the passage of time, the impact of the "outer layer of the egg" may subdue but events may trigger their re-emergence.

As we have discussed earlier, communication has consequence and such consequence cannot be retrieved from the emotional memory of the receiver no matter how hard we try. So, for however vociferous the attempt to take the impacts of our words back, what has left the peripheral of the mouth as speech, the mouth cannot by speech render impact less. Be careful what you say and be mindful of how you say it to people so that you don't have to "eat your words."

Communication is a natural human ability

If you revisit the definitions we have for communication, you would realize that it is something we have to learn to do; it does not come to us as an inherent, innate human quality. Communication is a learned skill just as leadership, basketball, and carpentry. The fact that you have a piano at home does not make you a good piano player. What makes one a good piano player is the knowledge and the practice, which will translate to proficiency skill in piano playing.

The more you become familiar with the principles of communication, the more you gain proficiency in the learned skill of communicating. As you learn to speak in various situations and put yourself in the public arena to perform, the more you would become familiar with what works and what does not in the art and practice of public speaking. Becoming a competent communicator requires gaining relevant knowledge of the principles and theories of communication. In addition, you must have the willingness to translate your knowledge into practical skills that you will employ in your everyday communicative acts. Moreover, when performing these skills, at first, you may feel awkward, but with persistence, you will become proficient through repeated practice of the desirable skills. So, you may have the natural ability to produce sounds and to gesture, but those do not make you a competent communicator.

Figure1.1/Impact of Communication on the Receiver

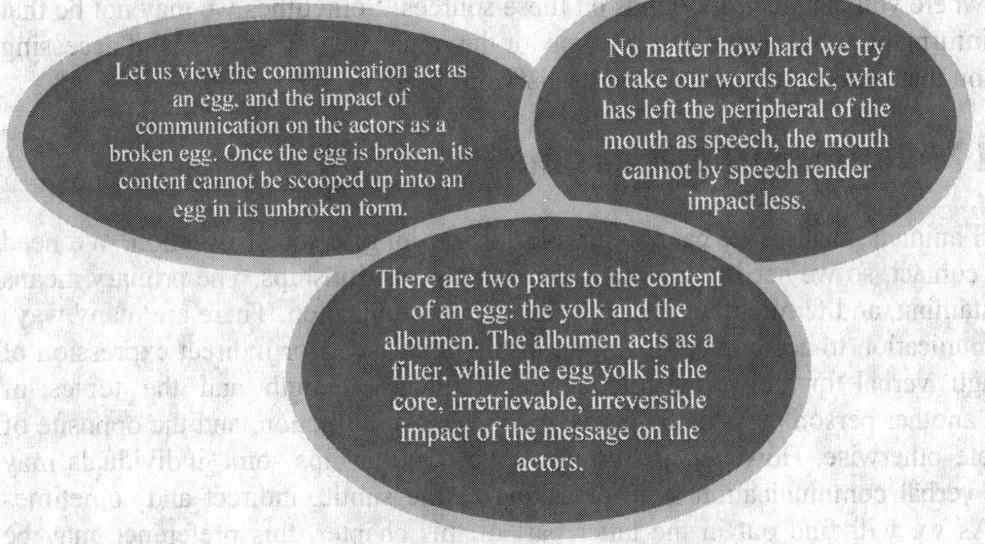

Let us view the communication act as an egg, and the impact of communication on the actors as a broken egg. Once the egg is broken, its content cannot be scooped up into an egg in its unbroken form.

No matter how hard we try to take our words back, what has left the peripheral of the mouth as speech, the mouth cannot by speech render impact less.

There are two parts to the content of an egg: the yolk and the albumen. The albumen acts as a filter, while the egg yolk is the core, irretrievable, irreversible impact of the message on the actors.

Why Do We Communicate?

It is apparent that humans communicate with one another for a host of reasons. These reasons underscore why we study the art and science of communication, which is to gain mastery of the nature and the processes of the phenomenon, so that we can do a better job of meeting the needs or reasons why we engage in the activity of communication in the first place.

Needs Satisfaction

Fundamentally, we humans use communication to satisfy our needs (Redmond, 2000). The diverse human needs which have been identified and described as Maslow's Hierarchy of needs, include physiological, safety, belonging and love needs, self-esteem needs, and self-actualization, (Maslow, 1982). To satisfy each of these needs, the common denominator is communication. For example, to satisfy physiological needs of food and sex, one must reach into oneself (intrapersonal communication) to determine means (message) that will form the basis of interaction with others and inform them of the desire for cooperation to meet these needs.

Gathering and Gaining Information

Decisions that lead to needs satisfaction are based on available information; therefore, humans seek information, which forms the basis of such decisions. Sometimes we may scavenge for information because having such information may be critical to the immediate satisfaction of our needs. Imagine that you're about to graduate from college, but you need only one speech to fulfill all of the requirements in your Public Speaking course. In order to pass this course, the professor had mandated that you needed to cite two particular sources in writing your speech on your chosen topic of "Genocide in the Darfur Region of Sudan". Certainly, you would seek information as to where you can get your hands on these sources! Sometimes we may not be that active in seeking information, but regardless, one way or the other, we devise means of accessing relevant information that we need to maintain and satisfy our basic needs.

Forming and Maintaining Relationships

Humans are social animals, that is, we cannot survive for too long in social isolation. We need prolonged human contact, so we need to maintain long lasting relationships. The primary means of initiating, maintaining, and terminating relationships is communication. There are many ways we may use communication to accomplish the relationship goal: direct or indirect expression of the desire, through verbal or nonverbal messages. Frequency, length and the topics of conversation with another person may be indicative of likeness or attraction, and the opposite of which may indicate otherwise. However, in forming love relationships some individuals may prefer the active, verbal communication style of asking to the subtle, indirect and sometimes nonverbal style. As we will find out in the latter part of this chapter, this preference may be cultural.

Pleasure and Entertainment

When grandma and grandpa sit on the porch and talk endlessly about a seemingly unimportant topic or issue, the purpose of the interaction may not necessarily be to gain information, but the act itself may allow for emotional outlet for both of them. It is certainly pleasurable to talk with a loved one who is always willing to listen. When new lovebirds talk endlessly on the telephone about nothing really, it is the pleasurable act of 'talking' that leads them to incur huge phone bills and not the act of sharing information. Again, we like listening to stories either told to us directly or captured on television or in the movies. The real business of Hollywood is indeed packaging pleasure and escape rather than making movies and organizing hit parades!

Self-Confirmation and Validation

We derive a sense of self through what others say or do to us. Imagine that on a morning, as usual, you dressed up for work, grabbed your breakfast and off you went through the door yet for another day of work. But what's different this day is that the very first person that saw you ran away from you! Then, the second and the third... How would you feel about the people and yourself? We are who we are because others confirm that we are. And in the face of disconfirmation, we tend to doubt self. Daily, we receive and give communication that confirms us all- communication that values us or that values others. A simple hello or a simple nod, or a simple smile tells me I am accepted and that I am human.

Managing and Coordinating Tasks

One communication function that acts as the basis for human performance is the organizing function. With organizing, comes coordination of actions, especially to achieve a common goal. The act of giving and following instructions that leads to the coordination of human efforts is communication. Humans are organized into hierarchies of tasks in the human organization and, as such, an organization has been described as a collection of individuals exerting influence on one another, for the purpose of achieving a common goal. The unifying force for the managing and coordination of functions is communication.

Persuasion

All that we need to satisfy our needs and desires cannot be produced and supplied by individuals working alone. All humans are interdependent. And if we cannot obtain what another has by force, we need to engage them in the act of persuasion. Since persuasion is the currency of human exchange, we engage others in persuasive communication all of the time. Whether asking for directions, asking for a date, asking for a raise or even interviewing for a job, we are engaged in the act of influencing others through the manipulation of signs and symbols. In order to gain their agreement with us, we use various communication tactics to secure acceptance of our values, beliefs, opinions, and behavior.

We may argue that we do not do a very great job of communicating to meet all of these needs adequately and that gives us an understanding why humans are faced with myriads of social problems. Although communication will not solve all of human problems, it certainly plays a great role in mitigating many of them.

Why Study Communication?

The need to study something, be it a subject or a craft, is derived from a desire to understand such a thing and to become skillful in it by mastering its principles, its techniques, and its nature. The reasons we learn about communication are to understand its nature and to become proficient in practicing it. But what benefits do accrue to someone who has gained a mastery of these communication competencies? As stated earlier, we study communication for instrumental reasons, that is, as a means to an end. These ends are professional/career, marital and educational success. Much research has been done to identify the critical life skills that leaders in education, business, and industry believe are must have for employees at all levels. Seiler and Beall (2007), confirm that recent studies emphasize that employers want workers at all levels that have the ability to communicate effectively. Here are the recommendations of these studies:

- Ability to speak effectively.
- Ability to listen carefully and efficiently.
- Ability to think critically.
- Ability to get along well with others.
- Ability to be aware of and sensitive to differences in cultural perspectives.
- Ability to make good decisions individually and in groups.

It is apparent from the list that the required competencies of potential employees are communication skills and not computer or technical skills. These technical skills can be acquired on the job. And as some personnel directors have demanded, "Send me people who know how to speak, listen, and think, and I'll do the rest" (Seiler and Beal, 2007).

The lesson here is clear: study communication and gain communication competencies and you will greatly increase your chances of succeeding in your professional career. In addition to this, your acquired skills will be of great use in your personal and professional relationships as well as in your education. Good communication study should engage students in all of the competencies identified. The greater focus of this book is the number one listed competency: Effective Public Speaking. By understanding the different principles of communication, you will gain mastery of the different aspects of the subject and you will become an effective communicator.

Ethical Communication

In addition to studying communication for instrumental reasons, there is the need to communicate appropriately and ethically. While ethics is not morality per se, it draws from the prevailing moral code of a culture. Communicators have to adhere to the moral code of the society in which they operate. For example, while it is reasonable to express one's freedom of speech, such a freedom has its corresponding responsibility.

There are moral, ethical, and legal constraints on our freedom of expression.

Plagiarism is the act of using another person's intellectual property or work of art or performance without due credit- be it by permission, mention or financial reward. Plagiarism carries stiff penalty for any violator, be-it a college student, professor, artisan, politician, and ordinary apprentice.

Slander is communication designed to damage the reputation of another person, based on phantom or malicious reasons. Of course, slander is actionable in many, if not all courts of law all over the world.

Incendiary speech is communication that leads to the disturbance of peace and may directly or indirectly cause injury to others. A popular example is shouting in a public place that there is fire when in fact there is no fire! The stampede that the bogus claim would cause may lead to the severe injury to others.

Credible communicators are ethical communicators. The act of public speech imposes on the speaker a huge ethical responsibility that if followed, results in the speaker being believed, accepted and trusted. Politicians are not trusted because of their perceived unethical behavior. It is generally believed that they are a breed of people who cannot be trusted because they would say anything and do anything to be elected.

Aristotle, the Greek philosopher and scholar argued that for a speaker to be successful, he or she must be mindful of three important tenets namely: Ethos, Pathos, and Logos.

Logos is generally referring to logic. A speaker's argumentation must be logical because humans are logical and analytical beings (Aristotle wrote extensively about Logic). In addition, humans are also emotional beings and, as such, the speaker must appeal to people's emotions or pathos as well.

Most importantly, the speaker, to be accepted and believed, must be credible to the listeners. That is the speaker must be ethical (from ethos) in his or her enterprise. (Read more about Aristotle' ethos, pathos and logos in part three of this book).

Multicultural Communication in a Global Village

The American communication philosopher, Marshall McLuhan, predicted the telecommunication explosion that we are witnessing today several decades ago. He popularized the term 'global village' when he used it to describe what the world is becoming because of the ease of telecommunication and unprecedented access to information around the world. So, the era of instantaneous communication with any remote part of the world is ever possible today, such that the far-flung locations across the world have been geographically and virtually brought into contact with the rest of the world. The increase in international trade and ease and rate of international travel increased the possibility of cross-cultural contact and infusion more than ever before. Indeed, the world is becoming smaller and smaller every day, thus making inevitable intercultural communication and making imperative international and multicultural understanding.

What happens in one part of the world now has far-reaching consequences across the world. Therefore, public communicators must now be versed in intercultural communication and, perhaps, learn other international languages in order to communicate effectively to the global audience. The far-reaching influence that public communicators exert has led to the maxim that we should "think globally and act locally in the new global village."

In a multicultural world, ethical responsibility takes on a new dimension. Not only are public communicators responsible to the local audience, but also to the global audience. Ethical standards now must pass the international litmus test such that what is not acceptable in the United States should not be acceptable behavior in Mexico, Sri Lanka or Nigeria. Sensitivity to the international community means being sensitive to cultural practices and differences across the world and being aware of the rules that govern ethical communication is the starting point.

Communication in the Age of Exploding Technology

The combination of telecommunications development and the invention of the computer microchip have brought a revolution to human communication. Now more people than ever before have access to information and are able to communicate rapidly across the world in little time from practically anywhere in the world. Now there is instant messaging, e-mailing, teleconferences, telecommuting and other innovations that have ensured that we remain connected to others in a virtual, instantaneous, and complex world of digital transmission. The caveat, though, is that people are becoming social isolates because as we access more information and the opportunity to connect virtually increases with speed, the "need to be there" is becoming outdated, thus reducing our interaction to medium- to- medium and not person-to-person. The need for face-to-face contact, though very important, is becoming less and less significant. Therefore, the McLuhan global village is here, but with mixed consequences for humanity.

The impact of the technological explosion on the practice of public speech is immense. Picking a topic and researching your speech topic is no longer a daunting task of laborious literature search and copious note taking. While research is very important and taking notes is essential in writing and organizing your speech, the easy access to information on the internet has made it possible to access unbelievable amount of information at the click of a button and, referencing your materials done automatically through web software. The presentational aids are easy to access and use, and the use of webcams allow you to deliver your speech remotely to an audience of thousands if not millions across the globe.

We can summarize the reasons why we study communication in practical terms that emphasize the importance of communication and state the fact that communication is essential. Studying communication comprehensively offers at least seven advantages (Pearson et al, 2011).

By studying communication you can:

1. Improve the way you see yourself.
2. Improve the way others see you.
3. Increase what you know about human relations.
4. Learn important life skills.
5. Help you exercise your constitutionally guaranteed freedom of speech.
6. Help you succeed professionally.
7. Help you navigate an increasingly diverse world.

Elements of Communication

Communication as a system constitutes a set of interrelating parts operating within sets of boundaries with rules of engagement that moderate the nature and the activities of the integral parts.

The elements of communication are:

1. Sender/Receiver (Communicator)

Using the term sender and receiver may not be appropriate when we see communication from the transactional perspective. The term *communicator* is appropriate because to send and receive messages is to communicate, to be involved in the process of jointly creating meaning and understanding. Though it is understood that communication does not start or end with a particular person, because a message, usually, is prompted by a previous stimulus or experience, we bring ourselves to accept, for purpose of study, the idea of freezing the communication process in time and space to identify a sender and a receiver. This is like taking a still photograph of an event- a process, in order to examine it and understand the event. Really, anything can be a source of messages: A barking dog, a rattling snake, a crying baby, a speeding car, an ambulance, etc. This book is concerned with human communication, the exchange of messages among humans.

2. Channels

When communicators exchange messages, they have to do this using some means that would allow such messages to be received. These are called *channels* and there are different forms of them. When two people, for instance two lovers, engage each other they may use their voice to send messages back and forth, they may smile at each other to express their love for one another, they may pat each other on the back, and they may spray nice smelling perfumes and cologne on each other. These actions employ different channels to convey the message of affection. The communicators in these instances see the message, hear the message, use touch and smell to send the message, and can sometimes taste the message as well. The channels of interpersonal communication, therefore, can be considered as the five human senses. Though we humans predominantly use the senses of sight, hearing and touch to send and receive messages, we also employ that of taste and smell.

In mediated communication (communication aided by technology), the intervening technology becomes the medium. In Mass Communication, for instance, the channels of sending messages from a centralized position to a large, widely scattered, diverse, and anonymous audience are generally referred to as mass media. These are radio, television, books, magazines, newspapers, movies, billboards, internet, and special events. These different media ultimately extend a human sense or combination of human senses with written and spoken words, still images, as well as, moving images. In Organizational Communication, the channels of exchanging messages in the human organization include meetings, memos, notice/bulletin boards, newsletters, employee handbook, intranet, etc.

3. Messages

The contents of communication are referred to as messages. These are the meanings and understandings you're trying to convey or share with another person or set of individuals. Messages can be shared in many different forms: as spoken or written words, as mode of dressing, gestures, facial expressions, choice of music, space maintained with another, one's time orientation, among several others. Indeed, anything you can see, hear, taste, smell, touch, and experience can be considered a message.

The message is made up of the ideas and feelings that a sender-receiver wants to share and… these can only be communicated if they are represented by symbols (Hybels and Weaver, 2001). Messages are understood if only they represent meanings shared by the communicators. Language is a very important means of conveying such meanings; therefore, language in its verbal and nonverbal sense is symbolic. Words are symbols and, as such, constitute a symbolic system that facilitates communication. And more importantly, words do not contain meaning, as meanings are imposed on them by the users. As words are symbols, they represent what the speakers of any particular language choose for them to represent. Meanings, therefore, are in people not in words. Consequently, there must be commonality of meaning among communicators for their symbolic exchange to convey meaning and to create understanding.

There are two dimensions of communication messages: these are content and relational. The content is what is said and the relational dimension refers to the relationship that exists between the communicators. The real meaning of a communication exchange therefore is in the context of communication- the relational, cultural, temporal, and physical situations in which communication occurs. This is explained further under the sub-topic of contexts.

4. Noise

Noise as a term used in communication is referred to as anything that impedes or interferes with any of the elements in the communication process. This is not necessarily sound that is being referred to here, but anything at all that may influence negatively the process of communication. There are different types of noise generally classified as deriving from internal and external sources.

There is **physical noise**- loud sound, physical, observable occurrence external to the communicators that may influence the sending and receiving of messages.

Psychological noise occurs inside the communicator, when he or she engages in daydreaming instead of listening to the sender or engages in thoughts other than those related to the ones being shared. Generally, this type of noise is associated with internal feelings and thinking of the receiver.

Physiological noise has to do with the biology of the communicator, especially relating to the senses. When a receiver is hard of hearing, has bad eyesight, experiences hunger or illness, it is difficult to receive and process messages effectively.

Semantic noise is attributable to the assigning of different meanings to the words being shared by the communicators. It is common that both communicators experience words differently, thus assigning different connotative meanings to them. Sometimes the meanings of the words may be missed completely by the communicators. Imagine what happens when people share meanings using words for which they both do not share same meanings. This situation is referred to as communication noise that occurs through **bypassing**. Differences in culture and general backgrounds of the communicators can constitute noise in the communication process.

5. Context

Communication does not take place in a vacuum; it exists within certain contexts, situations, or environments and these influence the type of communication that takes place and exert different meanings on messages being shared.

Scholars have identified basic aspects of the context in which people communicate.

The physical context is the physical place in which communication takes place. The nature and content of the communication that takes place in a church, synagogue, or mosque is quite different from that which occurs in a movie theatre or nightclub. Communication is influenced by the physical context in which it takes place, be it an auditorium, a small room, a large indoor football arena or a funeral parlor.

The social–psychological context has to do with the level of familiarity or intimacy between the communicators. The more familiar the sender and receiver are, the less formal their communication. Again, the type of relationship between the two influences their degree of self-disclosure, and how seriously the participants take one another. A relationship between two individuals that starts with the formal use Mr. or Ms. to address one another may grow to the use of first names and later to the use of pet names, depending on the level of intimacy. See how the nature of communication may change with changes in the social relationship that exists between the two of them.

The temporal context is the time dimension as it influences the nature of communication. As the popular saying goes, "timing is everything" and there is no phenomenon that is as greatly influenced by time as communication. To get a pay increase on your job depends on when you ask for it or when you're due for it. Most people would mind a telemarketer calling at 12 mid – night. Of course, it is strange to ask a friend out to a party soon after receiving terrible news of a sibling involved in a fatal accident. Again, some people function better at different times of the day and, would be greatly influenced by the time of the day you want to engage them in any type of activity.

Different cultures view and use time differently and, as such, are influenced by how they organize events and how much time is devoted to different activities. Some cultures' view of time is described as **monochronic**, while another view is described as **polychronic**. Monochronic people, generally speaking, are far too governed by time and schedule; they engage one thing at a time would frown at interruptions and, would rather have someone's undivided attention. On the other hand, polychronic people are generally more tolerant of interruptions, they engage many things at the same time, treat time as always being available; hence, and there is no need to rush things and people. These two general cultural orientations lead to the different perception of time and the consequent different use of time.

The historical context situates the communication experience based on antecedents. The past experiences that communicators share, influence their current attempt at exchange of meaning. Meaning may be buried in the past such that familiarity with such past episodes does influence and structure present interactions. Familiarity of communicators in the historical context does really "breed contempt," as prior encounters may lead to informality of interaction among participants.

6. Feedback

A literal translation of this concept may suggest something coming back to the originator or the sender. In communication, however, if this is a conscious return or response to a previously sent message, it may be interpreted as yet another message returning from the receiver, who is now a sender, back to the former sender, who now is a receiver. So, feedback is a form of message. It may also be described as the unconscious return to the sender, a reaction to the behavior that was previously generated. Many scholars agree that this is a gut reaction, an unconscious behavior that the receiver sends to the sender, who now must adjust his or her message to incorporate this gut reaction of the receiver. Feedback may be positive or negative, verbal or non-verbal, vocal or non-vocal.

In any communication situation, when feedback is positive, it is a sign that your message is getting through or it is well received. The sender should therefore continue to improve upon the message that is generating such positive reaction. On the other hand, if the feedback is negative, the sender must be sensitive to the fact that the message is not getting through or it is not being well received. It needs to be changed, modified, or reworked one way or another to reduce the noise. In public communication situations as in public speaking, the speaker must constantly monitor the reactions of the audience to the speech being given, to gauge the comfort level and disposition of the audience not only to the content of the speech, but the personality of the speaker, the environment and the style of delivery. The concept of **feed-forward** is very important to communicators, especially public speakers. This is the warning message you send before your primary message. For example, you tell an audience what the main points in your speech are before you actually get to tell them the details of the main points.

7. Encoding

Usually before you start to speak, you first think of what it is you want to say and how best to say it. This is referred to as engaging your mind before you engage your mouth. This process is called encoding, that is 'putting information in your mind into a send-able form, to that which can be understood by the receiver. You choose the appropriate code with which to send your message relative to the receiver of the message. Depending on your receiver, you may speak in jargons, mainstream language or just use hand gestures or a raised voice to convey your message or meaning. Since language is a code, what you're actually doing when you speak your language to another person is that you're encoding your thoughts into language – thus the term encoding.

When you use non-verbal signals, you're also sending codes to a receiver who must decode them in order to understand their meanings. The term actually comes from the telecommunications/mathematical model of communication in which a form of energy is encoded into another form to adapt to the nature of the available technology. For example in broadcasting, sound energy is encoded into electrical energy in order for it to travel the long distance necessary to reach a large and widely scattered audience. But humans cannot hear electrical energy! It has to be converted back to the original sound energy; hence, the use of a transistor or demodulator that converts one form of energy into another. This conversion is referred to as decoding.

8. Decoding

Decoding in the human sense is translating a message or code into meaning. When you receive a message, you have to make sense of it, you have to translate it into meaning, and you have to decipher or decode it. It makes sense that if the sender translates a message into a send-able form, the receiver has to decipher it in order to make sense of it. One popular code of sharing meaning is human language. Language as a code must be encoded and decoded in the process of using it to share meaning. Sometimes, the coded information may not be decipherable by the receiver because of the nature of the coding- perhaps the encoder used esoteric codes, unintelligible codes, or simply that the rules governing such codes are not followed. Deciphering a grammatically incorrect message may pose a problem, or when the pronunciation is off, it may present a problem of misunderstanding the code. In other words, noise is the primary reason why encoding and decoding may present a problem in the process of communication.

9. Effects

Communication has been defined as action and, we believe that for every action there is a reaction. Sometimes the effects of communication are calculated to happen and sometimes communication may have unintended effects. Communication may be designed to help people, to teach and learn, to relate, to influence and to play. A public speech may be designed to entertain, to inform and to persuade, but ultimately, a speech to entertain may inform and as well as persuade, and a speech to inform may invariably entertain and persuade, while a persuasive speech has to inform and may also be entertaining. Communication always has consequences, be it positive or negative, on the communicators. These are the effects of communication. Communication is real and so are its consequences. These consequences may also be positive or negative. Effective communication has been linked to marital and relational success, educational success, and job success. On the other hand, lack of or ineffective communication is linked to failed relationships, negative educational experience and, of course, lack of success on the job.

FIGURE 1.2/ KEY TERMS IN DEFINING COMMUNICATION

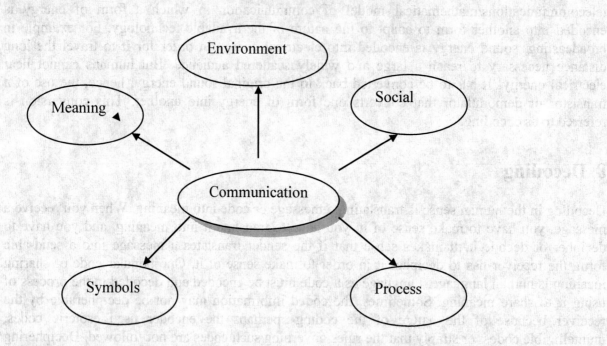

Source: West, Richard and Turner, Lynn H. (2007). *Introducing Communication Theory: Analysis and Application (3rd ed.).* Boston, MA: McGraw-Hill.

From the figure above, we can attempt to define communication by using the elements identified as relevant to defining the concept. Communication is a dynamic process that occurs in an environment where people share social meanings using symbols. All the elements are interconnected in a system that regulates itself and that imposes rules of engagement on the participants. In addition, all of the elements occur not in a perfect state, but in which there are interferences of different kinds.

Can you think of other elements that may be added in defining the concept of communication?

Levels of Communication

Communication occurs in different contexts, involving varying numbers of people, who may combine verbal or nonverbal behaviors in the process of achieving somewhat different goals. On these bases, scholars identify different types and levels of communication. Therefore, communication involves exchanging messages with oneself, with another person or persons in informal/formal settings, with three or more people in a small group. It may also occur in a formal setting when one person is designated speaker, interacting with an audience and, it may occur with technologies as intermediaries between senders and receivers.

Intrapersonal Communication

Before we speak, usually we first engage our minds and encode what it is that we would like to say and how we should say it. Normal human communication starts with engaging the mind or oneself before engaging the external or other human beings. The process of this internal interaction or thinking is referred to as Intrapersonal Communication. Cognitive Psychologists are concerned with what goes on in the human mind when we engage ourselves in the process of thinking. As we experience the world, we store such experiential information in our brains and, such is associated with present events in the process of encoding reactions to external stimuli. Intrapersonal communication is very complex and includes "diverse internal activities as thinking, problem solving, conflict resolution, planning, emotion, stress, evaluation, and relationship development"(Seiler and Beal, 2008). Understanding intrapersonal communication would require the study of such topics as self, perception and their connection to the verbal and non-verbal messages that we humans share.

Interpersonal Communication

The word inter suggests, with another or connected to another. Communicating with another human being, face-to-face, is considered interpersonal interaction. Scholars use the term **dyadic** to refer to interaction involving two people. As if communicating with oneself is not complex enough, consider communication with another human being, who engages in his or her own complex intrapersonal communication. Interpersonal communication, therefore, is **the complex process whereby two people exchange meaning to create understanding between them**. This may be informal interaction with people -a stranger, family member, adult, child, clergy, doctor, etc; or a formal interaction in an interview with potential employer, school counselor, or police.

Interpersonal Communication is not limited to two individuals however; it also occurs among group members of three, four, five, or more. In this case, the quality interaction among these members is what is referred to as being 'personal.' The opposite of this personal, quality interaction is impersonal, cold, rather 'official' interaction. Therefore, dyadic communication is only a part of the total experience of interpersonal interaction, which also could occur in small-group communication contexts.

The foregoing explains the two perspectives of interpersonal communication, which are **quantitative and qualitative perspectives**. The first perspective is concerned with the number of people involved in the communication exercise, while the latter is concerned with the quality of interaction that occurs in different communication contexts.

Quality, interpersonal relationships is characterized by a number of factors. Qualitative relationships are rather unique in nature because they occur between individuals who forge a one- of -a -kind relationship that cannot be replicated. Therefore, such relationships create a sense of interdependency and as such what affects a member affects another. In essence "at the most basic level, the fate of the partners is connected (Adler and Proctor, 2007).

Small Group Communication

A group is described as a set of individuals interacting and exerting influence on one another to achieve a common goal. That is, a number of people who share a common objective of meeting a goal by making joint decisions that will result in accomplishing a task that will lead to the goal. The interactional nature of groups suggests the sharing of information and/or meaning for creating a common vision or agreement that will underscore the joint production of results.

To distinguish this level of communication from interpersonal communication or dyadic communication, a group has at least three members and an uncertain maximum number of members. However, there are two basic rules of thumb that guide the operation of a small group: 1.The smaller the number, the better the quality of interaction, and 2. An odd number of members is preferred to an even number of members. This is because an even number of members can sub -divide itself to even subsets with the possibility of perpetuating conflict in the absence of a tiebreaker. In any case, five to seven members are considered ideal for a small group.

A small group can be organized for a number of reasons and purposes; hence, there are different types of groups defined according to their set goals. According to Engleberg and Wynn (2007), each type of group can be recognized by observing its setting and its membership.

Primary Groups meet individual primary needs of belonging, affection and social approval. Membership consists of immediate family members and long-term friends whose primary goal it is to provide each individual with support, sense of belonging and immediate identity. This becomes the foundational relationship upon which other relationships are built; hence, other group types are secondary in nature, as they meet other human needs beyond the family.

Social Groups as its name suggests provide opportunity for people to socialize and to provide the platform for members to share and enjoy each other's company. They provide an outlet for members to meet their need for emotional release and ego massaging. Such group members confirm one another and create an enabling climate in which to socially thrive.

Self -Help Groups come together to help solve specific problems that members may be facing. An example of this is Alcoholics Anonymous, whose focus is helping each other break the cycle of dependency on alcohol. This suggests that when people who share a common experience, in this case, a negative one, come together in self-help groups, it shows they need each other to lean on and to understand how they feel, and to jointly proffer a solution to that common experience and common situation they find themselves in.

Service Groups provide services that will bridge the gap between self-help and government help. "Service groups are dedicated to worthy causes that help other people both within and outside the group." Joining with others to perform civic duties is an example of service groups. Other examples include neighborhood associations, labor unions, Volunteer Fire Fighters, Parent-Teacher Associations and professional clubs.

Learning Groups exist to fuse members' efforts directed at understanding a particular subject, topic, or issue. This is common among students and company managers and staff. When a company changes its computer operating platform into another, there is need to form learning groups to learn and understand the new system. The goal is to jointly learn and gain working knowledge and mastery of the new system upon which their company operations and their jobs depend.

Work Groups are classes of people who jointly perform some duties or individuals in a particular line of work in a corporation or organization. Work group members are charged with particular functions that they perform on a permanent or periodic time frame. In the human organization, there are three general classes of work groups: management, supervisors and employees. Though their duties may differ, their performances are directed at achieving the overall objectives of the organization.

Public groups function in the public sphere and usually exist to serve a larger, more public purpose. The members come together in public and their deliberations are subject for public consumption and criticism. Such groups may be organized to gather information from the public, to deliberate on issues of public concern and, to make decisions on behalf of the larger public. Examples of public groups are panel discussions, forum, and symposium.

The Nature of Small Groups

Basically, as social animals, humans have a need to associate with one another. Though the basis of the attraction or coming together may differ, it forms the foundation of human cooperative effort. Usually geographic proximity often determines who we choose to associate with to form a group. It may also be due to similarity or perhaps complementary needs or just plain interpersonal attraction. Regardless of the basis of attraction, there are some underlying characteristics of small groups that distinguish this form or level of communication from others. These are interaction, interdependence, common goals, size, cohesiveness, commitment, norms and culture.

Interaction is a requirement for group existence and functioning, and without it a group cannot come into being. The sharing and exchange of ideas and feelings through communication is central to the group members' ability to jointly create meaning and understanding that form the basis of their existence. Commitment, cohesion, interdependence are all extensions of interaction or communication in the small group. The interaction of group members may be face to face or it may be mediated as in virtual interaction on the internet.

Interdependence is one member depending on another such that there is mutual dependence of all members in the group. Without mutual dependence members would not find a compelling reason to remain in the group because there would be no apparent value in membership if a member cannot benefit from the experience of others in reaching group goals.

The desire to work to accomplish a common end such that one member's experience would complement the other to the extent that the result is superior to that of an individual working alone is motivated by interdependence.

Common Goal is the driving force of any group. Without a common goal, there is no unifying element to necessitate group formation in the first place. Groups derive their essence from their desired goals such that individuals are willing to exert influence on others and otherwise be willing to follow others in order to achieve that common goal. This leads into **Cohesiveness** and **Commitment.** With a common goal, there is a collective desire and willingness to stick to the goal, to see it to fruition or completion. And this generates a form of bonding for the group members that creates liking and attraction to group membership and its rewards.

Group Norms emerge as members spend time together and begin to impose on one another 'rules of engagement that outline acceptable and unacceptable behaviors within the group. Norms create boundaries of behaviors for group members; essentially these are the dos and don'ts that characterize each unique group. According to Patricia Andrews, norms are 'sets of expectations held by group members concerning what kinds of behavior or opinion are acceptable, good or bad, right or wrong, appropriate or inappropriate."

TABLE 1.1/ TYPES AND PURPOSES OF SMALL GROUPS

Group Type	Group Purpose	Examples
Primary	To fill basic needs of inclusion and affection with others	Family Close friends Co-workers Neighbors
Secondary	To accomplish a task or achieve a goal	Decision making Problem solving Committee Learning group Therapy group

Source: Seiler, William J. and. Beall, Melissa L (2008). *Communication: Making Connections* (7th ed.). Boston: Allyn and Bacon.

Public Communication

The word **public** suggests an aggregate of people organized either loosely or firmly around a common issue, idea or thing. A common motivating factor or unifying force brings the public to a common place where they are exposed to a common set of information presented by a lone speaker or series of speakers. Although the field of public communication has grown beyond just public speaking, it still dominates the mindset of scholars and people attempting to define and explain the meaning of the two words: Public Communication. Perhaps this is so because its formal study dates back to ancient societies of Egypt and Greece where the power of public persuasion gained its pre-eminence. It was over four-thousand five hundred years ago in

Athenian society, that Rhetoric or public speaking was classified as one of the original seven subjects of the academy. At the prompting of his friend, Alexander the Great, Aristotle classified the disciplines of his time as including what he called Rhetoric and defined it as the "faculty of discovering in any particular case, all of the available means of persuasion." In fact, the ideas contained in Aristotle's *Rhetoric*, a book he published in 333 BC, are still very relevant to the field today.

Public speaking is the process whereby one person is designated as speaker, attempting to communicate a set of information to an audience of people, who are present physically to witness and receive the set of information otherwise referred to as a speech. The speech act, which is a collaborative act between speaker and audience, is a means of achieving three basic human communication needs: Giving and obtaining information for educational purposes, giving and receiving information for persuasion purposes, and giving and receiving information for entertainment purposes. The three general purposes for public speaking, therefore, are **to inform, to persuade and to entertain.** Apart from these broad goals, speeches are also presented to introduce, to pay tribute, to accept, and to welcome, (Seiler and Beal, 2007).

Public speeches by nature are rather formal and structured because they are directed at many different people who do have different, but sometimes overlapping environments. In order not to disaffect any member of the audience, public speeches are designed to use mainstream, formal language that will appeal to most members if not all of the audience. In addition, because of the nature of human listening, an organized speech is easier to follow and understood, just as it is easier for the speaker to present. It is usually all-inclusive, because through careful preparation, a speaker usually anticipates the information needs of the audience and presents them in the speech to an audience that usually does not have the opportunity to interrupt the speaker with questions and need for clarifications until the end of the exercise. The speaker must adapt himself or herself to the speaking situation and the nature of the audience in order to be successful.

Students and teachers of public communication are concerned with the principles that guide researching, organizing, writing, and presenting effective speeches. The issues of effectiveness of persuasive techniques, structure and logic of arguments, credibility, and the nature of information processing dominate scholarly research in the field.
In the following chapters of the book, you will learn about the early beginnings of the art of public communication; you will also learn of the different speech types, the different presentation styles, and the different speech structures or patterns. Also, you will learn about choosing appropriate speech topics, researching speech topics, and developing the basic parts of the speech. Not only these, you will also be presented with some theoretical information that informs the different practices of informative and persuasive speeches.

Mass Communication

As the word "mass" suggests a large number of people, mass communication, therefore, can be described as the process of **communicating to widely dispersed, large, and diverse groups of people, from a centralized position, using mass media**. The traditional centralized position is the newspaper organization, the radio station, and the television broadcasting station. This suggests disseminating information, images, and packaged contents for mass appeal through the mass media. The distribution of contents to remote locations was made possible with the invention of the printing press that allowed for mass production of prototype books and newspapers. In the same vein, Radio and Television became reality with the discovery of the electromagnetic spectrum and the possibility of transducers changing sound energy into electric energy that is capable of traveling via long distances.

Today, however, the fusing of the computer and telecommunications technologies has revolutionized mass communication. No longer is mass communication limited to a centralized, fixed position, it can originate from multiple positions anywhere across the world. The McLuhan Global Village is all a reality today! Not only do we have real time, instant feedback as in **synchronous** communication; we also have **asynchronous** mass communication, whereby the receiver can access the mass mediated message at any time. In this instance, feedback is delayed unlike in the synchronous mass communication and other types of communication such as interpersonal and the small group where feedback is instantaneous.

The business of mass communication is facing a number of challenges due to the telecommunication revolution that the world is witnessing. Competition is emerging from all fronts as traditional mass media are challenged by emergent mass media. Today we know of satellite radio, digital books, video streaming, podcasting, and the like. The mass media can be identified to include both traditional and modern. A list of these media would include: **Radio, Television, Books, Magazines, Movies, Billboards, Internet and other Telemedia, and Special Events**. There are mass media events that can be described as mess media because they have become means of reaching a widely scattered and dispersed audience. These special events may include the World Cup (Soccer), The American Super Bowl, The Olympics, Hollywood Awards and many others.

Practitioners of mass communication are indeed very powerful people in society because of the influence of their actions and the effects that their portrayals have on the consumers of mediated messages.

Mass media organizations are owned by the government in some countries and by the powerful and rich in some others. Not only is it argued that the mass media reinforce cultural stereotypes about race and identity (Wood, 2008); it is also believed that they perpetuate the power of the ruling class and thus, the social stratification in society.

Because of finite space and time, media practitioners, especially journalists and editors, use certain predetermined agenda to identify what is news and what is not. They also determine the prominence they give to certain issues, thereby determining what is kept in or out of the frame of reference of the consumers.

Wood, 2008, posits that "because mass communication surrounds and influences us, we have an ethical obligation to be responsible and thoughtful consumers." To do this, consumers must develop media literacy and respond actively to the media. The goals are to assess media's influence, identify methods of the media, in order to actively question media messages. More importantly, exposure to different sources of information would provide balanced perspective of information.

Organizational Communication

This type of communication occurs among the different levels of people functioning in the human organization. Because there are different levels of individuals and classes of people in the human organizations, their communication processes are usually highly complex, formal and structured. Yes, there exist other forms of communication in complex hubs, such as interpersonal, group, mass and intercultural, but the complexity of the webs of formal, business-oriented organizations gives way to formalized and sometimes prescriptive lines and flow of communication, to allow for controlled and efficient communication among the constituent groups.

There are two broad categories of people in the organization- the employees and management. In the middle are the supervisors, who act as liaisons or information and policy gatekeepers between employees and management. The dominant class is the management. While it is the duty of the management to establish organizational goals and objectives and to organize the means for achieving them, the employees must be consulted and their opinions must be factored into decision making in order for them (the employees) to feel a sense of belonging in an organization that requires their cooperation to achieve its goals. As communication in the organization has been described as a management function by Cutlip and Centre (1971), its relevance today places a responsibility on sophisticated management to use the communication resources at its disposal for the generation of employee support for, and 'identification' with the organizational goals and objectives. This is not claiming that management and employee goals, expectations, and objective are the same, but rather a merging of perspectives to the extent that both groups of people become vested in achieving organizational goals.

The hierarchy of positions and power in the organization has led to the different types and channels of communication that exist in the organization. There are employee, management, and supervisory communications. Management communication dominates in the organization environment and it usually starts from the top and **flows downward** to the employees, whose **upward** communication may hardly get across to the management. The openness and style of management definitely influences the flow of such information. The **laissez-faire** management style allows free- flowing unrestrained interaction among the constituent members, thus allowing for free-flow of information. **Autocratic** organizations allow for the dominance and control of the channels of communication by a few top leaders, who must approve of the sources of information within the organization, but the **democratic** organization, on the other hand, is positioned in the middle of these previous extremes.

Channels of communication in the organization include face-to-face meetings, memos, telemedia (faxes, intranet, internet, and audio/video conferencing), company publications (including newsletters, brochures and handbooks), bulletin boards, and the grapevine.

According to Awodiya (2005), there are differences in the perceptions of management and employees concerning the relevance of different channels of organizational communication, and so are perceptions different regarding the effectiveness of information sharing. In both cases, the views of management often contradict those of the employees and the effectiveness of the exchange of information is often positively exaggerated by management while often negatively exaggerated by the employees.

Intercultural Communication

Intercultural communication is the process whereby people of different cultures engage in the process of sharing ideas, feelings, and thoughts for arriving at a level of common understanding. In a world that is increasingly becoming a "global village," there is more intercultural communication going on around us than we realize. In a typical American classroom, there are divergent cultures represented because of the increasing multicultural nature of the American society. Assuming that the classroom is made up of students of the same culture, especially that the instruction is in English, is the primary source of misunderstanding and miscommunication in the American classroom. Usually the classroom is not mono-cultural, but multi-cultural; therefore, a good deal of intercultural communication takes place in the culturally diverse classroom.

Why is culture important? Scholars would argue that cultural differences translate to differences in values, beliefs, attitudes, expectations and behavior. This means that because of the cultural group we belong to, we see the world through different prisms and we do behave and communicate differently. The appreciation and adaptation to these differences becomes the first step in the process of jointly creating meaning for mutual understanding. To better understand the influence of culture, we should examine cultural characteristics that would inform us of the causal nature of the webs that humans spun around themselves. Some cultures are described as **Individualistic** and others **Collectivistic.** And as previously identified, a culture may be described as **monochronic or polychronic.**

Basic Communication Models

The conceptual and abstract nature of communication makes it a good subject to adapt to models. Models are graphical or diagrammatical representations of ideas and processes with the aim of simplifying and concretely explaining such otherwise abstract ideas, processes or phenomena. Models are used to complement attempts to define communication and capture its dynamic nature. The use of models offers a number of advantages over just describing ideas and verbally explaining them.

Models aid our understanding of ideas because they attempt to explain them; they aid creativity because in configuring them we often view what we are trying to represent in different ways, thus opening up our vista about the concept or idea. Models present ideas to us in simple, but rather inclusive ways that may capture the essence of the idea being presented without losing the fact that the idea may be dynamic and, as such, is constantly changing. With the foregoing we can surmise that models help save time as well, in that we can capture an array of ideas with a simple graphic representation. Because models can be tested and reworked or extended and reconfigured, we can conclude that models too can help generate new ideas. A good idea must not only survive the test of its utility, it must meet the test of usefulness and relevance over time.

In defining and explaining the concept of communication, scholars over the years have modeled their ideas in incrementally sophisticated ways, starting with the linear to interactive and the transactional models of communication.

Linear Models

Linear suggests 'like a line'- a one-way straight line. This is the earliest representation of the idea or process of communication by scholars who thought of communication as one person exerting influencing or sending messages through some channels to a receiver who is the end point of this enterprise. This suggests the transmission of information from one person who acts on the other. There are a number of things we know now that may make this linear model idea seem rather simple, incomplete, and unrepresentative of communication as we now understand it.

First, it does not acknowledge communication as an ongoing phenomenon; it does not suggest that communication is at least interactional; and, it does not identify the presence of **noise** in the process. In 1949, Harold Lasswell suggested the linear idea we now commonly refer to as the Lasswellian formula of Who Says What? To Whom? In What Channel? With What Effect? This represents communication as what someone does to another- otherwise referred to as the **actional model**.

An improvement to the Lasswellian model came through Shannon and Weaver when the two were working on a model to explain how the telephone functions and thus were concerned with channels of communication. **The Mathematical Model**, as their model was referred, added the presence of **noise** in the linear representation of communication. The concepts of source, message, receiver and channel were used to identify elements in the Linear Model of Communication. (See previous discussions on these concepts, especially on the types of noise).

This idea was seminal for its time, but we can identify some of its flaws. West and Turner (2007) contend that the model presumes there is only one message in the communication process and that communication does not have a definable beginning and ending. They conclude that the

Shannon and Weaver's model presumes a **mechanistic** orientation that oversimplifies that complex communication process.

FIGURE 1.2/Linear Model of Communication

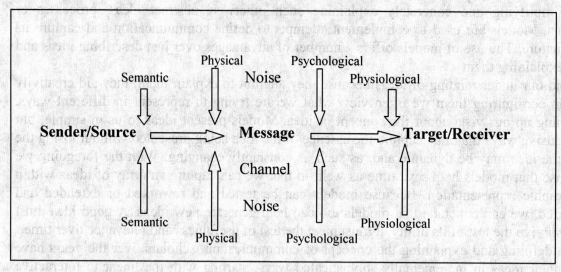

Source: Adapted from Shannon & Weaver, 1949.

In this model, Shannon and Weaver diagrammed their idea of how the telephone system would work. The elements they identified are the **source** of communication- who sends a **message** and the **receiver**, who is the receptor of messages. **Channel** is the conduit for sending and receiving messages and **interference** or **noise,** which is experienced in the process of **sending** and receiving information. Types of noise identified by the model are **physical** or **external**, **physiological**, and **psychological** noise.

Interactional Model

The interactional model of communication views communication as the sharing of meaning, with feedback that links the source and receiver (West and Turner, 2007). This model examines the relationship between the participants in the communication process; it is concerned with the returned behavior of one to another. The idea of feedback suggests that communication is not a one-way street, but a two-way street. Inserting feedback into this model, (Wilbur Schramm, 1954) suggests that communication is an on-going circular process that may not necessarily terminate at either end of the motion. As discussed earlier in the chapter, feedback may be verbal, nonverbal, or vocal, or non-vocal. However, feedback takes place after the message has been received by the receiver who reacts to the message. **It may be described as involuntary or gut reaction to the message**. An awareness of feedback in the communication process will go a long way in improving our communication with one another. Valuation of feedback should lead the sender to modify his or her message accordingly either by rephrasing, repeating or changing the channel of communication.

The fields of experience of the communicators are depicted in the interactional model. These are the backgrounds, be it experiential, cultural, interests, educational, of the sender and receiver. The fields of experience or backgrounds of the communicators often overlap, and this creates opportunity for and aid to understanding. In some cases, though, the experiences of the communicators do not overlap, thus making it rather difficult to create understanding. As we now understand in the definitions examined earlier in this chapter, the interactional model also has its shortcomings: It identifies the sender as performing a different and separate function from the receiver in the communication process, whereas, in real life situations, both participants are senders and receivers – all acting simultaneously. This is the distinguishing element of the transactional model.

FIGURE 1.3/Interactional Model of Communication

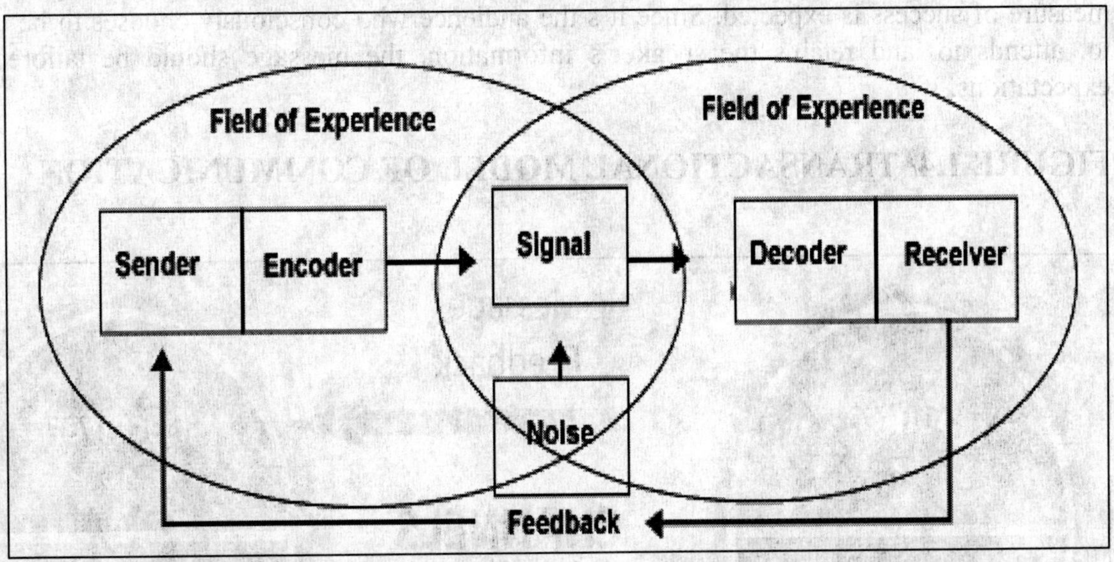

Source: Adapted from Wilbur Schramm, 1954.

Transactional Model

As discussed earlier, a transaction is a simultaneously occurring exchange of values such as a business transaction in which the participants exchange one value for another. As such, both the sender and the receiver are both sending and receiving messages all at once. If this is so, then both communicators are senders and receivers since they are interchanging roles constantly. The idea of a transaction suggests that communication is a cooperative process whereby the sender and the receiver are mutually responsible for the effect and the effectiveness of communication (West and Turner, 2007). These participants occupy different environments that may sometimes overlap, that is, their interests, backgrounds, orientations, expectations, cultures, gender, etc., may be different yet may be similar in some cases. The important thing is that the environments of the communicators influence the meanings being shared to the extent that a common environment produces understanding, while dissimilar environments create misunderstanding.

Is speech making a linear process, interactional process, or is it transactional? A far superior understanding of communication is presented through the transactional model of communication, which best represents, the speech process. Public speaking has been described as a collaborative effort between speaker and receivers, therefore, the participants in this exercise are simultaneously sending and receiving messages. The speaker delivers a speech in addition to other non-verbal messages that he/she may be sharing with audience. The audience members, on the other hand are not only receiving messages from the speaker, they are equally giving feedback to the speaker. Often, the speaker reacts to these signals and adjusts his/her speech accordingly to accommodate the audience members. Much of the feedback is nonverbal, however, because the etiquette of public speaking does not allow audience members to speak back to the speaker while engaged in the public speech act.

As public speakers, we have to understand that the speech act is a transactional process, whereby the environments of the receiver should greatly influence the choice of topic, the contents addressed, and the style of presentation. Since it is a formal interaction between the sender and the receivers, a careful analysis and understanding of the audience's sociological, demographical, and psychological information should influence the entire speech process, if a measure of success is expected. Since it's the audience who consciously chooses to be exposed to, attends to, and retains the speaker's information, the message should be tailored to its expectations.

FIGURE 1.4/ TRANSACTIONAL MODEL OF COMMUNICATION

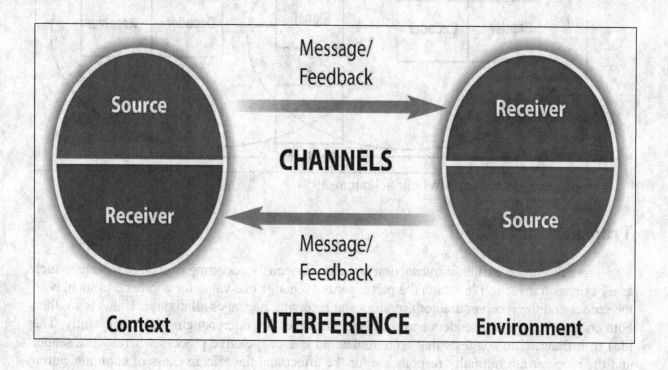

Review Questions

1. How would you define communication?
2. Why do people communicate?
3. What are the reasons why people study communication?
4. Identify and describe the basic principles of communication.
5. Identify, describe, and give examples of each of the nine elements of communication.
6. Describe, with examples, each of the different levels or types of communication.
7. Identify and describe the five misconceptions about communication.
8. What are the differences among the linear, interactional, and transactional models of communication?
9. How would you define communication competence?
10. What is ethics and what is ethical communication?
11. What is culture and why is it important to the study of communication?

Chapter Two

Perception and Listening

The human brain is a repository of information gathered by the five senses and stored according to some classification system for ease of access. Each experience is filed away into a category system of related information to be retrieved and interpreted in conjunction with current information. The human reality consists of myriads of interpretations attached to layers of information stored in the archival system of the brain. But the quality of interpretation and evaluation is dependent on the quality and type of information received and stored, in addition to the quality of the interpretation process itself. This is what makes human perception unique as well as somewhat unreliable. Everyone perceives the world from his or her vantage point and that, in itself, is biased as it is self-serving.

Since communication involves the sharing of information and experiences, such sharing of selective, highly biased and often erroneous experiences, nonetheless, constitutes the reality humans know. Therefore, when the collective experiences of a people informs them that something is real and consequential, so it is in all its ramifications. In other words, perception becomes reality, as it is the only way humans know to sense, assess, and interpret our world.

What is Perception?

Perception is a process of making sense of human reality. It involves selecting, organizing, and interpreting information in order to give personal meaning to the communication we receive (Seiler and Beal, 2008). Perception, therefore, is **an activity that involves the selection of certain impinging stimuli in the human environment, organizing such stimuli into patterns based on predetermined schemes, and imposing meaning on that which has been so organized in the process of interpretation.** As Woods (2007) reiterates, **perception is the active process of creating meaning by selecting, organizing, and interpreting people, objects, events, situations, and other phenomena.**

Human communication is greatly influenced by perception as perception is greatly influenced by communication. Human experience is an assortment of perceptions that are translated into meaning or messages that are shared with others. When we encounter others, we form impressions of them, and it is such impressions that represent the reality about them that we hold and subsequently share with others with whom we interact. Communication, therefore, is the process of encapsulating human experience into messages that are continually reproduced and shared with others. Such packages of impressions and interpretations are fraught with error and misinterpretations. But in the joint exercise of creating meaningful social realities with others, we influence and are influenced by our perceptions. According to Elizabeth Janeway as quoted in Julia Woods (2007), **the social world that we share with others is a world we have imagined together, and agreed with each other to believe in.**

The Perception Process

Awareness and Selection

With our senses we become aware of our surroundings—we see, hear, taste, touch, and smell. Because we are predisposed to making sense of the world in which we live, in our unique ways, we pay attention to certain stimuli at the expense of others. The selected stimuli are stored in our consciousness and mentally organized into meaningful patterns. Selection is a natural process of identifying what are of interest to us and of paying attention to them in a wide universe of endless stimuli. But why do we become aware of certain stimuli and pay attention to them over others? Though there are huge amounts of stimuli competing for our attention, we humans are capable of attending to a fraction of such stimuli because our senses are limited in their capacity to attend to all the impinging stimuli; hence, the need to select. Moreover, our expectations and predispositions inform our readiness to pay attention to some items over others. These predispositions are themselves influenced by our past experience, training, culture, gender, age, social status, among many variables. Again, some stimuli may impinge on our senses more intensely than others; as such, things that stand out capture our attention. So, for biological, psychological, and physical reasons, we favor certain stimuli over others.

Selection Process

The entire perception process is highly selective because our primary means of sensing the world- our basic five senses, are extremely limited relatively speaking in a nebulous universe of complex stimuli. Awareness of this limitation has led humans to selectively process information.

The process of stimuli selection in perception is three fold: selective exposure, selective attention, and selective retention. **Selective exposure** occurs when we deliberately choose to entertain certain messages and not others. For example a student may choose to attend a workshop presentation on "Financing College" and not the one on "Planetary Movements." Constantly we make choices of what information we want to let into our consciousness and which ones we do not want to bother with. This is based on the desire to satisfy immediate needs conforming to formed interests and habits. When students prefer to take classes with certain professors and not some others, they are using the principle of selective exposure.

Selective attention occurs when after exposing oneself to a particular information source, one pays attention to aspects of such information deemed important, further narrowing what set of information is eventually processed. Human attention span is equally limited; therefore, to cope with such limitation, we listen for relevant information out of the entire information presented say by a speaker or professor. For instance when a professor is lecturing in class, not everything that comes out of her mouth is important, so we select which information to pay attention to. This is what students do when they take notes in class- they write down important aspects of a lecture rather than the entirety of the professor's presentation.

Figure 2.1/The Perception Process

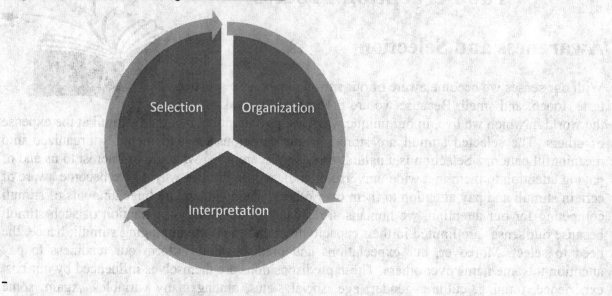

Based on the same selection principle, **selective retention** is deciding what aspects of information that we pay attention to are worth storing in our short and perhaps long-term memory. Because we judge such information as crucial and relevant, we repeat and rehearse them until they are permanently stored away in our minds. More important to this process is that individuals do not adjudge the same set of information as important. Therefore, what information individuals expose themselves to, attend to, and retain in their memories greatly differs. It is for this reason that we believe that perception is highly personal, selective, biased, and subject to error.

Organization

Stimuli organization is the storing, sorting, and association process that take place in the mind of the perceiver after receiving and accessing stimuli. As the computer's brain creates folders and files for categorizing and storing information, the human brain does the same thing by sorting and categorizing information in mental structures or templates referred to as schemas. In the process of interpersonal perception, scholars have identified four schemas we use to make sense, categorize, and interpret our experiences. Kelly (1955) and Hewes (1995), as quoted by Woods (2007), identified these schemata as **prototypes, personal constructs, stereotypes, and scripts**.

Prototype is the dominant representation of something- a true friend, a great teacher, or an ideal wife. The ideal is the prototype from which there can be variations according to our judgments of the others we encounter.

Personal constructs are mental measures that we usually apply in a bi-directional measure such as good - bad, intelligent-unintelligent, interesting- uninteresting. The bi-polar categorization forces labels on people, though they may not fit tightly into such extreme categories but somewhere along the continuum.

Stereotypes are generalizations or conclusions about a group of people, though such may be based on incomplete or insufficient information. Stereotypes allow us to categorize people based on our previously determined conservative criteria, which may lump people together indiscriminately, even though we acknowledge that people are unique and should be treated as individuals.

Scripts represent information gleaned from our knowledge of how people are, how they behave in certain situations and how they interact with one another in different contexts given certain variables. A script is a guide to action, and it consists of sequences of activities that are expected of us and others in particular situations (Wood, 2007).

We also sort or organize received stimuli according to the basic principles of psychological **closure**, geographic closeness or **proximity** and **similarity**. Often when humans receive information from the environment, there exists the psychological tendency to supply missing pieces to complete the idea or image. There is the readiness to perceive the whole rather than the bits and pieces that make up the whole, whereby we generally complete or invent embellishments to present coherent experiences or enhance our perception. The medium of television is described as a medium that taps into the **psychological closure** tendencies of viewers. For example, right on the production set, a couple opens and enters a prop door and pretends to engage in a romantic exchange and within seconds emerges from the same door, but this time with untidy clothes that they are desperately trying to put on properly. Our mental shortcut presents the information as a complete story of a couple that has just gone into a room to have sex, whereas nothing of sort happened. This principle is always at work when we try to make sense of events, people and ideas we form in our heads.

We also have the tendency to group things that are close geographically together as having equal qualities and characteristics. This is organization by **proximity**. The assumption is that such closeness presupposes sameness, but nothing could be further from the truth. We tend to generalize about people who live in certain sections of the city or those who live in the suburbs as against those in the city. For example, whenever I ask my students of their opinions of those who live in the Hamptons- a high class area of Long Island, New York, the opinions are generally that everyone who lives there is rich!

Similarity works also like proximity. Primarily people believe that others are just like them and, as such, should like what they like and, perhaps have ability to do just as they do regardless of whether they are so gifted. This form of organization, groups like terms together, be it shapes, sizes, colors and other characteristics. And the assumption is that because people and things are similar they must also share other similarities, maybe behave same way, dress same way, and perhaps have the same abilities. Such classification is applied to people of other cultures, races, and religion. No wonder that we are suspect of human perceptions because of their inherent fallibility. One day I had to visit the hospital because of some excruciating pain I was experiencing in my stomach. Of course my wife contacted some of my relatives who met us at the hospital concerned about what could be wrong with me. The attending physician, upon seeing many Africans congregated around me at the emergency room, thought they could only be there for one thing and one thing only: to interpret her English to me because she assumed that I did not speak English. How wrong she was, but I excused her assumptions because it probably was based on her experience. No, all immigrants to the United States are not similar!

Interpretation

After receiving and classifying information according to predetermined schemes, we still have to infer meaning to the messages received. **Interpretation** is the process whereby we pass judgment on information received in order to make sense of it in light of our past experiences and expectations. Interpretation is a form of conclusion we arrive at based on the associations of stimuli already stored in the schemata. When we assign meaning to such stimuli, we do so according to identifiable principles such as **past experience**, **opinions of others** and **current situations**.

Perception Figure One

Do you see the young or the old lady?

Perception Figure Two

What do you see: Vase or two faces?

Perception Figure Three

How many legs does the elephant have?

Perception Figure Four

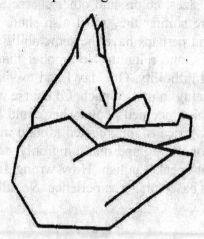

What is this?

Table 2.1/ Perception Activities and Processes

Mental Activities	Processes
Selection	Selective Exposure
	Selective Attention
	Selective Retention
Organization	Closure
	Proximity
	Similarity
Interpretation	Residual past experience
	New experience
	Social influence

Perceptual Errors

Perception is a private, individual process; therefore, it is subject to individual whim and caprices. Personal biases built into perception of objects and people makes the process highly tainted and subjective. Our perceptions of reality are, therefore, subject to error. If perceptions are individual and unique, then the organization and evaluation of information and meaning is private and thus subject to error. When we share these subjective views of reality with others in the process of communication, we are sharing our unique views of that reality. Though we may assume these to be accurate and reliable, this is not necessarily the case. Our communication with one another is replete with assumptions and perceptual errors unwittingly surmised as untainted evidence or information. Everything about us- our culture, physical characteristics, experience, and state of mind, influences our views of reality.

Why do individual perceptions differ and why do we look at the same event and come away with different and sometimes contradictory versions of the event? There are some human tendencies and other factors that influence our views of reality.

Perceptual Set

Past experience provides us humans with the foundation or platform with which to judge events and people. We, therefore, bring a previously determined, fixed way of viewing reality to current events and people. We tend to see the predetermined reality in the currently observed situation. How do students view examinations? The majority if not all sees examinations as personal evaluation and believes that examinations are rather testy if not difficult by design. So, whenever a teacher talks of giving an examination, this evokes in the students the previously fixed negative mind set about examinations as a dreadful experience to be avoided if at all possible. This mindset may prevent the students from actually seeing how easy a particular examination may be.

Seiler and Beal (2008) aptly summed the nature of perceptual set when they wrote that a perceptual set allows our past experiences to focus our perceptions so that we ignore information that is different or has changed about an event, object, or person. It is this mindset that informs a speaker of the pre speech credibility that he or she has among the audience members. Even before listening to a speech, audience members have predetermined evaluation of the speaker's competence, appearance, and believability. This mindset may be positive or negative, right or wrong, and this is why speakers should monitor where they stand with their audience before, during, and after their speeches to accurately gauge their effects on the audience. As previously discussed in Part I of the book, **stereotypes** are a fixed way of looking at categories of things, events, and people. Just like perceptual set, they lead to conclusions that are based on inconclusive information. However, for ease of classification and interpretation, we project such insufficient or inconclusive information on groups and classes of events, things, and people to categorize them. Based on your previous experience with some Chinese men or depictions of Chinese men in film and literature, you may want to classify all Chinese men as possessing the characteristics of the ones you know. What a leap of judgment, but we all do it. Informed perceivers know not to judge people by the standards of a few because of the dangers it portends. They know that individuals are unique, so it is a fallacy to prejudicially categorize them.

Psychological State

This factor easily captures how we humans tend to color and influence what information we take in through our senses based on how we feel at any given time. Is it not easier to attract friends when we are happy than when we are sad? You're still the same person physically when you experience different emotions and psychological states, but your mood leads to see things in a different light and for others to see you in a different light.

Therefore, our state of mind acts as a gauge of the theater of the mind, where events, things, and people are observed, categorized, and interpreted positively or negatively. It is your psychological state or mind-set that informs you whether "the cup is half-full or half-empty." Sometimes psychological states can be prolonged long enough to have a significant effect on perception and our communication to such extent that a situation may be classified positive or negative depending on the orientation. **Self-Esteem** is a part of your self-concept that represents your feeling of self worth. With a negative sense of self, the world is a lot more unfriendly than it usually is and the opposite is the case with a positive sense of self. Your self-esteem influences the way you receive and process information to the extent that you feed such into your messages with others. We can conclude that your state of mind influences your perception of the world just as it influences your interaction with others. As communication is the means through which the interaction is made possible, then your communication is influenced accordingly.

Attribution Error

This is another factor that influences human perception. Attribution is the attempt to explain human behavior. It is an explanation of why people behave the way they do. In this attempt to attribute human behavior, an error in judgment is observed in humans. This is that we tend to judge our own behavior more charitably than that of others. In fact, we tend to explain away or justify our own behaviors while we usually blame others for perhaps the same behavior. Explained another way, people tend to attribute the cause of their negative behaviors to external, environmental, or situational factors while they praise their personal inborn traits as responsible for their positive behaviors. That is people tend to praise themselves for their positive behaviors, but distance themselves from their own negative behaviors. However, when it comes to explaining or justifying others' behaviors, people tend to attribute internal factors or personal traits as the cause of others' negative behaviors and, perhaps, external factors for their positive behaviors. We tend to praise self but blame others.

Physical Characteristics

People are different not only in the way they perceive reality, but also in appearance and physical features. This world is full of variegated individuals in terms of height, weight, skin color, sex, health, strength, etc. These differences in people not only influence the way we view them, they also influence the way they themselves perceive the rest of the world. A tall person has a unique view of people in his or her environment, while a short person also perceives the people and the environment differently. A man is anatomically different to a woman- this alone accounts for the different ways they view each other, not to disregard the influence of cultural socialization. A person who sees himself as thin has opinions about another who he perceives to be obese. On the other hand, an obese individual sees those who are thin and forms a unique opinion about them. The way you look influences the way you perceive the world and in return the way the world perceives you.

You are familiar with the term Napoleon complex. What Napoleon lacked in height he compensated for in the art of bravery and warfare. What about the stereotype that short female bosses are rather difficult to work for. Though not scientifically valid, the fact remains that people perceive something different in people of different sexes, heights, and of other numerous physical characteristics.

Is beauty truly in the eye of the beholder?

Culture

What is culture and why does it influence our perceptions of the world? Culture is described as the total way of life of a people. It is the content of education as well as the teacher of knowledge; it is the totality of what a people, who occupy a set boundary with a sense of community, thinks, eats, and prays with and to. It is their language, values, belief systems, family structures, and religions, modes of dressing, music, government, education systems, and collective histories. According to Samovar and Porter (2007), "...you are born with all the anatomy and physiology needed to live in this world, but you are also born into a world without meaning. You do not arrive in this world knowing how to dress, what toys to play with, what to eat, which gods to worship what to strive for, or how to spend your money and your time." They conclude that "culture is both teacher and textbook."

The point is that we are not born with culture but we are born into it. We learn the elements and nature of our culture through agents in society that socialize us to the ways of our people. The family being the primary agent in the transmission of culture serves as the foundation that presents to us cultural identity, values, customs, belief systems, etc., of the society we call our own, as embodied in the education, religious and governmental systems. The reality is that there are thousands of cultures across the globe, which prepares us differently to survive in the same physical but socially different world. And when we experience the different socializations, we behave differently, because we perceive differently. Moreover, because we perceive differently, we communicate differently, using different languages and creating different meanings. Cultural identity, therefore, causes humans to be different in what they value, what they believe, and what picture of the world they carry in their heads.

People are evaluative by nature; we judge self and others and their practices. There is the tendency to want to judge one's culture as better than another's. There may be so much pride in self-identity that we may be blind to the realities of others. If we are exposed only to our own cultural reality, the tendency is to want to view our cultural values as "superior" and to see other's as "inferior." This means we use our values as the standard for judging other's values. This is what social scientists call a learned belief labeled **ethnocentrism**, which is a result of **cultural myopia**. Myopia is short sightedness and when we prefix this with culture, then it means to be culturally short sighted. The opposite is to adopt the principle of **cultural relativism**, which suggests the acceptance of different cultural values as different and not to evaluate them on the superior- inferior dichotomy.

Gender

The social construct of gender is not to be confused with biological sex. Although the anatomical differences in people may lead us to see women and men differently, it is another thing to assume that such biological differences would cause men and women to perceive differently. Gender, on the other hand, is based on observable behaviors of individuals regardless of anatomical sex. Since behavior classification is a better measurement of behavioral expectations, we can then claim that gender influences behavior and perception.

Women have been socialized largely to act feminine and men masculine, but there are men who take on feminine characteristics and women whose behaviors can be classified as masculine. Again there are some behaviors that are undifferentiated (neither masculine nor feminine) or androgynous (a combination of male and female behaviors). The different sexes are socialized into different role categories in society and this influences how we perceive people who play roles outside of the norm or expectations. As observed by Adler, Proctor, and Towne (2005), "gender roles are socially approved ways that men and women are expected to behave… After members of a society learn these customary roles, they tend to regard violations as unusual-or even undesirable."

The phrase: "what a man can do a woman can do too," underscores the relevance of role socialization and not sex in behavioral expectations. Therefore, the role an individual plays in society influences how he or she perceives society and in return, how he or she is perceived.

Gender roles are classified into eight different types.

Table 2.2/Gender Roles

	MALE	**FEMALE**
Masculine	**Masculine males**	**Masculine females**
Feminine	**Feminine males**	**Feminine females**
Androgynous	**Androgynous males**	**Androgynous females**
Undifferentiated	**Undifferentiated males**	**Undifferentiated females**

Source: Adler, Proctor, and Towne (2005) *Looking Out Looking In* (11th ed.) Belmont, CA. Thomson Wadsworth.

Media

Media are the conduits for disseminating information simultaneously to a mass of people, thus creating overlapping societies of consciousness that have common mindsets and perceptions. The pervasiveness of media influence in society requires examination because the media do present a slanted reality according to their different agendas, thus presenting society with a view that is manufactured to serve certain interests. So, the dominant powers of society, the political practice and the nature of media ownership in a society lead to certain types of influences in society. Consequently, in the process of reporting a reflection of societal reality, the media construct a certain type of reality that influences society accordingly. Media reality becomes societal reality and through the prism of the media, people form images in their minds and hold attitudes and opinions about events, things, and people. The challenge this presents is that the gatekeepers of the media are humans whose perceptions and constructions are as biased as they can be fallible.

Improving Perception

Perception influences communication and communication influences perception. We know that human perception is subject to error because we are easily influenced by the obvious; we cling to first impressions; and we expect others to be similar to us. All these suspect tendencies render our views of reality subject to error. And how do we ensure that we improve on our perceptions when now we realize how subjective they can be? Improving perceptions is a process that involves three different stages:

1. **We must verify and check our perceptions**. To really understand something, you need to question what you observe and know about that thing; you need to examine its different parts to affirm that what you think you know is all that is there to know. The awareness of the inaccuracies in your perceptions, which will lead you to ensure the accuracy of the process, is the first step toward a better perception of things, events, and people.
2. **We must become active information seekers in the process of perception**. Perceptions are based on available information and since we often short circuit the process or engage in premature closure of inquiry, it behooves an active perceiver to seek more relevant new information about the object of perception. Available information will reduce uncertainty or error in judgment when we arrive at conclusions about our observations.

3. **We must realize that perceptions are bound by space and time and, therefore, do not represent the total situation or person.** People and situations are subject to change, so we must adjust our perceptions accordingly. Just as communication, perception is a dynamic process and perceivers should treat their perceptions as temporary and must be willing to adjust in time and in various locations and under varying circumstances.

Situational **perception checking** also involves three processes that are somewhat related to the above. In order to ensure the accuracy of our perceptions on a situation-by-situation basis, we must do the following:

1. **An attempt must be made to describe to oneself any observed behavior.**
When you describe an event or a behavior observed to yourself, you're not only re- enacting that behavior under the prevailing circumstance, you're equally putting yourself in the position of the object of your perception, and that can be self-correcting in itself, thus ensuring some level of accuracy in your perception.

2. In every situation where we have to judge people's behaviors, **we must have at least two interpretations of such observed behaviors.** This is because an attempt not to rush to a conclusion is an attempt not to rush to make an error in judgment about observed behaviors. This also speaks to having an open mind and not to prematurely rush to an erroneous conclusion about our observations.

3. Within an appropriate cultural setting, **we can resort to asking questions to verify and validate our observations and consequent judgment derived from them.** The object of this is to affirm from the "horse's mouth" what the meaning of the observed behavior or utterance really is.

Test your perceptual set. What is this individual doing here?

Understanding Listening

The most important aspect of communication is, perhaps, the ability of the receiver to receive information sent, decode it, interpret it, and evaluate its meaning. Without adequate listening, the communication process cannot be complete. More importantly, even when the message is adequately received, it must be interpreted, evaluated, and responded to. If any of the stages in this process is compromised, effective communication cannot be achieved. So, if you remove listening from the communication and public speaking process, then you have nothing. In the public communication context, if a speaker fails to gain the attention of the audience, then nothing can be achieved beyond that point. The primary responsibility of the speaker, therefore, is to gain the attention of the audience to ensure that they listen and understand the message being shared with them. The audience also has some responsibility in this enterprise. Persons listening to a speech have to ensure that they listen and avoid distractions when they are engaged by a public speaker. Listening, indeed, is a collaborative effort between speaker and listener and the success of the speech enterprise depends greatly on the collaboration of the sender and receiver.

To understand the impact of listening on the communication process, we have to understand what the phenomenon really is. Contrary to popular belief, listening is much more involved than ordinary hearing. You may hear a sound, but may not pay attention to it, let alone understand it. So hearing as a biological function is something that all non-hearing- impaired individuals experience. Listening, on the other hand, is more involved and takes a lot of deliberate effort on the part of the listener. The consequences of effective listening are many. Because effective listening leads to understanding, we can see how it would lead to success in relationships, especially marital relationships, success on the job, and, most importantly, educational success. The opposite becomes the case when we don't listen effectively. Poor relationships, lack of empathy, misunderstood instructions on the job and the like, are examples of the result of poor listening.

Are we humans naturally good listeners? Considering all of the communicative activities we engage in (writing, reading, speaking, and listening), we spend more time listening than all the other three combined? Because we do it more often, we have taken the activity for granted, and rather than listen, we prefer to speak because it is advantageous to do so. We become the center of attention, we focus on our own issues and we gain some social recognition by being the speaker rather than being the listener. As we have seen, listening is a very important component of the communication process, but we humans are not naturally good listeners- we have to acquire good listening skills in order to become better at it. Baker (1971) summarized research that indicates that immediately after we hear something we remember only half. Eight hours later we remember only 35 percent, and two months later we remember 25 percent. All of these are based on the fundamental assumption the listeners were paying attention to the message in the first place and, that the message was short and simple.

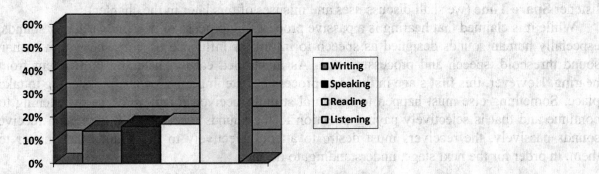

Figure 2.2 / Distribution of waking hours spent on four communication activities per day.

Source: Barker et al., "An investigation of proportional Time Spent in Various Communication Activities by College Students, "*Journal of Applied Communication Research* 8, 1981, pp.101-109 Reproduced in Tubbs Stewart L. and Sylvia Moss, (2000). *Human Communication*. Boston: McGraw-Hill.

So, what exactly is listening? Listening is a process that involves different stages. The behavioral approach to listening leads us to identify the six stages of listening, which are Hearing, Understanding, Remembering, Interpreting, Evaluating and Responding (Brownell, 2002). These stages, though separate, are integral parts of a system, all interacting as a whole. This underscores the interrelatedness of the elements and the fact that the sum of these elements diminishes in comparison to the whole. **Listening can be summed up as an active behavioral process of receiving stimuli from the environment, constructing meaning from such stimuli, and responding to such stimuli using a combination of spoken and nonverbal messages.** The final arbiter of the message received and the meaning constructed from it is the receiver, who is influenced by a number of factors such as past experience, culture, context, motivation, expectations, among a host of other influences.

Components of the HURIER Model of Effective Listening

Hearing

This is the physiological process of receiving aural stimuli. Sound energy impinges on our hearing sense, the ears, and the energy becomes sound cues that we can make sense of. Without being too technical, there are certain sound frequencies that we humans can hear, that is, there are certain frequencies below which sounds become inaudible to us or above which sounds become too loud and intolerable. This is the human sound threshold. There is also the human speech rate; this is the number of words that the average human can utter per minute. And if speech is rushed or too slow, the consequence is that the receiver would not be able to process it as expected. Goss (1982) posits that the average person can process up to 500 words per minute depending on the complexity and organization of the message, while the average individual speaking rate is 100 to 150 words per minute. The difference, which is ratio of 1-4, is termed the listener **Spare Time** (we shall discuss uses and misuses of this later in the chapter).

While it is claimed that hearing is a passive process, the process of hearing particular sounds, especially human sounds designed as speech to inform or influence us, must be within human sound threshold, speech and processing rate. As mentioned earlier, listening is different from hearing. However, this first stage in the long process of listening must occur for listening to take place. Something else must happen to the aural stimuli received for the process of listening to continue and that is selectively paying attention to the sounds received. While we can receive sounds passively, the receivers must desire to attend selectively to the sounds that matter to them, in order for the next stage, understanding, to occur.

Understanding

When we hear and pay attention to messages, the next step is that we attempt to process the information received. We ask ourselves the question: what is this and what can it possibly mean? The mind dips into its templates of past experiences to assign meaning to such stimuli received. The attempt to understand the sounds or messages received is what makes the difference between hearing and listening. But when we attempt to understand the message received, we are equally evaluating and judging the message, either accepting or rejecting it. And when we are unable to suspend judgment while we try to understand messages of others, we create barriers to interpersonal understanding. "If we can focus more of our listening effort on trying to understand the meaning that the speaker was intending to convey, temporarily withholding our tendency to judge or evaluate the message, we should considerably improve our ability to listen more effectively," Tubbs and Moss (2000).

To give a message accurate meaning, the message itself must be audible, clear, and grammatically correct and the receiver must understand the intent of the speaker taking into consideration the content and context of the message.

Remembering

With unprecedented availability of information in this technological era, keeping up with the myriads of information available is the challenge. Yes, we can always go to the laptop or the desk computer to retrieve information, but there are situations whereby depending on technological storing devices may not only be impossible, but also inappropriate. Imagine you're on a second date with someone who is beginning to fall in love with you and the occasion arises for you to mention the person's name and you cannot remember it. Would you open your blackberry at this point to rescue you? Effective communication depends on our ability to remember some levels of information and failure to adequately remember may jeopardize our relational, professional, and scholastic success.

Remembering involves recalling information from memory. Scholars agree that there are two different types of memory: short and long term. Short-term memory aids us to remember immediate things for utilitarian value. Shortly after we have used the information stored in this short memory bank, we find less use for it and less need to keep it in the bank. But for other information, we find them interesting, relevant, important and crucial to our perceived survival that we repeat and rehearse them in our minds until they are imprinted and transferred from short term to our long-term memory.

Is memory often recalled or is it constructed? It is often believed that we recall from memory, but do we actually store information verbatim in our memory or do we have some associational techniques that aid our ability to store like matters together and use such technique in retrieving stored information?

Figure 2:3/The Process of Listening Model

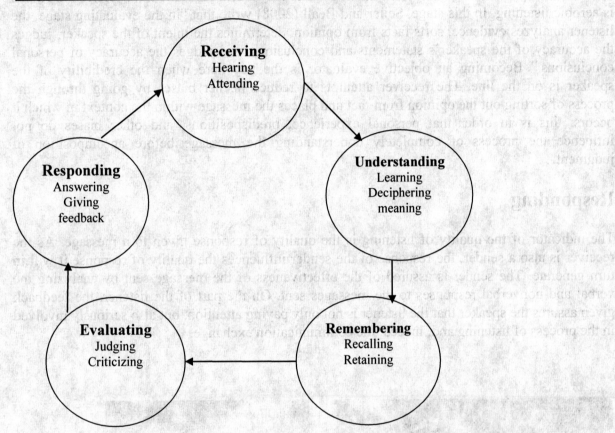

This model combines the ideas of scholars about the process of listening. The five steps process is a combination of the models of listening by different scholars (Alessandra, 1986; Barker, 1990; Brownell, 1987; Steil, Barker, & Watson, 1983).

Source: Joseph DeVito (2006). *The Essential Elements of Public Speaking, (2nd ed.)* Boston, MA: Allyn and Bacon.

Interpreting

When a speaker offers an explanation of some point that he/she is trying to get across, the receiver attempts to understand the message, not from his/her perspective, but from the sender's perspective- this is interpretation. Seeing the point from the sender's perspective is offering an interpretation that may be contrary to one's understanding, but the purpose is to see a situation from the other perspective. In order for this occur, the total communication message and context must be taken into account including all other variables that may influence meaning such as the intent of the speaker, nonverbal gestures of the speaker and other environmental factors. More importantly the listener must let the speaker be aware of his/her understanding of the message as intended by the speaker.

Evaluating

This stage emphasizes that effective listening is not easy work. As some have referred to it, this is aerobic listening. In this stage, Seiler and Beall (2008) write that "in the evaluating stage, the listener analyzes evidence, sorts facts from opinion, determines the intent of the speaker, judges the accuracy of the speaker's statements and conclusions, and judges the accuracy of personal conclusions." Becoming an objective evaluator is the key here when the credibility of the speaker is on the line. The receiver attempts to reduce his/her biases by going through the process of sorting out the opinion from fact and places the message within the context in which it occurs, this is in order that personal experience, predispositions, and other biases do not influence the process of completely understanding the message before an imposition of judgment.

Responding

The indicator of the quality of listening is the quality of response given to a message. As the receiver is also a sender, the response of the sender influences the quality of response it will in turn generate. The sender is assured of the effectiveness of the message sent by analyzing the verbal and nonverbal responses to the messages sent. On the part of the listener, the feedback given assures the speaker that the listener is not only paying attention, but also seriously involved in the process of listening and, indeed, the communication exchange.

Figure 2.4 / A Model of the Six-Component HURIER Listening Process.

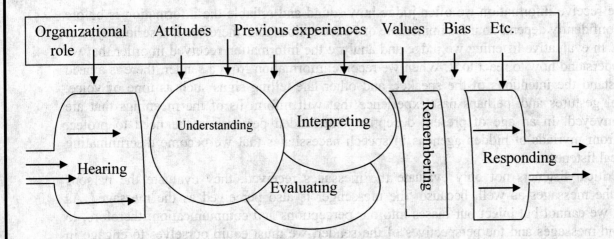

Source: Judi Brownell (2010). *Listening: Attitudes, Principles, and Skills*, 4th ed. MA: Allyn and Bacon.

Types of Listening

The different types of listening there are would depend on the different purposes for which we listen. Obviously everyone listens to obtain information, but sometimes we do this more critically and discriminatingly. Sometimes we listen for enjoyment purposes and oftentimes to empathize with others in order to provide comfort and understanding in times of emotional distraught. Depending on the purpose for listening, we employ different skills to the type of listening we engage in.

Listening to a conversation about a movie a friend just saw would depend on the purpose for such listening exercise. If you were to watch the movie for a class assignment that required you to write a paper on the movie, then you would listen more intently, critically and evaluate the information more closely. But if you have no such assignment and your friend's movie discussion is of less importance to you, listening in, therefore, becomes a casual thing- just for pleasure.

Listening to Obtain Information

Everyday living requires a lot of information that we seek out from others or different sources. To begin your day in the morning you might rely on your alarm clock to wake you up and, to determine how to dress for the day, you turn to your weather channel on television or radio for information and you seek out traffic information to help you navigate the roads. You listen to your teachers for educational instructions and to your mates for information about current events and sporting activities. The list is endless. We humans cannot survive our everyday living without listening for and obtaining information.

Evaluative Listening

When we receive information we often judge how sound and reliable the information is before we can confidently depend on it for immediate or future action- this, therefore is a serious type of listening. In evaluative listening we judge and analyze the information received in order that we might understand how to react to it. When we receive information from a sender, there is a need to understand the intentions of the speaker, and other tale-telling signs such as tone of voice, nonverbal gestures and, perhaps past experience that will inform us of the meanings that are being conveyed. In an age of present deception and hidden persuasion, the need to protect oneself from myriads of hidden agendas in speech necessitates that we become discriminating and critical listeners.

Critical listeners not only evaluate the messages received, they evaluate the persons sending the messages as well, because 'the messenger is also perceived as the message.' As Humans, we cannot but inject our biases into our perceptions and communication; therefore, to understand messages and the perspectives of the sender, we must equip ourselves to engage in critical listening. However, we should become aware of our own biases in the process.

Listening to public speeches requires critical listening, not only do listeners have the obligation to listen effectively to a speaker, they also have the responsibility to listen critically to understand the message, the
messenger, and the impact of the exercise on
both speaker and audience.

Empathic Listening

Empathy means to feel for, to have understanding for, and to have compassion for something. Empathic listening suggests listening to feel and understand the other person, that is, to really understand. To completely understand another person may be a tall order, but an attempt to really understand requires that we suspend judgment and the need to respond to the literal meanings of the words and messages coming out of another and focus on completely understanding the speaker. We are to listen to the emotions underlying the message to the extent that we understand a cry for help and not mistake it for a request for advice.

Interpersonal relationships thrive on empathic listening, which promotes "the opposite frame of mind required for critical listening… It implies a willingness not to judge, evaluate, or criticize but rather to be an accepting, permissive, and understanding listener," (Tubbs and Moss,

2000). Empathic listening promotes a concern for the thoughts and feelings of another, which underlie the real meanings they are communicating with us. Therefore, to listen empathically is to engage in effective listening and communication.

Pleasurable Listening

Seiler and Beall (2008), describe this type of listening as listening for pleasure, personal satisfaction, or appreciation. When older people sit for hours reminiscing about the past, the purpose is not to sit for an examination about the past, but to share something pleasurable. There is something inherently pleasing in sharing fond memories with other people. Some type of talk, therefore, is pleasurable listening. When we create time for activities such as watching movies and plays, going to concerts, pleasure is the ultimate goal. Although this may not mean suspending other types of listening, they become byproducts of listening for pleasure.

Barriers to Effective Listening

As we have discovered earlier in the book, humans are poor listeners partly because we assume that since we have been "listening" since birth, we have developed the skills for effective listening. Nothing could be further from the truth. But we are good listeners in some situations, concerning some people and certain topics. As effective communication requires a set of skills that we have to hone to become proficient, so also is listening. Listening is a learned activity and to be good at it, we have to acquire the set of pertinent skills to do so. The beginning is admitting our listening deficiency, then understanding and acquiring the skills needed and, subsequently practicing the skills. Now, let us examine some of the reasons why people don't listen effectively.

Woods (2008) classifies the obstacles to effective listening as situational and internal. The situational obstacles have to do with the communication context while the internal obstacles are within the communicators.

The situational factors include **information overload and information complexity**. With the explosion of telecommunication technologies, especially the internet, the opportunity to be exposed to information is greater than ever before. When we are faced with too many choices and too much information, we become overwhelmed and confused. Too much information may lead to a sense of helplessness that culminates in lack of attention and interest. It is advisable, therefore, for communicators to size up their audience and to give them adequate information within a reasonable time limit so that they are not overwhelmed by excessive details and long-drawn argumentation. The audience on the other hand should not attend to too much information at the same time. Trying to take on too many tasks is the same as attempting to listen to many sources at the same time. Human attention span and ability to attend to many sources of information all at once is very limited. The result is poor communication arising from information overload. For instance, a student cramming at the last second for an important examination or taking too many courses in order to meet a graduation deadline will experience a case of information overload.

Complexity has to do with how tedious the reasoning required to decipher the information is. If the information requires specialized reasoning and intricate analysis to adequately understand it, the average listener will be bored with it. Avoidance of jargon, breaking down of complicated information (semantic noise), and slow paced presentation may induce listeners to listen effectively, even when the material is complex. Situations like these require both the cooperation of the speaker and the listener. The listener should be prepared to pay attention and sustain such throughout the presentation, while the speaker is to do all possible to make sure the listener is drawn into the listening experience without unnecessary complications. After all, the duty of the competent communicator includes adequate consideration of the nature of the audience in the communication enterprise for effective communication to take place.

External distractions are other situational factors that impede effective listening. We are familiar with the concept of noise in communication. This is described as anything that causes distraction or that impedes the communication process and prevents adequate reception, interpretation, and understanding of messages sent and received. In this case we are referring to physical noise, that which is external to the communicators. Imagine two individuals attempting to have a conversation close to a live rock band. The external noise would be so much that it would be practically impossible for them to hear each other let alone understand the meanings of their exchanges. While some people read while playing music or when the television set is blaring, normal human listening cannot accommodate such cacophony.

Much of the factors influencing listening are **internal** to the communicators and these include hearing **problems**. When the hearing sense is defective physiologically, there is little one can do to hear properly. Since listening starts with hearing, this is a serious problem, which will impair reception of aural stimuli adequately to lead to understanding. Luckily there are myriads of hearing aids that medical technology has made possible to improve the limitations of impaired hearing.

Another internal factor is **Rapid Thought**. This occurs when the mind is preoccupied by many unrelated thoughts that shift attention from what is going on that requires our concentration. A restless mind jumps from one concern to the other and is not able to focus. The preoccupation drowns us and we are unaware of details required in a specific given situation say to complete a task and the end result is inadequate listening. This is linked to what we discussed earlier in chapter one which is the idea of **spare time. The difference between the speaker's rate and the processing rate of the listener is one to four.** This means that the listener can process information faster than the speaker can deliver such, thereby resulting in listener **spare time.** This spare time can be used in unnecessary preoccupation and as such becomes a liability rather than an asset in the listening process.

Prejudgment is a factor mitigating effective listening. Rather than hear people out, we rather prejudge them even before they complete what it is they have to say. The readiness of mind to complete others' thoughts for them and interpret them accordingly is a problem in many interpersonal relations. This kind of mind reading does not give adequate chance to the others; rather, it gives the listener the liberty to arrive at conclusions based on preconceived biases. "…Mind reading is assuming we know what others feel, think, and are going to say, and we may then fit our messages into our preconceptions. This can lead us to misunderstand what they mean because we haven't really listened to them on their terms" (Woods, 2000).

Effective Listening, as we know now, takes a lot of deliberate effort to accomplish. But when we **consider the speaker or the topic of discussion to be uninteresting**, we are not motivated to put in the required effort to listen effectively. Someone you consider boring and uninteresting may have information that will help you succeed on the job, pass an examination, or save a lot of money or avoid some grave mistakes. The duty of a competent listener is to focus on the content of the message rather than prejudging the messenger. An open mind is really an asset to the smart, effective listener.

Oftentimes listeners **pay attention to the speaker and criticize his or her appearance and speech mannerisms** rather than pay attention to the message. The listener focuses on mispronunciations, accent, and other possible distractions and not the content of the message. As distracting as all these things may be, the competent listener overcomes them by looking beyond the secondary nuances and focus on the primary goal of getting the complete message.

Other hindrances to effective listening include the different types of poor listening that we engage in because of our lack of listening training and willingness to practice it skillfully. **Ambush listening** is listening for the bit of information with which to attack the speaker. Rather than listen completely to the speaker and take into consideration the context in interpreting meaning, ambush listeners listen for an opportunity to grab a piece of what the speaker has to say as the basis of attack. **Insensitive listening** is literally interpreting a speaker's words or accepting such at face value without the necessary consideration of the factors that affect and influence meaning. Sometimes we **listen just for the facts** or only **for the emotions** exuded in a speech rather than listening for both. Listening to either emotions or just facts denies the combination of both in communicating meaning. What about **pretending to listen** when in reality our minds have wondered off? This is a common problem, especially when we find the speaker or the topic of discussion unappealing. Again, when it is obligatory to listen, say to a boss because of job requirements, many find it an opportunity to fake attention rather than listen intently. Alternatively, we may **listen selectively**, picking on information we deem interesting or important, leaving out what may be the critical message of the speaker. The opposite of selective listening is when a listener **intensely focuses on every detail of a speech being received and not the main ideas.** Since speakers are advised to break up their ideas into main points for ease of listening, it may not be necessary for the listener to focus on every detail surrounding the main points because usually what is remembered after some passage of time are the main points of a speech not the minute details explaining them. **Defensive listening** occurs when the listener perceives personal attack coming from a speaker and this arouses defensive mechanism from the listener who maintains the posture of "war" in receiving the information which in turn will be used to expose the intensions of the speaker and possibly to engage in a counter attack!
People of different cultures communicate in diverse ways and this includes different listening styles. Just as we have identified cultures as high context and low context, the communication characteristics of these different cultures influence their listening behaviors as well. As we are mindful of the different communication styles of people of different cultures, **we are less mindful of their listening behaviors,** behaving as if these differences do not exist. The problem of recognizing and failing to adjust to the different and diverse listening styles of diverse cultures and social communities has been identified as a major hindrance to effective listening, (Brownell, 2002).

Being mindful of these different pitfalls in our listening habits will lead us to become more aware of the impediments to our ability to listen effectively and lead us to finding ways to improve on this very important human communication skill.

<u>Table 2.3/ Ineffective and Effective Listening Habits</u>

Bad Listener	Good Listener
Thinks that topic or speaker is of no interest	Finds areas of interest-keeps an open mind
Focuses on the speaker's appearance and delivery	Concentrates on the presentation and overlooks speaker characteristics-stays involved
Listens only for details	Listens for ideas
Avoids difficult material	Exercises the mind-prepares to listen
Is easily distracted	Resists distractions
Fakes attention	Pays attention

Source: Seiler, William J. and. Beall, Melissa L (2008). *Communication: Making Connections* (7th ed.). Boston: Allyn and Bacon.

The Importance of Active, Critical, and Empathic Listening

Different situations and circumstances call for different approaches to listening. Often we listen to obtain information that we may have to retrieve and use in our everyday lives or that we may depend on to perform some tasks or that we may have to use in fulfilling some obligations. Students listen to lectures, someone seeking directions will listen for instructions, etc. In order to do all these effectively, we have to engage in active listening, which includes "making a mental outline of important points, thinking up questions or challenges to the points that have been made, and becoming mentally involved with the person talking," Hybels and Weaver (2007).

Critical listening involves active listening and an attempt to 'judge the accuracy of the information presented, determining the reasonableness of its conclusions, and evaluates its presenter, "Seiler and Beall, (2008). A critical listener is a critical thinker, who is aware of persuasive efforts and communication attempts directed at him or her to influence his/her judgment, which may result in the investment of time and expenditure of hard-earned resources. No wonder the need to be evaluative, judgmental, and critical not only of the message, but also of the speaker or source of such information.

A situation that calls for critical listening may not require empathic listening or vice versa. As we have discussed already, empathic listening involves an attempt to understand the feelings behind the message and that of the speaker. It purports a sort of identification between speaker and receiver that reflects an emotional connection of sorts. Table 2.6 clarifies the distinctions among these types of listeners such that an effective listener would be mindful of the differences and when to apply them to appropriate listening situations.

Table 2.4/ Active, Critical, and Empathic Listening Compared

Active Listening	Critical Listening	Empathic Listening
Identifies the central idea	Determines motives	Identifies the emotion(s)
Forms a mental outline	Challenges and questions ideas	Listens to the story
Predicts what comes next		Let the person work out the problem
Relates points to your own experience	Distinguishes fact from opinion	
Seeks similarities and differences	Recognizes your biases	
	Assesses the message	
Asks questions		

Source: Hybels, Saundra and Weaver, Richard L. (2007). *Communicating Effectively* (8th ed.). Boston: McGraw Hill.

Guidelines for Effective Listening

Knowledge of the principles and elements of listening serves to instruct both senders and receivers on what they must do to bring about effective communication. Trentholm (2005) identifies message design elements (strategies and tactics) the sender should be mindful of in order to make messages easy to process for the receiver. This is more so applicable to the public speaking situation where senders are trying to inform or persuade an audience whose expectations and orientation may be at odds with that of the speaker's. The goal of the speaker is to first gain the attention of the receivers, encourage receivers' interpretation and comprehension of message received, and to ensure they retain information they have received.

The following are the precepts of Trenholm (2005) for effective speaking and listening.

Precepts for Effective Speaking and Listening

To the Speaker:
Design Messages That Make Messages Easy to Process

Elements that Capture Attention
1. Increase voluntary attention by tying messages to receiver's goals, needs, and plans.
2. Increase involuntary attention by creating intense, novel, complex, or incongruous message elements; when speaking, present concrete, easily visualized ideas.

Elements that Enhance Interpretation by Increasing Comprehension
1. Relate new material to familiar material.
2. Adapt messages to the learning and interest levels of your audience.
3. Provide opportunities for feedback.
4. Use repetition.

Elements That Enhance Interpretation by Ensuring Acceptance
1. Relate proposals to receivers' current beliefs.
2. Offer receivers an incentive for accepting your proposal.
3. Encourage audience members to make positive cognitive responses; increase their active involvement in processing your message.

Elements that Increase Retention
1. Use active rehearsal and repetition.
2. Make information personally relevant to the receivers.
3. Associate recall with appropriate triggers.
4. Provide a simple, vivid summary of main ideas.

To the Listener:

Ways to Improve Listening Performance

To improve Attention
1. Focus only on relevant details.
2. Have a clear purpose for listening.
3. Use extra time to summarize content and review structure.
4. Keep a positive attitude; don't assume you'll be bored.

To Improve Interpretation by Increasing Comprehension
1. Pay attention to content, not peripheral cues.
2. Separate inference from observation.
3. Prepare yourself by knowing about the topic.

To Improve Interpretation by Increasing Acceptance
1. Control your emotions.
2. Acknowledge your biases and delay final evaluation.

To Improve Retention
1. Decide what information needs to be stored.
2. Mentally rehearse and review material to be stored.
3. Use mnemonic devices or special memory aids.
4. Seek out feedback; paraphrase or ask questions.

Source: Trentholm, Sarah, (2005). *Thinking through communication: An introduction to the study of communication* (4th ed.). Boston: Allyn and Bacon.

Review Questions

1. What is perception?
2. What are the elements of perception?
3. Explain the idea that perception is highly selective.
4. Why is perception subject to error?
5. How does one's mindset influence the selection, organization, and interpretation of stimuli?
6. What are the different factors that influence perception?
7. What is perception checking and how can you use it to improve your perception of others?
8. What is listening?
9. What is the difference between listening and hearing?
10. How can you improve your listening?
11. What methods can you use to ensure that you remember what you hear?
12. What is empathic listening and how can it improve your relationship with others?

Chapter Three
Verbal Communication

The ability of we humans to create and use words is one factor that separates us from other close relatives in the animal kingdom. Not only do we create words, we arbitrarily assign meanings to them for ease of exchanging such meanings in our communication with one another. Language production is a rather complex human activity but one with great consequences. We feel emotions, we have thoughts in our heads, we have opinions and we have needs to cooperate with others to tackle the challenges and opportunities of life. And how do we get all of these across to another human being, but through the use of language?

Our feelings, ideas or thoughts that occur in the human mind and items in our physical and imagined realities are given descriptive labels. Such labels allow us to characterize our experience such that they can be shared with others. So, humans interact through the use of symbols, which represent the real meanings we are trying to share with one another. A symbol is simply anything that represents something else and that which it represents is the referent, i.e. an idea, feeling or thing. Words, therefore, are symbols and language is a symbol system. Language is a set of stored information (in symbolic form) in our mind that represents our codified experience and, to make such experience external or to share it with others, we translate it into speech. Effective human communication depends on the meanings we assign to words, signs and marks. Because such meanings can be very complex we should examine language, its structure, nature, and development, so that we can further improve on our sharing of meanings through codes.

Seiler and Beal (2008) define language as **"a structured system of signs, sounds, gestures, or marks that is used and understood to express ideas and feelings among people within a community, nation, geographic area, or cultural tradition."** This is a rather comprehensive definition that suggests a number of things about the nature of language. First is that language is structured, which means that it is governed by specific rules and that it is not haphazard. Second is that language is not only verbal, that is, it uses words, but it also includes gestures, sounds and marks. So the way you sound when you speak words create additional meaning to those of the words being used. Your facial expressions, hand gestures, appearance, etc, constitute a set of cues without words, that is, nonverbal. Marks are punctuations used to structure the written word to give it form and meaning; for example, they signify complete and incomplete thoughts and are used to indicate feelings depending on where they are placed in the text. The exclamation point, for instance, is used to emphasize or underscore a point. Marks surely add significant meanings to our verbal communication. Third, is the idea of mutual understanding. The assigned meanings of words must be accessible to a community of people who understand and speak the language. Thus, a tongue can be classified as language if there is a considerable number of people (linguistic community) who have access to and uses it.

There are several thousands of languages in the world representing different cultural traditions and this fact makes cross-cultural exchanges very difficult. Communication through the exchange of ideas and thoughts that have been encoded in different languages and dialects is practically impossible except if one has acquired some proficiency in the codes used. Even when that is the case, there are still nuances of language that will bypass the users. Let's look at the English language for example. English is widely spoken across the world by different peoples either as primary or secondary language. Not only are some English words different in pronunciation from region to region, their meanings also are different. Even within a country such as the United States, there are different forms of English spoken by different groups such that one may sound foreign to the other.

Language is a powerful tool of communication that creates an identity for its user; it may confer prestige or it may denigrate. Language may facilitate communication or it may hinder it; it may create problems or it may solve problems. We can use language to divide people or to unify them, just as we can use language to endear others to us or to ensnare ourselves. In essence, language is not a neutral tool of communication; it speaks volumes of both speaker and receiver as it can change thoughts, views and action. Therefore, language is a very powerful, but subjective tool of communication.

So much is riding on our understanding of language and our ability to think and use it accurately. The goal of the communicator, in this case the public speaker, is to understand the language of his/her audience and to cleverly use such to present information and argumentation that will inform and persuade the audience as well as enhance the speaker's credibility. The rest of this chapter is devoted to some relevant aspects of language that will aid us in our attempt to communicate effectively with others.

> *Language is a set of symbols that a cultural group has agreed to use to create meaning. The symbols and their meanings are often arbitrary.
> *Language allows people to express and exchange ideas and thoughts with others.
>
> ...*Samovar, Porter, McDaniel & Roy*

Verbal Language

Language is a distinguishing factor between higher-order and lower-order animals. Humans, as far as we know, are the only ones capable of abstracting words from reality for the purpose of sharing meaning. But how did we develop the ability to invent and use words? Hybels and Weaver (2007) identify three factors that influence how humans acquire language and these are 1) native architecture, 2) cognitive development, and 3) environmental influences.

Native architecture refers to the presence in humans, among others, of the FOXP2 gene "which enabled the emergence of behaviorally modern humans (those with ability to use language) somewhere between 120,000 and 200,000 years ago." The FOXP2 gene creates in humans inborn language transmission and acquisition devices that aid in the structure of and development of language.

The schemas of the brain allow for storing and organizing of information that aid thinking. **The cognitive system** organizes and labels language, imagery, reasoning, problem solving, and memory development, among others. The process of creating pathways to store information in the brain is said to develop well before birth. This idea may support the claim of Piaget (1962) that child language is initially egocentric, because the primitive ability to coordinate thought and thinking is yet to be fully influenced by socialization, yet the ability to speak or communicate is present. The child's instinctive ability to communicate through language initially manifests as primordial sharing, but with interaction and the passage of time the speech becomes socialized- conscious adaptation of communication through language to another.

As the child encounters events, people, and myriads of experiences in his/her environment, new experiences/images that need labeling are stored in the brain. These **environmental influences** become language content or 'language-acquisition support system.'

In order to better understand the verbal message, let us clarify the different forms of language or symbols. As discussed earlier, there are two kinds of symbols: verbal and nonverbal and these can be subdivided into two further categories of vocal and nonvocal. So in human communication, we can identify four types of messages: **verbal vocal** messages, **verbal nonvocal** messages, **nonverbal vocal** and **nonverbal nonvocal** messages. See table 3.1 below.

Verbal simply means with words and if it is vocal, then it includes sound. This is the spoken language or speech. Verbal nonvocal of course has to do with words, but without sound production. This is the written word or writing. Nonverbal suggests without words. As we now know we can communicate without using words at all and, as a matter of fact, much of human communication is nonverbal. That is, when one compares the share volume of verbal vis-à-vis nonverbal forms of communication, the evidence points to predominance of nonverbal symbols (See the next section for more details). When we share nonverbal vocal messages, we share sounds such as groans, laughter, cries, and other vocalizations to convey meaning, but nonverbal nonvocal messages include gestures, facial expressions, eye movements, posture, appearance, distance or space, etc.

Table 3-1/Types of Communication

TYPES OF COMMUNICATION	VOCAL COMMUNICATION	NONVOCAL COMMUNICATION
VERBAL COMMUNICATION	Spoken words	Written words
NONVERBAL COMMUNICATION	Tone of voice, sighs, screams, voice qualities (loudness, pitch, etc.	Gestures, movement, appearance, facial expressions, etc.

Source: John Stewart and Gary D'Angelo (1980) *Together: Communicating Interpersonally (2nd ed.)*. Reading, MA: Addison-Wesley.

The focus here is translating language into speech, which is the vocal form of language. Let us examine the elements and dimensions of language as they affect human communication.

The Elements of Language

Language elements include sound, words, grammar, and meaning. These essentially constitute rules that govern the use of language. How words should sound, what they mean, how they are to be strung together, and how to properly use them in social settings constitute the rules of language. Here we are going to examine each of these rules.

Phonological Rules

As its name suggests, phonics has to do with sounds. These are the sounds we make that depict and distinguish the words we speak. The ability to produce sounds does not lead to the ability to communicate effectively through speech; therefore, we invent rules that guide how sounds are combined to form words. The rules of pronunciations allow for effective coding and presentation of words so that we may infer the desired meaning from the words spoken. But people sound differently even when they speak the same language. Geographic region, culture and other factors influence speech patterns of people, thus producing dialects.

Syntactic Rules

Formed from the word syntax which means structure, syntactic rules of language have to do with the order of words and phrases to convey meaning. It determines the shift in meaning when punctuation marks are used at different places in sentences, and it organizes language into parts of speech. This is, essentially, the rule of grammar. The rule of grammar as it pertains to the English language identifies the combination of subject and predicate to form a sentence; it orders the conjugation of verbs; and it recognizes past, present, future, and continuous events. Adherence to both phonological and syntactic rules of language facilitates our understanding of one another in the realm of symbolic exchange.

Semantic Rules

You have heard the expression: "it's all semantics!" This is probably when someone is trying to use different words to represent what meaning is being conveyed. **Semantics has to do with the meanings of words**. Do words really have meaning? The answer is no. Words are symbols that represent events, objects, concepts, contexts and ideas. The word is not the 'thing,' but the referent for which it represents. It's humans who assign meanings to words and we do so arbitrarily. There is no rhyme or reason to the process of assigning meanings to words.

"The word you choose to call something is initially arbitrary, an invention, but once that designation has been made, there must be common agreement (Conventionality) to use the word for that referent with some consistency" (Rothwell, 2000). For communication to take place there must be agreement of meaning as to what a word represents. It is a fallacy to think that words contain meaning; however, the meanings that words represent are twofold: **connotative and denotative.**

Denotation

What a word denotes is the objective meaning of the word, the primary, descriptive meaning that can be found in the dictionary. It is the surface meaning of the word without any user association. It is "the primary association that a word may have for most members of a linguistic community." That is when denotative meanings are used, they are readily understood. But people do not usually use words in this sense; much of word usage is private- having private meaning. The words we use represent our feelings and associations and thus we attach connotative meanings to them.

If you study a foreign language by learning the meaning of the words from the dictionary, the interpretations of the words as you understand denotatively would definitely not equate that of the native speakers whose conversational level of the language would be much deeper than the foreign learner. When I first came to America in the mid eighties, I found it hard to understand the colloquialisms of Americans and surely they found it rather difficult to understand my textbook usage of English words in conversations. My education in Nigeria included studying the grammatical forms of the English language as well as mastering English idiomatic expressions and memorizing 'big' words. To my chagrin, my American colleagues could hardly understand me!

Connotation

What a word denotes is not what it usually connotes. This is the conflict of private and public meanings. Connotation is the secondary, private, personal, emotional and subjective meanings of words. It is the "secondary association that a word has for one or more members of a linguistic community." Seiler and Beal (2008) describe it this way: The connotative meaning is based on the context in which the word is used, how the meaning is expressed nonverbally (tone of voice, facial expression, of the speaker, and so on), and the understanding of the person who is receiving it."

The personal experience of the speaker and the receiver influences the meanings they assign to symbols. For example the word *boy* does not connote the same meaning to an American couple who does not have a preference for the gender of its child, than a Chinese couple who prefers to have a male child and who, by law, is not allowed to have more than one child. What about a young man who describes his newly rented apartment in Manhattan, New York as large and roomy to a friend who lives in Plano, Texas? Certainly, large in New York is not the same as large in Plano.

Word connotations could be positive or negative depending on the experience that informs the association a hearer has for the word. Connotations can incite emotions either positively or negatively. How would you feel if someone calls you fat, ugly and old? The meanings you'll associate with these words depend on how you perceive yourself and in turn perceive the sender. Words invoke personal meanings in the hearers and such meanings may not represent the meanings of the sender.

Pragmatic Rules

This is really a set of rules guiding the appropriate use and interpretation of language within certain socio-cultural contexts. It is using language and its interpretation to negotiate the social terrain in which the users must traverse and achieve practical goals of which survival is the most fundamental. A speech may be correct grammatically and may appropriate meaning effectively, yet it may fail the test of pragmatism in that it may offend and it may be disrespectful depending on who is doing the interpreting. A children's rhyme goes thus: "Please say please and don't forget to say thank you…" The etiquette inherent in this poem captures the need for this rule of behavior.

There are pragmatic ways a speech can be adapted to its receivers for maximum effect. Also, the sophisticated receiver evaluates messages, mindful of its context. Awareness of context and sensitivity to the nature of the communicators are necessary to avoiding pragmatic blunders in social exchanges or the "coordinated management of meaning."

Uses of Language

Verderber and Verderber (2008) identify four purposes that all languages serve. Regardless of the variations in words, grammar and syntax systems used in different linguistic communities, the languages of humans serve four basic purposes.

1. **We use language to designate, label, define, and limit**.

   So, when we identify music as "techno," we are differentiating it from other music labeled rap, punk, pop, goth, or grunge.

2. **We use language to evaluate**.

   Through language we convey positive or negative attitudes toward our subject. For instance, if you see Hal taking more time than others to make a decision, you could describe Hal positively as "thoughtful" or negatively as "dawdling." Kenneth Burke, a prominent language theorist, describes this as the power of language to emphasize hierarchy and control (1968). Because language allows us to compare things, we tend to judge those things as better or worse, which leads to social hierarchy or a pecking order.

3. **We use language to discuss things outside our immediate experience**.

   Language enables us to talk about ourselves, discuss things outside our immediate experience, speak hypothetically, talk about past and future events, and communicate about people and things that are not present. Through language, we can discuss where we hope to be in five years, analyze a conversation two acquaintances had last week, or learn about the history that shapes the world we live in. Language enables us to learn from others' experiences, to share a common heritage, and to develop a shared vision for the future.

4. **We can use language to talk about language**.

We can use language to discuss how someone phrased a statement and whether different wording would have had a better outcome or a more positive response. Think of the power of language when we can communicate about how we are communicating [Meta communication]. For instance, if your friend said she would see you "this afternoon," but she didn't arrive until 5 o'clock, and you ask her where she's been, the two of you are likely to discuss your communication and the different interpretations you each bring to the words "this afternoon."

Forms of Language

Language takes different forms depending on a number of factors; it may be a mixture of two tongues, one dominant and the other less dominant; it may be a variation of a particular dominant language; or it may be an official language.

Jargon/Argot

These are specialized and/or technical terms whose meanings are easily understood by those initiated into the professions and academic disciplines that use them. The use of these terms to communicate with those who are not initiated into such professions and academic disciplines will result in misunderstanding. Why? This is because such words would constitute 'noise' to the receivers. As you know now, the word 'noise' has specialized meaning to students and scholars of communication, thus it is a communication jargon. 'Myocardial Infarction' is a term used by those in the medical profession to describe a heart attack and the word 'arson' does not represent an ordinary fire, it is a legal term suggesting a fire deliberately set by a person, which is a crime.

Use jargons sparingly in your speeches to a general audience. If they must need a specialized dictionary to interpret your message, then your message to them will be lost. Always ask yourself these questions when choosing words for your speech: Do I really understand the meaning of these words? Will my audience understand the meanings of the words? Will using these words help achieve the purpose of my speech?

Slang

This is a form of informal language designed to create a parallel linguistic community within a larger one for the purpose of hiding the meanings, interpretations of words, and their usage from outsiders. Informal vocabularies are created to confer status on the users and to create social identity. Thus, slang creates a society of 'insiders' and 'outsiders' at the same time. According to Verderber and Verderber (2008), "the simultaneous inclusion of some and exclusion of others is what makes slang popular with you and marginalized people in all cultures."

A trend that demonstrates this exclusion can be found in Computer Mediated Communication. In the virtual world of 'texting', e-mailing and the like, a new lingo is developing, creating a digitalized speech community that is different from the traditional. Not only are new words being created, words are spelled phonetically now in 'texting,' just as new abbreviations of words are surfacing. The advice here is that when using slang, make sure your audience understands and uses such slang; it will be inappropriate to speak slang to a group of people who does not have an understanding of the words being used. You cannot communicate effectively with an audience when your language, which is your vehicle of sharing meaning, is not understood by them.

Pidgin

When two languages are combined for ease of communication, the resultant form of language is called pidgin. This is a mixture of a dominant language, usually that of a colonizing country and a local language of the colonized. Throughout Anglophone West Africa the English pidgin is spoken as a convenient language that mixes the local language with the language of the British Empire. In Haiti, the local language is combined with the French language to form the Haitian pidgin that is popularly referred to as Creole. Joseph (2010) further explains that ... as far as the Haitian Creole, it was originally a pidgin, but it has become nativized- claimed as a community's first language.

Creole

This is pidgin (mixed languages) that has been spoken by a linguistic community over a long period of time. Therefore Creole is a permanent pidgin.

Lingua Franca

An official language of a region adopted to facilitate commerce, educational instructions and ease of governance. The official language of many African countries is English because of the difficulty and politics of choosing one of the local languages as an official language. In addition, English is the second most widely spoken language in the world and perhaps the most dominant. The status of English in the world as the language of commerce, and science and technology has prompted many national education systems to encourage the teaching and speaking of English by their nationals.

There are two hundred and fifty identifiable languages and linguistic communities in Nigeria, a country that is a little bigger than the State of Texas in the United States. The use of English as the official language of the country speaks to the conflict inherent in choosing one of the languages of the different rival groups as the national language. For many Nigerians, English is the primary language while their local tongue becomes their secondary language.

Dialect

In any linguistic community, there exist many sub- linguistic enclaves as a result of geography or a unifying common experience. The evidence of such subsets of a linguistic community is the variations observable in the language the people speak. These within language variations result in dialects. "A dialect is the habitual language of a community. It is distinguished by unique grammatical structures, words, and figures of speech," (Hybels and Weaver, 2007). Diverse cultural backgrounds, education levels and social class are identifiers of community members who speak dialects.

When should you use dialects? When you are speaking to people who speak the same variation of grammar, words and figures of speech, it is appropriate to use your dialect because there is linguistic agreement or convergence. The more similar the communicators, the easier the process of understanding and such will engender effective communication. However, it may be inappropriate to use your dialect when speaking to a diverse audience of people, many of whom may not understand your language usage. If your dialect is perceived by many to be more acceptable, when you do speak it, you have to be mindful of the limitations of understanding this may impose on your audience. Adaptation is the key to better understanding and communication whenever possible.

Those who speak different codes, either as a variation of a particular language or as an entirely different language, should be mindful of the advantages and disadvantages of **Code-switching**. This is changing from one form of a language to another or from one language to a different one in everyday speech. The sophisticated speaker should be able to switch his or her codes whenever the need arises. In that social setting where slang is widely spoken and understood, there is no problem engaging others in the choice of language form. But in a formal setting where a more formal language is expected, the ability to switch codes is imperative- that is the mark of a sophisticated and competent communicator.

Message Encoding: Language and Thought

The language one speaks is so intricately intertwined with one's thought processes that one may wonder what the relationship between the two may be. Encoding is described as putting information in the mind into a send-able form. So if language, which itself is a code, is internal and speech becomes a means of bringing it out, is the thought process constrained or influenced one way or the other by the language one speaks?

If you want to greet someone, you have a number of choices. One, you may say hello or hi, or you may wave at the person or simply nod your head. All these are encoding choices. You have thought of what message you wanted to send and you have encoded it in a way you deemed appropriate at that time. But are your choices confined by the limited array of the verbal and nonverbal codes available to you? Again, if you have never experienced something, can you have words to describe that experience? Do our physical and cultural environments impose on our language development? Can we really think outside of the language we speak? These are plausible questions that we must attempt to answer about the relationship of thought to language.

FIGURE 3.1/Examples of Dialects in the U.S.A.

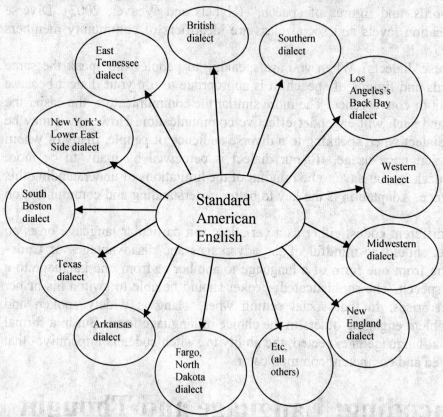

Source: Saundra, Hybels and Richard L. Weaver (2007). *Communicating Effectively (8th ed.).* Boston: McGraw Hill.

The Sapir-Whorf Hypothesis

One idea that has generated much debate about the nature of language and its relationship to thought is the Sapir-Whorf hypothesis. Developed by Edwin Sapir and popularized by his student Benjamin Whorf, the hypothesis posits that language influences our thought processes to the extent that we are captive to the language we speak and that communities of different cultures and languages do perceive the world differently and, it is the language spoken that perpetuates such perceptions. The conclusions are twofold: one, that language determines thought and the other, that language influences thought. This is referred to as the strong and weak determinism or linguistic determinism and relativism respectively. The deterministic perspective has drawn so much criticism and has been deemed rather controversial.

According to the Sapir-Whorf hypothesis, the world is perceived differently by members of communities and that this

According to Whorf (1956), our perception of reality is determined by our thought processes and our thought processes are influenced by our language and, therefore, the language we speak shapes our reality.

perception is transmitted and sustained by language (See Tubbs and Moss, 2000).

That cultural tenets and practices are different cannot be argued and that language is ultimately a product of culture is not controvertible. If we accept the fact that language is the primary vehicle of culture, then we tacitly agree that the language a cultural community speaks plays a role in creating such differences; therefore, we can conclude that the language we speak represents our reality and it perpetuates that reality.

Tubbs and Moss write that:

"Whorf supported this theory with findings from studies of Native American languages. In English, he points out, we tend to classify words as nouns or verbs; in Hopi words tend to be classified by duration. For example, in Hopi "lightning," "flame," "wave," and "spark" are verbs not nouns; they are classified as events of brief durations. In Nootka, which is spoken by the inhabitants of Vancouver Island, categories such as things and events do not exist; thus it is said that "A house occurs" or "It houses."

Rothwell (2000) argues that the differences in grammatical structures of human languages reflect differences in cultures and they do not prove that such differences in language cause differences in thought, perception, and behavior. Also cultures differ in the array of words they have in their respective languages to describe objects and events, and he summarizes a number of examples thus:

The Massai of Africa, for example, have 17 terms for cattle. The Hanunoo of the Philippines distinguish 92 kinds of rice. Trobriand Islanders have dozens of terms for yams. Italians have more than 500 terms for different types of pasta. Arabic has more than 6,000 words for what most of us think is simply your basic ill-tempered camel, its parts, and equipment, and American English has an extensive color vocabulary for house paint.

Rothwell further argues that "these are interesting differences in languages, but an elaborate vocabulary for an object merely reflects the degree of importance given to this object by the culture." But it is agreed that availability of words in a cultural lexicon can serve as an aid to recognizing events, objects and ideas that may not be readily available to other speakers; and more importantly the availability of words would serve as aid to memory. The question does arise as to whether we can retrieve a reality that has not been experienced and codified and stored in the language memory.

The importance of examining the relationship of thought to language is rested in the truths about the relationship. Though strong determinism may be difficult to prove, there is validity in the relativism perspective to say the least. Language influences thoughts and perception because it **defines** and it **frames.** We use language to define self, others, events, relationships, and feelings. The perception of self is largely derived from others and the vehicle for such definition is language. When in the U.S. one is described as an "Alien," that separates and reduces, it affects the way the labeled views him or herself. Being a naturalized American myself, I chuckle at the use of the words "Legal Alien" to describe me. I always respond jokingly that I must be a native of the planet Mars originally! The use of the term not only affects me in particular ways and it does so

Consider these statements…

Change your language and change your thought
-------*Karl Albrecht*

The limits of my language mean the limits of my world
-------*Ludwig Wittgenstein*

Language is the roadmap of a culture. It tells you where its people came from and where they are going
------*Rita Mae Brown*

because of my estimation of the mindset of someone who chooses to label me as such. What happens when the news describes an accident as involving two adult males one, an African American and the other a White man? What happened to European American? Prejudices are feelings and thoughts stored in our linguistic memories and such thoughts manifest as speech.

Framing occurs when we use language to influence meanings for others. When you ask two kids who are fighting to describe what led to the fight, each would frame or punctuate the antecedent events differently. This is framing- imposing a perspective or mindset on our communication. This is of great practical value to the public speaker who must frame his or her speech in particular ways to influence the audience one way or another.

Another lesson from the foregoing is that **self-talk,** the messages going on in our heads, framing and defining our personal experiences, have an influence on our perceptions and actions, to the extent that negative and positive self–talk influence our feelings and perception of self accordingly. As quoted in Tubbs and Moss, Whiteman et al. puts this succinctly: "The difference between a really good day and a really awful day is not in what happened but in what you tell yourself about that day." (Please see **self-fulfilling prophecies.)**

Verbal Communication Styles

The notion that culture influences language use and influences the perceptions of such users is affirmed by scientific findings supporting the mild version of the Sapir-Whorf Hypothesis. It is important then to examine different cultures and their impacts on the communication styles and structures of their members.

There exist different cultural contexts and such contexts impose acceptable patterns and styles of communication on their members; especially, such contexts regulate the act of speaking itself. Some people use **restricted codes** while others use **elaborated codes**. In other words some cultures communicate in great detail, elaborating and pontificating with words, while others say little and express themselves in greater detail using nonverbal codes and depend on the context of communication to supply inherent meanings. Klopf and McCroskey (2007), expanding on the work of Basil Bernstein on restricted and unrestricted codes, write that "elaborated codes make use of accurate and sophisticated grammatical structures. It employs a large range of adjectives and adverbs in a relatively large vocabulary. [The context] involves no shared assumptions between speakers and listeners, taking little for granted." Essentially the speakers of elaborated codes are explicit and depend less on the added meaning of context in using verbal language, thus assigning little role to nonverbal communication. On the other hand, restricted codes use short, grammatically simple, and often incomplete sentences usually of poor syntactic structure. Its vocabulary is small with limited use of adverbs and adjectives. Context-bound, it relies on many shared experiences between speakers and listeners and depends heavily upon nonverbal channels to carry its messages" (Klopf and McCroskey, 2007).

Edward Hall (1959) expanded Basil Bernstein code classification to include context. Thus he classified cultures according to the two variations of **Low-context** and **High-context,** essentially an extension of the elaborate and restricted code dichotomy.

People described as belonging to low-context cultures use language primarily to express thoughts, feelings and ideas as clearly and logically as possible. Low-context communicators look for the meaning of a statement in the words that are spoken, (Adler and Towne, 1999). Meanings are hardly dependent on the context; therefore, every meaning must be verbalized and every thought must be codified in verbal form and explicitly expressed for the perception of understanding to occur. In the United States, a low-context culture, people are expected to toot their own horns because no one would do it for them. It is customary, therefore, to expect people to speak up and not doing so, leads to some assumptions about the non-speaker.

People who live in high-context cultures are not given to verbalizing all of their meanings in communication exchanges because the context plays a great role in the determination of such meanings. That is, "much information is drawn from surroundings" and "little must be transferred explicitly." See figure adapted from Klopf and McCroskey (2007).

Writing about the cultural importance of speaking, Klopf and McCroskey contrast Western and Eastern orientations toward speaking. In illustrating the Eastern approach, they quote the fact that "Zen Buddhists maintain that language limits peoples' capability of thinking, thereby curbing imagination and tainting judgment." Also, "they meditate without language and communicate beyond language." This de-emphasizes the use of words as opposed to the tradition of the West which stresses speech. 'The East puts credence in mental unification with the other person to achieve total understanding. Oneness with the other, or total harmony, represents the position of the principal Asian religions, especially Taoism, Buddhism, and Confucianism (Yum, 1998).

The teachings of these Asian religions admonished the followers to speak rarely, and when they do, they should be weary of "fancy words and embellished styles." In essence, these teachings emphasized the virtue of silence over speaking. In the Western world speaking is encouraged; however, the emphasis is on logical, rational and critical thinking when speaking. Such were the foundations laid by Socrates, Plato, and Aristotle.

Gender and Language

The languages of the sexes also vary. Because men and women are socialized differently in society, their language uses follow their socialization routes. In patriarchal societies, where men are dominant, there is discernible male domination built into the language and, in contrast, the language of women function to serve the maintenance of such structure. Feminine and masculine languages differ in many ways. The contents of their communication vary; their reasons for communicating vary; their conversational styles vary; and they use nonverbal cues differently.

Surprisingly the contents of male talk and female talk differ. Studies conducted on the variations of male/female conversation topics about 80 years ago and those conducted recently revealed similar findings, report Adler and Towne, (1999). Certain subjects and topics are common to both men and women are work, movies and television. The talk about sex and sexuality is reserved for same sex conversation, rather than cross-sex conversations.

Table 3.2/Where Different Cultures Fall on the Context Scale

HIGHER CONTEXT	Higher-Context Cultures
Asian Arab Southern European South American African	(Much information is drawn from surroundings. Little must be transferred explicitly) • favor nonverbal communication • Relate information freely • Use physical context for information • Take into account environment, situation, gestures and mood • Maintain extensive information networks • Are accustomed to interruptions
LOWER CONTEXT	Lower-Context Cultures
Northern European Australian North American Scandinavian German Swiss	(Information must be provided explicitly, usually verbally) • Are less aware of nonverbal cues, environment, and situation • Lack well-developed networks • Need detailed background information • Tend to segment and compartmentalize information • Control information on a "need-to-know" basis • Prefer explicit and careful directions from someone who "knows"

Source: Klopf, Donald and James C. McCroskey (2007). *Intercultural communication encounters*. Boston: Allyn and Bacon.

Adler and Towne (p. 193) identified the dissimilarities between men and women clearly: "The differences between men and women were more striking than the similarities. Female friends spent much more time discussing personal and domestic subjects, relationship problems, family, health and reproductive matters, weight, food and clothing, men and other women. Men, on the other hand, were more likely to discuss music, current events, sports, business and other men."

Both men and women gossip, but they gossip on different topics. While men would talk about sports figures and media personalities, women would talk about close friends and family.

The purposes for communication also are different. Men are reported to **like** talking, but women reported **needing** to talk. The difference is that talk is something central to the existence of women in relationships and according to Julia Woods, talk is the essence of relationships. In a relationship, therefore, women are more likely to request a need to talk to affirm the relationship and to confirm their place in it. The need to maintain relationships positions women to be socially oriented toward needing to talk. Men's reasons for communicating are not the same. Men are more oriented toward achieving specific goals and accomplishing tasks through language rather than to nourish relationships.

Women, more than men, are reported to use **powerless language**; whereas men use more **powerful language** than women. A powerful speech is considered effective and powerful because it contains limited errors. The factors that may render a speech powerless are negative speech mannerisms of interjecting a speech with **hesitations** ("you know" "uh," "em," "well") and the language forms of **Hedges** ("kinda," "I think"), **tag questions** ("Let's go, ok?), **disclaimers** ("do not say I told you"). Others are **intensifiers and polite forms of language.** The removal or minimal occurrences of all these in a speech will make people perceive the speaker and speech as powerful and effective. Tubbs and Moss, in reporting the research of Bradac and Mulac (1981), which analyzed seven message types of differing power, report the finding thus: "in general, communicators who use a powerful style are considered more competent and attractive. Legal situations are different, however; plaintiffs and defendants using more powerful style are also considered more blameworthy, perhaps because they seem "in control' of themselves. Less powerful speakers are more often seen as victims."

Feminine styles of language typically use words of empathy and support; emphasize concrete and personal language, and show politeness and tentativeness in speaking. Masculine styles of language often use words of status and problem solving, emphasize abstract and general language, and show assertiveness and control in speaking, (Woods, 2007). In the same vein, Deborah Tannen, a sociolinguist confirmed the differences in the communication styles of men and women. Tannen (1990) refers to women conversational language as **rapport- talk** while that of men is **report- talk**. Women use language to build rapport and maintain relationship through language use, but men on the other hand use language to express their expertise and to announce their knowledge, status, and to maintain control. Also, women tend to use language to empathize and identify with feelings of another person, but men would rather use language to solve and fix problems. In terms of public verbalization, women would rather not get involved in public verbal conflicts or boisterous speech, but that is the purview of men. All these are as a result of socialization and the perpetuation of such by language and culture.

The Language of Responsibility

Table 3.3/Pronoun Use and its Effects

	Advantages	Disadvantages	Tips
"I" language	Takes responsibility for personal thoughts, feelings, and wants. Less defense-provoking than "you' language.	Can be perceived as egotistical, narcissistic, and self-absorbed.	Use "I" messages when other person doesn't perceive a problem. Combine "" with "we" language
"We" language	Signals inclusion, immediacy, cohesiveness, and commitment.	Can speak improperly for others.	Combine with "I" language. Use in group settings to enhance unity. Avoid when expressing personal thoughts, feelings, and wants.
"You" Language		Can sound evaluative and judgmental	Use "I" language during confrontations.

Source: Adler, Ronald B. and Neil Towne, *Looking Out Looking In.* (2002) p.205. Orlando : Harcourt College Publishers

Language Problems

Language is a means of communication, an instrument of thought and meaning; however, there are inherent problems attending the use of language. Thus language can be thought of as bridge- bringing people together and enabling them to share meaning and to socially construct their realities. But it can also be a barrier- creating misunderstanding and confusing the process of sharing meaning, further creating a gulf among the users, negating its primary purpose.

The following are some of the problems besetting language use and the ways such problems can be reduced to a manageable level. These problems revolve around what you want to say, how you want to say it, to whom you want to say it, and what other messages are being sent in addition to your original message.

Abstract Language

As we have identified, language is an abstraction from reality; it is a creation used to represent ideas, objects, and thoughts in our consciousness. However there are two classes of words- abstract and concrete. **Abstract words** are words representing ideas, qualities, and relationships. "Because they represent things that cannot be experienced through the senses, their meanings depend on the experiences and intentions of the persons using them," (Seiler and Beal, 2008). At best the meanings of abstract words are vague, therefore subject to different interpretations by their receivers.

Let's consider some vague words and the different interpretations they may provoke because of their lack of specificity. When someone describes something or a situation as **perfect,** many different meanings are inferred. Perfect, in what sense? What does perfection mean in that context and how might the receiver perceive the state of perfection as intentioned by the sender? Consider the statement: the boy is **good**. What does the word good mean? Do the communicators have a common interpretation for the word? What is the boy good at or is he just good generally speaking? Words such as **freedom, justice, beautiful, and the like convey** different meanings to their users. Obviously the use of abstract words can confuse and lead communicators to misunderstand the meanings of their verbal messages. So, abstract words may constitute noise in the communication process and to minimize such noise, communicators are encouraged to use more concrete words.

According to Seiler and Beal (2008), **concrete words** "are symbols for specific things that can be pointed to or physically experienced (seen, tasted, smelled, heard, or touched)." These words represent tangible things, thus having multiple interpretations of what they stand for is greatly reduced as their users are quite clear of what they stand for. Because of their specificity, concrete words may not lead to the misunderstanding that comes with vagueness of meaning. Examples of concrete words are **child, desk, moon, cell phone,** and **shirt**. These words can be made even more specific. This is my only child, or my desk at work is brown in color, are more specific statements. When these concrete words are used metaphorically, that is, used to compare unlike terms, or when they are used in idiomatic expressions, their meanings become even more complicated. Consider these statements: He is more than willing to give the **shirt** off his back or the old man is a **child**.

Figure 3.4/The Ladder of Abstraction

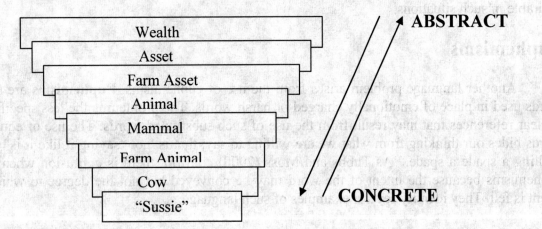

In this figure S. I. Hayakawa's (1964) ladder of abstraction illustrates opposite poles of concrete and abstract words. As one climbs the ladder, each rung of the ladder presents the same idea or thing in a more abstract and less specific manner until the last rung of the ladder that gives the most abstract, often confusing word to represent the same thing that the concrete word represents. For example, in the ladder of abstraction shown in figure (3.4) the most concrete reference to a cow is a particular horse named "Susie." And when she is referred to as "Asset" or "Wealth," these descriptions are far removed from the real thing that the reference is not understood. Wealth or asset can refer to almost anything of value or economic importance as such, the reference is very vague or abstract.

Equivocal Language

Sometimes we use words or make statements that are subject to more than one interpretation. The problem lies in not understanding which meaning the sender wishes to convey and which is the meaning interpreted by the receiver. Adler and Towne (2000) identified some amusing newspaper headlines that are equivocal:

Family Catches Fire Just In Time

Man Stuck On Toilet; Stool Suspected

20-Year Relationship Ends at the Altar

Trees Can Break Wind

The ambiguities in these statements are rather clear to the reader who would be surprised as to what they really mean.
Equivocal language is very common in our everyday conversations, but we can reduce the misunderstanding that comes with its use by being aware of the receiver's feedback and for the receiver, by asking for clarification from the sender. The general idea of perception checking becomes relevant in every communication situation where ambiguity of meaning is perceived. The assumption here is that clarity of meaning should be the goal of communication. However, sometimes the goal is to manage impression and to save face. Ambiguity of meaning becomes desirable in such situations.

Euphemisms

Another language problem arises from the use of euphemisms. **Euphemisms** are milder words used in place of emotionally charged or harsh words. The problem is the less specific and unclear references that may result from the use of such substituted words. The use of equivocal words hides our thinking from what we are willing to say; that is, not "saying it like it is" or not "calling a spade a spade." As Tubbs and Moss (2000) confirm, there is confusion when using euphemisms because the intent of the word may be conveyed but not the degree to which the intent is felt. They identify several examples of such language:

"Campaign of disinformation" is substituted for "Smear Campaign."
"Security review procedure" for "censorship."
"Discomfort" for "pain."

> "Memory garden" for "cemetery."
> "Powder room" for "bathroom."
> "Attack" for "rape."
> "Portly", "stout" and "heavy set," for "fat."

In the attempt to be nice and not to offend, we often forego clarity and specificity for obtuse language. Well, honest descriptions of persons and events may not be easier to handle than the misunderstanding that may come from using less specific words. In other words, there is a place and purpose for euphemistic language in our communication because we are not only logical, but emotional beings as well. The users of less blunt or less offensive words and phrases must be aware of the possible misinterpretation that may result from such usage. The users must also be aware that such words or phrases may obscure, distort meaning or even misrepresent it totally, thus bordering on lying.

Doublespeak

Sometimes language is used to deliberately mislead the receivers. The deception comes from the intentional use of words that give ambiguous meaning in order to confuse the receiver or to cloak the portrayal of situations and ideas the speakers determine may not be well received. This is language used by lawyers, government officials, advertisers and the like to deceive the reading public. According to Luntz (1987) doublespeak is language "designed to distort reality and corrupt thought." This he believes is very harmful because it makes something inappropriate or negative to appear to be appropriate or positive. Examples of doublespeak abound in government reports, newspapers and legal documents. How would you interpret the meanings of these words and phrases? "Structural adjustment," "revenue enhancement," "inordinate ordinance," "collateral damage," "de-hired," "involuntary conversion."

How do we avoid doublespeak? Just don't use it. To the unsophisticated listener, it leads to confusion, and to the sophisticated listener, it leads to suspicion. In essence, doublespeak constitutes noise in communication and, in most cases, our communication with others is improved when we reduce noise to its barest minimum. By a stretch of it, we can consider the deliberate misuse of words as unethical because the intent is deceitful manipulation.

Inferences/Facts Confusion

As language is symbolic, we are able to define and evaluate situations symbolically. That is, we can talk about events that we have not witnessed, we can reflect on ideas that are not concrete and make pronouncements about their nature, though the experience with such may be indirect. Inferences are conclusions that we claim to be true though we may not have the bare facts and evidence to back them up. Because they result from the interpretation of evidence and assumptions, we often confuse inferences with facts. Adler and Towne (2000), claim that arguments often result when we label our inferences as facts. For example, examine the following discussion they used to illustrate their claim:

A: Why are you mad at me?
B: I'm not mad at you. Why have you been so insecure lately?
A: I'm not insecure. It's just that you've been so critical.

B: What do you mean, "critical" I haven't been critical….?

Observed behaviors can be described as factual because there is observable evidence about that behavior, but the interpretation of that behavior becomes inferential. This is a reaction to the observed behavior and the interpretation may not be borne out by the facts. Let's imagine that I am thinking about something that I have to do in a short while and I wear a pensive look on my face. If you describe my look as focused, direct and blank, that would be correct. But if you conclude that I must be sad, disturbed, and or mad, then that would not be correct. As the above conversation goes, we can see how common this occurs in our communication.

How do we reduce fact/inference confusion in our communication? Well, let us consider the process of perception checking. Whenever you observe a behavior, the first step in ensuring accuracy of your observation is to describe what you observed. Secondly, if you have the open mind to accept that there are different interpretations possible for our behaviors, then you must be willing to entertain at least two possible interpretations of the observed behavior. Thirdly, what better way to clarify your perceptions than to verify your information from the perceived? Always be willing to ask for clarification whenever possible. This will minimize the misunderstandings that fact /inference confusion may bring in our interactions with others.

Dichotomies/Polarization

Dichotomy or polar are opposite values and as applied to language, suggests having two extreme and opposing meanings. The extreme or opposite meanings of words and phrases introduce yet another dimension of problems to our language use. We often use the 'either, or' descriptors to depict people. That is, if A is not one way, then he must be the other. The preclusion of the middle point or variations of values in-between bi-polar words does not allow for adequate or precise reference in describing and symbolizing intended meaning.

Semanticists who are concerned with how meanings are portrayed through words believe that some languages are "two-valued," while others are "multi-valued." The English language is believed to be a "two-valued" language because of the preponderance of bi-polar words or adjectives and the lack of adequate words to describe the in-between meanings of such bi-polar words and phrases.

The Scale of Dichotomies by Blake and Mouton (1970), attempts to create shades of meaning and descriptors for the meanings between sets of bi-polar adjectives. In the same vein the Semantic Differential Scale of Charles Osgood is designed to identify the connotative shades of meaning between sets of bi-polar words. The reactions of people to words can be measured and a scale of connotative precision can be developed.

The two scales identified seven shades of meanings in-between a set of bi-polar adjectives, that otherwise would have been ignored. A continuum of meaning is developed to capture the possible variations that people have in their minds, but for which there are no words to describe. So, the inadequacy of the English language to provide for words and phrases and for categorizing experiences as mutually exclusive has prompted a need for a scale of dichotomies.

Figure 3.5 /Scale of Dichotomies

			X					
Success	------	------	------	------	------	------	------	Failure
Brilliant	------	------	------	X ------	------	------	------	Stupid
Handsome	------	------	X ------	------	------	------	------	Ugly
Winner	------	------	------	------	X ------	------	------	Loser
Honest	------	------	------	------	X ------	------	------	Dishonest
Black	------	------	X ------	------	------	------	------	White

Source: Robert Blake and Jane Mouton, "The Fifth Achievement," *Journal of Applied Behavioral Science* 6, 1970, 418. Herbert M. Johnson, Publisher. As contained in Tubbs, Stewart L and Moss, Sylvia (2000), Human Communication (8th ed.) Boston: McGraw Hill.

Figure 3.5 illustrates the problem with bi-polar and dichotomous words. Take for example the placement of each of the Xs. Can you possibly invent words to adequately capture the shades of meanings the Xs represent? Let's look at these pairs of words by asking the following questions:

1. If one is not successful by some relative measure and by the same measure one is not a failure, what might you call that person?
2. If you're neither brilliant nor stupid, what might you call yourself?
3. What do you call a person who is neither a winner nor a loser?
4. Is a person who is not handsome or ugly average? Average is a term mathematically representing the sum of series of scores divided by the number of such scores, that is (n); therefore, it is not a dimension of handsomeness or ugliness.
5. What name is appropriate for a person who is half way on the continuum of honesty and dishonesty?
6. Someone who is between two poles of white and black should be called what?

The difficulty presented by these questions illustrates the dilemma of using a language that is described by scholars as "two-valued." By identifying the placement of their meanings, albeit, connotative on the scale of dichotomies, the user is closer to being precise than otherwise presented by ordinary use of the language without the scale.

Indiscrimination

Often when we use words, we tend to lump categories of things and people together. This lack of discrimination among objects and people confuses the listener, who is led to believe that all of the referenced items and people are the same. This creates a mindset that neglects the differences in personalities, nature and attributes of things, and people, to the extent that individual characteristics are overlooked. Indiscrimination, therefore, is the over emphasizing superficial similarities of objects and people and a de-emphasizing of the unique differences among these objects and people. The end result of indiscrimination is a form of generalization referred to as stereotypes. This is the over amplification of superficial attributes of a group of people, of events, and of things. As we already know, stereotypes can be both positive and negative. So, we can use language indiscriminately to perjure or promote undeservedly. The salient point is that individual qualities are overlooked in this characteristically lazy evaluation and categorization of people, events, and things.

According to Seiler and Beall (2008), "nouns that categorize people (*teenager, divorce, student, professor, African American, southerner, liberal, friend, government official, politician, sales-person)* encourage us to focus on similarities. And statements such as "Politicians are crooks," "All men are dogs" and Students cheat in school," may be interpreted as all politicians, students and men, instead of some politicians, men and students. But there are ways to forestall indiscrimination in our everyday language use.

Indexing and **Dating** help reduce the problem of indiscrimination. Indexing is an identification system that points to the uniqueness and differences in categories of people, events, or things. Through **indexing** we can identify the person, idea, event, or object that a statement refers to. By being specific in referencing the unique individual or event or thing being talked about, indiscriminate lumping is reduced if not totally eliminated. **Dating** is the idea of identifying a time frame within which something occurs. By dating, the time of an event or an observation is factored into the interpretation of meaning in that the time reference becomes a context of meaning. When we sort people, events, and things into time frames, we discriminate along that basis and allows for a clearer understanding of events, things and people with limited generalization.

Sexism and Racism

Another language problem is sexism. Differences between the genders can be emphasized through language and this can place one or the other in an inferior position. When there is a conscious or otherwise use of gender differences in language for the purpose of putting one above of the other or insinuating superiority or inferiority, this is language induced discrimination. Racism in language operates the same way. According to DeVito (2008) racist language expresses racist attitudes. It also contributes to the development of racist attitudes in those who use or hear the language. He claims that racist language emphasizes differences rather than similarities and separates rather than unites members of different cultures.

The point is that racist and sexist language exposes the prejudices of the users toward the recipients and do not bode well for race and gender relations. Seiler and Beal point to a goal of gender-inclusiveness in our language use, but add that the English language is structured with an inherent bias in favor of men. They claim, for example, that there are no singular gender-neutral pronouns in the English language. Therefore, the traditional masculine pronouns (*he, him, and his*) have been used to refer to people in general, both men and women. Again, words with positive connotations are used to describe men, while words with negative connotations are used to describe women. Men are described as *independent, logical, strong, confident, and aggressive.* Females on the other hand are described as *dependent, illogical, weak, gullible, and timid.* Sexist and racist languages emphasize and perpetuate sexism and racism in our society as they reinforce stereotypes and prejudices.

Racist and sexist attitudes influence language just as they influence listening. DeVito (2008) claims that in this type of listening you only hear what the speaker is saying through your stereotypes. This is based on the assumption that whatever the speaker has to say is influenced by his or her sex, race, or affectional orientation regardless of whether this is justified or not.

Using Language Effectively

With many of the language problems identified, we need to look into how to communicate more effectively by trying to avoid the pitfalls inherent in language use. While effective communication requires more than effective use of language, it is by all consideration the major source of misunderstanding in our communication as we have found out in the preceding pages. We all use language differently- women, men, adults, children, people of different educational backgrounds, of different ages and cultures. We also all differ in our ability to use language effectively and efficiently. By identifying the language problems in this chapter, we have begun a step in the direction of effective language use, which usually requires study and years of practice.

Seiler and Beal (2008) identify important variables that influence effectiveness of language use. For language to be effective, it must convey the meaning the user is trying to convey accurately; it must convey it vividly or clearly; it must convey the passion of the sender; and it must be appropriate to the situation and the receiver. The understanding of meaning is aided when comparisons are drawn between what is being said and experiences that the receiver can relate to. Especially the comparison of unlike terms draws attention to the contrasting ideas to the extent that it illuminates the imagination of the users. The final variable being referred to here is metaphor. Let us examine each of these five variables.

Accurate Language

Words in and of themselves do not contain meaning; it is the user who imposes meanings on words. Again, words are representations of things, events, and ideas in our everyday reality. And if we are to communicate effectively with one another, we must choose words that best represent the ideas we are trying to convey. The choice of words brings specific experiences together in the mind of the receiver and if the right words are not chosen, then the right experiences are not brought to focus, thus leading to confusion of meaning, misunderstanding and, oftentimes, conflict. As Seiler and Beall (2008) emphasize: "using accurate language is as critical to a speaker as giving accurate navigational directions is to an air traffic controller."

Using accurate words would ensure that you are precise in your exchange of meaning; it would ascertain that no room is left for misinterpretation and confusion. In order to have access to a variety of words to describe situations and convey meanings accurately, you obviously have to study the dictionary and practice the use of new words. The more your arsenal of words expands, the more readily can you phrase and rephrase your ideas to use the right words to convey the right ideas. But you have to be mindful of your receiver. Using words that are alien to the receiver, even though accurate, will not achieve your goal of effective communication. Again stringing words together to impress may not achieve your purpose of *linguistic convergence* through effective and accurate sharing of meaning.

As public speakers we should not alienate our audience by use of inaccurate or misleading words. Not only should we use accurate words, we should use words that are familiar and have concrete meanings than abstract and esoteric words. When words are subject to more than one interpretation, your duty is to clear it up by rephrasing and identifying your meaning. Punctuation marks should also be used accurately because a wrong coma here and a misplaced period there can convey a different message than the one intended. Just as when we speak, wrong emphasis on the wrong word, may convey unintended messages. There is a world of difference between *Therapist and The rapist*!

Vivid Language

Language that excites the imagination of the hearers will make them pay more attention and process the information received. Vividness has to do with "active, direct, and fresh language that brings a sense of excitement, urgency and forcefulness to a message." Such language extends more than one of the hearer's senses. Vivid language is not abstract, it is concrete and active; that is, it points to action or what is happening now in an interesting manner. And according to Hybels and Weaver (2007), "Vividness is the aspect or characteristic of style by which a thought is so presented that it evokes lifelike imagery or suggestion,"

Good radio writing is described as vivid writing and this is because though there is no opportunity to show through radio, descriptive writing compensates by being direct, imaginative, active, and fresh. It is not enough to say that it is hot out there today; it is much better to capture the effect of the sun on people-that is the reason for giving the weather report. So*, it is agonizingly hot out there as the sun is biting hard on people's skin.* This brings out the impact of the sun on those under its power and this would be "felt harder" than the plain statement about being hot today. Stories are often remembered because they usually capture the mood of the moment, the description of the setting, and the movements and intentions of the characters. Plain language can be likened to an action movie without sounds. There is no hearing of the crashes, the booms, and the bangs, and all of the razzmatazz- the essence of the screen play.

Trite expressions or clichés do not excite because they are overused, so, avoid using them. As persuasive speakers, you run the risk of not being persuasive with your audience if you do not develop the habit of using active and vivid words. This is because communication scholars have found that vivid language influences people to listen more attentively and to retain information more.

Immediate Language

When we speak, we project our dispositions toward the subject matter to the receiver. When we are excited about an issue, our emotions show through our choice of words, the volume of the voice, the tone, and other paralanguage. The same goes for when we are not excited about an issue. If the speaker is not excited about the subject matter, it is hard to get the listeners excited and involved.

Verbal immediacy is a term that captures the feelings and mindset of the speaker as he/she communicates with a receiver and such immediacy captures the imagination of the receiver and causes a feeling of inclusion and relevance. High verbal immediacy level directly connects the speaker to the event and the receiver; there is a sense of belongingness and connectedness between speaker and receiver.

According to Bradac, Bowers, and Courtright, as quoted by Seiler and Beal (2008), verbal immediacy influences the speaker as well as the receiver because it makes the speaker appear relaxed, confident, competent, and effective. The receiver, on the other hand, tends to view messages characterized by immediacy as similar to their own beliefs more readily than those cast in language unrelated to the speaker, topic, or receiver.

Here are some examples of sentences demonstrating levels of immediacy:

1. It is a good thing to have a good friend to depend on.
2. I am happy I have a good friend in you to depend on
3. I am glad you and I have each other to depend on as good friends.

The first statement sounds so distant that it could be said of anyone, connecting with no one in particular. The second statement expresses feelings toward a particular person, "you" and as such is preferred to the first, as it connects with "you." The third statement is most immediate as it connects the speaker and the receiver in the context of their relationship.

Appropriate Language

The rule of pragmatics in communication guides the use of language to navigate social relationships. It is about adaptation to the social contexts in which language is used to appropriate meaning. The social context imposes rules of appropriateness of language use. There are expectations about the choice of words, tone of voice, loudness of voice and general linguistic comportment when we encounter others of different statuses, gender, age, education and the like. As competent communicators, you have to adapt your language to the situation, person and event. For example, you would not address the president of the United States by his first name- Barack! Neither would you refer to your friend in an informal conversation involving the two of you in a private setting as Dr. so and so. It is not expected of you to hurl expletives at your pastor or spiritual leader. Again, in certain formal settings it is not appropriate for you to use slang, idiosyncratic verbiage, and bad grammar.

Breaking the rules of appropriate use of language has consequences. One, you as a speaker runs the risk of losing credibility and believability-- that is if you're not ignored in the first place. Using inappropriate language draws attention to your language and diverts the attention of your listeners. In other words, this constitutes noise in your communication and reduces your effectiveness as a sophisticated and competent communicator.

Metaphorical Language

If there were a means for getting your point across to your receivers in a way that mirrors their experience and creates a vivid picture in their minds that would influence their perceptions in the desired direction, would you not use this and quite often? Metaphors are a form of comparison or analogy that liken something being described to another that may have no semblance or relation, but that can create an understanding by making the object of comparison clear and vivid. So, the goal of using the metaphoric figure of speech is to make something clear and vivid in order to facilitate understanding.

For communication practitioners, ***metaphors are a breath of fresh air***. This example of a metaphor use clearly explains how the writer views metaphors. Fresh air is good and invigorating and so are metaphors in language use. Should The United States be a ***melting pot or a salad bowl***? To anyone within the mainstream culture of the United States, what the question is referring to is quite clear- it is about immigration and the new immigrant assimilating into the American culture or maintaining different cultural identities while still remaining American. This expresses the point that metaphors are products of culture just as languages are; therefore, the meanings of metaphors are culture bound.

Ethics and Language

Language conveys meaning and intentions, but what happens when a speaker deliberately sends the wrong message in order to disguise his or her intention? Since we are not mind readers, the sender owes the receiver some level of decorum and, therefore, should expect the sender to not knowingly mislead for manipulative reasons. The ethical implications of messages speak to their being moral, immoral, truthful, untruthful, just or unjust.

But what are the motivations for deceptive communication? One person may desire to gain some reward over the other by lying. Advertisers that are accused of misleading promotions and outright exaggeration of product and service capabilities are engaged in such deliberate deception for financial gains. Often our ego is in the way of truthful communication, so we lie to protect self and our self esteem. Often liars tell inaccurate stories to avoid punishment; however, some communicators lie to protect a third party- a parent can lie about the behavior of a child to school authorities or a teacher can protect the identity of an unruly student in his or her class for whatever reason. Whatever the motives, lying is considered unethical, but there are situations that may compel an otherwise ethical communicator to lie. Can you think of situations where lying may be justified or even ethical?

The article on the following pages by Professor Nimi Wariboko illustrates how language can be used to demean and assault another human being. The victims are not only the receivers of disrespectful and inhumane speech, but also the ones with vitriolic utterances, who expose their inhumanity and depravity and moral deficiency and, whose mouths are an open cesspool of overflowing rubbish. These people need communication training that would inform them of the impact of their practice and how they can improve and live in harmony one with another.

Language, depending on how it is used, could have either positive or negative effects on the receiver. In this article, Dr. Nimi Wariboko, decries upper class Nigerian's speech assault on their subordinates.

Speech Index and Human Dignity
By Nimi Wariboko

One of the interesting and provocative areas of social ethics is the valuation of human life. What level of dignity does a given community accord to human life? What is the price a society is willing to put on a human life? The calculated monetary value of human life varies across regions of the world. Is the life of an American worth the same value as that of a person in the Global South? The differences in valuation of life within a given society and between societies naturally raise questions of social and historical context of the valuation. There are political, racial, and imperial dimensions of valuation of human lives. Also valuation often intersects with modes of political economy and forms of imperial power. So it is of interest to understand ethics of valuation of human life.

While economists have narrowly focused on the value of life-time income stream or risk compensation to grasp the worth a society places on human life, I have always believed that there are many more ways of finding out the value and respect for human life. I stumbled on one recently. I just came back from a five-week visit to Nigeria and one more indicator became clear to me. Speech, interpersonal communication, is a good index for assessing the value of human life. I observed and listened to many conversations, talks, and interlocutions and I was appalled at the way Nigerians talk to one another.

Relentlessly, Nigerian speech jarred and wracked my sensibilities. Nigerian talk is full of disrespect and inhumane language. No one appeared to trust any form of speech. Nigerians now regard anything that you say as a "419" (The code number for economic or financial fraud in the Nigerian penal code) attempt. Hardly anyone believes what he or she hears. It is not only trust that has been thrown overboard. Politeness has become a casualty. Nigerians scream at one another- the loudness and ferocity of the voice correlating to the social status of the person on the receiving side. We lose our tempers easily. Indeed, I observed that one way people show their status is the ease with which they lose their tempers. Big men and women are quick to take offence at the slightest sign of perceived disrespect.

Political leaders from the top to the bottom generously dole out "shut -up" "stupid", "idiots" to fellow, but poorer, adults. Their language afflicts, enflames, and menaces their listeners. Listen to government officials talking to any citizen and you will be surprised to learn that it is some angry deity addressing some helpless, hapless supplicant groveling in abject dust. Listening to gun-trotting policemen talking to a driver; once they open their mouths and their guns ferociously pointed at a driver, the poor fellow is expected to fall on his face into the dust.

They always appear very angry that the driver did not immediately do so. If this was not their expectation, then I do not know why they always looked so angry. Listen to the bosses, minor or major, talking to their subordinates and you will get the feeling that they are not talking to humans but some creatures below the rank of roaches. They bark, shout, and scream at those below them. There is no civility in giving orders, no decorum in communication, and no appreciation of the humanity in the subordinates in even the simplest speeches. Nigerian big men and women have gone mad, at least a good number of them.

Their speech is violent. It is an unimaginable attack on the humanity and character of those receiving it. Several times, I cringed and became sad as I heard the raw, foul words that they freely flowed out of people's mouths. These were words that eroded, effaced and emptied the humanity in the persons they were directed at and also to anyone within hearing range. Our speech does not add grace to situations. The oppressive, poverty stricken, and corruption-laden economy has so reduced human dignity that everyone is behaving as if human life is worth nothing. Our speech reflects all this and further pollutes our surroundings.

Our daily speech hangs over all of us as a poisonous, virulent, vicious air over the whole country. At all times many mouths are spewing a miasma of toxic words. Morning, afternoon, and evening, tongues are on assassination mission. Often I imagined the words that propelled out of oga's or madam's mouth as violently lifting up people into the mid-air and flinging them down with such force and ferocity that I saw their humanity walking away, crying and weeping. Our language is killing us and we do not know it.

The masses have been so beaten down that they now see the insults emanating from searing speeches of the elites as a necessary appurtenance of survival in a sick society.

Their sick bosses and leaders revel in foul, gruesome speech in a macabre dance of raw power display. One inevitably gets the impression that foul-mouthed big men and women draw some kind of energy from vitriolic attacks on the poor. Wait a minute! It is not only the neglected masses that are afflicted. Even among the elites all politeness has completely broken down.

Someone told me that I would not like to hear how spouses talk to one another in bedroom-moments. Romance has not been able to blunt the edges of violent words even in the softest exchanges of emotions. Violence runs deep in the fabric of all relationships. Indeed, we are living through sick times and the level of violence in our inter-personal communication is only one veritable indicator of the death and decadence that have gripped our country for too long. The use of violent language is not limited to interpersonal communication.

I found the imageries and metaphors used in newspaper articles and columns suggestive of violence. Our prayer language drips with blood and violence; the voices of prayer- warriors thunder across the face of the earth as they speed towards heaven; tongues hauling firebombs to targets, and the mouths projecting glistering swords at enemies. My near five-week stay has left me with two nagging questions. First, how many Nigerians seriously take the scriptural revelation that human beings were created in God's image and thus have inalienable respect? Second, how can we develop our economy and lifestyle when we do not value one another as full human beings? I think speech reform and re-orientation of psyche with regard to how we value human life are necessary precursors to our national socio-economic development.

Culled from *The Guardian* (Nigerian) of May 2, 2007

(*Dr. Wariboko is an ethicist, theologian and pastor in Boston, Massachusetts*).

Review Questions

1. What is language?
2. How do verbal vocal messages differ from verbal-nonvocal messages?
3. What does it mean to say that language is rule-governed?
4. How does language influence perception?
5. Describe the many different ways you can improve on your language use?
6. Does language determine or influence thought?
7. How does male/female language differ?
8. What are the semantic and syntactic rules of language and how can they affect our communication?
9. What are bi-polar words and how do they hide and confuse meaning?
10. Explain this phrase: "Meanings are in people, not in words?"
11. Phonologically speaking, everyone speaks with an accent. Do you agree?
12. Describe how you could use metaphorical language immediate language in your communication with your friend.

Chapter Four

Nonverbal Communication

Human communication has two broad categories - verbal and nonverbal. Nonverbal communication comprises the messages we send without the use of words. Communication without words could be nonverbal-vocal or nonverbal-nonvocal. Nonverbal communication may be communication without words, but it also includes communication through some vocal varieties, that is, the sounds we produce which convey meanings to others, including the sounds that accompany words.

Scholars argue that much of human communication is nonverbal. As much as 93% of human communication is nonverbal argues Mehrabian (1972), but Birdwhistell (1970), estimates it to be 65%. Nevertheless, much of our communication is without words, thus making it imperative to understand these messages in explaining the total communication experience of people. In another vein, people do claim that action speaks louder than words, suggesting that nonverbal behavior is more believable than verbal behavior. Again, scholars agree that when verbal and nonverbal messages contradict, we tend to give credence to the nonverbal portion. Why? It is believed that nonverbal messages are not easily faked. Yes, we can lie through our teeth verbally, but the body is believed to reveal the "truth" even when we attempt to lie by faking the body language. Whenever we communicate face –to- face we are not only sharing verbal messages, we also send nonverbal messages and often times the unspoken messages are not only preponderant, they also weigh more in the interpretation of meaning than the words we speak. According to Burgoon and Bacue (2003), as much as 60% of the social meaning we share in face-to-face communication is a result of nonverbal behavior.

What are the different types of nonverbal messages otherwise referred to as body language and what are their characteristics and why are they so important to human communication?

The Nature of Nonverbal Messages

Nonverbal messages by nature are ever present in our communication. Whether we intend to or not, we cannot stop sending nonverbal messages because they are there, always, wherever we are. As long as you can see, feel, hear, touch or taste, your senses are constantly bombarded by these nonverbal messages. Therefore, **nonverbal messages occur constantly and are ever present in face-to-face human communication.** We judge people based on a number of factors regardless of whether they are aware of it or not. We draw meanings from people's appearance, facial expressions, physical characteristics such as weight, height and skin color, quality of voice, etc. If you speak, obviously you're sending messages and if you don't, you are equally sending messages.

Based on the foregoing, we can conclude that the first signals or messages received about a person are usually nonverbal. When you enter a room, the people already in the room evaluate you based on how you look, how you walk, and how you comport yourself- all these while you have not said a word. **Nonverbal messages are, therefore, the primary means of expression.** Our reaction to situations and the communication of others is primarily through nonverbal means. Our emotional dispositions are easily read on our faces; whether we are happy or sad. The first indication of that is what we communicate through our facial expressions and other body language.

As noted before, we tend to believe what we see over what we hear, so action speaks louder than words. Nonverbal messages are believed to be largely spontaneous and involuntary compared to verbal messages that we usually consciously and carefully construct. The often unintentional, subconscious nature of nonverbal messages places them higher on the human scale of believability than verbal messages. Because it is rather difficult to control our emotions and even when we do, it is believed that our body will "leak" out the true feelings. So, whenever nonverbal messages signal a message that is contrary to the verbal message presented, we tend to believe the nonverbal. **In essence, nonverbal messages are more believable than verbal messages.**

Sometimes we smile and laugh when we are sad, but sometimes when we are happy, we cry. By monitoring the facial expressions of people we encounter, we may not accurately determine how they really feel on the inside based on our outward reading of their gestures. We must rely on the context in which nonverbal communication takes place to attempt accurate interpretations of their meanings. Nonverbal messages can be abstract, intentional, and arbitrary. **Nonverbal messages are rather ambiguous or subject to different interpretations.**

Context of communication yields additional meaning to messages being sent; therefore, without considering the influence of context on meaning, the specific meaning of nonverbal signals may be difficult to deduce. Contexts of communication include existing relationship between or among communicators, time, culture, place and more. All of these influence the interactions of communicators and the meanings ascribed to the messages they share. How would you interpret a nonverbal communication scenario whereby two women or men hold hands "joyfully?" What about two very old couple kissing passionately in public? Again, what about a tribesman, who is happily eating some insects? **The meaning is in the context. The meaning of nonverbal messages depends on context.**

People across the world differ in their use and interpretation of nonverbal communication; just as languages vary, nonverbal languages are also varied. It is customary in some cultures to greet acquaintances with kisses to both cheeks while in another a hug is just fine. In Arab cultures, it is observed that people maintain less space between each other during conversation than White Americans and Europeans in general. In South Africa, it is confrontational and disrespecting to look authority figures directly in the eyes, but in the United States of America, such behavior is encouraged. In my Yoruba (Nigerian) culture, especially in Ilesa my home town, it is offensive to face your palm toward someone with fingers spread out. While this may mean stop in some cultures, to us it means f---- your mother and your father and your entire family. Cultural norms lead people of different cultures to enact and interpret nonverbal messages differently, so **nonverbal messages are related to culture.** Though there are universal gestures such as a smile and a frown, much of our nonverbal communication is culture bound.

Functions of Nonverbal Messages

What roles do nonverbal messages play vis-à-vis verbal messages? The stream of nonverbal messages do not exist in isolation, they usually co-exist with verbal messages. As a matter of fact the verbal and nonverbal signals are co-dependent as they co relate. Therefore, interpreting one in isolation of the other may not present a complete picture or complete message. While interacting with one another, the nonverbal messages being shared among participants regulate their behaviors and indicate the level of the relationship that exists among the communicators. And to ignore the nonverbal in interpreting meanings being shared among communicators is to ignore the pertinent source of meanings being shared in such relationship. Many textbooks of communication identify functions of nonverbal messages as complementing, repeating, regulating, substituting and contradicting.

Complementing

To complement is to add to. Nonverbal messages add to verbal messages as they can be used to describe what has been said, complete what is being said, or to accent what is being said. A smile may complete a morning greeting and the tone of voice may underscore the importance of a message. Enthusiasm of the speaker is often portrayed by use of accenting nonverbal devices. According to Seiler and Beal, "if used correctly in a public speech, that is, if accenting gestures and changes in tone of voice appear natural and flow smoothly with the message, they can be especially effective ways of making a point clearer to an audience."

Repeating

To repeat is to go over again. Some nonverbal messages just repeat what has been verbalized. Why is there a need for this repetition? Redundancy is good in communication. This is trying to say that if you do not hear me, perhaps you will see me. Repetition is good for gaining attention and ensuring message reception. Coming at the receiver from at least two sides ensures that the message is clear and is received without ambiguity. When you tell a child to sit and motion the same command to the child, there is no mistaking your expectations (and the expected behavior) of the child.

Regulating

To regulate is to control. Some nonverbal cues are directed at regulating or controlling the communication flow between communicators. In a conversation, you may signal your willingness to talk by raising your hand slightly to indicate to the other person that it is your turn to speak and when you want to yield your turn to another person, you may lower the volume of your voice to indicate that you're coming to the end of your contribution. But then you may raise your voice to indicate to someone who wants to interrupt you that you're not done talking. All of these are regulating behaviors that we accomplish using nonverbal cues.

Substituting

To substitute is to replace. Nonverbal cues are sometimes used to replace verbal messages- this is using gestures and cues that directly translate into words or the use of nonverbal cues that have equivalent meanings in our verbal language. An elaborate form of this is sign language that substitutes for words and phrases of a language. Substituting becomes necessary because of the inability of participants to speak, or the desire not to speak in certain situations. When you receive a thumbs-up, the sender is actually saying "good job" to you in the American context.

Contradicting

Contradicting is going against or presenting the opposite of something. Sometimes when we feel something, we voice the opposite, though we may do so subconsciously. A visibly angry person shouts that "I am not angry." And a nervous date proclaims that she is cool and calm. But which message comes out stronger? As has been stated earlier, people tend to put greater premium on nonverbal cues. There are reasons for these contradicting "double" messages. Adler and Towne (1996) claim that these reasons include "to cover nervousness when giving a speech or in a job interview, to keep someone from worrying about us, or to appear more attractive than we believe we really are."

Public speakers should be mindful of the contradicting messages they are sending to their audiences because of the fact that audiences put more emphasis on nonverbal cues than on words to decide whether speakers are honest (Hale and Stiff, 1990). On the other hand, the audience also uses nonverbal behaviors to judge the character of speakers as well as their competence and composure; and differences in nonverbal behavior influence how much listeners are persuaded by a speaker (Burgoon, et al, 1990).

Types of Nonverbal Communication

Generally there are five categories of nonverbal messages we send to others either consciously or otherwise. These are body motions or movements, the use and management of space, the use of the voice as sounds that accompany speech, the philosophical orientation to and use of time, and self-presentation cues. It is important to note that these messages or cues influence the way we are perceived and the way we perceive others; consequently, a great deal of attention should be paid to these cues in order that we may identify what they are and how they influence our communication.

Kinesics

The study of body movements and body positioning is referred to as Kinesics. Such body movements and motions that people observe and give meanings to would include facial expressions, eye movements, hand gestures, posture, body positions, and touching behaviors.

Facial Expressions

These are the voluntary and involuntary movements of the facial muscles used to communicate what we feel on the inside, that is, they are used to communicate emotional meaning and to express our reactions to external stimuli or cues. The face is believed to be the number one source of nonverbal cues because of the variety of ways that the contours of the face can be manipulated and the countless meanings they may reveal. When we encounter others, usually we observe the face the most, therefore, we have learned to communicate numerous messages through our facial expressions and receivers, on the other hand, have learned to read messages off of people's faces. "The face is the image of the soul" as Cicero, the Roman orator and politician observed; it is also a fertile deposit of nonverbal cues.

The common categories of emotions we express through the movements of the contours of the face are: anger, fear, happiness, sadness, surprise, and disgust. While it is believed that every human across cultures has the same expression for these categories of emotions, people may choose to mask or control their feelings and fake some others such that the facial expressions may not accurately depict their feelings. (Please see Table 4.1) Often this is due to cultural expectations which vary immensely across the globe. Again, with the understanding that emotions are rather like colors- some are primary while countless others are blends, we cannot limit the emotions revealed through facial expressions to just the basic six identified here, because the possibilities are immeasurable.

Seiler and Beal (2008) confirm that "facial expressions have an extremely powerful role in communication and relationships." And if they are the number one source of nonverbal messages, and we agree that nonverbal messages are more believable than verbal messages, then we cannot overemphasize the importance of facial expressions in human communication. The perceptions and interpretations we ascribe many different aspects of a person's behavior may indeed be attributable to the interpretations derived from the person's facial expressions. So, judgments about a speaker's credibility, likability, warmth, approachability and others may be dependent on facial cues.

When communication is not face-to-face, how do the communicators compensate for the inability to read each other's facial expressions? Or does such communication suffer from inadequate cues from which complete meaning can be deduced? The need to compensate for the lack of **affect displays** (as facial expressions are often referred) in computer mediated communication, has led to the invention of sketches or typed symbols (**emoticons**) to represent the emotions of the communicator. This is typical of online e-mail sharing where, unable to see the receiver, the sender uses emotion symbols to express how he or she feels.

Here are examples of some emoticons and their meanings:
}{ meaning face-to-face
☺ Smile
☹ Frown
:-1 Straight Face.

TABLE 4.1/ Facial Management Techniques

Technique	Definition	Example
Intensifying	Exaggeration of expression to meet other's expectations	You receive a gift and try to look completely surprised, excited, and delighted.
Deintensifying	Understatement of reactions to meet other's expectations	You receive an A on a speech, a friend receives a C. You tone down your elation, just in case your friend feels bad about receiving a lower grade.
Neutralizing	Avoidance of any emotional expression in a situation-"poker face" shows no emotion	You show no fear or sadness when fear or sadness may be justified but you don't want to show your emotions.
Masking	Replacement of one expression with another considered more appropriate for the situation	Smiling when a friend wins a scholarship and you don't, even though you think you deserve it.

Source: Seiler, William J. and Melissa L. Beall (2008). *Communication: Making Connections*, 7th ed. Boston: Allyn and Bacon.

Eye Movements

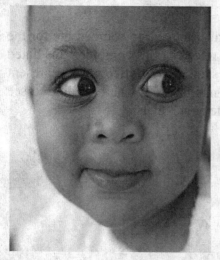

You've heard of the expression: "if looks could kill." What is it about the eyes and the way we humans can use them that can cause others to feel either damned or appreciated? It's all in the eyes. Though we think that we use our eyes to receive visual information from our environment, the way we gaze at others, roll our eyes at them, or even avoid eye contact with them, all communicate important messages. The roles of eye contact in interpreting human communication and behavior are so important that scholars study eye movements and their impact on interpersonal relations. The term **Oculesics** is used to describe the study of such eye behavior, especially eye contact.

When we engage others in communication, the first thing we notice is the eyes; they can signal acceptance and they can give notice of disapproval. In general, "eye messages provide turn-taking signals in conversations that regulate interactions. They indicate attentiveness, involvement, immediacy, and connection to other," Hybels and Weaver (2007). But the use of eye contact varies from culture to culture. Its use is strictly governed by cultural norms and values. While it is acceptable and even encouraged in the United States for people to look each other straight in the eyes while interacting face-to-face, this is a taboo in many other cultures. Looking at elders straight in the eyes is disrespectful in many African cultures, especially in South Africa and Nigeria. So, while the Nigerian mother admonishes her wards not to look people straight in the eyes because it is confrontational and shows lack of respect, the American mother, on the other hand, charges her wards to look people straight in the eyes when interacting with them, regardless of their age, because it shows respect, interest and attention. She might also add that it is disrespectful not to look people straight in the eyes when talking with them.

Understanding the uses of eye contact and its effects on receivers can prove very useful to all communicators, especially public speakers. Eye behavior can serve important communicative functions according to Dale Leathers (1986).
These functions include to:

1. Influence attitude and change perception
2. Indicate degree of attentiveness, interest, and arousal
3. Express emotions
4. Regulate interaction
5. Indicate power and status
6. Form impressions in others.

For public speakers to gain the attention of their audience, they have to maintain good eye contact with them. This is true in other cultures, in addition to those of the Western world. In Nigeria, for example, The Yorubas have a saying that literally claims that "talk is in the eyes." In other words, if something is important and worth deliberating upon, it is better done face-to-face, "eyes to eyes!"

Attempts to change attitude and perceptions are easier when the speaker maintains good eye contact with the listeners, who will look into the speaker's eyes and estimate his/her credibility, interest and passion. Listeners who, on the other hand, avoid eye contact with the speaker are probably not paying attention, not interested, or not aroused.

Body Movements

There are numerous body movements that we humans use to convey our emotions, information about our personality traits and attitudes and a host of other messages. We gesture with our hands (some more than others), head, and the whole body. These different gestures, however, can convey different meanings across cultures. Klopf and McCroskey, in explaining varied cultural meanings of gestures, used Axtell's (1991) analogy of a man going into the bathroom where a young lady was bathing and asked the question: How would the young lady react? Women from various cultures were asked this question to get their reactions.
It is reported that a Mohammedan lady would cover her face. A Laotian would cover her breasts. A pre-Revolutionary Chinese would hide her feet. A woman from Sumatra would cover her knees. A Samoan would hide her navel. A Western woman would cover her breasts with one hand and her genitalia with the other. Which of these gestures seems more sensible to you? Axtell submits that the Mohammedan's gesture seems more reasonable, because how would the stranger be able to identify her later?

Posture

Posture is defined as the position and movement of your body and from your posture, others interpret how attentive, respectful and dominant you are (Verderber and Verderber, 2008). So, when we take a stance on something we use our posture to show our position on that issue. You sit up when you're eager to get involved in something, but you sit back to enjoy a great moment. Your body positioning tells a lot about your expectations, your self-esteem and your perception of others in relation to you. If you consider yourself to be of a higher social status than someone else, your body position "tells" that you feel superior to this other person by say, for example, how you put your hands on your hips and how you cock your head. But when you turn your back on somebody, that displays your disapproval of this person's behavior or attitude toward you-it's a form protest. This is referred to as **body orientation**, which describes your body position in relation to another.

Monitoring your posture and body orientation, especially in the communication situation is very important, because your audience will interpret your attitude toward them and the topic based on your posture and positioning in relation to them. Again to quote Verderber and Verderber, "when you are making a speech, an upright stance and squared shoulders will help your audience perceive you as poised and self-confident. So when you're giving a speech, be sure to distribute your weight equally on both feet so that you maintain a confident bearing."

The numerous body movements have been classified for ease of identification and functions. Ekman and Friesen (1969) identify five categories of body movements as:
Emblems, Illustrators, Regulators, Affect displays, and Adaptors.
The next table identifies these categories and gives their characteristics with illustrative examples.

Table 4.2/Categories of Body Movements and Facial Expressions.

Category	Characteristics	Example
Emblems	Translate directly into words and are used for specific words or phrases. Meanings of emblems are like those of words- arbitrary, changeable with time, learned, and culturally determined	A hitchhiker's extended thumb, the thumb and circle sign for "OK," the peace sign
Illustrators	Accent, reinforce, or emphasize a verbal message	A child holding up his hands to indicate how tall he is while saying, "I'm a big boy;" an instructor underlining a word on a poster to emphasize it
Regulators	Control, monitor, or maintain interaction between or among speakers and listeners. Cues that tell us when to stop, continue, hurry, elaborate, make things more interesting, or let someone else speak.	Eye contact, shift in posture, nod of the head, looking at a clock or wrist watch
Affect displays	Body movements that express emotions. Though your face is the primary means of displaying affect, your body may also be used.	Sad face, slouching, jumping up and down
Adaptors	Helps one feel at ease in communication situations. Are difficult to interpret and require the most speculation.	Scratching, smoothing hair, playing with coins, smoking, hands in front of the face, moving closer to someone

Source: Seiler, William J. and Melissa L. Beall (2008). *Communication: Making Connections* (7th ed.). Boston: Allyn and Bacon.

Haptics

Haptics is the study of the use of touch in communication. Using our hands and other parts of the body to touch another human being communicates some social meaning. We pat each other on the back, we kiss, and we slap, pat, hug, shove, stroke, hold, embrace, and punch others. Usually we use these different touches to express how we feel toward one another, but each touch may depict different emotions. We may hold someone tenderly or firmly or in a lock to prevent escape; we may punch to inflict pain or to gingerly show affection; a slap across the face is provoking while a slap on the buttocks may be interpreted positively depending on who is doing the touching and who is being touched! Two things are clear about the interpretation of the use of touch: the meanings depend on the relational and cultural contexts in which it takes place.

The touching behaviors of men differ from that of women; the touching behaviors of children differ from that of adults; and different cultures use and interpret touch differently. Edward Hall (1966), in regard to touching behavior, identifies two broad categories of cultures- one that is **contact culture** and the other that is **noncontact culture**. In contact cultures, people touch more, communicate in closer proximity, face one another squarely and use more eye contact. Whereas, people in non-contact societies, touch less, maintain more space between one another when communicating. Contact cultures include most Arab countries, Mediterranean and Jewish people, Eastern Europeans, Russians, Hispanics, and Indonesians. Non-contact cultures typically are found in Northern Europe, Japan, China, Korea, and other Far Eastern countries (Casteel, 1992). The United States presents a unique case because of the ethnic diversity of her citizens. The different ethnic groups from different countries and parts of the world reflect their different cultural practices, which include different touching and other communicative behaviors.

Functions of Touch

McCroskey and Richmond (1996) classify touch into five functional categories:
functional/professional; social/polite; friendship/warmth; love/intimacy; and sexual arousal.

1. **Functional/professional.** These are touches that we cannot avoid because the person or persons doing the touching has a job to perform by touching us. A doctor's examination, a barber's touch, and a tailor's touch are examples of this type of impersonal touch that does not indicate an invasion of privacy because of the job, or task that has to be performed.
2. **Social/polite.** We touch one another in a gesture to communicate acknowledgment, recognition, and generally a welcoming greeting; the most common of which is a handshake.

3. **Friendship/warmth**. This is a type of touch used in close relationships to communicate affection and fondness. A pat on the back, hugs and casual kisses among friends and family members express the feelings of respect and esteem that these people share.
4. **Love/intimacy**. This type of touch goes beyond friendship and warmth; it expresses deep, more intense emotional and relational connection. Lovers embrace and kiss each other passionately and cuddle as if they are one.
5. **Sexual arousal**. This is the most personal type of touch that expresses not only love and intimacy, but also physical attraction.

From the foregoing we can see that there are rules, albeit, unspoken, that govern the use of touch in our everyday interactions. Often times, there are touch behaviors that do not follow these guidelines and thereby offend the recipients of such "unwanted" or "unwarranted" touch. The relationship between the communicators and the cultural contexts within which touch behaviors occur serve to regulate such behaviors. We are all familiar with sexual harassment cases that were brought about by inappropriate touches between males and females, bosses and employees, students and teachers, caregivers and children.

Communicators must be aware of conventions and guidelines for the use of touch in different settings and among different groups in order not to offend and run afoul of relationships dos and don'ts.

The use of physical touch in communication has another dimension to it. Studies suggest that touch can lead to liking, compliance, and healthy development, especially in babies. In laboratory experiments that measured impact of touch on liking, partners that were touched more, were evaluated more positively, (Burgoon, et al., 1992).

Touch also increases compliance-getting people to do what you expect of them. In the different experiments, verbal requests were accompanied by touch and the findings confirmed the impact of touch as influential in gaining compliance (Kleinke, 1977; Willis and Hamm, 1980; and Crusco and Wetzel, 1984).

Use of Space (Proxemics)

How we use space and the distance we maintain with one another communicate meanings that can be interpreted by others, though we may not be totally aware of it. The study of the use of space and the distance we maintain with others is referred to as **Proxemics.** Each of us uses physical and psychological space to indicate the type of relationship we have or would like to maintain with others. In a classroom, for example, the instructor is given more space and usually has a bigger desk and more comfortable chair than anyone of the students. What does this suggest? It speaks to the instructor's power in relation to his/her students. In an office, the person who occupies the room with a view is usually the boss, while the other workers are put in open rooms that have many cubicles, thus giving less privacy to the occupants. Again, we all have a bubble surrounding us that we claim to be an extension of our person, the psychological space surrounding us into which others may not intrude; and if people accidentally invade this space, they usually apologize for doing so. So, we humans and other animals have and use space to communicate social meanings to others. It is true that we are all territorial creatures.

Territoriality

The study of animals in their natural surroundings (**Ethology**), suggests that animals possess and have controlling attitude toward spaces and objects they claim to be theirs. Such spaces are marked and delineated with territorial markers to lay claim of ownership to such spaces and ward off encroachment by others. While humans use white picket fences to mark their properties, animals, on the other hand, may urinate to mark such territories. Altman (1975) identified three types of territories: **primary, secondary,** and **public territories.**

Primary territories are such that you have exclusive rights to. Examples are your house, car, bedroom, and locker. You usually control access and use of these spaces and may allow others into it if you grant the permission. Secondary territories are habitually occupied by you though they do not belong to you. But because you've used them for so long they are assigned to you. Examples are your lockers at school or in a sports arena, desk and chair at school, or "your chair" at a local restaurant or place of worship that you habitually occupy. Public spaces belong to everyone and you use them on a temporary basis. The Public Park, movie house, beach, and restaurant are good examples of this type of territory.

Personal Space

Your personal space, as stated earlier, is the bubble that surrounds and acts as a buffer between you and others as you interact with them. This psychological space is mobile as it goes with you everywhere you go. But people of different cultures perceive and use this space differently. While interacting with my students in the classroom, they operate on the basis of their cultural experience by "getting too close" to me. While this makes me feel very uncomfortable, the students are oblivious of the fact that they are invading my personal space. I do believe that, being a Black African, I have been used to a larger "bubble" than the "invaders" realized.

Anthropologist, Edward Hall (1959, 1966) studied how Americans use space in their social interactions and identified four zones of space. These are **intimate distance, personal distance, social distance,** and **public distance.** See table 4.3 for details of far and near phases of the social distance zones.

Intimate Distance

As the name suggests, this is the space that extends from our skin outward to about eighteen inches. This is the space we reserve for those who are emotionally close to us, usually our loved ones such as our spouse, children, parents and those we permit to be intimately close to us.

Personal Distance

According to Hall, this stretches from eighteen inches after the intimate zone to about four feet. This is the "bubble" that we own. The near phase of this distance is reserved for those who are very close to us, those with whom we have some social relationship, but the far phase is for casual interaction. Far enough to put them at "arm's length," but close enough to regard them as acquaintances.

Social Distance

This extends from four feet to twelve feet and it is the kind of space you would maintain with someone you're meeting for the first time and for business conversation. If someone you're meeting for the first time moves closer to you - say into your personal space, you'll become uncomfortable; whereas if a friend maintains social distance with you, you're equally uncomfortable. We expect our friends to be closer and non-friends to stand a little farther away.

Public Distance

This is the farthest distance for social interaction and it extends from twelve feet and beyond. This is the kind of space a speaker would maintain with an audience in the public speaking situation. Again, an example of this space would be found in auditoriums and movie theaters where the podium and the screen are usually twelve feet away from the first row of the audience.

TABLE 4.3/ Social Distance Zones

Distance	Description of Distance	Vocal Characteristics	Message Content
0-6inches	Intimate (close phase)	Soft whisper	Top secret
6-18 inches	Intimate (far phase)	Audible whisper	Very confidential
1.5- 2.5 feet	Personal (close phase)	Soft voice	Personal subject matter
2.5 – 4 feet	Personal (far phase)	Slightly lowered voice	Personal subject matter
4-7 feet	Social (close phase)	Full voice	Nonpersonal information
7-12 feet	Social (far phase)	Full voice with slight over-loudness	Public information for others to hear
12-25 feet	Public (close phase)	Loud voice talking to a group	Public information for others to hear
25 feet or more	Public (far phase)	Loudest voice	Hailing, departures

Source: Hall, Edward T. (1981) *The Silent Language*. Doubleday, Random House.

Vocalics (Paralanguage)

The interpretation given to our spoken words is not necessarily based on the meanings of the words spoken, but on the many other subtle messages that accompany the words. The gestures we make, the volume of the voice, intonation, pitch, rate and even the quality of our natural voices- all these send additional messages to the real message intended by the words we speak. The study of such additions to our original messages, which usually come in the form of sounds, is termed **vocalics** or **paralanguage** or **paralinguistics**. The vocal cues are nonverbal though they are sounds because they do not include words. So they can be described as nonverbal/vocal cues.

Pitch

This represents the highs and the lows (frequency) of sounds that we produce or hear. We attach meanings to these sounds and label the source according to our expectations of the association we have for such sounds. Generally women and younger people are expected to have higher pitched voice than men or older people. When the voice pitch does not match our expectations, other meanings are inferred. According to Tubbs and Moss (2000), most untrained speakers use a pitch somewhat higher than their optimum pitch, but it has been found that lower pitches are most pleasant to listen to.

Rate

This represents the fastness and slowness of speech or how rapidly or slowly one speaks. When someone speaks to you in a rapid rate of speech, this may indicate to you a number of things; that the speaker is rushing and does not have time, or is not patient, or is fearful or angry, or is not sure of what to say, hence the need to rush to cover for the deficiency. The list of insinuations is endless just as when one speaks with a lower or low speech rate. The reality is that people perceive you differently based on your speech rate.

The rate of speech can be measured in terms of how many words are delivered in a time frame of usually one minute and the average human speaking rate is about 125 to 150 words per minute Tubbs and Moss (2000). And since there is no perfect speech rate, the advice is that each speaker adapts his/her speech to the context and the receiver.

Fluency

A fluent speaker is one who speaks with minimal speech errors, especially vocalizations such as "um," "er," "ah," and "you know." These interrupt and cause breaks in speech and render it less fluent and less effective. While calculated pauses here and there in a speech may enhance the effectiveness of the speech, unplanned pauses and vocalizations however are disruptive and detrimental to the speech purpose, especially given the listening habits of most listeners.

Volume

How would you react to a speaker whose voice you can hardly hear? Apparently adequate volume is a primary requirement for hearing and listening to a speech. A speaker whose voice volume is low can hardly maintain the attention of the audience, let alone involve them in the collaborative effort of speech performance, thus becoming the source of noise in the enterprise.

Different cultures perceive different **loudness of voice** as adequate in public encounters. According to Hall (1959) in social distance encounters, the American voice is below that of the Arab, the Spaniard, the South Asian Indian, and the Russian, and somewhat above that of the English upper class, the Southeast Asian, and the Japanese. So what is considered loud in one culture may not be perceived as such in another. The best measure of the adequacy of one's speech volume is its gauge by the audience to which one speaks.

Quality of Sound

How is it that we are attracted to certain sounds and not to others? Or more appropriately, how come we prefer a certain speaker's voice over another's? The answer is in the quality of the sound. Each of us has our distinctive voice tone and quality which is a product of our vocal chords, and size and shape of the body. These allow the human voice to resonate in unique ways to produce the sounds that come out of the mouth when we speak. And as with human perception, some human sounds are received more favorably than others. In the American culture, some voice qualities that are considered unpleasant include **hyper nasality** (talking through the nose), denasality (which sounds as though the speaker has a constant head cold!), hoarseness, and harshness (or stridency), Tubbs and Moss (2000).

Pronunciation, Enunciation, and Articulation

The way we pronounce, enunciate, and articulate words constitutes other vocal cues. The perceptions associated with correct pronunciation, enunciation and articulation makes these nonverbal but vocal phenomena important to our communication. Those who can effectively combine the elements are perceived to be effective, good and believable communicators. The opposite of this is that a speaker who mispronounces and cannot articulate appropriately is perceived to be ill-prepared, lack education or training and, therefore, is unbelievable or less credible and may not be able to hold the attention of the listeners for too long, if at all.

Pronunciation is the uttering of syllables and words to produce sounds identified within a linguistic tradition as appropriate. In other words, it is saying and sounding words correctly.

Enunciation has to do with the combination of good pronunciation and clarity of the voice in order for the receiver to adequately distinguish among the words being uttered.

Articulation involves shaping the mouth, placing the tongue and teeth into position to produce sounds that the receiver would understand. Vocal cues are important indicators of the body type, age, gender, appearance, height of the speaker- all variables that influence the way someone sounds. According to Pearson and Nelson (2000), people often associate a high-pitched voice with someone who is female; someone who is younger; and someone who is smaller, rather than larger. ...We visualize someone who uses a loud voice as being tall and large or someone who speaks too quickly as being nervous. People who speak slowly and deliberately are usually perceived as being of high status and having high credibility.

Silence

Is silence ever good in communication? Yes, a vocal pause here and there in a speech sends a message. Silence can be used to draw attention to a point, to emphasize an idea or to underscore an argument. Silence can be used as a punctuation mark to justify a previous point or that which is to follow. A prolonged silence can seem awkward in a public presentation, but the speaker can stylistically use it as a presentation strategy to draw in the audience or to jab at them. But a break in presentation that is not calculated as a means of gaining attention or drawing particular attention at something, can, indeed, mar the presentation because it may convey the message that the speaker is ill-prepared or is uninformed and, perhaps, is not competent to talk on the speech topic. The audience's perception of the speaker's credibility may become negative as a result of misplaced or prolonged silence. So, sometimes silence can, indeed, be golden! That is, if used appropriately.

Use of Time (Chronemics)

The study of how we use time and make time references to human life is called chronemics. Different people and cultures perceive and use time differently. Cultural teachings lead us to value and have different orientations to the use of time. While some cultures have developed an orientation that values schedules that devote a period of time to a single activity and does disapprove of interruptions that may change the schedule as in **Monochronic time orientation**, some other cultures have developed an orientation that does not superimpose schedules on human relations; they perceive time to be fluid and adaptable and, as such may engage in many activities at any given time as in **Polychronic time orientation**. In these cultures an interruption to a planned activity is taken in stride because "time and schedules are made by man and not the other way around." In a multicultural environment, however, it is apparent how the different orientations toward time may result in conflict.

When someone of a Polychronic time orientation interacts with another of a monochromic time orientation, misinterpretation of their different attitudes toward time may result in some conclusions that may irrevocably damage their relationship. Imagine the misperceptions that may occur between a boss and an employee who are of different time orientations. A boss, who is Polychronic, may ask an employee who is monochronic to engage in multiple tasks all at once and expects results immediately, without the benefit of scheduling and prioritizing. Upon all, the same boss, may want the employee to stay after "work time" to do the job until it is finished without regard for the needs of the employee and the contractual working agreement.

The students that I have come across over the years have had to answer the time orientation question. If I, the professor, were to invite you to my family member's wedding that is slated for, let's say ten o'clock in the morning on a Saturday, and you would want to honor my invitation, what time would you be there? Many of the European American students would rather be there at some time before ten or at ten o'clock, give or take a few minutes. Many of the Spanish American students would arrive at some time after ten, maybe fifteen to thirty minutes after. Many of the African American students like the Spanish American students would arrive about fifteen to thirty minutes after the scheduled time and some would rather give themselves about an hour "after everything must have started before they make an entry!"

I do not characterize these different orientations as late or on time because the answers reflect cultural influences that are ingrained in the natures of these categories of people. The dominant, mainstream American culture, which is European, continues to influence the cultural orientations of the different co-cultures present in the United States.

Self-Presentation

The expression that 'appearance maketh the man' speaks to the perceived importance of appearance and self- presentation in interpersonal and public communication. The first impression or information gleaned from us when we encounter others is through our physical appearance, clothing, grooming, and our physical environment. And to make a good first impression or self presentation, some people go to greater lengths than others; they become obsessed with their weight, height, complexion, and general health.

Physical Appearance

Your physical characteristics are partly determined by your heritage and personal alteration. Exercise and diet can influence the way you look and so can plastic surgery. People form stereotypic impressions of us based on our outward physical body types. According to Verderber and Verderber (2008) "**Endomorphs**, who are shaped round and heavy, are stereotyped as kind, gentle and jovial. **Mesomorphs**, who are muscular and strong, are believed to be energetic, outgoing, and confident. **Ectomorphs,** whose bodies are lean and have little muscle development, are stereotyped as brainy, anxious, and cautious." While these are stereotypes, they have consequences in terms of how people react to and judge us. Consequently, we try all we can to control what people see and react to about us.

The concern for outward appearance is for a good reason as research findings would confirm. People are often attracted to others they perceive to be attractive, Wells and Seigel, (1961); both males and females are strongly influenced by attractiveness, but males are more responsive to appearance than females, Collins and Zebrowitz (1995). Numerous research studies indicate that attractive people, when compared to unattractive people, are perceived to be more popular, successful, sociable, persuasive, sensual, and happy, Seiler and Beal (2008). The implications of these findings include the issue of credibility. Speakers who are perceived to be credible are well received by the listeners, and are more likely to be persuasive and successful in the speech enterprise.

Clothing/Grooming

People make their choices of what to wear based on their perception of what looks good or what they look good in, thereby sharing a conscious set of cues they hope others will interpret appropriately and favorably. These conscious cues influence the judgments that others pass on how we appear to them and their estimates of our personality, character and sociability. Such cues and their interpretations influence our job choices, dating choices and other relational choices. But the question is: Can clothing make a man?

The answer is a resounding yes! As confirmed by Thourlby (1978), clothing conveys at least 10 types of messages to others and these are:

1. Economic level
2. Educational level
3. Trustworthiness
4. Social position
5. Level of sophistication
6. Economic background
7. Social background
8. Educational background
9. Level of success
10. Moral character

Artifacts

The articles and materials we acquire and the way we use them to decorate our physical spaces tell a lot about who we are, our personality, character, social status, educational level, etc. Teenagers are in the habit of decorating their rooms with posters and pictures of their favorite artists and admirable persons. Why would a teenager have a Michael Jackson poster on her wall while another has that of Bob Marley? Why would the larger than life poster of Britney Spears adorn a teenager's wall and another that of Shakira?

Objects and artifacts are used to communicate messages to others as well as confirm to ourselves what we like and value. A fifty –year old man may prefer the quintessential American sports car, the Corvette, in red while another fifty-year old man would prefer the same car in white! The first man may be perceived as trying to act young or may be going through some mid-life crisis; while the latter may be said to be acting his age. The way furniture is arranged may invite others to seat or speak loudly to them not to even try!

Improving Nonverbal Messages

As we can see, nonverbal messages are rather ambiguous, are multi-channeled, continuous, culture- based, and may be unintentional; therefore, accurately interpreting their meanings portends some challenges. We have seen how we attach stereotypes to verbal cues and misjudge people. But how can we as effective communicators reduce the problem of misinterpretation when it comes to nonverbal cues in order that we may judge behaviors more accurately? As with human perception, the basic ways to ensure accurate perceptions are to have a clear description of the messages sent, to have at least two interpretations of the message to preclude prejudgment; and to ask for clarity whenever possible.

Verderber and Verderber (2008) identified ways to improve both the quality of the nonverbal messages we send to others as well as the interpretations of the nonverbal messages we receive. In sending nonverbal messages, they advise us to be mindful of the following:

1. Be conscious of the nonverbal behavior you are displaying.

2. Be purposeful or strategic in your use of nonverbal communication.

3. Make sure that your nonverbal cues do not distract from your message.

4. Make your nonverbal communication match your verbal communication.

5. Adapt your nonverbal behavior to the situation.

In interpreting nonverbal cues, they admonish us to do the following:

1. When interpreting others' nonverbal cues, do not automatically assume that a particular behavior means a certain thing.
2. Consider cultural, gender, and individual influences when interpreting nonverbal cues.
3. Pay attention to multiple aspects of nonverbal communication and their relationship to verbal communication.
4. Use perception checking.

Review Questions

1. Describe what is commonly referred to as body language?
2. Describe the nature and characteristics of nonverbal messages.
3. What are the functions of nonverbal messages and how do they influence your communication?
4. What are the consequences of this statement: Nonverbal language is ambiguous?
5. What is paralanguage and how does it help us to communicate?
6. What is haptics and how does it influence your communication?
7. How is Chronemics important to intercultural understanding?
8. Edward Hall identified four zones of space. What are they and when do you use them?
9. What are the ways you can improve your nonverbal communication?
10. How does culture impact nonverbal communication?

SECTION TWO

Interpersonal Communication

Chapter Five
The Self in Interpersonal Communication

How would you answer the question: "Who are you, really?" The question suggests reaching deep into oneself to come to an understanding of self and to describe that understanding in ways that the listener would understand. The real question is: Do we really know ourselves? Do we have the lexicon with which to describe who we are? An awareness of self and the ability to describe that understanding will go a long way in improving our interpersonal relationships.

Interpersonal communication involves understanding the nature of the relationships among communicators whether in a two-person, small or large group context. The quality of the relationship, on the other hand, is influenced greatly by the perceptions the individuals hold of themselves. This is because who you are, according to Adler and Proctor (2011), both reflects and affects your communication. Imagine how the following personal characteristics and traits may influence your interaction and communication with others.

The following, adapted from Adler & Proctor (2011) with major alteration and addition (table added), if answered and summarized, will constitute a profile, a sort of self-concept of the respondent.

Table 5.1/ Elements and Descriptors of Self-Concept

Elements of Self	Sample Descriptors
Moods or Feelings	Frustrated, anxious, afraid, angry, friendly
Appearance	Slender, tall, attractive, short
Social Traits	Shy, outgoing, aggressive
Talents	Athletic, musical
Intellectual Capacity	Precocious, smart, slow learner
Beliefs	Deeply religious, vegetarian
Social Roles	Student, parent, teacher, priest
Physical condition	Overweight, healthy

What is Self-Concept?

Your idea of who you are is, basically, your perception of yourself. How do you see yourself or what or who do you see yourself to be? To answer these questions, you have to sum up your perceptions of yourself over the years, and describe such to others' understanding. The key word is perception. Your sense of self is an estimation of who you think you really are. And with perception being subject to error, your estimation of who you are may be deflated or inflated.

Self-concept is defined as the images you have formed in your head about yourself; it is your perception of yourself. This is the **Self-Image** dimension of your self-concept. **Your self-concept also includes how you feel about yourself, your likes and dislikes, strengths and weaknesses, and what you think about your feelings, physical condition, social traits, appearance, beliefs, talents, and intellectual capacity.** Self-concept has physical and psychological dimensions. It is one thing to be tall and muscular, but another thing to feel good about being tall and muscular! This introduces the concept of **Self-Esteem, which is a part of your self-concept that indicates your feeling of self-worth.** And as it is with feelings, they are rather dynamic—they may change depending on the situation, the event, and the time.

The definitions given by Adler and Proctor (2011) make the distinctions of semi- permanency and fluidity clear between Self-concept and Self-esteem. To these scholars, Self-concept is the **"relatively stable set of perceptions you hold of yourself"** and your self-esteem **"describes your evaluation of self-worth."** Seiler and Beal (2008) also claim that **"self-concept is a person's perceived self, which consists of an organized collection of beliefs and attitudes about self." Self-esteem**, on the other hand, is **"a person's feelings and attitudes toward himself or herself."** The conclusion is that the beliefs, attitudes, feelings, and judgments you hold toward yourself are not fixed and, how they change from situation to situation and at different times, will greatly impact the way you see yourself and, consequently, the way you communicate with others. This is the **social identity perspective** to self-concept—**the changes in the perception of self as a consequence of different situations and time**. The umbrella concept is commonly referred to as the **personality-social continuum.** On the personality extreme of the continuum, a person sees himself or herself as a unique individual and the other extreme, he or she is perceived as a member of a group or a larger culture. As the contexts change so do the perceptions of self and the communication engaged in to enact that perceived self. Apparently, self- concept, perception, social influence, and communication are interwoven and may not be separable.

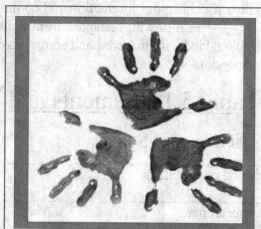

Figure 1: A Yoruba proverb states that: "The human fingers are not equal!" Can you relate this proverb to self-concept?

How Self-Concept is Developed

When Mary was asked "who is she, really," she responded by saying that she could only go by what others said she was, but quickly added that they might be 40% correct. In other words, what others see her to be has influence on how she sees herself, but that they may not see her complete self. There are other sources or influences on self–concept other than the opinions of others. **Self–concept actually develops from unique individual abilities and personality traits, cultural teachings, social comparisons, and opinions of others.**

Individual Unique Abilities and Personality

One fact that we humans have come to terms with is that we are all different biologically. Two siblings may be raised in the same household by the same set of parents, but may exhibit diametrically opposed behaviors and personality traits. We are, therefore, not only products of our genetic makeup, but also of our environment. This is what Adler et al (2011) call the biological and social roots of self.

Our genetic makeup influences our personality which, even with socialization, remains relatively stable over time. So, who you perceive yourself to be, is an approximation of the observable conditioned ways you approach events and people over time — your personality. And your personality will program you to communicate in predictable patterns. The sum is that your personality will predispose you to act in particular ways, and your actions will lead you to see yourself as someone who acts in such particular, predictable ways. As such, you will come to the conclusion that you are your actions. Scholars have confirmed that biology accounts for as much as fifty percent of some communication-related personalities traits, including extroversion, assertiveness (Cole &McCroskey, 2000), shyness (Heisel, McCroskey & Richmond, 1999), verbal aggression (Wigley, 1998) and overall willingness to communicate (McCroskey, Heisel, & Richmond, 2001).

In addition to personality are unique skills and talents that individuals may have that would separate them from the pack. Awareness of such unique gifts would influence one's perception of self. Michael Jordan, with his unique basketball skills, would think of himself differently than some of his teammates who did not receive popular acclaim during their tenure with the Chicago Bulls. Unusual musical talents, intelligence, and other gifts would give a sense of uniqueness to individuals who possess them and thus influence their perceptions of self.

Personality and unique gifts are usually influenced by experience and socialization. This means that your personality trait is not a sentence because it is not a fixed entity, but that which can be polished and controlled through practice. In addition, you probably have personality traits that cut across the five major personality types identified by psychologists. So, you can adapt yourself to different situations through concerted effort.

Table 5.2/The "Big Five" Personality Traits

Extroverted Sociable Fun-loving Talkative Spontaneous	Introverted Reserved Sober Quiet Self-Controlled
Open Imaginative Independent Curious Broad interests	Not Open Unimaginative Conforming Incurious Narrow interests
Conscientious Careful Reliable Persevering Ambitious	Undirected Careless Undependable Lax Aimless
Agreeable Courteous Selfless Trusting Cooperative	Antagonistic Rude Selfish Suspicious Uncooperative
Neurotic Worried Vulnerable Self-pitying Impatient	Stable Calm Hardy Self-satisfied Patient

Adapted from Adler, Ronal B. and Proctor II, Russell F. (2011). *Looking Out Looking In* (13th ed.) Ohio: Cengage.

Cultural Teachings

Culture is the total way of life of a people who share the commonalities of language, religious traditions, social organizations, and who occupy a geographic territory. Through **acculturation**, the cultural traditions are passed from generation to generation, thus ensuring the continuation and perpetuation of that culture. Although individuals are unique, the cultural influence on each member of the social unit ensures commonly held beliefs, values, and prevailing attitudes. The result is a guiding set of norms that influences the perceptions of self and behaviors.

Culture influences the perceptions of self, others, and how one communicates with natives and non-natives. The reciprocal influences of culture on communication necessitate understanding the nuances of culture and how cultural differences may lead to different perceptions of self and others. Hofstede (2001) attempted to study variations in the norms of different countries of the world by examining their five value dimensions of **individualism/collectivism, uncertainty avoidance, power distance, masculinity/femininity, long-term/short-term orientation.** (See chapter thirteen for a detailed treatment of Hofstede's cultural value dimensions, adapted from a book he co-authored in 2004 titled *Cultures and Organizations: Software of the Mind*.)

As "software of the mind," cultural dimensions program how we see, feel, think, and act. For example, the socialization of the American child includes lessons in the central/dominant American values, which include orientation toward individualism, expression of individual freedom, equal opportunity, material acquisition, science and technology, progress and change, work and play, and competition. In describing self, therefore, it is expected that the American child will see himself or herself as an individual who feels free to voice his or her opinions, someone who enjoys hard work and fun times as well, and who enjoys unfettered competition and values progress and change, especially through the advancement of science and technology.

> *Your beliefs become your thoughts.*
> *Your thoughts become your words.*
> *Your words become your actions.*
> *Your actions become your habits.*
> *Your habits become your values.*
> *Your values become your destiny.*
>
> **Mahatma Gandhi**

The roles that people play in society also influence the perceptions of self. If we look at societies from the broad categorization of masculinity/femininity, one of the five value dimensions of Hofstede, we can see sharp differences in the reserved roles for the sexes. Gendered roles, which are expected behaviors and role specifications for women and men in society, differ and as such influence perceptions of self. In many societies, a man is socialized to be strong, assertive, and provide for the family. Therefore, the man's sense of self encompasses these expectations. On the other hand, women in many societies are socialized to see themselves as fragile, courteous, supportive, and to be taken-care of. If you are taught to see yourself as a second fiddle, there is no doubt that would influence your self-image and, consequently, self-esteem.

The Looking Glass Self

As we have discussed earlier, no one lives in isolation, but in a social environment where the opinions and perceptions of others create a set of expectations that one must fulfill. Often, we perform in public to meet social demands and the dictates of the situations in which we find ourselves. We, therefore, see ourselves through the eyes of others. What people say to us about us becomes the way we see ourselves, thus affirming that "*we are not only our brother's keeper; in countless large and small ways, we are also our brother's maker*."

The people that we live in close proximity to and whose opinions we value, we use as mirrors to reflect back to us what they perceive us to be. This is the "**reflected appraisal**" phenomenon developed by sociologist Charles Cooley in 1912. In many different ways we use our **"significant others"** as an evaluative mirror whose reflections of us influence the way we see ourselves. So, we develop self-concepts that mirror the way we think others see us. Such ways could be in the comments our "significant others" may constantly share with us such as:

"You are a kind person;" "you are lovable;" and "you are the smartest person I know." The comments may be negative rather than positive. If a mother constantly tells a child that he is "a good for nothing kid just like his father," what do you think the child would believe about his father and himself? That, perhaps, mother, who would know better, is right! Negative or positive reflections or opinions from important, relevant people to us, go a long way in influencing the perceptions of self, especially in the formative years to adolescence.

There is the possibility that "reflected appraisal" may be too positive or negative and may not reflect reality. The result of this will be an exaggerated sense of self either positive or negative. If your "significant others" do not see anything good in you, or see you as the best thing to ever happen to humanity, then you need a re-appraisal of the reflected appraisal. While a good self–esteem is desired, an exaggerated sense of self may prove detrimental, just as a low self-esteem. There are safeguards to ascertaining a "realistic" sense of self which we shall discuss in the following pages.

Social Comparison

Psychologist Leon Festinger (1956) developed the concept of **social comparison** to identify the process by which humans gain a sense of self through comparing themselves to others. In a sense, we gain an understanding of self through the characteristics we see in others and how such compare with the same characteristics, if they are equally present in us. It is by evaluating ourselves in comparison to others that we gain a measure of self as smart, beautiful, aggressive, rich, fat, talkative, and dependable. The degree to which we see ourselves as different from or equal to others depends on with whom we compare ourselves. The social comparison concept includes the dimensions "inferiority-superiority" and "same as or different from."

In a media-saturated society such as the United States, where "ideal images" pervade the screens and air waves, unrealistic expectations are developed and these lead to frustrations and, often times, disappointments. A negative self-concept may result from comparing self or one's situation and condition to the "ideal states" and "make-believe realities" created for mass consumption in the media. Often the result is a perception of self as inferior to and negatively different from others.

Just as with the "significant others," comparison "reference groups" influence whether an individual acknowledges his or her differences or caves in to the social pressures of the group. If a reference group attaches importance to certain features such as body weight, mode of dressing, and manner of talking, then these become important in their social judgment of others and have real consequences on those who accept the judgment of such reference group.

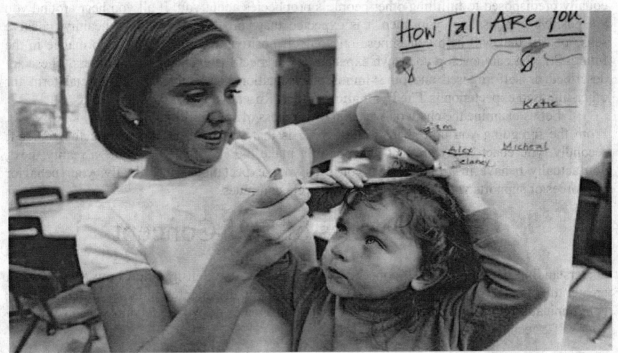

Do you measure up to your own expectations or your parents'?

The Influence of Self-Concept on Communication

Adler and Proctor (2011) claim that the self-concept is such a powerful force on the personality that it not only determines how you see yourself in the present, but also can actually influence your future. By this, these authors are alluding to the impact of your self-concept and self-talk on your behavior. The way you see yourself will influence the way you talk about yourself and possibly will influence the way you will see yourself in the future. Based on your self-concept, which is your perceived self, you may predict the outcome of your future behavior and would confirm such expectations because you tend to fulfill your own expectations.

Self-Fulfilling Prophecy

A prophecy is a prediction, a look into the future for what will likely happen. **Self-fulfilling prophecy, therefore, is the enactment of a prediction that you have made about and for yourself.** The predictions are based on how you see yourself now (self-concept) and your subsequent behaviors will be based on those predictions, thus making the predictions more than likely to occur. For example, if you are set up for a blind date and your self-concept prevails on you to predict that your date will probably not like you because you perceive yourself as not likeable or lovable, then you would behave in a way to confirm your self-doubt and affirm the expectation that your date would probably not like you. You may also listen to the appraisals that others have of you that they frame in the form of expectations. For example, your professor may say to you that: "I expect you to be one of those who would score an A on the coming test." Or "you have an inquisitive and intelligent disposition, so I know you will succeed in your academics." How would these statements influence your perception of self and your behavior?

You are predisposed to fulfilling your own predictions and, as a matter of fact, you're equally predisposed to fulfilling other people's prophecies about you. If all you hear around you are positive appraisals of you, then it is expected that you would develop a healthy, positive sense of self that will help you impose on yourself positive and successful performance in the future. So, you can develop your own expectations or meet the expectations of others. These are described as self-imposed and other-imposed expectations respectively. The special term for other-imposed expectation is **The Pygmalion Effect** (Rosenthal and Jacobson, 1968).

Let us examine the chain of events in the process of self-fulfilling prophecy.
From the foregoing you note that the first thing is that you hold an expectation for yourself; secondly, you enact behaviors that will possibly make the expectation become a reality; next, you actually behave in a manner that confirms your expectations; and, finally, your behavior reinforces or supports your expectation, so the cycle continues.

Characteristics of Self-Concept

Understanding the nature of self-concept will help you to have insight into how and why you create the mental pictures you have of yourself, how the mental pictures influence your communication and relationships, and how you can create a positive self-image and improve your self-esteem.

Self-Concept is Subject to Error

From our understanding of perception, we understand that human perception is rather subjective than objective. That is, our perceptions may be biased and self-serving. So it is with our self-concept. Because your self-image and self-esteem are based in perception, then they are subjective in nature and may not be factual. How you see yourself may not be congruent with the reality. You may perceive yourself as very good socially—that is, in your ability to get along well with others, but a verifiable record of your performance may contradict your report. Again, because perception is self-serving, we tend to exaggerate our abilities and qualities, especially more positively than may bear testimony.

One time or the other, we have come across people who have the tendency to exaggerate their qualities and abilities. But when they are observed in real moments, their self descriptions may not match the observed, verifiable performance. We do have friends or family members we describe as "all mouth" because of their tendency to boast of their capabilities, but which we have known to be a "stretch of the truth." How many times have we been bombarded with boastful claims from professional boxers who predict that their opponents would hit the canvas in a particular round, only for them to suffer ignominious defeat in the hands of the opponent they had underestimated? In other cases, the exaggeration may be negative. There are people who often downplay their abilities or underestimate their capabilities, not as a gesture of modesty, but a genuine lack of an accurate estimate of their real selves.

Self-concept is influenced by many variables that are themselves rather dynamic, in that they change over time. The state of mind of a person or his or her psychological condition can be a positive or negative influence on the perception of self. Sometimes someone may have a brief spell of self-doubt because of prevailing circumstances and may result in a negative distortion of the self-concept. The opposite may be the case because a spell of self-confidence may equally result in distorted self-concept.

Adler and Proctor II (2011) confirm four critical reasons why self concept is subjective and they are: *distorted feedback, obsolete information, emphasis on perfection, and social expectation.*

Distorted feedback is biased or inaccurate information gleaned from the "reflections of significant others," given to a particular individual. This arises from the subjective nature of person perception. Friends may be too critical of you, or your parents may be too supportive of your work and, without factual evaluation, distorted self- esteem may result.

Obsolete information is out dated or old information. When someone still sees himself or herself in the light of old, inaccurate information, the result is wrong self perception. Let's imagine that when in high school, you were considered the smartest kid in the subject of Mathematics, but that was then. Now, in college, you're competing with the best students from different high schools and, suddenly, you are one of many smart students and you no longer enjoy the accolades of high school. But if you still have the high school mindset, you're relying on obsolete information to gauge your sense of self.

Emphasis on perfection is an irrational expectation because "no one is perfect," and if you expect perfection in all that you do, then, you're setting yourself up for failure. All you will get are disappointments that would further deflate your self-esteem and self-image.

Sometimes social conventions and societal expectations may cause one to downplay one's abilities and achievements because a label of immodesty may be placed on someone who "blows his own horns." On the other hand, it may be socially acceptable to exaggerate one's confidence and, in essence one's self-concept, because that is the expectation or norm. The reality may be that the individual may actually experience internal self-doubt and lack of confidence. Hardly could one find an American soldier who would claim in public that he or she is very afraid of fighting a war that has been declared by the American government. The American populace on the other hand is always expressing a support for the troops and do have the perception of America's superiority over other countries in art and science of warfare. This exuberant confidence may lead us to get into wars unnecessarily. This is the same with individuals who take on responsibilities beyond their strength and capabilities because of the need for social approval.

Self-Concept Endures

Once we have formed our impressions, such images resist change. That is, just as we cling to first impressions, we cling to our self-concept. This is because we resist or avoid information that contradicts the impression we have formed of ourselves. As a matter of fact, we tend to expose ourselves to and accept information that supports our sense of self. This tendency has been aptly described as **cognitive conservatism** by scholars.

Self –concept is enduring regardless of whether it is positive or negative, because we act in many conservative ways to emphasize and maintain the old sense of self. We tend to associate with people who would confirm our self-concept.

It is reported that college students and married couples with high self-esteem seek out partners who view them favorably, but those with negative self-esteem would likely interact with people who view them unfavorably (Bower, 1992; Swann, 2005).

This awareness of the nature and nuances of self-concept should help you in realizing the need to constantly evaluate your strengths and weaknesses and to associate with those who would lift you up rather than those who would beat you down. Again, it is necessary to be realistically positive about other's evaluations of you so that you do not have an overtly exaggerated sense of your abilities and capabilities. This leads us to the subject of **self-awareness.**

Self Awareness and Self-Disclosure

Understanding yourself is very important to your communication with others. How you see yourself, influences how you communicate with others and, how you communicate with others influence the way others see and act toward you. Now, you know that how others see and act toward you influences your self-concept. There is further need, therefore, to gain self-knowledge in order to understand better who you are and how you can better communicate with others and improve your relational and professional success.

A useful model for examining and understanding self and for becoming more self-aware is called the **Johari window.** The window is a model of the self as containing four panes like most home windows. In essence, **Joseph** Luft and **Harry** Ingham (1984), the creators of the model, see the self as having four different parts—**the open self, the hidden self, the blind self, and the unknown self.** The key to understanding the Johari window is that the entire window represents all the information about a person. When divided into four separate parts, two parts are **known to self,** but **not known to others,** while the other two parts are **known to others,** but **not known to self.** See the figures that follow.

Self- Disclosure

Do you have a secret that you have sworn never to tell anyone? Do you have a friend that you trust completely and that you have told what you had declared not to tell anyone? **This revelation of private information, that is otherwise unknown to others, is described as self-disclosure.** This usually occurs in quality relationships where the communicators feel at ease with each other and do feel obligated to reveal significant information one to another. Obligation is not compulsion; therefore, revealing private information to another person is by choice and therefore is deliberate. **Self-disclosure is deliberately revealing to another person, significant and previously unknown information about yourself.**

Characteristics of Self-Disclosure

Self-disclosure usually happens in one-on-one dyadic encounters. This suggests that it is more comfortable for individuals to reveal personal information to another person in a one-on-one context rather than in a one-to-many context. As a matter of fact, it has been found that the more you reveal information about yourself to another person, the higher the likelihood that such a person would self-disclose to you as well. This is called the **dyadic effect.** Because you know the person to whom you are revealing your pertinent information and that you trust this individual to some extent, the risk is far less than the need to self-disclose. But when there are more people present, because you may not have the same level of trust for each of them, you would rather not self-disclose in public. In this case the risk far outweighs the benefit of self-disclosure.

Self-disclosure occurs in small increments. Any interpersonal relationship has different stages in its life cycle and, at the beginning stage, self –disclosure is rather small. But in time, trust and confidence in the other person develops, as well as the level of self-disclosure. We can think of self-disclosure resulting from interpersonal confidence—the greater the confidence, the greater the self-disclosure. **Self-disclosure is relatively uncommon in mature relationships.** When a relationship has stood the test of time and has witnessed incremental revelation of information by both parties, there is not much left to be disclosed, except for crucial or special occurrences. This is unlike relatively new relationships where the persons are just getting to know one another.

Self-disclosure is better received or handled in positive relationships. When a relationship is positive, participants feel good and confident about their relationship and themselves to the extent that any new information, even if it is negative, will be better presented and received. This is because the positive nature of such relationships has strengthened the confidence of the participants and has instilled in them a sense of selflessness without hidden agendas. For example, if your friend knows that you will always love her and that you do have her utmost interest at heart, then it will be easier for you to tell her what you really know and how you truly feel about her new boyfriend. Likewise, it will be easier for your friend to accept your evaluation of her new boyfriend.

Figure 5.1/The Four Selves of the Johari Window

The Open Self	The Hidden Self	The Blind Self	The Unknown Self

Known to Self Not Known to Self

The Open Self	The Blind Self	The Hidden Self	The Unknown Self

Known to Others Not Known to Others

Figure 5.2/The Johari Window

Known to Self	Not Known to Self	
1 *Open Self* *Information about self that is known to self and others*	*3* *Blind Self* *Information about self that is not known to self but known to others*	**Known to Others**
2 *Hidden self* *Information about self that is known to self but that others do not know*	*4* *Unknown Self* *Information about self not known to self as well as others*	**Not Known to Others**

Box number one contains information about yourself that you know of and that others interacting with you also have knowledge of. This is common knowledge about you such as your love for football, and your fear of flying.

Box number two contains information about yourself that you know, but that others do not know about you. This is information you have deliberately kept from those who interact with you. You may have a crush on your best friend and he doesn't even know it! Or that you have a fear of rejection, but you "mask" it from your friends.

Box number three contains information about you that others know of, but that you do not know. This may include behaviors and mannerism that you're unaware of, but that you engage in and, that others know too well about you. Example: You may be a conversational narcissist (someone who dominates others in conversation because he or she enjoys being in the spotlight always) and may not be aware of it.

Box number four contains information that neither you nor others know about you. These are your capabilities that you have not yet realized and that others are unaware that you are capable of. May be if you try your hand at piano playing as if your life depended on it, you may surprise yourself and others as to how good you may become.

As you may have discovered, the Johari Window model can be used to measure your willingness to disclose information about yourself to some people and not to others. You can actually construct your own Johari Window to reflect the variations in the different window panes, depending on whom you are interacting with. For example, a married couple may have different sizes of panes in their windows, representing their degrees of **self-disclosure** one to another.

Is someone whose life is an open book a good candidate for a trusting relationship? *Explain the following different Johari Window models and the different implications these may have on the communicators.*

Known to Self	Not Known to Self
Open	Blind
Hidden	Unknown

Figure 5.3

What kind of relationship would exist between you and someone whose Johari Window looks like the one above? This person has a rather open quadrant, a small blind quadrant, and a larger hidden quadrant than the unknown quadrant.

Known to Self	*Not Known to Self*
Open	Blind
Hidden	Unknown

Figure 5.4

What kind of relationship would exist between you and someone whose Johari Window looks like the one above?

In answering the questions above, you would have come to the conclusion that it is a good thing to be self-aware and that it is even better to relate to others who have a good understanding of who they are. To increase self-awareness, you must increase knowledge of self such that you would have a larger **Open Self**. You should seek more information about yourself and listen more to others in order to reduce your **Blind Self,** and by trying new things and discovering new abilities, you will reduce your **Unknown Self.** In order to reduce your **Hidden Self,** you should learn to reveal more of yourself to others, without which you would be able to have trusting friends or people who would be more open to you in return. **You should realize that self-disclosure begets self-disclosure.**

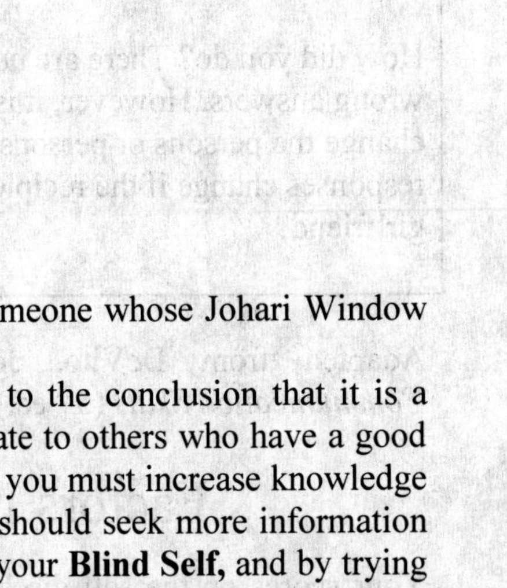

Why is it that people who meet on the train are more than willing to self-disclose to strangers?

Take the Self-Disclosure Test

How Willing to Self-Disclose Are You?

Instructions: Respond to each statement below by indicating the likelihood that you would disclose such items to, say, other members of this class.

Use the following scale: 1 = would definitely self-disclose, 2 = would probably self-disclose, 3 = don't know, 4 = would probably not self-disclose, 5 = would definitely not self-disclose.

_____ 1. My attitudes toward different nationalities and race.
_____ 2. My feelings about my parents.
_____ 3. My sexual fantasies.
_____ 4. My past sexual experience.
_____ 5. My ideal mate.
_____ 6. My drinking and/or drug-taking behavior.
_____ 7. My personal goals.
_____ 8. My unfulfilled desires.
_____ 9. My major weaknesses.
_____ 10. My feelings about the people in this group.

How did you do? There are no expected responses here because there are no right or wrong answers. However, it is believed that your responses would change if you were to change the persons or persons you are self-disclosing to. For example, would your responses change if the recipient of your disclosure is your close friend, boyfriend or girlfriend?

Adapted from DeVito, Joseph A. (2003). *Messages: Building Interpersonal Communication Skills* (5th ed.) New York: Allyn and Bacon.

Factors Influencing Self-Disclosure

Your scores on the self-disclosure test may be influenced by a number of factors. The influences on your self-concept formation also will influence your expression of self. **The factors that influence self-disclosure are personality, culture, gender, your listeners, and the topic under discussion.**

Personality

Remember the five personality categories identified in the beginning of the chapter? **People with different personality types have different tendencies to disclose or not to disclose.** Extroverts tend to be more sociable and do self-disclose more than introverts.

Also, those who experience less communication apprehension tend to self-disclose more than those who are apprehensive about communicating and self-disclosure. Self-confidence plays a great role in influencing the tendency to self-disclose. What gives self-confidence? These can be identified as perceptions of expertise and, sociability, less apprehension about self and a positive self-worth. Because of their positive perception of self, competent people tend to self-disclose more and feel less apprehensive about disclosing negative information about self. According to McCroskey & Wheeless (1976), self-confidence may make people more willing to risk possible negative reactions.

Culture

Culture is another determining variable in the degree of self-disclosure. People from different cultures tend to self-disclose differently. While some may feel obliged to disclose personal information in public, others may think it a taboo to do so. The differences can be drawn from the value dimensions of the different cultures as enumerated by Hofstede. In masculine societies, the disclosure of emotions and inner feelings may be considered a sign of weakness. Among some groups, for example, it would be considered "out of place" for a man to cry at a happy occasion such as a wedding, whereas in some Latin cultures that same display of emotion would go unnoticed (DeVito, 2005). Japanese culture socializes the citizens to see revelation of personal information to colleagues as undesirable, but in the (mainstream) U.S. culture such revelation is expected (Barlund, 1989; Hall& Hall, 1987). In many West African cultures, it is unusual for a woman or a man to talk freely about being a single parent, because the belief is that it is a personality failure not to be able to maintain a home with whom one has a child. So, people would describe a person who professes single parenthood in public as uncultured and shameless. Again, these are cultures where polygamy is practiced, so it is expected that if you "really want a husband or wife," you could get one.

In the American college classroom, the differences between American students and foreign students are easily discerned with the way the American students feel free to discuss issues and even give personal experiences to buttress their points. On the other hand, Middle Eastern students and their Oriental counterparts hardly ask or answer questions unless asked specifically to do so. And when they do answer, they hardly give lengthy and anecdotal information. For more information on Hofstede's value dimensions, review the early part of this chapter and the chapter on intercultural communication.

Gender

The stereotype about the non-expressive male and the overly expressive female may have some validity in it after all. All of the research findings that have been cited in this book about gender differences and communication do point to the fact that women tend to be more expressive than men. **So, women self–disclose more than men, as such, gender influences self-disclosure.**

Women, according to Sprecher (1987), disclose more than men about their previous romantic relationships, their feelings about their closest same-sex friends, their greatest fears, and what they don't like about their partners. Also, research has confirmed that women increase the depth of their disclosures as the relationship becomes more intimate, but men appear not to change their self disclosure levels even with increased intimacy in the relationship. In addition, men tend to have more taboo topics that they would not disclose to their friends than women (Goodwin and Lee, 1994).

As it is with gender comparison studies, there are always exceptions to the rule. In online dating encounters reported by CNN.Com in 2000, boys have been found to more than likely disclose family information than girls on the internet. In an earlier study by Derlega, Winstead, Wong, & Hunter (1985), in the initial encounters, men will disclose more intimately than women. This is done by men "in order to control the relationship's development."

Listener

That who your listener is will determine your degree of self-disclosure is basic common sense. You are more likely to self-disclose in small groups and in dyads than in public contexts. Not only that, you probably will self-disclose to people you like and trust and, more than likely the people you disclose to would tend to like you.

Imagine how you would disclose, if at all, your personal encounter with your boyfriend or girlfriend to your mother or father. Would a young man or woman in the American culture ever disclose his or her first kiss with the dad? Who your listener is will definitely influence your self-disclosure.

Sometimes, though, you may find yourself in a brief encounter that would lead to some significant sharing of information. This is what usually happens on the train, at conferences, and other situations that you may be "stuck with someone for long hours and the ensuing talk would lead to some unexpected revelations. The understanding is that you would disclose to such a stranger because you understand that you would never see that person again or that there is no chance of a further relational development with the person. And if there should be such a chance, we would become rather embarrassed for having been an "open book" during the initial encounter.

The Topic and Channel of Communication

As we have discussed earlier there are some topics that men would rather not discuss with their friends and that may be considered taboo. It is common sense, again, to note that there are some topics that are off the table when you're talking to a stranger, just as there are some issues you may not wish to discuss with your spouse, parents, teacher, and church members.

Studies have found that the channels of communication used to send messages with another person may play a significant role in your degree of self-disclosure. The fact that you see your listener face-to-face may influence your disclosure. Again, if you cannot see the person you are interacting with, would that influence your willingness to self-disclose? Reciprocal self-disclosure has been found to occur more quickly and at higher levels of intimacy online than in face-to-face interactions (Levine, 2000, & Joinson, 2001).

Appropriateness of Self-Disclosure

Self-disclosure comes with benefits and dangers. We make the decision of how much information about ourselves we will reveal to others based on how we evaluate the cost and benefits of such self-disclosure. The process by which we make the determination to conceal or not conceal private, significant information about ourselves to others is known as **privacy management** (Petronio, 2007). As we will find, we use self-disclosure to form stronger ties with others in some case, while in other cases, we may use it to drive others away.

Advantages and Disadvantages of Self-Disclosure

The rewards of self-disclosure include emotional release, encouraging others to self-disclose in return, understanding and clarifying one's feelings and position on issues, self-affirmation, image and relationship management, and social control.

    Emotional release or catharsis is a great reward of self-disclosure in that you have the opportunity to tell someone what might have been bothering you for sometimes, and when you finally let it out, you experience a sort of emotional release. So, you may self-disclose to maintain your emotional well-being.

    As pointed out earlier, "**self-disclosure begets self-disclosure.**" The tendency is that **self-disclosure is often reciprocal** and, as such, you can use it to form and maintain relationships with others. This is because as you reveal information about yourself, the other person naturally feels obliged to share private information of his or her own with you, thereby creating some level of trust and commonality. We can also conclude that self-disclosure is a function of trust and intimacy, which are the basic requirements of qualitative relationships.

    Sometimes you may not be able to clearly articulate your feelings, attitudes and opinions toward issues and persons until you share them with other person(s). **Through such declaration and articulation, you become aware and come to terms with your predispositions on such issues and persons.**

    Self-affirmation is another benefit of self-disclosure. When you reveal your privately held beliefs, attitudes, and perhaps actions to someone, you may be seeking the person's agreement and validation of such beliefs and actions. With another's stamp of approval, you may feel justified in your action and become less afraid or apprehensive of your status, orientation or actions as the case may be.

    We all have public and private selves and for reasons of presenting a particular image of self to a love interest, for instance, you may decide to reveal the fact that "you had never been so madly in love before." Such a revelation may stir greater interest for you in the other person because of the perception that you must have a genuine love interest in him or her.

    Often, we strategically drop information about ourselves to entice others to form and maintain relationships with us. **Such continued revelation of private, significant**

information has been found to help maintain self-images that promote relational satisfaction and success.

When you want others to feel that you are not helpless and that you have choices or, perhaps that you are in control of the prevailing circumstances in which you find yourself, you may use self disclosure to confirm that. Telling someone on your job that you have two good job offers you are considering when others are under the fear of massive lay-off on the job is a control or power strategy. This is that you are above the exigency that others may be facing and, such stance may earn you social prominence and other social rewards.

Revealing information about self has its attendant risks. There is no telling how others may react to your self-disclosure. On one hand your image and relationship may be enhanced, but on the other hand you may suffer rejection, loss of influence, negative impression, and you may end up hurting someone you love. **The risks of self-disclosure can be classified into three categories: Personal risks, relationship risks, and professional risks** (DeVito, 2003).

Personal risks of self-disclosure include **rejection by loved ones**, especially family members. What do you think would happen to you if you told your friends and family that you were the serial rapist sought by the police or that you have a highly contagious disease such as AIDS?

Relationship risks could arise from total self-disclosure because, usually, the information may be "too much to handle" by the recipient. As succinctly put by DeVito (2003), self –disclosures concerning infidelity, romantic fantasies, past indiscretions or crimes, lies, or hidden weaknesses and fears could easily have such negative effects.

As for professional risks, telling your boss of your attractive job offers while you're still working for him or her may lead to a doubt of your loyalty and you being fired before your presumptuous leave. Professional practitioners who "confess" to past sharp practices may lose respect and possibly may be faced with professional misconduct prosecution. In all, self-disclosure may result in social and personal rejection, professional and financial/material loss.

The Social Penetration Model of Self-Disclosure

Not all information disclosed to another person is equally significant, nor is it of the same depth. Some information that you reveal about yourself to several others cannot begin to scratch the surface of the deep, private information that you withhold and, that you rarely discuss with others but a significant few. In other words, our communication can be more or less disclosing depending on whether it has significance or it is about our deep, personal, private lives.
It is possible, therefore, for you to talk at length with some without actually revealing any personal, significant information about yourself.

How much of yourself have you revealed to someone else when you share stock phrases and ritualized communication with them? These are often superficial exchanges we share with others beyond which, we will cross to the level of facts about ourselves. Facts are verifiable, personal information about self that, in this case, you intentionally share with another person. Now you're yielding a little depth of yourself to that person. Even deeper are the opinions you hold on certain issues, persons or events. The deepest information we reveal to others have to do with our feelings. You must note that the deeper you are revealed to others, the more vulnerable you become, but since self-disclosure and trust co-relate, such revelation is not expected to be used to your disadvantage.

The **social penetration** model of social psychologists Irwin Altman and Dalmas Taylor (1973) reveals the degree of self-disclosure we share with others using the criteria of **breadth** and **depth** of the information shared. **Breadth of information has to do with the variety and extensiveness of the topics one person may discuss with another. Depth, on the other hand, is how significant, private, and intimate the information may be. Social penetration is the degree to which we are willing to share significant and private information with others.** In essence, we can assert that social penetration reveals the degree of intimacy in a relationship. Stenberg (1998) describes **intimacy as the feelings that promote closedness, bondedness, and connectedness.** These are the measures of the types of relationships we may have with other individuals. With casual friends we share breadth of information, but with intimate ones, we share both breadth and depth of information.

Figure 5.6/The Social Penetration Model

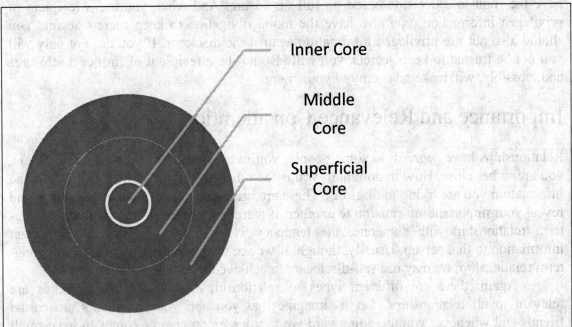

The social penetration model is represented here by three concentric circles.

*The innermost circle represents the most personal and significant information we may be willing to disclose to others. **(Depth)**

*The middle core represents information of lesser degree of significance, but still personal that we may want to disclose to others. **(Semi- Depth/Semi- Breadth)**

*The outer core or the superficial outer layer of the circles represents the breadth of information that we may disclose to others. **(Breadth)**

Guidelines for Self-Disclosure

The question is not whether or not one should disclose, but how one should do it! We are now aware of the great benefits of self-disclosure and, of course, its risks, but if one could learn how to do it appropriately, perhaps the risks can be minimized. The many guidelines for disclosing yourself to another person include the following considerations.

Ethical and Moral Consideration

We make decisions based on available information to us. But if we are not informed of a situation or condition that may be factored into our decision-making, then the person who refuses to disclose such important information to us has taken away our right to make the right decisions for us. We and others do have the moral and ethical obligation to self-disclose to others in order not to preclude them from making an informed decision. Would you want to know if a man who is proposing marriage to you is currently married to another woman? Also, would you want to know that a child that you are trying to adopt has mental illness? Would you, also want to know that your spouse of several years has just contracted HIV? These issues present dilemmas that can be resolved by moral and ethical responsibility—the significant others, who stand to be affected gravely, do have the right to a decision based on full disclosure. And when you are a recipient of privileged information, you also have the moral obligation to keep secrets secret. You should also not use privileged information against the discloser. If you do, not only will you not be trusted to keep secrets, you will also not be a recipient of further disclosures and, possibly, will make an enemy of your friend.

Importance and Relevance Consideration

Relationships have degrees; to some people, you're a casual friend, but to some others, you are rather close. How important to you is the other person and how significant is the information you are trying to disclose? These are important issues to consider before you reveal your important information to another. If there is no chance of an intimate or long-term relationship with someone, the tendency is not to reveal critical, important information to that person. Usually, though, if we see the possibility of an intimate, long-term relationship, we may use self-disclosure to achieve that goal.

Again, there are different types of relationships and, not all disclosures are relevant to all relationships. Let us imagine that you and your neighbors are casual friends and whenever you are doing yard work, your friend always comes to have small talk with you. Would you be willing or is it appropriate to reveal to him or her, the fact that your childhood friend, who lives in another state is cheating on her husband. How would your neighbor process this information? That you yourself are considering having an affair, or that you suspect the neighbor of having an affair... The motivation behind your self-disclosure might be misjudged and you may no longer have a friend to engage in small talk with depending on how your irrelevant disclosure is judged.

Appropriateness Consideration

This relates to the previous consideration of how important the other person is to your relationship. The amount and type of information you disclose to another person depends on the status of that relationship. Adler and Proctor (2010) do claim that, it is usually a mistake to share too much information too soon in a relationship and that, when you decide to disclose your pertinent information to another individual, you should share both positive and negative information. This provides a sense of natural balance because hearing only negative information may be discouraging. Let us also add that hearing only positive information about you may lead to suspicion as well.

When you disclose information you have " kept close to your chest" to someone who is practically a stranger, you run the risk in the short-run, of possibly scaring the person away or, in the long-run, of losing your most prized possession, your self – concept and self-esteem, especially if the relationship does not last. As we have confirmed through research, self disclosure is incremental in most relationships (Duck and Miell, 1991). At the initial stage of the relationship, most of the exchanges are ritualistic and superficial information which may be expansive, but certainly lacking in depth. The degree and importance of information disclosed increase as the relationships move to the deeper, more intimate stages in its development.

The Risk Consideration

Revealing your "secrets" to another person for whatever purpose, comes with a number of risks. While you can be considered candid in revealing that you don't particularly like your boss, this may not sit well with your boss, who may not find it "necessary" to appreciate your work, let alone to promote you. Office politics requires that you judiciously measure the risks against the benefits of revealing personal feelings and thoughts. If not, what you say and do not say may come to haunt you. As noted by Rosenfeld and Gilbert (1989) revealing personal thoughts and feelings can be especially risky on the job.

When you self-disclose you open yourself up for judgment either positive or negative. This is why it is necessary to measure the trustworthiness and reliability of the recipient of your disclosure. If the other person has a hidden agenda, then your information can be used against you, but if the person is supportive and understanding, then you can consider you and your information safe. You have to balance the risks and benefits of self disclosure either in office or personal relationships. If others are not saying much, find out why, and if you are the one always running your mouth, you have to be more self-aware. Remember the Chinese proverb that states that: "When you speak, I have the advantage and when I speak, you have the advantage."

The Effect Consideration

All self-disclosure has effects, either positive or negative. Were it not for the effects of disclosure on self, the other and the relationship, we would not have to consider the guidelines for self-disclosure. You have to consider how easily emotionally disturbed your receiver can be by your disclosure and how sensitive the issue at hand is. Everyone is a psychological being with different ranges of emotional tolerance. While your girlfriend may envy the fact that all the men around you are attracted to you, your boyfriend may not appreciate that fact and you should know whether to tell him or not, whenever any of man propositions you. While you may think this would make him feel lucky for having you, it may also indicate to him that his relationship with you will always be competitive.

The Reciprocation Consideration

As we have noted earlier, self-disclosure begets self-disclosure. This suggests that when you self-disclose to another, it is expected that the receiver will self-disclose back to you. If you are the only self-discloser, then the recipient may be overly cautious of self-disclosing back to you for a number of reasons we have discussed. However, there are situations where one-way disclosure would be the norm. For example, an interview for a job or a personality television interview would qualify as a one-way self disclosure. The purpose of the interview is for you to reveal who you are to the interviewer in order to determine your suitability for a given position. And a media personality interview is to expose you and your nature, experience, strong points, weaknesses, and other background information necessary to provide human interest and motivation to the viewing audience.

Responding to Disclosures

Just as the discloser has considerations and responsibilities, the receiver also has responsibilities. After all, the discloser chose to reveal pertinent information to a specific person and not the whole world for a reason. As such, the receiver of disclosed information has the responsibility of understanding the information, lending support to the discloser and, most importantly, the obligation not to carry a megaphone to announce the disclosed information to all.

Active Listening Responsibility

As we know (Chapter Two), there are different listening habits—some bad and some good. It is desirable to listen to understand and to empathize with the disclosers to the extent that we fully comprehend whatever the message is that they are trying to share, as well as the impact on them. DeVito (2005) charges the receiver to "listen actively, listen for different levels of meaning, listen with empathy, and listen with an open mind." To be sure that you understand what the speaker is saying, you should put them into your own words as you repeat what you have heard, and verify that understanding by asking questions. It is a disservice to the speaker if you should misrepresent the meaning and purpose of the disclosure, especially by not actively listening to understand him or her completely.

Support or Affirmation Responsibility

When someone self-discloses a rather painful experience to you, the least you could do to help this person is to offer emotional support and positive reassurance of: "I am always here to help and support you." After disclosure of embarrassing information, the discloser would feel a sense of vulnerability that you the receiver can help to defuse by affirming and supporting with your understanding and reassurance. You should remember that self-disclosure is often based on trust and confidence and you should act in a manner that would justify such reposition of trust and confidence in you.

Confidentiality Responsibility

How would you feel if what you said in confidence to a close friend has now become public knowledge to everyone around you, many of whom you would never tell much about yourself to, let alone some deep feelings and thoughts? This is the issue of confidentiality. If you cannot keep a secret, not many people would find you a reliable friend and you would not have many to depend on, either. When you are given privileged information, you have the responsibility to keep it confidential and not broadcast it all around to others for whom it was not meant.

Improving Self-Concept and Self-Awareness

One characteristic of a competent communicator is the recognition, desire, and capacity to adapt to situations in which he or she may be found. Now that you have great insight about self-concept, self-esteem, and self-disclosure, you can now recognize how to objectively view yourself, improve your self-worth, and manage your personal information appropriately. Although we have recognized the impact of your genes on your self-concept, you are not imprisoned by these biological determinants, because "you have the power to change a great deal of your communication traits" (Seligman, 1993)). Again, self-concept itself is a dynamic process that keeps changing over time and through different experiences.

Would you like to be more assertive in your communication with others? Or would you want to explore yourself more so that you may reduce your blind self? Changing and improving your self-concept to improve your self-awareness and bring about personal growth, no doubt, will take time, determination, skill, and practice. Whatever the focus, there are guidelines you can follow to improve your self-awareness and communication.

Adler and Proctor (2011) present some guidelines that can be followed to improve your self-concept. These guidelines are that the individual should:

- **Have a realistic perception of him or herself**
- **Have realistic expectations**
- **Have the will to change**

- **Have the skill to change**.

Seiler and Beal (2008) also present a set of similar guidelines for improving the self. The guidelines are as follows:

- **Decide what you would like to change or improve about yourself**
- **Describe why you feel the way you do about yourself**
- **Make a commitment to improve or change**
- **Set reasonable goals for yourself**
- **Decide on the specific actions you are going to take**
- **Associate with positive people whenever possible.**

Focus on how you perceive yourself and go through both of the guidelines above and suggest different ways you can improve your sense of self.

Identity Management

Your perception of who you are can be described as your identity. And, as we know, your identity is influenced by a number of factors. Your social environment plays a great role in who you perceive yourself to be, just as your genetic make-up has its influence on your person. We compare ourselves to others to see how we measure up or how they measure up; we use others as our mirrors to reflect back to us what and who they perceive us to be and; our cultures socialize us to see ourselves through the cultural prisms. We, therefore, tend to perform or play the roles of the perceptions of our assigned self in society, just as we also tend to display our natural traits.

Consequently, "identity is partly a *characteristic* (something that you possess), partly a *performance* (something you do), and partly a *construction of society* (Duck & McMahon, 2012).

The performance of self-concept or identity is an expectation based on assigned roles and statuses in society. When we enact these societal expectations we are presenting an image to others who are equally performing their roles. Often, society frowns at the non-performance of assigned expectations because the performer is not conforming and, as such may receive unfavorable sanction even though largely social. Sanctioned behavior may run counter the **perceived self** (who you see yourself to be in moments of self-examination—a reflection of your self-concept), thereby necessitating a need to present another self that is more acceptable and that would receive positive evaluation. Your **presenting self** is the performed public image that you believe would create the desired impression you want others to have of you at a particular point in time.

The strategic presentation and creation of desired impressions for other's consumption, for the purpose of their positive evaluation of you is called Identity or Impression Management. It can also be described as something you do to make others feel good or comfortable around you. In all, the activities we engage in to present ourselves differently in different situations and to different people for different purposes is called identity management.

We all engage in self and other enhancement. We present different identities to other people for different purposes. What we do to perform these different identities is what sociologist Erving Goffman (1959) refers to as **facework**. These are the **verbal and nonverbal behaviors we engage in to influence how we and others are perceived.**

Why We Create Different Identities

Can you recall when you had to present a different image of yourself to another person and for what reasons? We present different images or identities of ourselves to others for different reasons. This may be to start up a relationship or maintain an ongoing one; it may be to gain the agreement of others; it may also be to save the face of another person (creating an image so others may be seen in a particular light) and; it may be to create new selves, a creative exploration of new dimensions to ourselves to improve self-perception and the way others perceive us.

Imagine that your friend has invited to your house another friend whose affection you desire. This is a chance of a lifetime to make a positive impression on this person. Scholars agree that you could do one or a combination of three things to create the desired impression: **Change your attitude, the setting, and your appearance.** To enhance your appearance, you could get a new haircut, a new set of clothing and shoes, and a new deodorant, cologne or perfume. This means you will do something to your physical appearance that will endear you to the person. Also, you may manipulate the setting of the event. You could clean up your house, re-arrange some on the wall, place a flattering picture of yourself conspicuously on your coffee table, etc. You could also enhance your new identity by changing your demeanor and attitudes. This is the time you may want to appear gentlemanly, cultured, and sophisticated both in language and deeds.

We have confirmed that we all manage our identities for different reasons and in different ways. We also have different abilities to manage our identities. Some of the characteristics of impression management would suggest that it is a dynamic process.

The Nature of Identity Management

Each Person has Multiple Identities

The previous picture on "Identity Management" page and the one on the next page to this are pictures of the same lady, who displays some of her identities. To different people and in different contexts, she performs and presents different images of herself. Just as the lady in the pictures, we all have multiple identities; we play different roles in society and have different personalities; we also have the need to adapt ourselves to different situations for different purposes.

Among your friends you may present yourself as the talkative, happy-go-lucky person, but in your college classes, you're the quiet one who rarely asks questions. You may be the confident, fast-talking, and sometimes rude person at home with your parents, but with your intimate friend, you're a timid, unsure, but careful person. Immigrants to the United States who speak other languages often find themselves in situations where their fluency and accent would be an asset rather than a liability. In police encounters, some may pretend not to understand English while others would emphasize their accent to present themselves as powerless victims to attract sympathy or favorable consideration.

Politicians on political campaigns have mastered the art of presenting different selves to different political crowds in order to identify with them. Before blue collar workers, they roll their sleeves and appear to be "one of the people;" but before corporate icons and leaders of industry and the professions, politicians adapt not only their mode of dressing, but their lingo as well.

Each Person Manages His /Her Identity Differently

As personalities differ, so are personal styles and idiosyncrasies. The same goes for how we manage our identities. While some people are more aware of themselves, others are less aware of the images they present or their observable characteristics to the extent that they are less skillful at managing their identities.

Self-monitoring is the process through which you observe and monitor your behaviors and the impressions they create. High self-monitors have the ability to pay attention to their own behavior and others' reactions, adjusting their communication to create the desired impression (Adler and Proctor, 2011). The opposite is true for low self-monitors who have less caution in expressing their emotions and thoughts and the way others may perceive them.

Sometimes, though, high self-monitors may over analyze situations and miss out on enjoying the moment in interpersonal relations. We can question whether someone who is so overly conscious of the images he or she presents out there can really enjoy close, unfettered, spontaneous relationship with others. On the other hand, low self-monitors may have a rather simplistic view of self and others and may not be able to adapt sophisticatedly to situations that are rather less unambiguous and complicated.

YOU MAY HAVE HEARD OF "SCENE KIDS."
By Lori Ilardi

What is "Scene?" *Scene* is a stereotype given to people like me for dressing and acting the way we do. It's not all about the way I dress that makes me *scene*; being *scene* is just who I am. Many people who are stereotyped as *scene* have qualities that put us into that category such as teased hair that's many different colors, short skirts with knee high socks, and our "IDGAF" attitudes. Some people may ask:

"What makes a person *scene*?" Here's the answer: You can't make someone scene-- you either are or you're not. Scene people have a very strong attitude because they don't care about what people think or say about them. We are usually obsessed with little things. Most scene girls are in love with Hello Kitty. I, on the other hand, have a strange obsession with cupcakes, dinosaurs, and zebras. Scene hair is mostly having razor cut jagged hair that's either black or multi colored. Sometimes, like in my case, even both. Many scene girls like to tease their hair such as I do. And to complete the hair, we add bows of all different colors and sizes depending on our outfits. Clothing of a scene person is very out of the ordinary. We wear bright neon colors along with black to make the neon stand out more. The bows usually always match the neon color on the clothing. Leg wear usually only consists of skinny jeans and miniskirts with knee high socks on.

Many scene people also have something called a *scene* name that they are referred to as instead of their actual name. For instance, my nickname is Nightmare and my *scene* name is Lori Vanity. These names are not to be attention seeking, they're to be known as a special label to the scene people of this decade.

The music we listen to is mostly crunk-core bands, such as some of my favorites: "Blood on the Dance Floor" and "Brokencyde." Most of us love going to concerts all the time just to watch bands who are trying to make it and watch the bands we love play. *Scene* is a style that not everyone can fully understand because no one really understands why we do what we do. Being *scene* is just who we are and we like ourselves because of it. No one can fully understand any style but this one seems to confuse people the most. I would like to know why. Also, a lot of people hate us because we're scene. They don't realize that it's just us showing ourselves for whom we really are and that we don't care about what other people say about us. Like my idol, Dahvie Vanity, always says: "Haters Make Us Famous." And that's what they are doing. Not everybody who has some of these qualities is *scene*. Every *scene* person is different and has his or her own way of being *scene*.

Every stereotypical thing people say is what makes *scene* kids *scene* when, in reality, we all have our own ways of being *scene*, and we each have our own way of expressing it. Each day, the *scene* population grows and each day our small minority of a stereotype grows into a majority of how people want to be. We are who we are and our attitudes and clothing are what make us *scene*. People either love it or hate it, and if you hate it, we don't care. *Scene* is who and what I am and I won't change for anybody.

To learn more about "scene" kids, please visit the following websites:
http://www.urbandictionary.com/define.php?term=scene
http://www.urbandictionary.com/define.php?term=scene+kid

Identity Management is Situational

We have already identified that identity management varies from person to person and from situation to situation. Would you be more guarded when dealing with friends than strangers? Would you be more conscious of the images you present to a new girlfriend or boyfriend than your ex-girlfriend or boyfriend? When I was presented as a new hire to the payroll department of my college, the person attending to me looked me over and commented on how well dressed I was. I took that as a compliment and, then, she added that I should not change my mode of dressing as soon as I settled into my position at the college because she had seen many such new hires that came well-dressed to their interviews and their orientation programs at the college, but who, over a short while had changed their appearance. Needless to ask if the change had been for better or worse!

Somehow we can see that "familiarity breeds contempt," in impression management. But research confirms that the gender of the person is significant. When interacting with familiar persons of the same sex, we tend to be less concerned with impression management than when interacting with less familiar people of the same or opposite sex (Leary, Nezlek et al, 1994).

We Engage in Conscious and Subconscious Identity Management

Here is another question: Do people present different identities in situations where there are no people present to observe the changes in the identities? We may get so used to performing for the public that we unconsciously engage in impression management behaviors even when others are not available to monitor or view the performance. Think for a moment on the reasons you engage in flirtatious eye movements and facial expressions when you're talking on the phone with your lover. Are you aware of your behaviors or have such behaviors become a part of you that you engage in them subconsciously? The answer is both. Some impression management activities are rather deliberate while others are public performances we engage in as second nature.

We Are All Participants in the Game of Identity Management

We are all in the boat of identity management together. To paraphrase Shakespeare: All the world is a stage and everyone is an actor and has his or her entrances and exits. As actors on the world social stage, we are all aware of the parts others are playing just as we follow our own scripts in the same play. Impression management is, therefore, a collaborative enterprise. You are expected to present a "front" and others do know that you're presenting a 'front," and are busy presenting their own fronts simultaneously. This is because you are all actors in the same play of impression management.

Ervin Goffman's metaphoric theatre suggests that in the drama of identity management, each of us is a playwright who creates and performs roles that meet others expectations. The others are part of the drama as well; they are audience members who are equally creating and performing their characters designed to impress others.

Imagine yourself in your college class. Your professor expects certain behaviors of you just as you expect the professor to behave as expected. There are other role expectations for you and your colleagues in the class. You're to submit assignments on time, ask questions in class, and should not in any way disturb others' right to a pleasant class exercise. What if you have an unruly student in the class who constantly talks about events and stories not related to class work, and does so in a rude manner disrespecting the professor and the other students. How do you suggest the professor should handle such a student and would you handle the situation as someone who is impacted by the selfish behavior of the lone student? Now imagine that the professor lashed out on the student and rained expletives on him. Is this appropriate? Would you also "curse out" this student? All the actors in this scenario do have an image to maintain and present. While truly the professor may want to say some nasty things to the student, often, the social expectations forbid his doing so. So, what he would do in the "front stage" may not be what he would actually do in the "back stage."

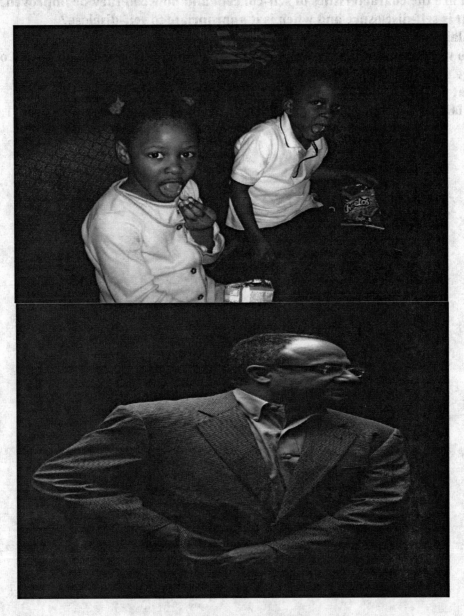

Does age influence identity management?

Review Questions

1. What is self-concept and how is it different from self-esteem?
2. Identify five self-concept descriptors you would use to describe who you really are.
3. Identify and describe four major contributors to self-concept development.
4. Identify and describe each of the 'big five' personality types.
5. To what extent does cultural teaching influence your self-concept?
6. What are the major differences between the looking-glass self and social comparison theories of self-concept formation?
7. How does self-concept influence one's communication?
8. What are the characteristics of self-concept and how can they be improved?
9. What is self-disclosure and when is it appropriate to self-disclose?
10. Explain the idea of the Johari Window?
11. Who would you rather be friends with: A person with a large hidden self or a large unknown self?
12. What are the factors influencing self-disclosure?
13. Explain the social penetration model of social psychologists Altman and Taylor.

Chapter Six
Human Emotions

What are emotions and how do they influence human behavior? Any observable changes in human behavior will, undoubtedly, influence interpersonal relations, which will have to accommodate and adjust to the changes in the behavior as it affects the expectations and enactment of such relationships.

Often, what we characterize as emotions are the bodily reactions that are observable and not the instigator or causes of the reactions. We describe emotions as feelings, things that happen to us and that make us react in some perceptible ways. But are emotions reactions to events or thoughts, or are they the causes of reactions or thoughts? Studies over the years have progressed from seeing emotions as causes of reactions, as results of reactions, and as both. The latter is more acceptable today because we have come to understand that when we experience external stimuli, there are bodily changes that do occur that, then lead to the arousal of feelings. On the other hand, your emotional memory will cause you to cognitively interpret certain situations in particular ways and such will lead to the experience of certain emotions.

Psychologist Charles Morris offers an inclusive definition of emotions as **"a complex affective experience that involves diffuse physiological changes and can be expressed overtly in characteristic behavior patterns."** This shows that emotions are complex feelings we experience that involve changes of our internal tissues that manifest in secretion of hormones, and that cause observable behaviors. This definition implies the presence of external or internal stimuli that trigger internal changes in humans, that lead to cognitive interpretations and, that lead to behavioral reactions that are apparent and, therefore, observable.

Credit: Bill O'Connell

The link of emotions to interpersonal relationships and communication is better understood when we realize that any observable behavior is a result of complex reactions to both external stimuli and the physiological changes that result from the stimuli. Your actions, either verbal or nonverbal, influence the feelings and behaviors of others. You may influence others positively or negatively, to love or to hate, to stay or to flee. So, understanding what emotions are, their sources, how they are expressed, will improve our understanding of interpersonal relationships. Not only that, success in our interpersonal relationships is dependent on our ability to understand and to manage our own emotions and to be sensitive to the feelings of others. This is what Goleman (1995) described as **emotional intelligence**. The importance of emotional intelligence is demonstrated when it is identified as having a positive association with self-esteem, life satisfaction, and self-acceptance (Carmeli, Yitzhak-Halevy, & Weisberg, 2009). Emotional intelligence has also been linked with healthy conflict management and relationships (Smith et al., 2008).

Components of Emotions

From the definition offered us by Morris (1976), we see that there a number factors involved in understanding human emotions. **There are external stimuli, physiological changes, observable verbal and nonverbal reactions or behaviors.** Let us examine each of these components of what we understand as constituting human emotions.

External Stimuli

Whenever we are confronted with external stimuli of different kinds, there are attendant mental and bodily reactions. When you see your girlfriend or boyfriend, the sense of sight is aroused and signals are sent into your brain that instructs instinctively how you should handle the situation depending on your prior experience or conditioning. When you witness vehicular accidents, the sights affect you one way or the other. The same principle informs us that what you see, hear, touch, taste, and smell, will register in the brain where instructions of how to react is given. Although these may occur in imperceptible moments of time, nonetheless they do, and subsequently will lead to our experience of certain feelings.

The fact that what you sense or receive through your senses does influence, one way or another, is demonstrated in the need to control what people are exposed to in the media. For instance, movies are rated G, R, or X for a reason, and this is because of people's expected reactions to the contents of the movies. Accident victims are quickly covered from public view; pornographic scenes are blocked from public view; and the laws about indecent exposure exist because of the assumption that what people see will influence their thoughts and reactions, that is, their emotions.

Physiological Changes

Whenever someone feels an emotion, many bodily changes do occur (Rochman & Diamond, 2008). The term **proprioceptive stimuli** is used to denote the process whereby the internal tissues secret hormones into the blood stream, thus causing internal changes of increased heart rate, blood pressure, adrenalin flooding, increased blood sugar level, etc.

> ***Proprioceptor:***
>
> *A sensory nerve ending in muscles, tendons and joints, that provides a sense of the body's position by responding to stimuli from within the body.*
>
> Dictionary.com

External Reactions

When physiological changes occur in the body as reactions **to external stimuli**, there are also corresponding external reactions. Feelings manifest externally as blushing, sweating, different facial expressions, shaking body, twitching hands, varied postures, high or low tone of voice, increase or slowed rate of speech, etc.

Cognitive Interpretations

The mind also plays a role in what type of emotion we feel and how we express the feelings. As a matter of fact, we cannot be certain of what type of emotion someone is feeling by observing the external, observable nonverbal manifestations of such emotions. Sometimes we cannot distinguish between the nonverbal manifestations of excitement and fear. Sometimes we cry when we are happy or sad; we sweat when we are afraid or elated.

In essence, because the secretions that flood our body are the same for many of the emotions we feel, and the external reactions may be ambiguous, it is rather difficult to be certain of the emotions we feel by just observing our external nonverbal behaviors.

The interpretations that we give to external stimuli will influence the type of emotion we feel. Imagine that someone you know and respect, without forewarning, started to hurl expletives at you. How would you feel? Your feeling depends on how you interpret the situation. Strange as it may be, you may consider your assailant as someone who is on the brink of emotional breakdown or is at the onset of mental disorder. Or you may consider that this person is of a sound mind and must find you or your actions deplorable to have warranted such outburst. These are two cognitive interpretations of a situation which will result in feeling different emotions. The first interpretation will cause you not to take offence at the expletives being hurled at you; rather, you will feel **pity, compassion and concern**. The second interpretation may cause you to feel **hurt, annoyed, and sad.** Apparently, cognitive interpretations of external stimuli influence the emotions we feel. The lesson here is that whenever you're feeling certain emotions, be it good or bad, we must examine why that is so. May be a **reappraisal** of the interpretations we give to stimuli will reduce the emotional impact of such on us. And if we do this in our interpersonal encounters, perhaps, we can begin to reduce the tensions that we feel and create a positive mindset that will not only grow relationships but make them less stressful.

What is love?

Types of Emotions

Emotions have been likened to colors: some are primary while others are blends. **The most common and typical human emotions have be identified as anger, fear, joy, and sadness**. Regardless of culture, gender, class, and roles played in society, these emotions have been found to be universal.

Plutchick (1962) identified eight basic categories of emotions, which he claims are derivatives of basic human and animal instincts. These emotions are **destruction, reproduction, incorporation, orientation, protection, deprivation, rejection, and exploration**. Plutchick emphasizes that it is **intensity** that differentiates one emotion from another. Considering "deprivation," for instance, its intensity moves along a continuum in descending order from grief, sorrow, sadness, dejection, gloominess, and pensiveness. All the emotions we feel represent a lack of something in our lives--from money, shelter, to love and sex. Although scientists have added new dimensions to the ideas of Plutchick, the recognition of emotion intensity has become a part of our understanding of emotions.

In the following three-dimensional model of Plutchick's emotion categories, intensity of emotions is represented by the vertical dimension, ranging from maximum intensity at the top to a state of sleep at the bottom. The model tapers inwards at the bottom to indicate that emotions are less distinguishable at low intensities (Morris, 1976).

Figure 6.1/Plutchick's Three-dimensional Model of the Emotions

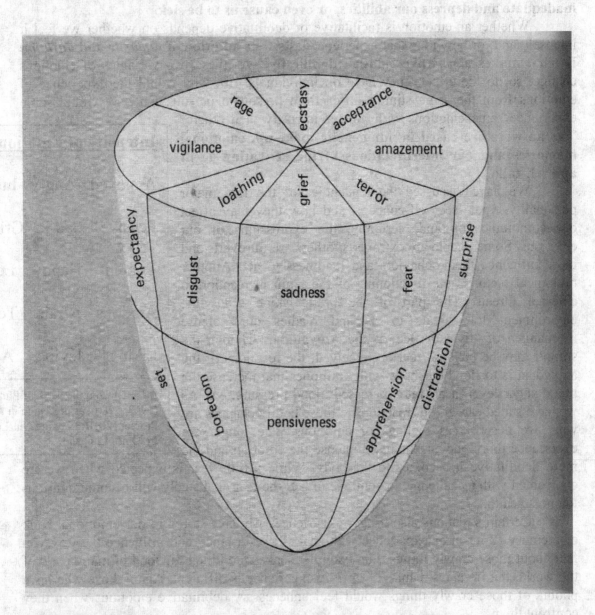

Adapted from Plutchick & Robert (1962). *The Emotions: Facts, Theories, and a New Model*. New York: Random House.

Facilitative and Debilitative Emotions

Apparently, some emotions can be classified as good or bad, but neither can be totally good or bad, considering that emotions are reactions and we can choose how we react to emotion inducing agents. Sometimes we feel great and at other times we feel terrible about the same event. But some emotions are felt more intensely than others and for a longer duration. This is the distinction between strong and mild emotions. Emotions can also be classified as **facilitative and debilitative.** In other words, **some emotions are good because they help us to achieve greater ends, rather than cause us to feel inadequate and depress our abilities, or even cause us to be sick.**

Whether an emotion is facilitative or debilitative depends on whether we feel it intensely and for how long that experience lasts. **The addition of *intensity* and *duration* is what makes a negative emotion debilitative.** As these two variables of emotions change, so do the effects they have on individuals. But why would the experience of emotions from the same stimuli differ from person to person, and why would some experience same emotions with greater intensity than others? **The answers are based in our genetic make-up, emotional memories and our interpretations of the activating agent and self-talk.**

We have discussed the tendencies of the five major personality types (see self-concept) and how they may affect our communication and, certainly, the expressions of our emotions. Some people are extroverts, others are introverts and these influence their behaviors and readiness to act. Another biological factor is the functioning of the brain in reaction to external threats. The part of the brain which scans the environment for threats to us and readies our defense mechanism of "fight or flee" is the **Amygdala.** Though the stimuli may be physical/real or perceived, the reactions of the amygdala is to flood our body with hormones that increase the blood sugar level, heart rate, increased blood pressure, etc. As we have stated earlier, our reactions to these bodily changes are what we describe as feelings or emotions. The longer we experience this flooding, the more intense the emotion and the more debilitative it becomes to the body. While a little fear is expected when we are confronted with a challenge, to continue to feel the fear unabatedly will become injurious to one's health.

Intensity of Emotions		
Annoyed	Angry	Furious
Pensive	Sad	Grieving
Content	Happy	Ecstatic
Anxious	Afraid	Terrified
Liking	loving	Adoring

Adapted from the work of Plutchick (1962, 1980), as presented in Adler & Proctor (2010) Looking Out/Looking In. Ohio: Cengage.

Certain situations also trigger experiences we have stored in our emotional bank or memory. Your prior experience with snakes, for instance will influence the way you feel about those crawly things. For example, snakes are killed for food in many parts of the world, but in mainstream U.S. A., the experience is different. Again those who have phobia of those crawly things would feel unnecessary debilitative emotions when they confront them.

As we have also mentioned, your interpretations of situations and events will influence how you react to such events and situations. Self-fulfilling prophecy is a situation whereby we make our predictions come true having confessed such and convinced ourselves of their being real. **In essence your thoughts and self-talk would cause your feelings**. If you agree with yourself that you'll not like the person you're set up on a date with, you'll probably not going to come away with a good impression of that person. Often, debilitative emotions derive from our irrational thoughts and, yes, we experience several of them from time to time. (See "Fear of Public Speaking" for more on irrational thoughts).

Credit: Bill O'Connell

Can you identify what emotions this lady is experiencing: Facilitative or debilitative?

Factors that Influence Emotional Reactions

Personality

As we have discussed under self-concept and self-disclosure, your personality plays a great part in how you see yourself and your willingness to open up communication with other people. Your personality also affects the way you perceive and express emotions.

Culture

In addition to the biological disposition of personality is the influence of cultural environment on emotional reactions. Different cultural experiences produce different human reactions and expectations. While some cultures may frown at a cheating husband, another may frown at why a man would be restricted to only one wife. Some cultures eat certain foods that may cause others of a different culture to puke.

The experience of communication varies from culture to culture, in that some value open expression of feelings while others are less expressive. Comparison of Asian American and Hong Kong Chinese and European Americans, for instance, would reveal that European Americans favor "high arousal positive affect" such as excitement to Asians' preference for "low arousal positive affect" such as calmness.

The Yoruba of Western Nigeria value expression of emotions in public, especially when mourning the dead. If someone does not express such sorrow visibly, many negative interpretations are alluded. Perhaps this individual did not love the departed or, perhaps, had a hand in the death of their departed beloved. It is interesting to note that these days, pall bearers are hired to not only convey the dead to its final resting place, but to also display loud outburst of painful emotions to "show how deeply loved" the departed was to the relatives. Mind you, the emotional mercenaries are adorned in the same attire as the family members of the departed, such that a distinction between the hired help and the family would not be apparent.

The impact of culture on emotional expression cannot be more apparent than in the distinction between church services in the African and African American on one hand, and the European American communities on the other. When we play church in the African and African American communities, it is a festive occasion marked by singing, dancing, outbursts of catchphrases, and call-response. In the European American church, there is less of visible excitement of the worshippers. Hardly would anyone go "out of line" to interrupt the preacher, who in a subdued manner preaches to a stoically attentive audience. We know that the Christian God of the African is not different from that of the Europeans! Culture is the determining variable here.

Gender

Gender variation and biological sex also influence emotional reactions. Across cultures, women are believed to be more attuned to their emotions than men (Canli et al., 2002; Merten, 2005), just as men and women in different cultures are encultured to react differently to the emotions they experience. In certain situations, men are expected to suppress their emotions, especially in public, while it is permissible for women to express such in public. There are several other such social conventions or unwritten rules that guide the reactions of men and women to the emotions they experience. In the United States, for instance, it is unconventional for the President to breakdown and cry in public! Men are not supposed to display such fragility in public, let alone the Commander-In-Chief of the world's greatest army.

Several studies have contrasted men and women's emotional reactions of which some of them are reported by Adler and Proctor (2010) as follows. Research confirms the common saying that men are unexpressive while women are more expressive (Kunkel & Burleson, 1999). Women, collectively, are more likely than men to express positive emotions (love, liking, joy and contentment) and feelings of vulnerability (including fear, sadness, loneliness, and embarrassment). But men are more willing to reveal their strengths (Goldsmith & Fulfs, 1999). Women are also more likely than men to use **emoticons** to indicate their feelings online. Also, research confirms that power differences among communicators does influence who is more likely to be more sensitive

> ### EMOTICONS
>
> Emoticons are nonverbal images/messages created, using computer keyboards, to convey emotions and feelings of communicators online.
>
>

to the emotions of the other. Obviously, the more powerful have less need to be more sensitive to the emotions of those that are less powerful.

The different observable behaviors of men and women regarding emotional reactions and expressions are more likely a result of socializations and roles played in society than biological differences. Although biology plays a great part in emotional reaction as it relates to differences in personalities, we cannot say categorically that women are more emotional than men, but can affirm that the sexes are oriented differently and such orientation manifests in different ways of expressing our emotions.

Social Expectations

What happens if a man chooses to display his emotions in public in a culture that prides itself on male dominance, pride, confidence, and certainty? Loss of favor, respect, and recognition may be the fallout of such unconventional behavior. The fear of these social consequences may influence the emotional reactions of men. Even if they feel certain emotions, the fear of social condemnation will prevent their emotional self-disclosure.

Social expectations can be described as norms or rules that guide behavior and, there myriads of such that govern the expression of emotions from culture to culture. On banal television shows such as The Maury Povich and The Jerry Springer shows, when women and men confront each other with marital infidelity or relational faux pas, the men can only talk sharply at the women but not hit them, even in the heat of raw emotions. But the men are free to hit each other and often encouraged to do so for ratings. The women on the other hand, are frequently seen hitting the men in addition to hurling unprintable expletives at the men. What controls these behaviors, even in a banal situation such as these shows, is the established norms of behavior that govern emotional expression.

Guidelines for Expressing Emotions

We experience emotions with degrees of intensity, so we must express the differences in intensity with different words for others to understand how we truly feel. Again, scholars have affirmed that we find it rather challenging to express our feelings, just as we lack the vocabulary with which to truly express our feelings.

There are hindrances to expressing our emotions. We just identified the influence of power on expressing emotions; in addition to that, the type of relationship we have with others will facilitate or constrain emotional self-expression such that we will censor ourselves. Also, there is a distinction between feeling, thinking, and talking. The fact that you feel something does not necessarily mean that you should say it. Although you may hate your dear friend's husband, it is not your place to verbalize this to your friend or the husband. Again, there are certain feelings you may have about your employees that would be insensitive to verbalize and share with others.

Overall, though, it is a good thing to know how to communicate our emotions appropriately to others. The real task is to know how much, what level, how, and with whom to share the appropriate emotion. A good balance of this is good for our health as research has confirmed the physiological as well as social psychological advantages of appropriate emotional self-disclosure and expression. According to DeAgelis (1992), under-expression of feelings can lead to serious ailments to the extent that inexpressive people, who value rationality and self-control, try to control their feelings and impulses, and deny distress, are more likely to get a host of ailments, including cancer, asthma, and heart disease.

How then can we do the best job of expressing our feelings so that others may know how we feel and understand how to react to such feelings? Better still, how can we appropriately share our feelings with other without social or physiological repercussions? Let us examine some of the guidelines for expressing emotions.

Recognizing the Activating Agent

In order to express our emotions accurately, we need to identify the source(s) of such emotions. What are the activating agent(s) and how can we evaluate such sources of stimuli? If we understand the source as inconsequential, then our reactions should not be perturbing. If it a friend, then we have to find rationales for the behavior, and if it an unexpected source, then further evaluation is necessary. Understanding the why of the activating behavior will go a long way in determining how appropriately we should respond to it.

Recognizing and Describing Our Feelings

Identifying the behaviors that might have triggered your feelings is not enough; we have to be able to recognize what feelings we are experiencing and how deeply we are experiencing them. The problem with describing our emotions as we have dimensioned, is the fact that we lack the vocabulary with which to describe how we truly feel. Ask someone who is feeling terrible about a meeting that went awry, "How did it go?" The answer would usually be the emotional stock phrase of "not so good" or simple "alright," with a tone of voice that suggests everything is not alright. Perhaps, more appropriately he should have expressed the following emotions: Disappointment, annoyance, anxiety, concern, frustration, etc. The list could continue.

The point is that when we express our feelings, we should not only be certain of the emotions we feel, **we should share multiple emotions** as well. We all experience multiple emotions at any giving time and it will be inadequate to state only one or two of them when, as a matter of fact, they are many feelings rolled into one.

Claiming Ownership of Your Emotions

You cannot blame others for your emotions--they are yours. No one can make you feel any emotion, because emotions are your reactions to external and internal stimuli, to the extent that the other person may choose to react differently to the same stimuli. So, you have to state your emotions as yours, using "I" language and not "It" or "You" language.

"I" language is a language of responsibility, while "It" language is an indirect way of placing blame on another without directly stating so; it appears neutral, but it is not. The "You" language is as good as pointing an accusing finger at another person. Can you imagine that you have to change the way you accuse others when you say: "You make me mad," or "you make me sick," How is that possible if we are still referring to how we feel? It is better to state that: "I feel terrible for what happened," "I am happy you came, or "I am terrified of snakes." Note how each statement identified the feeling, its source, and who is responsible for the feeling.

Developing Your Emotion Vocabulary

As we have learned, many people do not have access to the vocabulary with which to describe how they feel. This is why we have to expand our vocabulary of emotions in order to be able to purge ourselves of our innermost feelings and by so doing, we relieve ourselves of the psychological burden of unexpressed emotions, which as we have learned, can be debilitating to our health. Floyd (2002) enumerates the consequences of low and high affection communicators and confirms that when compared with low affection communicators, high affection communicators (those who are able and do express their feelings) are:

1. Happier
2. More self-assured
3. More comfortable with interpersonal closeness
4. Less likely to be depressed
5. Less stressed
6. In better mental health
7. More likely to engage in regular social activity
8. Less likely to experience social isolation
9. More likely to receive affection from others
10. More likely to be in satisfying romantic relationships

You should look up the descriptors below (Table 6. 1) in the dictionary to become familiar with their meanings in order to be able to describe your feelings more accurately.

Table 6.1/Common Human Emotions

Afraid	Concerned	Exhausted	Hurried	Nervous	Sexy
Aggravated	Confident	Fearful	Hurt	Numb	Shaky
Amazed	Confused	Fed	Hysterical	Optimistic	Shocked
Ambivalent	Content	Fidgety	Impatient	Paranoid	Shy
Angry	Crazy	Flattered	Impressed	Passionate	Sorry
Annoyed	Defeated	Foolish	Inhibited	Peaceful	Strong
Anxious	Defensive	Forlorn	Insecure	Pessimistic	Subdued
Apathetic	Delighted	Free	Interested	Playful	Surprised
Ashamed	Depressed	Friendly	Intimidated	Pleased	Suspicious
Bashful	Detached	Frustrated	Irritable	Possessive	Tender
Bewildered	Devastated	Furious	Jealous	Pressured	Tense
Bitchy	Disappointed	Glad	Joyful	Protective	Terrified
Bitter	Disgusted	Glum	Lazy	Puzzled	Tired
Bored	Disturbed	Grateful	Lonely	Refreshed	Trapped
Brave	Ecstatic	Happy	Loving	Regretful	Ugly
Calm	Edgy	Harassed	Lukewarm	Relieved	Uneasy
Cantankerous	Elated	Helpless	Mad	Resentful	Up
Carefree	Embarrassed	High	Mean	Restless	Vulnerable
Cheerful	Empty	Hopeful	Miserable	Ridiculous	Warm
Cocky	Enthusiastic	Horrible	Mixed	Romantic	Weak
Cold	Envious	Hostile	Mortified	Sad	Wonderful
Comfortable	Excited	Humiliated	Neglected	Sentimental	Worried

Adapted from Adler, Ronald B. &Proctor, Russell F. (2011) *Looking Out/Looking In* (13th ed.) Boston: Wadsworth-Cengage.

Review Questions

1. What are emotions?
2. What are the common human emotions?
3. Identify and discuss the difference between facilitative and debilitative emotions.
4. What are the guidelines for expressing your emotions?
5. How might your emotions influence your communication?
6. Is there any difference in the way men and women express their emotions and why?
7. Why is it that humans find it challenging to express their emotions?
8. What does the word 'catharsis' mean and why is it important?

Chapter Seven
Interpersonal Relationships

Defining Interpersonal Relationships

The concept "interpersonal" suggests one with another, an exchange and acceptance of influence between two or more individuals that may result in quality relationships characterized by expectations and fulfillments of such expectations. All humans engage in one or more interpersonal relationships at any given moment in their lives. We all have friends, good friends, and intimate friends. This suggests that interpersonal relationships have levels, types, qualities, and characteristics that define them. The focus of this section is to identify the different types of relationships, their characteristics, and how they develop and possibly disintegrate. The lesson is to equip us with the understanding of the nature of relationships so that we may be able to form good relationships and recognize what may ail our relationships and to find ways to appropriately deal with the situations in which we may find ourselves.

According to Wood (2008), **a personal relationship is a voluntary commitment between irreplaceable individuals who are influenced by rules, relationship dialectics, and surrounding contexts.** This definition suggests a number of things. It suggests that an interpersonal relationship is unique because it involves irreplaceable individuals who treat each other as unique persons; it also suggests that relationships are governed by rules that guide the behaviors of the participants. Again, the definition points to the fact that relationships are influenced by different contexts and that it also has dialectics or tensions and dilemmas that the participants experience.

Another definition of relationship claims that it is **an association between at least two people, which may be described in terms of intimacy or kinship** (Seiler and Beal, 2008). Intimacy has to do with the degree of closeness while kinship explains biological or blood connection of the participants in a relationship. There are different dimensions to any relationship; they can last very long, they can be casual or intimate, and may be happy or unhappy. They may also be personal or impersonal, hateful or loving, private or public. To understand relationships, it is better to examine why they are formed.

The Need to Form Relationships

Have you ever wondered why you have the friends you have, and have you ever thought of what would happen to you if you had no friends at all? Humans have been described as social animals because we thrive in interpersonal relationships and cannot survive without human contact. There is, therefore, the need for humans to form social relations—webs of relationships from which we derive our identities and meet other physical and psychological needs. Apparently, we can only form a limited number of relationships, some of which may be satisfying and others less rewarding.

The following are the theoretical explanations why humans are motivated to form relationships. Here, we will examine uncertainty reduction theory, social exchange theory, and the fundamental interpersonal relations orientation theory.

Uncertainty Reduction Theory

As we interact with others, we seek information about them to give us a clue as to why they behave the way they do, and to increase our understanding of them. We want to get to know them better and reduce any uncertainty about them. The need to know stems from our desire to be able to control our choices and predict others choices as well.

The uncertainty reduction theory is a theory that suggests that when we meet others to whom we are attracted, our need to know about them, tend to make us draw conclusions from observable physical data (Berger and Calabrese, 1975; Berger, 1986). That is, the theory suggests that when we are attracted to others, we tend to want to know them better and, this need leads us to draw conclusions about them from the onset from their physical characteristics. This desire necessitates more communication from those with whom we want a relationship.

According to Berger and Calabrese (1975), the basic assumptions of the uncertainty reduction theory is that when strangers meet, they tend to seek to reduce uncertainties about one another. And the more attracted we are to the person, the stronger the desire to know more about the person. Uncertainty reduction principles manifest in interpersonal relationship development. The increased desire to know more about another person is a measure of the degree of attraction to that person.

The beginning or *entry phase* of an initial interaction is characterized by the exchange of **stock phrases** and **small talk** that do not let us into the deep knowledge of the other person. Therefore, much information is inferred from the physical, external features such as height, size, age, skin color, sex, general appearance and physical attractiveness (Seiler and Beal, 2008).

In the following **personal phase** of the initial interaction, communicators gain more latitude to probe and release more personal information than before. In essence, there is more disclosure of information relating to personal beliefs, values, and interests.

In the third stage which is described as the **exit phase** of the initial interaction, a level of trust and communication is established. This will dictate the direction that the relationship will take. This means that it is in this phase that the future of the relationship is ascertained. More importantly, the quality of the exchange that leads to uncertainty reduction between the communicators will determine the future of the relationship.

You have had the opportunity to meet someone with whom you desired a relationship. At first, you would attempt to determine whether there was a chance of a relationship by estimating such information from external indicators available to you. Upon meeting and interacting with the individual, you would confirm from the utterances and demeanor if you two had a chance at a relationship and, finally, you would evaluate the encounter and determine whether the effort was worth a try.

Social Exchange Theory

Exchange suggests trading value for value. When you value yourself, you place a worth or prize that another should pay for having access to what you have to offer. In other words, we constantly weigh the costs and rewards of our social and interpersonal relationships. Certainly, there are costs associated with our interpersonal involvement just as there are rewards.

Costs are considered the perceived negative outcomes that are associated with a relationship and **benefits** are the perceived gains associated with a relational involvement. As these are perceptions, they vary from person to person and from relationship to relationship.

According to Thibaut and Kelley (1986), the proponents of the social exchange theory, people deliberately evaluate the costs and benefits associated with possible relationships and seek those that are beneficial. Benefits in a relationship include pleasurable feelings, status, prestige, economic gain, and emotional satisfaction. Costs, on the other hand, include time, energy (physical and emotional), and economic loss. At the heart of these postulations is the underlying premise that individuals will think and act in self-interest.

The outcome of a relationship, therefore, is the difference between rewards and costs. In a formula we can put it this way:

Relationship Rewards – Relationship Costs = Relationship Outcome.
Or   RR – RC = RO.

There are three possible scenarios that can play out when relationship reward is measured against cost. Also, there are three possible outcomes for these scenarios.
For example:
Reward may be greater than the cost (R > C).
   1. Reward may be lesser than the cost (R < C).
   2. Reward may be equal to cost (R = C).
    Let us express this as a graph using reward and cost as curves.

Figure 7.1/The Relationship Reward/Cost Curve

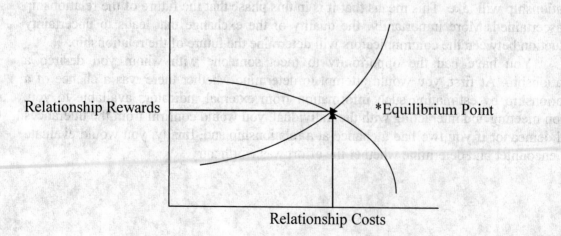

Relationship Rewards   *Equilibrium Point

Relationship Costs

*The intersection between benefits and costs is the tipping point of relational satisfaction.

What are the possible outcomes of these scenarios?

1. **When reward is greater than the cost of staying in a relationship, the logical expectation is that the relationship is satisfying and, as such, it pays to stay in the relationship.**
2. **When the reward is less than the cost of staying in a relationship, the tendency is for the participants to experience dissatisfaction and, as such, may not want to stay in the relationship.**
3. **When the reward derived from a relationship is about equal to the cost, this is an equilibrium state that suggests a 50/50 chance that the participants may stay or not stay in the relationship.**

The question is: Are we this calculating in our relationships? Perhaps yes and no! Because humans are logical, calculating beings, it follows that naturally if the cost outstrips the reward in a relationship, we may choose to leave. There is an assumption, however, that there are choices and other available relationships that may be more rewarding.

On the other hand, because humans are emotional beings, we tend to defy logic, sometimes, and stay in less rewarding relationships such as abusive and degrading ones. Perhaps the major factor, again, is the available alternatives. Many stay in relationships because they lack self-esteem and may believe that there are no better alternatives out there for them.

Fundamental Interpersonal Relations Orientation Theory

The theory proposed by Schutz (1966) claims that most of our interpersonal needs and behaviors stem from the desire to have affection with other people; to be included as part of social groups in order to increase our self-worth and significance and; to have control over our circumstances, especially to be able to predict others' behaviors in relation to us. This is the need to exercise some power over our surroundings, including other human beings.

Affection need is a desire for love- to love and to be loved. We have the emotions that motivate us to want to belong to others and for others to belong to us and to know that we are valued, respected, and more importantly desired.

As a human need, **inclusion** is being involved with others and being worthy of inclusion with others. We enjoy having others who are willing to acknowledge us by inviting us to join with them to work or play together. What is satisfying is the psychological recognition and valuing that comes with inclusion because it informs us of our identity and status in society. This is why we value being members of our families, local organizations, religious bodies, interest groups and work groups.

Control need has to do with the ability to influence our surroundings and the world we live in by doing something to present the world to us the way we want it to be.

But we cannot do it alone because there is so much to do and "one person does not make a forest."

Schutz explains that **human needs are bipolar**. On one hand, we need inclusion and, on the other hand, we need to include others in our lives. According to Schutz, there are three dimensions to the need for inclusion. Some people are **social, some undersocial**, while others are **oversocial.**

Social people do have a satisfied need for inclusion. These individuals are comfortable being alone or with others and do have the capability to be assertive if need be without any feeling of disaffection. Undersocial people on the other hand are apprehensive of being around others. These are shy individuals who experience communication apprehension when in social situations and find it challenging to initiate conversations with others, especially those they had never met. The opposite of undersocial is oversocial. People who fall in this category are extremely communicative; they tend to start up conversations even with strangers at will and, will find it difficult to stop talking or listen to others. As we learned in the listening chapter, these individuals seek attention and find it uncomfortable not to be at the center of attention.

The need for one to control others also yields to the need to be controlled by others. As a matter of fact, there are others who would rather be controlled by others. Schutz describe, again, three manifestations of the control need in people. Some are **autocrats,** some **abdicrats**, and others are **democrats**. Simply put, autocrats are always in need of control; they always manipulate themselves into a position of dominance over others. And because they need power, they could not be overly concerned with the impact of the quest for control over others. Abdicrats are rather submissive; they yield to others and are unwilling to take charge of situations. As Seiler and Beal (2008) describe them, they have little or no self-confidence, often perceive themselves as incompetent, take few risks, rarely make decisions on their own, and need much reinforcement to believe they are useful and capable. Democrats are in between the former two; they are satisfied with the degree of control they have over their circumstance, such that they are willing to lead or follow a group. As democrats, they are open- minded and are more accepting of others' perspectives without necessarily inflicting injury on self or others psychologically.

The need to show affection to others also includes the need to be shown affection. Some people are unable to fulfill this need in their lives and are described as **underpersonal** or **overpersonal,** while someone who has a balanced affection need is described as simply **personal.**

Schutz further explains that because these needs exist in degrees and, as such, may be deficient at times, excessive at times, and exist at a normal level in other times. As has been shown, individuals, therefore, will enter into relationships that best satisfy their needs and in which there is the best matching of needs with others. As with Maslow's hierarchy of needs, Schultz' needs are satisfied according to their prepotency (from most pressing to least pressing) and they follow the pattern of inclusion, followed by control, and finally affection.

Now, to better understand relationships, let us examine their characteristics.

Characteristics of Personal Relationships

Interpersonal relationships are unique, rule-governed, context- influenced, based on commitment and, experiences dialectics or tensions.

Personal Relationships are Unique

You have social contact with countless number of people over the course of a day, but these individuals are replaceable. You meet people on the elevator and you exchange pleasantries; you enter a cab and you engage a stranger in a discussion about the weather and even the political climate of the country; you also interact with a classmate to discuss the coming examination. These are examples of social relations rather than personal relations. This is because there is no strong connecting bond between the participants in the cases cited here.

Personal relationships are described as "personal" because of the special bond that exists between the participants, a kind of connection that only the two of them understand and experience. This is the uniqueness of interpersonal relations that exists between two individuals. Think of the unique relationship you have with your boyfriend or girlfriend. You love each other, but in a different way unlike the way you loved your previous partner. The relationship is romantic, but the experience with each person is different and when you should dissolve the relationship, there is no new friend or lover that can recreate the personal, unique nature of that past relationship. This brings to focus the **irreplaceability** of partners in personal, unique relationships.

Irreplaceability and uniqueness nature of personal relationships can further be explained by the type of relationship and love that parents of different children may have for their offspring. As each child is different so is the type of relationship each may have with the parents, who, also, relate differently with each of them. Indeed, no two interpersonal relations can be the same.

Personal Relationships Involve Commitment

Without commitment of time, emotions, thoughts, feelings, and materials, there cannot be a personal relationship. Remove all the variables of commitment from a personal relationship, and then it no longer qualifies as "personal," but a social relationship as discussed earlier. Though every relationship starts at the social level, when it moves on to the level of "personal," the difference is in the investment of self and time and material.

Wood (2008) describes commitment as the decision to remain with a relationship, while Beck (1998) and Ragan (2003) confirm that the essence of commitment is the intention to share the future. It is one thing to have passion for the other person, but such intense feeling cannot by itself sustain a relationship on the long run. That is why commitment goes beyond passion as it suggests a shared future which necessitates personal investment. Brehm, Miller, Perlman, & Campbell (2006) succinctly put it: the more we invest in a relationship, the more difficult it is to end it.

Relationships are Rule-Governed

Every relationship sets its own rules and boundaries to which partners adhere as long as they value the relationship. These are rules of expectations of behavior and communication in the relationship. Some of these rules are explicit and others are conventional-- unwritten, but mutually agreed upon rules of engagement.

Partners agree as to the frequency and contents of their communication (calls, personal contacts, and exchange of pleasantries and inquiries about what each person is up to). The meanings of these communicative behaviors are also enacted and a violation of the expectations will demand a need for explanation and justification.

There are two general rules that guide our communication—**constitutive** and **regulative** (Wood, 2008). **Constitutive rules define and determine how we interpret our communication.** The messages we share one with another do not have universal meanings, the interpretations are unique to each relationship, because the meanings are contextual and are within the individuals.

For example, Tavris (1992) & Wood (2001), state that some people count listening to problems as caring, whereas others count engaging in activities to divert attention from problems as caring. Another example could be the use of silence as a means of solving or averting problems. Whenever my wife and I do have a situation that would escalate to a conflict, one of us would become **silent**, yielding to the other. The understanding is that the issue is not as important for us to expend valuable time and energy on. This has become an effective way of avoiding unnecessary argumentation and an avenue to affirm ourselves and our relationship as more important than any inconsequential conflict.

Regulative rules govern interaction by specifying when and with whom to engage in various kinds of communication (Woods, 2008). Many couples do control their communicative behaviors by specifying what types of communicative behaviors are acceptable in public and in private. Many parents agree never to argue loudly before their children and never to yell at each other. Many of these rules are based on religious principles and morals such as the regulative rule not to fornicate or commit adultery; the rule to always put the family first and to provide for the welfare of the children, etc. Some of these rules are more important than others. So are the consequences for breaking them. While it is easier to forgive and overlook a yelling wife or husband, a cheating husband or wife may actually lose the relationship.

Contexts Affect Relationships

The acceptance of different kinds of relationships depends on the society or environment in which they exist. Certainly relationships do not exist in cultural and social vacuums; they are influenced by the different layers of social relations that encircle them. There are family expectations and influence on our choice of whom we can form a relationship with and the type of such relationship. Family also prescribes the nature of that relationship and sometimes imposes regulative and constitutive rules of engagement on our relationships. Some families do not encourage interracial dating while others do not frown at it; some welcome their children's boyfriends and girlfriends into their homes, while others prohibit such behavior. The words of Monsour (2002) confirm that our families of origin influence what we look for in people with whom we want close relationships. Our families pass on their views of the importance of social status, income, appearance, race, religion, intelligence, and others.

In the United States, it is common place to see and hear women proclaim their single motherhood, whereas in Nigeria, this is frowned upon. More and more, homosexual couples are becoming an acceptable reality in many Western cultures, but in many countries of the Middle East and Africa, while there is private acknowledgment of homosexuality, public acceptance is still not common. Another societal influence on relationships is the issue of how many children a couple may desire to have. When I tell my students that I am one of thirty-two children, they are surprised that anyone would even contemplate having that many children. Many questions that would follow include whether we were all born of one woman. Obviously not! Then, they would ask if polygamy is still practiced in my country of origin. Then, the fact that all of us, the children and the wives, lived under one roof was more perturbing than the number of children. How is this possible? They would ask. The answer is in the fact that contexts affect relationships. Culture is a context that influences relationships.

Relational Dialectics

A dialectical approach views relationships in terms of sets of contradictory or opposing impulses that create tension between two people (Tubbs and Moss, 2006). An individual who is raised differently and, who has different expectations and views life differently, and who wants to maintain a relationship with another, would experience a kind of dilemma or tension periodically in that relationship. In close relationships, the occurrence of opposing and continuous tensions is manifested in three dimensions of relational dialectics of **autonomy/connection**, **novelty/predictability**, and **openness/closedness**.

Baxter and Montgomery (2000, 1996) establish the assumptions of the dialectical approach as follows:

1. Contradictions are inherent in social life and are the basic 'drivers' of change and vitality in any social system.
2. There is a dynamic tension between stability and change in all social systems.
3. We are at once both actors and objects of our own actions. We make communication choices, but at the same time we are reactive.
4. We can understand phenomena "only in relation to other phenomena."

The Autonomy/Connection Dialectic

Autonomy suggests independence and separation, but connection is having a kind of bond with another. In our relationships, we often experience these contradicting pulls that result in tensions. We want to be connected to others and, yet, we want to be separate from them. When children come of age, especially in their teen years, they desire to be separate from the parents they had depended on for several years. These young adults crave their own identity and act in ways to establish their independence. However, because they have a connection with their parents, homes, and the nurturing of the need for belonging, they often find themselves torn between their desire for individuality and the overwhelming emotional connection with home.

Seeking connection and autonomy in our relationships is not atypical. According to Beck (1988) and Erbert (2000), most people in personal relationships experience a continuous friction as a result of the contradictory desires for autonomy and connection. However, the intensity of the 'pull and push' of relationships differs from person to person and the nature of the relationship.

The Novelty/Predictability Dialectic

What comes with stable relationships is predictability and routine. But people in relationships often seek dynamic, spontaneous activities, separate from the boring drag that often characterizes routine interpersonal relationships. Novelty is experiencing something spontaneous, new, different and, sometimes, unusual. But this challenges the desired stability we also seek in our relationships. The tension between novelty and predictability can manifest itself in dissatisfaction of partners if friends and romantic partners do not find a reasonable balance between the trust that a partner will always be there to depend on and the opposing desire of new exciting experience. This is the pull between certainty and uncertainty.

The Openness/Closedness dialectic

Partners in relationships, be it just friends or lovers, desire openness and trust of each other. The question is: Can we be totally open one with another? Better still, when we are candid with our friends and partners, can they really handle the truth? Although intimate relationships sometimes are idealized as totally open and honest, complete openness would be intolerable (Baxter, 1993, 2006; Petronio, 1991; Petronio & Caughlin, 2006).

Openness in relationships has to do with self-disclosure. How much of ourselves do we know to disclose with another? Certainly, we cannot disclose what we are blind to! Again, we all feel a need to hold on to some information about ourselves to retain some sense of our identity. How much of sexual desires can lovers truly share with each other without negative repercussions? How much of your sexual experience would you be willing to discuss with your new boyfriend or girlfriend? When a new lover asks of how many lovers you've had before him or her, how would you answer this question if at all?

> *Saving face is the process of attempting to maintain a positive self-image in a relational situation (Ting-Toomey, 2004).*

The need to maintain a level of privacy may contradict the desire for openness and candidness in relationships, but both are desirable; therefore, we should seek a balance of the two.

Types of Relationships

As we interact in different relationships, we adapt to their different nuances through communication. What communication style works in a particular relationship may not necessarily work in another. Unique relationships, therefore, call for unique communication strategies.

When relationships move from impersonal to personal and, ultimately to intimate, we should gain the understanding of the nature, type, and stage of the relationship for a better satisfying interpersonal relations. **People we relate to can be classified as acquaintances, friends, close friends or intimates, family members, and co-workers**.

Acquaintances

Acquaintances are people we meet per chance and with whom we engage in small, perfunctory or **face-saving** talk. The talk is usually related to the situation or context in which we met these individuals, without the revelation of any personal or intimate information. Many people we meet on the bus, in the train, and other social gatherings fall into this category of casual contacts with whom we chit-chat, but who we hardly know personally. This type of exchange we engage in with acquaintances is described as **impersonal communication. This is communication that lacks both breadth and depth because it is limited in range and personal self-disclosure**. Verderber and Verderber (2010) write that our goals when communicating with acquaintances are usually to reduce uncertainty and maintain face. Berger (1987) concurs that we engage in impersonal conversations to gain information that may help us to connect with other people by discovering that their beliefs, attitudes, and values are similar to our own.

Friends

Friendship often develops out of acquaintance relationships. This is the movement from impersonal to personal relationship where the players share more personal information and have formed a bond between them that is more satisfying. DeVito (2003) describes **friendship as an interpersonal relationship between two persons that is mutually productive and characterized by mutual positive regard.** As such, friendship cannot be destructive to either person, and once destructiveness enters into a relationship, it can no longer be described as friendship.

There are three basic characteristics of friendships which differentiate it from other relationships. **Friendship is based on trust, emotional support, and sharing of interests**. It agrees with reason that the more you trust someone, the more you rely on him or her and the more you share interests. **Friends provide security, ego support, affirmation, stimulation and are useful for problem solving**. That is, friends make you feel secure because they are generally supportive of you and your actions; they bolster your psychological self because they increase your sense of worth and competence; they agree with your choices and your personal value; and they provide an avenue for looking at the world, events, and other people differently.

The more friends grow close to one another, the more they become dependent on one another to the extent that they spend time together, develop common interests and may not enjoy pursuing individual adventures without the other. Ironically, the more interdependent friends become, the more independent they become of external influences.

There are three major types of friendship which are friendship of *reciprocity,* *receptivity,* **and** *association.* A friendship of reciprocity is the ideal type, characterized by loyalty, self-sacrifice, mutual affection, and generosity (DeVito, 2003). In this type of relationship, there is equality and both participants give as much as they take from their relationship. Receptivity suggests only receiving. In a relationship characterized as such, one person is giving and the other is receiving; or one person gives more than he or she receives. As long as the participants are satisfied with their roles, the relationship can be described as positive. Associations are rather like acquaintance relationship and are transitory in nature. This type of relationship is neither intimate nor intense, it is not marked by great loyalty, trust, or giving; it is simply cordial and less personal.

Close Friends or Intimates

Close friends or intimates are those few people with whom we share close, caring, and trusting relationships characterized by a high degree of commitment, trust, interdependence, disclosure and enjoyment (Verderber and Verderber, 2010). One major difference between this type of relationship and the others is the degree of intimacy. "Acquaintances are a dime a dozen," but close friends are few in number, and we let them into our inner core by self-disclosing pertinent and personal, intimate information about us to them. Because these close friends are privy to our secrets, we are more vulnerable with them; however, since trust and exclusivity are some of the hallmarks of such a relationship, we revel in the assurance that our secrets are safe with them.

Intimate relationships involve love, but intimacy is not the same as "love." Both **platonic** and sexual relationships may become intimate, but not all sexual relationships are intimate. Trust and commitment may be lacking in sexual relationships to the extent that we cannot describe them as intimate. Intimate relationships between men and women that do not lead to the expression of sexual desire do occur, but many argue that they are rare. The argument is that over time, with intimate self-disclosures, and time spent together, sexual attraction may develop. Often, though, people involved in such a relationship might have developed a perception of "brotherly love" or "sisterly love for one another," to the extent that they may see sexual attraction and desire and the expression of such as taboo.

Intimate relationships share other characteristics such as physical sharing or connection, intellectual sharing, emotional sharing, and shared activities. Intimate relationships may share some of these characteristics, but others may share a couple. Sometimes, though, intimates may be willing to withdraw at times rather than share all of their feelings and activities. All these characteristics are dynamic as they may grow or decline at various times in the relationships. The major lesson, however, is that "although no relationship is always intimate, living without any sort of intimacy is hardly desirable" (Adler and Proctor, 2011).

On April 29, 2011, Kate Middleton and Prince William became husband and wife after a relationship that started as platonic roommates at college. Their platonic relationship developed into intimate attraction that manifested in the desire to date as boyfriend and girlfriend. Of course, there are many such relationships between men and women, but the TV show "Will and Grace" exemplifies the complications of an intimate, roommate relationship between a homosexual male and a heterosexual female.

Types of Love

Love has three different components which are **intimacy, passion, and commitment**. Intimacy, as we have discussed it, involves closeness, bondedness, and connection (Tubbs and Moss, 2006).) Passion involves intense desire, physical, and psychological stimulation. To be committed to a relationship means maintaining desire and love for the other person over a long period of time. Each of these elements may occur in different degrees in love relationships.

Sternberg (1998, 1988) uses the figure of a triangle to represent the three dimensions of love. In some instances the triangles are balanced, that is, there are equal amounts of intimacy, passion, and commitment present in the love relationship he describes as **complete love**. But in other instances, the presence of commitment without passion or intimacy he describes as **empty love**. And a situation where passion is present, but not intimacy or commitment is described as **infatuation love**. **Foolish love**, on the other hand, is love which has passion and commitment.

A relationship in which passion is missing, but both commitment and intimacy are present is called **companionate love**. Sternberg states that this is a long-term, committed friendship, the kind that frequently occurs in marriages in which physical attraction has waned.

Figure 7.2/ Sternberg's Triangular Model of Love

Balanced Triangle of Love

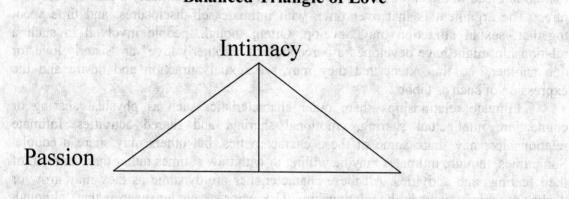

Lopsided Triangle of Love

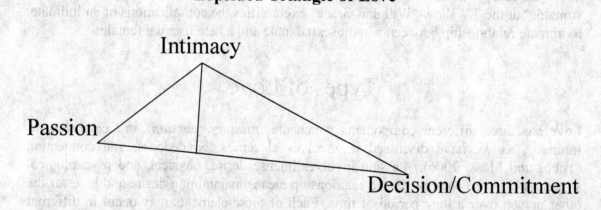

Adapted from: Sternberg, Robert J. (1998) *Cupid's arrow: The Course of Love Through Time*. New York: Cambridge University Press.
Hendrick, Clyde, Hendrich, Susan S. & Dicke, Amy (1998). The love attitude scale: Short form. *Journal of Social and Personal Relationships*, 15, 2: 147-159. Sage Publications.

Another theory about types of love was developed by Hendrich and Hendrick (1986, 1998) when they developed a "love attitude scale" questionnaire designed to measure the six different love styles originally identified in the work of Lee (1976). ***The different types of love are identified as eros, ludus, storge, pragma, mania, and agape.***

Eros: This is a passionate style of love that is characterized by deep emotions, strong eroticism, and strong commitment of each of the partners. The focus of this type of love is beauty and sexuality—physical attractiveness of partners. The attachment to physical beauty suggests that these lovers may not share the required intimacy characteristic of long–lasting relationships.

Ludus: This is seeing love as a game to be played without much seriousness, and the lovers are players who may outdo each other in the game of having fun. Emotions are controlled lest love got the better of you and commitment is kept low. DeVito (2003) writes that a ludic lover is self-controlled, always aware of the need to manage love rather than allowing it to be in control. As a ludic lover you would keep a partner for as long as the fun and amusement lasts and would not mind engaging in *extra dyadic* (beyond-couple) affairs and sex. Ludic lovers focus on entertainment and excitement.

Storge: The focus of storgic love is friendship that involves commitment and thus lasts long. This type of love develops slowly and without much passion. This is why sex comes at a later stage and is of less importance; the key is companionship based on shared interests and activities, peace and slowness.

Pragma: When you are practical about love and seek a traditional relationship that would work for you based on matching characteristics, your love style or type is pragma. Compatibility is crucial to this type of lover and considers social status as more important than personal qualities. Love to the pragma lover is a logical convenience that makes life easier. The focus is similarity, logicality and tradition.

Mania: This is a 'bipolar' type of love that swings from one extreme emotion to the other. This type of lover experiences elation and depression interchangeably. Insecurity moves the manic lover to jealousy and fear of losing a partner. This tendency leads to possessiveness and dependency. Manic lovers focus on love and are emotional, consequently they are insecure and experience less satisfaction in their relationships.

Agape: The examples of people who practiced this type of love are Jesus, Buddha, and Gandhi (Lee, 1973). Agapic love can be described as spiritual or philosophical type of love that is uniquely different from that which most individuals would have the capacity to practice. This is love based on selflessness, compassion, and humanity. It is love given without a desire for a reward; it is love based on altruism.

Table 7.1/Love Attitude Questionnaire

This questionnaire measures your style or kind of love. If you agree with statements 1-3, your love type is eros; if you agree with statements 4-6, your love type is ludus; if you agree with statements 7-9, your love style is storge; if you agree with statements 10-12, your love style is pragma; if you agree with statements 13-15, your love style is mania and; if you agree with statements 16-18, your love style is agape.

Please note that your love style may cut across some of these different types, and may change from time to time.

Indicate whether each of the following statements is True or False.

1.-------- My lover and I have the right physical "chemistry" between us.
2.-------- I feel that my lover and I were meant for each other.
3.-------- My lover and I really understand each other.
4.-------- I believe that what my lover doesn't know about me won't hurt him or her.
5.-------- My lover would get upset if he/she knew of some of the things I've done with other people.
6.-------- When my lover gets too dependent on me, I want to back off a little.
7.-------- I expect to always be friends with my lover.
8.-------- Our love is really a deep friendship, not a mysterious, mystical emotion.
9.-------- Our love relationship is the most satisfying because it developed from a good friendship.
10.------- In choosing my lover, I believed it was best to love someone with a similar background.
11.------- An important factor in choosing a partner is whether or not he/she would be a good parent.
12.------- One consideration in choosing my lover was how he/she would reflect on my career.
13.------- Sometimes I get so excited about being in love with my lover that I can't sleep.
14.------- When my lover doesn't pay attention to me, I feel sick all over.
15.------- I cannot relax if I suspect that my lover is with someone else.
16. ------- I would rather suffer myself than let my lover suffer.
17.------- When my lover gets angry with me, I still love him/her fully and unconditionally.
18.------- I would endure all things for the sake of my lover.

Adapted from "A Relationship–Specific Version of the Love Attitudes Test Scale" of Hendrick, Clyde, Hendrich Susan S. (1990). *Journal of Social Behavior and Personality, 5.* As contained in DeVito(2003). *Messages: Building Interpersonal Communication Skills (5th ed.).*Boston, MA: Allyn and Bacon.

VIRTUOUS WOMAN

10A wife of noble character who can find? She is worth far more than rubies.

11 Her husband has full confidence in her and lacks nothing of value.

12 She brings him good, not harm, all the days of her life.

13 She selects wool and flax and works with eager hands.

14 She is like the merchant ships, bringing her food from afar.

15 She gets up while it is still night; she provides food for her family and portions for her women servants.

16 She considers a field and buys it; out of her earnings she plants a vineyard.

17 She sets about her work vigorously; her arms are strong for her tasks.

18 She sees that her trading is profitable, and her lamp does not go out at night.

19 In her hand she holds the distaff and grasps the spindle with her fingers.

20 She opens her arms to the poor and extends her hands to the needy.

21 When it snows, she has no fear for her household; for all of them are clothed in scarlet.

22 She makes coverings for her bed; she is clothed in fine linen and purple.

23 Her husband is respected at the city gate, where he takes his seat among the elders of the land.

24 She makes linen garments and sells them, and supplies the merchants with sashes.

25 She is clothed with strength and dignity; she can laugh at the days to come.

26 She speaks with wisdom, and faithful instruction is on her tongue.

27 She watches over the affairs of her household and does not eat the bread of idleness.

28 Her children arise and call her blessed; her husband also, and he praises her:

29 "Many women do noble things, but you surpass them all."

30 Charm is deceptive, and beauty is fleeting; but a woman who fears the LORD is to be praised.

31 Honor her for all that her hands have done, and let her works bring her praise at the city gate.

Proverbs 31 (TNIV)

What type of love exists between the woman of Proverbs 31 and her husband?

Bases of Human Attraction

We have affirmed that we all have the need to form interpersonal relationships for a number of reasons. We are yet to find out why we form relationships with certain individuals and not others. What are the factors that influence someone's choice of an ideal mate, friend, or intimate companion? Scholars have examined the bases of human attraction and have found that diverse factors are responsible for why we are attracted to some people and not others and, why others are attracted to us, while we cannot get along well with others.

Have you ever wondered what some friends and, even married couples, find attractive about each other? Have you ever thought of why a person you consider unattractive - perhaps too short, too thin, too fat, too unattractive – is married to another person you consider to be very attractive and the total opposite of the other person? Or, have you wondered why a professional person would marry someone of little or no education and, possibly, without a trade? The following bases of interpersonal attraction will satisfy your curiosity. The bases of human attraction have been identified by scholars to include the following: **Physical appearance and personality, similarity, complementary needs, proximity, reciprocal attraction, competence, disclosure, and rewards.**

Appearance

This is the way a person looks on the outside; it is a person's height, weight, mode of dressing, complexion, and other physical features. At the onset of a relationship what is apparent and attracts people, one to another, are the physical appearance features. You yourself must have once commented on how beautiful and

attractive someone looked. Physical appearance formed the basis of your wanting to know and befriend this person to whom you are attracted.

A study to confirm appearance as the primary basis of human attraction was an organized blind date among several hundreds of men and women. Independent raters were asked to judge the physical attractiveness of the daters and, those who were rated as attractive were perceived to be more desirable and were preferred for second dates. The inference here is that the more physically attractive a person is, the more he or she is perceived as desirable, and the higher the preference for him or her as a friend or mate. When other factors that may influence interpersonal attraction at the initial stage of a relationship were compared, social skills and intelligence were not found to be influential (Walster et al, 1966). But as time progresses in a relationship, physical attractiveness will become less important. The caveat is that attractiveness opens the door of interpersonal attraction.

Similarity

We tend to be attracted to others who share similar values, culture, interests, race, and experience. This is because these variables provide bases for communication, the precursor of intimacy. Similar interests, values and others provide the common basis for your interaction with another person, to the extent that you have some things to talk about. Similarity, like physical appearance, therefore, would open the door of interpersonal attraction.

If you look around you where you live, you'll find that there are more people of the same race married to one another; more Christians married to Christians; more people of the same age bracket gravitating toward one another, etc. Because most people would value themselves more than others, they would therefore value others that share certain things in common with them. By so doing, they are valuing themselves. Such valuation supports the ego and affirms the person. If you like yourself, you'll likely like those who are like you. Consequently, for example, the more similar a married couple's personalities are, the more likely they are to report being happy and satisfied in their marriage (Luo and Klohnen, 2005).

Similarity begets attraction and there is no other place where this is more emphasized than on dating websites, where people look for those whose interests, backgrounds, and expectations match theirs. This is why friendship between similar people tends to last a long time (Ledbetter et al, 2007). The name of a popular dating website says it all: Match.com!

Complementary Needs

Sometimes opposites attract. When people who have differences, even of personalities, are drawn to one another, to the extent that one provides what the other lacks, you have the principle of **complementarity** at work. This is what happens when a person who is quiet and passive is attracted to another who is dominant and talkative. When a partner is better at a particular skills set than the other—be it money management or cooking—the roles they play in their relationship may fly in the face of societal expectations. These partners may choose roles that each has an edge performing in order to make their relationship work. In this regard, Adler and Proctor (2011) report that when successful and unsuccessful couples were compared over a period of time of twenty years, it became clear that partners in successful marriages are similar enough to satisfy each other physically and mentally, but different enough to meet each other's needs and keep the relationship interesting.

When a rich man, for example, marries a "trophy wife," they are both seeking to meet different complementary needs. One is seeking financial security and comfort, while the other is seeking physical and psychological pleasure or ego massage. Certainly, money attracts beauty and vice-versa.

Reciprocal Liking

When you like someone and the other person likes you in return, the feeling can be very pleasant. So, when you feel that someone you like likes you in return, you feel good about yourself and feel obliged to like the person in return. This is the perceived reciprocity basis of human attraction.

Finding out that another person likes you is rewarding because it increases your self-esteem and the "liking" behavior is a compliment that you often return with reciprocal liking (Tubbs and Moss, 2008).

For an example, now, imagine what happened to Tim, who had been in the same college course with Anya for about two months. Tim would once in a while talk with Anya, but never once told her that he liked her and would want to have a date with her. Unaware of Tim's desires, Anya agreed to go on a date with John who, without having talked with her at all in the semester, summoned the courage to ask her out. Anya, who had some liking for Tim, waited for Tim to hint at liking her, so she could jump at the offer, never heard such expression from him. So, realizing that John wished to date her, Anya was reassured that at least someone liked her and she thought to herself that "it was better to like the one who liked her than to wait for the one who did not." As soon as John and Anya started dating, Tim tried to express his desire for her, but was told he was too late, because Anya had given her love to the man whom she perceived to like her and she had returned the compliment.

Proximity

Proximity can be described as the physical, geographic closeness between individuals. When you live or work in close proximity to someone, the opportunity to see that person frequently is there and such situation lends itself to interaction and communication. After all, without the opportunity to meet and to communicate with someone, a relationship might never be formed. Proximity, therefore, provides a platform for relationships to be initiated and for communication to be used to maintain them. Proximity also brings familiarity and as Zajonc (1968) suggests, familiarity by itself may likely increase liking.

Consider the number of people you know who are involved in long distance relationships and those in close distance relationships. Without doubt, the latter category far outnumbers the former. Studies confirm that you're more likely to marry someone who is geographically close to your home or school than to someone who is geographically remote from your location.

An old Oprah Show provides anecdotal information on the import of proximity to interpersonal attraction, dating, and marriage. Once, Oprah Winfrey had a show about men in Alaska who were eligible bachelors, who had shared a common desire to be married, but expressed the lack of available, eligible women in the State of Alaska. The reasons there was a drought of eligible women in Alaska were that it was far from mainland U.S.A. and that the weather was not so friendly. Therefore, not many women would want to relocate to the state and not many would want to stay. The Oprah Winfrey Show showcased the men for match-making with women in the mainland. These were men who otherwise would have been married were it not for their geographic location far from eligible women.

There are two confirmed theoretical conclusions to be drawn from this story. One theory is that if we know we are going to be in close proximity to someone—such as living next door or working side-by-side over a long period of time, we tend to minimize or even overlook that person's less desirable traits. This suggests that geographic availability trumps appearance, similarity, and other bases of human attraction. The second theory is that with proximity comes the opportunity to be attracted to someone and to communicate with that person. The more the opportunity arises, the more intense the liking will become.

Competence

Competence is the ability to excel in what one does, either for a living or for recreation. Competence attracts because others find competent people unique and desirable. We understand why star-athletes and rock stars attract legions of admirers. Partly because of complementarity, we are drawn to those who have the ability to do what we admire, but that which we are unable to do. However, as confirmed by Adler and Proctor (2011) we are uncomfortable around those who are too competent, probably because we look bad by comparison.

Disclosure

We have learned that we self-disclose to those we like and trust. Those to whom we self-disclose would feel compelled to self-disclose back—this is what is referred to as the **dyadic effect** of self-disclosure. This reciprocal self-disclosure reveals information that may reveal **similarity and common experience,** which in of themselves are bases of attraction. Read more about self-disclosure in the earlier part of the chapter.

Reward

 Reward derived from a relationship can be physical, economic, and social. The social exchange theory presupposes that humans are attracted to each other or form relationships based on the perceived rewards that would derive from the relationship. When on the outside looking in, potential partners may evaluate the costs and rewards of a relationship before they decide to get into the relationship. We have learned of the relationship costs-rewards curve and the possible scenarios that affect the decisions to form, stay, or leave a relationship. Please see social exchange theory for further discussion of this topic.

Theories and Models of Relationship Development

According to Park (2006) we develop relationships through communicating with others. But, overtime, we create, re-create, and sometimes even destroy our relationships, through communication. Scholars agree that relationships are unique, but that they all tend to move through stages that include beginning, developing, maintaining, and deterioration (Baxter, 1982; Duck, 1987; Knapp & Vangelisti, 2005; Taylor & Altman, 1987). There is an agreement that progression through the different stages of a relationship is not linear, but in a back-and-forth manner throughout the life cycle of the relationship (Honeycutt, 1993; Duck, 2007). Whether a relationship moves forward or backwards depends on the degree and quality of self-disclosure and feedback that occurs within it (Verdeber, Verdeber, & Sellnow, 2010). A healthy relationship is, therefore, characterized by an appropriate balance of self-disclosure and feedback as presented in the Johari Window.

Every relationship is dynamic because it goes through different evolutionary stages. As the stages change, so does the nature of the relationship. Every personal relationship develops at its own pace and in unique ways, but a majority of friendships and romances have some commonalities in their evolution (Wood, 2008). Indeed, all relationships, be it ordinary friendship, intimate, or romantic, all move along a continuum in their life cycle and all share birth, growth, and decline and, possibly regeneration. It is not expected that all relationships will move progressively along this continuum, rather, each relationship moves at its own pace and may go back an forth the different stages. Also, it should be noted that relationship development models are developed primarily for understanding and reflecting on the nature of relationships and not to prescribe how a particular relationship would progress.

A popular model of relationship development is that of Mark Knapp, who identified three distinct stages in the life cycle of a relationship: 1. **Coming Together 2. Relational Maintenance 3. Coming Apart** (Knapp & Vangelisti, 2006). The model identifies ten different stages in the life cycle of a relationship and they are: **Initiating, Experimenting, Intensifying, Integrating, Bonding, Differentiating, Circumscribing, Stagnating, Avoiding, and Terminating.**

Figure 7.3/Mark Knapp Stages of Relationship Development

Coming Together
Stages 1- 3

1. *Initiating*
2. *Experimenting*
3. *Intensifying*

Relational Maintenance
Stages 4-7

4. *Integrating*
5. *Bonding*
6. *Differentiating*
7. *Circumscribing*

Coming Apart
Stages 8 -10

8. *Stagnating*
9. *Avoiding*
10. *Terminating*

Coming Together Stages

Initiating

This is the stage you initiate contact with the person with whom you would want a relationship.

At this stage, you have the opportunity to form an immediate and lasting impression on each other such that the two of you would perceive a desire to continue to communicate beyond this initial encounter. Usually, after a simple greeting such as hello, you would initiate a conversation about common, sometimes impersonal things, such as the weather, the event that brought you together, or a current event, so that you two may have the opportunity to engage each other. As you are exchanging banal pleasantries, you're sizing each other up, especially examining each other's appearance and seeking other clues that will reveal enough information with which you would form an immediate judgment of the person's desirability or not for continued interaction. This stage may last as long as a brief moment or longer than a week, after which you are both ready to move on to the second stage in the model.

Experimenting

This is the stage where you try to find out what the two of you have in common that will propel the relationship forward. Here you move your conversation to a more personal level by asking information about interests, education pursuits, job interests, and recreational activities. All of these are in the effort to gain as much information about the other person in order to **reduce uncertainty**. You would expect the other person to reveal these information to you because they are easily accessible to others because as they are usually contained in the open quadrant of the Johari window. Since you are engaged in small talk, which is a common, often not too personal information to save face, it is expected that both of you would be willing to participate fully in this stage of the relationship. However, if the other person is reluctant to share any of the information, this may be a signal for non-continuation of the relationship. Other communication strategies may be employed to cut short a relationship at the experimenting level. You could change the topic of discussion; you could refuse to answer certain questions, or; you may answer some question rather sparsely, hinting at discontinuance. If the two communicators willingly participate in the experimenting stage, the relationship may move on to the next level.

Intensifying

At this stage the communicators start to spend more time together and they start to express their mutual feelings to each other. Quality interpersonal relations develop and more self-disclosure is experienced. Diverse communicative behaviors are engaged in to express desire and interest in one another at this stage. In addition to overt and direct expression of their feelings towards one another, participants at this stage more often use less direct methods of communication such as spending an increasing amount of time together, asking for support from one another, doing favors for the partner, giving tokens of affection, hinting and flirting, expressing feelings nonverbally, getting to know the partner's friends and family, and trying to look more physically attractive (Adler and Proctor, 2011).

The intensifying stage of a romantic relationship is that which is full of excitement and dreams, but which does not last very long. After emotions might have "settled down," the excitement though still may be present, is tempered and measured. Where the desire still remains, the relationship is about to move to its next phase.

The Relational Maintenance Stages

Integrating

Partners are now becoming like one person; they begin to see each other as belonging together as a unit and the people around them also start to see them as a couple. Trust and self-disclosure begin to intensify that they may share living quarters, properties, and even have common friends.

As the integration process continues, it is expected that partners will begin to lose their individual characteristics and take on shared identities as a social unit. And as a social unit, the sense of obligation one to another develops and the partners would share resources without second thoughts. The next level in this maintenance stage is to move on to the level of formalizing the union.

Bonding

Barely over a month ago, Prince William of England married his long-time girlfriend and college roommate, Catherine Middleton. The marriage was a public display and confirmation of the love the two have for each other to the extent that they engaged in public rituals that signal that a couple has moved to the level of a legal unit and, as such, should be sanctified in public. This is the bonding stage of Knapp's "coming together," but the second in the "relational maintenance stage."

Not all relationships at the bonding stage are labeled as marriage, because not only romantic relationships move on to the phase of bonding. Today, there are many different romantic relationships between same-sex partners, between individuals who may not necessarily choose to marry but co-habit. There could be a formal declaration by common law of the bonding between an adoptive parent and a child, etc.

As the partners settle into their relational roles, the need to assert themselves would start to develop. After all, as individuals, they have unique personalities and would see things differently and, perhaps, have different aspirations for self and the relationship. The extent to which the next stage in the relationship is well managed will determine the success of the relationship.

Differentiating

As partners start to exert themselves, they emphasize their differences and express desire to break the monotony of the "we" identity, to begin to intersperse it with the "me" identity. Relational tensions of this sort are expected in relationships and this does not necessarily have to spell the doom of the union.

Differentiating is exerting differences or pursuing individual agendas in a relationship and it is characterized by the communication of differences. Zeuschner (1997) writes that conversations begin to be dominated by what one person does, likes, thinks about, admires, or tolerates that is different from what the other does, likes, and so on. This autonomy versus dominance dialectic is inevitable in relationships, but a good management of this stage would balance the two opposing tensions for the good of the relationship. However, if this is not managed positively, it may further degenerate into negative communication climate that may eventually doom the relationship.

Circumscribing

This is the last stage of the maintenance phase of a relationship. In this stage, partners communicate less both in quantity and quality. This little exchange that goes on lacks depth and intimacy and we can call it **communication of convenience**. As partners share less information and become less intimate in their psychological and physical interaction, their interest and commitment to one another decrease. Rather than continue to integrate, the relationship tethers on disintegration.

Coming Apart Stages

Stagnating

Neutrality and lack of commitment is often evidenced in the *stagnation* communication of romantic partners. Endearing statements of the past are now perfunctory, desolate expressions of relationship rituals. While there are two individuals in the house, a partner may question: "Who left this stuff here?" Or, a statement such as: "I am going out," gets blurted out without an indication of where to, or what for. When this occurs, without restraint and reconciliation, the relationship, though has not collapsed totally, is on a free fall toward disintegration.

Some relationships may remain in this stage for a long time because of some external forces such as religious beliefs, family influence, social status, finances, children, and many more. When some of these influences ease, the next stage may set in.

Avoiding

Many couples avoid speaking to one another or avoid any form of interaction at all cost and would result to direct hostility and antagonistic behaviors to express their dissatisfaction with their partner. At this stage, partners alter their schedules to avoid each other; they sleep in different rooms or in the same room at different times; do not attend social functions together, or attend as separate individuals and seek new friends, partners, and lovers without the other's knowledge. If this goes on without abatement, the relationship is heading for termination.

Terminating

This is the formal dissolution of the relationship that had once flourished between partners. The communication between the two partners at this stage is a summary of how they view the relationship, and an indication of whether they are ending in good terms, sour terms, or possibly will end up in the court of law. "Well, it has been a ride—a rough one at that." "I know things cannot continue this way, so this is it for me!" "Anyway, we gave it a try, but we both know it should end." These are statements that may be used to sum the relationship before the final exit.

Not all relationships end up in termination. Surely, you know of friends who had been together "forever." Perhaps your grandma and grandpa had been married for 70 years! These go to show that not all relationships end up in termination, but all relationships go through different stages in their life cycle and many do mend fences and some go back and forth the different stages in Mark Knapp's model. Termination in particular does not occur in a progressive manner. Often, partners seek help and get their relationships on track. Some even re-marry after divorce. Again, some professional relationships never end. So, there is no way of telling what exactly will happen in your personal relationships, but the knowledge of the different stages in the life of a relationship is a foundation education for maintaining positive relationships with others.

A Further Look at Relationship Breakup

An examination of another model, this time of relational breakup, can also prove useful in understanding what really happens in the process of breaking up, the recognition of which will possibly help in knowing what to do to avoid such processes in the process of maintaining relationships. Communication scholars Duck (1982) and Rollie & Duck (2006) developed the model of relational break up. The focus of the Duck model are the five identified stages of relationship break up, which start with thoughts in one's head about dissatisfaction in a relationship to the final communication patterns that develop at the final end of the relationship. Rollie and Duck (2006) added a final stage (the sixth) in which former partners now get ready to form new relationships and move on with their separate lives. Particularly, this model focuses on the communication that occurs within and between the partners in the now six-stage relationship breakup process.

Figure 7.4/Breakdown Process Model

Breakdown   Dissatisfaction with relationship   **Threshold**   I can't stand this anymore
Intrapsychic processes   Social withdrawal; rumination; resentment   Brooding on partner's "faults" and on the relational "costs"   Reevaluation of possible alternatives to the present relationship   **Threshold**   I'd be justified in withdrawing
Dyadic Processes   Uncertainty, anxiety, hostility, complaints   Discussion of discontents, more time spent with partner "discussing stuff"   Talk about "Our Relationship," equity in relational performance, roles   Reassessment of goals, possibilities, and commitments to the relationship   ~~Threshold~~
Social Processes   Going public; advice/support seeking; talking with third parties   Denigration of partner; giving accounts; scapegoating; alliance building   "Social commitment," forces outside dyad that create cohesion within it   **Threshold**   It's now inevitable
Grave Dressing Processes   Tidying up the memories; making relational histories   Stories prepared for different audiences   Saving face   **Threshold**   **Time to get a new life**
Resurrection Processes   Re-creating sense of own social value   Defining what to get out of future relationships/what to avoid   Preparation for a different sort of relational future   **Reframing of past relational life**   What I learned and how things will be different

This figure is an adaptation of Rollie and Duck (2006) Model of Relational Breakdown Process as contained in Duck, Steve & McMahan, David T.(2012). The Basics of Communication: A Relational Perspective (2nd ed.). California: Sage.

Relational Climate: Confirming and Disconfirming Communication.

The defining characteristics of relationships include the physical and social/psychological contexts in which they exist; the nature of information sharing between partners; the degree of trust experienced; and the amount of quality time spent together. The social/psychological context of relationships is what is usually referred to as its climate. **Relational climate is the prevailing 'atmosphere' in a relationship that either fosters or hinders relationship growth. As a relationship develops, the prevailing attitudes and treatments of partners in the relationship will determine how it will develop and whether the members will be satisfied or not.** Consequently, how partners treat each other and make each other feel are central to the measures of their relational climate.

Communication contents and styles in a relationship reflect its climate. The dimensions of communication climate in a relationship include the tensions between confirmation and disconfirmation, and supportiveness and defensiveness. Sieburg and Larson (1971) define **confirmation as any behavior that causes another to value himself more.** Tubbs and Moss (2006) adds that it is any behavior that strengthens or reinforces the other person's self-esteem.

The communication responses among partners that are considered confirming are identified as *direct acknowledgment of partners, expressing positive feelings, clarifying response, agreement, and supportive response.*

The opposite of confirmation is disconfirmation. This is **any behavior that causes another partner to value him or herself less and; any behavior that does not reinforce or strengthens the self–esteem of another in a relationship.** The types of communicative responses that are classified as disconfirming include: *Tangential response, impersonal response, impervious or disregarding response, irrelevant response, and incongruous response.*

Your communication with your partner will make or break your relationship. When your messages elevate your partner, there is positive psychological disposition that encourages the partner to feel valued and to continue with the relationship. But when your communication reduces and objectifies the partner, the result is dissatisfaction and alienation. The following figure 1.10 enumerates the responses that are confirming and disconfirming. Do you consider your communication confirming or disconfirming to your partner and how can you improve on the social /psychological climate of your relationship?

Another measure of climate in a relationship is the degree to which partners engage in **supportive** and **defensive** behaviors. **Supportiveness occurs when you unconditionally accept and acknowledge another person for who he or she is. It is understanding why and how the other person is the way he or she is and to communicate such acceptance in a non-condescending manner.** Such understanding and response is referred to as **empathy, which** (Pearce and Newton, 1963) **describe as the perception and communication by resonance, by identification, by experiencing in ourselves some reflection of the emotional tone that is being experienced by the other person.**

Defensive behaviors are such that arouse our suspicion and which generate a need to protect ourselves from perceived offensive behaviors. This means that behaviors that are not supportive trigger our defensiveness because we perceive them as threat. And if you always put your partner on the defensive, an atmosphere of distrust is established that would not engender the flourishing of the union.

A foundational study by Gibbs (1961) on interpersonal trust identifies two opposing sets of behaviors that he labeled **supportive and defensive climates.** The six different behaviors and their possible problems are identified in figure 1.11. To Gibbs, trust is a determining variable in interpersonal relations. As such, he claimed that "when trust increases, efficiency and accuracy in communication also increases."

Awareness of the Gibb's dimensions of trust as exhibited in positive or negative responses of supportiveness and defensiveness respectively, will enhance our understanding of relational dynamics and help us in facilitating supportive climates in our desired interpersonal relationships.

Table7.2/Confirmation and Disconfirmation: Some Ways of Responding

Confirming Responses	Disconfirming Responses
Direct acknowledgment **"Yes. I see where you're coming from."** *This says I respect you and I see you as relevant.*	**Tangential response** **["Do you know what I mean?"] – "Yes, I'm thinking of going to the movies."** *This is a diversionary response.*
Expressing positive feeling **"That's a good idea."** *This also affirming the other person directly as valuable and a source of good ideas.*	**Impersonal response** **"Well, that's one way of thinking about it."** *This does not respect the idea of the partner; hence seems to reject it as just another way of looking at the issue without personally addressing the source.*
Clarifying response **"Could you explain? I'm not sure I understand."** *It is the person you value that you want to understand clearly.*	**Impervious or disregarding response** **"Have you seen my computer case?"** *This happens when you think what you have to say is more important than responding to another's message. The other person cannot get across to you.*
Agreement **"You're absolutely right."** *Nothing could be more ego boosting than thinking of another's idea as worthy of value and acceptance.*	**Irrelevant response** **["I am afraid I might lose my job."]- "I wonder if he's going to ask me out?"** *When you don't address the content of another's message, but shifts focus to something irrelevant, you're snobbish.*
Supportive response **"I'm sure you'll make a good decision."** *Expressing confidence in the other person will not only boost the ego, but performance as well.*	**Incongruous or mixed response** **"Of course, it's your decision. It's up to you." (Contradictory facial expression and tone of voice)** *When you send mixed messages, you're sending a clear message of distrust or lack of confidence in your partner.*

Adapted from Tubbs, Stewart L. & Moss, Sylvia (2006). *Human Communication: Principles and Contexts (10th ed.)* Boston: McGraw-Hill.

Table 7.3/Supportive and Defensive Communication Climates

Defensive Climate	Problem Created	Supportive Climate
Evaluation—*This is judging another person, which is perceived as a personal attack.*	**Feeling judged increases our defensiveness.**	**Description**---*Describing what happened and not questioning the judgment or the decision will not arouse defensiveness.*
Control—*Everyone is born with a measure of dignity and freewill and resists dictation and control by another.*	**We resist someone trying to control us.**	**Problem orientation**—*Focusing on the problem rather than control of the person's behavior is preferable in problem solving.*
Strategy—*Calculating to have an edge arouses suspicion of taking advantage of.*	**If we perceive a strategy or underlying motive, we become defensive.**	**Spontaneity**--- *If you have no ulterior motive, you will not be hesitant and calculating in your responses.*
Neutrality---*How can you not favor the one you love? Bias is necessary in favor of the one with whom you have an intimate relationship.*	**If the speaker appears to lack concern for us, we become defensive.**	**Empathy**---*Social identification and emotional connection leads to perception of care.*
Superiority---*When you feel more important than your partner, then you consider him or her as less important.*	**A person who acts superior arouses our defensive feelings.**	**Equality**---*Love is not proud.*
Certainty—*If you think you know it all, then, you think the other does not know anything.*	**Those who are "know-it-alls" arouse our defensiveness.**	Provisionalism---*The opposite of certainty, presupposes that no one should presume he is always right.*

Source: Gibb, Jack R.(1961). Defensive Communication. *Journal of Communication, 11: 3 pp.141-148. Italicized statements are those of the author.*

Review Questions

1. Why do human have a need to form relationships?
2. Explain the need to reduce uncertainty in relationship formation.
3. Explain the social exchange theory of relationship formation.
4. Explain Schutz' fundamental interpersonal relations orientation theory.
5. What are the characteristics of personal relationships?
6. Identify and explain the three major dialectics of relationships.
7. Identify and explain the different types of relationships.
8. Identify and explain the different types of love.
9. Explain the relationship you have with boy/girlfriend, using Steinberg's triangular model of love.
10. What are the bases of human attraction?
11. Explain Mark Knapp's stages of relational development.
12. What can you do to improve the climate of your relationship with your significant other?
13. Explain, with examples, supportive and defensive communication.

Chapter Eight

Managing Interpersonal Conflict

Credit: Bill O'Connell

A staple of interpersonal relations is conflict. This is a natural occurrence that results from individuals asserting their claims to their opinions, desires, and expectations. As two opposing interests struggle for recognition in a particular situation that calls for a single choice, the arising tension between the choices will have to be resolved in one or a combination of different ways. Interpersonal relationship is, therefore, an interaction of forces or mutually agreed alternatives. Sometimes, though, agreement is not achieved especially when one person wants to upend the other.

What is conflict and what are its different characteristics? How can conflict be minimized, negotiated, or resolved in our interpersonal relationships? We shall attempt to answer these questions in this chapter.

A widely quoted definition of conflict is that of Wilmot and Hocker (1998) which claims that it is **an expressed struggle between at least two interdependent parties who perceive incompatible goals, scarce resources and interference from others, in achieving their goals.** There is interdependence of partners in a relationship and this dependence does not often lead to unity of ideas and goals. Hence partners perceive interference from the other person and struggle to balance the contending forces of both interdependence and interference. The scarcity of resources includes the unavailability of other equally satisfying relationships, such that the idea of foreclosing one's unique, intimate relationship is not contemplated. But partners would rather stay in the relationship to negotiate their needs and iron out their differences.

To further analyze the elements of conflict identified in the above definition, let us look at its important constituting concepts.

Conflict as Expressed Struggle

To express is to make known, and a conflict that is not expressed, either verbally or non-verbally is not perceived as a conflict. The parties to a conflict must be aware of the contention between them. Maybe through a stern warning, a rolling of the eyes, a stinging letter, or a punch in the face--there must be awareness of disagreement for it to matter.

Conflict as Interdependence

The expression: "It takes two to tango" is appropriate here. You need to be my friend for you to place demands on me in terms of time and other relational expectations. Apparently, the more involved we are in a relationship, the deeper and more intimate the expectations become and the greater the perceived conflict when expectations are not met. Conflict cannot exist between two individuals who are not interdependent.

Perceived Incompatible Goals

Sometimes conflicts arise because there is no middle ground for achieving individual goals. When the satisfaction of someone's goals results in the total loss of the accomplishment of another's, then there is conflict. If there is a compromise, such that each person realizes to some degree his or her goals, the conflict diminishes and, possibly, ceases to exist. When goals are perceived to be incompatible, they are mutually exclusive, in that it produces a win-lose situation where one person's desire is met at the expense of the other.

Perceived Scarce Resources

Scarce resources in human relations are money, time, quality friends, and land. Many human conflicts revolve around these elements because of the competition that always surround their availability and use. Many people that we form relationships with demand our time, but there are only twenty-four hours in a day. So, we contend with one another on the use of our time: It's whether we spend so little or so much with one person and not the other; or spending time on things others do not see as important. The same goes for money—there's never enough to go around satisfactorily. As with land, this is the only resource that is inelastic. As human population grows, so does are need for land, but he supply is never expanding, but always shrinking as people acquire their portion of it.

Perceived Interference

When someone interferes with your goals, needs, and expectations, it means that he or she stands in the way of your ability to accomplish your goals. And when another person has that kind of power to preclude you from your set goals, it is expected that conflict would arise. Trenholm and Jensen (2008) summarize the nature of conflict as beneficial and natural to interpersonal relations. Their ideas are paraphrased as follows:

* Conflict suggests interdependence and the resolution of which will lead to further cohesion in the relationship.

* Conflict signals a need for change; it is an opportunity to become more adaptable and creative.

* Conflict allows problem diagnosis; it is a safety valve that allows problems to be aired before escalating.

Types of Conflict

There are different discernible conflicts, from superficial ones to critical ones. The superficial ones are based on momentary misperceptions, while some are based on deep-rooted differences in values. A good enumeration of conflict types is that of Verderber, Verderber, & Pitts (2010). The scholars identify the type of conflict as **pseudo, fact or simple, value, policy, ego, and meta.**

Pseudo Conflict

This type of conflict occurs when there is a difference in the perceptions of an issue, event, or idea between partners. This is easily resolved because it is not deep-rooted as it is based on perceptions which are known to be fallible, biased and that can be corrected. This occurs when partners interpret words differently, or when partners perceive their goals or needs to be incompatible, when in reality the differences are minimal and can be accommodated. It is a result of banal behaviors of partners.

Fact or Simple Conflict

A fact is verifiable information or the truth about something, but when partners disagree as to the accuracy and truth of a piece of information, conflict may arise. If your partner does not remember that you paid for a service on her behalf sometime ago, the dispute in fact will translate to a dispute in the relationship. Often the act of not remembering or disputing a fact can be more painful to partners than the loss of material or anything of value.

Value Conflict

Values have been described as shared ideas about what is true, right, and beautiful, that underlies cultural patterns, and guide society in response to the physical and social environment (Nanda and Warms, 1998). Not only do we believe values are true, we also accept them as the truth; therefore, conflicts that arise from value differences are deep-seated and may not be easily resolvable. Can you imagine negotiating the idea of multiple wives with your husband, who does not see anything wrong with it? You may think it is morally wrong and are convinced that it should never be allowed, but others would argue the opposite, to your chagrin. Again, you value a college education, but your life- partner does not and argues that the education your children really needs is a high school diploma.

Policy Conflict

Policy is action orientation; it's decisions made or line of action proposed to be taken. Policy conflict, therefore, is a disagreement over an action taken or a course of action proposed. Your wife plans to withdraw your children from schools because she claims she can do better by home-schooling them. But you disagree with her for a number of reasons. Or your husband spends your credit card money to by a man-toy that he craves when there are other more important things to incur such a debt on.

Ego Conflict

The word "Ego' can also be referred to as the "self." Ego conflict, therefore, is the disagreement that occurs as a result of wanting to protect self in many different ways. It is the expression of the need to feel superior to the other, to be more entitled than the other, and to want to be the "winner" in the contest of "selves." Actually, it is ego defense that causes the conflict because the person who wants to be the "winner" is selfish, just as the other person who may want to defend his or her ego. In order not to feel inferior, you may go on ego offensive or, if at the receiving end, you may engage in ego defensiveness to shield self from the perceived attack of the other person.

Meta Conflict

Metacommunication is simply interpreted as communication about communication. Meta conflict, therefore, is conflict that results from the conflict process. It is conflict that result from the process of communicating about the conflict at hand. For example, while arguing about a problem that arose between you and your boyfriend, you raised your voice to shout at him while trying to explain yourself. The resulting meta conflict is his objection to your shouting on him. The conflicts are now two.

As you can see, there are different types of conflict and, while we define them separately, they are nonetheless dynamic and, therefore, not mutually exclusive. Ego may play a part in pseudo or value conflict, just as simple or fact conflict can result into meta conflict. Differences in values can result in different types of conflict.

Levels of Conflict

We can categorize conflict by looking at its various sources. Conflict first arises in the individual, after which it may become something we experience with another individual. Individuals within groups may experience conflict, just as independent groups may experience relational tensions. From the foregoing we can identify **intrapersonal, interpersonal, intragroup, and inter group conflict levels.**

Intrapersonal

This is within-self conflict that arises due to contending attitudes, beliefs, emotions and other biological instincts. Sometimes we are confronted with choices and choosing may create some internal tensions. At a practical level, you may have to choose which of your two girlfriends to dump. You love both of them dearly for different reasons and each complements you in a unique way. But you must give up one of them because, at least in the U.S.A., you cannot marry two women at the same time.

There is no doubt that your ruminating over which choice to make will affect your demeanor, and may manifest in ways that will influence your relationship, not only with your girlfriends, but also with other people that you relate with. Intrapersonal conflict may not fit into the definition of conflict that we have identified in this section because it is experienced within and not as an expressed struggle over scarce resources; however, Losoncy (1997) identifies the connection between intrapersonal and interpersonal conflict by stating that the more an individual is conflicted within, the more the likelihood of interpersonal conflict.

Interpersonal

All humans in relationships experience interpersonal conflict. Tensions at the interpersonal level may arise from perceptual differences (**pseudo**), accuracy contentions (**fact or simple**), differences in beliefs, attitudes, and values (**value**), course of action taken or to be taken (**policy**), **self-defense (ego)**, and nature of communication during conflict (**meta**).

Intragroup

As personalities interact in a group, there are manifestations of different orientations, interests, and expectations, which may result in conflict. While some group members may focus on the charge or task of the group, others may be preoccupied with anti-group activities. Divergent focuses and preoccupations of members within the group can also lead to conflicts. See the chapter on Group Processes.

Intergroup Conflict

Groups are formed based on similar orientations and expectations, to the extent that different groups may have different conflicting expectations. The National Rifle Association is a group of people who uphold and fiercely defend the rights of Americans to bear arms. This stance is definitely at odds with the anti-gun lobby groups, who vehemently decry the proliferation of arms and use of such to solve disputes in the U.S. What about the "Pro-Choice" and the "Pro-Life" movements who are the opposite ends of the abortion debate? When leaders of antagonizing groups meet to debate their positions, value positions are fiercely debated and defended. Often, though, the disagreement may escalate to physical and, sometimes, deadly confrontations. This was the case when "Defenders of the Rights of the Unborn," took matters into their own hands to kill so-called abortion doctors.

Conflict can occur at these different levels and may progress from the intra to the interpersonal, to the intra-group and intergroup levels.

Negotiating Conflict

As we have noted, conflict is inevitable and can be positive or negative for our relationships. Without relationships we cannot have conflicts; therefore, the necessity of interdependence makes conflicts unavoidable. From its inception to escalating, and resolution levels, tensions in a relationship confirm the persons in the relationship and may unearth sources of disagreement. It also leads to proper diagnosis of problems and suggests need for change or infusion of new and dynamic orientations.

Since conflicts are inevitable, the best we can do to maintain our relationships is to negotiate and/or resolve the conflicts that would always be in attendant as long as humans continue to be the social animals that we have been described to be.

Credit: Bill O'Connell

Negotiating Needs in an Interpersonal Relationship

People have different interests and expect them to be met. An individual cannot always get all of what he or she wants in a healthy association because it takes two to maintain a relationship. Having your way all the time suggests that the other person is always losing out. When the other person does not get his or her own needs fulfilled, dissatisfaction results, which would threaten the foundation of the relationship. Negotiated interests will accommodate partners in a relationship to the extent that each feels satisfied. After all, negotiation has been defined as the process of resolving differences through mutually acceptable tradeoffs (Walker & Harris, 1995).

There are ways you can communicate the goals of meeting your needs, desires, and expectations without necessarily putting the other person at a disadvantage. These behavior strategies include the **passive approach, the aggressive approach, and the assertive approach.**

Passive behavior is to avoid confronting another to ask or demand that our needs be met. Verderber & Verderber (2010) describe passive behavior as **not expressing personal preference or defending our rights because we fear the cost and are insecure in the relationship, have low self-esteem, or value the other person above self**. This is certainly not a healthy way to maintain a relationship in that such passivity will further negatively affect one's self-esteem and erode the security yearned for, and promote other's dominance over oneself. If we submit to others' desires over ours all the time, this becomes a lopsided relationship that is better described as servitude.

On the opposite end of passive behavior is **aggressive behavior**, which is **a forceful claim of our rights and privileges without consideration for others' feelings and rights in the relationship**. This can be seen as a selfish and anti-social way of dealing with issues that are better handled with mutual respect. Dissatisfaction is inevitable in such relationships where one or both members engage in aggressive behaviors as a method of achieving their desires, needs, and preferences.

The preferred alternative behavior for communicating our needs, desires, and expectations in a healthy manner is **assertive behavior**. This is communicating our needs and desires in a manner that establishes our individual rights and freedoms without infringing on the rights and privileges of others. Assertive behavior is an affirmation of one's needs in a manner which further develops our relationships. **The bedrock of assertive behavior, especially when exhibited by both partners, is mutual respect and appreciation.** It is expected that the needs established through assertive behavior will not infringe on the desires of the other but, if it does, it must be as a result of willful yielding by the other and not by compulsion.

Negotiating differences and conflicts can be achieved in six identifiable steps documented by Walker and Harris (1995). The steps or stages in the process of conflict resolution are: **analyzing the negotiation situation, planning for the upcoming negotiations, organizing, gaining and maintaining control, closing the negotiation, and continuous improvement.** Here, these stages or steps are presented in a table format for you to have a snapshot of the ideas of the scholars.

Table 8.1/Walker & Harris Six-Step Negotiation Process

1. Analyzing the negotiation situation
This is the problem or conflict analysis stage when you try to understand what it is that you are really negotiating for and what objective you want to meet. Here, you have to evaluate the prevailing circumstances that may impact the outcome that you desire. You must also consider the needs of the other party and determine the range of acceptable alternatives for the negotiation. Be ready to have a best alternative to the negotiated position.

2. Planning for the Upcoming Negotiations
Goals for the negotiation are set at this stage. You should consider setting goals for the major issues that need resolving, which are usually money, people and timing. Communication strategy and tactics to employ should be planned and, ahead of the negotiation, the outcome should be anticipated. The possible outcomes are win-win, win-lose, or lose-lose. In addition, the logistics of the negotiation should be planned ahead and this includes location of negotiation, the people to be invited, the time of the meeting, the format of the meeting, how many meetings, and how the records will be documented and presented.

3. Organizing
At this stage, the negotiating team should be identified, the objectives for negotiation should be established and a total game plan devised. Order the offers, strategizing from least to the most important or maximum offer able point. Practice is key at this stage, so, the negotiating team should conduct dry-runs or mock negotiation sessions with observers to give feedback. Finally, always have alternate plans for all of the strategies because negotiations can be unpredictable and may need quick adaptation to new conditions and strategies during the actual session.

4. Gaining and Maintaining Control
If you get the partners in conflict to agree to the terms of the negotiation, before the actual meeting, some level of control has been gained. Escalating emotions and shouting matches do not augur well for conflict resolution, and that is why you must control everything that can possibly be controlled in the negotiation setting and process. An agenda is the controlling force of the negotiation session, as such, you should get the both parties to agree to the agenda and the need to adhere to such, even before the actual program. An agenda would include the following negotiated items where and when necessary: *date, time, location, attendees, list of topics, order of topics, time allotted to each topic, start and end times, and ground rules for the sessions*.

5. Closing the Negotiation

This is similar to closing the deal in sales or business transactions. When there are minor issues left unresolved in a prolonged negotiation, creative means can be invented to close the deal. Do not over flog the issues when agreement is near or has practically been reached. A little concession worth 2% of the negotiated value of a transaction can create a win-win solution to a protracted conflict. There is always a price to pay for negotiated struggle or transactions or relationships.

6. Continuous Improvement

This is the evaluation stage of the whole negotiation performance. Every step of the negotiation process should be evaluated with the possibility of improving on the performance. The questions you should ponder to fulfill this stage are the following: Was the problem thoroughly analyzed and was the negotiation adequately planned? What about the organization, is there room for improvement? Were you able to adequately gain and maintain control of the negotiation agenda? And, how effective was the negotiation closing?

There are several precepts offered for handling negotiations in the utmost effective manner. An evaluation of many of these suggestions indicates that most, if not all are communication-based. The suggestion is that effective negotiation involves effective communication and that competent communicators will make good negotiators.

Examine the following guidelines for negotiation presented by Tubbs and Moss (2006) which they adapted from the work of Deep and Sussman (1998), and determine which of them are based on communication competencies addressed in the first chapter of this book.

In negotiating, you should try the following guidelines:

- *Establish a cooperative tone at the outset*
- *Strive for a win-win outcome.*
- *Ask lots of questions and really listen to the answers. Knowledge of other person's needs, expectations, preferences, pressures, and strategies will help you reach an understanding.*
- *Find a line of reasoning that meets your need while also meeting the other party's needs at the least cost to you.*
- *Know your "bottom line." Don't give away more than your maximum or accept less than your minimum.*
- *Stay calm. If you feel you are losing your temper, call for a break.*
- *Don't appear too anxious for a solution. Avoid snap judgments.*
- *If you reach an impasse, either suggest a recess or restate the consequences of not reaching an agreement. You may also suggest a trade of items from each party.*

Conflict Resolution Methods

Individual differences are reflected in the manner in which different people handle conflicts. Note that we identified the different types of conflict and one of them is ego-based. Our experience, background, culture, personality, type of relationship, the level of intimacy, the cost of the relationship, all influence the way we choose to resolve our conflicts. As Kilmann and Thomas (1975) note, individuals may have a preferred style and method for resolving conflicts. In a model they developed about the different styles for resolving conflict, there are five identifiable methods, which are **avoidance, competition, compromise, accommodation, and collaboration.**

This conceptual model cannot exhaust the array of methods used by all individuals, but the ideas presented capture the typical behaviors of people in conflict situations. In practice, the dividing lines among the different methods are blurry, just as each of the methods is not self-sufficient. People would find it useful to combine some of these ideas in resolving their conflicts over time.

Avoiding (Lose-Lose)

We have confirmed that conflict is inevitable and that it is not a bad thing for a relationship. This is because a relationship grows when the interdependence of the partners has been tested by conflicts that allow the areas of tensions to be articulated and discussed. Conflicts signal a need for change and allow for growth of relationships.
Conflict is, therefore, something not to be avoided, but to be understood and resolved whenever possible. However, there some people whose conflict resolution style is avoiding or withdrawing. Rather than confront the conflict head-on, they choose to avoid it both physically and psychologically. Tactics used by conflict avoiders include, avoiding certain discussion topics, changing the topic of discussion, reducing conversations to jovial matters, and physically removing themselves from the venue of interaction to avoid having to deal with their conflict.

The misunderstanding is that if you avoid a problem, it will go away. Not so, because when conflicts are avoided, they are unresolved and resentment builds up between partners. Overtime, the pent-up negative emotions would erupt into a far deeper conflict than before. Avoiding conflict will often exacerbate the issues in conflict and escalate the dissatisfaction in the relationship.

Stonewalling
The act of stone silence-- refusal to discuss a problem, or to physically avoid another person who disagrees, complains, or attacks us.

While you would agree that sometime it is preferable to avoid a problem, such as the bickering of a troublesome friend, it is not always advisable to withdraw from conflict in an enduring relationship. This is because "self-silencers" have more frustration when dealing their partners than those who face their problems and attempt to resolve them (Harper and Welsh, 2007). The frustration of not being able to think of good solutions to conflicts may justify the actions of conflict avoiders, but resolving to give up and hide is not a solution either.

Or, the goal of avoidance may be to postpone confrontation until a calmer time before dealing with it. But as time passes, the problem may even grow larger and the emotions run deeper. On the long run, "conflict silencers" in relationships both lose out of a rewarding, uncontaminated social climate.

As we can confirm now, in the words of Seiler and Beal (2008), withdrawal can be a useful strategy, but it is also limited in its ability to resolve the conflict itself.

Figure 8.1/Kilmann-Thomas Conflict Resolution Process

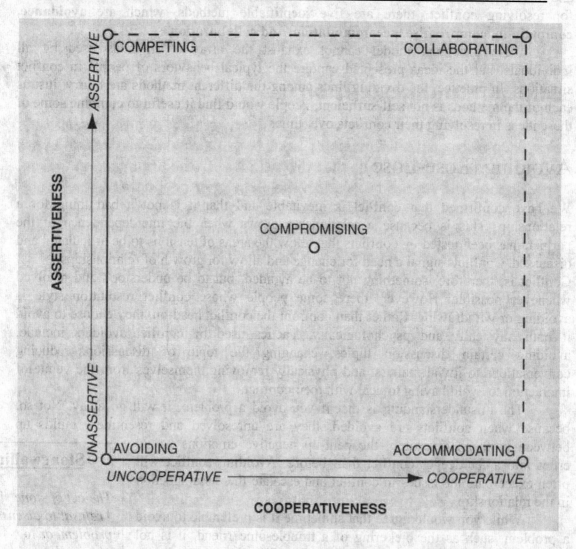

This model of conflict resolution behaviors is adapted from "The Kilmann-Thomas Conflict Model" as it appeared in Tubbs and Moss (2006) *Human Communication: Principles and Contexts* (10th ed.) New York: McGraw Hill.

Avoiding ultimately results in both partners' desires and needs not being met. This is why this method of conflict resolution is characterized by unassertive and uncooperative behavior and, as such, is classified as a **"lose-lose"** result for the partners. Can you think of events, situations in which you applied this method to resolve some of your conflicts with your friends and loved ones?

Accommodating (Lose-Win)

Rather than avoid conflicts, some people prefer to yield to the demands of the other person. This occurs when one person unassertively allows another to have his or her way, perhaps in an argument, or in decision making. This suggests that the individual values him or herself less, especially when it comes to the issue in conflict, and is willing to lose out for the other person to win.

Sometimes, an accommodating partner is willing to strengthen the relationship by genuinely yielding to the other person for the sake of the relationship. This is all well and good, but if the motive is not a genuine act of love, generosity, or magnanimity, then this is not considered a good way to resolve conflicts. A "doormat" of a person can never be that loving of those who trample upon him. Usually those who habitually yield to others lack good self-esteem, desires to be loved rather than share love with another, and would often in private complain and whine about being used or dominated.

Accommodating tactics according to Sillars and Wilmot (1994) include giving up or giving in, disengagement, denial of needs, or a desire to get along. When you give up or give in, another person gains something at your expense; when you disengage, you empower another over you to take charge. And when power sharing is lopsided in a committed relationship, the imbalance causes dissatisfaction. If you are always accommodating because "you have no choice," then, your desire to get along is actually motivated by your incapacitation in your relationship and, that cannot be a healthy situation to be in.

Cultural orientations may play a great role in whether someone avoids or accommodates, or engages in any of the conflict resolving methods discussed in this section. When we compare collectivist and individualist cultures, a marked difference is found in their communication of conflict resolution. Collectivist cultures value social cohesion and the authority of the in-group, to the extent that members of this cultural orientation would not exert their individual rights and privileges, rather, they would promote the group and avoid anything that may bring disrespect and shame to the collective. The result is not vehemently arguing their points of view with another, not defending an issue that would bring shame to another, because winning an argument is putting another person to shame! Such people would be described as "pushovers," "spineless," and "fool" in a low-context, individualist culture such as that of mainstream U.S.A.

Have you ever had to accommodate your partner in certain situations? Are you always accommodating your partner in decisions made or are you the one who always demands that the other person yields to you in your relationships?

Competing (Win-Lose)

Competition is a contention of wills and of means. The result is that one person wins at the expense of another. Conflict is seen as a battle to be won and by all means. We can relate to runners outrunning one another or pugilists out-boxing one another, or two football teams gunning for the Super Bowl-- the prize is one and you either win or lose. Many social relationship situations are rather competitive where partners issue "**threats, criticism, confrontational remarks, or extreme language choices**," to gain an upper hand over on the other and to win. Tubbs and Moss (2006), confirm that in the competition style of conflict, one party tries to use aggression or power to beat the other party.

The tactics used (**Sillars schema**) to achieve an edge over the other in a relationship, be it between husband and wife, parent and child, co-workers, and family members, will include **faulting, hostile questioning, hostile joking, presumptive attribution, avoiding responsibility and prescription** (Sillars, 1986).

To point to the fault of another person is to personally criticize that person and such an act leads to defensive behavior. That is if your person is attacked, you have to defend yourself.

Presumptive attribution is making statements that attribute to the other person feelings, thoughts, or motives that he or she does not acknowledge (Tubbs and moss (2006). This is saying that someone feels one way because of a particular reason that may not be true. For example: "You're always copying what I do because you lack originality." "I know you think 'am not smart enough." These are statements that speak to the competitive mindset of partners in a relationship or, why else would a husband say such statements to his wife if there is no underlying competitiveness?

The prescription strategy of competitive conflict management involves issuing threats, demands, or arguing for a prescribed behavior, without which some consequences are also prescribed. For example: "If you don't get your act together, I will leave this marriage." "If you don't clean your room, you'll not get your allowance for the week."

Competition in a relationship is not always a bad thing. In competitive situations, partners can bring out the best in each other that can lead to a measure of regard among them, thereby enhancing their relationship. Couples can compete in exercising to lose weight to the extent that the "bigger loser" is accorded some respect for his or her achievement. But all this could backfire if the partners don't take competitive loss lightly and do engage in attitudes and behaviors to get even.

If you watch enough of Ice hockey, basketball, soccer, and other competitive sports, you would agree that competition often gives birth to aggression. In interpersonal relationships, just as in sports, **aggression may be direct and physical or passive**. Direct aggression could be verbal or nonverbal, which Infante (1987) identifies to include character attacks, competence attacks, physical appearance attacks, malediction (wishing others bad fortune) teasing, ridicule, threats, swearing, and nonverbal emblems. Indirect or passive aggression occurs when subtle means are used to display aggressive feelings toward another person. A front of politeness is maintained but there is underlying hostility that is expressed indirectly because either the person is unwilling to directly or overtly show his or her displeasure or is unable to do so. This kind of behavior has been labeled **crazy-making.**

Compromising (Partial Lose-Lose/Win-Win)

When both partners in a relationship opt to yield some of their expectations, desires, and goals such that each gains some and loses some, this is what is described as compromising. Partial satisfaction of goals is perceived to be the better alternative to lose-lose or win-lose, and lose-win conflict styles. In this situation, the partners engage each other to negotiate their needs and goals and do settle for a mutually satisfying compromise.

This style of conflict resolution may be perceived to be better than some of the methods already discussed, but there is a great danger in compromising certain things in a relationship. What if partners compromise their religious values or even individual values? Should compromise extend to marital morality of monogamy? Again, can we compromise our need for a clean, tidy home with a spouse who is less willing to clean up after him or her? When it comes to certain issues, we cannot see compromise as a good thing.

Compromise as a conflict resolution method is usually not the first option of contending partners, but may be the workable solution in many cases of conflict, especially when the parties involved wield equal power. It could be more satisfying if deep values are not compromised and if other more permanent solutions can be found.

Without compromise, it will be difficult to achieve harmony in our many relationships with others. Certainly, in a market economy, compromise on prices of goods and services is key to success, because the seller cannot charge arbitrarily high prices for goods, higher than the buyer is willing and able to pay--they both have to meet at the equilibrium point which economists describe as the intersection of demand and supply. As long as both are satisfied, compromise can, indeed, be a good conflict resolution method.

Collaborating (Win-Win)

This is the ideal method of resolving conflict. When parties of different needs and desires collaborate rather than compete, the result is the maximization of their potentials. The focus of collaborators is not on their individual goals, but the respect for and satisfaction of each other's goals. When everyone realizes his or her goal within the context of interpersonal relationships, everyone wins.

Imagine the needs of two lovers to spend time with each other and the conflict that may arise if they want to do this by watching a movie together, which on of them does not like. If they should compromise, then they both would watch the same movie, but one of them will be left unsatisfied. Watching the choice of movie of one person will be at the expense of another. But how can this be resolved? The goals are twofold: the lovers want to spend time together, and watching a movie would together would achieve this. If they go to a movie theatre, they can as well watch separate movies and meet afterwards for dinner, or they could both watch each other's movies together. Two movies compared to a movie and dinner will result in different outcomes. What about someone's choice of a movie and dinner for one outing and another's choice for another outing? These are all creative attempts to put the relationships above individual choices. Partners in a collaborative relationship would feel a sense of equality and respect, which are two elements that promote healthy relationships. Ultimately, **different situations, relationships, goals, and the persons involved in a relationship will call for different styles of conflict resolution**. One method does not fit all problems with all people, and in all situations. There is value in each of the methods discussed here and, at times, they can be combined to achieve the best results possible for the unique problems that people may have. In the following table, Wilmot and Hocker (2010) enumerate which factors to consider when choosing the most appropriate conflict style.

Credit: Bill O'Connell

Table 8.2/When to Choose the Most Appropriate Conflict Style

Avoiding (Lose-Lose)
1. When the issue is of little importance
2. When the costs of confrontation outweigh the benefits
3. To cool down and gain perspective.

Accommodating (Lose-Win)
1. When you discover you are wrong
2. When the issue is more important to the other person than it is to you
3. When long-term cost of winning isn't worth the short-term gain
4. To build up credits for later conflicts.

Competing (Win-Lose)
1. When there is not enough time to seek a win-win outcome
2. When the issue is not important enough to negotiate at length
3. When the other person is not willing to cooperate
4. When you are convinced that your position is right and necessary
5. To protect yourself against a person who takes advantage of noncompetitive people

Compromising (Partial Lose-lose)
1. To achieve quick, temporary solutions to complex problems
2. When opponents are strongly committed to mutually exclusive goals
3. When the issues are moderately important but not enough for a stalemate
4. As a backup mode when collaboration doesn't work

Collaborating (Win-Win)
1. When the issue is too important for a compromise
2. When long-term relationship between you and the other person is important
3. To merge insights with someone who has a different perspective on the problem
4. To develop a relationship by showing commitment to the concerns of both parties
5. To come up with creative and unique solutions to problems

Adapted from Wilmot, W.W. & Hocker, J.L. (2010) *Interpersonal Conflict* (8th Ed.).
New York: McGraw-Hill

Review Questions

1. How would you define conflict?
2. Identify and describe the different perspectives of conflict.
3. What are the different types of conflict and how might you resolve them?
4. Explain the methods of resolving interpersonal conflicts.
5. Describe the process of negotiating conflicts.
6. What are the differences among assertive, aggressive, and passive behaviors?
7. Discuss the advantages and disadvantages of the five conflict resolution methods developed by Kilmann and Thomas.
8. Why is compromising considered a win/win—lose/lose, conflict resolution method?

Toxic Relationships

By William O'Connell www.williamoconnell.net

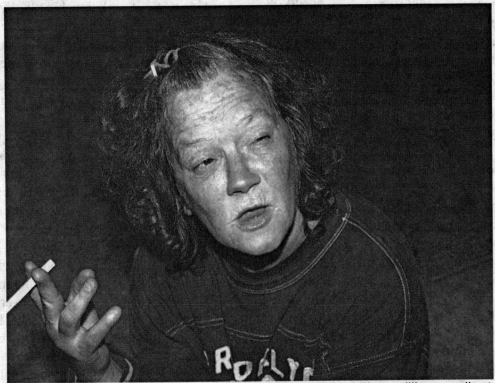

(Photo William O'Connell/www.williamoconnell.net)

"Crazy Mary," toxic to herself and others while being filmed for *Voices in the Sand* on Venice Beach.
She has been arrested nearly 200 times.

American culture has seen a dramatic increase in domestic violence cases. Toxic relationships are not limited to friendships that go sour or intimate relationships that become debilitating. These damaging relationships take place in the workplace and in the home.

The rise of domestic violence has heightened the need to understand relationship climate and how to identify whether or not our relationships are healthy or toxic. A sign of escalating interpersonal abuse is the more than 600 domestic violence abuse shelters in the United States, which are not in short supply of clients. To say that toxic relationships are a big part of American culture would be an understatement.

We must understand how these types of negative relationships can ruin lives, careers, families, and our future.

In this article, you will learn what defines a toxic relationship and the difference between a healthy and toxic relationship. You will also come to understand how a relationship becomes toxic and what the **seven toxic signs** in a relationship are? Finally, we will examine how we can get ourselves out of toxic relationships.

A healthy relationship occurs when your partner respects your independence, time, and personal space.

Collaboration, trust, loyalty, love, and mutual understanding are what make relationships successful. There are crucial signs to understanding the differences between a healthy, compatible relationship and a toxic one. Understanding these signs can help you to attain emotional growth, confidence, and expert problem solving skills, as well as the ability to be mindful of the relationship you want, so that you can be happy with the partner you chose. The same can be said about toxic relationships. If you knew what your partner was like when the mask was not on, perhaps you could have leveraged self-control in the relationship such that you would not have allowed another to control you. Having a sense of independence in a relationship is important for the relationship to maintain a healthy level. When that mask comes off, always question actions rather than words like love, respect, and whether or not your relationship has

stability. We allow ourselves to the point of toxicity in our relationships.

Perhaps one of the most important steps a person can take to avoid a toxic relationship is by not jumping into a relationship after just ending one. Relationship addiction is a problem. Since we are creatures of patterns and habits, taking time to get to know our self is crucial. For example, take the necessary time to heal after dissolving your broken relationships by rebuilding your self -worth, confidence, and by challenging yourself to DEMAND respect. When we disrespect ourselves it gives everyone else the right to disrespect us. So, we have to start with positive self- concept and self-worth. Be aware of who you are within, especially your strengths and limitations.

Toxic relationships often end in physical abuse, including death! Imagine the following statistics: 25% of women experience domestic violence their lifetime, reports the National Coalition against Domestic Violence.

Consider these relationship-related data.

An estimated 1.3 million women are victims of physical assault by an intimate partner each year.[1i]

- 85% of domestic violence victims are women.[ii]
- Historically, females have been most often victimized by someone they knew.[iii]
- Females who are *20-24 years of age* are at the greatest risk of nonfatal intimate partner violence. [iv]
- Most cases of domestic violence are never reported to the police. [v]
- Witnessing violence between one's parents or caretakers is the strongest risk factor of transmitting violent behavior from one generation to the next. vi
- Boys who witness domestic violence are "twice as likely" to abuse their own partners(s) and children when they become adults.
- 30% to 60% of perpetrators of intimate partner violence also abuse children in the household. vii
- Nearly 7.8 million women have been raped by an intimate partner at some point in their lives. viii

- Sexual assault or forced sex occurs in approximately 40-45% of battering relationships. Ix

How do we recognize a toxic relationship?
Below are some ACTION signs.

1. The Head-Over Heels beginning: (OMG I am in love! Yeah, with their looks! Slow down. Make him/her earn it—don't be so easy!)
2. Possessiveness and Repetitiveness: (The She/he belongs to me stage.)
3. "Clicking the Switch" (Dr. Jekyll and Mr. Hyde)
4. Verbal Abuse (Geez, he/she never used to call me that before we had sex.)
5. The Blame Game (Baby, I did this for you—I didn't mean to cheat.)
6. Indifference to Humanity (Life's a B*&^ and then you die.)
7. Physical Aggressiveness (Let the beatings begin.)

The Head Over Heels Beginning

Toxic relationships' *Head Over Heels Beginning*.

Lexi came to me a few years ago saying, "If I only knew that he beat his last girlfriend. I would have never gotten involved in this relationship." The relationship began with a "Head over heels" beginning whereby Lexi fell in love with Morgan's good looks, charm, and physical appearance. Morgan's mask is still on. Lexi never knew Morgan was coming out of a relationship where he cheated on his ex-girlfriend to be with Lexi, and that Morgan hit his last girlfriend. He was physically aggressive toward her more than once. Lexi did not know that Morgan's ex-girlfriend had to file an Order of Protection against him because she felt unsafe. She never knew what would happen when she wanted out of the relationship, and she didn't see the writing-on- the-wall that Morgan's repetitive behaviors signaled the possibility of developing a toxic relationship that would soon affect Lexi. Why? Morgan lied to Lexi. She took for granted that Morgan was telling the truth about his past. This method of manipulation and behavior had Lexi feeling sorry for her newly found boyfriend, Morgan who Lexi became intimate with within three weeks. How well can we know a person in three weeks? Lexi never knew that Morgan had a bad temper, that he was possessive, that he had rage, or that his interpersonal incompetency or, most important, his controlling and jealous behaviors would be the root of his destructive personality. And, he saw Lexi for her body, her beauty, and her submissiveness as a way to mold and manipulate her into what he wanted in a woman. Drama!

In the early stages of a relationship, people are usually at their best performance or are on their best behaviors because to get to the next stage, we have to make a positive impression. When someone asks for more than a kiss on a first date--be careful. Likewise, be careful when a person seems too good to be true. Be critical by testing the relationship rather than rush into anything. Don't worry, if he or she likes you, he/she will be back. The model below contains relationship timeline suggestions. This is a challenge

to see how long you can wait in your next relationship before becoming intimate.

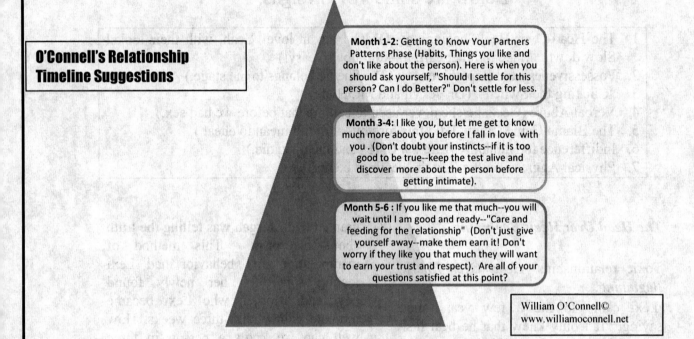

O'Connell's Relationship Timeline Suggestions

Month 1-2: Getting to Know Your Partners Patterns Phase (Habits, Things you like and don't like about the person). Here is when you should ask yourself, "Should I settle for this person? Can I do Better?" Don't settle for less.

Month 3-4: I like you, but let me get to know much more about you before I fall in love with you . (Don't doubt your instincts--if it is too good to be true--keep the test alive and discover more about the person before getting intimate).

Month 5-6 : If you like me that much--you will wait until I am good and ready--"Care and feeding for the relationship" (Don't just give yourself away--make them earn it! Don't worry if they like you that much they will want to earn your trust and respect). Are all of your questions satisfied at this point?

William O'Connell©
www.williamoconnell.net

Possessiveness

Let's take an empowering look at *Possessiveness*. 81% of women stalked by a current or former intimate partner are also physically assaulted by that partner; and 31% are also sexually assaulted by that partner. [xi] Possessiveness is considered one of the most important signs of a toxic relationship to understand. It is a huge Red Flag. A person who understands signs of possessiveness can avoid falling into the trap of being controlled.

Lexi said that she became concerned when her handsome boyfriend, Morgan started with the "You can't put pictures of yourself in those clothes on *Facebook*" command. Then he made her delete any male acquaintances she had on her page. Some of these male friends

she knew since early childhood. Now she had to weigh the costs and rewards of the relationship. Had she understood the Exchange Theory and its connection to toxic relationships, perhaps she would have leaped out of the relationship at this point. It didn't end there. Morgan wanted Lexi to close her *Facebook* page after less than six months of meeting him. This was an important toxic relationship sign which Lexi completely missed. She lost her freedom to be herself. Having the handsome boyfriend at her side made Lexi's friends jealous because their boyfriend's where not as physically attractive as Morgan.

Lexi was in a state of denial that Morgan loved her for who she is. You have probably heard the cliché that "as you make your bed, so you will lie in it." Possessiveness is a behavior that presents clear and toxic danger in relationships yet people do not recognize it and often times they ignore the signs. When someone uses the phrase, "You belong to me or if I can't have you nobody can," it creates the "Monster" within the toxic person to be further possessive and obsessive. In other words, we enable them. Lexi only created the "Monster" within Morgan to fuel his next toxic step and negative behavior in the relationship. This pattern will not go away. Now is the time to get out of the relationship. Demand respect and do not let the relationship continue. This is easier said than done, however, but in reality this measure of toxicity using this model will enable you to remain in control of your actions and the climate of the relationship.

"Clicking the Switch" (Dr. Jekyll and Mr. Hyde)

After being in a relationship for so long and after reaching the "couple stage," be aware of deterioration in the relationship described as "The Switch" stage, which interlinks potential toxic signs in the relationship. A simple example of the change would be to look back at how your partner treated you up until the couple stage. Everything that was respected i.e., your opinion, value as a person, may no longer be valid when a toxic person shows his/her differences and true face. In other words, the mask is off. Suddenly the toxic person, who appreciated you up until this stage, now disrespects or disregards your feelings, to manipulate the relationship and situation outcome to satisfy his/her own ego.

After realizing that a partner might be lost, many people have make-up sex to rectify and please each other's feelings as a way to apologize for the hurt they cause each other. Demand that you need time to evaluate the relationship. Make your partner understand that his/her behaviors hurt your feelings and will not be rewarded with sex. Understand that people wear masks. It's all about tolerance and how much drama each individual is willing to accept.

Verbal Abuse

Another pattern is verbal abuse. Patterns of behaviors help to make predictions about a person. For example, if someone was constantly fired from his/her job, it is a signal to an interviewer that the candidate has trouble keeping a responsible and stable position in the workforce. The same goes for relationships. When a person has trouble nurturing a positive relationship, it says something about the character of that person. Once the verbal abuse begins and we allow it, it is an open door to repetitive behavior. The abuse will not end here. Sometimes as children we watch our parents verbally abuse each other. They are our teachers at a young age, so we learn to behave likewise. In the case of Lexi, Morgan was now calling Lexi names because he thought she was looking at other man. This verbal abuse continued, yet Lexi enabled Morgan by staying in the relationship.

The Blame Game

The Blame Game is when a person stages events such as pseudo arguments to try to make the partner feel guilty. Lexi said that Morgan was accusing her of cheating. Here she had been completely loyal to what she thought was her "dream" guy. And now he was accusing her of cheating. **Double-standards are part of any toxic relationship.** It was okay for Morgan to stay out late with his friends, but when Lexi wanted to, it became a heated argument about what she was allowed to wear, who she could go out with, and even what time she had to be home. Morgan had control. Lexi abided because she did not want to lose the relationship and in her submissive way, allowed Morgan to continue to control her. Morgan also continued to blame Lexi for the relationship being *stagnant*. If you have ever asked yourself why people stay in relationships like this, it is clear that people like Lexi did not take the time necessary to truly get to know Morgan the way she should have. Morgan continued to drive Lexi's emotions and terrorize her into believing that without him she could not make it. He had total control over her emotions and only made her feel guilty whenever she went out with her friends.

Indifference to Humanity

Lexi had lost her father at a difficult time in her life. Morgan first showed indifference to humanity when he told her, "we all have to die sometime." Then days later, when Morgan hit a dog with his car and killed the dog, Lexi said: "Morgan showed no emotion at all. He just ran over a dog and killed it without even stopping. I was afraid of him at this point in the relationship. As I was crying and yelling at him, we broke out into such an argument that he slapped me in the face and told me to shut up! This was the first time I was ever hit by a guy."

This is *Physical Aggressiveness*. Yet, Lexi stayed in the relationship. She lost all of her friends by this point because Morgan found flaws in every one of them and he now controlled who Lexi was allowed to be friends with. She also became distant with her own family.

This is not love—this is a toxic relationship. All this time Lexi did not know Morgan was a toxic human who manipulated his girlfriend and tossed her around like a toy. His ego, size, and mental toughness were not something that Lexi was going to challenge or change. He no longer had a soft side. Morgan has now exposed his other side by coming full circle, bringing Lexi into the toxic relationship with him. Toxic people are hard if not impossible to change.

So how do we grow and learn from these individuals?

ACT/REACT

First, use intellect over emotion. Learn from your relationships. If you are coming out of a broken relationship, you need to take time to heal the emotional wounds of losing a partner. Some people rebound quickly from relationship termination. Others take six months to a year, and even longer depending on your self-control. The point is, heal! Realize you have been bruised and the ego needs time to regain a comfort level that redefines your relational worthiness. Don't be fooled into a new relationship even if you have been cheated on. Set rules as to when you will become sexually active in a relationship. Don't worry about losing the person. Don't be pressured! Demand respect!

Foresee the Mask Off

If you are fresh out of a relationship, create and manage a timeline so that you do not rush back into a relationship that can hurt you again only to repeat the same negative behaviors. Be in control!

On every level be sure you get what you want in a partner. Begin with a timeline;

seek respect, integrity, character, in a person who synergizes your dreams with his/her own and not some controlling, selfish person, who has the ability to ruin

your life. Set the tone, control the tone and you will be in charge of the relationship   your   way

.

1. Tajden, patricia & Thoennes, Nancy. National Institute of Justice and the Centers of Disease Control and Prevention, "Extent, Nature and Consequences of Intimate Partner Violence: Findings from the National Violence Against Women Survey," (2000).

[2] Costs of Intimate Partner Violence Against Women in the United States. 2003. Centers for Disease Control and Prevention, National Centers for Injury Prevention and Control. Atlanta, GA.

[3] Bureau of Justice Statistics Crime Data Brief, *Intimate Partner Violence, 1993-2001*, February 2003.

[4] U.S. Department of Justice, Bureau of Justice Statistics, "Criminal Victimization, 2005," September 2006.

5U.S. Department of Justice, Bureau of Justice Statistics, "Intimate Partner Violence in the United States," December 2006.

[6] Frieze, I.H., Browne, A. (1989) Violence in Marriage. In L.E. Ohlin & M. H. Tonry (eds.) *Family Violence*. Chicago, IL: University of Chicago Press.

[7] *Costs of Intimate Partner Violence Against Women in the United States*. 2003. Centers for Disease Control and Prevention, National Centers for Injury Prevention and Control. Atlanta, GA.

[8] Campbell, et al. (2003). "Assessing Risk Factors for Intimate Partner Homicide." *Intimate Partner Homicide*, NIJ Journal, 250, 14-19. Washington, D.C.: National Institute of Justice, U.S. Department of Justice.

[9] Campbell, et al. (2003). "Assessing Risk Factors for Intimate Partner Homicide." *Intimate Partner Homicide*, NIJ Journal, 250, 14-19. Washington, D.C.: National Institute of Justice, U.S. Department of Justice.

[10] Tjaden, Patricia & Thoennes, Nancy. (1998). "Stalking in America." National Institute for Justice.

Chapter Nine
Interviewing: A Specialized Interpersonal Communication

An interview is a two-way communication in which two or more persons, trade questions and answers for a predetermined purpose. The specific purpose for which an interview is organized is what makes it a specialized exchange. The questions are often structured to meet the predetermined goals of the exchange.

The purposes for which interviews are conducted include: Information gathering, information giving, persuasion, and evaluation.

Information Gathering

Information is necessary to bring general and specific awareness of issues, events, and agenda to individuals; it is also necessary for decision making. The profession of journalism thrives on information gathering and dissemination to large audiences, the purpose of which is to satisfy the psychological urge that people have to be aware of what is happening around them and to make informed decisions.

The primary tool of the journalist for gathering information is the interview. The practitioner develops relevant questions to guide and structure the exchange of information with another person. In the case of breaking news, a journalist would use the interview format of the **"Five Ws and H"** to interview eyewitnesses to collect relevant information about the event. The "Five Ws and H" represent the beginning letters of the different types of questions the journalist, as an **interviewer,** will ask the eyewitnesses, who are the **interviewees.** The first question is about **What** happened; the second is about **Where** the event happened; the third is **Who** was involved; the fourth is **When** the event happened and; the fifth is **Why** the event happened. The **How** the event happened is what the "H" stands for. So, when you read the news in your newspaper or listen to the news on radio and watch it on television, you should realize the interview techniques that have been used to collect the relevant information that are pieced together to satisfy your need to know. In addition to newsgathering, journalists also interview notable individuals to obtain background information for stories and personality profiles.

College students and scholars also interview sources to collect first-hand information about issues, topics, and events. Research studies depend largely on the interview as a means of polling participants, respondents, and research subjects. In writing papers, writing speeches and reports, the interview becomes indispensable.

Medical practitioners also use the interview as a means of taking the "history" of their patients. This is the background information of the patient, including medical history, that will help the attending doctor in evaluating the patient's current condition and help in determining what line of treatment to follow. The line of questioning has become routine to medical practitioners that they follow the structured interview in a somewhat interactional style. But the goals are predetermined because there are specific areas of interest of the patient's history that the Doctors have specific questions to elicit.

Information Giving

When attending one-on-one information sessions, students are on the receiving end of the information giving exercise of their counselors. The counselors have access to information that the students do not and by means of an interview such information is made available to the recipients. Doctors and pharmacists also give information on drugs, their functions, and their possible side effects to their patients. Managers in job orientation situations also give information to their orientees.

Persuasion

Often the goal of an interview is to present an idea, product or person to the other person for acceptance, purchase or a favorable vote. The persuasive interview is designed to change or maintain attitudes, to influence opinion, and to induce action. Sales interviews qualify as a persuasive exchange where the seller asks questions of a potential buyer to "qualify" his/her needs in order to meet them by purchasing the products or services provided. Also, persuasive interviews can take the form of a neighbor who comes to your door to canvass for a change in the home owner's association in order that he may install a larger than acceptable swimming pool. A political candidate for office who comes to your door to canvass for support is also an example of a one-on-one persuasive interview.

Evaluation

Interviews to evaluate can take many different forms depending on the specific purposes for which they are to serve. **Performance appraisal interviews** are evaluative because the purpose is to evaluate the performance of an individual or groups of person in a set of activities in order to identify areas of deficiencies and opportunities for growth.
 Exit interviews are also evaluative exchanges because the interviewer is attempting to obtain the objective evaluation of a departing employee regarding the culture and conditions of service and any other relevant information that may help the interviewer to evaluate the job process and the working conditions of the current workers. **Employment interviews** also qualify as evaluative because they are designed for the employer to examine and judge a potential employee's qualifications and experience, to ascertain their suitability for an available position. **Counseling interviews** are evaluative to the extent that they may provide information with which to evaluate the social-psychological state of an individual, for the purpose of understanding and resolving the problem. Obviously, one of the participants is in need and the other, the counselor. However, there are situations whereby individuals or groups of people may meet to exchange information to

get to the root of the problems that they may be facing, with a view to resolving such problems. This is referred to as **problem-solving interviews**.

There are other forms of interviews that can be better subsumed under any of the four general headings above, just as some of the interviews types identified can fall under more than one of the classifications.

The Structure of an Interview

An interview usually fields questions that would probe into the personal and professional lives of the interviewee. The process involves an opening, middle or the body, closing, and follow-up.

The Interview Opening

This is the stage when the interviewer 'breaks the ice' with the interviewee. It is characterized by small talk designed to set a tone and climate for the interchange of messages to follow. A very brief introduction is done and the purpose for the interview is restated and the protocol for the meeting is established. The interviewer should preview the different types of topics/questions to be posed and their purpose, suggest the time frame for each of the questions, and determine how the exercise would flow. As soon as all these are done, it is time to get to the body of the interview.

The Interview Body

This is also referred to as the substantive stage of the interview when the structured questions are posed as the interviewer has organized them. In the case of a job interview, this is the stage to examine the applicant's background experience, qualifications, and motivation for applying for the job. All the types of questions designed to get the best information out of the interviewee are deployed at this stage. Open-ended questions are asked to allow the applicant to generally state opinions and to present his or her prepared **self summary.** The general questions are followed with **close or forced-choice questions** to clarify statements, opinions and positions on issues being discussed.
At this stage, the interviewee also has the opportunity to pose his or her own questions and give reasons for such questions. The agenda, as stated in the introduction, should be adhered to. If some of the questions are not covered by the interviewer, the respondent has the opportunity to ask and give relevant answers. This shows a high level of preparation as well as effective listening on the part of the respondent.

The Interview Closing

A good interviewer will present a summary of the interview to reflect the adequate coverage of all the elements previewed in the agenda presented in the introduction. A good summary of each of the answers of the respondent's should be summarized with a view to ascertaining their veracity and not to misrepresent the ideas of the candidate.

Opportunity is giving to the interviewee to correct any misrepresentation, after which the interview will wind up.

Now, before exiting the interview finally, the interviewer should state what he or she has accomplished or learned from the interview and offer thanks for the opportunity for the exchange and give a possible follow-up plan after the meeting, if any. Both the interviewer and the interviewee should leave the conversation with a positive sense of accomplishment, even if the candidate would not be offered the position.

The Interview Follow-Up

Prior to leaving the interview, the respondent should have contact numbers and addresses of people to contact within the organization to write or call to thank them for the opportunity given to interview for the position or to exchange your opinions on an issue as the case may be. In the case of a job interview, this is the opportunity to ask when you should expect the result of the interview and to ascertain if a decision has been made and if you are being considered or not for the position.

Types of Interview Questions

Examining different interview questions, one would find the different types below.
Often, these questions are combined in many different forms, as the case may be, to suit the type of interview organized. The questions serve to elicit specific responses that are the bases of the decisions sought by the interviewees.

Sociological Questions

These are questions that identify the characteristics an individual may have in relation to other members of society, and are easily observable with appearance, except for a few of them. These are also referred to as demographical questions which relate to age, income, gender, race ethnicity, location, etc. While some of the questions may not be relevant (may even be illegal) to the employment situation, they are very useful to meeting the purposes of many other interview types. A personality interview will benefit from all of the aforementioned sociological variables and so is the news or journalistic interview, which seeks to acquire as complete a vitae as possible from the respondent.

These sociological variables are identified by scholars as predictive variables in that people's attitudes, opinions, values, and actions vary because of their age, gender, location, race, ethnicity, income level, interest, education level and religious affiliations. As we will learn in the next interview question type, the sociological variables are predictors of the psychological variables.

Psychological Questions

These are questions that elicit individual attitudes, opinions, and beliefs. The questions address the mindset of the respondents, their internal states, rather than the external.
When someone asks your opinion about a governmental policy program such as "Welfare" or "Affirmative Action," what he or she is doing is soliciting your psychological responses (feelings) toward those programs. All the questions that start with "what do you think," what is your take on," "How do you feel about," "in your own opinion," are all psychological questions.

Interviewers know to always include both sociological and psychological questions in their interview questions because of what we have confirmed earlier that, if we want to cross reference opinions and attitudinal responses to the sociological characteristics of respondents, we will find a predictive relationship among them. In other words, sociology predicts psychology.

Open or Non-directed Questions

Interviews usually open with general questions to which the interviewee is free to be general in his or her response as well. But skillful interviewees use the opportunity to their advantage by steering their answers to issues, qualifications, experiences that show them in good stead before the interviewer. A common open question is the "Tell me about yourself," question. Specifically respondents should itemize three to four specific things about themselves that they should know that the interviewer wants to hear and for which they are proud and stand to gain competitive edge over others who may not have such unique background. Another general question is: Considering that we have interviewed several candidates for this position, why should we make you our number one choice? Your answer should include your exceptional skills, including interpersonal skills, unique work experience and ethic, ability and willingness to learn new things to improve yourself and the business of the organization.

Focused or Directed Questions

Whenever you are asked a question that requires a specific answer such as yes or no, you have been asked a direct, focused question. The purpose is to be as specific as possible and, especially after a general question has been asked or when a premise has been laid to precede the question. For example, you have been asked this question: What do you think about the laws banning cigarette smoking in the work place, bars restaurants and other public places? The follow-up to this may be a focused, direct question such as: Do you smoke cigarettes? The opportunity for a wiggle room is not available to the interviewee in this situation. If the atmosphere is assessed to be against smoking and smokers, as it is in many places today, you should tell the truth if you do smoke and indicate how that will not affect the well being of others. Perhaps, you should quit smoking, not for the job, but for your own good health.

Funnel Questions

These are questions designed to move the interview process from general to specific. The general questions are to make the interviewee comfortable and relaxed, to open up to the interviewer and, from the general exchange, the interview can get more specific and directed, hence the use of the term funnel. A funnel has a wide opening and a narrow discharge spout. Also, the questions are structured strategically to weed out certain irrelevances and to save time in the interview process. How? From the general questions the respondent can make enough general statements from which the interviewer could determine the suitability of the candidate, there by focusing on specific areas that will explore further such areas of strengths or weaknesses.

Mirror Questions

During the interview, as the respondent answers questions, the interviewer may attempt to summarize the ideas of the respondent by paraphrasing what he or she heard. The attempt is to clarify information and to seek elaboration on some issues raised that are not clear or that may help the interviewer to understand the interviewee's perspective.

Probing Questions

General questions usually always precede probing questions, which dig underneath to unearth new information and gain perspectives that the respondents may not think necessary or may be reticent to share. Whenever interviewers feel that their answers have not been adequately answered, they use probing questions to encourage the respondent to provide further, fuller information. For example, if you are asked your opinion about homosexual marriage and you answer: "To each his own." This is definitely not an adequate answer. So, the probing or follow-up question would be: What do you mean by that phrase and why? The probing could continue until the interviewer is satisfied. What about when James was asked about his former supervisor at a job interview? He answered: "I would rather not talk about that woman!" Do you think the interviewer would do John's bidding and move on to another question? Do you think John has set himself up to fail at the interview? How can you best handle the situation even if you hated your former boss so much?

Hypothetical Questions

Hypothetical situations are imagined but not real situations. Scenarios are created and the respondents are asked questions based on the typical hypothetical case. The purpose of the questions is to evaluate the critical thinking ability of the respondent, usually in an employment interview. As an informed person, a critical thinker can handle imagined situations or issues at the spur of the moment to show to a potential employer that he or she possess the ability to think quickly and find relevant solutions to impinging situations.

These questions mimic what happens in many scientific endeavors where simulations of actual events are undergone in closed environments to prepare for the real time troubleshooting. By creating hypothetical scenarios, the interviewer is creating a simulation scenario for the potential employee to respond to as if it were real. It is common in a teaching interview for potential teachers to be asked to tell what they would do in the case of "a rude student who does not appear to care for the rights of others in the classroom and who is always asking the teacher to cater to his personal needs at the expense of the whole class." Or, they may be asked to respond to a scenario whereby a student bickers about his grade and threatens the teacher to change the grade or else." These are hypothetical scenarios that a quick thinking and experienced teacher would know how to handle.

Leading Questions

The opposite of leading questions are neutral questions. Leading questions are suggestive of the answers expected of the respondents. Depending on how they are stated, they may encourage positive or negative answers. "All our hardworking sales counselors earn well over $100, 000 a year. Do you think you will be able to make that kind of money? How else are you supposed to answer this question? Do you wish to say that you are not hardworking and, as such, will not be able to make that kind of money? This type of question may not be useful is soliciting honest, candid information from an interview, but that may not be its purpose. The interviewer may use leading questions to suggest agreement with the interviewee and to indicate how well the interviewing is progressing. The real meanings of leading questions can be deduced from the climate of the interview experience itself as it happens and the participants should measure the temperature of the environment to determine the right answers to leading questions. Here, reference is made to employment interviews, however, in research study interviews, the use of leading questions is not permissible because such questions would elicit biased responses and, consequently contaminate the study.

Unethical and Illegal Questions

There is an ethical difference between asking personal and private questions. The equal opportunity and employment commission regulates what are appropriate and inappropriate questions in an employment interview. While you can be asked of your opinion about certain issues, it is illegal for an employer to ask questions about age, race, sexual orientation, religious affiliation. As a matter of fact, we should be aware that these characteristics do not have any bearing on how well an employee would perform on the job; as such, they are irrelevant to the interview process.

Guidelines for Handling an Employment Interview

An employment interview is an encounter in which communication strategies play a determining role in whether the interviewee is successful or not. The hiring has a need for a suitable, skillful, affable, and dutiful employee and it is your duty as a job seeker to communicate all of these qualities successfully to the potential employer. Those who are successful at this are the ones who get hired and not necessarily the most educated or skilled. Presentation of who you are and what you know and what you can do is the determining influence on the employer. Let us examine some of the general guidelines you should be aware of in applying, interviewing and landing a job.

A Foot in the Door

You have to be invited for an interview for you to have the opportunity of getting the job. In order to get called for an interview with a company, your **resume** must precede you. With a cover letter, the goal of your resume is to present you, your qualifications, experience, and overall suitability for the job in a persuasive manner to the hiring company.

Writing an effective **cover letter** requires some knowledge of the company and the agent or person with whom you will be communicating within the organization. In addition to these, you must know the detailed job requirements of the position that you are applying for. So, the process starts with research, which will include the history of the company, its operations, and plans for the future. Most organizations have websites that you can visit to access the information you'll need. Knowing the key personnel of the company is also helpful, because your reference to what they are currently engaged in, as reflected on the website, may signal to the employer that you're a diligent person who is highly interested in what the company and its people do.

Your cover letter should be short and direct attention to your interest and qualification for the job advertised, particularly, you must highlight the special qualifications you have that would make you the best fit for the job. You must write clearly, concisely, and correctly, and present a good first impression that would persuade the first contact inside the company to shortlist your name for further consideration.

Your cover letter should provide your contact information, including phone numbers and you should indicate that they should contact for an interview and that you are looking forward to hearing from them. In all, your cover letter should not be more than three paragraphs. There is not enough time for a personnel director to peruse all of the applicants' cover letters, so if yours is rather long, it will not be read.

Your **professional resume** should speak for you as it presents the required information about you to the company. Most resumes would include the following information: Contact information, career objective (usually a sentence), employment history, education experience, relevant professional affiliation, special skills, volunteer activities, military service, extra-curricular activities, and references. See the sample resume for additional information.

After You Have Been Invited

Now, you have a foot in the door because you have been invited for a face-to-face- or electronic interview as the case may be. This is when **to increase your search for information about the job, its requirements**, and about the activities of the company itself. You will gain great insight about the company by accessing its literature and possibly talking with someone within. If the company is not doing well and the plan to open new branches or satellite offices has been scrapped, it will be 'shooting yourself in the foot' if you should state your interest in that satellite office which has already been foreclosed.

Often, the number one question you will be asked at the interview is to speak about yourself. So, **prepare information about yourself** and identify three to four key things you would say that would sell you completely to the interviewer. Remember that this is strategic communication at play and the rule is that you should be relevant at all times.

You must be ready to **ask your own questions** at the interview. If you should be asked if you have any questions, you should present some of your own. It shows that you are engaged, interested, and prepared---especially to take on the job if offered. As you prepare your questions, you must be ready to adequately answer the interviewer's questions. **You must rehearse the interview session**. This means that you should prepare practice questions to which you would have prepared answers. Practice makes perfect, so when you do much interviews, you would have access to your prepared answers and not be intimidated by the interview process. Again, you would have the opportunity to strategically structure your answers to present you in the best possible way to the company. Below is a list of frequently asked interview questions (Verderber & Verderber, 2010) that will help you in your mock interview.

Performance at the Interview

Now that a date has been set for the interview, you should get a good night rest before that day and plan to **arrive on time**, possibly 15-20 minutes earlier. Now that they will see you face- to-face, your appearance is critical your acceptance. **Dress appropriately** to match the dress code of the company or to match the generally acceptable interview wear which is formal dressing. It is better to be overdressed than underdressed for a job interview. You can certainly take off your jacket and loosen or remove your tie if the atmosphere calls for casual appearance. Black or gray suit with white shirt is standard

Common Interview Questions

- In what ways does your transcript reflect your ability?
- Can you give an example of how you work under pressure?
- What are your major strengths and weaknesses?
- Can you give an example of when you were a leader and what happened?
- Tell me a time when you tried something at work that failed. How did you respond to the failure?
- Tell me about a time you had a serious conflict with a co-worker. How did you deal with the conflict?
- What have you done that shows your creativity?

American formal wear, so be prepared for this. **Bring with you to the interview relevant supplies** including copies of your resume and cover letter, reference letters, and your questions.

Stay involved throughout the interview session by practicing **direct eye contact, active listening, speaking eloquently, and immediate responses** to the questions asked. Your active listening skills will help you to listen critically to the questions asked and to discern the real motive behind them so that you may answer them tactfully and appropriately.

You should be aware of the difference between private and personal information. Should the interviewer ask you to reveal information that is private to you and which should be off limits to the interview, you should **tactfully assert your right not to answer private and, often, illegal questions.**

Duck and McMahan (2012) enumerate illegal questions in the context of a job interview and provide alternate legal questions that may be asked during an interview. The following table is a representation of their ideas.

Table 9.1/Avoiding Illegal Questions

Age
Illegal questions
- How old are you?
- What year were you born?

Legal questions
- Are you 21 years old or older, and thereby legally allowed to accept this position if offered?
- Are you under the age of 60 years old, and thereby allowed to accept this position if offered?

Marital/family Status
Illegal questions
- Are you married or living with a partner?
- Are you pregnant?
- Do you have any children or plan on having children?

Legal questions
- There is a great deal of travel involved with this position. Do you foresee any problems with this requirement?
- Will the long hours required of this job pose any problems for you?
- Would you be willing to relocate if necessary?
- Do you have any responsibilities that may prevent you from meeting the requirements of this position?

Ethnicity/national origin
Illegal questions
- What is your ethnicity?
- Where is your family from?
- Were you born in the United States?

- What is your native language?

Legal questions

- Do you have any language abilities that would be helpful in this position?
- Are you authorized to work in the United States?

Religion

Illegal questions

- Are you religious?
- What religion are you?
- Do you worship regularly at a church/mosque/temple?
- Do you believe in God?

Legal questions

- Are you able to work on Saturday evenings/Sunday mornings, if necessary?

Affiliations

Illegal questions

- What clubs or social organizations do you belong to?
- Are you a Republican or a Democrat?
- Are you now or have ever been a member of the Communist Party?

Legal questions

- Do you belong to any professional organizations that would benefit your ability to perform this job?

Disabilities

Illegal questions

- What is your medical history?
- Do you have any disabilities?
- How would you describe your family's health?
- What resulted in your disability?

Legal questions

- This job requires that a person be able to lift 100 pounds. Would you have any problems fulfilling that requirement?

An interview is a specialized interpersonal communication that is characterized by skillful exchange of questions and answers. As a communication exercise, the success of the participants depends on their communication competency. Therefore, the communicative choices of the interviewer and the interviewee will determine how successful they will be.

The interviewer's goal is to hire the best candidate possible and failure to do just that is placed in the inability to ask the right questions, to listen actively to the answers supplied, and to critically evaluate such responses to see if they match established expectations. The interviewee on the other hand is to present him or herself as positively as possible by presenting a **professional resume and cover letter,** being enthusiastic in the interview session, assessing the intent of the questions and answering them appropriately and critically, speaking eloquently while maintaining good eye contact and in professionally attire.

A study by Einhorn (1981) outlines six key differences between successful and unsuccessful interviewee communication. The following table is a presentation of these six ideas as it appears in Duck and McMahan (2012).

Table 9.2/Learning From Successful and Unsuccessful Interviewees

Clearer career goals

Successful interviewees are able to clearly articulate their career goals and explain how those goals relate with the position for which they are interviewing

Unsuccessful interviewees, on the other hand, provide no clear career goals or how those goals might relate to the position for which they are interviewing.

Identification with employers

Successful interviewees mention the organization by name often and exhibit knowledge of the organization.

Unsuccessful interviewees rarely mention the organization by name and demonstrate little or no knowledge of the organization.

Support for arguments

Successful interviewees provide illustrations, comparisons and contrasts, statistics, and even testimony from colleagues, supervisors, and instructors.

Unsuccessful interviewees provide little evidence or support material when answering questions.

Participation

Successful interviewees are actively involved in the development of the interview throughout the entire process and spend a great deal of the interview talking.

Unsuccessful interviewees play a passive role in the development of the interview and talk very little during the interview.

Language

Successful interviewees use active, concrete, and positive words along with technical jargons associated with the position.

Unsuccessful interviewees use passive, ambiguous, and negative words while using little or no technical jargons.

Nonverbal delivery
Successful interviewees speak loudly and confidently while also using vocal variety and avoiding nonfluencies. They incorporate meaningful gestures and support interviewer comments with positive nonverbal feedback such as nodding and smiling.

Unsuccessful interviewees speak softly and provide little vocal variety while including longer-than-appropriate pauses. The use few gestures and engage in distracting mannerisms such as rubbing their hands or shaking their legs. They also engage in little or no eye contact with the interviewer.

<u>Sample Student Resume</u>
Clyde Richardson,
423, West 76 Street,
Boston, MA 01741,
(123)-456 9890.

Professional Objective:
Seeking for the position in nursing that best utilizes skills obtained from clinical experience and academic study.

Education:
University of Kentucky, Lexington, KY
Bachelor of Science in Nursing, May 2007
GPA: Nursing = 3.4   Overall = 3.2 / 4.00
Academic Honors:
- Dean's List, Three (3) semesters
- Inductee, Sigma Theta Tau Nursing Honor Society, 2005
- Recipient, Student Nursing Scholarship, 2004
- Recipient, Bloustein Scholarship, 2003

Licensure:
First Aid and CPR, 12324, expires 12/2011

Professional Preparation:
Sunrise Hospital and Medical Center, Springfield, KY
Nurse Extern (9/2007-12/2008)
- Accountable for the direct personal care of patients including dressing, bathing, feeding, oral hygiene, and elimination.
- Communicated with professional staff regarding pertinent observations concerning conditions of patients.

Clinical Rotations:
Student Nurse - Six (6) semesters as follows:
- Pentagon Memorial - Pediatrics
- Congregation Beth Israel - Maternity/Nursery
- Northside Hospital - Psychiatric Nursing
- Finger Lakes Visiting Nurse Service - Community Health
- Rochester General - Medical/Surgical

Affiliations:
Treasurer, Queen's Nursing Society, 2007 - Present
Secretary/Member, Queen's Nursing Society, 5 semesters

Technical Abilities:
Bilingual: Spanish / English
Efficient at using Microsoft Office: Word, Excel, PowerPoint, Access
References:
Professional and academic references available upon request.

Review Questions

1. What are the important steps to consider in preparing for a job interview?
2. What are the different types of interview questions and why are they important for you to know?
3. What are the guidelines for handling an employment interview?
4. What are unethical and illegal questions and how can you avoid them in a job interview?
5. Why is it important to have a professional resume when applying for a job?

SECTION THREE

Public communication

10. *Defining Public Speaking*

11. *Relating with and Gathering Audience Information*

12. *Identifying, Researching, and Managing the Speech Topic*

13. *Organizing the Speech: The Strategic Introduction, Body, and Conclusion*

14. *Delivering the Speech*

Chapter Ten
Public Speaking Defined

The synonyms of the word "public" capture the nature of the enterprise described as public communication. "Public" is a community of people, it's communal in nature, belonging to all; it is free, open, and unrestricted. In comparison to other forms of communication, especially interpersonal and group, public communication may as well be all of the above with some modifications. It may not be unrestricted, because of some of the rules that guide its conduct, but in a general sense, the descriptions capture the essential nature of it.

The nature of public communication or public speaking is different from the other forms of communication. It is a public rather than private performance; it is usually organized in advance; and it has a set of rules that governs the behaviors of the participants.

Here, one person is designated the sender and others the receivers, who are collectively referred to as the audience. The public speaking situation imposes on the speaker a lot of constraints. The speaker cannot be too personal or focus on an individual as is the case in interpersonal communication because of the number of people involved. The message cannot be designed to appeal to a segment of the audience; it must appeal to everyone in a deliberate and organized manner. The language has to be formal, it has to be understandable by all involved and, it must be devoid of personal or private slang and other restrictive codes.

Unlike mass communication though, public communication is face-to-face and interpersonal. It is performed before a "live audience," who listens, watches the speaker and evaluates his or her gestures, verbal and nonverbal mannerisms as well as the prepared message itself. In terms of power, the public speaker engages in a non-egalitarian act because much of the attention is focused on the speaker. Not only that, the speaker in most cases chooses the topic and directs the agenda of the speaking event. As we have noted earlier, the receivers look more at the speaker than the other way around, so the speaker enjoys more popularity and visibility than the receivers. The public speaking situation provides an opportunity for the speaker to control, inform and persuade as the case may be with little or no challenge until the end of the exercise, in which case much of the information must have been received and processed and stored by the recipients one way or the other. The public speaker is a powerful gatekeeper of ideas and influence.

Griffin (2003) contrasts public speaking with other levels of communication and identifies the distinguishing factors that separate the public speaking enterprise from all of the rest. These are that public speaking creates a community, it is audience centered, and it encourages dialogue. Public speaking is often perceived as an isolated act, but it occurs because "individuals belong to a community and are affected by one another. We speak publicly because we recognize this connection. We create a community when we speak because we are talking about topics that affect ourselves as well as each member of the audience." The issue of audience centeredness is understood as intellectually empathizing with the values, beliefs, and interests, and feelings of the audience while adapting the speech to them. Public speaking promotes topics and issues to the public sphere thus generating discussions and sometimes stimulating public opinion to public action. As Griffin noted, "Public speaking encourages dialogue because speakers want the people who hear the speech to be able to engage others, and perhaps even the speaker, in a conversation about the topic or issue after the speech is given."

Sprague and Stuart (2000), claim that a book about public speaking is a contradiction because it may not adequately represent the nature of the specific act. They defined public speaking as: "… a lived, performed, embodied event that draws its special qualities from the immediate context, the personality of a particular speaker, and the response of a certain audience."

The Unique Demands of Public Speaking

Tobbs and Moss (2000) summarized the ten unique demands of public speaking of Hart et al.1975 p.25) as follows:

1. *The message must be relevant to the group as a who*le – not merely to one or a few individuals in that group. In public communication, the "common denominator" must be constantly searched for by the speaker.
2. *"Public" language is more restricted*, that is , it is less flexible, uses a more familiar code, is less personal in phrasing, and is filled with fewer connotations than is "private" talk.
3. *Feedback is more restricted*, since it is limited to subtle nonverbal responses in many instances.
4. *There is greater audience diversity to deal with*. In public communication we face the difficulty of entering *many* "perceptual worlds" simultaneously.
5. As the size of the audience increases, there is greater chance of *misinterpreting feedback*, since there is so much to look for.
6. The speaker must do a much complete job of speech preparation, since there is so little direct moment-to moment feedback to guide his or her remarks.
7. The *problem of adaptation* becomes paramount since one message must suffice for many different people.
8. *Audience analysis is more difficult* and necessarily more inaccurate when many people are interacted with simultaneously.
9. It is sometimes *difficult to focus attention* on the message because of the great number of distractions a public situation can entail.
10. A greater amount of change is possible in public communicative settings since the message reaches more people in a given unit of time.

Purposes of Public Speaking

Public speeches vary according to the purpose they are organized to serve.
The traditional purposes of public speeches are: **To inform, To persuade, and To entertain**. These three categories are not mutually exclusive because a speech designed to entertain may be informative as well as persuasive; and a speech designed to persuade definitely must inform. An informative speech may persuade in that it may lead to cognitive restructuring that will facilitate change of attitude and perhaps opinion and behavior.

When you have unique knowledge and experience about a given topic, sharing it with others makes you an informative speaker. This is presenting information that is otherwise unknown or presenting familiar information in a new and enlightened manner to an audience. You become the teacher who has information (knowledge) to share with your students (audience). And when you hold a point of view or do believe in a particular cause, you may want to align your thinking with that of an audience and that of the audience with yours. In this case, you engage in persuasive speaking- appealing to the logic and emotions of the audience members, albeit in a manner that makes you credible and believable to them.

In classical times, a different classification mode was used. Aristotle identified three types of speeches according to their distinctive purposes. Speeches that argue about decisions concerning the future are referred to as **deliberative speeches**. These are speeches that present premises as to why things are the way they are, and that if things are expected to change in the future, a particular line of action should be followed. But speeches that focus on decisions about the past, (especially in the courts) to correct a line of action, a failure of good judgment, are referred to as **judicial speeches**. **An epideictic speech** often has either praise or blame as its purpose.

There are other speech classification types. These include the evocative speeches, invitational speeches, introductory speeches, commemorative speeches, and acceptance speeches. This list may not be exhaustive, either because more speech purposes can be identified, though they can all be subsumed under the mentioned categories.

Griffin's (2003) delineation is useful here.

Speeches are presented to fulfill a number of purposes, which include:

To inform:	describe, clarify, explain, define
To invite:	explore, interact, exchange
To persuade:	change, shape, influence, motivate
To introduce:	acquaint, present, familiarize
To commemorate:	praise, honor, pay tribute
To accept:	receive an award, express gratitude

Source: Griffin. Cindy L. (2003). *Invitation to public speaking*. Belmont, CA: Wadsworth

Public Speaking and Society

The bedrock of any democratic enterprise is the ability of citizens to share relevant information with each other in a free and unfettered way. Democracy only survives in an atmosphere of dialogue and debate, without which autocracy will replace freedom of choice and freedom to engage in dialectics. It's the freedom to advance one's ideas, and the right of others to critically examine such ideas before accepting or rejecting them that characterize the successful democracies of the Western world.

One of the means of initiating and maintaining public dialogue is public speaking. When individuals engage others in sharing ideas and persuading them, this is possible because there is an atmosphere that allows for ferment to take place in public discourse. And in the words of Griffin (2011), "when we share ideas and information and consider questions and possibilities with others, we are creating a civil community….We create a community when we speak, because we are talking about topics that affect us and each member of the audience."

Apart from creating a civil society, public speaking helps to develop a sense of honesty, equity, and ethics. It is the expectations of honest performance in the sharing of truthful information and in the ethical debate that it generates that a speech acquires its import in a civil society.

There must be constant on-going dialogue in society and it is public speaking that provides the platform for this to happen. Indeed, giving a speech "is a natural way to enter the public dialogue because it gives us a chance to clearly state our own perspectives and to hear other's perspectives" (Griffin, 2011). Griffin captures the essence of public dialogue by quoting the narrative of Kenneth Burke (1941) describing the nature of conversation:

> Imagine that you enter a parlor. You come late. When you arrive, others have long preceded you, and they are engaged in a lively discussion, a discussion too passionate for them to pause and tell you exactly what it is about. In fact, the discussion had already begun long before any of them got there, so that no one present is qualified to retrace for you all the steps that had gone before. You listen for a while, until you decide that you have caught the tenor of the argument; then you put in your oar. Someone answers; you answer them; another perspective is shared. The hour grows late; you must depart. And you do depart, with the discussion still vigorously in progress.

Model of Public Speaking

As we have confirmed that public speaking is a form of or level of communication, its diagrammatic model, therefore, would include the elements identified in the process of communication. The discernible difference is the number of people involved in the public speaking act. It is important to note that, just as any form of communication is a collaborative act between sender and receiver, so it is in the case of public speaking. But the cooperation now is among the audience on one part and between the audience and the speaker on the other.

The elements of the model of public speaking include: Speaker, Speaker Background, Message, Channel, Audience, Audience Background, Situation, Feedback, and Noise.

Figure 10.1/ Model of Public Speaking

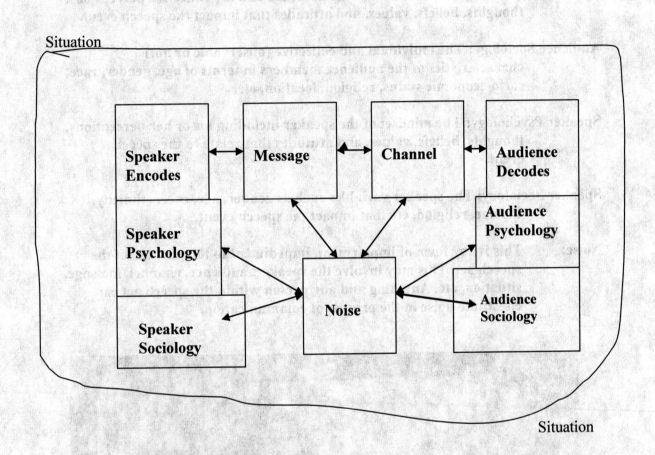

Speaker: This is the person designated as the sender who speaks to an audience.

Encoding: Organizing information into an understandable or decipherable form to an audience.

Audience: A group or collection of individuals for whom a speech is designed and to whom it is presented.

Decoding: Breaking down a piece of information (speech) into meaning or making sense of a message.

Message: The content or meaning that is meant to be deciphered and understood by the receivers.

Channel: The means by which the information is conveyed or delivered to the

Audience (The spoken word/non-verbal messages/the human senses).

Situation: This is physical place where the speech event occurs or the psychological state of both the sender and receivers.

Audience Psychology: The mindset of the audience and the collective perceptions, thoughts, beliefs, values, and attitudes that impact the speech event.

Audience Sociology: The individual and collective (observable or not) characteristics of the audience members in terms of age, gender, race, socio-economic status, religion, location, etc.

Speaker Psychology: The mindset of the speaker including his or her perceptions, thoughts, beliefs, values, and attitudes that relate to the speech event.

Speaker Sociology: The speaker variables such as gender, age, race, ethnicity, income, religion, etc that impact the speech event.

Noise: This is any form of impairment, impediment to the purpose of the speech act. This may involve the speaker, audience, channel, message, situation, etc. Anything and any person within the speech act can constitute noise in the process of communication.

The Rhetorical Tradition

Perhaps more akin to our understanding of public speaking is the **Rhetorical Tradition** of communication theory, which studies communication as an art. An art is an expression of personal qualities or skills, a showing of talents and a gift embedded in creativity and practice. The Greeks and the Romans studied this art and applied it to practical issues of legal defense and political persuasion. Emphasis was placed on the speaker and his ability to manipulate language beautifully to influence the audience. Speech was considered a powerful art equal to that of the ability to wage war, because of the understanding that words can "make a heaven of hell and hell of heaven." So much power was placed in the ability to engage in oratory that anyone who possessed such powers was equally accorded political power. The study of contemporary public speaking benefits from the message and speaker- oriented Greco-Roman rhetorical tradition. The rhetorical traditions examined in this section are explanatory as they are prescriptive in nature.

Rhetoric Defined

In ancient times, especially in Greece, the study of rhetoric was accorded a high level of significance because of the part it played in society; it was actually one of the original seven liberal arts, which included dialectic, grammar, music, arithmetic, geometry and astronomy. This meant that an educated person in ancient Greece must be schooled in the art of argumentation and persuasion and must acquire the all too important skill of oratory.

As the Greeks discovered that success in politics required public persuasion and participation through the speech act, the ability to speak and to use words effectively became very important. This gave rise to the study of rhetoric, **which is the strategic use of the spoken and the written word**. Aristotle describes rhetoric as **"the art of discovering, in any given case, the available means of persuasion."** In a slightly different manner, Bryant (1953) offers an important definition of rhetoric as **"the art of persuasion, the art of using symbols to adjust ideas to people and people to ideas."** Rhetoric, therefore, is the combination of effective use of language for argumentation and persuasion purposes. As we can see, rhetoric is what we refer to as the art of persuasion today.

Why study classical rhetoric? This is to understand how language works orally and in writing, "in adjusting people to ideas and ideas to people," and to be able to apply the nature or nuances of language in one's speaking and writing.

Rhetoric is not only concerned with what is being said and how it might be said, but also pays attention to the understanding that the form or style and the content are interwoven and, as such, inseparable in their impact on the audience.

Ancient Rhetoric

Otherwise referred to as classical rhetoric, this tradition can be divided into two epochs with Socrates as the dividing seminal figure. Because of the importance of the works of the philosopher on rhetoric as exemplified by the writings of his protégé Plato, periods and figures in classical rhetoric are classified as Pre Socrates and Post Socrates. The personalities identified here do not necessarily fully represent these eras, but are the main thrusts. The pre-Socrates are Homer, Corax, Protagoras and Gorgias, and the post-Socrates are Plato and Aristotle. The Roman rhetorical figures of the era are Cicero and Quintilian.

Egyptian Rhetoric Precepts

Quoting Gray (1946), Jaffe (2007), documented the relevant content of "the oldest book in existence:" *The Precepts of Ke' gemni and Ptah-hotep* (ca.2100 BCE) containing clear instructions to young Egyptians on how to speak and listen.

Rhetoric Precepts:
1. Speak with exactness, and recognize the value of silence.
2. Listeners who have "good fellowship" can be influenced by the speeches of others.
3. Do not be proud of your learning.
4. Keep silent in the face of a better debater: refute the false arguments of an equal, but let a weaker speaker's arguments confound themselves.
5. Do not pervert the truth.
6. Avoid speech subjects about which you know nothing.
7. Remember that a covetous person is not a persuasive speaker.

This is evidence of formal study and recognition of the art of rhetoric pre Greece and Rome. It must be noted that Western civilization identifies Greco-Roman influence as its cradle rather than Egypto-Greco-Roman.

Aristotle's Rhetoric

The early beginnings of rhetoric can be traced to ancient Greece and to a seminal figure of that time in the person of Aristotle. Charged with responsibility of charting and developing the typology of epistemology by his friend Alexander the Great, Aristotle classified Rhetoric as an integral part of academe. Rhetoric or the art of persuasion was an art that was extensively written about and such skills that were required of politicians and leaders were widely taught by sophists- the teachers of the art of persuasion.

Aristotle wrote many books including *Rhetoric*- a classical book on persuasion. The principles and ideas presented in the works of Aristotle on persuasion are still very relevant to the study of the subject of persuasion today, in that many schools use his works as the foundation to the theories of persuasion. Not only that, many of these principles are fundamental principles that influence the contemporary practice of not only persuasion, but subjects and professions such as marketing, advertising, public relations, public speaking, sales, etc.

Unlike his mentor and teacher Plato, Aristotle did not see rhetoric as a 'sham art,' a kind of artistry best fitted for charlatans and con artists. Far from it, he presented four major arguments to reinforce his belief that rhetoric is indeed very useful. Benjamin (1997) presents these arguments as follows:

1. Aristotle argued that truth will prevail if given an equal chance, and it is the art of rhetoric that gives both sides an equal chance.
2. Rhetoric could teach people who are not trained to follow the complicated syllogisms and close dialectical argumentation advocated by Plato. That is rhetoric could be used to popularize important issues.
3. Rhetoric is valuable because it does not judge a case- it is an art that can be used by both sides in a dispute.
4. Rhetoric is useful in defending oneself against attacks. This is the art of verbal defense that was necessary in ancient Greece because citizens had to defend themselves against any accusations by the state or fellow citizens in the public arena.

Aristotle recognized three dominant persuasion contexts, that is, situations and occasions where the use of rhetoric become important. The first is **Forensic Discourse**— this applies to situations of allegations of past wrong doing in the legal arena whether the speaker will have the opportunity of self-defense, using all of the available means of persuasion to prove one's innocence. The second is **Epideictic Discourse**—applies to present situations that are often ceremonial focusing on praise or blame. This happens when you have to give a toast to someone at his or her birthday, or give eulogy at a funeral. These are emotion-laden occasions that call for appeal to the natural expectations of blame or praise as the case may be. Courtesy often overtakes at such ceremonies such that praise is what we usually hear. Except that blame may be appropriated in clever euphemism and satire. The third is **Deliberative Discourse**--which deals with future policy, with special attention to the legislative and political realm. When President Barrack Obama presented his health care reform bill to The US House of Representatives and The Senate, a lot of debate and argumentation characterized the deliberation on the future of health care in America. One could recall the heated shouting matches at political rallies of the Green Party/Tea Party and the town hall meetings of Senators and Legislators with their constituencies. Often, these debates/meetings became shouting matches that jettisoned the measured civility that usually characterize such encounters among highly-placed leaders of the country.

Aristotle's ideas are prescriptive in nature for practitioners of persuasion. By giving insight into the nature of audiences, especially that they are both emotional and logical beings, he recognized the need for audience-centeredness of persuasive arguments. He identified that one approach to persuasion did not fit all audiences. Each approach must be customized to fit each situation and target audience. By so recommending, he recognized the concept of **segmented audiences** which is dominant to the practice of public speaking, marketing, and other professions mentioned earlier.

According to Aristotle, listeners have **a common universe of ideas** which the speaker can promote. The common ground technique (Topoi) identifies places or topics of argument that are a good way to establish common ground with the audience. Speaking to a common universe of ideas promotes 'identification' with the audience and offers opportunity for the speaker to establish rapport with the receivers. Speakers can speak against things that destroy happiness but in favor of things that bring happiness.

Aristotle identified such common appeal topics to include:

Having One's Independence
Achieving Prosperity
Enjoying Maximum Pleasure
Securing One's Property
Maintaining Good Friendships
Producing Many Children
Enhancing One's Beauty
Attending to One's Health
Fostering One's Athletic Nature
Promoting One's Fame, Honor, and Virtue.

Aristotelian common universe of ideas speaks to audience analysis, whereby the speaker becomes cognizant of issues, topics, and events that affect humans because such speak to the human condition. What better way to interest people in a discourse than to speak to issues that concern them and that will motivate them to think, speak, and act? It behooves the speaker, therefore, to adapt the speech topic, content, and presentation to the nature of the audience. Without such adaptation, the speaker runs the risk of alienating the receivers and thus scuttling the speech purpose.

To Aristotle, the available means of persuasion includes two broad classes of proof—**artistic and inartistic proofs**. Inartistic proofs are evidences that can be used to present an argument that is physical and incontrovertible because the art of rhetoric did not produce them. Physical proofs will include a murder weapon, a dead body, blood stained clothing of an assailant, gun powder residue on a piece of clothing, etc. These are physical evidence that you cannot use the power of logic and the effective use of words to wish away. However, the other class of proof can be used to argue artistically, stylistically as to whom the physical evidence belonged to. The second class of proof is the province of rhetoric and there are three types of such proof that if well organized and presented to the audience, will help the speaker achieve the purpose of effectively moving the audience to a desired position on an issue. The three kinds of proof are **logos, ethos, and pathos**.

Recognizing that humans are not only logical, but also emotional beings, Aristotle believed that appealing to the emotions and logic in people will move them to agree with the speaker. The third factor to consider is the ethical stature of the speaker, believing that a logical and emotional appeal's success is dependent on the ethical status of the speaker. Ethical stature refers to the **trustworthiness, expertise, and character** of the speaker. It's also the image or reputation and friendliness of the speaker. The combination of these elements amounts to how believable a speaker is to the audience. Ethical standard is important because Aristotle believed that trust (an element of ethos or credibility) has moral superiority over logical argumentation and emotional appeal. He argued that falsehood was not acceptable. So, persuasion by all available means does not include sharp practices as we see today in political and other public discourse.

Logos is presented in the line of argument in the speech where logical reasoning is used to advance a position and supported by generalizations and examples. Logos appeals to the intellect, or to the rational side of humans. Aristotle suggested two types of rhetorical reasoning: **reasoning by enthymeme and by example**. Reasoning by enthymeme is an abbreviated syllogistic reasoning; it is a rhetorical form of deductive reasoning in which an audience is asked to draw a conclusion about a specific situation or case from a generalization. In such reasoning, a major premise is advanced, a minor premise follows, and the third is a conclusion drawn from the two.

Reasoning by example on the other hand, is a rhetorical inductive reasoning which proceeds from specific cases, situations or instances to general.

Example of Deductive Reasoning

Major premise: **All politicians are usually economical with the truth**
Minor premise: **Alex Dorito is a politician**
Conclusion: **Alex Dorito is usually economical with the truth (Meaning—Alex Dorito does not usually tell the truth.)**

As an enthymeme, there is no need to spell out all the three statements. Stating the major and minor premises is enough to lead the listener to arrive at the conclusion by themselves. Note that the major premise is a general statement that includes all politicians and a conclusion can be drawn from the general to the specific case of Alex Dorito.

Example of Inductive Reasoning

Inductive reasoning allows speakers to cite specific cases or examples and induce from them that such will be the case if the example were to be copied and applied in another instance. Consider the following:

Government–run healthcare works in Canada.
We should adopt the Canadian healthcare system in the United States.

The unstated argument in this case is the conclusion that if government-run healthcare succeeds in Canada, then it should succeed in the United States. In this case, however, the speaker must be careful not to compare "apples to oranges." Similarities or dissimilarities in the two countries must be considered in making such an analogy.

Reasoning by enthymeme and example allows the speaker to draw in the audience in the process of speech delivery. These allow the audience to participate in the process by drawing conclusions for themselves on issues, rather than the speaker urging them to do so. And if you partake in a decision making process, it is usually found that you're more likely to adhere to the decisions and even argue in its favor.

Pathos refers to the emotions of the audience and the use of such by the persuader. It is not enough to appeal to the logic of the audience; persuasion should include evoking the emotions of the audience as well. We all feel emotions and when invoked they tend to influence our thinking and action. Aristotle paid attention to some of human emotions such as anger, mildness, love or friendship, fear, shame, hatred, envy, shamelessness, etc. The key is to identify the relevant emotions to the situation and to make an appropriate appeal to them accordingly.

Language is important to logical argumentation. Aristotle encouraged the use of active, lively metaphors because, 'it's from the metaphor that we can best get hold of something fresh."

Cicero

Reference to ancient rhetoric is never complete without mentioning the contributions of the Romans, who continued the Greek tradition of writing about and practicing the art of public oratory. Of the Roman contributors to the study and practice of rhetoric, **Cicero (106 B.C. - 43 B.C.)** was the most significant figure. A famous politician and orator, Cicero's theoretical works on persuasion and speech performances still generate scholastic examinations in the field today.

Cicero and the Romans had a practical approach to the art of persuasion through public oratory that they "sought to systematize the art of persuasion to make it easier to employ, and [they] are credited with having organized the concepts of rhetoric into **five "canons"** or bodies of principles: invention (*inventio*), organization (*dispositio*), style (*elocutio*), delivery (*pronuntiatio*), and memory (*memoria*)," (Benjamin, 1997). (It must be mentioned here that the authorship of the book, *Rhetorica ad Herennium*, that delineated the elemental parts (canons) of the persuasive process, so credited to the Romans, is in doubt.)

The canons of rhetoric provide a framework for developing and delivering speeches, which is still in use today. It is pertinent that a speaker selects a topic, determines the purpose for speaking, and invents ideas to be communicated to the audience about the topic. Then the generated ideas are to be organized into a presentable structure that the audience can follow with ease. Style has to do with the use of vivid, immediate, and effective words that resonate with the audience, and as for delivery, the existing oral culture of the Greeks and the Romans appreciated the power of the voice and the body in delivering speeches so passionately. The speaker who has memorized the contents of his or her speech is not encumbered by any script and, as such, can perform the delivery with drama and engage the audience in a rhythmic dance. Memory as a speech cannon looks into strategies or devices to use in aiding memory when delivering the speech, an idea that is guided by the ability to perform to the utmost in performing the speech act before a judgmental audience who would expect to not only be informed, but also to be charmed by the performer.

Managing Public Performance Anxiety

What is speech anxiety? All speakers experience some form of speech anxiety or the other, but how each deals with it will determine whether it becomes a motivation for greater performance, or a debilitating experience that grinds the speaker to a halt, and makes the experience unbearable and that which is to be avoided at all cost.

Public speaking anxiety is known as **speechophobia**, (Berko, Wolvin and Wolvin, 2001). It is a serious problem for a large number of people and has been found to affect career development as well as academic performance (Ayres and Hopf, 1993). These authors state that it is a phobia because it meets the criteria for phobias which are:

1. There is a persistent fear of a specific situation out of proportion to the reality of the danger,
2. There is compelling desire to avoid and escape the situation,
3. The fear is unreasonable and excessive,
4. It is not due to any other disorder.

Speaker anxiety is a normal, physiological reaction that can actually help us in our speaking tasks. It is said to involve physiological symptoms such as rapid heartbeat, butterflies, shaking knees and hands, quivering voice, and increased perspiration (Bebe, Bebe, & Ivy, 2001).

On the other hand, speech anxiety, better known as stage fright, arises from negative emotions that come from our irrational thoughts. It is our self talk that results in our feeling of anxiety. Not all emotions are bad. Adler and Rodman (2000) identify both **facilitative and debilitative emotions** as sources of positive motivation and sources of extreme negative anxiety respectively. They added that facilitative stage fright can help improve one's performance. Using the analogy of a musician or an athlete, Adler and Rodman claimed that the totally relaxed athletes or musicians aren't likely to perform at the top of their potential , speakers think more rapidly and express themselves more energetically when their level of tension is moderate. On the other hand, it is only when the level of anxiety is intense that it becomes debilitative, inhibiting effective self-expression.

The result of intense fear is two-fold. First, it is intense fear that keeps one from thinking clearly (Borhis and Allen 1992). The result of not thinking clearly may be poor preparation, researching, planning, and writing a speech. The second result of intense fear is the urge to do something, anything, to make the problem go away. This, for example, will lead the speaker to rush through the speech, consequently making more speech errors Adler and Rodman (2000).

In order to understand the impact of debilitative stage fright on speakers and begin to recommend ways to reduce or manage them, it is useful to explore the reasons why people are afflicted with the problem in the first place. Adler and Rodman (2000) identify the sources of debilitative stage fright as **previous negative experience and irrational thoughts.**

The adage says: "Once beaten twice shy," meaning that once you experience something, especially with a negative result, it will be difficult to fall prey to that circumstance again. If you have had a negative public speaking experience, it is rather difficult for you not to feel apprehension, again, when you are to relive the experience all over, again. The old defensive attitude kicks in and you're frightened stiff. It is the fear of negative evaluation by others that exacerbates the problem, because, naturally humans do not like to be evaluated. So, when giving a public speech, you become the focus of all the audience members, who are judging your skill, competence, and intelligence. In response, your defense mechanism spurs changes in your physiology causing increased heartbeat, blood rush, perspiration and the like. This is the feeling of déjà vu that what went wrong in your previous experience would go wrong again. It is also fulfilling your own prophecy that if anything would go wrong it will.

Psychologists would submit that events do not cause irrational, debilitative emotions but, rather, our mindset or set of beliefs about those events. It is also true that no single event or person causes another's reaction; rather, it is our mindset that causes us to react to such external stimuli in different ways. Ellis (1977) identifies some of our unfounded beliefs which result in debilitative emotions. Because they are unfounded, they are equally referred to as irrational thoughts. Here are Psychologist Albert Ellis' list of irrational or illogical thinking as documented by Adler and Rodman:

1. **Catastrophic Failure**: This is an irrational expectation of a terrible thing happening whenever you're to perform in public. This is a mindset that if anything bad can happen that it probably will happen. This feeling or thought serves as a fulfilling prophecy that becomes reality because of the convincing self talk that dominates the mind of the person who engages in this kind of unfounded fear. Self-consciousness and self-deprecation would lead such a person to think of failing in the act of public performance. And the common thoughts relating to catastrophic failure of public speaking that would come to mind, for example, are:

   "I will make a fool of myself when I speak before the audience."
   "I will probably not meet the expectations of the audience."
   "I don't really have anything of importance to say."
   "What if I forget what I want to say?"
   "After my subpar performance, I will become the laughing stock of the people."

   Negative self-evaluation is a terrible thing to do to oneself, let alone doing it before the actual performance of a speech. The expectation of catastrophic failure may be as a result for fear of judgment or evaluation of our person and performance by others. But the reality is far from the unfounded expectations. The audience members have been found not to be as judgmental as speakers may want to believe; as a matter of fact, the audience is more empathetic and sympathetic toward the speaker. This is all about nervousness. Nervousness has been found to be more apparent to the speaker than to the audience (Behnke, Sawyer, & King, 1987).

2. **Perfection:** This is the expectation of perfect performance. Speakers who have this mindset believe that their public performance should be perfect without any blemishes of any kind. To expect flawless performance in an interactional, social performance is to impose an undue expectation on oneself. Such an expectation will generate the feeling of inadequacy if there is any indication of slightest imperfection in the preparation of the speech. People who put this idealistic pressure on themselves often experience debilitative emotions whenever they are to perform in public. Anxiety dominates their lives to the extent that their behavior can be classified as neurotic. The simple counter-point to this neurotic state of mind is that the audience is not perfect and does not expect other people to be perfect—and that extends to the act of public speaking.

3. **Approval:** This is the fallacy that a public speaker should gain the approval of every member of the audience and, that it is desirable and vital to do so. Nothing could be further from the truth. Because the issues that public discourse deals with are controversial, polar issues, total agreement among your listeners on them is an unreal expectation. You are to identify those who agree with you and reinforce their agreement and, at the same time do your best to win the others, but do not expect that everyone will be pleased or approve of your point of view and arguments.

4. **Overgeneralization:** To generalize is to arrive at a conclusion based on some insufficient information. When you have this fallacious thought, you tend to exaggerate your inadequacies and minimize your strong points. To you your cup is half empty and not half full. If you can't remember something you just went over, you generalize by saying: "Oh, I am so stupid!" And if you miss a point in your presentation you tend to generalize that you're "good for nothing!" As you can see, you're your own worst enemy with these fallacies, but you can turn things around for yourself.

Again, many Communication writers have compiled the precepts that serve as guidelines for managing speech anxiety or stage fright. Here we are going to state some of them and, hopefully, by practicing the recommendations given, you will begin to arrest your fear of public speaking and be on your way to effective public performance.

Adler and Rodman (2000) claim that there are four simple ways to overcome debilitative stage fright:

1. **Be Rational:** This speaks to the list of irrational thoughts that are listed above. You have to contest your irrational thoughts with yourself. Argue if these thoughts are based in reality or are based on fear of public speaking. Then listen to the internal voice that calms you down and points to your irrationality.

2. **Be Receiver-Oriented:** If you concentrate on your audience and try to meet their expectations, then you'll not have the time to worry about yourself. Your purpose

is to inform or persuade and you should focus on whether you have done what is necessary to focus your audience's attention on your topic, create the necessary atmosphere to maintain their interest and move them along the path you want them to go with you.

3. **Be Positive:** You're to view yourself, the audience, your speech and the entire process of public performance in positive light. After all, it is an opportunity for you to be heard and to make a positive difference in other people's lives. If you view the public speaking event as a positive occurrence, it is easy for you to see success ahead of you. As indicated earlier, you fulfill your own prophecies. **Positive visualization and positive confession** help you to put yourself at the end point of your speech when the audience would feel satisfied and pleased to have had the opportunity of listening to you, and, you can dwell in the moment of success—all in your mind's eye. Along same line of thought, Adler and Rodman quote three statements communication consultants believe should help you stay positive when giving a public speech and these are:

I'm glad I'm here.
I know my topic.
I care about the audience.

4. **Be Prepared:** This book is all about getting focused and prepared in planning, researching, writing, and presenting your speech. If you spend adequate time on these processes, the speech event would be something you look forward to rather than something to cause you to **hyperventilate**. You must write your speech out and section it into the three major parts of introduction, body and conclusion. If you know what you are to say, and have evidence to support your claims, and have developed strategies to capture and maintain the attention of the audience, and you have strategized your conclusion, then, the rest is easy! Don't forget the adage that: "practice makes perfect." There is a difference between a well written speech and a well presented speech. The difference, of course, is practice. It is through practice that you know that certain words and ideas don't sound right where they are placed; it is through practice that you know that your introduction is not polished enough to achieve its intended goals. All of these require due diligence, that is hard work, without which you are likely to experience debilitative stage fright.

The explanations of these ideas are of this author, with some paraphrasing of the ideas of the original author.

Beebe, Beebe, & Ivy (2001) also suggest ways you can manage anxiety which are listed below. Compare their suggestions with those of Adler and Rodman.

1. **Know how to prepare a speech.**
2. **Be prepared.**
3. **Focus on your audience.**
4. **Focus on your message.**

5. **Be constructively self-aware.**
6. **Take advantage of the opportunity to speak.**

Ayres and Hopf (1993) offer the following precepts for dealing with speech apprehension. Again, compare these suggestions with those of the other authors stated here.

1. **Use relaxations techniques.**
2. **Use visualizations.**
3. **Prepare**
4. **Do not use relaxation drugs (some use Paxil, but must be doctor prescribed. This is because some people do have medical conditions associated with neurotic and more grave social anxiety behaviors)**
5. **Accept that you're experiencing anxiety**
6. **Do not shy away from giving public speeches**

Many of the suggestions from the many authors of public speaking books are somewhat the same with minor variations here and there. That there is great overlap of all of these ideas suggests the agreements among scholars as what is necessary to overcome your speech anxiety. As we have discussed earlier, speech anxiety is normal, but what is abnormal is debilitative fright. We are to turn the mild anxiety into strength by being mindful of the useful suggestions that have been listed here.

ASSESS YOUR PUBLIC SPEAKING ANXIETY

Take this test to self-assess your anxiety regarding public speaking. In the blank beside the statement, write the number of the response that best reflects your feelings.

0 = Strongly disagree
1 = Disagree
2 = Agree
3 = Strongly agree

----- 1. I begin to get nervous the moment the speech is assigned.
----- 2. I feel panicky because I don't know how to create a speech.
----- 3. I usually feel nervous the day before I have to speak.
----- 4. The night before the speech, I can't sleep well.
----- 5. I'm afraid people will think I'm dumb or boring or weird in some way.
----- 6. On the morning of the speech, I 'am really tense.
----- 7. I find it difficult to think positively about giving a speech.
----- 8. I think my physical reactions are greater than those that other people experience.
----- 9. During my speech I actually think I'll faint.
----- 10. I continue to worry even after the speech is over.

Add Your Scores

-------- Total Score
0 – 5   You are virtually fearless.
6 – 15   Your level of anxiety is fairly normal.
16 – 25   Your level of anxiety may give you problems.
26 – 30 Consider making an appointment with your professor. Go back and look at the areas that bother you the most, and develop specific strategies to help you with your unique stresses.

From Jaffe, Cecelia (2007). *Public Speaking –Concepts and Skills for a Diverse Society*, (5th ed.). Belmont, CA: Thomson-Wadsworth

Communication and Ethical Considerations

What is Ethics?

Ethics is a branch of philosophy that deals with issues that individuals and society consider good or bad, honest and dishonest, acceptable and unacceptable, moral or immoral. Usually the issues of ethics attract societal sanctions be they positive or negative. There is positive acclaim for ethical speaking and, of course, negative reward for unethical speaking. Ethics requires an understanding of whether communication behavior meets agreed-upon standards of right and wrong (Johannesen, 2002).

The concern for ethical public speaking is not new. Over two thousand years ago, classical rhetoricians such as Plato, Aristotle, Quintilian, and others were concerned with the issue of speaker credibility and the demonstration of ethos in public speaking. A good speaker must speak to the truth according to Plato. He lamented that practitioners of the art of rhetoric at a time before Socrates did not teach the truth, but the appearance of the truth. To Plato, the art of rhetoric was a sham art that could make the truth appear bad, the important seem unimportant, the guilty appear innocent (Benjamin, 1997). He believed that the practitioners of his days did not seek the ultimate truth which was discernible in every situation. His emphasis was on unraveling the ultimate truth (Truth with the big T) through public discourse. On the other hand, Aristotle, a student of Plato, identified three elements of **artistic proof** that must be employed by the speaker to make him or herself believable and these are Logos (logic), Ethos (ethics), and Pathos (passion).

The question of ethics or ethos as Aristotle termed it, is central to the responsible performance of a speaker. The speaker is advised to be trustworthy and of good character, and to have the interest of the audience members at heart. Failure to do this will lead the audience not to be endeared to the speaker and not to put any premium on the believability of the messages conveyed through the speech. What Aristotle referred to as character of the speaker, Quintilian represented as "a good man skilled in speaking" (Little, 1951). He offered to public speakers the advice that "speech should not be used as an accomplice to crime, serve as the foe to innocence, or act as the enemy of truth," Gamble and Gamble (1998).

Ethics is an integral part of public discourse and communication in general; it guides what can be said and what is better omitted, what evidence can be presented and which would constitute falsehood. Moral uprightness is a desired quality of the speaker – and the listeners. This is better articulated through the words of Gamble and Gamble (1998) that eloquently summarized the necessity of ethics in communication thus: "[w]hen speakers and receivers practice ethical communication, critical thinking replaces cynicism and callousness, the careful processing and evaluation of ideas replaces the careless handling of ideas, and cultural understanding replaces cultural disregard."

As noted, the issues of ethics relate to both senders and receivers in the communication process. Just as speakers have their obligations toward the listeners, so do the listeners owe some obligations to the speaker.

Below (in guideline format) are the ethical obligations of speakers and receivers as articulated by Gamble and Gamble (1998). While the issues with the speaker are content or message-related, the obligations of the listeners are listening-related.

The Ethical Speaker: Receiver Expectations

When functioning as a speaker, you should:
1. Share only what you know to be true.
2. Fully prepare yourself to present.
3. Consider the best interests of your receivers.
4. Consider whether you have made it easy for your receivers to understand you.
5. Refrain from using words as weapons.
6. Not wrap information in a positive spin just to succeed.
7. Respect the cultural diversity of receivers.
8. You are accountable for what you say.

The Ethical Receiver: Speaker Expectations

When functioning as a listener, you need to:
1. Give the speaker a fair hearing.
2. Be courteous, attentive, and honest with the speaker.
3. Be speaker-centered, not self-centered.

This appeared originally in Gamble, Teri Kwal and Gamble, Michael W. (1998) _Public Speaking In the Age of Diversity_, 2nd ed. Boston, Mass: Allyn & Bacon.

In like manner, Berko, Wolvin and Wolvin (2001) itemized the dos and don'ts of an ethical public speaker. Even a cursory look will confirm to you that many of these ideas overlap.

The Dos and Don'ts of an Ethical Public Speaker

An ethical public speaker:
- Speaks with sincerity.
- Does not knowingly expose an audience to falsehoods or half-truths that cause significant harm.
- Does not premeditatedly alter the truth.
- Presents the truth as he she understands it.
- Raises the listener's level of expertise by supplying the necessary fact, definitions, descriptions, and substantiating information.
- Employs a message that is free from mental as well as physical coercion by not compelling someone to take an action against his or her will.

- Does not invent or fabricate statistics or other information intended to serve as a basis for proof of a contention or belief.
- Gives credit to the source of information and does not pretend that the information is original when it is not.

Originally appeared under "The Ethics of Public Speaking" in Berko, Roy M., Wolvin, Andrew D. and Darlyn R. Wolvin (2001) *Communicating*, (8th ed.) Boston, MA: Houghton Mifflin.

Ethical Issues in Public Speaking

Plagiarism

Plagiarism is presenting another person's language or ideas as one's own (Lucas, 2007). It involves both misrepresentation and lying (Gamble and gamble, 1998). Either done intentionally or otherwise, there is no excuse for copying another person's intellectual work without giving credit to the originator.

Plagiarizing says a lot about the perpetrator as a selfish, lazy, indecent, and unreliable communicator. Selfish because of the disregard for the original author and the audience of the stolen information; lazy because the offender did not put in enough time to identify the source and to credit such accordingly. Indecent because it is not a nice thing by society's and personal ethical standard to take what does not belong to one, while the antidote is just due diligence of crediting the original author. The plagiarizer is unreliable, because a plagiarizer cannot be relied upon to present accurate information faithfully.

Lucas (2007) identifies three categories of plagiarism that would be identified here. When the entire work of another author is lifted verbatim and passed on as one's own, this is referred to as **global plagiarism**. When a speaker lifts materials from different sources and patches them up as one single idea emanating from him or her, this is labeled **patchwork plagiarism**. The third category is called **incremental plagiarism**, which means failing to give credit for particular parts of a speech that are borrowed from other people. The lessons here are to attribute whatever is borrowed or quoted directly from another to that person by means of acknowledgment. And in the case of paraphrasing someone else's ideas, there is still need to credit the person whose original work is being summarized even if it is done in the paraphraser's own words.

In the late 1980s, Joseph Biden, United States Senator from Delaware had a near-successful run at becoming the Democratic Party's nominee for candidate for president of the United States. This was until press reports surfaced citing his plagiarism past. It was reported that Biden had presented an address that had earlier been delivered by a British politician, Neil Kinnock, without given credit to this original author. Also, it was found that he had copied some part of a speech by Senator Robert Kennedy, without giving him credit either. Digging deeper, reporter unearthed information that while he was a law student, Biden had plagiarized. Needless to say that Biden lost his chances of becoming president because of these accusations that led to his withdrawal from the race.

The consequences of using another's intellectual property without giving credit can be dire. It may lead to loss of power, prestige and recognition. It may prevent one from aspiring to higher office or resign from one because of the indication of unethical disregard for the audience or the populace as the case may be. Point blank, plagiarism is theft and thieves are not respected in society.

Fabrication

The power to persuade is the power to mislead (Benjamin, 1997). One might add that the power to communicate in general is the power to mislead. Communicators do, however, have the responsibility to engage in ethical communication, which includes presenting truthful, non-misleading information to their receivers. This would also mean that speakers are not supposed to fabricate or make up information they think would influence the audience one way or the other, or information that would serve the ego of the speaker and not fulfill the obligation of speaker to listener. While many believe erroneously that numbers don't lie, the speaker is ill-advised if he or she should make –up evidence and data in a speech. Manipulating of fabricating information to justify your position or to damage the arguments of another is unacceptable in ethical public speaking.

Discussion question: Do polling and election prediction surveys prejudice voting behaviors of the audience? Do you think some pollsters fake their data for political reasons?

Slander/Libel

Slander is the legal term for spoken communication that is designed to injure, disparage another person by bringing him or her to ridicule in the presence of other witnesses or hearers. The evidence of slander lies in the act being deliberate, and the intention being to damage the reputation of another and, it must be done not only for the consumption of the person slandered, but before a group of people who would see the slandered person in bad light. Because a speech is designed for and presented before an audience, there are hearers of such damaging information who would testify to its slanderous content. It is, therefore, not ethical and, as a matter of fact, illegal for a speaker to deliberately use words to injure members of the audience. Slander is an actionable case, because it can be taken before a court of law for adjudication and possible punishment of the offender.

The distinction between slander and libel is basically how the information is presented. If you give speech extemporaneously and you don't have the disparaging comments written down for others to read and possibly duplicate, then it is slander. But if the information is in print and it is available for circulation either in print or electronic forms, then it is libel. Originally crafted for newspaper and other print publications, libel laws cover disparaging and damaging information in print and in some form of retrieval system. It, therefore, extends to public speeches that are documents that can be widely circulated.

Table 10.1/Checklist for Ethical Public Speaking

Yes/No	Have I examined my goals to make sure they are ethically sound? 1. Can I defend my goals on ethical grounds if they are questioned or challenged? 2. Would I want other people to know my true motives in presenting this speech?
Yes/No	Have I fulfilled my ethical obligation to prepare fully for the speech? 1. Have I done a thorough job of studying and researching the topic? 2. Have I prepared diligently so as not to communicate erroneous or misleading information to my listeners?
Yes/No	Is the speech free of plagiarism? 1. Can I vouch that the speech represents my own work, my own thinking, my own language? 2. Do I cite the sources of all quotations and paraphrases?
Yes/No	Am I honest in what I say in the speech? 1. Is the speech free of any false or deliberately deceptive statements? 2. Does the speech present statistics, testimony, and other kinds of evidence fairly and accurately? 3. Does the speech contain valid reasoning? 4. If the speech includes visual aids, do they present facts honestly and reliably?
Yes/No	Do I use the power of language ethically? 1. Do I avoid name-calling and other forms of abusive language? 2. Does my language show respect for the right of free speech and expression?
Yes/No	All in all, have I made a conscious effort to put ethical principles into practice in preparing my speech?

Lucas, Stephen E. (2007). *The Art of Public Speaking*, 9th Ed. New York, NY: McGraw-Hill

The checklist for ethical public speaking and other precepts for ethical performance by the speaker and attendant listener responsibility can be summed into three categories: Ethical considerations of the source of information or the speaker, ethical considerations of the message or speech contents, and ethical considerations of the receivers of the message.

Public speaking is not only a deliberate act; it is a collaborative act between speaker and the audience. The intentions of the speaker should be examined in the context of its ethicality as it relates to the receiver. The message as an instrument of information or persuasion should also be examined in terms of its meeting prescribed ethical standards.

Ethics and Sources

The rules and precepts guiding the ethical behavior of the source of information can be condensed into four ethical principles represented by the acronym TAGS, Benjamin (1997). The source or, in our case, the speaker, should *Tell* the truth, *Acknowledge* others, *Give* sufficient information, and *Show* the consequences.

Tell the truth is a self –evident statement that mandates the source of information not to bend or mend the truth in any shape or form. Speakers should present facts and explanations to the audience with all sincerity. The credibility of the speaker is on the line when the audience members examine the veracity of the information provided as fact or truth. Falsifying information is not only unethical, it is a criminal act.

Acknowledge others, refers to the rule that you must not plagiarize others' intellectual property (See preceding pages for the different types of plagiarism.)

Give sufficient information means that you as a speaker should not 'conveniently' omit information that may not support your claim while playing up part or incomplete information that does. To this point Benjamin (1997) writes that "leaving out critical information, failing to put quotations in their proper context, or omitting contradictory evidence, deliberately or accidentally, are detrimental to the source's integrity and the integrity of the group the source represents."

Show consequences of your message, is the speaker's mantra. Messages do have effects and the speaker should explicitly intimate the audience with the consequences of applying or relying on the information given to them. When the motive of the speaker is not clear or hidden, that is when the audience's suspicion is roused and may lead to total rejection of an idea that may otherwise benefit them.

Ethics and Messages

Ethical consideration of messages has to do with making sure that messages say exactly what they purport to say. Over the years scholars of communication and persuasion have identified messages that represent pseudo logical representation of ideas that appear logical to the unsuspecting receivers, in that they appear to be genuine and valid but come from illogical or fallacious reasoning. The danger lies in the appearance of being logical and sound in argumentation, but are in effect defective reasoning and should be labeled as fallacies.

There are two categories of fallacies: **Content errors and process errors**. Content has to do with the content of the informative or persuasive messages, while process refers to the order of thinking. Many ideas are presented as one leading to or causing the other, or one presenting a condition that must precede another, giving an impression that the occurrence of one necessarily leads to the other. But these may not be apparent to the non-critical information consumer. (For more, please see "Faulty Reasoning" under Persuasive Speaking).

Ethics and Audiences or Receivers

As the issue of ethics concerns the speaker, it equally concerns the audience because, as mentioned earlier, the speech process is a collaborative act. The audience members have an important role to play in making sure that unscrupulous speakers or sources do not take them for a fool and misrepresent ideas and lead them to conclude wrongly at their own disadvantage. Therefore, the receivers have the ethical responsibility not to be deceived by a clever source.

The receiver should be critically minded in evaluating messages and analyzing the contents and motives of speakers. Critically listening involves not only understanding what the speaker is saying, especially from the speaker's perspective, but also knowing the agenda or motives behind the message. The receiver of information is the buyer who should beware—*caveat emptor*. So, the source and the listener should equally be sensitive to the ethical responsibilities of their roles in the communication process. To this end Anderson (1984) has proposed that both the speaker/writer and listener/reader should be each 100% liable for the ethicality of their communication, thus introducing what he called the **200% theory of responsibility**. Benjamin quotes Anderson as saying

> "In evaluating our activity, typically we accept responsibility for the impact of our communication efforts both on ourselves and on other people. We thus are (or should be) willing to assume 100% responsibility for the action and impact of our communication effort….
>
> As we think of ourselves in the role of receiver we certainly wish to exercise our own judgment. We want and need to assure ourselves that actions urged, means employed, and effects eventuated will meet our ethical requirements. Thus, in our role as receiver we will surely wish to assume responsibility, 100% responsibility, for our decisions/actions."

Two professional codes of ethics of practitioners of the art and science of communication are included in the appendix of the book. These enumerate the agreed-upon principles of right and wrong that guide the practice of professional communication. These codes, as they are usually identified, become the test for professional and ethical performance of the practitioners and serve as the premise for professional sanction of practitioners' misconduct. All ethical provisions are obligatory precepts for practitioners enforced by the governing council of the profession, but some of the provisions have legal implications and, as such, can lead to civil or criminal liabilities.

Culture and Public Speaking

Public speaking is a cultural experience; it is an enactment of a culture's mode of sharing information. The act alone is a reflection of the acceptable structure of communication exchange that pervades a cultural milieu. The language used is a product of culture as much as the content is a cultural construction. Undoubtedly, there are sets of beliefs, attitudes, values, and feelings held by different cultures about the nature and purposes of public speaking, the speaker, the audience, and the messages being shared in the public arena. The goal here is to examine the differences in cultures and show how such cultural differences impact the mythos of public speaking.

Mythos is a set of interrelated beliefs, attitudes, values, and feelings held by members of a particular society or culture (Griffin, 2011). The connection between mythos and public speaking, especially with the goal to persuade becomes apparent when Griffin further writes that "when we appeal to mythos, we call into mind history, tradition, faith, feelings, common sense, and membership in a community or culture… In doing so, we tap into a rich reservoir of emotions, attitudes, and values." All of these are elements that play important roles in our attempt to speak to a people, especially in the context of one person speaking to an audience at a particular location. The connecting elements are both language and the cultural realities that language conveys.

> *Human beings draw close to one another by their common nature, but habits and customs keep them apart.*
>
> **Confucius**

Mythos separates one cultural group from another because it varies from culture to culture. And this makes the task of a cross-cultural public speaker daunting, because he or she has to speak to the mythos of the audience in order to make the exercise relevant to them. Take for example the use of proverbs in communicating common experience with an audience in a particular culture. Proverbs provide insights into a culture using colorful, terse, and vivid prose or poetry. These succinct, wise sayings capture the mythologies, wisdom and native intelligence of a people, and act as anchors between their past and present. A stranger to these "words of wisdom and of the elders," will not be successful at adequately representing logic and reason, mysteries and generalities to the people, thereby missing an important component of the enterprise of public communication.

As the McLuhan world is now a reality, there is more and more cross-cultural communication taking place in the sphere of trans-border business and cross-cultural training, to the extent that becoming a competent intercultural communicator is inevitable in what has been described as **glocal** communication. Thinking globally and acting locally is the maxim of our modern world of constant intercultural communication. We have to communicate effectively to the audience with whom we speak regardless of its culture or location in the world. This is just as we should communicate effectively to a local audience whose culture we are part of and, especially, whose language we share as our own.

A **competent intercultural communicator** has been described by Samovar et al. (2010), as one who has the ability to interact effectively and appropriately with members of another linguistic-cultural background on their terms. The components of such competence are identified as **motivation or personal desire to communicate effectively with people of a different culture; acquisition of required content and procedural knowledge about the rules of behavior of another culture; and mastering the skills to listen, observe, analyze, and interpret to perform specific cultural behaviors with the purpose of achieving one's goals of effective communication. Other competence elements are sensitivity to the cultural traditions and behaviors of others, and demonstration of good character, that is, goodwill, sincerity, honesty, honor, and altruism to people that are culturally different (see figure 13.1).**

Figure 10.2/ Elements of Intercultural Competence

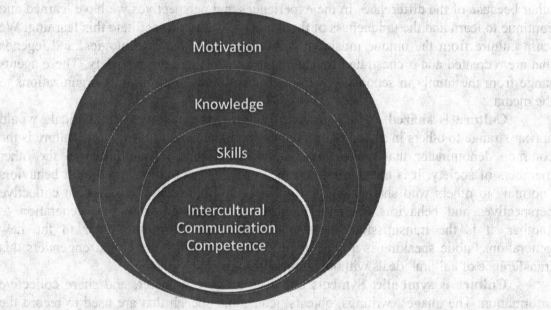

What is Culture?

Understanding what culture is will help us not only to be aware of the nature of the concept, but also to appreciate why culture is a determinant of the variations in people, their ways of life, values, and behaviors. As communication is behavior, the influence of culture on communication is of great importance to public speaking. As we will see, communication and culture are intertwined and are inseparable. This is why the study of culture and the awareness of cultural differences is central to inter-cultural public speaking.

Let us examine the definition of culture offered by Triandis (2000):

> **Culture** is a set of human-made objective and subjective elements that in the past have increased the probability of survival and resulted in satisfaction for participants in an ecological niche, and thus became shared among those who

could communicate with each other because they had a common language and they lived in the same time and place.

From this definition we can deduce that culture is learned and that it includes objective and subjective elements. The objective elements are physical things created by a people that reflect their adaptation to their ecological niche or environment. The subjective elements are values, beliefs, attitudes, and mind sets that influence the behaviors of the people. Culture is shared or preserved through the use of common language and creates a sense of satisfaction among those who share it. Culture galvanizes a people and gives them a sense of direction and purpose as it ensures their adaptation and survival.

Culture is learned. The process of cultural assimilation starts from cradle and ends when death comes. The experiences we share, the perspectives that direct our realities, all are learned and internalized. Every cultural group is different one from the other because of the differences in the experiences and perspectives we have learned and continue to learn and the uniqueness of the language we use to facilitate this learning. We learn culture from the unique music, art, proverbs, folktales, mythologies, and legends that are recreated and orchestrated by the agents of socialization in society. These agents range from the family to schools, government institutions and religious organizations to the media.

Culture is shared. Without shared cultures, the actions of individuals would appear strange to others in a society. In fact, as Haviland et al. (2005) put it: culture is the common denominator that makes the actions of individuals intelligible to the other members of society. It is the sharing and the commonness that make cultural behaviors "normal" to others who share them and derive a cultural identity from such collective perspectives and behaviors. Cultural identity is transmitted from one generation to another; it is the transmission of "social inheritance" from the older to the new generation. Public speaking is a part of the communication process that engenders this transference of cultural ideals without a break from the old to the new.

Culture is symbolic. Symbols allow us to store, transfer, and share collective information. The images, writings, objects, icons, and speech that are used to record the objective and subjective elements of culture are the symbols that represent the essence of such culture and that allows for the storage, portability, and permanency of cultural heritage. The most important cultural symbol is the language that is spoken or written by the group. It is language that allows for the coding of experiences, reflections, and insights. Through language we can reach into the past realm of accumulated knowledge, exert influence on the present and, forecast the eminence of years to come. According to Bates and Plog (1990),

Language thus enables people to communicate what they would do if such-and-such happened, to organize their experiences into abstract categories ("a happy occasion," for instance, or an "evil omen"), and to express thoughts never spoken before. Morality, religion, philosophy, literature, science, economics, technology, and numerous other areas of human knowledge and belief—along with the ability to learn about and manipulate them—all depend on this type of higher-level communication.

When we engage in the public speaking act, we are employing a cultural instrument of language to share meanings with others and because languages differ and, also that meanings differ, the public speaker should be mindful of the elements and characteristics of culture which create the discernible differences in peoples' worldviews, if we are to be successful at cross-cultural sharing of meaning.

The Importance of Language

Language is not only a means of communication; it is the defining element of our perception. What we experience directly, we put into words but we can also describe vicarious experiences. Our choice of words, the intonation of our voice, both indicate our feelings and perceptions of the object of our description. In the same vein, our perceptions shape our language. We tend to perceive people who speak a different language than us differently. Often, they are seen as separate, different and described as the "other," with a subtext of superior- inferior imbued in our preconceptions.

Such differentiation brought about by linguistic differences, is often orchestrated and maintained through the language we speak, to the extent that stereotype and prejudice are built into our language. The Sapir-Whorf hypothesis (**see chapter three for more on the Sapir-Whorf hypothesis and Language**) presupposes linguistic determinism. That is, the language we speak influences or determines our thought processes and structures. The affirmation that people of different cultures who speak different languages, perceive the world differently, speaks to this deterministic nature of language. According to Whorf (1956), our perception of reality is determined by our thought processes and our thought processes are limited by our language and, therefore, that language shapes our reality. This can be better understood by looking into the nature of language.

Linguists study the nature of language and examine the four major rules that govern the use of language which are **phonological, syntactic, semantic, and pragmatic rules (**see chapter three for a detailed discussion of these rules). Languages are for the best part unique because of the peculiarities in the four rules identified here. Let us examine each of these rules and see how they may cause challenges in intercultural public speaking.

Phonology is the study of the sound system of a language and focuses on the units of sounds that are called phonemes, and on the pronunciation of words and speaking in different languages. We know that different languages use different sounds and that it is rather difficult for a nonnative speaker to pronounce words in a particular language as native speakers; therefore, we are to be mindful of these differences and to check the tendency to want to equate nonnative accent as inferior or perhaps an indication of the inferior intelligence.

Many nonnative speakers of English may be challenged by the "th" or "v" sounds just to cite a few examples. Among some Nigerian English speakers, it is common to hear the sound of "da" when they attempt to pronounce the "th" sound in "father." Or, one may hear the sound "fe" as in "ferry" when they mean to say "very." On the other hand, Americans always find it difficult to pronounce the "gb" sound in the Yoruba word of, say "gbogbo." What I hear when they attempt to do this is the "g" or "b" sound separately because the English language does not have the "gb" sound. Imagine what you would hear if you should ask an American to say the equivalent of the phrase "all of you" in Yoruba language. This is written as "Gbogbo yin." So, French speakers have problems pronouncing some English words, just as English speakers have problems pronouncing some Spanish words. Such are the variations we experience in linguistic phonology.

Syntactic rules govern the structure of word and sentences to produce meaning. English sentences are structured differently than French sentences; indeed, no two languages are syntactically the same. That is, no two languages arrange words the same way to express feelings and convey meaning. For example, let us look at the structure of the English sentences in expressing subject-verb-object arrangement, expression of plurals, possessives, and gender forms. The examples used by Martin and Nakayama (2011) are useful here.

> To express possession in English, we add an "*s*" ("John's hat" or "the man's hat"). Other languages, such as Spanish, express possession through word sequence ("the hat of John" or "the hat of the man"). In English, the subject or actor is usually placed at the beginning of the sentence ("The girl ran"). By contrast, in Spanish, the subject is sometimes placed at end of the sentence ("ran the girl").

The lesson here is to learn not only the words of a language or its common expressions, but also to learn the rules that govern the structures of words and sentences to convey meaning.

Semantic rules govern the meanings of words and phrases in a particular language. When we want to communicate our meaning to another, we have to use the words that best represent this meaning, hoping that we are successful in effectively sharing our intended meaning with the receiver. But our use of words to convey meaning is fraught with interference otherwise called **semantic noise**. While native speakers understand the shades of meanings of words and phrases as well as the different words that mean the same thing, foreigners, who have not mastered the foreign language, may not have access to such meanings. Not only that, there are unique wisecracks, culture-based jokes, and idiomatic expressions, which may be totally strange to the non-native. Even among people who speak the same English language, the differences in the words they use to depict things and ideas may lead to confusion and miscommunication. For example, look at the different sets of words that British and Americans use to refer to the same things in table 18.1(Genzer, 1987-1988).

Table 10.1/British-American Word Usage

British	US
Jersey	sweater
Pants	underwear
Pumps	tennis shoes (sneakers)
Trousers	pants
Biscuit	cookie, cracker
Chips	French fries
Crisp	potato chips
Twigs	pretzels
Cooker	stove
Rubber	eraser
Loo	toilet (bathroom)
Carrier bag	grocery sack

Pragmatics is the appropriate use of language to navigate social settings, their rules, and customs. It is using language to achieve goals in social settings--goals that are acceptable to both receiver and sender. Different social contexts produce different meanings and expectations in the communicators. This is really a set of rules guiding the appropriate use and interpretation of language within certain socio-cultural contexts. It is using language and its interpretation to negotiate the social terrain in which the users must traverse and achieve practical goals of which survival is the most fundamental. A speech may be correct grammatically and may appropriate meaning effectively, yet it may fail the test of pragmatism in that it may offend and it may be disrespectful depending on who is doing the interpreting.

Pragmatics is not usually taught in schools, but it is acquired through daily usage and thoughtful guides of adults and other sophisticated users of the language, who are adept at the social expectations inherent in a people's use of their language. A non-native speaker may study a foreign language and become proficient in the semantics and syntactics of the language, but may be ignorant of the appropriate social rules that govern the use of that language. For example, in the Yoruba language that is spoken in Nigeria, West Africa, the words "come here," is "wa n'bi" or just "wa." While you can say "wa n'bi" to a person and he or she would understand what you're trying to say, but if that person is older than you, this becomes an insult because it is rude for a younger person to say the equivalent of the word "come" directly to an older person. But if this is exchanged among equals, there is certainly no offence taken.

In the United States, where informality is the dominant style of communication, pragmatic rules also apply. There are certain things you cannot say to certain people in certain places. You cannot call the President by his first name in a public, official setting; you are expected to code switch to mainstream English in official, corporate or educational setting. As much as you may like to spit out profane language that may draw applause from your friends, it is not an appropriate choice of language in certain settings where decorum and comportment both in action and speech is expected. It takes someone who has been immersed in a culture to understand the rules that govern language, especially pragmatic rules. Without such knowledge, at best the speaker may be laughed at and not taken seriously, but worse still, he or she may be considered rude, unschooled, and incompetent.

Verbal Communication Styles

We already learned that some cultures use **restricted codes** while others use **elaborated codes**. In other words, some cultures communicate in great detail, elaborating and pontificating with words, while others say little and express themselves in greater detail using nonverbal codes and depend on the context of communication to supply inherent meanings. Klopf and McCroskey (2007) expanding on the work of Basil Bernstein on restricted and unrestricted codes wrote that "elaborated codes make use of accurate and sophisticated grammatical structures. It employs a large range of adjectives and adverbs in a relatively large vocabulary. Essentially the speakers of elaborated codes are explicit and depend less on the added meaning of context in using verbal language, thus assigning little role to nonverbal communication. On the other hand, restricted codes use short, grammatically simple, and often incomplete sentences usually of poor syntactic structure. Its vocabulary is small with limited use of adverbs and adjectives. Context-bound, it relies on many shared experiences between speakers and listeners and depends heavily upon nonverbal channels to carry its messages," Klopf and McCroskey.

Edward Hall (1959) expanded Basil Bernstein code classification to include context. Thus he classified cultures according to the two variations of **Low-context** and **High-context,** essentially an extension of the elaborate and restricted code dichotomy.

People described as belonging to low-context cultures use language primarily to express thoughts, feelings and ideas as clearly and logically as possible. Low-context communicators look for the meaning of a statement in the words that are spoken, (Adler and Towne, 1999). To them, meanings are hardly dependent on the context; therefore, every meaning must be verbalized and every thought must be codified in verbal form and explicitly expressed for understanding to occur. In the United States, a low-context culture, people are expected to toot their own horns because no one would do it for them. It is customary, therefore, to expect people to speak up and not doing so, leads to some assumptions about the non-verbally explicit speaker.

People who live in high-context cultures are not given to verbalizing all of their meanings in communication exchanges because the context plays a great role in determining such meanings. That is, "much information is drawn from surroundings" and "little must be transferred explicitly." Writing about the cultural importance of speaking, Klopf and McCroskey (2007) contrast Western and Eastern orientations toward speaking. In illustrating the Eastern approach, they quote the fact that "Zen Buddhists maintain that language limits peoples' capability of thinking, thereby curbing imagination and tainting judgment." And that "they, meditate without language and communicate beyond language." This deemphasizes the use of words as opposed to the tradition of the West which stresses speech. 'The East puts credence in mental unification with the other person to achieve total understanding. Oneness with the other or total harmony represents the position of the principal Asian religions, especially Taoism, Buddhism, and Confucianism, (Yum, 1998)

The teachings of these Asian religions admonish the followers to speak rarely, and when they do, they should be weary of "fancy words and embellished styles." In essence, these teachings emphasize the virtue of silence over speaking. But we know that in the Western world, speaking is encouraged and the non- speaker is looked upon negatively.

Nonverbal Communication Styles

Cultural influences on public presentations include not only verbal cues, but the use of nonverbal cues as well. There are nonverbal variations among people of different cultures, especially in their use of facial expressions, hand gestures, mode of dressing, use of time and space. All these will introduce consequential differences into the public speaking exercise.

Culture and Public Speaking

From all we know about cultural differences of the peoples of the world, it is little wonder that people from different cultures may not respond to persuasive strategies or efforts the same way. The influences on people are derived from the cultural contexts of language, social structures, and other social symbols, as such; the logical presentation of information and the evidence-based argumentation of the Western world may not appeal to some people of other cultures. For example, Gamble and Gamble (1998) write that the oral tradition from which African Americans draw ... leads them to prefer **analogical speaking style,** which relies on the telling of an analogy story, or parable from which receivers can derive an implicit or explicit moral. They add that this pattern of persuasive speaking is often emotional and dramatic.

The analogical speaking style of the African Americans, contrasts with that of members of White American culture, who, according to Gamble and Gamble, view explicit "facts" or physical evidence rather than analogies or stories as the highest form of evidence. This group of people prefers the use of **quasilogical style** which relies more on statistics and expert evidence to support an assertion and to arrive at a logical conclusion.

Black churches in the United States are venues for the display of the different communication style of the African American. The minister does not preach to a quiet audience, but to an audience that engages in the speech act with the speaker through the phenomenon called call-response communication. This means that the audience gives responses to the calls or proclamations of the speaker, who expects such responses and performs to the cues of the audience. This call-response communication style is evident in Rap music when rappers engage themselves in an "exchange" of lyrical messages and, to which the audience responds in a collective exercise of griotic exchange. The root of this is in West Africa where it is common practice for griots to engage themselves in a competition of praise singing to honor natural, spiritual leaders and the nobility. This call-response performance can go on for hours and, the effect is the inflated egos of the recipients of the praises who, in appreciation, would give money to the performers. This antecedent experience is evident in the communication cultures of Africans in the Diaspora. Martin and Nakayama (2011) write that [t]his form of call and response arises from the values or priorities identified in many African American communities: the importance of religion; the participatory, interrelatedness of people; the connectedness of spiritual and secular life. Also, public speaking is viewed as a communal event in which speakers are supported and reinforced.

The different communication style of African Americans may cause European or White Americans to view the call-response style as interruptions of the speech process and, as such, create listening problems. On the other hand, an African American speaker may think of the European American receiver as not involved, uninterested or not listening to his speech.

As we will see later in the chapter, people of different cultures view the public speaking event differently and, as such, have different expectations of both the speaker and the audience. Take, for example, the event that happened on the campus of Howard University in Washington D.C. in the summer of 1987 when Kenneth Kaunda, the then president of Zambia, was a guest speaker at a forum organized in his honor. When the President was invited to the podium after a well-crafted and befitting introduction, the guest speaker brought to the stage several chorus singers, who backed him in rendering some of the native songs of his people. Can you picture President Obama doing that in England, France or even Kenya? The public speaking event is perceived differently and performed differently by peoples across the world. I am sure that the host of the occasion, President Cheek, was pleasantly surprised- to put it lightly- to hear a President sing instead of give a "speech" as he was accustomed to.

Take a look at these two speeches (examples given by Martin and Nakayama, 2011) that further illustrate cultural differences in public speaking. These speeches were given by the opposing heads of State at the onset of the American invasion of Iraq, otherwise termed "Operation Iraqi Freedom."

George Bush:

My fellow citizen: At this hour, American and coalition forces are in the early stages of military operations to disarm Iraq, to free its people, and to defend the world from grave danger.

On my orders, coalition forces have begun striking selected targets of military importance to undermine Saddam Hussein's ability to wage war. These are the opening stages of what will be a broad and concerted campaign (Bush, 2003).

Saddam Hussein:

Oh great Mojahed people.
Oh sons of our glorious nation.
Oh men, bearers of arms and the honor of resistance. God's peace be upon you as you confront the invaders, the enemies of God and humanity, the transient blasphemers with chests brimming with faith and love of God....

Seize the opportunity, the pride of Iraq and the nation. It is the opportunity to become eternal and a long life for the living and glory unparalleled.

Strike at them, fight them. They are aggressors, evil, accursed by God, the exalted. You shall be victorious and they shall be vanquished....

Fight them everywhere the way you are fighting them today and don't give them a chance to catch their breath until they declare it and withdraw from the lands of the Muslims, defeated and cursed in this life and the afterlife (Hussein, 2003).

Hofstede's Cultural Value Dimensions

There are cultural dimensions that manifest in how people reason or think, respond to criticism, learn, cooperate, view power, view their relationship with nature and one another, and communicate. These cultural dimensions have real consequences on all of the activities people engage in, especially their communication. So, people learn differently because they are accustomed to different cognitive processes; they focus on individual achievement and competition with one another because their culture has taught them that way of life; they learn to accept inequality of power and have great respect for authority figures; they would rather speak up and care less about "face saving," because they are not accustomed to doing otherwise. These are cultural traditions that influence us all in our interactions with people of different cultures, who may wonder why we do things the way we do, and reason the way we reason. The communication act of public speaking in this sense, therefore, is a form of cultural expression that people of different cultures will perform differently because of the different cultural dimensions that manifest in their social cultural lives. Awareness of the consequential cultural dimensions that influence our communication and other activities is necessary in order to understand the cultural influences of the differences inherent in our behaviors.

Hofstede (1991) identifies four cultural value dimensions that affect the way people of different cultures perceive, are oriented, and influenced. The first of the dimensions is the individualism/collectivism dichotomy. Individualist cultures view the individual as separate, unique members of society, who pursues his or her individual interests, goals, and achievement, including that of the immediate, nuclear family. Primary to this culture is individual freedom, rights, and success. In collectivist culture however, the individual is an integral, inseparable part of close-nit social-cultural group from cradle to grave. Rather than pursue individual goals, the members of a collectivist culture would value group affiliation, loyalty, and cohesiveness over individual goals and success. As Calloway- Thomas et al (1999) put it, a collectivist society is tightly integrated; an individualist society is loosely integrated.

What are the resulting behaviors of the collectivist and individualist dimension of culture on the people? In individualist cultures, people are supposed to speak up and defend their opinions and do not mind if others lose face in the process. It is acceptable to have open, public debate or confrontation. After all, if you don't defend your ideas and, indeed, yourself in public, who will? Speaking up will advance the cause of the individual because this act is tied to self-respect, competence, success, and advancement in life. But in collectivist cultures, open, public confrontation is seen as an affront and, consequently, is injurious to the ego of the "defeated." Harmony is the underlining tenet of these cultures, therefore, public argumentation and "tooting one's horns" is rather selfish and should be avoided. There exists an environment of noncompetition and cooperation that allows for sharing of resources, ideas and information that some might have used to have an advantage over others. In the view of Calloway-Thomas et al. (1999), this is the reason why, for example, Mexican children, because of their culture emphasize cooperation, allow others to share their homework or answers... If an American student shares his or her homework, he or she is seen as dishonest, perhaps even a cheater!

In terms of public speaking, engaging in political debates to argue a candidate's position as better than the other, may be well suited for the individualist cultures of the United States and The United Kingdom, but certainly not to that of Mexico, Nigeria, or Pakistan. Presenting oneself as the connoisseur of information that can be used in making independent decisions may not be that of an advantage in a culture where competitiveness is perceived as self-serving and should be avoided. A speaker or a leader is not speaking for him or herself in a collectivist society but for the collective, the group and, as such, should not have a sense of being better than the rest.

Another of Hofstede's value dimensions is the concept of **power distance**. This is the degree to which individuals in society are accepting and consider normal, the inequalities of power and position in society. There are societies where there is **low-power distance**, that is, the distance between the powerful and those who are aspiring to positions of power is rather low. In the United States, for instance, practically anyone born in the country can aspire to become president or, in the least, become a millionaire, a senator, or an important member of society, regardless of race, creed, or gender! At least we know that there are no provisions in the constitution of the U.S. that approve of the demarcation of people according to variables of class, or race or gender. In England and other monarchies around the world, on the other hand, only members of the royal family can aspire to become King or Queen. In other words, in low-power distance societies of the world, by and large, leadership is by achievement, while in **high-power distance societies**, leadership is by ascription.

Different behaviors characterize different degrees of power distance in society. In low-power distance societies, authority figures do not see themselves as all powerful persons that cannot be questioned or brought to defend their stand on issues. The other members of society can and, indeed, question authority figures and demand answers to their queries. Equality of members engenders debate, open and fair consideration and treatment of all, such that the focus is on sound arguments and ability to persuade others in order to advance a cause and not the use of autocratic, non-democratic means. In **high-power distance** societies, on the other hand, the authority figures and the powerful in society dictate policies and establish criteria for directing the affairs of The State and the less powerful have little or no say. As a matter of fact, they cannot question their leaders, let alone demand answers to their requests.

In terms of public speaking, in a low-power distance society, audience-centeredness is necessary for success in the sphere of public opinion and policy because, if the audience members are not fully informed and satisfied, they have the collective power to shape the structure of public opinion and power in such societies. Leaders are more responsive and sensitive to the requests of the citizenry who, invariably control the leaders. Speeches are to be well reasoned, researched and designed to move the audience rather than dictatorial. The nature of the practice of public speaking, argumentation, and debate in the Western world attests to the underlining nature of power distribution in these largely democratic societies.

In high-power distance societies, the practice of public speaking serves the purpose of informing the populace of what has been done or is proposed to be done by those in position of authority. The purpose is not to stir debates that will result in collective problem solving that will end in policy decisions. Consequently, there is little or no need to engage in prolonged, systematic presentation of evidence to support an assertion or proposition because the purpose of public presentation is not to engineer public consent, but rather to inform the public as a courtesy. This is because the citizens cannot challenge the powerful, and the powerful do not answer to the citizens. As a form of cultural belief, the authority figures have "wisdom" that they can exercise on behalf of all of society. These are value positions, so we are not saying that one way or the other is better; they are just different ways of doing things. And if the members of the different societies are accepting of the distribution of power in their societies, then we are to examine how that is and with what consequence.

Another value dimension that separates one culture from another is the idea of **uncertainty avoidance.** Certainty means to be sure, predictable, and not dynamic; and to avoid uncertainty is to prefer the certain, the predictable, the balanced state of affairs that do not challenge the order of things much. **Uncertainty avoidance** is the extent to which people within a culture are made nervous by situations that they perceive as unstructured, unclear, or unpredictable, situations that they therefore try to avoid by maintaining strict codes of behavior and a belief in absolute truths (Calloway-Thomas, 1999). We can differentiate between **low-uncertainty avoidance** and **high-uncertainty avoidance cultures**. If a society is described as having the weak or low uncertainty avoidance characteristic, it means that that society thrives on the unpredictable, the dynamic, and the challenging. A society with high or strong uncertainty avoidance feels comfortable when the order is predictable, when there is less conflict and, when there is little or no competition. Again, in the words of Calloway-Thomas et al (1999), cultures with strong uncertainty avoidance are active, aggressive, emotional, compulsive, security seeking, and intolerant. (Whereas) cultures with weak uncertainty avoidance are contemplative, less aggressive, unemotional, relaxed, accept personal risks, and are relatively tolerant. Examples of cultures with strong uncertainty avoidance are France, Chile, Spain, Portugal, Japan, Peru, and Argentina. The United States, Great Britain, Denmark, Ireland, and India are characterized by weak uncertainty avoidance.

In terms of public speaking, weak uncertainty avoidance cultures compared to those that are not, will be more accepting of speech topics that challenge the status quo, and would not frown at suggestions of new ideas that may challenge the establishment and present a new paradigm or perspective of viewing seemingly unchallengeable mindsets. Again such people would not believe that one person has all the answers to issues, rather, that each person presents a perspective that can be challenged and improved upon. Citing evidence from non-established, but insightful sources will be more acceptable and the new will present opportunities rather than challenges to weak uncertainty avoidance cultures. What about conflict and competition avoidance? These characteristics will question the basis for debate and public speaking as a form of competition among opposing forces, such as the Republicans and Democrats in the United States. The implications of these dimensions are many and varied. You should consider all of them in your attempt to gain intercultural competence as a public communicator.

The fourth dimension of Hofstede's culture classification is **masculinity and femininity**. This has to do with the clear delineation of what the sexes can do and not do in society. Societies classified as sharing masculine values, emphasize such values as assertiveness, strength, competitiveness, ambition and material success. These are values that they ascribe to men in such societies, because they believe that women should occupy and perform nurturing roles and duties in society such as catering to the weak, children and the nonmaterial things. Feminine cultures are more accepting of overlapping roles for men and women in society. Men and women can engage in nurturing and nonmaterial, nonpolitical endeavors and such would be valued by society. Masculine societies emphasize material success whereas feminine societies value quality of life and social relations; nonetheless, in both societies, the dominant values are those of men.

Are there some speech topics that women will be naturally perceived as having a greater credibility if they should speak about them? Are there such for men as well? Consider your immediate reaction (mindset) to the following topics and questions:

   a. Women should be allowed to serve in combat positions in the military.
   b. Breast milk is the most important source of nourishment for the newborn.
   c. After several years of debate, the U.S. military has decided to allow women to serve in the submarine fleet.
   d. Is it not time for a female President of the United States?
   e. Are men well-suited for taking care of babies?

TABLE 10.2/ HOFSTEDE'S CULTURAL VALUE ORIENTATIONS

Power Distance	Low power distance Less hierarchy is better	High power distance More hierarchy is better
Femininity/Masculinity	Femininity Fewer gender-specific roles Values quality of life, support for the weak or unfortunate in society	Masculinity More gender-specific roles, Value achievement, ambition, acquisition of material wealth
Individualism/Collectivism	Individualism Individual is separate, unique members of society, who pursues his or her individual interests, goals, and achievement, including that of the immediate, nuclear family	Collectivism Members of a collectivist culture would value group affiliation, loyalty, and cohesiveness over individual goals and success.

Uncertainty Avoidance	Low uncertainty avoidance Dislike rules, accept dissent, and new Less formality	High uncertainty avoidance More extensive rules, limit dissent More formality
Long-Term/Short-Term Orientation	Short-term orientation Truth over virtue Prefer quick results	Long-term orientation Virtue over truth Value perseverance and tenacity

Adapted from Hofstede, G. & Hofstede, G.J. (2004) Cultures and organizations: Software of the mind (2nd ed.). Boston: McGraw-Hill

These are general overview of the cultures studied by Hofstede and, by no means, are the classifications exhaustive and represent every member of the societies so classified. Communication styles differ from culture to culture. Some are more formal than others; some favor indirect rather than direct communication; others value impulsivity, but others reflectivity; some are topic-centered and others are topic associating. **Topic-centeredness is focusing on a particular topic, say, under discussion or analysis, when solving a problem**. Euro American and African American students have been identified to have contrasting problem-solving methodologies. According to Au (1993), Euro-American children tend to be topic-centered. Their accounts of events focus on a single topic or closely related topics and are ordered in a linear fashion and lead to a resolution. The topic-associating style, often used by African American children, constitutes a series of episodes linked to some person or theme. These links are implicit in the account and are not stated.

We have learned of the logical-deductive reasoning of Europeans and Americans, which were reportedly developed in ancient Greece and Rome and, in the same vein, we are familiar with the circular reasoning of the Africans, as documented in communication and sociology literatures. Little surprise then about the comments of Au (1993) about the different ways the children of these culturally different peoples approach problem solving. The practice of logically presenting arguments with supporting materials to bolster credibility and believability is not a cultural universal; rather, it is a practice that may be foreign to some other people with a different reasoning and problem-solving process. Consequently, the structures of a speech and the different manners of structuring speeches that are presented in this book have a cultural bent which is Euro-American. Nonetheless, we must acknowledge the dominance of the Eurocentric approach because of its dominance and pervasiveness across several spheres of cultural influence, especially education and the media.

Culture and Public Speaking
Nausheen Qureshi
Intercultural Communication
High and Low Context Cultures

Every culture in today's society has high and low-context aspects of communication. High-context and low-context communication pertain to how much speakers rely on things other than words to convey meaning. In each culture, members have been handed over the specific "filters" that make them focus on what the society demands. Cultures that favor low-context communication will pay more attention to the literal meanings of words while cultures who favor high-context communication will be more aware to the context of the surroundings. High-context and low-context cultures differentiate from each other and they can be seen in many cultures.

Context can be defined as "the information that surrounds an event; it is inextricably bound up with the meaning of the event" (Samovar & Porter, 76). It is important to remember that every society has characteristics of both high-context and low context communication. It is not the choice of an individual to be high-context or low-context; it is contingent on his cultural beliefs and his background. High-context cultures emphasize interpersonal relationships. According to Hall, these cultures are collectivist, which prefer group harmony and consensus to individual achievement. Knowledge in high-context is situational. The use of verbal explicit is not high. There is more internalized understanding of the conversation like knowing an inside joke. High-context communication is used in well-established relationships and is conducted personally face-to-face. These types of cultures have a strong understanding of "insiders" vs. "outsiders". Trust builds up slowly and is usually stable. An individual's identity depends on his family, culture and work status.

High-context cultures use non-verbal elements like tone of voice, facial expressions, gestures, and eye movement. These elements carry the most important parts of the conversation. For example, when the police are about to raid a house, they use high-context communication to send their messages. They do not use any verbal communication. Most of the verbal communication is indirect; a person has to talk around the situation to emphasize his point. Disagreement is personalized; it needs to be solved before work can progress. Most societies learn their high-context culture from observing others in their society. Most situations involve a large group and the accuracy of the information is valued (Wilson, 2009). Examples of high-context culture include small religious congregations, a party with friends, family gatherings, expensive gourmet restaurants and neighborhood restaurants with a regular clientele, undergraduate on-campus friendships, regular pick-up games, hosting a friend in your home overnight. Low-context cultures are usually rule oriented. The knowledge is considered to be more public, external and accessible. The durations of the conversations are shorter because everything is stated to the point. The knowledge can be transferred through words unlike, high-context cultures, knowledge is observed. The situations are task-centered and decisions are focused on what needs to be done.

In low-context cultures, relationships begin and end quickly unlike, high-context, where the relationships build on trust. Many people can be inside one's circle or outside the circle. There are no boundaries. Most of the tasks get done by following procedures and paying attention to the goal. Unlike high-context cultures, the person's identity is rooted in oneself instead of his family and culture. Responsibility is not concentrated to one authority figure, social structure is decentralized. Conversations are carried more by words than by nonverbal means and the verbal message is direct. Communication is seen as a way of exchanging information, ideas, and opinions. Disagreement is depersonalized; a person can withdraw from a conflict with another and progress work (Wilson, 2009). The solutions to problems tend to be more rational instead of personal. Unlike high-context cultures, there is only one source of information instead of having a whole group providing information. Focus is on detail. Speed is valued and instead of accuracy the efficiency of how something is learned is more important. An example of low-context communication is between a student and a teacher. A teacher explains everything word to word when she is teaching the student. The student has no background information on the topic. Other examples include large US airports, a chain supermarket, a cafeteria, a convenience store, sports where rules are clearly laid out, a motel.

High context cultures are more common in the Eastern nations than in Western, and in countries with low racial diversity. Cultures where the group is valued over the individual promote group reliance. High context cultures have a strong sense of tradition and history, and change little over time, such as tribal and native societies. For instance, a person from an Arab culture may assume that the listener knows the background information about their topic of discussion; therefore, when an American tries to explain something to the Arab, he may feel humiliated and think that he's being made fun of.

An individual from a high context culture has to be accommodated when shifting to a low context culture. High context cultures expect small close-knit groups, where professional and personal life are interrelated. Therefore, when an individual moves to a low context culture, that individual is more likely to ask questions than attempt to work out a solution independently because people in this culture work with word to word explanation of any situation. High contexts can be difficult to enter if you are an outsider because you don't carry the context information internally, and because you can't instantly create close relationships (Wilson, 2009).

When individuals from high-context and low-context cultures collaborate, there are often difficulties that occur during the exchange of information. These problems can be separated into differences concerning "direction", "quantity" and "quality." For example, employees from high-context cultures like China and France share very specific and extensive information with their "in-group members" (Samovar & Porter, 77). In comparison, low-context cultures like the United States and Germany prefer to limit communication to smaller, more select groups of people, sharing only that information which is necessary.

It's easy to see how these very different styles can cause misunderstandings and even complete failures in the communications process. High-context and low-context cultures have been a part of our society.

Every culture or every cultural situation has its high and low dimensions. Often one situation will contain an inner high context core and an outer low context ring for those who are less involved. Both high-context and low-context cultures differentiate in many ways.

References:

Wilson, Brian. "High-Context and Low-Context cultural styles." Business Communication Online. 2009. College of Marin. October 6, 2009 http://www.marin.edu/buscom/index_files/Page605.htm

Samovar, Larry, Porter, Richard E. & McDaniel Edwin R. (2007) *Communication Between Cultures*. (6th ed.) Belmont, California: Wadsworth,

PUBLIC SPEAKING: AN IMPERATIVE SKILL
Daniel Olawale Awodiya

Imagine that you were alive about four thousand years ago in ancient Greece and you had a run-in with the law. And your case was brought before the Congress of citizens at the town square for hearing. You would think that you, an affluent Athenian, would be able to buy the best defense lawyer in town who would argue successfully against your spending, at best, the next thirty years in incarceration or worse still, being put to death. Guess again! You would have to advocate for yourself! Because at a period in time in Athenian society, lawyers were banned and individual citizens had to defend themselves against accusations, either real or trumped up, brought against them by the City State.

At this time in Greek history, the measure of truth was based on how eloquently a speaker was able to advance artistic and inartistic proofs in his/her defense oratory. This meant that an accused person must be able to eloquently present factual evidence and cleverly dribble with words and move the passions of the audience, to convince them of his innocence. Consequently, much of a speaker's believability or credibility is based on presentation-including acceptable speech presentation buffered with passionate performance. How would you do this if you had no training in forensic Oratory?

Needless to say that the Greeks spent a great deal of time studying the Art of Oratory and Persuasion in order to be able to argue eloquently against any charge by the authorities. Over three thousand years ago, the Greeks understood the importance of Public Address and Persuasion that Aristotle, the great Greek philosopher and scholar of Rhetoric, at the bequest of Alexander The Great, classified the field of public speaking, as we call it today, as one of the original disciplines of the academy. Imperative was the art of Rhetoric to the Greeks that many teachers of the art (Sophists) earned good living teaching endless numbers of students who wanted to become proficient in the art of public presentation and socio-political influence. The power of eloquent oratory bestowed on people political and economic power. Political leaders had to be great orators before they could become potentates who inspired war and conquests. As a matter of fact, the power of oratory was equated with military prowess in ancient Greece!

Proficiency in public speaking is needed more in contemporary times than ever before. In the age of mass education, instantaneous access to information, and expansive interconnectedness of the peoples of the world, there is greater contact and exchange of values, meanings, and products, which impose on us the need for understanding through efficient communication. It is obvious that the more means of communication we have access to and the more rapid human access to information becomes, and the more globally we communicate, the more are the chances for misunderstanding through miscommunication, especially if we are not equipped to handle such communication exigencies through adequate training.

Persuasion through communication is the currency of human exchange and not force or coercion. So, a nation to excel economically and politically must deploy sophisticated individuals with great mastery of public address, negotiation, and persuasion to spread its influence both within and internationally. This public speaking efficacy starts with the number one citizen- the president, on to the rank and file of government functionaries.

One of the important means of human communication is speech- translating ideas into symbolic representations, so adequately articulated to warrant understanding and possible co-creation of meaning. And this, as humans, is what we do every day, though often with great failing. There arises the need for one to engage a small group, perhaps a large group, or even a mammoth crowd in public address. This we have to do as Teachers, Students, Politicians, Athletes, Farmers, Engineers, Doctors, Lawyers, Bankers, etc. We all need to understand and hone our public speaking skills. This we need to do to engage one another with critical reasoning and employ civil debate and argumentation to advance our opinions, perspectives, and the rationales for the choices we make. Absence of this will invite intolerance, rash autocratic decision making, and ill-informed choices- all the vestiges of oppression that we should concertedly jettison in a nascent democracy as Nigeria's.

The Greeks recognized the need to teach the art of public speaking then, but many of the Nigerian higher education institutions do not include it in their course offerings now. This is perplexing because it is difficult to fathom why those who are in need of these skills the most to advance the enterprise of critical thinking, writing, and speaking, do not yet recognize the need to include it in their college curriculum as a requirement for graduation.

The Western world identifies Greece as the cradle of its civilization and no wonder the art of public speaking is widely accepted in these societies as a necessary skill from cradle to grave. The American child is taught earlier on in life that the power to remain politically free rests on one's ability to express oneself clearly and assertively, in order to defend one's rights and privileges as a citizen, thereby preserving the philosophies and the tenets of democracy. Democracy, it is argued, imposes on those who want to remain free, the responsibility of civic participation and this can only be sustained through free and (eloquent) speech. But there is more to speech than stringing words together and performing passionately.

Credible communicators are ethical communicators. The act of public speech imposes on the speaker a huge ethical responsibility that if imbued, results in the speaker being believed, accepted and trusted. Politicians are not trusted because of their perceived unethical behavior. It is generally believed that they are a breed of people, who cannot be trusted because they would say and do anything to get elected.

Aristotle argued that for a speaker to be successful, he or she must be mindful of three important tenets of successful oratory referred to as artistic proofs: Ethos, Pathos, and Logos. Logos is Logic and critical argumentation. A speaker's argumentation must be logical because humans are logical and analytical beings (Aristotle wrote extensively about Logic). In addition, humans are also emotional beings and, as such, the speaker must appeal to people's emotions as well. Most importantly, the speaker, to be accepted and believed must be credible to the listeners. Scholars have for long been preoccupied with the concept of speaker credibility, identifying many factors that encompass credibility and how each and all of such factors sway the audience or receivers of messages.

Aristotle's teacher, Plato and Plato's teacher, Socrates are seminal figures when it comes to the study of Classical Rhetoric, but there were other scholars of this subject even before Socrates! The Romans are not to be left out either. The Roman politician and orator, Cicero and others were believed to have canonized the elements of Rhetoric. Quintilian (35-100 AD), a Roman lawyer, argued that an orator should be a good man skilled in the art of speaking and he wrote that speeches are designed to inform (educate), move (persuade), and please (entertain) the audience. He started the *Institutes of Oratory* that published twelve books exploring the proper education of an orator.

A student of Public Speaking can explore the early beginnings of Rhetoric and compare it to modern Public Communication today and would surprisingly find that nothing is really "new' in this field! We may now have Power Point and the Internet and other human communication extensions, but the speech form is still very basic. The means may be different and the forms variegated, but the purpose is still the same and so are the tactics. Many notable leaders of modern times either read directly the writings of ancient rhetoricians or were greatly influenced by such writings vicariously.

The inclusion of Speech, especially Public Speaking in the American undergraduate education as a required course is informed by the foregoing. Generally, though, Universities and Colleges in the United States mandate a broad-based education for their students, in addition to the students' areas of specialization. This broad-based, multidisciplinary education is usually referred to as General Education Requirements of which Speech Communication is an essential part. The general education courses constitute about a half of the requirements for an undergraduate degree.

The goals are usually articulated as "encouraging students to come to an understanding of themselves, their society, the physical world, and the life-long nature of learning itself." The curricula are structured such that each academic program specifically includes "courses which develop oral and written communication skills; encourage thinking skills and creativity; foster appreciation for scientific methodology; promote an understanding of self, nature, and society and its historical context, and a heightened awareness of personal, social and aesthetic values." These courses will run the gamut of the arts, social sciences, history, music, speech, physical sciences, medical sciences, etc. Some of these are mandated within certain disciplines and others are unrestricted.

There is no doubt as to the need to acquire Public Speaking skills by anyone who wants to succeed and lead others in any society. This is a skill that is expected of all who have acquired, in the least, a High School education let alone a college education. Ability to speak effectively, ability to listen carefully and efficiently, and the ability to think critically are the measures of an educated mind and a sophisticated, responsible member of society.

There is a caveat though, everyone experiences public speaking apprehension. However, in a world where such ability is imperative for success, there are practical ways of managing this phobia. Studying the nature of public speaking and understanding how to structure and deliver a good speech would go a long way in attenuating the ever present speech anxiety. As I admonish myself and my students, and those who consult with me, I will state the obvious maxim here, which is often handy whenever one is to give a public speech and this is: practice, practice, practice and rehearse, rehearse, and rehearse!

Review Questions

1. Define public speaking.
2. How is public speaking different from other levels or forms of communication?
3. Why is ethical consideration important in the enterprise of public speaking?
4. Identify and discuss the different purposes for public speaking.
5. Identify and discuss three ways in which public speaking contributes to a civil society.
6. Identify, describe, and discuss the elements of the public speaking model.

Speech Anxiety

1. Define and describe what you understand by speechophobia.
2. Why is some level of speech anxiety good for the public performer?
3. What are irrational thoughts and how can they influence public performance negatively?
4. What are the different ways you can overcome public performance anxiety?
5. Why is it not a good idea to shy away from public speaking?
6. Assess your public speaking anxiety level by taking the survey at the end of this chapter. How would you interpret your score?

Ethics

1. What is ethics and why should it matter to public communication?
2. Define and explain the three types of plagiarism.
3. What are the expectations of an ethical speaker?
4. What are the expectations of an ethical listener?
5. Under the topic of ethics and sources, what does the acronym TAGS stand for?
6. How is slander different from libel?

Culture

1. What is culture and how does it influence public speaking?
2. What are the characteristics of a competent intercultural communicator?
3. How are language rules different from culture to culture?
4. Explain the importance of phonology to intercultural public speaking.
5. What are Hofstede's four cultural dimensions and how do they impact intercultural public speaking.

Chapter Eleven

Relating with the Audience

The elements of the public speaking process are the same as those of the communication process. These elements are: speaker, message, channel, audience, and noise. Mindful of all of these elements, the public speaker, in order to connect with listeners, must choose a topic that is relevant to the audience to whom the speech is to be delivered; the audience must find the information or message relevant, useful, and be motivated to retain and use such in the short term. The speaker must relate to the audience truthfully by giving complete information that is supported by verifiable and relevant evidence. The speech is designed for an audience, as such, the speaker must find out as much information about this set of listeners in order to tailor the speech to their situation, purpose, expectations, mindset, and knowledge level. As a speaker, you have to listen to your audience just as you expect them to listen to you. All of these start with the process of audience analysis.

Audience Analysis

An audience is a collection of individuals who have come together to watch or listen to a speech (Seiler and Beal, 2008) Essentially, this group of people share a common interest of wanting to receive information for the purpose of educating and or persuading themselves about certain topics, issues, persons, and events. As public speaking is an audience-centered exercise, it behooves the speaker to identify what the audience thinks of the topic of a speech meant for them. Also, it is important to recognize the diversity in the audience members because such differences lead to divergent perspectives and opinions.

The practice of examining the nature of the audience in terms of its demography and psychology, and adapting the result to the speech process to communicate effectively with the audience is called **audience analysis**. In this process, the speaker evaluates available information about the audience and the speaking situation prior, during, and after a speech, with a view to constantly adapting the speech to the audience, just as the audience members also continually modify their impressions of the speaker, before, during and after the speech.

A good way to start studying the audience of your speech is to identify the different types of audiences there are and identify what motivate them. Clella Jaffe (2007) asks a set of relevant questions to provide clues about an audience's motivation and purpose. Why do audiences gather? What attracts them? And what holds them? Audiences can be segmented in many different ways. In analyzing who is listening to your speech, Jaffe quoted Hollingsworth's (1935) six audience types:

Types of Audiences

1. **Pedestrian Audiences** randomly and temporarily come together because something grabs their attention—perhaps a salesman's flashy demonstration of a food processor, the impassioned voice of an activist in an outdoor forum, or the humorous stories of a sidewalk entertainer.

2. **Passive audiences** listen to speeches in order to accomplish other goals. For instance, some teachers attend job-related workshops not because they're fascinated by the topics, but because their principals insist they attend. Most speech classes consist of passive listeners who attend class not just to hear speeches, but also to receive academic credit. For these audiences, you should select an interesting topic and help your listeners understand its relevance to their lives.

3. **Selected Audiences** voluntarily and intentionally gather to hear about a topic (for example, wind surfing) or to hear a particular speaker (such as a famous author). A **homogenous audience** is composed of members who share an attitude, whether positive or negative. Speaking to an audience with a positive attitude can be fun, but you must develop your ideas clearly, so that listeners understand and accept them. Facing a negative or **hostile audience** presents an entirely different set of challenges.

4. **Concerted audiences** voluntarily listen because they basically agree that the subject is important but don't know what to do about it. They need someone to motivate them and provide specific directions. For example, students, parents, and educators gather at the state capitol to protest cutbacks in education funding. There, speakers urge them to organize letter writing campaigns, coordinate additional protests, and so on.

5. **Organized audiences** already know about the topic and are motivated and committed to act but need specific "how-to" instructions.

6. **Absent audiences** are intentional listeners separated in distance and time who are reached through various media. These are listeners to mediated messages, who gather to watch and listen to a president's inaugural speech or a movie star's personal announcement.

Within these categories of audiences are sub categories that may be worth identifying, depending on the speech purpose and the desired specificity of the speaker in addressing certain issues directly to certain sub groups of an audience. As the case may be, the speaker should be careful not to stereotype audience members in an attempt to segment them. General characteristics observed are influenced by situation and time, and do not totally capture the entire nature of each audience member, who may share various attributes within and outside their identified sub group.

Audience Sociology

Audience members can also be classified demographically, that is, they can be categorized based on their membership in certain population groups. The assumption is that these different categories or groupings may and often lead to variations in attitudes, beliefs, and, perhaps behaviors. Regardless of the variations you may find in an audience two facts remain. According to DeVito (2006), among all the qualities that might be said to characterize today's audiences, two stand out: uniqueness (no audience is like any other audience) and diversity (audiences are never truly homogenous).

Sex/Gender

Audience members or listeners can be categorized as males and females, which is biological differentiation of the sexes based on physical and anatomical differences. Gender on the other hand is a social classification that measures social behaviors rather than a person's biology. This means that a person can be female, but may exhibit masculine tendencies and behavior, while a male may exhibit the opposite which is feminine. As communication is classified as a humanity and social science and since the subject of study of social scientists is behavior and social-cultural tendencies, the **masculine- feminine** classification is more appropriate. This leads us to other social tendencies that may be a combination of both feminine and masculine traits—the **androgynous** classification. There is also the **undifferentiated** classification, which portrays the behaviors that cannot be grouped as either feminine or masculine. For audience analysis purposes, we should note that more females are identified with feminine tendencies and more males with masculine tendencies according to cultural labeling. In other words, cultural socialization processes orient boys and girls into different roles and expectations in most societies, though there is considerable change in and blurring of these roles in contemporary societies.

Race is another demographic or social variable that may and often lead to different perceptions and expectations of audiences. Although race represents external features such as skin and facial structures of people distributed in different clusters in regions of the world, scientists believe that humans internally, albeit genetically are 99.9% the same. Often considered along with race is **ethnicity**, which is a subset of race that represents the cultural heritage of a people. This is a more consequential classification for audience–speech adaptation than race. Here we believe that culture influences perception, beliefs, and opinions. There is the danger, though, of generalizing about the nature of cultural groups, in that we may assume that everyone from such a culture, behaves the same way or would have the same opinions as other members within the cultural heritage. In other words, while attempting to segment audiences on the basis of cultural heritage, we should not stereotype such audience members. For example, one cannot assume that all Chinese love rice, or all Irish like to drink alcohol, or that all Italians are gangsters, or that all Nigerians are fraudsters.

Avoid ethnocentric condescending as well. This occurs when the speaker subtly or even ignorantly measures others' cultural practices against his or hers and deems such to be inferior or less sophisticated. It helps to understand that one's culture is relative, unique and different, not necessarily inferior or superior to another.

Age is an important variable in classifying audiences. Age ranges represent generational differences that may predict shifts in interests, preferences as a result of changes in beliefs, values, and even behavior. If the 'times are changing,' so are the views of people of different times: they are equally changing.

The recent result of the American election that puts Barack Obama, the first African American President, in the US White House, is a testimony to the relevance of age in decision making. People of different generations think and act differently. The

Obamites are relatively young people, many of whom are college educated Americans who have transcended the barriers of race, gender and partisan politics.

Speaking to an audience of Generation Xers or the Face book generation requires a different level of understanding than that of, say the Baby Boomers. If you're asked to speak about the Ailing American Economy to two different groups of students, one consisting of elementary school children and the other, graduate students, using age as the denominator, you would have to prepare two distinctly different speeches.

Audience classification on the basis of age is not new. Marketers and advertisers classify customers or consumers based on this variable and develop behavior patterns that typify them in order to develop and tailor relevant and appropriate persuasive messages that will induce them to buy products and services.

Culture is an all-encompassing phenomenon; it is the way of life of a people, who occupy a geographic space and, who have spurned a way of life, which is clearly distinct from another. The elements of culture include language, type of government, marriage traditions, education experience, clothing, food, music, religion, artifacts, and belief systems. The import of culture is derived from the directing and controlling influence it has on the members of such social construction. It separates and differentiates insiders from outsiders in terms of appearance, orientations, and expectations. These influences of culture on people call for its evaluation when one is to speak to different cultural groups. In the American communication tradition, it is acceptable and advised that a person should voice his opinions even in public when one is in disagreement with someone else's ideas and stand on issues, regardless of the age and status of that individual. But in many oriental cultures, it is disrespectful for such public display of "discord" or dissension in public. Such a public "outburst" will cause the other to lose face, especially the older person. There are attitudinal and behavioral variations in people and culture becomes the determinant variable. As such, the identification and evaluation of cultural differences would allow the speaker to be more sensitive to the needs of culturally diverse audiences and consequently communicate more effectively with them.

The **Education** level of the audience member is important to know so that the speaker's message may be tailored accordingly. Different speech topics appeal to audiences of different educational backgrounds. Again, education level would determine the liberty with which the speaker may use sophisticated or simplistic language in conveying a point or presenting an argument within the speech.

The ultimate goal of the speaker is to reduce as much noise as possible in the process of communication and, as such, should be mindful of the role of semantic noise in confusing and losing an audience. Semantic noise occurs when communicators do not interpret the words being exchanged within the same sphere of understanding, such that one may be at great variance with the other. The speaker can certainly not afford to disaffect the audience with restricted and esoteric words, and in the same manner, cannot afford to insult the intelligence of the listeners, who have some measure of high level education, with rather simplistic argumentation or illustration in a speech.

Occupation. The social or occupational roles people play in society influence how they think and perceive others and how they themselves are viewed and perceived by others. Therefore, a person's occupation presents a purview from which to evaluate and categorize him or her either psychologically and or socially. Presenting a speech about the latest research findings in medicine to a group of medical practitioners will generate more interest among them than if the same speech were to be given to a group of non-practitioners. There are speaking situations where differences in the occupation of the audience will be a salient factor in audience analysis and in others, it may not. However, there are usually common threads of influence among those who have shared a common practice, experience, and or training. This is also true of **Socio-economic status** as it is a unifying force of some audiences as differences in socio- economic levels would suggest differences in perceptions and expectations. In all, awareness of commonalities and differences is central to knowing, adapting, and to motivating a speech audience.

The reasons why people join groups should be considered important factors as well in stratifying an audience for the purpose of effectively communicating with its members.

Group affiliation or membership results from a number of factors such as similarity, complementary needs, interpersonal attraction and proximity. So membership in a group suggests solidarity, identification with group ideals, values, interests, and loyalty to the group. All these may influence the orientation and how willing to receiving new information a group member is and, perhaps, how susceptible to change that member may become. The speaker identifies the shared values and interests of the group members and speaks to such to generate a common mindset- a "we are one stance," to endear the audience to the speaker and the subject of the speech.

People who live in close proximity to one another may share more than some geographic commonalities. So, the **Regions/location** of the country where an audience comes from matters in estimating the socio-psychological dispositions of such listeners.

Audience Psychology

Psychology is the study of the human thought processes and behavior; it focuses on the individual and not the group. Audience psychology has to do with individual mindsets of an aggregate of people who form an audience. This mindset may be measured prior to or after a speech experience. This relates to the belief set, values, and attitudes of the listeners that embody how they may see and react to the speaker as well as the speaker's message. It is important to develop the audience's psychological profile in order to be able to relate and adapt such to the speech experience. After all, a speech is designed for an audience. Awareness of the audience's mindset would inform the speaker of how to proceed with organizing, and presenting her message content to bring about its desired effect. But this will be impossible if the speech is misaligned with the audience's belief and value system and general cognitive expectations. "The audience of a speech is likened to a piano and one has to know which key to play," Al Capp, as quoted in Metcalf (2000).

According to Metcalf (2000), there are five principle factors that can significantly influence listeners' reactions to a speech and these are: The audience's perception of the speaker, their perception of the topic, their needs and emotions, social groups to which they belong, and the occasion. All of these create a mindset in the listeners that significantly inform their attitudes, values, and beliefs about a particular speech experience.

Prior to the speech experience, the listeners or audiences have preconceived ideas about a speaker based on direct or precarious experience. So, a reputation of sort, either positive or negative, has been established of the speaker. This impression carries over to the speech situation and, as the case may be, influences the speaker's credibility positively or otherwise. Audience members do have an opinion regarding the topic of the public discourse. For example, the issue of health care reform in the United States is a volatile issue that has drawn much virulent debate and confrontations from proponents and opponents of the reform at town hall meetings throughout the country. The Democrat and Republican town hall meetings to promote or denigrate the healthcare reform proposed by President Barrack Obama witnessed stiff opposition with vociferous boos and negative cajoling that often drowned out the speakers. Although this is extreme reaction to an issue that calls for debate, it does speak to the need for organizers and speakers to gauge the audience's perceptions of the issue at hand in order to carefully plan, organize, and present such in a strategic manner to the audience.

Benjamin (1997) writes that it is difficult to make generalizations about audience psychology because of the diversity of receivers, but he identifies some general truths about audiences and lists them as:

Ten Generalizations About Receiver Psychology

1. Receivers expect rational support.
2. Audiences respond to emotions.
3. Receivers react to both source and the message.
4. Receivers expect a source's ideas to fit with their own experiences.
5. Receivers respond to other receivers.
6. Receivers generally want the source to succeed.
7. Receivers will cooperate with the source.
8. Receivers need structure.
9. Receivers will tend to go on mental holidays.
10. Receivers need stylized redundancy.

These generalizations will help you achieve great success in the public speaking enterprise if you take cognizance of them. After all, a speech is meant for the audience and if you have insight into their psychology, as elaborated by these generalizations, you will become knowledgeable in adapting your speech to the audience in order to adequately inform, persuade, and entertain them. Let us take a look at each of these audience psychology principles.

Generalization one claims that the audience expects rational support. That implies that because humans are logical and rational beings, they are biased in favor of logical and rational argumentation and decision making. They expect rational arguments based on evidence, either verbal or physical, to support any assertion or claim made by the speaker. As Toulmin would argue, it is not enough to present evidence to support a claim, you also need to link the evidence to the claim by the use of warrants. These are statements connecting the evidence to the claim. In other words, a claim must be based on evidence and evidence must be categorically linked to the claim in terms of warrant(s).

Rational decisions are usually slow, painstaking and systematic; therefore, the appeal to rationality must be to reason through evidence that will be examined carefully by the receivers. Aristotle was so aware of the need for rational argumentation in public speaking that he devoted great attention to writing extensively on logic and rational argumentation that he referred to as logos.

Again, Aristotle identified three kinds of proof in rhetoric and these are ethos, logos, and pathos. A combination of these will endear a speaker to an audience and cause them to accept the claims or arguments of a speaker. Here, *the second generalization has to do with audiences responding to emotional proof.* We humans are both rational and emotional beings. We are not always calculating and rational and business-like in every situation, but we are swayed also by emotions. Speakers are to present messages that not only appeal to human logic, they should also use human susceptibility to emotions advantageously. Taking stock of feelings, being aware of prevailing emotional status of the audience, and tapping into them will not only ease the perceived distance between speaker and audience, it will also connect with the audience's humanity by creating a link between the audience and messages that trigger positive connotations in them. You should not forget that an audience usually has positive disposition toward success, parents, children, good life, happiness, common good, freedom, individual rights, justice, equity, good health, having money, etc.

The third generalization is that the receiver reacts to both the source and the message. This is the proverbial messenger and message where the messenger is the speaker and the content of the speech, the message. It is advised that one should not crucify the messenger but the message. But how can you crucify the message and be totally at peace with the messenger? The lesson was taught by Aristotle and other scholars who have written extensively about the impact of the speaker on the message and its perception by an audience. Ethos is understood to be the speaker's believability by the audience—it is the sender's expertise, trustworthiness and attraction. All of these speaker credibility elements influence the receivers' perceptions of the speaker's message.

The lesson is that the speaker has the responsibility of presenting his or her content in the manner that will enhance his or her credibility. We have learned from speaker credibility studies some important lessons about this third generalization, and they are that:

1. High-credibility sources are generally more persuasive than low-credibility sources.
2. High–credibility sources often enhance the impact of high-quality evidence.
3. High-credibility sources may be more important in situations advocating substantial changes from currently held positions.
4. Strong arguments can work in the favor of a source with low credibility if the receiver remembers the argument.
5. Similarity, gender, and attractiveness (physical attractiveness, prestige, social standing, and influence) also influence persuasibility.

The fourth generalization is that receivers expect a source's ideas to fit with their own experiences. We all live in the real world where values, beliefs, and traditions rule our daily routines, and create a mental homeostasis or balance with which we comfortably navigate our complex world. Anything that will disturb this seemingly comfortable and balanced state of existence will be challenged and resisted. Therefore, a speech is expected to present arguments and ideas that will fit into the receiver's worldview. For example, our mindset is that the earth rotates on its axis in a clockwise direction, but if a speech were to suggest the opposite, it will take the dislodging of several years of concrete evidence and learning, and the presentation of incontrovertible evidence to begin to have people even take a second look at established facts. This may be a farfetched argument, but to suggest that there is evidence of water on the moon can be supported by recent probe discoveries that there is stone ice on the earth's satellite's surface.

The fifth generalization claims that receivers respond to other receivers. I call this the 'sowing a seed' phenomenon. When you're speaking to an audience or teaching a class, the moment one or some of the students or audience members start a complaint about say, how complex the information is, the complaint by the few has sown a seed that will "bear fruits" by spreading across the audience members. The same happens when an audience member expresses an emotion, either positive or negative; sooner, the whole audience will 'catch' the feeling. Emotions are rather contagious because as an audience member expresses it, it spreads.

Politicians are aware of this phenomenon and often use it to their advantage by 'hiring' touchy-feely listeners as members of their audience at political rallies. These are people who, on cue, react to every statement the politician utters with exaggerated approval and applause, and to which the other unsuspecting audience members would chorus either cheerfully or reluctantly because they do not want to contradict the prevailing mood of the audience. Benjamin states that "if a few people in the audience give a performer a standing ovation, we feel the urge to rise to our feet as well, even if we didn't think the performance was *that* great."

Receivers generally want the speaker to succeed is the sixth generalization. Often those who attend speech events are usually not vehemently opposed to the speech topic or they would not be there. Except if they are forced to attend, and this is a rare situation, audiences at worst will be apathetic to the speech topic rather be totally opposed to it. Our knowledge of cognitive dissonance informs us that if a situation is going to present uncomfortable stimuli, often we avoid such rather stay and be cognitively 'assaulted.' So in most of the cases, audience members really want the speaker to succeed. Again, audience members can empathize with the speaker putting himself or herself on the line to present a case, and rather than being hostile, they side with and wish for the effort to succeed.

Receivers will cooperate with the source. We all have witnessed situations whereby a speaker, who is relatively a stranger to the audience members, asks them to engage in certain behaviors in other to prove a point. And without much resistance and in the spirit of cooperation the audience would oblige the speaker. Why is this so? Does it have to do with group behavior? Benjamin puts it this way: "persuaders can count on the cooperation of the audience as long as the request is reasonable and does not single out an individual." The lesson here is that the speaker should engage and invite the audience to participate in the speech event because they are more willing to help the speaker in the process of informing or even persuading themselves.

Understanding the nature of perception will further help you to understand how humans impose structure on the information they receive. Not only is our exposure to information selective, our attention and retention of information are also selective processes. After stimuli selection, we tend to organize them according to the principles of *closure, similarity, and proximity*. Then we interpret information so organized according to three principles: past experience, new situations, and opinions of others. All these point to one fact, that *the receivers need structure* in the information they receive, and the speaker should, therefore, present information in capsules and logical manner to them. If a speech lacks structure, it will confound the listeners; if it lacks orderly flow, the audience will induce theirs and that may not be congruent with what the speaker intended. How many times have you followed a movie from plot to plot and scene to scene oblivious of the passage of time? What about watching a movie that you find its storyline difficult to follow? It is torture!

Receivers' information processing rate is put at about 400 words per minute while the average American speaker's rate is put at about 125 to 150 words per minute. The difference of the speaker's rate when contrasted with the receiver's rate is roughly a ratio of one to four. This difference is referred to as 'spare time.' Now, spare time can be an asset or liability depending on how it is put to use. *A listener who can process information faster than the speaker can deliver it has ample time to daydream and go on mental holidays.* Although a receiver may be looking straight at the speaker, there is no guarantee that he or she is listening because listening is a biological and internal process. As a matter of fact, the speaker may think that a listener is paying rapt attention to his speech, whereas the listener is far away in never land enjoying the images and sounds of nothingness—all these while pretending to listen.

There are strategies a speaker can use in the speech to utilize the listener's spare time positively. First, are devices within the speech to interest and keep the audience from engaging in external rapid thought. You should develop a good speech introduction with means of gaining the audience's attention such as a riveting story, a rhetorical question, alarming statistic, or a gripping quotation. You can preempt rapid thought by occupying the listener's spare time with a forecast of your main points which are to come in the speech. This will help them to anticipate what is to come in the speech instead of escaping into the oblivion. A transitional statement from the introduction to the body of the speech helps the listeners to structure and follow the speech in their minds. While in the speech body, engage them by previewing what to come, reviewing what they have been told, and announce signposts along the way to direct their minds according to your speech process traffic.

The way you word your ideas is also critical to the audience's ability to follow your line of thought and argument. We have already discussed the manner in which you present your main points and your supporting materials. Speech main points are claims and as such should be presented in short, easy to understand declarative sentences. Verbal evidence should be easy to follow and should create distinct images in the minds of your listeners. Statistical evidence should be broken into simple understandable percentages, ratios, and, perhaps, charts for ease of recognition. Complex numbers can be rounded off and large numbers can be reduced to percentiles. Remember that a combination of visual and auditory channels of presentation will keep your audience alive and interested in your presentation. Good articulation, enunciation, varied rate of speech and other paralinguistic cues will attract the attention of your audience. You should also not underestimate how you may use eye contact, gestures, good appearance, and other nonverbal variables to your advantage. In all, create interest in your speech by introducing something that is novel, relevant, and understandable to your audience.

Receivers need stylized redundancy. What is redundancy? This is not just repetition of materials just for the sake of it, but strategically repeating information in the course of the speech to recapture audience members you might have lost at any given time in your speech to inattention, random thought, or physical noise. As you have learned in this chapter, you present your speech in three segments: The introduction, body, and conclusion. If you follow the requirements of the introduction, you'll discover that in it you have to announce to the audience what you will tell them in the body of the speech. In the body of the speech, you tell them what you had announced to them that you will tell them. Even in the course of revealing to them what you had promised to tell them, you retell each main point by offering a quick summary of what you have told them so far. And in the conclusion, you remind them of what you had told them by summarizing, again, what you had told them and then reconnect with your opening and thesis statement.

As you repeat your ideas, you must vary them, you must make them appear fresh and immediate each time so that each time they hear it again, it is new and interesting. As you can see, the speech process is filled with repetition, strategic redundancy—all designed to cater to the poor listening habits of the audience.

Photoright: Whitehouse

"We must start from the simple premise that Africa's future is up to Africans... I say this knowing full well the tragic past that has sometimes haunted this part the world."--**President Barack Obama, Speaking to Ghana Parliament, on July 11, 2009.**

Table 11.1/ Points to Consider When Determining Speaking Role On a particular Occasion

1. Do your topic and general purpose suit the occasion?

2. What is the order of speaking, and where is your speech in that order?

3. What time of day do you speak- morning, afternoon, or evening?

4. What is the time limit of the speech?

5. Who is the featured speaker?

6. Will you be introduced to the audience, or must you introduce yourself?

7. How is the ceremony organized?

8. Is someone clearly in charge of the event?

9. Are there any customs or traditions associated with the event that you will be expected to know or to perform?

Source: Metcalf, Sheldon (2000). *Building A Speech* (4th ed.). Orlando: Harcourt Inc.

We know that people's needs motivate them to hold certain beliefs and such may propel them to hold certain views, values and consequently behave in a particular way. Knowledge of the needs and motivation of the audience will go a long way in intelligently adapting the speech—its claims and arguments to the audience.

Oftentimes, audience members are influenced by the social groups to which they belong. Such membership in social groups exemplifies their core beliefs, values and perceptions to the extent that they resist contrary beliefs, values and opinions. As we will learn more in the following chapters, an individual's decisions are influenced by both individual and social normative components. That is, a person's decisions are not solely his or hers, but are greatly influenced by the social pressures and influences he or she allows from significant others whose opinions are considered valuable to the individual. Therefore, a successful speech is that which speaks to the needs and motivations of the constituent social groups that audience members belong to. Social organizations such as MADD-Mothers Against Drunk Driving, NRA-National Rifle Association, and Religious organizations exert great influence on their members' perceptions.

The occasion for which a speech is designed also influences the mood of both the speaker and the audience, and will dictate the tone and language of the speech content. How might a speech given to commemorate the event of September the Eleventh (9/11) be different from a speech to mark the independence day of the United States? What about a speech at a wedding compared to that at a funeral? A speech at a birthday ceremony is (epideictic) and cannot be expected to castigate the celebrant. Metcalfe (2000) puts it best by writing that: "audiences attending events have certain expectations of speakers. They expect a graduation speaker to be warm and congratulatory. They expect a minister or priest to reinforce beliefs and include references to moral and spiritual values. They expect politicians to be more responsive to social and governmental concerns."

Gathering Audience Information

Information about the audience will reveal pertinent insights that a speaker would need in order to adapt to the nature of such audience in informing them. Such knowledge would be employed in managing the process of persuading the audience and, overall, be employed in structuring and presenting the speech to attain the maximum desired effect on the audience. Audience information is, therefore, critical in selecting a topic, narrowing the topic to the specific nuance of the audience, developing the speech thesis and main points and, selecting the type of evidence to use in supporting the claims of the speech.

Collecting audience information may be done in a number of ways. If the audience of a speech can be identified beforehand, then the speaker can research information about them from indirect **secondary sources** such as newspapers, books, magazines, or general descriptors available to those who invited the speaker to speak. Prior knowledge of the category of listeners can be further researched to apprise the speaker of the characteristics of such group. If they consist of educators, be it at the college or high school or elementary levels, there are secondary sources available where detailed information can be accessed about them. For instance, if an audience consists of community college professors, a quick visit to the website of some community colleges will yield descriptors of their professors, where they received their training, their income level, age range, tenured or non- tenured status and their areas of expertise.

On the other hand one can collect direct, primary information from the audience by asking them questions (**Survey Questions**) relevant to the speech topic and /or purpose, to which they will supply answers to be analyzed and used in the speech process. In some cases, a **personal interview** can be conducted. This is a research situation whereby the interviewer asks direct questions from the respondent and has the opportunity to probe inadequate answers, face-to-face, to obtain the desired information. This is a rather time consuming process and it does not allow for surveying a pool of people who usually constitute an audience.

A rather economical way to collect large pool of information from a large number of people within a short period of time is the structured, often self-administered survey. The instrument for collecting such data is called the **questionnaire**. It contains different types of questions including two general categories of demographical or **sociological questions**, designed to elicit information such as age, income, ethnicity, education levels, interest, membership in various organizations, religion, geographic location, and general socio-economic status data. The second category is the opinion or **psychological questions**, designed to gauge attitudes, beliefs, values, and general mental orientation of the potential audience members.

Scholars combine sociological and psychological questions in their studies because of the relationships that have been established between the two. Sociological variables of age, income, religion, ethnicity, and the like are reasonable motivators that influence values, opinions, and beliefs of people. In other words sociological data serve as premises that predict psychological responses. In more analytical and predictive studies, responses to these two types of questions are cross-validated and their correlations calculated through sophisticated statistical measures.

Types of Questions

Within each category of questions, there are different types. There are **open-ended, close and scaled questions.** Open –ended questions invite the respondent to freely give an opinion without restraint—this allows for a quick study of the general orientation of the audience members toward the speech topic. It also allows for collecting background information on the possible motivations that can be used to influence (in case of persuasive speeches) the audience. The key to this is that the interviewer may control the wording of the question, but not the variety of ways the audience may respond to such. For example, general open-ended questions about "Gun Control" may include the following:

1. What is your opinion about the rights of individuals to carry weapons?
2. Should the government limit the rights of individuals to bear arms.
3. Do you believe the idea that "guns don't kill, but people do"?
4. Is any form of gun control necessary in today's society?
5. How can the society protect itself from gun related homicides?

The answers to these questions can be analyzed into different themes as they have been designed to estimate the respondents' positions on "Gun Control." Easily the interviewer can assess the prevailing attitude of the audience toward this topic and plan the speech to address, confirm, refute, or reinforce these attitudes.

Close-ended questions are designed to elicit specific responses from the interviewee, especially on a topic that is as polarizing as "Gun Control." The researcher designs close ended questions to elicit specific answers that will help determine specific values, valence or weight, either positive or negative, of the opinions of the respondents. It is one thing to be generally against gun control and another to answer no or never to "any attempt to restrict access to guns." As you can see, this type of question forces the respondent to answer yea or nay, thereby firmly committing himself to a position on the issue. Here are some examples based on the set of questions used above:

1. Do individuals have the right to carry weapons. Yes or No?
2. Government should not limit the rights of individuals to bear arms. Yes or No?
3. "Guns don't kill, people do, True or False?
4. Gun control is not necessary in today's society. True or False?
5. Society has a right to protect its members by limiting access to guns. Agree or Disagree?

While these types of questions may be good in obtaining specific information from the respondents, you would be hard pressed to find people whose responses are so clear cut on issues of much debate and argumentation.

In order to solve the problems associated with **forced response questions** or close-ended questions scaled questions allow respondents to choose a position that they agree with the most among several choices or, better still, place a value on their level of agreement. Attitudes are measured along a continuum or scale as in the **Likert Scale or The Semantic Differential Measurement** of Charles Osgood, et al (1957).

Likert Scale Example:

Directions: Identify which position you're most comfortable with when it comes to the issues in the questions below.

The Topic is Gun Control

1. Individuals have the right to bear arms.
    _____ Strongly Agree
    _____ Agree
    _____ Undecided
    _____ Disagree
    _____ Strongly Disagree

2. Government should not limit the rights of individuals to bear arms.
    _____ Strongly Agree
    _____ Agree
    _____ Undecided
    _____ Disagree
    _____ Strongly Disagree

3. Guns don't kill, people do.
    _____ Strongly Agree
    _____ Agree
    _____ Undecided
    _____ Disagree
    _____ Strongly Disagree

4. Gun control is not necessary in today's society.
    _____ Strongly Agree
    _____ Agree
    _____ Undecided
    _____ Disagree
    _____ Strongly Disagree

5. Society has a responsibility to protect its citizens by limiting access to guns.
    _____ Strongly Agree
    _____ Agree
    _____ Undecided
    _____ Disagree
    _____ Strongly Disagree

As mentioned earlier, Likert (1932) developed an answer to the overly restricted two-choice answers of "Yes or No" by developing a scale that offers variety of responses, specifically five on a variety of topics, thereby allowing for the different grades of attitudinal responses to be identified for such questions. According to Gass and Seiter (1999), "a Likert scale consists of a series of declarative statements, pertaining to some attitude object, followed by a continuum of choices ranging from "strongly agree" to "strongly disagree."

The advantage of this scale lies in its major tenet which is that there is equal distance between each of the scales, making for mathematical calculations to be possible, thereby allowing for statistical comparisons of respondents attitudes. On a 5-point Likert Scale, attitudes can be graduated such that a "strongly agree" or "strongly disagree" response can attract the value of 5 while "agree" or "disagree" may attract 4, etc. The average value of the responses can be added to provide an aggregate value of a group of respondents' reactions to a question as in the above example.

As Gass and Seiler (1999) observed, 'specialized versions of this scale have been developed to measure teaching effectiveness, job satisfaction, marital satisfaction, ethnocentrism, verbal aggressiveness, homophobia, dogmatism, and communication anxiety." It is needless to say that all of these topics are possible public speech topics.

Semantic Differential Scale Example

Directions: Check your exact position on the scale relating to the issue identified below.

Gun Control

Good	_	_	_	_	_	_	_	Bad
Responsible	_	_	_	_	_	_	_	Irresponsible
Constitutional	_	_	_	_	_	_	_	Unconstitutional
Achievable	_	_	_	_	_	_	_	Unachievable
Important	_	_	_	_	_	_	_	Unimportant
Constructive	_	_	_	_	_	_	_	Destructive
Positive	_	_	_	_	_	_	_	Negative
Acceptable	_	_	_	_	_	_	_	Unacceptable
Futuristic	_	_	_	_	_	_	_	Retrogressive

Charles Osgood, Percy Tannenbaum, and George Suci, in 1957 developed this scale for measuring attitudes, in essence, the denotative interpretations of respondents to bi-polar adjectives or opposite words, usually separated by seven spaces of equal value. The respondents identify the exact "semantic" space on the continuum between the sets of opposite words where they place their "meaning" or overall attitude in regard of the subject, issue, or person being evaluated. The different positions of each respondent are summed up as an average overall attitudinal disposition to the topic of study. Because it is easy to assign numerical values to these different positions in-between a set of opposite words, and because the semantic spaces are assumed to be equal, mathematical calculations can be made about the general attitudes of respondents to the topic of a speech, thus yielding statistics that can be incorporated into the speech. Again, as the middle point across all of the elements in the scale is the undecided, responses that cluster to either side of the scale can indicate approval or disapproval of the topic under measurement.

Sample Survey Questionnaire

Usually, a questionnaire will combine all of the different types of questions in one survey, making it a rather efficient way to collect audience information. However, there are guidelines to follow when using such an instrument.

- Survey questions must be brief and address one single issue at a time in order not to confuse the respondent.
- Questions must be worded clearly in simple easy to understand manner (The respondent must not require a dictionary to understand what it is asking)
- Questions must not lead the respondent to a predetermined answer that the respondent desires.
- The questions must be ordered in a progression that would be easy to follow.
- The entire survey should not take too much time to complete.
- There must be space enough for the respondents to indicate their answers.
- Must include demographical and psycho graphical questions
- Must include the different types of questions and scales.

Sample Combined Questionnaire

Name (Optional):_____

Age_____ Sex_____ Political Party_____ Education Level_____

Please check your answers in the following questions:

1. Do individuals have the right to carry weapons?
    _____ Yes _____No _____Not sure
2. Government should not limit the rights of individuals to bear arms.
    _____ Yes _____ No _____Not sure
3. "Guns don't kill, people do."
    _____ True _____ False _____Not sure
4. Gun control is not necessary in today's society.
    _____True _____ False _____Not sure
5. Society has a right to protect its members by limiting access to guns.
    _____Agree _____Disagree _____Not sure

Directions: Identify which position you're most comfortable with when it comes to the issues in the questions below.

The Topic is Gun Control

6.   Individuals have the right to bear arms.
        ____ Strongly Agree
        ____ Agree
        ____ Undecided
        ____ Disagree
        ____ Strongly Disagree

7.   Government should not limit the rights of individuals
        to bear arms.
        ____ Strongly Agree
        ____ Agree
        ____ Undecided
        ____ Disagree
        ____ Strongly Disagree

8.   Guns don't kill, people do.
        ____ Strongly Agree

9.   Gun control is not necessary in today's society.
        ____ Strongly Agree

_____ Agree
_____ Undecided
_____ Disagree
_____ Strongly Disagree

10. Society has a responsibility to protect its citizens by
limiting access to guns.
_____ Strongly Agree
_____ Agree
_____ Undecided
_____ Disagree
_____ Strongly Disagree
_____ Agree
_____ Undecided
_____ Disagree
_____ Strongly Disagree

Directions: Check your exact position on the scale relating to the issue identified below.

Gun Control

Good	__	__	__	__	__	__	Bad
Responsible	__	__	__	__	__	__	Irresponsible
Constitutional	__	__	__	__	__	__	Unconstitutional
Achievable	__	__	__	__	__	__	Unachievable
Important	__	__	__	__	__	__	Unimportant
Constructive	__	__	__	__	__	__	Destructive
Positive	__	__	__	__	__	__	Negative
Acceptable	__	__	__	__	__	__	Unacceptable
Futuristic	__	__	__	__	__	__	Retrogressive

The Personal Interview

Interviewing is an exchange of information during a conversation between an interviewer and an interviewee. It is designed to gain valuable information from a competent source about a subject of study or a speech topic. Journalists use interviews to collect information from eye witnesses to provide different views to balance their news stories. Public speakers use the interview as a research tool to gather necessary expert ideas, testimonies, and declarations and stories, which they will incorporate into their speeches.

An interview is a face-to-face interaction involving the exchange of questions and answers on topics of interest to both the speaker and the expert source. The process of the interview is rather complex and requires some know-how to make it a success. This process can be divided into three parts: Necessary activities before, during, and after the interview. The following are a series of advice a speaker should heed when conducting an interview to solicit information to be incorporated into a particular speech.

The most important consideration before you set out to interview your source is to determine the purpose of the exercise. This will direct you as to which questions are necessary to ask and why. Doing prior research helps you to acquire some information about the subject of your interview, and some necessary information about the interviewee. Determine which questions are not necessary to ask because you can easily find answers to them by consulting available documents and other secondary sources. Do not waste your time and that of your interviewee by asking irrelevant questions.

As an interviewer, you're supposed to be as neutral as possible, not biased and confrontational. Avoid **leading questions** as well as **loaded questions** and remember that you're a researcher and not an interrogator.

At the onset of the interview, you should establish rapport with your respondent because he or she will be more than willing to reveal information to you if she feels comfortable with you and the interview process. Stay focused and attentive in the process of the interview, probing insufficient answers and asking follow-up questions to clarify points and ideas. If you both agree to the use of a tape recorder, record the interview for ease of reference and accurate quotations.

At the end of the interview, thank the interviewee for collaborating with you in your effort to present accurate and reliable information to your audience. You have a duty to transcribe your interview accurately and to adequately represent the expert's opinions as contained in the interview. Reference must be made to the source's expertise when you quote information from the interview in your speech. The format for **verbal referencing** of sources in your speech is as follows. Let us imagine that your expert is Dr. Steven L. Epstein, a professor of Communication at Suffolk Community College, whom you interviewed for s speech on "The Internet as a Source of Scholastic Information." At the appropriate point of reference in your speech, you can quote what he said in the interview in this manner:

According to Dr. Steven L. Epstein, a professor of Communication at Suffolk Community College in New York, *"the internet is a great source of information for research, but much of the information on the web, unlike such in the library, has not been edited or sourced by reputable contributors."*

In the written reference page of the speech, an interview source can be cited in different ways depending on the citation style used. To reference your interview with Dr. Epstein, you should format it this way:

MLA: Steven L. Epstein. Personal Interview. 16th Oct. 2009.

APA: S. Epstein (Personal Communication, October 16, 2009).

Considering the Speech Situation

Environment

Having information about the audience is not an end by itself, but adequately using it to shape and direct the speech is paramount. Of great importance also is information about the environment in which a speech is to take place. If you are invited to give a speech, you may want to inquire about the location. Is the venue an auditorium, a classroom, a hall and how big is it? Will the audience fit perfectly into the environment or are many of the seats going to be empty? What about sound amplification? Does the auditorium have a public address system and if so, will it be functioning properly by the time you're to speak? Are the lighting and ventilation systems working normally? The audience as well as the speaker must feel comfortable in the environment where they are expected to engage in the acts of speaking and listening. You must ensure that the venue is appropriate, has minimum noise, is large enough (relative to the audience size) and does not in any way impede the speaking exercise.

Time

There are many dimensions to be considered when giving a speech. The first time consideration has to do with the timeliness of the topic. It is of no use spending valuable time and resources discussing issues that are out of date and time, an issue whose relevance has run its course. Events may preempt the timeliness of a speech topic, for example, giving a speech to group of high school students on "**How to Prepare for and Ace the ACT Examination**," just after they sat for the examination is rather misplaced in terms of time.

Another consideration is the time of day the speech is to take place. From my experience as a college professor, I find that my early morning students respond differently to my lectures than my midday and evening students. The midday students are in their last class before lunch time and are unwilling to cooperate with me should the class run very close to the end of the assigned time. The evening students on the other hand are somewhat lethargic, feeling heavy having just had lunch. Needless to say that my early morning students are more alert and take me little or no effort to motivate than my other students. Again, this is coupled with the fact that I am fresher, more alert in the morning as a professor and this may also play a great role in my perception of the different students I see at different times of the day. Speeches have to be adapted to the time of day it is to be given to ensure maximum participation of the audience who may be motivated differently by the time of the day an event takes place.

The third consideration is a phenomenon called **cultural time** (see part one of the book). People of different cultures, even co-cultures perceive and use time differently. Different time orientations mean that people would behave in consonance with their group's conception, perception, and performance expectations. Generally, Americans are considered **monochronic** people, who are governed by schedules, and who view time as commodity to be used wisely, hence every minute counts! But not every culture is so driven to use time as Americans do. Many countries of Africa, Middle East and South America have a more relaxed view and use of time. Why is this important to you as a speaker? Well, imagine that you're to give a speech to a culturally diverse group of people who include the different nationalities mentioned above. Some would arrive at your speech location some fifteen minutes before it starts, while others would not find it inappropriate to "join the speech" twenty minutes after you had started!

Audience Size

The size of your audience matters to the success of your speech. How large the location of your speech is directly relates to the number of people who are going to fit into that location. The size of the audience will affect your ability to directly connect, face-to-face with them. A large crowd can easily be distracted because many of them will not have intimate relation to the speaker because of distance to the speaking podium and lack of direct eye contact with them. Such large crowds would require a functioning public address system and display materials large enough to be seen from the back of the auditorium or the back of the crowd. But the speaker can turn the situation around by varying the location from where the speech is delivered, and from time to time connecting with audience members in different sections of the crowd to make them a part of the experience rather than just speaking to and maintaining rapport with those audience members who are in the front rows of the location.

Review Questions

1. **Identify and discuss three reasons why knowledge of the audience will prove useful to the public speaker.**
2. **What are the differences between primary and secondary data?**
3. **What is a questionnaire and why does it usually contain both sociological and psychological questions?**
4. **Describe the advantages and disadvantages of open-ended, forced response, and scaled questions.**
5. **Compare the Likert Scale to the Semantic Differential Scale.**
6. **Develop a combined questionnaire for your speech audience analysis.**
7. **Why is the speech situation analysis necessary before you give your speech?**

Chapter Twelve

Identifying and Researching the Speech Topic

Audience consideration is very important to the success of a public speech and the one thing that is most important in ensuring the interest of the audience is a relevant topic. There is no amount of preparation and strategizing that may be employed within the contents of a speech to entice and keep the audience. If the topic is of no importance and relevance to them, the speaker labors in vain. This is to emphasize the importance of selecting a topic that is of interest to the listeners. A speech topic that suits their purpose, interest, desire, will motivate them not only to pay attention, but also to actively participate in processing and retaining the information garnered. Indeed, there is no substitute for a relevant and appropriate topic in the success of speaking to inform, persuade and possibly entertain.

The speech topic must meet three important criteria: *It should suit the occasion perfectly and be relevant to the prevailing circumstances; it must appeal to the audience, either directly as something that impinges on their values, beliefs, and general human nature, or something that resolves a conflict or answers a question in their mind, and; it should get the speaker to become more knowledgeable of the speech topic and motivate and instill confidence in the speaker's position on the topic.* A speech topic should present something new, fresh, and engaging to the audience; it should expand their horizon and prime their desire to know. A topic may be commonplace, but it must present a new twist to something or a new nuance that will attract the audience. For example, we all know the Honey Bee, but a speech on this common creature could expose the audience to something about the honey bee that is not so common after all. The speech may be titled: **The Secret Lives of the Honey Bee**. This is as intriguing as it is novel.

Choosing a speech topic is like choosing a town in which one wants to live. Everything you do and become in the town is dependent on the fact that you chose to live there in the first place. A good speech, therefore, starts with a good, relevant topic. A speaker should naturally go from the known to the unknown. A topic that you have some knowledge about is a good place to start. This is because it provides a base from which you can launch into other not too familiar areas. Familiarity with the topic grows the speaker's confidence and saves the time and anxiety that accompanies the search for a brand new topic. On the other hand, you may choose a topic for its novelty value—it's new and interesting and useful. Therefore, the first thing to consider when choosing a speech topic is who you are and what you know.

Questions to ask yourself when choosing a topic according to Gamble and Gamble (2010) will include:

Is the topic worthwhile?
Is the topic appropriate?
Is the topic interesting?
Is there sufficient information on the topic?

Brainstorming

This is the practice of accessing information about yourself in your mind and jotting it down as fast as you can. What are your hobbies, job experience, skills, interesting people you have met, a unique experience you've had, and things that are fascinating to you? Do you live in an urban area, suburb or a farmland? Do you watch television or go to the movies; read newspapers or surf the net? What political party do you belong to and why? Do you particularly enjoy drinking milk or coffee? The list goes on.
When you write all these ideas down without attempting to analyze them, you usually will come up with a handful and from this list, one or two will appeal to you the most.

Consider Your Academic Experience

Students of public speaking usually do not take just one course in college; their academic experience is rather eclectic in that they take courses in different academic areas from which they can draw speech topics. From Biology and Genetics is the issue of the human genome; from Philosophy is the discourse on ethics and religion; History has different stages in human development; Mathematics and physics speculate about the existence of several dimensions other than the commonly known three. Anthropology has exotic places and cultures to explore while Sociology has personalities such as Pareto, Emile Durkheim and Economics has topics such as capitalism, economy of scale, international trade, etc. Indeed, every college endeavor has potential topics that are inexhaustible.

The 'Bucket List' Method of Choosing Speech Topics

In the comedic movie the *Bucket List*, starring Morgan Freeman and Jack Nicholson, as Carter Chambers and Edward Cole respectively, fate places these seemingly different men together in the same hospital room where they are receiving treatment for the same ailment. terminal cancer. This is Edward Coles' hospital, which he had built and that had made him a billionaire. Carter is an auto mechanic, who had to drop out of college to take any job he could find because his wife was expecting a baby. Carter's two scores plus years of work as a mechanic has its reward of a loving, happy, and healthy family. Whereas, Cole has had four failed marriages and is estranged with his only daughter.

As the adventure of the two men continues in the hospital, Edward notices

Carter scribbling what Carter calls a **"bucket list,"** a reference to an assignment a teacher once gave him in college, which asked the students to make a list of things they wanted to do before they died. Wealthy Edwards decides that this list is something the men can accomplish together. Carter, reticent of the idea of two cancer-infested, terminally ill old men embarking on such an adventure to accomplish the to-do list before the end of their lives, resisted the wild idea. Well, persistent Edward convinces Carter, and against the stance of Carter's livid wife, the old men set out to accomplish the bucket list.

When my colleague, Alyssa Kauffman, informed me of the 'bucket list' assignment she gives to her Intro. to Communication students, and showed me some of the lists the students came up with, I quickly realized that they are, indeed, very good speech topics. And we both thought of this as a good method for students to use to generate their speech topics. This is a good method for two reasons: One, students will enthusiastically and quickly identify five or ten things they would like to do before they die as in the 'bucket list.' Two, these must be items the students are passionate about and would be more than willing to research and present speeches to inform or persuade or even entertain on.

Newspapers, Magazines and the International News on Television

Newspaper headlines tell stories that can be developed into speeches. Consider the following:

"Iran Defies the World—Tests Long Range Missiles"
"Agriculture in the US has Become a Labor of Love"
"Ghadafi Engages the World in a Ninety-minute Speech"
"Mob Kills Teen in Chicago."
"Drone Kills Insurgents Near Tora Bora"
"War Persists in Darfur"

These are possible headlines you could find in a day's supply of newspapers and magazines. And if you're literate about international affairs, you have access to a fountain of topics on international events, politics, diplomacy and competition. Often, audiences are intrigued about events happening in foreign lands because they often open up their vista to the rest of the world and inform them of the humanity of other people from other places.

Reference Materials

Reference materials are available to you to search for topics on almost anything you're interested in. Encyclopedias, The American Heritage Dictionaries, and other periodical database are great sources for speech topics. You can begin your search by selecting a letter of the alphabet and record topics and titles that you can find in any of these source materials. You will be surprised as to how quickly you can generate several potential speech topics.

Other sources of possible topics and materials for a speech are library computer software programs such as Infotrac and Periodical Abstract Ondisc, in which magazine titles and summaries are stored.

Internet Search

The internet has really revolutionized access to information in the modern electronic age. The global network of computers that contain databases is referred to as the World Wide Web shortened as WWW. There are search engines which provide various forms of information that you can easily access. Especially useful are topic-related search engines which can yield relevant information on any topic you might be interested in. The common search engines are:

Lycos (www.lycos.com)
Go.com (www.go.com)
Alta-Vista (www.altavista.com)
Google (www.google.com)
Yahoo! (www.yahoo.com)
Excite (www.excite.com)
Info seek (www. the frontpage.com/search/infoseek.html)
Ask (www.ask.com)

Meta search engines include:

Dogpile (www.dogpile.com)
Mamma.com (www.mamma.com)

Note that these web addresses are usually referred to as uniform resource locators (URLs).
A common source of speech topics online is www.ablongman.com/devito

You have to be aware of some of the dangers of using materials sourced from the world- wide web. Websites are databases –electronic storage facilities for information— which are usually not subjected to critical, academic vetting by a committee of learned individuals from the appropriate discipline, as it is usually the case with works found in academic journals and books by reputable authors and publishers. Almost anyone can post information on the internet, thus posing a challenge for the user, who must verify the accuracy and validity of the information before use. As a speaker, credibility is your watchword and, as such, you cannot risk presenting inaccurate information to your audience.

A critically minded student would develop a way of evaluating the quality of information accessed on the internet in order to isolate the valid and the reliable. Epstein and Barr (2007) identify the criteria for evaluating website content and these have to do with the following:

- Accuracy: How reliable is the information?
- Authority: Who is the author and what are his or her credentials?
- Objectivity: Does the website present a balanced or biased point of view?
- Coverage: Is the information comprehensive enough for your needs?
- Currency: Is the website up to date?

Additional criteria are:
- Publisher, documentation, scope, audience, appropriateness of format, and navigation.
- Judging whether the site is made-up of primary (original) or secondary (interpretive) sources.
- Determining whether the information is relevant to your research.

Epstein and Barr further expand on the relevant questions to ask when examining website information. These questions are the traditional ways to verify a paper source, but can be applied to web-sourced information as well.

To determine the **Accuracy** of web -sourced information, the questions to ask are the following:

- Is the information reliable?
- Do the facts from your research contradict the facts you find on this web page?
- Do misspellings and /or grammar mistakes indicate a hastily put together Web site that has not been checked for accuracy?
- Is the content on the page verifiable through some other source? Can you find similar facts elsewhere (journals, books, other online sources) to support the facts you see on this Web page?
- Do you find links to other Web sites on similar topic? If so, check those links to ascertain whether they back up the information you see on the Web page you're interested in using.
- Is a bibliography of additional sources for research provided? Lack of bibliography doesn't mean the page isn't accurate, but having one allows further investigation points to check the information.
- Does the site of a research document or study explain how the data was collected and the type of research method used to interpret the data?

To determine the **Authority** behind the information source on the Web, you should ask the following questions:

- Who is responsible for the content of the page? Although a webmaster's name is often listed, this person is not necessarily responsible for the content.
- Is the author recognized in the subject area? Does this person cite any other publications he or she has authored?
- Does the author list his or her background or credentials (e.g., Ph.D. degree, title such as professor, or other honorary or social distinction)?
- Is there a way to contact the author? Does the author provide a phone number or email address?
- If the page is mounted by an organization, is it a known, reputable one?
- How long has the organization been in existence?
- Does the URL for the Web page end in the extension .edu or .org? Such extensions indicate authority compared to .coms (.com), which are commercial enterprises. (For example, www.cancer.com takes you to an online drugstore that has a cancer information page; www.cancer.org is the American cancer Society Web site.)

Objectivity questions to ask are as follows:

- Is the purpose of the site clearly stated, either by the author or the organization authoring the site?
- Does the site give a balanced viewpoint or present only one side?
- Is the information directed toward a specific group of viewers
- Does the site contain advertising?
- Does the copyright belong to a person or an organization?
- Do you see anything to indicate who is funding the site?

In terms of **Coverage** the questions to ask are:

- Does the author present both sides of the story or is a piece of the story missing?
- Is the information comprehensive enough for your need?
- Does the site cover too much, too generally?
- Do you need more specific information than the site can provide?
- Does the site have an objective approach?

In terms of **Currency** the questions to ask are:

- Does the site indicate when the content was created?
- Does the content contain a last revised date? How old is the date?
- Does the author state how often he or she revises the information? Some sites are on a monthly update cycle (e.g., government statistics page).
- Can you tell specifically what content was revised?

- Is the information still useful for your topic? Even if the last update is old, the site might still be worthy of use *if* the content is still valid for your research.

In terms of **Relevance** to your research: primary versus secondary sources, the questions to ask are:
- Is it a primary or secondary source?
- Do you need a primary source?
- Does the assignment require you to cite different types of sources? For example, are you supposed to use at least one book, one journal article, and one Web page?

A shortcut to finding high –quality Web sites according to Epstein and Barr (2007) is using subject directories and meta-sites, which select the Web sites they index by similar evaluation criteria to those just described.

Narrowing Your Topic

A speech topic must be manageable within the timeframe given to deliver it. A topic too broad can hardly be adequately dealt with to the satisfaction of both the speaker and the audience. Whether you decide to speak or you're invited to speak, you need to tailor your speech to the time allotted and to be specific as much as you can in the range of issues and ideas you cover in the speech.

Narrowing the speech topic to a manageable form achieves two goals: the audience can anticipate specific contents of the speech and are motivated to pay attention and listen. Again, the speaker has a specific road map to follow and, with adequate preparation, can gain mastery of the specifics which will aid in the delivery of the speech.

Imagine a speech assignment on the general topic: "The United States of Africa." What is this topic all about and what does the speaker intend to do with this broad subject? The answer is in narrowing the topic and focusing it on some specifics. "The Arguments In Favor of the United States of Africa," is a more focused title as its goal is advancing arguments in favor of the Union. But 'arguments in favor' are several and will take an awful long time to flesh out. Now, this can use further focusing if a number of arguments are identified and not just 'general arguments." "The Three Major Arguments in Favor of The United States of Africa" is a better manageable topic because it is mindful of how protracted an argument can be, so it is limited to three. As the case may be, the topic could be refocused as "The Major Challenges of a United States of Africa." Again, the problem here is the classification of challenges: are they political or economic challenges? Mindful of the limited time to present a speech and the need to be specific in order to direct and control the attention of the audience members, the final speech topic in this example should read like this: **"The Three Major Economic Advantages of A United States of Africa."**

To reiterate an illustration used earlier in the book, let us review the narrowing of the topic such as **"Cancer: A Deadly Disease."** Suffice it to say that there are different forms of cancer, such as ovarian, pancreatic, brain, breast, lungs, etc. So, which form of cancer is the speech focusing on? The topic should be focused on specifics forms of cancer or the title be worded to narrow its scope. The title can then read: **"The Deadliest Forms of Cancer."**

At the onset of the speech exercise, identifying the purpose for speaking will help in narrowing the speech topic by focusing on what the speaker wants to achieve by giving the speech. As has been noted earlier, the **general speech purposes are to inform, persuade and entertain**. By keeping your purpose in focus, you can specifically identify the major ideas you want to present and how you will adapt them to the nature of your audience. The **specific purpose** will direct your speech in terms of seeking relevant supporting materials, organizing, and outlining the speech. It is when you know exactly where you are going and why that you can begin to find out specific information about the place, recognize the challenges along the way, and map out the best course for your journey. Informative speeches are billed to describe, define, explain, and sometimes demonstrate. Persuasive speeches on the other hand are designed to change attitudes, reinforce existing values and attitudes, and sometimes alter behavior. Speeches to entertain usually contain relevant jokes and stories to present ideas in the lighter mood to the audience. As the case may be, it is the **thesis statement or central idea** of your speech whether informative or persuasive, that will declare the essence of your speech.

Figure 12.1/Ladder Technique for Narrowing a Topic

Worldwide Poverty

Poverty in the Western Hemisphere

Poverty in the United States

Poverty and the homeless

The impoverished homeless
in our state

The impoverished homeless
in our city

The impoverished
homeless in
our public schools

Source: Gamble, Teri Kwal and Michael W. Gamble (2010) *Communication Works*. (10th ed.)New York, NY: McGraw Hill.
(Select a topic and place it at the top of the "ladder." Then subdivide the topic into constituent parts; that is, break it down into smaller and smaller units. The smallest unit should appear on the lowest step of the ladder.)

Gathering Information about the Speech Topic

Once the speech topic has been selected, the next task is to find as much information as possible on it. A number of resources will help you in this process.

The Library

The library is the common reference point for finding information on any topic you might choose for your speech assignment. In the traditional sense, the library is a physical place you can go to access data and resources. But in the modern sense, it can be a virtual place where you can access electronically stored information. Online library can be accessed at-- http://w.w.w.lpl.org/ref.

The library contains print and online references to data referred to as catalogs. These provide subject, title, and author information on books, journals, magazines and reference electronic materials. Traditional card catalogs reference materials by titles, authors, and subject matters. Online sources as identified earlier, allow for database searches by subject, author, and titles, as well as allow for selective key word and subject searches.

Databases

These are electronically networked information sources that are readily easy to access both because they organize topics and subjects alphabetically and also, because they can be accessed by typing key terms, words, names or titles within a short period of time, in some cases minutes. Databases are of two kinds: **Bibliographic databases and Full text databases.**

Bibliographic databases organize published materials in indexed reference forms that allow for ease of access. Here you can access alphabetized annotated information (**abstracts**) about books, periodical articles, government reports, statistics, patents, research reports, dissertations and conference and workshop proceedings and communiqués.

Full text databases store actual, complete texts of periodicals such as newspapers, magazines, and journals. Others include encyclopedias, court cases and reports, research reports and other important publications.

Government Documents

The government is a purveyor of information. It collects information on virtually every topic you can imagine. The different departments of government have specialized responsibilities on which they collect information that they file into databases. The government documents include information on population distribution, growth and changes, employment data, funding of programs, findings on pertinent issues affecting the economy, political trends and voting records. The government also conducts research of various kinds on multiplicity of topics and the data collected and interpreted are contained in government reports, congressional records, and the like.

In this age of the internet, all of the departments of the U.S. government have specialized internet websites where the general public can access relevant information about that arm of the government. There is a U.S. government web portal (USA.gov) where information seekers can browse all government web sites and conduct general and specific topic or word searches. Of great importance for research purposes is the Library of Congress (loc.gov), where all of the published works in the country are archived.

Reference Works

Your job as a researcher has been simplified by those whose job it is to gather and organize relevant information, drawings, and pictures on specialized or general subjects into reference works such as Almanacs, Atlases, Biographical Dictionaries, Dictionaries of Modern Quotations, Language Dictionaries, Encyclopedias, Gazettes, and Handbooks. Your job is to know which reference material to consult for your speech topic and to make sure you acknowledge the source(s) of the works you referenced in order to prevent plagiarism. For expanded work on plagiarism, please see the chapter on ethic and communication.

Review Questions

1. Describe the process of identifying, researching, and managing the speech topic.
2. Identify and discuss the four major questions you should ask yourself when choosing a speech topic.
3. Discuss the criteria for evaluating the quality of information accessed on the internet.
4. Describe the ladder technique of narrowing speech topics.
5. What are the relevant sources of information for speech topics?
6. Suggest ways to narrow this sample speech topic: "The United States of Africa."

Chapter Thirteen
Organizing the Speech

According to Dictionary.com, to organize means: "to form as or into a whole consisting of interdependent parts…" or "to systematize… and "to give organic structure or character to." The parts of a speech are organized into systemic parts whereby the whole is greater than the sums of these different parts. The interdependent parts breathe organic life into a performance as it is to an audience that is billed to appreciate the performance and consequently is informed and or persuaded by its contents.

A speech is, therefore, like a piece of music with an entry note or a beginning, middle, and an end or conclusion. But a good piece of music sounds like a coherent whole, without any note being out of place and the harmony pleasing to the ears. Audiences are used to such organized and systematized presentations and expect nothing less of speeches. And because speeches appeal to people's listening desire and ability, organization is favored. Research has indeed confirmed that listeners learn more from an organized speech than from a disorganized one (Spicer and Bassett, 1976).

Listeners prefer organized speeches to haphazard ones because the former are easier to follow, understand, and follow the nature of human perception which favors organization. Unorganized speeches cannot command and arrest attention of the listeners let alone aid their recall of the information so presented. So, a speech is organized into three interdependent parts that present information to the listener in a systematized manner that will encourage their attention, motivate their interest, and aid their memory of the contents.

Navigating a structured speech is easier for both speaker and the audience. The speaker would find it easier to move from the speech introduction to its body, and then to its conclusion. Within each of the three sections, there are some strategizing that goes on that further helps the speaker to present the speech and for the listener to follow the speaker.

How you organize your speech in terms of what you include and what you leave out, what you pay attention to more or less, what you present first or last, and how you perform these different parts, will inform your audience of your interest, purpose and expectations. A good speech is coherent in both organization and delivery.

The Strategic Introduction

This section is titled strategic introduction because it is organized through **conscious choices** of what are believed to be beneficial to both speaker and audience. It takes into consideration the nature of the audience, their ability to listen and for how long, their motivation and desire to open themselves up to the ideas of another, and how to secure the best result for the speech exercise.

The beginning of a speech or the introduction is designed to accomplish several objectives for the speaker. It is designed to introduce the topic or subject of discussion to the audience, but while attempting to do this, **the first order of business of the introduction is to first gain the attention of the audience members**. Audience members may appear to be paying attention to a speaker, but if the speaker makes no attempt to draw them into and maintain their attention in the speech process, no other objectives of the speech can be accomplished. Once their attention is gained, audience retention must be maintained throughout the speech. Next, **the speaker should introduce the topic/title of the speech and state reasons (purpose of the speech)** why the audience should not only be interested in the speech topic, but also in the speaker. Here, **speaker credibility should be established**. At least a statement of the speaker qualification and experience with the topic should be stated in a manner that the audience would find the speaker not only believable or credible but also reliable and dependable. The information presented in the speech would be accepted as complete and expert information.

After knowing the topic, the purpose, and the credibility of the speaker, at this point **the audience should know where the speaker is going with the topic in terms of the thesis statement of the speech or its central idea.** This speaks to the essence of the speech; the thesis directs the speech and identifies the mindset of the speaker regarding the topic. Oftentimes, the speech thesis directly translates to the main point of the speech, but it is not to be assumed that the thesis is enough to intimate the audience with the main points to be discussed in the body of the speech. **Next in the introduction, therefore, is the forecast of the body of the speech. The speaker enumerates the specific aspects or points of the topic to be discussed later in detail in the body of the speech**.

The idea is to familiarize the audience with what they are going to be paying attention to later in the speech. Also the idea of previewing serves the purpose of preoccupying the minds of the listeners, thus maintaining their attention or specifically positively using their "spare time." For example, the speaker may say that **"today we shall examine the causes of performance anxiety, its symptoms, and the many new treatments that are being developed for it today."** After the audience has been informed of what are to come in the speech, **usually the last thing in the introduction is to transition to the first main point in the body of the speech.** Continuing with the Performance Anxiety topic, the transitional statement can be worded like this: **"now let us examine the many causes of performance anxiety."**

Sample Informative Speech Worksheet
By Amy Lynn Herman

Topic: Performance Anxiety.

Specific purpose: To inform my audience about the causes, symptoms, and
treatments of Performance Anxiety.

Central Idea: Performance Anxiety is sometimes called stage fright and is an
exaggerated fear of performing in public.

Main Points:

I.   There are many causes of Performance Anxiety.

II. Performance Anxiety has a wide variety of symptoms.

III. There are many new treatments for Performance Anxiety
that are being developed today.

Sources:

1. Emmons, Shirlee and Alma Thomas. *Power Performance for
Singers.* New York: Oxford University Press, 1998

2. McPherson, Gary E., Richard Parncutt. *The Science and
Psychology of Music Performance.* New York: Oxford
University Press, 2002.

3. Miller, Carole B., Performance Anxiety.[Online}
http://www.mostlywind.co.uk/performance anxiety. html,
April 2004

Sample Informative Speech Worksheet
By Maxine Navarro

Topic: Global Warming
Specific Purpose: To inform /educate the audience of the causes, effects, and
                        solutions to global warming.
Thesis: Global warming is a very serious and dangerous issue in our
                        lives, the lives of our children, and the future of the world and
                        must not be taken lightly.
Main Points:

   I.   The major causes of global warming are increasing carbon
           dioxide levels in the atmosphere and deforestation.

   II.   Global warming has caused many changes in our climate and
           earth.

   III.   There are several solutions to global warming.

Sources:

   1. http://www.epa.gov/climatechange/ (last updated: 6/23/2009)
   2. http://www.climatehotmap.org/index.html/ (last updated: 1999)
   3. http://www.worldviewofglobalwarming.org/ (last updated: 2008)
   4. Gore, Al.(2007)*An Inconvenient Truth: The Crisis of Global Warming.*
      New York: Penguin Books.

Gaining the Audience's Attention

Through practice and research it has been found that a number of techniques can be used to gain the attention of the audience—to motivate them to feel and become a part of the collaborative act of speech making.

The attention of the audience can be gained by **telling a relevant story.** Story telling is the primary means of communication in the early beginning of human history. People gather around camp fires and or in the open under the moon light to listen to oral presentations of elders and sages alike. Often the listeners pay rapt attention to the lines and messages or lessons of the stories because such stories also embodied the history of the people and present sociological webs that acculturate the locals. Stories take the listeners on a journey, an escape, and a treatment that compels attention. That is why the technique is so useful in gaining the attention of an audience at the beginning of a speech and may be used during the speech to continue to gain and sustain the interest of the audience. The key word here though is relevant. It must relate to the topic and frame of reference of the listeners. If cleverly done, the story can weave purpose and the thesis of the speech together, while even suggesting the main ideas to be presented in the speech.

You can open a speech by **telling a relevant joke**. Jokes present ideas in a lighter mood. While jokes relax the hearers and may cause them to laugh, they also help achieve the goal of focusing their mind on the topic of the joke. A relaxed mind is certainly a fertile place where ideas can access and germinate. Even if the topic has to do with a life-and- death issue, telling a joke about it would certainly put people at ease and make them more willing to pay attention to a speaker who, while talking about a serious issue, does not take him or herself too seriously.

Quoting a relevant and alarming statistic at the beginning of a speech would surely rouse the listeners because the numbers may present a rude awakening, surprise or disturbance to them. Again, a statistic, which is numerical summarization of information, would appeal to the audience members because of the attraction that people have developed for them. Often, people believe that statistics are facts represented in numbers, not realizing that a statistic is as reliable as its author wants it to be! If the study that produced the statistics is not valid and reliable, then same goes with the findings regardless of the fact that they are presented in numbers and formulas.

Sometimes **asking a rhetorical question** is the ploy used to gain the attention of the audience members. A question usually is a probe to which people engage their minds to provide answers to. But a rhetorical question by nature is such that the audience is not required to answer and to which the speaker must provide an answer in the course of the speech. Or the entire speech may be the answer to the rhetorical question. For example a speech about "Immigration and The United States" may start by the speaker asking a probing rhetorical question that: What is the current population of the United States and which racial group's population is growing the fastest in the country? Of course, the current population of the U.S. officially is put at about 306 million people and the fastest growing racial group is the Hispanic population, which constitutes about 14 percent of the total population of the country.

One way of gaining the audience's attention and maintaining it is through story telling. (See an example of a compelling story below).

The Art of Story Telling

Story telling is one of the oldest art forms of message presentation. It's interesting how stories appeal to our sense of social integration and connectedness. A good story is not only awe-inspiring; it can be didactic as well. A good story relaxes and stimulates at the same time; it draws the listener in and keeps him or her in a state of ecstatic expectation, wanting to hear more, the entirety of the story, without which the listener would feel a sense of incompleteness, a sense of loss.

A story is a narrative of events couched in potent language presented before an audience. Usually a story has a major lesson or point that the story teller wants to get across to the listeners. Stories capture history, human epochs, and may reveal or recreate cultural scripts that bound people together.

As it is with all speeches, a story has structure; it has an opening, a body, and an end. Because it is woven around events, places, and people, it must treat the setting, develop the characters, and establish central and peripheral themes. A story will be void without a focus; therefore, it is imperative that the storytellers focus on the reason(s) for the story. In drawing attention to the reasons, the supporting cast of characters should be described in immediate, concise and vivid language. Metaphors help listeners connect their personal experiences to the story. Concrete words are not confusing, they illuminate. Immediate language on the other hand captures the passion and enthusiasm behind the story. Concise words help stories come alive and focused just as they help economize time and words. The advantage of vivid language is in its helping the listeners to visualize the events, persons and settings being described.

The Richest Woman I've Ever Met
By Matt Arnold

I stood in the old woman's living room on a Tuesday in December of 2004. I wasn't used to being invited into the homes of strangers, but there was something special about this lady. I figured it was safe enough, so I accepted the invitation and stepped foot into the home of the richest woman I've ever met. But it wasn't money and wealth that had made her so rich; it was happiness and contentment.

Growing up, I had lived a life where I had everything I needed, and then some. My parents were rarely short on giving me what I asked for. I knew there were those who didn't have as much as I did, and I was fairly content with everything I had. But nothing changed my attitude towards life more than this sunny December afternoon. However, this wasn't the same December sun I was familiar with. I was on an ATV tour of the

Dominican Republic. My family was staying in an all-inclusive hotel, and along with beachside drinks and fantastic dinners, my dad booked an ATV excursion for my brother and I that included a beautiful countryside tour. As I would find out, the expedition included a bonus sight not many experienced.

My father had asked the tour guide to stop at a poor person's house to teach my brother and I a lesson. I had no knowledge of this, and figured that we were heading to a place with a bathroom. We pulled up to what looked like a small hut for farm animals. But when I saw an old woman's face pop out of the front door, I realized it was her home. The woman smiled the toothiest grin I've ever seen. She looked like a hag that you might see depicted in a Disney movie, except for her wide smile. I walked through the front door and tried not to stare. The woman's raggedy clothing and screeching Spanish made a character I will never forget. To my left was a twin-sized bed with clothes hanging above it. Our translator stated that two other people lived in the home with the old woman. To my right was a sink with dishes and a small stove. I walked about three feet and found a room with another twin bed, no door, also with clothes hanging above it. Apparently, the clothes had been hand-washed and were drying. Another two feet and we were out the back door. The entirety of the house was no larger than my dorm room.

After exiting the back door, I found the woman's water system. When it rained, water came down the drain and into a bucket. The water was used for drinking and washing clothes. I asked the woman, in Spanish, where her bathroom was. She pointed to the woods. I saw a few chickens running around and learned that she sold their eggs at a market, where she then bought food. I was in absolute amazement that anyone could live this way.

What was astonishing to me was this woman's happiness. The entire time I was there, she was smiling, absolutely thrilled that someone wanted to meet her, and that she had the opportunity to show off her home. She didn't have much, but was extremely proud of what she did have. Sitting in my room that night, I almost felt guilty that I had air conditioning and this woman didn't. But I decided that from that night on, I was going to be happy with my circumstances. Whenever I worry about my money situation or what will happen to my fiancée and I after college, I think of the old woman and her home. I have so much! But if I realize that happiness doesn't come with wealth or possessions, I might one day be as rich as that elderly woman.

Establishing Speaker Credibility

It is desirable for a speaker, right at the onset of the speech, to provide a reason for the audience to pay attention, believe the assertions to be made in the speech, and to have assurance in the veracity of the contents of the speech. Credibility can be viewed as believability because it is linked to the expertise of the speaker. Therefore, the speaker's statement of connection, experience and, or involvement with the topic will lead the listeners to have confidence or otherwise in the speaker's message. For example, a professional soccer player who gives a speech on the game of soccer should be received and perceived as credible in terms of his expertise, passion, and experience with the game. In the classroom, however, credibility of a student speaker can be derived from experience, passion or interest in a given topic. However, in the case of little or no experience, statement of having done research on the subject matter will go a long way in establishing the student's credibility. The question is: why should I listen to you, the speaker? Why should I believe in what you're telling me? And what level of confidence should I repose in you as a reliable person who can be trusted to present truthful and complete information on your subject?

Although a student may not have direct experience with the issue of teenage pregnancy, directed research on the topic can make the speaker become greatly knowledgeable and, as such, credible to the audience.

Speaker credibility has other dimensions. The enthusiasm of the speaker toward the topic, and physical appearance, go a long way in endearing the audience to the speaker. What would be the result of a lost credibility or little or no credibility of the speaker in the speech situation? This would mean a defeated or futile exercise for the speaker because the goal of informing or persuading the audience cannot be achieved with lack of credibility.

Speakers should know that there are three levels of credibility, categorized as **extrinsic, intrinsic, and terminal.** A speaker may have high or low credibility prior to the speaking engagement because of known or unknown prior reputation on a particular topic or as a result of position occupied in society, or as a result of professional affiliation, etc. If a medical doctor is billed to talk on health issues, the audience would assume that the speaker is competent on such matters. If a prominent art historian talks about "the changing face of art," her credibility on such subject would be expectedly high. **This is extrinsic credibility.**

Hopefully in the course of giving the speeches used as examples here, the speaker will demonstrate such expertise to the audience and confirm the audience's expectation. This is not usually the case, though. Some speakers may have high extrinsic credibility, but in the judgment of the listeners, such expectations may not be met in the course of the speech, thus the demonstrated credibility would suffer. Perhaps the medical practitioner took the topic for granted and did not prepare well for the speech, or did not bother to know the level of education of the audience members, who may ask rather technical questions to which the medical doctor may not provide up-to–date and satisfactory answers. The audience is always looking for evidence that the speaker is knowledgeable, especially that the knowledge in fresh and complete. The result of diminished credibility is lack of interest and of believability on the part of the audience. **Intrinsic credibility is that which a speaker demonstrates or establishes in the course of the speech.**

When the speech is over, the overall credibility the speaker has is a result of the evaluation of extrinsic and intrinsic credibility, coupled with the knowledge the audience has of the speech topic and of the speaker. Particularly, the audience expects the speaker to demonstrate expertise, use evidence to support claims, to be passionate about the topic and to deliver the speech with a great level of confidence. **This final, overall judgment of the speaker and the speech by the audience is referred to as terminal credibility.** As time goes by, you may come across new information that would enhance your understanding of a topic that a speaker once spoke about. This new understanding may contradict the evidence provided by your speaker and, as a result, you become less confident of the expertise of the speaker. So, extrinsic reputation may precede a speaker, but the final, terminal reputation would linger and continue to shift and possibly diminish over time.

Enhancing Ethos or Credibility

In the *Communication Handbook*, Joseph DeVito (1986) suggests several ways a speaker can enhance ethos.

To increase one's competence he suggested that sources should:

- **"Tell the audience of your special experience or training that qualify you to speak on your topic**
- **"Cite a variety of research sources**
- **"Stress the particular competencies of your sources if your audience is not aware of them**
- **"Demonstrate confidence with your materials and with the speech situation generally**
- **"Demonstrate your command of the language**
- **"Do not needlessly call attention to your inadequacies as a spokesperson."**

To demonstrate one's trustworthiness or character, DeVito recommends that you:

- **"Stress your fairness**
- **"Stress your concern for enduring values**
- **"Stress your similarity with the audience, particularly your beliefs, attitudes, values, and goals**
- **"Demonstrate your long-term consistency**
- **"Demonstrate a respect and courtesy for audience members**
- **"Make it clear to the audience that you are interested in their welfare rather than simply seeking self-gain"**

In conclusion, DeVito provides four suggestions to improve dynamism or, as he terms it, charisma:

- **"Demonstrate a positive orientation to the public speaking situation and to the entire speaker-audience encounter**
- **"Demonstrate assertiveness**
- **"Be enthusiastic, and**
- **"Be emphatic."**

Source: DeVito, Joseph (1986). *The Communication Handbook*. New York: Harper & Row. As presented in Benjamin, James (1997). Forth Worth, Texas: Harcourt Brace & Company.

Stating the Purpose and Thesis

As noted earlier, there are three basic speech purposes—reasons why a speaker may engage an audience. These delineations are identified by Aristotle as **forensic, deliberative, and epideictic.** Forensic speeches have to do with pleading a case before a judge whereby an appeal is made to the judge or jury to convict or clear an accused as the case may be. Such speeches are organized to appeal to logic and human passions to evoke feeling of guilt or innocence. An epideictic speech, on the other hand, is designed to praise or blame—to elevate or to bring down. Deliberative speeches as the title suggests, deliberate on a course of action –arguing as to whether or not a course of action is desirable or not. A more common categorization of speech purposes simply identify what speakers have to do, that is, **to inform, to persuade, to motivate, and to entertain**. To apprise the audience on the purpose of your speech is to dictate which direction you are going with the topic and what expectations the audience should have of the outcome. This also answers the question that is usually in the minds of the listeners:

What is this about? Why is it so? And, what is in it for me?

Identifying the speech purpose in the introduction will help focus the speech for the speaker, as well as gain the attention and fulfill the expectations of the audience.

Hybels and Weaver II (2009), suggest five guidelines for constructing your specific purpose:

1. *Make it clear, complete, infinitive phrase, not a sentence fragment, and not a question:*
   To inform listeners of the value of home schooling.
   To persuade listeners to become educated consumers.

2. *Phrase it in terms of the effect you want to have on the listeners:*
   To inform listeners of ways they can help people with disabilities.
   To persuade listeners of the negative effects of binge drinking.
   You should also be able to rephrase your specific purpose from a listener's vantage point. At the end of your speech, listeners will refrain from binge drinking or be able to explain specific ways they can help people with disabilities.

3. *Limit the statement to one distinct idea only.* For example, a specific purpose that reads "To inform my audience about the value of daydreams and how to

use them to escape and relax," would need to be rephrased to focus on either their value or on how to use them to escape and relax.

4. *Use specific language*:
   To inform listeners of the negative effects of alcohol on the body.
   To persuade listeners that they should help control drunk driving.

5. *Make certain your purpose meets the interests, expectations, and levels of knowledge of your listeners.*

The Speech Thesis

The speech thesis statement presents a terse summary of the essence of the speech and announces the speaker's perspective on the topic. It provides a more focused direction than the purpose statement. For example, an informative speech on Breast Cancer may deal with a variety of sub issues such as causes, symptoms, and treatment. But a clearly stated thesis may further narrow the scope of the speech. For example, the thesis may state as follows: **The major causes of cancer are genetics, diet, and environmental factors**. This speech is therefore narrowed to just the causes of breast cancer and excludes the symptoms, and treatment. Another thesis statement may focus on the symptoms and another on the treatments. For example: **The treatment of breast cancer includes chemotherapy, radiation, and surgery.** Think of the relationship of the speech purpose to the speech thesis this way: purpose tells you the how, but thesis states what is to be said and why.

Lucas (2009) provides a checklist to guide the effective phrasing of the speech central idea or thesis. If you can answer all the following questions in the affirmative, then you have written an effective central idea for your speech.

Answer "yes" or "no" to the following questions:

1. Is the central idea written as a complete sentence?   Yes___ No___

2. Is the central idea phrased as a statement rather than a question?   Yes___ No___

3. Is the central idea free of figurative language?   Yes___ No___

4. Does the central idea clearly encapsulate the main points to be discussed in the body of the speech?   Yes___ No___

5. Can the central idea be adequately discussed in the time allotted for the speech?   Yes___ No___

6. Is the central idea relevant to the audience?   Yes___ No___
7. Is the central idea appropriate for a nontechnical audience?   Yes___ No___

Connecting With the Speech Body

Now the audience is sufficiently oriented toward the speech topic, its essence, and expected outcome. The next task is now to preview the major points to be developed in the body of the speech. This is when to announce the specific main points to be discussed in the body of the speech. As the Breast Cancer example goes, the thesis statement or central idea of the speech suggests clearly that the focus of the body of the speech is causes of breast cancer which are genetics, diet, and environmental factors. This translates to the three main points of the speech which can be presented as follows:

Main Point I. **A major cause of breast cancer is genetics, which is the passing of diseased genes from one family member to another.**

Main Point II. **Poor diet, especially of treated foods, has been linked to Breast Cancer.**

Main Point III. **The presence of carcinogens in the environment has been linked to increased incidence of Breast Cancer.**

Each of these main points is to be treated as a separate but equal topic in the body of the speech. Separate because each is distinct from the others and equal because each is equally important. It is expected that each main point is accorded saliency in terms of treatment and space allotted to it. In other words, one cannot be thought to be more important than the other to the extent that limited time is allotted it in the speech. If it is identified as a main point, then it should be treated as such. After all, so much thinking and evaluating has gone into identifying the main points of the speech, so symmetrical treatment of each of them is expected.

Aware of what is expected in the body of the speech should now be followed by a direct transition into the body of the speech. So much has gone into the speech introduction that now that the audience has been teased of the main points, next is to connect now and transition into the speech body where much of the speech information is presented. The first connective is to the first main point of the three and in our case, this is the link of genetics to Breast Cancer. For example a transitional statement could read as follows:

First, let us explore genetics as a major cause of breast cancer.

This statement marks the end of the introduction and the beginning of the body or, more appropriately, the first main point in the body of the speech. The element that connects the introduction and the body of the speech is the **transitional statement**, which is a sort of a bridge or traffic control that signals the end of a part of a speech and heralds the beginning of another.

The Strategic Speech Body

The body of the speech is where the bulk of information in the speech is presented. But the presentation must be systematic- must follow a pattern that will encourage the listener to follow the presentation from the beginning to the end and, in the end, be able to remember the main points and arguments presented. The speech body must be presented strategically.

First, the speech body is developed into sometimes mutually exclusive sub parts that can be treated as separate or stand-alone topics. In order to show continuity, the main points must be arranged in a manner that naturally allows one to flow into another using the organizational method that is appropriate to the topic. Though the main points may be treated as stand-alone topics, they are still a part of a whole that must be coherently organized to form a single presentation.

The main points of a speech are strategically connected to the thesis statement of the speech as well as its specific purpose. A well-defined speech sub parts will inform the specific purpose of the speech and will clearly meet the goal set out to accomplish in the exercise. Connecting all these will formulate a coherent, easy to follow, and interesting speech.

In the example of the speech on "Breast Cancer," the topic has been developed into three sub parts that are the three major causes of cancer. Having identified these main points, the specific purpose of the speech is clear: **To inform my audience of the major causes of breast cancer.** The thesis statement also can be easily developed from the identified main points. For example:

a. **There are three major causes of breast cancer.**
b. **The major causes of breast cancer are genetic, diet, and environmental factors.**
c. **Breast cancer is a serious disease that can be treated if its major causes are identified and examined.**

Each main point identified in a speech must be supported with evidence. If a main point is stated as a statement of claim as usually the case, the claim must be based in evidence and proof. For example, if a main point on a speech titled: **The Three Most Important Yankee Players of All Time** states that: The number one Yankee player of all time is Derek Jeter, the speaker must be ready to present the criteria used for determining this assertion and the evaluation process of such criteria must unequivocally support the claim.

Not every idea can be used as a main point in a speech. Primarily, a thorough study and elimination process would help the speaker to determine the salient issues to discuss in a speech and which ones to eliminate or, perhaps, use as minor ideas to fully develop the main points. Every idea cannot be a main point, because if it were, none of them would merit the importance attached to it. In other words, if everything is deemed important, then nothing really is! The point is that the speaker should identify an appropriate number of main points suited for the occasion and the time allotted to the speaker.

Navigating the Speech-The Connectives

Mindful of the attention span of the audience, perhaps more importantly the audience's listening tendency, the speech is organized to make it easy for the audience to follow and to understand. It is only if they follow the propositions, arguments, reasoning being laid out in the speech that a speaker can achieve the goals of informing or persuading them.

This can be likened to modern day GPS technology that aids travelers to move from one point to the other to locate an address that has been programmed into a Tom-Tom or Garmin and other such devices. If the traveler misses a turn as indicated by the address locator, the device alerts of such and re-routs the mapping to lead to the programmed address. By voicing "recalculating," the map is altered to put the traveler on the right track! The GPS is a travel guide just as speech connectives are listening guides.

In the case of speech making, though, the human GPS is the speech maker who incorporates the connective devices into the twist and turns of the speech to aid the audience in receiving, following, and interpreting the information provided. When the information presented is complicated, it is broken into smaller pieces for ease of consumption. When the information is long, it calls for reviewing and rephrasing and, when the sub parts are many, transitional statements of location (where the speaker is in the course of the speech) are made to direct "the traffic" along the way. Eventually the goal is for both the audience and the speaker to arrive at the location desired by the speaker. Here are some of the speech connectives used for various purposes in the course of a speech.

Transitional Statements

As the name suggests, transitional statements connect one part of a speech to another. Clearly there are three parts to a speech and each stage is connected to the others by means of transitional statements or verbal signposts. These verbal signposts direct listening traffic and cue the audience of a shift or a different focus in the speech. For example, **"having discussed the positive impact of supply-side economics, let us now look at its possible drawbacks."** This statement clearly cues the audience for a change in the focus of the speech from the positives to the negatives of supply-side economics and verbally directs their attention to the two-sided evaluation of the topic, which is often required of audiences in public discourse. Should the speaker not use transitional statements, the speech will become a long, boring, and tedious exercise. Ultimately, the purpose of transitions is to present a speech as having different parts that are connected as seamlessly as possible as a whole. Thus they make speeches flow better and stimulate the audience to hear a coherent and easy to navigate piece.

Gamble and Gamble (1998) identify the four Cs of transitions:
Chronological transitions aid the listener to follow a sequence of events and ideas as they are presented in the different main points of the speech. References to time in speechmaking connectives include the use of words and phrases such as *after, at the same time, while, in the meantime, and finally.*

Contrasting one idea to the other means showing how they differ. Such phrases and words that indicate contrast include *but, on the other hand, in contrast, in spite of and, as against.*

Causal transitions lay out the cause and the result of something. Before making a causal statement, however, you must be sure of the validity of the relationship and be able to exclude other causes. The cause-effect relationship is established by such words as *because, therefore, and consequently.*

Complementary transitions allow the speaker to add more ideas to already stated ideas. The examples of complementary transitions include the use of **also**, *in addition to, and likewise.*

Previews (Internal and External)

A preview is like a movie trailer. It informs the audience of what they will see in the full-length movie by highlighting the most inviting and memorable parts of the movie. Speech previews are statements introducing the audience to materials, ideas, proposition, or arguments that will be presented especially in the body of the speech. This is usually presented at the beginning of each main point of the speech when the speaker apprises the audience of what to expect in that particular main point.

The external preview is done before going into the main point while the internal preview is used as a mini break within the point to take a breather, then a quick introduction of the remaining ideas within that main point. Often this is done when the ideas to be covered are more than two to three so that the ideas within the main point may not drag on and lead to audience "drop off."

Summaries (Internal and External)

As noted in the listening section of the book, human attention span is very short indeed and it behooves a good speaker to strategically manage this human deficit and turn it into an advantage by summarizing ideas after they have been presented to the audience. This allows for transient listeners an opportunity to capture whatever they might have missed and to recap the main ideas for those who were listening in the first instance. If done properly and strategically, this redundancy tactic is good in the communication process because it reinforces what was heard and ensures effective reception and possible understanding.

Internal summaries are reviews done within a main point after so much material has been covered. If this is done after the completion of the main point, it is considered external as it is done "ipso facto." This helps the speaker to emphasize what has been said and to prepare the audience to follow what is to come.

Signposts

When traveling on the highways of this country, there are signposts at strategic intervals on the road indicating where the traveler is and how many miles a town or site is away from that location. Speech signposts are locators, usually in the body of the speech, and they tell the audience exactly where the speaker is in the course of the speech, and locate other important ideas on the way. This helps the audience to keep track of the progression of the speech and to anticipate what is to come next. Examples of signposts are: **"There are three important parts to a speech, the first of which is the introduction." "After the introduction, the most significant part of the speech is its body where the main points are developed." "The last part of a speech is its conclusion."**

Supporting the Speech Claims

We now know that speech main points are stated as matters of fact. Often these are categorical statements of claims that must be substantiated. If a speech's main point states that "there are three known causes of road rage," then the speaker must be ready to answer questions that may come to the mind of the listeners that they might not be able to ask directly during the course of the speech. These questions would include: how does she know this? What expertise does she have that qualifies her to make this statement? And what evidence can she show to prove this point? Especially when a speaker is making a causal claim, there must be ample evidence to lead to the conclusion of such statement of causality. The listener as we know is a logical and affective being, as such, claims in the speech must not only agree with reason it must also ring through and stimulate human motives. **The speaker must use facts!** These are verifiable information through multiple observers (empirical facts) and which observations are consistent regardless of the observer (established facts).

To meet the expectations of the audience, the speaker must use materials of support to illuminate and prove the veracity of her claims. She needs to use a variety of tactics, ideas, and support building evidence to buffer her declarative assertions as based in logic, critical analysis, experience and research. **Materials of support in speeches are examples, quotations and testimonies, statistics, definitions, stories, and comparisons and contrasts.** Others are anecdotal experience, observation, and role playing.

Choosing the right supporting material for your speech is important. This may depend on your topic, your audience, and other considerations that may determine the appropriateness of the support material. Also, the reputation of these supporting materials is equally important. Materials must be sourced from competent and credible sources, who are experts on the topics and who have direct experience or relation to the topic of your speech. Another factor to consider is the timeliness or recency of the materials used in building an argument in a speech. If the presented information is out of date, the audience would not value it and may perceive the speaker as less credible, though the aim of a reliable and current material of support is to bolster the credibility of the speaker.

Use Examples

Examples are particularly good supporting materials because they illustrate the point that the speaker is getting across to the audience. Lucas (2007) describes an example as "a specific case used to illustrate or to represent a group of people, ideas, conditions, experiences, or the like." It is the representation that rings through with the audience. When a speaker uses an example to represent a rather abstract idea or situation, it brings it home and helps the audience to visualize what is being spoken about.

There are three general types of examples and they are **brief or specific examples, extended examples and hypothetical examples.** Brief examples are usually mentioned in passing referring to a specific instance that can buttress a point for the speaker. The extended examples on the other hand are longer narratives or illustrations, and are sometimes stories of events relevant to the point the speaker is illuminating. Unlike factual examples, hypothetical examples are made- up or imaginary stories to demonstrate what happens or will occur should someone be placed in a position or situation. Examples concretize the speech assertions for the audience; they help them to visualize the events, ideas or situations described and place them right in the topoi of the speech.

There is a method to using these examples effectively. If they are not placed at points in the speech where they can make the maximum illustrative impact on the audience, or be used strategically to reinforce, clarify, and personalize your ideas, then their use is misplaced. Lucas (2007) provides us with a checklist for using examples and it is presented here as a guide for you whenever you are building support for your speech claims.

Checklist for Using Examples
Yes__No__   1. Do I use examples to clarify my ideas?
Yes__No__   2. Do I use examples to reinforce my ideas?
Yes__No__   3. Do I use examples to personalize my ideas?
Yes__No__   4. Are my examples representative of what they are supposed to illustrate or prove?
Yes__No__   5. Do I reinforce my examples with statistics or testimony?
Yes__No__   6. Are my extended examples vivid and richly textured?
Yes__No__   7. Have I practiced the delivery of my extended examples to give them dramatic effect?

Use Narratives

Narratives are stories we tell to illustrate our points and arguments in a speech, to bring it to life and create a vivid image of what is being portrayed. Story telling is one of the oldest art forms of message presentation. A good story is not only awe-inspiring; it can be instructive as well. A good story relaxes and stimulates at the same time; it draws the listeners in and keeps them in a state of expectation. The listeners would want to hear more, the entirety of the story, without which they would feel a sense of incompleteness, a sense of loss. It's interesting how stories appeal to our sense of social integration and connectedness.

A good story is a narrative of events that must be couched in potent and immediate language before an audience. Usually a story has a major lesson or point that the story teller wants to get across to the listeners. Stories capture history, human epochs, and may reveal or recreate cultural scripts that bound people together.

Like a speech, a story has structure; it has an opening, a body, and an end. Because it is woven around events, places, and people, it must treat the setting, develop the characters, and establish central and peripheral themes. A story will be void without a focus; therefore, the story teller should focus on the reason(s) for telling the story. In drawing attention to the reasons, the supporting cast of characters should be described in immediate, concise and vivid language. Metaphors help listeners connect their personal experiences to the story. Concrete words are not confusing, they illuminate. Immediate language on the other hand, captures the passion and enthusiasm behind the story. Concise words help stories come alive and focused just as they help economize time and words. The advantage of vivid language is in its helping the listeners to visualize the events, persons and settings being described. It is because of all these stated advantages that narratives should be used in supporting speech claims.

Narratives can be **brief,** sometimes called **vignettes,** or they can be **extended** in nature. The brief narrative can be used to illustrate a point or two in the speech, but the extended narrative can be woven into the entire speech to illustrate several points. Griffin (2003) advises that whatever the length of the story, it should organize the events you describe in your speech, flesh out characters, and tell of actions, settings, and plots." Cindy Griffin also itemizes four criteria for using narratives as supporting materials in your speech:

- Use Narratives to Personalize a Point

- Use Narratives to Challenge an Audience to Think in New Ways

- Use Narratives to Draw an Audience in Emotionally (See the speech on Cancer)

- Use Narratives to Unite the Speaker and the Audience.

Use Statistics

We live in the age of science where evidence is necessary to prove any claim or to make predictions about the future. A useful tool for obtaining evidence is research- a process of systematically unraveling prevailing situations objectively and making claims and predictions about such situations. And a tool of research is statistics, which is the numerical representation of information. It is using numbers to summarize information or research verbal data that otherwise would have been rather voluminous to present in reasonable time frame. Statistics offer economy of time and words to users as they present evidence to support claims and to predict a trend. While narratives, quotations, examples may present verbal data or evidence, statistics present processed numbers representing data.

Often, the summary of data are numbers that represent the most frequent cases, the typical cases, or the most likely to occur. These are what researchers call **measures of central tendencies.** Indicators of central tendencies are **mean, mode, and median**. Other useful **statistics** are range and **ratios.**

Range is the difference between the lowest and the highest scores in a set of numbers. It may help in showing the difference between classes of people, incomes, examination scores, etc. The mean represents the average case, which is the sum of all the scores under measure divided by number of cases of the measure. Mode is the most frequent number in a set of numbers, thereby identifying which number repeats itself the most in a series of numbers. The median is a more sophisticated measure than the mode in that for it to be identified, the set of numbers being studied must be rank-ordered to locate the middle point between the highest and the least scores. So the median is the middle point, but the mean gives us the most accurate midpoint because not only does it allow for summing of all the scores, it also allows for the dividing of all the sum of the scores by the number of cases under study. It is, however, sensitive or influenced by extreme numbers in a set of numbers. Extreme because they may be unusually higher or lower than any of the numbers in the set, thus artificially increasing or decreasing the average number as the case may be.

These statistics are usually presented in the form of percentages, which are measures per hundred (for every 100 cases) commonly understood by many when large information is reduced to numbers. Often percentages are presented as a ratio thus using raw numbers in appropriate situations to indicate the rate of occurrence of something. For example, it could be reported that 1 in every 2 marriages end up in divorce in the United States instead of stating that about half of marriages in the United States end up in divorce. Ratios are more appropriate in situations whereby the percentage information may be very small, so using the raw numbers in a ratio may bring the numbers alive. For example, stating that .0001 percent of cars in the United States have manual transmission may not be clear to the audience. This is the same as saying that 1 in every ten thousand. But the usefulness of each of these measures depends on the type of data being summarized and the purpose the numerical data will serve in the speech. There are situations when the use of average numbers is useful evidence in a speech, especially because averages are more representative of the central measures in a set of large cases; they thus reduce the effect of the extreme low or high numbers on the overall statistic presented.

Listeners have a fondness for numbers because not only does their use save time, they also present evidence that people perceive to represent valid data from reliable research! This is the reason why many people are taken by statistics and why many are suspicious of their use. And the more reason why speakers should use statistics carefully, making sure they are borne out of reliable and valid studies.

Reliability of studies has to do with how dependable the instruments or methodologies used in collecting the data from which statistics are drawn. Is the instrument dependable to the extent that if it is reused with the same population of study or, perhaps at another setting, it will yield an accurate measure of what it is supposed to measure? In other words is the data reliable and to what extent can you depend on them? Validity, on the other hand, has to do with the extent to which a study is actually measuring what it is supposed to measure. That is, the findings of the study can be attributed only to the manipulations of the objects and subjects of study and not caused by any other or external factors. The issues of reliability and validity of studies are interwoven when one considers the use of statistics in a speech. Since many speakers will conduct minimal first-hand studies by themselves, the examination of certain issues concerning secondary sources (Data from published and unpublished studies of other sources) is very important in determining how useful, reliable and valid the data may be.

Speakers should examine:

- The qualifications of the source of the statistics they are to use in a speech. What is the expertise of the author(s)?
- How appropriate is the instrument used in collecting the data which formed the basis of the statistics?
- How old is the study or the data? If it is not recent, you should affirm that the passage of time has not rendered the data obsolete.

There are many advantages to using statistics in your speech, but you must use statistic when appropriate and necessary. When you quote statistics all over your speech, you run the risk of boring your listeners to death. Several statistics cited in a speech will not only confuse the listeners, it will make it harder for them to process and remember the speech. But important, startling, clarifying statistics will make your speech more interesting, easy to understand and memorable.

Tips for using statistics more effectively in your speech include the following:

- You should use statistics when words alone would not be sufficient to tell a compelling story.
- You should quote relevant statistics
- You should help your listeners by summarizing your data into manageable forms
- You should round off your statistics to a whole number or percentage
- You should interpret your statistics
- You should relate your statistics to your audience
- You should present your statistics in graphs or charts (Pie, bar, pictorial, etc)
- You should quote up-to-date statistics.
- You should state source(s) of your statistics, including their qualifications and affiliations
- Use statistics honestly

Where to Find Statistical Information

Sources of statistical information include arms of government's publications, and statistical year books, the examples of which are: *The World Almanac and Book of Facts, Information Please Almanac, Statistical Abstracts of The United States, Vital Statistics of The United States, The UN's Statistical Yearbook, The Guinness Book of Records.*

Use Testimony

In our daily conversations with friends and family, we make several statements of claim without realizing how often we do so. Once in a while we get a friend or two who would query some of our careless assertions by asking "where did you hear that," or "who said that," or how do you know that?" Indirectly, they are asking us to support our claims. This is also the case when we are speaking to an audience. They want to know how sure you're of what you're saying, especially on a topic that is consequential to them. This is because they want to rely on your information and it is important for them to ascertain the veracity of what you are telling them. The audience needs testimony either in direct quotation or paraphrased, expert or peer to lend credibility to your speech and its claims.

There are two types of testimony: **expert and peer testimony**. Expert testimony is using the informed pronouncement and claims of an expert to support your own claims in the course of your speech. Expertise is derived from study, professional development, practice, and experience. It is best to use known personalities who have excelled in their various fields of endeavor as experts, recognizing that their popularity stems from their expertise, excellence, and experience. To use the example we had used before, speaking on the topic of Breast Cancer would require that a testimony is quoted or paraphrased from a reputable *Oncologist* and not just any doctor. A good research of the topic should have yielded records of papers presented, articles written, interviews granted by such experts in professional journals, newspapers and magazines, or, if possible, in direct conversation between the expert and the researcher. Again, the use of expert opinions is useful when the topic of your speech draws arguments and is polarizing. Some speech topics that are controversial are: The Right to Abortion, Immigration in the United States, Global Warming, and Health Care Reform in The United States. Can you think of many more?

Peer testimony is finding support for your speech from the testimonies of ordinary people who have had firsthand experience with your speech topic and whose experience can provide a real time direct experience for the audience. Again, to our example of Breast Cancer, how might your audience be influenced by the testimony of a male student who has undergone chemotherapy for the disease? The impact is without doubt comparable if not much more than what an oncologist might have said on the occurrence of breast cancer among men! Peer testimonies are the stuff that prime time television and newspapers news are made of. They so abound in the arena of public information that a conscientious speaker would find it easy to access such information. What about the internet? Just Google your topic and you'll find tons of peer testimonies.

There are some basic guidelines for using testimony in your speech. First, a decision has to be made whether to quote your source verbatim or to paraphrase his or her statements. Paraphrasing is revising, summarizing a source's ideas and restating them in one's own words and to quote verbatim is to directly present word-for-word, a source's ideas. Lucas (2009) advises that the standard rule is that direct "quotations are most effective when they are brief, when they convey your meaning better than you can, and when they are particularly eloquent, witty, or compelling." However, he claims that paraphrasing is better than direct quotation in two situations: (1) "when the wording of a quotation is obscure or cumbersome, as is often the case with government documents; (2) when a quotation is longer than two or three sentences." The argument is a compelling one that a long quotation from another source would interrupt the flow of your own speech and cause the audience to miss the links. As such, a long quotation should be paraphrased into the speaker's own words.

Guidelines for Using Testimony

- Quote or paraphrase ideas that are relevant to your speech claims
- Quote or paraphrase ideas from qualified and recognizable individuals.
- Quote or paraphrase others ideas accurately
- Quote or paraphrase others' ideas within and not out of context
- Quote and paraphrase the source's most current statements on the topic
- Paraphrase others' ideas without losing their meaning
- Identify and quote the sources of your testimony accurately
- Identify the bias (if any) of the source of your testimony

Use Definitions

Language can be a bridge to understanding ideas and events through the symbolic sharing of meaning. However, it is its very symbolic nature that can make it a barrier to understanding meaning. When individuals interchange meaning through words and do not attribute similar meanings to the words being exchanged, then there is misunderstanding, which scholars label as **bypassing**. When presenting a speech on a topic not too familiar to an audience, or when you're presenting a new way of looking at old ideas, there is a need to clarify the meanings you associate with terms and jargons you use in the speech. In order to clarify, simplify, and establish common understanding of terms with their audience, speakers make good use of definitions, which are the exact meanings of words, usually as found in the dictionary and established through common usage. Although there may not be a "proper meaning" for the words we speak, but agreeing to a common meaning will create effective communication.

As noted in the earlier chapter on Effective Use of Language, a word has two types of meaning: **denotative and connotative**. Denotative meanings are the primary, common, dictionary, and objective meanings of words, while connotative meanings are private, unique, emotional, and subjective meanings of words. The speaker must understand that the public meaning of words may not be the individual meanings held by audience members, but it is good to establish a common definition for terms used in order to have a collective viewpoint regarding the concept or word being clarified. At times, it is useful to establish a **working definition** for a technical term in a speech if it is to be used in a rather peculiar and imaginative manner. Clearly the speech context would provide the interpretation and use of such terms and the particular purpose for its use.

In all, the speaker should use definitions for specific purposes in the course of the speech. If a listener would have any reason to wonder what a word or term used in a speech means, there is need to define that word. The key is to simplify everything as much as you can so as not to confuse the audience with difficult to understand words. Tips for using definitions according to Griffin, include:

- Use Definitions to Clarify and Create Understanding.
- Use Definitions to Clarify an Emotionally or Politically charged word.
- Use Definitions to Trace the History of a Word (Etymology).
- Use Definitions to Illustrate What Something Is Not.

Use Comparisons and Contrasts in the Speech

There are times when showing differences between two situations or events will illustrate your point better to an audience than when you present only one situation or describe a singular event. At other times, showing similarities may be the epiphany or eureka moment in your speech for your audience. This is because showing such similarities of causes, effects, and traits, for instance, will connect well with the audience. In turns, the audience will buy into your argument and agree with your proposal or claims. **Comparisons by definition show similarities and contrasts show differences.**

Comparisons and contrasts are usually referred to as analogies and there are two types: **Literal analogy and Figurative analogy.** Literal analogies provide comparisons of things of like terms such as two colleges, two political figures, two empires, etc., while figurative analogies compare things, events, situations that on face value are apparently dissimilar, but through comparisons, their similarities and contrasts are brought to life.

When using comparisons you must be careful to compare events, things, situations that share similar characteristics, traits, and principles. That is you must compare "oranges to oranges" and not things that do not share some commonalities, thus making the comparison illogical, not feasible and, therefore, unbelievable. Is it logical to compare Health Care in Canada to that of the United States? Though larger in terms of land mass, Canada's population is 1/6th of that of the U.S. Not only that, the political histories of the countries are dissimilar, the economic structure of the U.S. is much complex, and the cultural traditions are equally at variance. Gamble and Gamble (2003) confirm that 'it is important that the essential similarities inherent in the analogies you use must be readily apparent. If you strain to create analogies, audience members may conclude that your analogies are far-fetched, inappropriate, unbelievable, or unpersuasive."

Whenever appropriate, it is better to combine both comparison and contrast in a speech, meaning that the speaker will show both similarities and dissimilarities of events, issues, and situations. This will reduce the error in judgment that is usually associated with either comparing or contrasting alone.

The Strategic Speech Conclusion

Managing the speech event includes managing both the topic and the audience, especially in the delivery of the speech. After all a speech is designed for an audience, therefore all strategizing is done with the audience in mind. The conclusion of a speech needs careful planning and structure in order to achieve maximum effect on the audience members. As had been stated before, repetitions or redundancy are a useful thing in communication. Why? A speech is fleeting and to help the audience to catch what they might have missed, in case they misused their **spare time** in the course of the speech introduction and body, **the conclusion offers a recap or summary** of what had been presented in the speech. This is definitely not a place to introduce new ideas to the audience because they are not now psychologically willing to take in new ideas that need further expatiation. Here the speaker enumerates the main points and possible sub points of the speech and neatly ties them together for maximum effect as a reminder to the audience of all too important ideas that had been presented to them.

The conclusion section of a speech offers an opportunity for the speaker to tie or connect the beginning of the speech to its final exiting point, where the speech now becomes a coherent whole- a complete story or presentation, just as a piece of music is stylistically connected to its beginning score. So, **the conclusion connects the beginning to the end** to give a sense of completeness to the audience and, prepares the audience for the final exiting narrative to follow. Shakespeare wrote that "all is well that ends well." Same goes for the exiting statements of a speech. **The exiting phraseology should present a sense of completion, a lasting impression, and a final bang** that would compel the listeners to want to applaud the speaker or speech for having attained its desired goals.

Speech Organization Patterns

The speech body can be organized into several well-known patterns and these are:

Topical

When the speech topic can naturally be sub divided into its different constituent parts as in the example of the Causes of Breast Cancer. The three causes fall into three separate sub topics that distinctly form three different main points of the speech. Usually a speech that naturally forms into the topical organizational pattern can best be presented using the pattern, but it may be adaptable to other patterns. See the example of a speech outline written by Taylor Karp below:

Topic: Body Building

Specific Purpose: To inform my audience about the three major aspects of Body Building.

Thesis: **The three major aspects of bodybuilding are proper weight training, nutrition, and rest.**

Main Points:

I.   **Weight training is used to rip muscle fibers, hoping they heal bigger than before.**
II.   **In order for the muscles to heal properly, they need certain nutrients.**
III.   **Rest allows these nutrients to repair the muscles adequately.**

Time –Sequence Pattern

This is also referred to as the chronological speech pattern. As the name suggests, the topic is developed following a timeline. Following the time sequence of occurrence enables the audience to follow the time trend and demarcate the speech into time phases that they can easily follow and remember. Chronological progression or regression is followed usually to reveal a process or stages in the life of something. Following the progression of an event allows the speaker to order relevant information into periods that will discourage haphazard, disorganized presentation.

Example:

The Mayan civilization has three time periods:

1. **The first is the Pre-Classic Period spanning from 2000B.C to 250 A.D.**

2. **The second is the Classical Period which spanned from 250 A.D. to 900 A.D.**

3. **The third is the Post-Classic Period which spanned from 900 A.D. to 1500 A.D.**

Spatial Pattern

This organizational method is used to present ideas and topics in terms of space relationships. Spatial orientation has to do with directions, physical surroundings and distances. Speeches that describe, enumerate in terms of these properties orient the listeners spatially. Sports topics can be developed using this type of pattern because, usually sports are played in geographical environments. For example, a speech on the Different Positions of Players in The Game of Soccer is appropriately adaptable to the spatial order pattern when ordering the main points. Other examples of topics adaptable to the spatial pattern are: The Continents of the World or The Planets or A description of the Globe.

Example:
Topic: **Significant Geographic Locations on the Globe**
Specific Purpose: **To describe to my audience the three significant geographical locations on the globe.**
Central Idea: **The three significant geographic locations on the globe are the Arctic, Equator, and Antarctica.**

Main Points.

    I.   **The Arctic region is located in the extreme northern pole of the globe.**
    II.   **Equator is the exact mid-point or centre of the globe.**
    III.   **Antarctica is at the extreme southern post of the globe.**

Problem-Solution Pattern

Speeches that identify problems or needs usually proffer relevant solutions to such problems or suggest appropriate action to meet such identified needs. The main points automatically become the problem and its solution. Even if there are different aspects of the problem, they are enumerated and treated under the main point-problem; while same goes for the solution main point, which may contain several solutions but will be enumerated under the singular coverage of solution(s). For a problem to be adequately resolved it must be thoroughly understood and the solutions must adequately resolve it and show how the solution will work. Consequently, a lot of critical thinking goes into developing a speech into the two main points of Problem-Solution pattern. According to Seiler and Beal (2009), the problem-solution pattern, usually include three of the following:

1. A definition and description of the problem, including its symptoms and size
2. A critical analysis of the problem, including causes, current actions, a requirements for a solution
3. Suggestions of possible solutions, including a description of each solution's strengths and weaknesses
4. A recommendation of the best solution, including a thorough justification of its superiority over other proposed solutions
5. A discussion of the best solution put into operation, including a description of how the plan can be implemented.

Example:

Definition:

Global warming is an average increase in the Earth's temperature caused by both natural and human activities.

Problem:

Increased human activities in the last three decades have significantly increased the rate of global warming, the results of which are extreme and deadly weather conditions.

Solution:

There are several steps everyone must take immediately to reduce the negative effects of global warming.

Cause-Effect Pattern

Using this pattern suggests that the speaker has done adequate research on the cause of an identified problem, especially isolating and linking this cause directly to observable effects or consequences. It is problematic to determine that something is the cause an effect where there is no link of such causality. A reverse of this pattern can be used as well. The effects of a problem can be enumerated before the causes are identified. This is a linear view of events and their causes, which dominate Western thinking. As you will read in chapter on intercultural communication and public speaking, other cultures do not necessarily follow the logical-deductive pattern of reasoning.

Example 1:

The major causes of poverty in Haiti are lack of education, deforestation, and poor farming practices.

This is a statement of claim which links some causes to an effect. In this case, poverty is linked to three major causes. Each point must be fully examined to justify the claim of causality.

Example 2:

The major consequences of illegal immigration in the US are increasing healthcare costs, rising wave of crime, and lower standard of education.

Example 3:

Binge drinking on college campuses often results in unplanned sexual activities, vandalism, recklessness, and DWI.

Alternative Patterns

The Climax or Anti Climax Order

The climax order calls for the suspension of the story punch line, or the most important argument that the speaker is trying to make until the end of the speech in order to make the utmost impact on the audience. This is much like storytelling, whereby the moral of the story or what eventually happened to the hero or heroine of the story is saved for last. This is a tricky thing to do in that the speaker assumes that the audience will stay with the story till the end to find out the punch line. Karlins and Abelson (1970), advise that "if your audience is favorably disposed to your speech, you can afford to save your strongest argument for last… And if the audience is in opposition, it is better to state your strongest argument first.

Other alternative speech patterns are the **wave, spiral, and the star**. These are various patterns that are not commonly used in the Western world, but are used in many parts of the world, especially Africa.

Review Questions

1. Identify and discuss three major advantages of organizing a speech.
2. Identify and discuss the components of a speech introduction.
3. Describe with examples the different ways you could gain the attention of the audience of a speech.
4. Identify and describe the components of a speech body.
5. Identify and describe the components of a speech conclusion.
6. What are speech connectives and what roles do they play in the speech?
7. What are speech materials of support and what roles do they play individually in the speech?
8. What is speaker credibility?
9. Discuss the different types of speaker credibility.
10. Examine and discuss the different ways a speaker could enhance his or her credibility.
11. What is a speech thesis or central idea? Give some examples.
12. Discuss the uses and misuses of statistics in a speech presentation.
13. Identify and describe the advantages of each of the speech organization patterns.

Chapter Fourteen
Delivering the Speech

Most speeches are prepared ahead of their delivery time and are usually scripted in one form or another. A speech may be written out as an essay or it may be scripted in a speaking or preparation outline format. Ultimately a speech has to be vocalized before an audience and there are different methods of accomplishing this task.

There are situations whereby a scripted speech has to be read verbatim before an audience; there are also situations that call for a memorized delivery, when the speaker speaks directly from memory without the use of any form of notes. But there are events that call for the spur of the moment speech making, especially at social gathering where, for example, one may be asked to toast a friend or give a vote of thanks. This type of speech making is dubbed the impromptu speech. A mixture of memorization and script reading is termed extemporaneous speech delivery. This is when a speaker memorizes important parts of the speech through extensive practice and copies important, not-easy-to-memorize information on index cards. The speaker then speaks from memory and relies on the index cards to jar his or her memory about these important points during delivery.

As a rule, apart from impromptu speeches, a speech has to be painstakingly researched, organized, written and practiced before delivery. As has been stated, a speech is a public performance before an audience and, as such, should be delivered with authority and elegance. Only careful planning and repeated practice can make the delivery an effective communication performance.

What is considered good delivery? The words of Lucas (2009) put it more lucidly:

> Good delivery does not call attention to itself. It conveys the speaker's ideas
> clearly, interestingly, and without distracting the audience. Most audiences
> prefer delivery that combines a certain degree of formality with the best
> attributes of good conversation-directness, spontaneity, animation, vocal and
> facial expressiveness, and a lively sense of communication.

The speaker is a performer, a dynamic communicator who is able to adapt to varying situations and demands of the speech act.

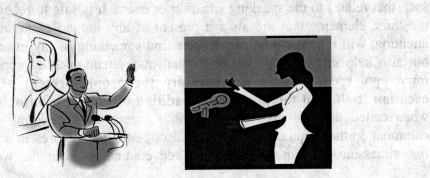

Methods of Speech Delivery

Manuscript Reading

Manuscript reading is speaking from prepared notes, often verbatim. Some speaking events require manuscript reading because of legal considerations or possible socio-political impact of a miss-statement. Conventionally The American President's State of the Union Address must be scripted and distributed to members of Congress as well as the press and others shortly before delivery. This allows for people to follow the speech as it is delivered and for accurate referencing in the press and in other related contexts. Such a speech, because it is available in print form, would not encourage misquotation as it may portend to policy statements and implementation. The President also needs to be deliberate in his statements and calculate the political implications of his words because a mistaken word, phrase or ambiguous references, may negatively impact world politics and economics. Because the manuscript is right there before the speaker, there is little apprehension as to what to say and whether it will be accurate or not.

The advantages of reading from a prepared manuscript also include an indication of preparation on the part of the speaker, who is perceived to have taken time to formally organize his or her thoughts before presenting it to an audience. This sense of apparent diligence may predispose the audience positively toward the speaker. The major challenge with manuscript reading is the possibility that the reader may not sound conversational in presenting the speech; again, there is the tendency to speak in monotone or not vary the voice tone for emphasis and other effects in the process of reading, thus disconnecting with the audience. There is also the tendency of the manuscript reader being glued to the script and not maintain some level of eye contact with the audience, but with good practice, the manuscript reader can sound conversational, direct, spontaneous and dynamic to the audience.

A good manuscript should contain concrete and easy to pronounce words, must be legible and contain delivery markers such as pauses, vocal variety, repetition, etc., that will guide the reader. The more natural a reader sounds, the easier it is for the audience to connect with the message and the speaker.

Impromptu

An impromptu speech is delivered at the spur of the moment with little or no preparation. The content of this type of speech is drawn from the speaker's life experience, especially such that relates to the speaking situation or event. It is safe to recognize that relating to the three elements that are always present at any human gathering that may call for attention, will not only help the speaker find something to say in an awkward moment, but also help in reducing the anxiety that may attend such an appointment to give an impromptu speech. **These elements are the people present at the occasion, the occasion itself, and the prevailing condition of the occasion or event**. For example, when called upon to give an impromptu speech at a wedding, it is appropriate to comment on the purpose of weddings, describe the people present and compliment them for witnessing such an occasion, and add comments about the weather or prevailing atmospheric condition- both psychological and physical. People can relate at any moment of giving an impromptu speech to these elements.

Memorized

This occurs when a speech is learned by heart and is delivered to an audience without any reference to a script. Of course, prior to delivery, the speaker must have written out a complete speech following the appropriate structure of introduction, body, and conclusion and support each of the claims in the main points with statistics, quotations, examples, comparisons, etc. Memorizing all these is a daunting task and that is why very few speeches are delivered from memory. Certainly, it is not easy to memorize a rather long speech, especially the US President's State of the Union Address, with its many quotations, statistical evidence and references. Since a memorized speech is recalled from memory, we need to understand the nature of memory and the devices that can be employed to effectively recall information from our memory bank.

After multiple deliveries of a speech, it is possible to file such away in the long term memory in the mind. This means that the speech has become second nature because it can be accessed effortlessly from memory and in the same token it has been imprinted indelibly in the memory of the speaker. **As has been noted earlier, repetition and rehearsal are what make the differences between materials stored in the short-term memory against those stored in the long-term memory.**

The techniques that help recall information from memory include **mental association**, the use of **acronyms** and **mnemonic devices**. For instance, a speaker may make a mental note of her ideas by using numbers to denote certain ideas in a speech. And when the number comes to mind, it triggers the idea or ideas that have been mentally identified with that number. A speech on the "Rise of the American Empire" can be organized mentally into three categories or simply stated as the three reasons why the American empire has flourished. Idea one is the spirit of the American constitution, two is the American mode of government, and three is the indomitable competitive spirit of individual Americans. In other words, the number one idea is the constitution; number two is the government, and three is the competitive spirit in that order. The speaker would have memorized these and have associated each reason with a number. It is easy to recall the numbers and ideas by simple association as one will stimulate the recall of the other. Mnemonic devices, on the other hand, are short cuts to memory, whereby words may be formed whose letters represent the beginning letter of each of the ideas the speaker is trying to recall from memory as in an acronym. Common acronyms include the Five Ws and H, referring to the journalistic news writing technique of identifying who, what, where, when, why, and how. There is also the Four Ps of Marketing, referring to product, placement, price, and promotion.

As challenging as memorized delivery may be, there are advantages to delivering a speech from memory. As a speech is a performance before an audience, the speaker is not encumbered by any script or reference materials during the speech and, as such, is free to perform before the audience, moving freely from position to position, gesturing, demonstrating, and presenting ideas to the audience.

Extemporaneous

Speaking extemporaneously involves partly speaking from memory and partly from prepared notes. Here a speech is written out completely, practiced and rehearsed, but the final speech will come at the spur of the speech moment, meaning that the actual wording of the speech comes as the speech is delivered. Often the speaker accesses more detailed materials from index or cue cards. This style takes advantage of the scripted material, which is at hand and the freedom of memorization, which is spontaneity. The advantages of this mode of delivery is that the speaker appears prepared with the availability of index cards and is re- assured of the veracity of the information being presented. Again, the speaker appears confident, especially that there are notes at hand to jar his or her memory during the speech presentation.

Table No. 14.1/ Methods of Delivery: Advantages and Disadvantages

	Advantages	Disadvantages
Impromptu		
	Spontaneous	No time for preparation
	Flexible	Can be inaccurate
	Conversational	Difficult to organize
		Can be stressful
Manuscript		
	Good for material that is technical or detailed or that requires complete preciseness	No flexibility Great amount of preparation time
	High accuracy	Difficult to adapt to audience response
	Can be timed to the second	
	Prepared	May sound technical Lack of eye contact
Memorized		
	Good for short speeches	Inflexible
	Speaker can concentrate on delivery	Requires practice and repetition
	Easier to maintain eye contact	Speaker can forget or lose place Difficult to adapt to audience response May sound mechanical

Extemporaneous

Organized	May be intimidating to
Flexible	inexperienced speakers
Conversational	
Prepared	
Great amount of eye contact	

Source: Seiler, William J. and Melissa L. Beall (2008). *Communication: Making connections* (7th ed.). Boston: Allyn and Bacon.

Table 14.2/THE SOUNDS OF ENGLISH

Consonants	Vowels
p as in *p*in	a as in p*a*t
b as in *b*in	ai as in p*a*rk
t as in *t*ank	e as in n*e*t
d as in *d*ank	i as in p*i*t
k as in *k*ate	ee as in f*ea*t
g as in *g*ate	o as in p*o*t
m as in *m*ope	au as in f*o*rt
n as in *n*ope	u as in p*u*t
ng as in di*ng*	oo as in b*oo*t
l as in *l*ight	uh as in b*u*t
r as in *r*ight	i as in ch*i*rp
f as in *f*at	a as in *a*bout
v as in *v*at	ay as in d*a*y
th as in *th*ere	ai as in m*y*
s as in *s*ap	oy as in t*oi*l
z as in *z*ap	ow as in p*ou*t
sh as in *sh*are	oa as in g*oa*t
zh as in a*z*ure	ee as in sm*ea*r
h as in *h*ear	ae as in st*a*re
ch as in *ch*eck	oe as in n*e*wer
j as in *j*amb	
w as in *w*inner	
y as in *y*esterday	

The English language consists of forty three meaningful sound units called phonemes. Adapted from Benjamin, James (1997) *Principles, Elements, and Types of Persuasion.* Troy, MO: Harcourt Brace.

> *Good speech delivery depends on good pronunciation, enunciation, and articulation. The starting point is being familiar with the sounds in your language. Here, the sounds of English are identified because English language has become the most widely spoken language in the world.*

Personality Traits, Vocal Variety, and Speaker Perception

Various studies have linked vocal variety and personality traits (summarized in Burgoon, J.K., Buller, D.B., and Woodall, W.G. (1989). Nonverbal Communication, The Unspoken Dialogue. New York: Harper and Row.

    a. Loud and fast speakers: self –sufficient, resourceful, dynamic
    b. Low and slow speakers: aggressive, competitive, confident
    c. Soft and fast speakers: enthusiastic, adventuresome, confident, composed
    d. Soft and slow speaker: competitive, enthusiastic, benevolent

- *People tend to form different perceptions of speaker intensity and speech rate in the public speaking context.*

Physical Aspects of Delivery

Lucas (2007) credits Herodotus for the maxim: "People trust their ears less than their eyes." This statement captures the nature and importance of nonverbal cues in the delivery of a speech. Although we can hardly separate the two sets of cues--verbal and nonverbal--in the process of speech making, because the stream of nonverbal cues co-exist with verbal, the functions that they perform sometimes may be at cross purposes, that speakers should be mindful of the nonverbal cues they give off in the process of public speaking.

    When we examine the functions of nonverbal messages, including vocalics, they are usually compared with or in reference to verbal messages. A speech can be well researched and written, but if not delivered appropriately, that is with some measure of calculated nonverbal skills, it may fail completely to achieve its purpose.

Many nonverbal factors impact the delivery of a speech and may result in the audience accepting or not, the speech propositions and evidence used in supporting the propositions. So, which is more important in the speech exercise: The content or the nonverbal delivery factors? They both are important, but as you will find out in the discussion to follow, the nonverbal factors (visual and vocal) influence the speech and its reception greatly more than its verbal content! This is not to diminish the relevance of good research and writing in the speech exercise, the point is that people trust their eyes more than their ears. Again this evidence is not to encourage sloppy preparation and writing with the hope that a brilliant performance in the delivery will compensate for lack of good structure, arguments, and evidence in the speech. As a matter of fact, the lesson is that a well written speech should also be delivered with brilliance for it to have the maximum desired effect. Lucas (2007) describes what good delivery is when he states that " good delivery does not call attention to itself. It conveys the speaker's ideas clearly, interestingly, and without distracting the audience." He added that "most audiences prefer delivery that combines a certain degree of formality with the best attributes of good conversation—directness, spontaneity, animation, vocal and facial expressiveness, and a lively sense of communication."

There are two classes of nonverbal variables that impact speech performance: visual and vocal delivery. Vocal delivery elements include volume, articulation, pitch, quality of sound, rate of speech, pronunciation, pausing, emphasis and phrasing (Fisher, 1975). Visual elements that impact public speaking include facial expressions, eye contact, appearance, gestures, body position and movement, and space.

The human voice is an instrument in delivering speeches. The quality of the speaker's voice (resonance, tone) volume, pitch, and rate, all communicate additional messages to the contents of the speech being delivered. Often times, the voice instrument becomes the major focus in the act of speech delivery. Audiences react differently to speakers with low or high pitch sounds; the more a sound pitch matches the expectations of the audience, the more endeared they will become to the voice of such speaker. Generally speaking, women have higher pitch voices than men. The loudness of the speaker's voice is equally important. The **volume** of the speaker's voice must be sufficiently loud for the audience members to hear the speech without straining their ears. If possible, a microphone should be used to augment the volume of the speaker. Not only should the speaker speak loudly enough, the speech **rate** must not be too fast or too slow; it must be within the normal human speech range of about 100 to 150 words per minute.

A speech that is delivered in monotone will bore the audience. Such a monotonic presentation would demonstrate enthusiasm and passion on the part of the speaker and the audience can sense this and not be particularly enamored by such a presentation. **Vocal variety is the key to making a speech interesting to an audience**. Sometimes a speaker's voice is lowered to draw in the audience and sometimes the voice is augmented for dramatic influence. This manipulation of the human voice keeps the audience on its toes, motivated and drawn into the participatory speech act. **Vocal variations are changes in volume, rate, and pitch in the speaker that combine to create an impression in the minds of the audience.**

A **pause** here and there in the speech brings drama and emphasis to the speech. It also commands the attention of the audience because it breaks the **fluency** of the speech and thus arouses attention and interest.

Another key vocal characteristic is articulation. This is using the tongue, palate, teeth, jaw movement, and lips to shape vocalized sounds that combine to produce a word (Verderber and Verderber, 2005). Articulation problems include: pronouncing words with extra sounds, omitting some sounds, and transposing sounds. Reading aloud and practicing one's speech would assuage some of these minor articulation problems.

Vocal Delivery Factors

Volume

The intensity of sound we humans produce from our vocal chords is referred to as Volume. Naturally, your voice should be loud enough for your audience to hear your speech delivery so clearly that they would not have to strain themselves to hear you. How would you react to a speaker whose voice you can hardly hear? A speaker whose voice volume is low can hardly maintain the attention of the audience, let alone involve them in the collaborative effort of speech performance. Thus, the speaker becomes the source of noise in the enterprise.

Depending on your speech location, you need to project your voice such that everyone, including those in the back rows of the speech location, could hear and pay attention to your speech. In some instances, the use of microphones and loudspeakers may be necessary to enhance the speaker's volume. The real impact of volume on the speech is its strategic increase or decrease in speaker volume to achieve specific goals in the speech process. Variations in volume can reflect variations in moods that the speaker wants to share with the audience. Sometimes speaking softly will get the audience to be drawn into the speech and sometimes a sudden loud voice may cause them to pay particular attention to an idea, a point of view or an event.

Different cultures perceive different **loudness of voice** as adequate in public encounters. According to Hall (1959), in social distance encounters, the American voice is below that of the Arab, the Spaniard, the South Asian Indian, and the Russian, and somewhat above that of the English upper class, the Southeast Asian, and the Japanese. So what is considered loud in one culture may not be perceived as such in another. The best measure of the adequacy of one's speech volume is its gauge by the audience to which one speaks.

Articulation

Articulation refers to clarity and enunciation of words, phrases, and sentences in a speech (Metcalfe, 2000). Articulation involves shaping the mouth, placing the tongue and teeth into position to produce sounds that the receiver would understand.

A common articulation problem is the elimination of vowels and consonants, resulting in running and mumbling words together. The meanings of words can only be clear to the hearers if they are articulated properly. Understanding is hindered when words are poorly enunciated.

The problem of poor articulation can be eliminated by simply consciously opening the mouth and speaking clearly by distinctly enunciating words. But in some cases where poor articulation is as a result of physiological deficiencies, speech therapy and other medical restoration of the vocal cord will be necessary.

Vocal cues are important indicators of the body type, age, gender, appearance, height of the speaker- all variables that influence the way someone sounds. According to Pearson and Nelson (2000), people often associate a high-pitched voice with someone who is female; someone who is younger; and someone who is smaller, rather than larger. …We visualize someone who uses a loud voice as being tall and large or someone who speaks quickly as being nervous. People who speak slowly and deliberately are usually perceived as being of high status and having high credibility.

Pitch

This represents the highs and the lows (frequency) of sounds that we produce or hear. We attach meanings to these sounds and label the source according to our expectations of the association we have for such sounds. Generally women and younger people are expected to have higher pitched voice than men or older people. When the voice pitch does not match our expectations, other meanings are inferred. According to Tubbs and Moss (2000), most untrained speakers use a pitch somewhat higher than their optimum pitch, but it has been found that lower pitches are most pleasant to listen to.

Quality of Sound

How is it that we are attracted to certain sounds and not to others? Or more appropriately, how come we prefer a certain speaker's voice over another's? The answer is in the quality of the sound. Each of us has our distinctive voice tone and quality which is a product of our vocal chords, and size and shape of the body. These allow the human voice to resonate in unique ways to produce the sounds that come out of the mouth when we speak. And as with human perception, some human sounds are received more favorably than others. In the American culture, some voice qualities that are considered unpleasant include **hypernasality** (talking through the nose), **denasality** (which sounds as though the speaker has a constant head cold!), hoarseness, and harshness (or stridency), Tubbs and Moss (2000).

Rate

This represents the speed of speech or how rapidly or slowly one speaks. When someone speaks to you in a rapid rate of speech, this may indicate to you a number of things; that the speaker is rushing and does not have time, or is not patient, or is fearful or angry, or is not sure of what to say, hence the need to rush to cover for the deficiency. The list of insinuations is endless just as when one speaks with a low speech rate. The reality is that people perceive you differently based on your speech rate.

The rate of speech can be measured in terms of how many words are delivered in a time frame of usually one minute and the average human speaking rate is about 125 to 150 words per minute Tubbs and Moss (2000). And since there is no perfect speech rate, the advice is that each speaker adapts his/her speech to the context and to the receivers.

Pronunciation

This is the uttering of syllables and words to produce sounds in a manner accepted within a linguistic tradition as appropriate. In other words, it is saying and sounding words correctly. This occurs when a speaker combines vowels, consonants, syllables, and accents to emphasize specific words in the speech (Metcalfe, 2000). A good source of information on English pronunciation is the dictionary- a source to be studied and become familiar with. Proficiency in correct pronunciation takes study and practice, but the end result is effective communication with the audience and that is the underlining purpose of public speaking.

Enunciation

This has to do with the combination of good pronunciation and clarity of the voice in order for the receiver to adequately distinguish among the words being uttered.

The perceptions associated with correct pronunciation, enunciation, and articulation make these nonverbal-vocal variables all too important to effective public speaking. Persons, who can effectively combine these vocal elements in their presentations, are perceived to be effective, good, and believable communicators. The opposite of this is that a speaker who mispronounces and cannot articulate appropriately is perceived to be ill-prepared, lacks education or training, and is unbelievable or less credible.

Fluency

A fluent speaker is one who speaks with minimal speech errors, especially vocalizations such as "um," "er," "ah," and "you know." These interrupt and cause breaks in speech and render it less fluent and less effective. While calculated pauses here and there in a speech may enhance the effectiveness of the speech, unplanned pauses and vocalizations however are disruptive and detrimental to the speech purpose, especially given the listening habits of most listeners.

Pauses

Momentary silences or breaks in a speech that separate ideas and thoughts for dramatic effect are called pauses. When used effectively, pauses can emphasize and bring about the meaning of a sentence in a speech; they can be used to create emotional response or to underscore the essence of statements, and to suggest how an audience should interpret an idea or thought. Unplanned pauses and vocal fillers in a speech will render the speech less fluent and indicate nervousness of the speaker and cause the listeners to lose interest or not pay attention to the speech.

Emphasis

The voice is a musical instrument that can be used to communicate variety of meanings. It can be consciously used to underscore, reinforce, distract from, and contradict what is said. If what is written and said in a speech were to be compared, the two sets of meanings might vary significantly. The variations in the human voice, the alteration of the speaker's rate, volume, and speech can alter observably the meaning of the written word and this is known as emphasis. Phrasing is similar to organizing words and ideas together to present a particular meaning or to make the meaning clear and easy to follow.

Examples are:

My brother is *twenty* years younger than me. That is twenty years *younger.*
It took me a *whole day* to locate my children. It took me a whole day to locate **my children.**

Visual Delivery Factors

Visual nonverbal nonvocal cues communicate messages that usually complement the verbal messages of a speaker to an audience. Oftentimes, the nonverbal nonvocal cues stand alone and do influence the audience's judgment of the speaker's credibility, interest, persuasibility and general reception of a speaker's message. Great attention should be paid to the elements of these nonverbal nonvocal cues in the speech process because of their confirmed impact on the speech exercise, especially on the perceptions the audience members have of the speaker and the message.

Scholars argue that much of human communication is nonverbal. As much as 93% of human communication is nonverbal argues Mehrabian (1972), but Birdwhistell (1970), estimates it to be 65%. Nevertheless, much of our communication is without words, thus making it imperative to understand these messages in explaining the total communication experience of people. Common folks, out of firsthand experience, do claim that action speaks louder than words, suggesting that nonverbal behavior is more important and more believable than verbal behavior. Again scholars agree that when verbal and nonverbal messages contradict (and they sometimes do), we tend to give credence to the nonverbal portion. Why? It is believed that nonverbal messages are not easily faked because they are produced involuntarily, representing how we truly feel on the inside. Yes, we can lie through our teeth verbally, but the body is believed to reveal the "truth" even when we attempt to lie by faking body language.

According to Burgoon and Bacue (2003), as much as 60% of the social meaning we share in face-to-face communication is a result of nonverbal behavior. Whenever we communicate face –to- face we are not only sharing verbal messages, we also send nonverbal messages and often times, the unspoken messages are not only more preponderant, they also weigh more in the interpretation of meaning than the words we speak. The nonverbal nonvocal delivery cues a speaker shares with the audience greatly impact them even more so than the words presented in the speech. These cues are categorized as eye contact, facial expressions, gestures, appearance, body positioning and movements. For fuller reference please visit nonverbal communication in Section One of the book.

Eye Contact

Connecting with the audience "eye-to-eye" is referred to here as eye contact. There is one speaker and several audience members. The speaker has the advantage of seeing all of the audience in front of him or her, but the audience members do not have this advantage. The speaker should maintain eye contact with all of the audience members as if he or she were the only person the speaker is addressing. This behavior acknowledges the audience member and makes him or her feel important and an indispensable part of this communication exercise. As has been confirmed by different cultural groups, truly the essence of speech is in "meeting eye-to-eye."

There are advantages to maintaining eye contact with your audience when you deliver your speech to them. Minimal reference to your script during your speech allows you to look directly at your audience to solicit their attention, build rapport with them, and track their reactions to your speech. By looking directly at your audience when delivering your speech you have the opportunity to use your facial expressions to convey the emotions and feelings you are trying to convey verbally, thus enhancing your delivery and confirming your passion and interest in ensuring that the audience receives and understands your message. Your credibility is further enhanced when you speak with minimal notes and with direct eye contact with your audience because it conveys the message to them that you have prepared well and have rehearsed your speech well to the extent that you have committed much of it to memory.

A good practice is to shift your gaze every now and then to different parts of the room or auditorium to connect with positive faces you can find and as you progress try to include all of your audience in this collaborative speech exercise. Do not neglect a part of the audience by just looking straight ahead of you without panning the room. Again you can look briefly at different parts of the auditorium to give the impression that you're actually looking at every member of the audience.

Remember that we become easily bored when the speaker avoids eye contact with us and reads from a prepared manuscript without looking up to create a connection with the audience. Put yourself in the position of the audience member, wouldn't you expect all that have been said of someone speaking to you? Also note that research evidence supports good eye contact between speaker and the audience in public speaking. There is scholarly evidence that poor eye contact will impact the audience's perceptions of the speaker and that poor eye contact may have a negative impact on the amount of information an audience comprehends during a speech (Chaiken, 1978).

Facial Expressions

The face is what people generally look at when communicating face-to-face. We humans have therefore learned ways to read expressions off of people's faces. In the public speaking exchange, therefore, the audience monitors the facial expressions of the speaker while the speaker also looks at the facial expressions of the audience for cues about how well or otherwise they are receiving the speech.

The face has several muscles that are and can be contorted to communicate specific messages. Through our facial expressions we can show anger, love, acceptance, sadness and many more emotions. We can frown in disapproval or we can smile sarcastically. Nonverbal messages, especially facial expressions are best suited to conveying emotions and feelings (Adler and Proctor, 2007). All these messages usually complement the verbal messages being exchanged by the sender and the receiver. So a speaker's message is reinforced by her facial expressions. But the facial expressions must send the appropriate message to complement the speaker's verbal message for the audience to accept and believe such. It is the congruency of these verbal and nonverbal messages that confirm meaning. If one should contradict the other, we already learned which one carries more weight with the listeners.

The spontaneity of nonverbal expressions is what makes them more believable and ingenuous to the audience. However, rehearsed and prototypical facial expressions will appear fake and will be easily detected. Researchers have confirmed that video cameras can detect micro facial expressions that are genuine from fake by studying the facial expressions of salespeople. This is to underscore the fact that your facial expressions should reflect your true state of mind and should match your verbal message.

Facial expressions are subject to abuse! You can frown at another person's message or smile wryly about it that it may cause another to lose respect in the eyes of others. The following story from Reuters (news agency) exemplifies the importance of facial expressions in consequential communication such as a political debate, when certain facial expressions are proposed to be banned by City Council officials.

PROPOSED SMIRKING BAN RAISES EYEBROWS

SAN FRANCISCO (Reuters)- A raised eyebrow, loud guffaw, smirk or other facial expressions could all be banned in future political debate under new rules proposed for the city council in Palo Alto, California.

In a bid to improve civility in the town's public discourse, a committee on the city council has spent hours debating guidelines for its own behavior.

"Do not use body language or other nonverbal methods of expression, disagreement or disgust," a new list of proposed conduct rules reads.

Another rule calls for council members to address each other with titles followed by last names, a formality not always practiced in laid-back California.

"I don't want to muzzle my colleagues," council woman Judy Kleinberg, who headed the committee that crafted the rules, told the *San Jose Mercury News*. But, she added: "I don't think the people sitting around the cabinet with the president roll their eyes."

Source: Adler, Ronald B. & Russell F. Proctor II (2007). *Looking out looking in* (12th ed.). Belmont, CA: Thomson.

Gestures

Gestures are the movements of the arms and your hands, which are used to support your verbal messages. They are used to illustrate the speech messages and allow the speaker to appear natural and not stiff in the process. Inexperienced speakers unconsciously engage in some awkward gestures such as folding arms on the chest or behind the back while speaking; they may also nervously bite their fingers, or rigidly put hands on their sides stiffly pointing downward as if to permanently control their motion. These can take away from your speech because they will distract the listeners or expose the speaker's nervousness.

The use of measured spontaneous gestures will relax you as a speaker, enhance your animation or dynamism factors, as well as project your mastery of the subject matter and confidence before the audience. There is really no need to master some set of specific gestures, but you can identify locations in your speech when you need to project images that can be created through the use of effective spontaneous gestures.

Appearance

You are familiar with the common expression that "you don't have a second chance to make the first impression." This is saying that people will judge you on the basis of your outward physical appearance before they have the opportunity to know the stuff you are made of. In like manner, the audience will estimate your trustworthiness, education level, level of sophistication, and even your moral character based on your appearance, especially clothing. Communicators who wear special clothing often gain persuasiveness (Adler and Proctor, 2007). This is not to say that the perceptions of the observers are accurate, but that they are made based on outward appearance. And we know that once people form their impressions about an event, idea, or person, it takes an effort to dislodge such impression.

Public speakers should be aware of the impact of their appearance on the audience and such subsequently impact on the message they want to share with that audience. Your appearance can make or mar your speech success. Adaptation is key. You have to be cognizant of the nature of your audience, their expectations, and the occasion, and to dress to suit the moment. This is what informs politicians' choices of wearing suits to some campaign events, and wearing T-shirts to others. Sometimes they roll up their shirt sleeves and do away with the tie to create the effect of 'identification' or 'convergence' with the audience. What about carrying and kissing babies and eating at McDonalds during campaign stumps? These are extensions of their appearance that they use to their advantage in creating impressions with the voters.

Imagine that you're to speak to your class or your fellow workers on the topic of "The Duties and Responsibilities of Our Local Police," and you dress up as a police officer. Will this enhance or detract from your speech? The police uniform should help the audience to identify with the speaker and see her in that role of an officer who, with a well prepared and presented speech, will gain the support of the listeners. In reference to a student who wore her uniform when presenting a speech about being a school crossing guard, complete with hat and badge, and whistle, Metcalfe (2000) writes that "the speaker's words and feelings conveyed commitment to the topic, while her appearance communicated authority and dedication on a nonverbal level."

Body Positioning and Movements

The way you stand before the audience, your posture, poise, and bearing and general body movements influence your communication and the judgments of you and your speech. Standing upright is a dominant posture than slouching or hunching over. Posture is defined as "the position and movement of your body. From your posture, others interpret how attentive, respectful and dominant you are" (Verderber and Verderber, 2008).

Your stance as you face toward your audience communicates your power, confidence or lack of it; it presents information about you with which the audience will judge whether you are a credible, assertive presenter who is assured of his/her knowledge and purpose. Your body positioning tells a lot about your expectations, your self-esteem, and your perception of others in relation to you. If you consider yourself to be of a higher social status than someone else, your body position "tells" that you feel superior to this other person by say, for example, how you put your hands on your hips and how you cock your head. However, your body movements should not attract attention to themselves, rather they should help emphasize your points and aid in your transitions within the speech.

Monitoring your posture and body orientation in the speech situation is very important, because your audience will interpret your attitude toward them and the topic based on your posture and positioning in relation to them. Again in the words of Verderber and Verderber, "when you are making a speech, an upright stance and squared shoulders will help your audience perceive you as poised and self-confident. So when you're giving a speech, be sure to distribute your weight equally on both feet so that you maintain a confident bearing."

Using Visual Aids/Presentation Media

Communication philosopher, Marshall McLuhan (1964), referred to the media of communication as the extensions of man because they are instruments or technologies used to enhance humans' ability to share meaning through the written words, pictures, sounds, and video. The importance of media is in their ability to convey messages in a significantly rich form that impacts not only the sender and the receiver, but also the message itself. This has led to the profound claim by McLuhan that, "the medium is the message." The nature of the medium used in conveying a message, allows it to do more than just acting as a conduit of information; it alters the meaning of the message considerably. This is such that the same message presented via two characteristically different media as radio and television, would impact the receiver in significantly different ways.

This understanding of the impact of media of information presentation has led to the use of many different audio-visual aids to enhance public presentations. What an ordinary speech cannot convey with maximum effect, can be presented with appreciable result through the use of audio-visual aids. This is because presentation media meet the diverse needs of different audience members, some of whom who are auditory, visual, or kinesthetic learners.

It is important to note that the use of visuals helps the speaker and the audience members to bypass the distortions of and limitations in using language because visuals act as '**language filters**.' If the meanings of the words employed by the speaker bypass the listener, visuals would help to convey a non-language-dependent meaning. This emphasizes the import of multi-sensory appeal in presentations, especially that of visuals. Not only does this help enhance the delivery of speeches, it equally helps the receiver to understand the meaning of the speaker. As Devereaux-Fergurson (2008) comments, visuals occupy the speaker and reduce stress and speech anxiety and help the listener to understand complex materials.

The phenomenon which is referred to as the '**pictorial superiority effect,**' gains paucity because people with visual intelligence learn best from videos, films, photographs, and other materials that appeal to this sensory mode (Gardner, 1983) and that people retain visual information better than verbal information (Alesandrin, 1983). To further support 'pictorial superiority effect' in speech delivery, Menzel and Carrell (1994 p. 17-26) claim that "visual support increases the perceived quality of speeches." And this is due in part to the fact that we are living in the age of digital television and the internet, when people expect sophisticated presentations and want to be entertained as well as taught. So, computer technologies (and the new media) have fostered expectations of interactive and dynamic content, filled with images, such that we judge the professionalism of speakers by their visual aids (Devereaux-Fergurson, 2008).

Yarberry and Epstein (2009) write favorably of visual aids when they claim that [y]our words obviously provide the "sound" element to the speech experience…Visual aids emphasize your content by helping the audience connect your content to something tangible. They summarize that, as a tool in public speaking, visual aids function to emphasize ideas through both sound and sight, to enhance your credibility, and to capture and hold attention through multimedia components. Also, they identify the unexpected benefits of visual aids to include helping to control stage fright, complement speaker notes, and help audience remember your speech.

"Presentation media are technical and material resources ranging from presentation software and real-time web access (RWA) to flip charts and handouts that speakers use to highlight, clarify and complement the information they present orally" (Cooper and Lull, 2011). As the name suggests, these materials aid the speech presentation by allowing the speaker to present complex ideas, new concepts, detailed and supplemental information, not only through speech but also through the use of audio and visual media. Therefore, using presentational aids must be to fulfill these supplemental or complementary purposes and not to detract from or overtake the speech itself.

The two categories of public presentation aids are audio and visual media. Audio materials are recorded sounds of persons and objects, pre-recorded sound effects, music on compact discs and other sound storing devices. Visual aids include overhead transparencies, flip charts and posters, whiteboard and chalkboards, graphs, charts, recorded images, video and movie recordings, modern computer technologies, and presentational software.

Table 14.3/How Visual Aids Affect the Retention of Messages

	After three Hours	After Three Days
Speech Alone	70%	10%
Visual Alone	72%	20%
Speech and Visual	85%	65%

When combined with speech, visual aids enhance retention of a message.
Source: Gamble and Gamble (1998) *Public Speaking in the Age of Diversity (2nd ed.)*.MA. Allyn and Bacon. Originally from Zayas-Baya, Elena (1977). "Instructional Media In the Total Language Picture." *International Journal of Instructional Media*, 5. pp145-150.

It does take some expertise to effectively use these presentation devices. As useful as any presentation media can be in enhancing the delivery of information to its receivers, it takes informed choices and guided use to employ them successfully. It is useful to know the different types of presentation media, but more important is the awareness of their different characteristics. To be aware of the different characteristics is to be aware of the appropriate media to employ to aid your presentation. Again, familiarity with the different effective guidelines for using these media will be of great advantage to the user.

According to Coopman and Lull (2011), just as any other part of the speech, you must have good reasons for incorporating media into your presentation and the suggested reasons are to:

1. Draw attention to your topic.
2. Illustrate an idea that can't be fully described by words alone.
3. Stimulate an emotional reaction.
4. Clarify a point.
5. Support your argument with a graphic display of facts and figures.
6. Help your audience remember your main ideas.

Types of Audio-Visual Aids

Otherwise called presentational aids, these are the objects and materials used as adjuncts to the speech itself. There are many different forms of presentational aids. The list is endless but your choice must be informed by relevance and suitability of the aids. In other words, presentational aids must not be employed in your speech just for the fancy of displaying the 'bells and the whistles' of the aid, but to help you deliver your speech more effectively beyond the capacity of just the words of your mouth.

Presentational aids include audio materials which are recorded sounds of persons and objects, pre-recorded sound effects, music on compact discs, video and movie recordings, and other sound and image storing devices. Others are overhead transparencies, flip charts and posters, slides, whiteboard and chalkboards, graphs, charts, tables, objects, models, drawings, photographs, modern computer technologies, and presentation software.

Audio and Sound Effects Recordings

You probably have heard and do understand the meaning of the expression: 'seeing is believing,' but you should also realize that in the world of radio storytelling, 'hearing is believing.' Because radio and storytelling extend our sense of hearing, the radio professional and 'griot' must present audio materials in ways most appealing to the listener in order to gain and maintain his or her attention. This is why sounds are creatively manipulated and presented in invigorating ways as major tools to aid listening in aural presentations.

Many broadcast studios have on record sounds of objects, events and persons, stored in their audio library that they use to complement their audio presentations in order to bring life and the impression of reality, immediacy, and freshness to their broadcast. As you present your speech, it is advantageous to both you and your audience to hear the sounds of objects, events, animals or people that are the subject of the speech. While you may not be able to bring a real lion to display before your audience, a recorded sound of a roaring lion would have great effect on the audience. Better still, if you can show a video of the lion in its natural habitat interacting with other lions or cubs, this would bring the reality of the animal to the audience and would aid in their understanding of the subject matter of the speech, in a more incisive manner than without the audio-visual material.

Audio recordings and sound effects are available on the internet for easy download to your CDs, MP3s players and other digital audio devices. And with the necessary USB cord you can transfer the sounds and amplify them to meet the requirements of the physical setting where the speech will be presented. So, you can incorporate into your speech sound effects such as the sounds of trains, percussion instruments, conversations, traffic, airplanes, etc., to extend the imagination of your audience beyond pictures and other visual aids.

Video Recordings

Usually video recordings capture the images and sounds of objects, events, and people that you can use to complement your speech. Nowadays, there are unprecedented devices that can record images and sounds fast, with great quality and in the most seemingly difficult to reach places –under the deep ocean, in the clouds above the earth and caves and crevices. So, the possibility of using video recordings to enhance your speech is very high as these video recordings are available in public and private collections that have been uploaded into the popular site "YouTube" for public use.

Recently in my Intercultural Communication class, the topic of discussion was "the world's five major religions," and the ease with which we accessed video materials online to illustrate and enhance our discussion was nothing short of 'miracle.' Just in seconds, we accessed on YouTube the tenets of each of the religions with video imagery of worshippers splattered across the projection screen. In minutes, we 'visited' Jerusalem, Bombay, Mecca, Jakarta, etc. Apart from online video sources, there are clips of movies you can 'drop' into a presentation, DVDs you can show, or personal recordings you can show to demonstrate or illustrate the points you're trying to make in your speech.

People, Objects, and Models

Most of public speeches are about people, events, ideas, and things. What better way to make an impression upon the audience members than to bring the real thing into the speech situation. People can be used to illustrate people, processes, events and ideas. A demonstration speech about talking with "Bata Drums" (Yoruba, West Africa) can better be accomplished through using a volunteer Bata drummer who would show the different steps and combination of hand beatings on the drum and its tensioning tongs, that would produce syllabic rhythm that combine to 'talk' to the hearers. People as we know can be used as props and performers in a speech, but the caveat is that they are to be used as adjuncts and should not become the main focus of the speech.

When people are not available or may not be effectual, we can use objects or models. These are things we can feel and touch because, as humans, they are three dimensional and, as a result, we can use them as props. Props are considered anything your mind can imagine that will get and keep attention focused on you and your subject and are considered by some to be among the best techniques for adding interest, humor, and variety to presentations and speeches (Epstein and Yarberry, 2009). While doctors use cadavers to teach anatomy and physiology in a teaching hospital setting, it is inappropriate and, perhaps illegal, to bring a cadaver to a speech setting. Therefore, a scale model of a human is certainly useful in your case in explaining the functions of the different parts of the human body. Again, while using live reptiles to illustrate your speech about different types of this animal may seem a good choice, models may be more appropriate because some members of the audience may be squeamish about crawly things.

Whenever appropriate, representations of objects such as models are useful in enhancing your speech. When the real thing is too large and cannot be easily moved, a skyscraper for instance, use a model; when the real thing is easily damaged and cannot be easily replaced, as in the remains of the boy king of ancient Egypt, King Tut, use a model and; when the real thing can suffer the stress of repeated demonstration, use a model. A good example mentioned by Epstein and Yarberry is the use of a dummy for CPR demonstration. Since you must practice your demonstration process several times to gain perfection and to be sure that you do it right before the audience (the only time that matters), how many times do you think you can compress a volunteer's chest before the volunteer starts to experience some discomfort? With a dummy, that is certainly not a problem. "Yes, you will certainly learn a lot from a dummy!"

Obviously you must realize that your model should be easily transportable, easily demonstrable, and easily seen from different parts of the speaking auditorium. In addition, you must follow the rules of visual aid use which include showing your object only when it needs be seen and to "fade to black" (TV production terminology) immediately after the showing. That is, the object must not be in public view after use because it may constitute a distraction from the other equally important parts of your speech.

Photographs

When using objects and models is not feasible, the next best things would be the two dimensional representation of those things in the form of drawings and photographs. The popular expression that "a picture is worth a thousand words," is true if the pictures are strategically used in the course of the speech. Of course pictures can create vivid imagery in the minds of the viewers, and can be used as concrete evidence as well as emotional proof to appeal to the audience. Imagine that you are to give a speech on the topic of "Pollination." You can describe the process of how birds suck nectars of flowers and move pollen grains from a plant to another to fertilize it, or you can actually show pictures of birds in the act of plant fertilization. Or how best can you show the unfortunate event commonly referred to as "911" in the US when terrorists brought down the Twin Towers in New York City to the ground, without showing the pictures of the towers after they had been destroyed?

Again, the emphasis here is how best to use photographs to your advantage in delivering your message to the audience. The advice for the appropriate use of photographs in speeches includes the following. You're to make sure the picture is large enough to be seen by everyone in your audience and, if possible, you should enlarge the photograph or use **document cameras** to capture and project the photograph onto a large screen. Pictures can distract your audience or may even prompt them to ask questions when you're not ready for them. Therefore, you are to refrain from passing the pictures around while your speech is in process and if you must for one reason or another, you must collect them back from the audience before you go on with your speech. Also, inform your audience of when you shall entertain questions on the pictures you have passed around. Finally, make sure that your pictures are tasteful and do not overly disturb the emotional balance of the audience. For example, you cannot show a nude picture of a person or individuals to an audience of religious people who have not been forewarned of the nature of the pictures before doing so. Yes, there are instances that you may have to do this, but apprising your audience would leave the choice to them to want to look or not at the pictures. Remember that for every liberty we have to enjoy, there are corresponding responsibilities (For more discussions on communication and ethics see Chapter Fifteen of the book).

Drawings, Diagrams, and Maps

Sometimes when you cannot get to show your audience photographs, you can choose to show drawings of what you're trying to portray. For example, we do not know what Jesus Christ looked like; however, there are multitudes of his drawings everywhere. Drawings can be as effective as showing the real thing, but the audience should know the difference between a drawing and the real thing. Drawings and diagrams can be used to explain the various stages in a process and to show relationships among ideas, things and events. For example you can use a drawing or diagram to show the process of food digestion in humans or the stages in the process of building a house.

<u>Figure 14.1/Example of a Map.</u>

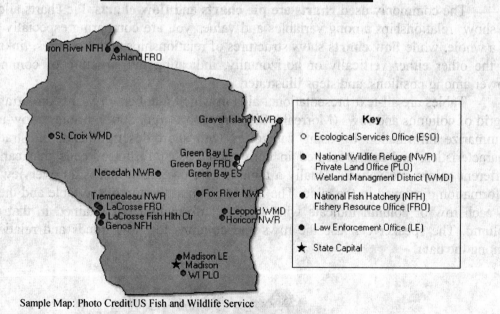

Sample Map: Photo Credit:US Fish and Wildlife Service

Encarta dictionary describes a map as a geographic diagram—a visual representation that shows all or part of the Earth's surface… Or a diagrammatic drawing of something such as a route or area made to show the location of a place or how to get there. So, when you're to give a speech about a place, or historical site, or about the geographical features of a State or country, you can show the map of the place with all of the major features indicated and, as such, you will transport your audience with you to that location for a surreal encounter. What about a speech on how to defend yourself in the Traffic Court? Surely, a map or diagram of the location, route, the direction of traffic, and major landmarks would map the territory in visual form to convince the judge of your arguments to win your case.

With several internet sources for maps, diagrams and drawings, it is easy to access the maps, drawings, and diagrams you want to use to enhance your public presentation. Especially with Google earth, you can access instantaneously any map of any location to show direction, important places, and general physical features of the area, all in real time.

Graphs, Charts, and Tables

Often, you have to present a lot of numerical information in your speeches and in order not to confuse your audience members, using summary of such data in the form of percentages or ratios would be useful. And when you present these numerical data in the form of graphs, charts and tables, your audience can easily see and understand the point you're trying to make with the data.

Graphs are visual representations of data, which enable you to summarize and organize numbers by comparing them, showing their patterns, trends, and they help to clarify otherwise cumbersome and boring statistics. The frequently used graphs are line and bar graphs.

The commonly used **charts** are **pie charts** and **flow charts**. Pie charts allow you to show relationships among variables and values you are comparing especially as part of a whole, while **flow charts** show structures of relationships and processes, linking one to the other either vertically or horizontally, indicating the structure of command or power among positions, and steps illustrated.

Tables are all-text presentational aids in which numbers or words are arranged in a grid of columns and rows (Morreale, Sitzberg, and Barge, 2007). Tables allow users to summarize information by using categories with short descriptions to illustrate their characteristics, and are presented in convenient visual forms of cells that can be of different colors and values. Usually a table is given a title which is an overview of the information displayed in the table. The title is given at the top of the table and the labels of each row or column indicate what type of information is contained in that row or column. The speaker can use the rows and columns to show trends and relationships among the data.

Figure 14.2/Sample Bar Graph.

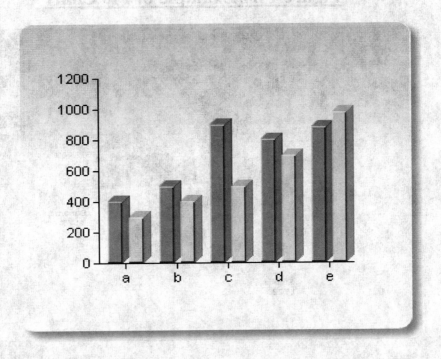

Figure 14.3/Sample Line Graph.

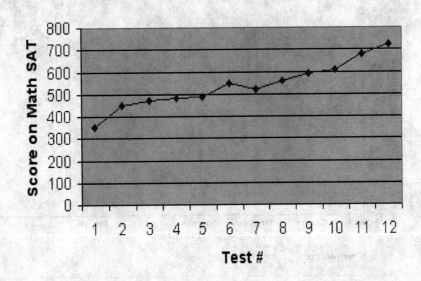

Figure 14.4/Example of Pie Chart

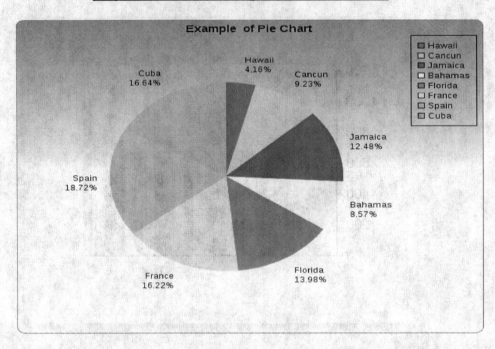

Figure 14.5/ Sample Double Line Graph to Show Comparison.

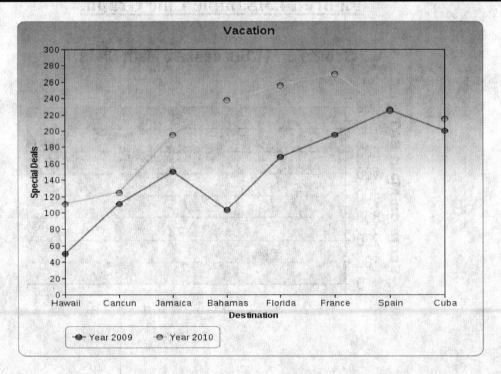

Figure 14.6/ Sample Flowchart

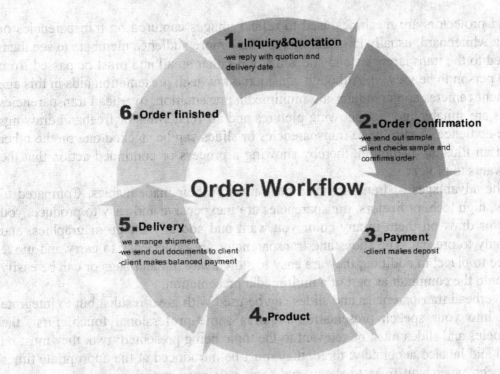

Document Cameras

This device functions like the overhead projector you are probably familiar with, but unlike the overhead projector that projects images from transparency sheets using light and mirrors, document cameras use video camera to capture and display images to a larger screen. The cameras are of high resolution that you can use to capture images from various sources such as photographs, books, magazines, slides, even objects with great detail and clarity. The ability to capture images through video cameras allows for ease of manipulation of the images captured and the different parts of these images can be highlighted, enlarged, detailed and stored digitally. These cameras are the modern overhead projectors because they are like a scanner, microscope, whiteboard, computer, and projector rolled into one (Jaffe, 2011).

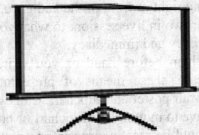

Portable screen for projecting images, including transparencies, pictures, and video.

Overhead Transparencies and Slides

Overhead projectors are machines used to reflect images captured on transparencies or slides to a whiteboard, usually large enough to allow more audience members to see them as opposed to the transparencies and slides that are rather small and must be passed from person to person to be viewed. Although considered low-tech presentation aids in this age of document cameras and computer-aid multimedia presentation, overhead transparencies and slides are suitable aids for showing pictures and art renderings or freehand drawings to a large audience. Again, these transparencies or slides can be stacked one on the other to project an illusion of motion, thereby showing a process or continued action that the speaker wants to project.

The advantages of transparencies far outweigh their inadequacies. Compared to other new, high tech. projectors, transparencies are inexpensive and easy to produce, you just copy or draw on them in any color you want and add any image or graphics, and you're ready to present. The slides and transparencies are rather easy to carry and move from place to place; in addition, they are easy to store away in hand bags or can be easily scanned onto the computer as part of a multimedia presentation.

Overhead transparencies and slides can be used with great results, but to integrate their use into your speech presentation requires some professional touch. First, the transparencies and slides must be relevant to the topic being presented; two, they must be numbered and labeled accurately; three, they must be introduced at the appropriate times in the speech when you refer to them; and four, you must practice and rehearse your speech with the transparencies incorporated at the appropriate times. In case you have to use your transparencies over a period of time, you have to follow the rules of presentation aids which include: "show them when you have to and fade to black or do away with them when you're done." This suggests that you should either cover the transparencies when you are not using them or to turn the machine off after you're done using it. Leaving the projector on with a transparency still in view or with a blank transparency projected to the screen is an avoidable distraction from the speech.

Flip Charts and Posters

A flip chart is a large pad of paper that rests on an easel, allowing a speaker to record text or drawing with markers during a speech (Coopman and Lull, 2011). When speakers ask for ideas from their audience in an interactive brainstorming session, there is need for immediate documentation of the ideas generated. The flip chart and/or posters are the objects that are used in this type of situation. Although the speaker might have prepared materials on the flipchart or poster ahead of the speech, usually they are useful for instantaneous writing or drawing right in front of the audience. To this end, it is advisable to always have to add a thing or two in live session, to what you had prepared beforehand to create the impression of currency and immediacy.

Whether you prepare them before hand or you write on them in front of the audience, whichever is the case, these means of presentation require some careful handling. Consider the size of your poster and flipchart. Can everyone see it from all over the speaking venue? Do you have to mount your flipchart or poster on an easel and where in the front of the audience would be most appropriate to place it? You must make sure not to turn your back on the audience when you're writing so that you may not break that all too important conversational rapport your are maintaining with your audience. Again, you must time when you "flip" the flipchart in the speech and when to remove it from public view. A good use of these manual presentation aids will prove of immense advantage to you in your speaking assignment.

Whiteboard, Blackboard or Chalkboard

Every classroom and every conference room seems to have one these days. Of course they are for writing on, but should you write on them during a public speech presentation? They serve the same purpose as flipcharts and posters and as such should be used sparingly because flipcharts and posters look more professional and, importantly, you do not run the risk of "board back," "back talk," and "board worthiness."

Board back occurs when you lean against the board and chalk or marker residue gets onto your shirt or dress. **Back talk** on the other hand is turning your back on the audience (a rude gesture in some cultures) when you are supposed to be facing them. And board worthiness has to do with your hand writing, this, as in all nonverbal messages can be very subtle, but have significant effects on the audience's perception of you as a sloppy writer, unprofessional person and speaker.

If you must use the whiteboard, blackboard, or chalkboard—whatever you call it—you must check the ability of the audience to see the board, their ability to read what you had written or will write, and when you must point to the board, you should not use your fingers. Get close enough before you point and please use a wooden or a laser pointer.

Handouts

Handouts are prepared written materials that you hand to the audience members to give them pertinent information that you want them to leave the speech situation with for their immediate use or for future reference. It is a means of continuing the speech experience for the audience members and the speaker as well. One, the handout may consist of the names, addresses, and e-mails of both presenter and the audience; it may contain references for websites to be consulted for the audience's use after the speech, and it may contain information about a process to follow to accomplish a task that was presented in the speech of which the audience may easily forget.

While handouts have their purpose, you must know how and when to use them. Determine whether you will distribute the handout at the onset, during, or after the speech. Know exactly when you need the audience to have the materials in the handout for use during the speech and you should have a helper who would do the distributing for you. Also, know this: If you distribute the handout at the onset of your speech, the tendency is for your audience to be preoccupied with its content, even when you have started speaking. Again, how would you prevent this distraction? Collect the handouts back until the end of your speech? No, that would look unprofessional! Better still, you should give handouts at the end of your speech so that they may serve the purpose of extending the speech experience and not distract from it.

Computer Technology and Presentational Software

Presentations these days are done with multimedia aid using presentation software such as PowerPoint to present your speech with a combination of text, graphics, audio, video, and animations. Who says you cannot "frazzle and dazzle" your audience with all of the media that are available to you today? I say you should not do so! You cannot afford to exhaust and confuse your and audience. Using too many of the applications without much tact will surely frazzle your audience. While you can use presentational technologies to enhance your speech, they must become your substitute. You're the speaker and not the presentational aids.

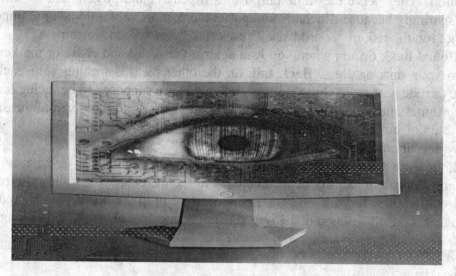

PowerPoint software allows you the user to use pre-designed templates, color backgrounds, stock photos, to create dynamic, professional presentation without all the frills. You have to follow some basic rules of presenting digital slides to enhance your speech. You must choose the right template for your speech, the right transitional modes, right images, less crowded bullets per power point page (three to four suggested), and you must not talk to the screen, but to your audience. More importantly, you must practice your PowerPoint presentation with your speech and make sure that everything works well before and during the speech.

Sometimes a speaker may make quite an impression by accessing online sources during the speech to bring a sense of immediacy and timeliness to the presentation. Using **real-time web access** (RTWA) has its advantages. With RTWA you navigate in real time through web pages associated with your topic…You can use it to demonstrate how to do something special on the web, such as researching an idea, checking current status of any topic, or displaying articles found on websites that support your purpose or argument. This **webidence,** gives your presentation an in-the moment feeling not possible with static digital slides (Bell, 2004). (Coopman and Lull, 2011) define **webidence** as web sources displayed as evidence during a speech, found by using real-time web access or **webpage- capture** software. They submit that because the audience members understand that you are functioning in real time, you can encourage their participation in your navigations or searches.

The lurking danger in using the computer to access materials online is twofold: one, the access speed of the computer is a factor in the timing of your speech. What happens when you try to access the web and your computer slows down to a crawl? What would the audience be doing when this happens and how can you best cope with the "technology moment"? During your practice session you should have discovered this problem and if that is the case, then you have to make a judgment call to use or not to use the web. Two, there is no telling that the website you're trying to access will be accessible at the time you're searching for it. This is an experience that will add to your already present speaking anxiety. However, with advancement in technology, computers are becoming more sophisticated and faster than ever before, so make sure that the computer (desk or laptop) you're using will work up to your desired speed. Use available computer software to your advantage and do not let it overtake your presentation and cause you more stress and loss of credibility.

Table 14.4/Advantages and Limitations of Presentation Media

TYPE	ADVANTAGES	DISADVANTAGES
Overhead Transparency	Technical simplicity; ease of use	Transparency placement and order; speaker tends to talk to screen
Flip Chart and Poster	Documents audience feedback and ideas	Lacks a professional look; may be hard for all audience members to see
Whiteboard and chalkboard	Records spontaneous thoughts	Writing takes away from speaking time; speaker may appear unprepared, rude
Document camera	Projects images with great detail; can zoom in, capture images, display 3-D renderings	Expensive equipment; complex to use
Video	Evokes emotions in audience; portrays examples	Interferes with speaking pace and audience focus
Handout	Enhances audience recall after speech; reinforces key ideas	Disrupts continuity of presentation; wasteful
Model	Provides specific references; helps audiences visualize materials and concepts	Can be too small or detailed; not suitable for large audiences
Audio media	Sets mood; triggers imagination	Decreases speaking time; distracting
Digital slide	Blends text, images, video, sound	Overused, boring, speech content neglected; speaker tends to talk to screen
Real-time Web access	Fresh, current information	Slow connections and download times; available systems can be unreliable

Source: Coopman, Stephanie J. and Lull, James (2011). *Public Speaking: The Evolving Art.* Boston, MA: Wadsworth.

Review Questions

1. Why should a speaker pay attention to how a speech is delivered?
2. Explain the statement that: "A speaker is a performer."
3. Is how something is said more important than what is said? Why?
4. Discuss the advantages and disadvantages of the four speech presentation styles.
5. What do you understand by the physical aspects of speech delivery?
6. What are the visual and vocal characteristics a speaker should be mindful of when delivering a speech?
7. What are the advantages and disadvantages of using audio/visual aids in speech presentations?
8. Identify and discuss the dos and don'ts of PowerPoint presentations.
9. Elaborate on the statement that claims that: "the medium is the message."
10. Discuss the different speech organizational patterns identified in this chapter.
11. Read the following passage and write a one – page reaction paper on the topic of Discourse Markers

---

Discourse Markers

Discourse markers are words and phrases used in speaking and writing to 'signpost' discourse. Discourse markers do this by showing turns, joining ideas together, showing attitude, and generally controlling communication. Some people regard discourse markers as a feature of spoken language only.

Example
Words like 'actually', 'so', 'OK', 'right?' and 'anyway' all function as discourse markers as they help the speaker to manage the conversation and mark when it changes.

In the classroom
Discourse markers are an important feature of both formal and informal native speaker language. The skilful use of discourse markers often indicates a higher level of fluency and an ability to produce and understand authentic language.

BBC/UK

SECTION FOUR

Informative and Persuasive Speeches

15. The Informative Speech

16. The Persuasive Speech

Chapter Fifteen
The Informative Speech

One of the goals of public speaking is to inform and educate an audience about an issue, a process, an event, a person, a concept or an idea. The ultimate goal is to provide information to enrich the understanding of the listeners. An electorate, for instance, would base its judgment of issues and persons on the level of information it has access to. The purpose of informative speaking, therefore, is to not only provide access to information, but also open up the mindset of the receivers through exposition, description, explanation, and analysis.

Democracy as a philosophy of governance thrives on the principle of access to and presentation of information. As such, informative speaking becomes a civic duty to ensure informed judgment in the polity. In the corporate sphere, information is an ingredient in the process of making strategic decisions, a conscious determination of choices among competing alternatives. So, information provides choice, allows for discrimination among choices and the determination of preferred choices. The quality of the choice the audience makes depends on the quality of information presented, the audience's capacity to process and understand information presented and, the relationship of such information to the different situations, interests, and expectations of the audience. The ultimate goal of an informative speech, therefore, is the accurate encoding and decoding of the content of communication. This will lead to information gain that will enable the communicators advance their causes.

We have heard of the constant reference to the fact that we live in the information age where the chief product is knowledge. We go to school to acquire knowledge, the know-how that will translate to marketable skills and serve as the basis for effective functioning in the community of the Knowledgeable. The professor, therefore, is an information merchant; the politician an information broker; and the doctor, a harbinger of specialized information. Surviving in the information age depends on seeking and having access to relevant information and we do these in corporate information sessions, educational settings, health fairs, political rallies, and from distilled sources of books, media, especially the internet, and from narratives told us by family members, clergy, and others.

Gaining access to and using information is not as egalitarian as we would want it to be because it costs resources to have access to and participate in the global information village. So, many people don't have resources as others to avail themselves of useful information to live by in the information age. There is, therefore, a **knowledge gap** or **information imbalance** in every society of the world, certainly greater in some than others. With the creation of the internet, access has become widespread, but there is still the phenomenon of the **digital divide**, describing the information haves and the have-nots. There is useful purpose for engaging the art of public speaking to spread information and to engender critical thinking and informed choices in the world we live in. But we should be mindful of the differences that naturally segment audiences and the social dimensions that persist and serve to separate people.

So, the audiences of communication, especially public speaking, are usually diverse in terms of their sociology and psychology. In other words, people vary in terms of their age, gender, race, socio-economic status, education, geographic location, interests, religion, and in many other aspects of culture. People, on the bases of these often observable differences, also have different beliefs, attitudes, and opinions. Consequently, the act of presenting information to an audience so varied must cater to its inherent differences.

There are basic theoretical assumptions that serve as the bases for the speech act of informative speaking. Assumption one is that people are receptive to and seek information that is relevant to their situations, their aspirations and interests. Secondly, people seek different levels of information and process information differently depending on their cognitive capacity; and, thirdly, people tend to benefit from receiving information as it is a means to education, learning and social integration. Therefore, access to information will produce a level of understanding that will bring the sender's and the receiver's spheres of understanding closer than they were prior to the informative experience.

The three basic principles to know when informing an audience are enumerated by Verderber and Verderber (2005) who summarize that (1) audiences are more likely to listen to information they perceive to be intellectually stimulating; (2) audiences are more likely to listen to, understand, and remember information that is presented creatively and; (3) audiences are more likely to listen to and remember information they perceive to be relevant. The questions to ask at this point are numerous and such will guide what we discuss in this chapter. What motivates the receiver to selectively access information? What factors influence the process of information reception? Which information is most likely to be processed and remembered by the receiver? What roles do language forms play in the process of information sharing? How are meanings constructed and shared? What are other message considerations in the process of informative speaking? What are the source factors that influence audience information processing? These and others are the relevant questions that will guide our thoughts when we focus on speaking to inform others. These critical questions are general research questions that guide theorizing about the process, patterns, structures, and consequences of public speaking.

The theories we are going to explore in this section, therefore, will deal with sources of information, that is, the characteristics of the sender that influence the message and its reception; the receivers of information, that is, how humans listen to and process information; and the message, that is, what type of presentation works best for which audience and, how should the message be organized and what type of contents interest the audience the most. Also, the influence of the channels of communication in the speech context such as semantics, kinesics, paralinguistics, oculesics, and others will be analyzed.

While these theories and principles are explored under the informative speaking rubric, they are by no means exclusive to this type of public speaking; they can be included under the persuasive sphere of speaking as well. Why? This is because the delineation of informative and persuasive is not mutually exclusive. An informative speech, without doubt, will lead to cognitive shifts in the receiver, thus qualifying as effecting a change in such mental structure which is a form of persuasion or a precursor to persuasion. A persuasive speech, on the other hand, must inform in other to persuade! The starting point in the process of persuasion is being informed of the aspect, object, or purpose of change; thus, both speaking traditions are intertwined.

The separate treatment of these two types of speaking is but an academic exercise. Though such classification may induce different reactions from the audience in that, if an audience is advised to listen to a point of view without being asked to accept the point of view, such experience may be classified as informative, but some theories of persuasion (e.g. Zajonc's **Mere Exposure Theory**) would claim that just exposing yourself to a particular perspective, influences one way or the other.

Information Defined

With our senses, we humans receive or actively seek stimuli from the environment. Sensing becomes the first stage in the process of knowing and knowing is dependent on information reception. The tendency to want to reduce uncertainty about our environment is the motivation to seek out stimuli or information; therefore, information can be referred to as that which causes us to reduce uncertainty (Dance and Larson, 1972). Reduction of uncertainty helps to predict the world we live in and have a measure of control and stability over circumstances in which we find ourselves. And Redmond (2000) writes that in essence, information is all the stuff we don't know, all the uncertainties that we possess. We can tell something is information because we recognize it as new to us."

When we have access to information we can use such to adapt to situations in which we have to function such as making decisions, solving problems, and judging events, ideas, and people. All of these are mental processes, all occurring in the brain; therefore, information reception and processing will lead to **cognitive changes** in people, the result of which is **understanding**. When actions are induced as a result of information received or understanding, then another facet of change is involved, which is **behavioral change**.

We can safely conclude that the purpose of informative speaking is mainly to provide information or new stimuli to people, who will receive it, analyze and interpret it, and adapt themselves to their prevailing circumstances, based on the learning and understanding garnered from such informational exchange.

Purposes of Informative Speaking

Jaffe (2007) states that the needs of the different audiences you may have to speak to vary, confirming that: "Listeners may have no information, a minimum information, forgotten or outdated information or misinformation." The different information states of the audience calls for different information strategies. Therefore, the speaker has to present new information, supplemental information, or counter information, as the case may be. The ideas of Jaffe (2007) regarding how to present information to meet these differences are outlined below.

These guidelines are in no way exhaustive of what you can do in these different situations, but they serve as foundation upon which your other ideas may be placed. Knowing the information needs of the audience presupposes that you had conducted an evaluation of the information level and need of your audience. This confirms the information already presented under audience analysis. You must know the audience to which you have to speak and determining the familiarity or lack thereof of your audience with your topic is the starting point. Then, an assessment of the accuracy, sufficiency, or adequacy of information known is undertaken in order to determine what your job as a speaker specifically entails in each situation.

Guidelines for Presenting New Information
1. Provide basic , introductory facts—the 'who," "what," "when," "where," and "how," information.
2. Clearly define unfamiliar terminology or jargon
3. Give detailed, vivid explanations and descriptions
4. Make as many links as you can to the audience's knowledge by using literal and figurative analogies and by comparing and contrasting the concept with something familiar.

Guidelines for presenting Supplemental Information
1. Dig into your research sources to discover less familiar details and facts.
2. Go beyond the obvious; add in-depth descriptions, details, and facts.
3. [Narrow a broad topic and provide interesting and novel information about just one aspect of it.]

Guidelines for Presenting Reviewed or Updated Information
1. Review material by approaching the subject from different angles and different perspectives.
2. Be creative; use vivid supporting materials that capture and hold attention.
3. Use humor when appropriate; and strive to make the review interesting.
4. For both reviews and updates, present the most recent available information.

Guidelines for Countering Misinformation
1. Prepare for emotional responses--often negative ones. Consequently, present the most credible facts you can find, and tone down the emotional aspect.
2. Look for information derived from scientific studies, especially quantification, when statistical or numerical support would be best.
3. Define your terms carefully; consider explaining the origin of specific words or ideas.
4. Counter negative prejudices against and stereotypes about a topic (such as a particular culture) by highlighting positive aspects of the subject.

Note: The guidelines are developed here into a table format, but were not presented as such in the original work by Clella Jaffe (2007).

Five Types of Informative Speeches

Informative speaking can be organized to describe, explain, demonstrate, and report. These are speeches about processes, events, ideas and concepts, people, objects, and places. The goal is to present accurate information that is clear, easy to understand, and meaningful about all the listed categories of informative speeches purposes listed above.

The speech designed to inform can fall into five categories. **These are speeches about processes, events, places and people, objects, and concepts or ideas**. These categories overlap because people are involved with ideas and concepts; also, processes are about events, places, objects and people. In any case, it is the specific purpose of your speech that will identify in which category your informative speech can be placed. These are the subjects and objects we usually need to acquire information about or be educated about as requirements of modern, daily, professional living.

Speeches about Processes

Processes are series of steps or stages in developing or accomplishing something. Many of the events and phenomena around us form in stages and over time. Life itself is a process and becoming a skilled public speaker takes time and involves series of activities. Manufacturing is a process; electing a president involves series of activities and stages that culminate into the inauguration day. So, speeches about processes are speeches about events, places, ideas, and objects. Speeches about processes describe how something is done, how something comes to be, or how something works (Griffin, 20011).

As professionals already or in training, your ability to describe or demonstrate how something works or is done, is a testimony to your knowledge and skills set that make you experts. As a student, you can gain familiarization with how something occurs or how it is done through good research, in turn becoming an expert when you're to present such information garnered to an audience that may not be familiar with what it is that you're informing them about. This is how the education process works either in the classroom, on the job, or through mediated learning methodology such as television, radio, the internet, etc.

Examples of speeches about processes are "Becoming a naturalized American citizen," "The process of launching communication satellite into orbit," "The stages of getting a professional tattoo," and "The stages of building a skyscraper." Whatever the topic may be, remember that you know something, either through direct experience or learning that your audience can benefit from. Often the audience may have insufficient, incomplete or outdated information about your topic. So, it is your job to conduct adequate **audience knowledge audit** in order to educate them beyond their current level of understanding, give them adequate information, and show them new ways of accomplishing what they may already know how to do. Your information must be fresh, new, offer new insights, and must be beneficial overall to the audience.

Speeches about Events

Events can be natural occurrences or human organized and enacted. The value of this type of speech is the significance of the event in terms of the effects on people and the people who are involved with it. This is the human interest angle to the event. An event is not significant if it does not impact the lives of humans, animals, and or institutions in a remarkable way. In other words, what and who of events and their effects, are what make them provoke the curiosity of people and, as such, make them worthy of being spoken about. If an event only touches the life of the speaker or a handful of people in society, it may become interesting and significant because of the manner in which it affects the lives of the few individuals. More importantly, the speaker may have to project such effects of the event both on the audience and on the rest of society as a whole.

An example of an important event was the earthquake that hit the country of Haiti in January, 2010, when over 200,000 people were killed and many more were displaced and the economy of the country left in total ruin. The people of Haiti and, indeed the world, would never forget the magnitude of the destruction to life, institutions, both social and physical, and the collective psyche of the people of the country. Other notable world events are: The disappearances of people and machine in the Bermuda Triangle, the inauguration of Barack Obama as the first African-American President of the United States, the assassinations of President Kennedy and Dr. Martin Luther King, Man's first landing on the moon, etc.

Events capture our imagination and appeal to our collective humanity. They shock us, they amuse us, and they inspire us. Speaking about events to an audience helps them to experience their common bonds as humans while they vicariously relive those sights and sounds and capture their impacts on society.

Speeches about People and Places

People and places are fascinating because human curiosity motivates us to want to know more of ourselves, other people, and especially of other places. These are excellent sources of informative speech topics due to their significance, their uniqueness and their ability to arouse people's curiosity.

As a speaker you want your audience to understand why this place or person is important or useful to them or their community, important historically, or just interesting and worth learning about (Griffin, 2011). When young people display unusual and unique talents, they are classified as prodigies. The emphasis is unusual and unique and that is why Mozart, Beethoven, Schubert, who were and still are musical giants, are fascinating informative speech topics. Bill Gates sits atop a giant computer company, Microsoft, and that makes him an interesting and unique speech topic. Barack Obama broke the barrier of racism and cynicism to become the first African to be elected to the presidency of the United States of America.

In terms of places, Afghanistan and Iraq fascinate Americans, especially because the U.S. has engaged the military of the two countries. There are many intriguing and unique locations across the world and in our solar system that would interest an audience. The surface of the Moon, The Florida Everglades, The World's Tallest

Building in Dubai, UAE, The Sahara Desert, Yellowstone National Park, The Pyramids of Egypt, The Taj Mahal in India, etc. are important locations and places that will interest people.

Speeches about Objects

Objects are things we can sense or perceive, but which are non-living. They are tangible and are elements of nature or are created by humans. The audience would inquire about the nature, components, characteristics, use and impact of such objects on their lives. Informative speeches about objects, therefore, describe and explain the objects' characteristics and how we may use them profitable and efficiently in our daily lives, or such speeches may show how these objects are made and how useful or dangerous they may be to humans.

Cultural artifacts are objects that fascinate Anthropologists and sociologists and they make good informative speech topics for the general population as well. Certainly, modern humans are fascinated with Airplanes, Submarines, Digital Cameras, Machine Guns, Nuclear Bombs, Hybrid Cars, Communication Satellites, Sun Glasses, Laptop Computers, etc.

Speeches about Concepts and Ideas

Concepts, ideas and mental thought products are rather abstract in nature. Because abstract ideas are rather challenging to grasp, a speaker must define, clarify, and concretize such ideas for the benefit of the audience's understanding. This is why speaking about concepts and ideas is also referred to as speeches of definition and explanation. Examples of concepts and ideas for informative speaking are Freedom, Affirmative Action, Malthusian Theory of Population, Polyandry, Democracy, Opportunity Cost, Myocardial Infarction, etc.

For the speaker to engage the audience on any of these topics, two steps must be taken: one, is defining the concept for a common understanding and reference for both the speaker and the audience and, two, explaining what the idea represents and its various dimensions. Definition is the key to understanding concepts because from that basic level of understanding, the audience can be taken on to a higher level of explanation that usually follows. But there are **two major types of definitions: logical and operational**. The logical definition is the primary associative meaning of the concept that identifies it as separate in nature and manner compared to others. This is also the dictionary, general or common meaning. The operational definition narrows and focuses the meaning of a concept for a particular purpose in a practical situation. Often, this is referred to as a working definition that explains how something is in a particular state or how it works in non-hypothetical situation.

According to DeVito (2006), you should use definitions when you wish to explain difficult or unfamiliar concepts or when you wish to make a concept more vivid or forceful. He offers strategies for effective defining of concepts and ideas.

Defining Concepts

When defining concepts, you can approach defining in these three major ways:

1. Use a variety of definitions.
   Here are the ways you could define a term:
   a. Define by etymology—tracing the historical or linguistic development of a term or concept.
   b. Define by authority—using the definition of an authority or an authority's view of the term.
   c. Define by negation—noting what the term is not; that is by negation.
   d. Define by symbolization—by showing the actual thing or a picture or model of the concept or idea.
2. Use definitions to add clarity--define only what needs defining and don't use extensive definitions that do not clarify. If the purpose of the definition is to clarify, then it must.
3. Use credible sources—use authority with credibility, expertise, and direct experience with the concept. In other words, link the authority's profile to the term. This is justification. Proceed from known to unknown.

Source: DeVito, Joseph A. (2006). *The Essential Elements of Public Speaking,* (2nd Ed.). Boston, MA: Allyn and Bacon.

Organizing Informative Speeches

As we have learned from the previous chapter, we know that public speaking favors organization and that a structured speech is easier to follow because it encourages not only audience involvement, but also aids its ability to recall information presented in the speech. It has also been noted in the previous chapter that the suitable organizing patterns for informative speeches are **chronological, spatial, topical, narrative, and cause –and – effect patterns.** A speech can be organized in more than one pattern depending on the topic, and what the purpose of the speaker is. Below, Griffin (2011) identifies the organizational pattern or patterns suitable for a variety of informative speeches.

Table 15.1/Type/Pattern of Speech Organization

Type of Informative Speech	Type of Organizational Pattern
✓ Speech about a process	Chronological organization
✓ Speech about an event	Chronological, topical, or causal organization
✓ Speech about a place or a person	Spatial, topical, or chronological organization
✓ Speech about an object	Topical, spatial, or chronological organization
✓ Speech about a concept	Topical, chronological, or causal.

Source: Griffin, Cindy L. (2011). *Invitation to Public Speaking Handbook*. Boston, MA: Wadsworth.

The following speech outline (***Evolution of Tattoos)*** could be organized in different patterns, possibly topical and chronological, but the speaker chose the topical method for her outline. Explain how you can develop the speech using the chronological pattern.

Sample Informative Speech Outline

Topic: **Evolution of Tattoos by Dawn Mount**

Specific Goal: To inform my audience about the evolution of tattoos.

Intro:

I.   I may be a little older, a wife, a mother of two, a professional, and an athlete but.....I love tattoos!

II.   I picked this topic because I myself have a lot of tattoos, and I wanted to learn where tattooing came from and how they have evolved to today.

III.   The dictionary defines Tattoo as the act or practice of marking the skin with indelible patterns, pictures, legends, etc., by making punctures in it and inserting pigments. (www.dictionary.com)

Thesis: From the very first tattoo to the present, changes have been made to the tattoo industry primarily due to ancient cultures, sailors, criminals and the circus.

Body:

I.   <u>Tattoos date back to ancient cultures.</u>
    A. Iceman Oetzi (<u>www.history of</u> tattoos.org)
    B. Russian mummies (see handout)
    C. Egyptian mummies (www.smithsonian.com)
    D. Maori culture

II.   <u>Tattoos date back to sailors.</u> (www.tattooarchive.com)
    A. Captain Cook
    B. Meanings

III.   <u>Tattoos date back to criminals.</u>
    A. Romans & Greeks
    B. Prison Tattoos (www.tattoo-designs.dk)
    C. Tracking criminals (New York Times)

IV.   <u>Tattoos date back to the circus.</u>
    A. Introduction of the first electric inking machine
    B. Circus freaks and sideshows
    C. Advertisement for tattooists

Conclusion:

I.   Tattoos have changed over the past 5000 years mainly due to ancient cultures, sailors, criminals and the circus.

II.   It doesn't matter what religion you are, what color you are, or how old you are....anyone can have tattoos.

Outlining the Informative Speech

As we have noted that audience members prefer and respond better to organized speeches, the speech outline, therefore, helps the speaker to organize the elements of the speech and order the progression of the speech such that the entire process is coherent, polished and, most importantly, easy to follow by the audience. The human body cannot stand without the skeleton that provides a frame on which it stands. Buildings cannot stand except they have frames and structures to anchor them; so is a bridge that requires its basic frames before the dressings of lanes and tar and dividers. A good outline highlights your speech's framework and displays your ideas and their relationships to one another (Jaffe, 2007).

Your speech cannot stand without its structure. Even if you commit your entire speech to memory, you still have to organize it according to some form of outline in your mind to jog your memory. For example some people use mnemonic devices of outlining ideas according to the first letter of the opening phrase of a main idea or point in the speech or some will create a song that they can easily remember to outline their ideas in their minds. I can still recall such technique taught us in my elementary school about the rivers of Africa. Imagine a speaker speaking about: The Rivers of Africa who would burst into a song, though in his or her mind, about the topic that goes like this:

The Rivers in Africa are—

The Rivers in Africa are—

Nile, Niger, Benue, Congo,

Orange, Limpopo, Zambezi.

The names of some of the rivers might have changed now, but remember I learned this in 1967.

There are different ways you could outline your speech depending on your purpose and experience. You could have a rough draft outline, a complete script or text, preparation or full sentence outlines, and speaking notes. In your **rough draft outline**, you document the different parts of your speech, but not outlines with proper format of alternation, coordination, and indentation. You're familiar with the idea of rough drafts and you know they are not usually the final draft, so your main ideas and the supporting evidence are identified in the different sections they belong to in the structure of the speech, but are not fully polished and ready for presentation.

The speech manuscript or **full script** is your speech containing the main points and supporting materials all fully developed and written out completely containing every word you would deliver in the speech. Writing a full script would suggest that you intend to read your script word for word, but it may also mean that you will use the full script for memorization practice, such that a preparation outline or speaking notes may be developed from it to help you deliver the speech extemporaneously. The **preparation outline** is the record of your major ideas and their supporting materials written out in full sentences relating one idea to the other from beginning to the end. The **speaking note** is the actual material you will take to the podium with you; it is the highlights of your speech with instructions to yourself on what to do, what to say, and how to say it at every juncture of the speech.

Preparation Outline

This is a fully developed speech written out in or full sentences detailing what will come under each of the major parts of the speech: The introduction, body, and conclusion. As an outline, though, the formatting is very important. The standard formatting for preparation outlines includes the use of headings, standard format of alternation, coordination, and indentation. See the sample speeches at the end of the chapter.

Heading

Writing your preparation outline starts with a heading or title, a general purpose, specific purpose, thesis statement, main points, and the organizational pattern used. (See the sample speech worksheet)

Sample Speech Worksheet

Topic: The Bermuda Triangle
General Purpose: To inform
Specific Purpose: To inform my audience about the origins of the legend, astonishing incidents, and the explanations of the Bermuda Triangle.

Central Idea: The Bermuda Triangle, also known as the Devil's Triangle, is a region in the western part of the North Atlantic Ocean in which numbers of aircrafts and surface vessels are alleged to have mysteriously disappeared.

Main Points:

    I. The origins of the legend of the Bermuda Triangle are from disappearances.
    II. The incidents of the Bermuda Triangle are truly astonishing.
    III. There are natural and paranormal explanations of the Bermuda Triangle events.

Sources:

    1. Kusche, Larry: Bermuda Triangle.
       http://en.wikipedia.org/wiki/Bermuda_Triangle
    2. Quasar, Gian J., Bermuda-Triangle.org
       http://www.bermuda-trinagle.org/html/introduction.html
    3. McGregor, Rob. Bermuda Triangle Odyssey.
       http://www.fatemag.com/issues/2000s/2005-08article la.html

See the speech on The Bermuda Triangle presented in the preparation outline format at the end of this chapter. As an exercise, you should compare the speech outline with its developed preparation outline format and see where one helps in the development of the other. A good speech worksheet will help you identify your topic, clearly articulate your thesis statement, identify your main points and state them in categorical, complete sentences. The preliminary sources you identify in the worksheet will help you find relevant information and supporting materials for your final speech.

Alternation

Alternation suggests mixing a number of things up and in this case it is a system of alternating Roman numerals, English alphabets, and Arabic numbers in labeling different types of ideas and parts of the speech such that it gives for varied and appealing appearance.

Each main point in the speech is identified with a Roman numeral (I, II, III), a sub-point with an English alphabet (A, B, C), and, a sub-sub point with an Arabic number (1, 2, 3). And if there is a sub-sub-sub point, it will be represented with small letters of the English alphabet (a, b, c,) in that order. So, you are alternating Numerals, alphabets, and numbers. See the Bermuda speech as an example of how this is done.

Subordination

The principle of subordination suggests that you put under a main point all the materials that support that main point and to arrange them in some fashion or structure. Some supporting points can be arranged in their order of importance to the main point, so they should be presented as such in such grades as A, B, and C, or 1, 2, and 3 as the case may be. Look at how this principle is used in the "Blood Diamonds" speech.

The main points are stated as encompassing statements and the ideas under them only serve the purpose of expanding and justifying their claims. It should be noted that the sentences in the subordinated points can be further reduced to single or shorter sentences that summarize the ideas that the speaker will deliver to the audience at the various points in the speech. In other words, the preparation outline format does not present all of the materials the speaker would deliver to the audience, but are sentence summaries of such materials.

Guidelines for Informative Speaking

Several authors of books on public speaking have presented different guidelines for effective informative speaking. Let us examine some of these ideas and, then, see how we can improve on these guidelines and possibly add new ones. Here I added comments to explain what the authors meant by the suggestions given.

Coopman and Lull (2011) offer the following suggestions:

1. **Keep your speech informative**
    (This implies that you should give information by offering explanation, defining, analysis, demonstration, and not by giving opinions or telling what the audience should do)

2. **Make your speech topic come alive**
    (This has been explained already in the previous chapter. You should be excited about your speech and your presentation nuances—both verbal and non-verbal should reflect your passion for the topic and for the opportunity to inform the audience. Your speech will come alive when you use vivid and concise language, when you relate the speech context to that of the audience, and when you use stories and other attention grapping methods to arouse and keep the interest level of your listeners up throughout the exercise.)

3. **Connect your topic to your audience**
    (To connect with your audience, you must have considerable knowledge about them, especially in relation to the topic of your speech. Your language must connect; your examples, narratives, statistics, and the overall tone must connect with the experiences of the audience. After all, a speech is meant for an audience and not the edification of the speaker.)

4. **Inform to educate**
    (The informative speaker should do more than just present information to the audience; she should show the usefulness of the information and how the contents relate to the lives of the listeners. This is why the purpose of the informative speech is outlined in the previous page. Your speech is to provide new and useful information; it should supplement current information they already have and; it should correct misinformation they already believe in.

5. **Use presentation media to inform**
    Presentations aids are flip charts, graphs, pictures, pictographs, etc. that you use to enhance your presentation. These presentation aids extend another sense other than the hearing sense and that tend to help the listeners' comprehension of the information presented them. See the guidelines for using presentation aids in the previous chapter.)

The important elements in the informative speech process include choosing a suitable topic and specific purpose, analyzing the audience, gathering relevant materials, choosing supporting details, organizing the speech, using words to communicate meaning, and delivering the speech. Lucas (2007) emphasizes that for an informative speech to be successful, all of these must be done effectively. Lucas suggests five guidelines for effective informative speaking:

1. **Don't overestimate what the audience knows.**
   (When you speak to an audience do not assume that your knowledge level about the topic is the same as your audience's. When you mention an event, and idea, or a concept in passing in your speech and you do not elaborate, you leave the audience wondering whether you would return to explain, elaborate, or elucidate what it is you are trying to inform them about. A good audience analysis will indicate whether your listeners have no knowledge, insufficient knowledge, or are misinformed about your topic.)

2. **Relate the subject directly to the audience.**
   (We have heard of this precept several times in this book. To be passionate about your topic is not enough, you must make the audience members like and be interested in your topic and your information should convey this interest and, the way to achieve this is to answer that question that every listener asks: what is in this for me? So, relate the speech to their experience, education level, concerns, and passions. Personalize your information by putting the audience in the description, role playing, and stories that you weave to convey your important points.)

3. **Don't be too technical.**
   As a professor, I always like to identify and define the special words in every one of my lectures. This is to proceed from a common understanding of these terms to reduce any uncertainty that may arise as a result of semantics—the use of words and the different meanings that they represent. It is the primary job of any speaker, any teacher, to breakdown the jargons that the listeners will encounter in the course of the presentation. Imagine that you're to explain the game of soccer to a group of people who are new to the game. Would you freely use such terms as penalty kick, off-side, two-three- five formation, etc. without having to explain in simple terms what these jargons mean? Or how many of you would call the emergency number 911 and report a big fire by stating to the telephone operator that "a conflagration is consuming a domicile?" Your job is to simplify the technical, specialized words you use in your speech, but if you do not, you stand to confuse rather than to inform.

4. **Avoid abstractions.**
   Abstract ideas are vague, unclear, and blurred. The opposite are clear words, precise ideas, descriptive and concrete stories which relate to real events and real people. Abstract ideas are stale and lifeless, but practical ideas relate to the realities and passions of people. Lucas (2007), states that to avoid abstractions speakers should use description, comparison, and contrast.

5. **Personalize your ideas.**
   Lucas describes the concept "personalize" in this way: to present one's ideas in human terms that relate in some fashion to the experience of the audience. This suggests that you should use stories about events and people to personalize your ideas; you should also cite examples that will make the experience real for the audience. Personal stories help you connect with the listeners who can project

themselves into the story plot, scene, act, and the entire drama—this will bring the message home, indeed. For example, imagine that you're to speak about Marijuana abuse among college students to your classmates. You open your speech this way:

How many of you are currently under the influence of some mood altering substances? Are you under the influence of alcohol, some pills, or marijuana as I speak to you? I do not intend to embarrass you or place you under any stress of having to publicly confess to your personal choices and that is why I do not expect any of you to answer my question. However, I will answer this question for you.

According to national studies and governmental data, in excess of 60% of college students admit to using marijuana on a daily basis. This information shows that if this classroom were to be a typical American classroom, then more than half of you in this class, right now, are under the influence of marijuana. But I know this class is not a typical American college classroom or is it?

I know a college student who has agreed for me to use his life history of marijuana abuse to explain to this class that marijuana is indeed a gateway drug as many experts have confirmed over the years. In the next two or three minutes, let me tell you the story of John, a college sophomore like any of you sitting in this class right now.

The following guidelines will be listed and you're to explain what each of them is trying to say to you as a speaker and if you've already come across the precepts before.

Upon the premise that an informative speech should be interesting and that it should gain the attention of the audience as well as be understandable by them Jaffe (2007) quoted the precepts of Rubin (1993) as guidelines for producing comprehensible messages:

1. Do an "obstacle analysis" of the audience.
   (What part of your speech may not be easy for your audience to follow? What words may sound strange to them? And what if you're to be on the receiving end of your own speech, would you be willing to pay attention to it and, better still, you would find it interesting and useful? All of these and many more constitute obstacle analysis of your audience, to the extent that dealing with them will help you do a better job of organizing and presenting a good speech.)

2. Organize the material carefully.
   (Apply all you have learned about organizing your speech here. Identify main points, use parallel structures among the main points, use transitional statements, internal previews, summaries, signposts, etc. Use appropriate structure such as chronological, topical, narrative, cause-and-effect, comparison-contrasts, etc.)

3. Personalize your materials for your audience.

4. Compare the known to the unknown.

5. Choose vocabulary carefully.

6. Build in repetition and redundancy.
(Repetition and redundancy are desirable in communication, especially in public speaking because of the nature of human listening. Stating something more than once allows the audience more than one opportunity to catch it and, redundancy refers to repetition in many varied ways so that you build in a buffer system into your speech, especially to emphasize salient points or arguments.)

7. Strive to be interesting.
There are many more guidelines presented in many different communication books, but they all state in varying ways the different ones already mentioned here. For more instructions on how to best organize and word your speech, visit Chapter Two where instructions are outlined on how to use language effectively and appropriately.

Example of a Speech Body in Preparation Outline Format

I. Examples of diamond's power and influence can be witnessed through a number of civil conflicts that have taken place in Africa over the course of the past thirty years.

   A. Such was the case in the Southern African country of Angola, which after gaining its independence from Portugal in 1975, erupted into a 27-year long civil war between government forces and guerilla rebels.

      1. The rebels' success in mining and selling diamonds abroad provided an illegal but lucrative trade to secure funds for their fight against Angolan government forces.

      2. To gain an understanding of how these diamonds trade hands on the black market, one manner of smuggling is described in the United Nations Fowler Report released in the year 2000, states that "a former DeBeers diamond company stockholder worked with the government of Zaire to provide military equipment to Angolan rebels in exchange for bushels of raw diamonds."

      3. Such under the table transactions provided billions of dollars in arms and capital that indirectly contributed to the deaths of nearly 600,000 Angolans and the displacement of nearly four million more over the course of their conflict.

      4. Although what I have just described may seem like a scene from a

Hollywood movie, conflict diamonds soon became African government opposition groups number one method of income for providing funds to carry on armed conflicts.

II. During a civil war that raged from 1991-2002 in the tiny West African nation of Sierra Leone, a rebel faction used profits from the sale of conflict diamonds, in an attempt to overthrow its country's government.

A. By taking control of government owned diamond mines, the rebels had a Near endless supply of investment capital in raw gem form.

1. These mines were worked by local residents, some as young as seven years old, who were often threatened with death or amputation for non-compliance.

2. The profits made from conflict diamonds sales granted the rebels an effective manner in which to fuel their insurgency. From purchase of arms from European weapons manufactures, to hiring of mercenaries to aid in their fight, diamonds offered a simplified but profitable alternative to methods of conflict that had been used in the past.

3. In his book: Blood Diamond: Tracing the Deadly Path of the World's Most Precious Stones, Greg Campbell states that, "the diamond industry trading centers in Europe funded these horrors by purchasing nearly $125 million dollars worth of diamonds per year from rebel groups within Sierra Leone."

Indentation

To indent is to space typed material or text on farther from the other to create an impression of one idea coming under the umbrella of another. The first idea may be indented five type spaces to the right while the second idea is indented ten spaces to the right and the third idea is indented fifteen spaces further to the right. Typed written texts are structured in the form of a series of steps, one lower or higher than the other. The clockwise movement on this ladder would mean stepping from a major idea down to a sub-idea and further down to a sub-sub idea. (See the example that follows).

Body I: The major causes of cancer are known to medical practitioners.

A. The American Cancer Society states that more than 87% of lung cancers are smoking related.
1. This means that not all smokers develop lung cancer. Quitting smoking reduces an individual's risk significantly, although former smokers remain at greater risk of contracting lung cancer than people who never smoked.

2. People who don't smoke, but who constantly breathe the smoke of others are also at high risk for lung cancer.

B. Besides smoking, there are many other risk factors for this disease.
1. According to www.cancer.org, cigar and pipe smoking are almost as likely to cause lung cancer as cigarette smoking.
2. Working with asbestos is another risk factor. If those people who work with asbestos also smoke, their risk is greatly increased.
3. Marijuana also has many cancer-causing substances. If it is inhaled deeply and held in the lungs for a long time, it will be harmful to the body. Other risk factors include a diet low in fruits and vegetables, air pollution, radiation treatment to the lungs, exposure to coal, gasoline and diesel exhaust, and one's personal and family history.

Balanced or Parallel Structure

As you must have observed from the examples of speeches presented in the preparation outline format, the main points are accorded equal weight and are in the same format. Each main point is stated as a full declarative sentence and not in different sentence structures. They should be worded similarly and, each main point is to be accorded roughly the same amount of time when presenting the speech.

For example, the three main points of a speech on Exercises and another on Vegetarianism can be presented as follows:

Main Points
I. Exercising benefits our body in many ways.
II. Exercising can be accomplished in different ways.
III. Exercising has to be done right it to be a success.

Main Points
I. Vegetarian diet has many health benefits
II. Vegetarianism has profound positive environmental effects.
III. Vegetarianism protects animals from cruelty and slaughter

Each main point is one complete sentence and not two or three ideas fused together. As a matter of fact, each of the main points should express distinct ideas that can stand alone even as a speech topic. From the examples above, the following topics can be developed:

The Benefits of Exercising,
The Different Forms of Exercise, and
Successful Exercising

Other speech topics from the main points are:

Health Benefits of Vegetarian Diet,
Environmental Effects of Vegetarianism, and
Vegetarianism and Animal Protection

Many students make the mistake of presenting main points as incomplete sentences or fragments, sometimes as questions, and often as two or more separate ideas fused as one, but labeled as one main point. The lesson here is to always phrase your main points to include only one idea and stated in one sentence of claim. This is both for the benefit of you, the speaker, and your audience. While you're preparing and organizing the speech, the parallel structure and one- idea, one- sentence main point will give you direction and focus and allow you to explore and develop your ideas fully. And when you present your speech to your audience, it will be easy for them to follow the progression of your thoughts and ideas and, by so doing, will enhance their listening ability.

Speaking Outline

This is a modified preparation outline in that it follows the structure and the visuals of the preparation outline, but it includes instructional cues and marks for the effective delivery of the speech inserted at every necessary juncture in the process of speaking. It is an aid to delivering the speech which helps the speaker to perform the speaking exercise with ease and punch. Equally it is an aid to memory because the different cues help jog the speaker's memory to recall and present practiced speech with spontaneity.

Lucas (2004) identifies four major guidelines for the effective use of a speaking outline. These are that the speaker should: 1. Follow the visual framework used in the preparation outline; 2. Make sure the outline is legible; 3. Keep the outline as brief as possible; and 4. Give yourself cues for delivering the speech.

Sample Informative Speech (1).

Speech Topic: **Conflict Diamonds**
By Daniel Bell

General Purpose: To explain the impact of Conflict Diamonds in Africa

Specific Purpose: To inform my audience about the uses of conflict diamonds to fund wars in Africa, the countries that have been significantly affected, and what is being done to combat their trade.

Thesis: Although diamonds are synonymous with love, commitment, and marriage in the Western world, in Africa illicit precious stone trades have funded bloody armed conflicts.

Introduction:

I.   What is smaller than a marble, owned by millions of Americans and, has inadvertently contributed to the death, mutilation, and displacement of millions of people throughout the continent of Africa?

   A. The answer to this question and the subject I will be speaking about is diamonds. But more specifically, conflict or blood diamonds as they are more commonly known.

   B. To clarify, a conflict diamond is defined as "any rough diamond that is used by rebel movements to finance their military activities, including attempts to undermine or overthrow legitimate governments."

II.   In the Western world, diamonds are viewed not only as a symbol of status, but also as the personification of love, commitment, and marriage.

   A. However, through copious research and an insatiable interest regarding this subject, I have learned to view these breathtakingly beautiful stones from an entirely new perspective.

III. Through this presentation, I will introduce you to the uses of conflict diamonds to fund wars, the countries they have affected, and what is being done to combat their trade worldwide.

(Transition: I will begin by examining how conflict diamonds came to change the course of modern warfare and where they were first widely used to fund such conflicts.)

Body:

I.   Examples of diamonds power and influence can be witnessed through a number of civil conflicts that have taken place in Africa over the course of the past thirty years.

    A. Such was the case in the Southern African country of Angola, who after gaining her independence from Portugal in 1975, erupted into a 27-year long civil war between government forces and guerilla rebels.

        1. The rebels' success in mining and selling diamonds abroad provided an illegal but lucrative trade to secure funds for their fight against Angolan government forces.

        2. To gain an understanding of how these diamonds trade hands on the black market, one manner of smuggling is described in the United nations Fowler Report released in the year 2000, states that " a former DeBeers diamond company stockholder worked with the government of Zaire to provide military equipment to Angolan rebels in exchange for bushels of raw diamonds."

        3. Such under the table transactions provided billions of dollars in arms and capital that indirectly contributed to the deaths of nearly 600,000 Angolans and the displacement of nearly four million more over the course of the conflict.

        4. Although what I have just described may seem like a scene from a Hollywood movie, conflict diamonds soon became African government opposition groups number one method of income for providing funds to carry on armed conflicts.

(Transition: I will now offer you a brief summary of another African conflict that was responsible for bringing the use of conflict diamonds before the general world public.)

II.   During a civil war that raged from 1991-2002 in the tiny West African nation of Sierra Leone, a rebel faction used profits from the sale of conflict diamonds, in an attempt to overthrow its country's government.

    A. By taking control of government owned diamond mines, the rebels had gained a near endless supply of investment capital in raw gem form.

        1. These mines were worked by local residents, some as young as seven years old, who were often threatened with death or amputation for non-compliance.

2. The profits made from conflict diamonds sales granted the rebels an effective manner in which to fuel their insurgency. From purchase of arms from European weapons manufactures, to hiring of mercenaries to aid in their fight, diamonds offered a simplified but profitable alternative to methods of conflict that had been used in the past.

3. In his book: *Blood Diamond: Tracing the Deadly Path of the World's Most precious Stones*, Greg Campbell states that, "the diamond industry trading centers in Europe funded these horrors by purchasing nearly $125 million worth of diamonds per year from rebel groups within Sierra Leone."

4. To illustrate the reality of the atrocities caused by the sale of conflict diamonds during this war, it was estimated by Amnesty International at the conclusion of the war that "between 50,000 to 75,000 people lost their lives, 20, 000 were maimed, and over 2 million were displaced as a result of this diamond funded war conflict."

(Transition: Now that I have given you a general understanding of what conflict diamonds are, their specific uses, and the human rights abuse they have caused, I will now inform you about what is being done to stop the sale of conflict diamonds on the world market.)

III: After many years of public debate on how to effectively curb conflict diamond sales, the international community of diamond traders gathered in Kimberly, South Africa to develop a monumental system called The Kimberly Certification Scheme to deal with the problem. This system was implemented in August of 2003.

A. This process requires that participating governments ensure that shipments of rough diamonds be imported/exported in tamper-free containers and that they be accompanied by a uniquely numbered government validated certificate stating that the diamonds are from sources free of conflicts.

1. Although this system is assumed to have resulted in a decrease in the number of conflict diamonds in circulation and is applauded by human rights groups worldwide, many international organizations feel as though a publicly monitored process would be more effective.

2. A report published in November, 2006 by non-governmental organization Global Witness, states that "although the Kimberly process has taken positive steps towards eradicating the sale of conflict diamonds, the practice still exists today throughout African nations such as Democratic Republic of Congo and Cote D'Ivoire." Global Witness further states that "with the positive steps already undertaken through the implementation of further restrictions regarding rough diamond sales, the trade in conflict stones could be successfully depleted to a fraction of the percentage it represents today."

Conclusion:

I. I hope that as a result of the information that I have shared with you today that you have gained a better understanding of the subject of conflict diamonds, their uses and the effects such illicit stones have on populations of their countries of origin.

II. I urge you all, on your own, to do a bit of independent research to gain an even better clarification as to how these polished stones of natural beauty may conceal, in their glimmer, the heartache and bloodshed of innocent victims spanning the African continent.

Bibliography

Campbell, Greg (2002). *Blood Diamond: Tracing the Deadly Path of the World's Most Precious Stones*. Westview Press.

Roberts, Janine (2003). *Glitter & Greed: The Secret World of the Diamond Empire*. pp. 223-224.

United Nations (2000) Fowler Report.

Global Witness Non Governmental Organization (2006). Retrieved 2007.

<u>Sample Informative Speech (2)</u>

<u>The Bermuda Triangle</u>
<u>*By Steve Damiani*</u>

<u>Introduction:</u>

I. There is no other place in the world that challenges mankind with so many extraordinary and incredible events. On average, four aircraft and about twenty ships vanish each year. More than 1,000 lives have been lost in the past twenty-six years, without a single body being found.

II. This is where far more aircrafts and ships have disappeared throughout recorded history than in any other region of the world's ocean, leaving no wreckage or bodies.

III. What's the name of this strange place? The name of this place and the subject that I will be speaking about is the Bermuda Triangle.

IV. The Bermuda Triangle, also known as the Devil's Triangle, is a region in the western part of the North Atlantic Ocean between Bermuda, Miami, Florida, and San Juan, Puerto Rico in which a number of aircraft and surface vessels are alleged to have mysteriously disappeared.

V. I have learned from reading such books as <u>Into the Bermuda Triangle</u> by Gian J. Quasar, and <u>The Bermuda Triangle</u> by Charles Berlitz, and from further research, the origins of the legend, the interesting incidents, and the natural and paranormal explanations of the Bermuda Triangle.

VI. Today, I will speak about the origins, incidents, and the explanations of the Bermuda Triangle.

(Transition: We'll start by looking at how the legend started)

Body:

I. The origins of the legend of the Bermuda Triangle are from disappearances.

    A. The Bermuda Triangle has many ways in which it received its name, but the main reason was the result of the disappearance of six Navy planes and their crews on December 5, 1945.

        1. On December 5, 1945, Flight 19 that consisted of five navy Avenger bombers with a crew of 14 mysteriously vanished on a routine training mission, as did a rescue plane of 13 men sent to search for them.

        2. Six aircrafts and 27 men, gone without a trace.

        3. After this incident, Vincent Gaddis is credited with putting the triangle "on the map". The term "Bermuda Triangle" was first used in an article written by Vincent H. Gaddis," which appeared in the February, 1964, issue of *Argosy*, an American pulp magazine.

    B. The other way the Bermuda Triangle received its name was because of the triangular flight plan.

        1. According to Gian J. Quasar, author of <u>Into the Bermuda Triangle</u>, Bermuda has been given its name principally because it was noticed at the time that the highest point of the triangular flight plan from Fort Lauderdale was in a direct line with Bermuda.

        2. Also partly because Bermuda seems to be the northern boundary of both earlier and later disappearances of ships and planes in very unusual circumstances.

        3. The Bermuda Triangle has been called "The Devil's Triangle," "The Triangle of Death," "The Hoodoo Sea," "The Graveyard of the Atlantic," and various other names due to all the unusual incidents that occur there.

        (Transition: Now let's look at the incidents of the Bermuda Triangle)

II. The disturbing incidents of the Bermuda Triangle are unknown.

    A. According to the website, Bermuda-Triangle.org, the incidents can be traced back to the time of Christopher Columbus in 1492.

        1. In 1492, shortly before making land in what Columbus called the West Indies, he recorded in his ship's log that he and his crew had observed a

large ball of fire fall into the sea and that the ship's compass was behaving erratically.

2. Estimates range from about 200 to 2,000 incidents in the past 500 years.

3. In 1973, the U.S. Coast Guard answered more than 8,000 distress calls in the area and more than 50 ships and 20 planes have gone down in the Bermuda Triangle within the last century.

B. There are many incidents of disappearing planes and ships.

1. According to Charles Berlitz, author of The Bermuda Triangle, a chartered DC-3 en route from San Juan to Miami, in the early morning of December 28, 1948, disappeared into the void with thirty-six passengers and crew.

2. Planes continued to disappear during the fifties. On February 2, 1952, a British York transporter, carrying thirty-three passengers and crew, vanished on the northern edge of the Triangle while on its way to Jamaica.

3. There have been many major ships lost in the Bermuda Triangle. In January 880, a British warship, Atlanta, left Bermuda for England with 290 aboard and vanished not far from Bermuda. On March 4, 1918, a U.S. Navy supply ship U.S.S. Cyclops, all 500 feet, 19,000 tons with 309 aboard disappeared with no radio messages and no wreckage ever found.

(Transition: Let's look at the explanations of the Bermuda Triangle)

III. There are natural and paranormal explanations of the Bermuda Triangle.

A. There are many natural explanations of the Bermuda Triangle.

1. A significant factor with regard to missing vessels in the Bermuda Triangle is a strong ocean current called the Gulf Stream. It is extremely swift and turbulent and can quickly erase evidence of a disaster.
2. The weather also plays its role. Hurricanes are powerful storms which are created in tropical waters, and have historically been responsible for thousands of lives lost and billions of dollars in damage.
3. The topography, which is a study of Earth's surface shape, plays a role in the explanations. The topography of the ocean floor varies from extensive sandbanks around the islands to some of the deepest marine trenches in the world.
4. It has been claimed that the Bermuda Triangle is one of the two places on earth at which a magnetic compass points towards true north. Normally a compass will point toward magnetic north. The amount of variation changes by as much as 60 degrees at various locations around the World. If this compass variation or error is not compensated for, navigators can find

themselves far off course and in trouble.

B. There are many paranormal explanations of the Bermuda Triangle.

    1. It is said that the "Bermuda Triangle" is one of two portals, used by the "human-like" aliens, to travel from their planet to ours. The "Bermuda Triangle" is not actually a triangle. When it is "in-phase," it is constantly in motion and in intensity about one to one and a half miles wide. The disappearances occur when airplanes or ships are caught in the center or within the first two outward radiating rings of the "Triangle" waters. It takes the aliens approximately 24 hours to travel from their planet to Earth.

    2. Another paranormal explanation is that Atlantis had been situated near the Bermuda island of Biminis. It is believed that Atlanteans possessed remarkable technologies, including supremely powerful "fire-crystals" which they harnessed for energy. A disaster in which the fire-crystals went out ofcontrol was responsible for Atlantis's sinking. If still active beneath the ocean waves, damaged fire-crystals send out energy fields that interfere with passing ships and aircrafts.

Conclusion:

  I. As we have seen, the Bermuda Triangle is still a mystery today.

    A. The Bermuda Triangle, also known as the Devil's Triangle, is a region in the western part of the North Atlantic Ocean in which a number of aircraft and surface vessels are alleged to have mysteriously disappeared.

    B. Although I have told you the origins, the incidents and explanations of the Bermuda Triangle, we still will never know what really the answers to all these mysterious disappearances are.

    C. So, therefore, the mystery continues.

Sources: 1. Kusche, Larry: Bermuda Triangle.
           http://en.wikipedia.org/wiki/Bermuda_Triangle
      2. Quasar, Gian J., Bermuda-Triangle.org
         http://www.bermuda-trinagle.org/html/introduction.html
      3. MacGregor, Rob., Bermuda Triangle Odyssey.
         http://www.fatemag.com/issues/2000s/2005-08article
         la.html

Sample Informative Speech (3)

Lung Cancer
by Lisa Giametta

Introduction:

I. On August 27th, 2004, my life was forever changed. Cynthia Galasso, a victim of lung cancer, passed away.
 A. To all of you, she might just be "some woman." To me, Cynthia was a second mother.
 B. She was the center of our town- a woman everyone knew, loved, and adored.
II. Upon meeting her about 7 years ago, I knew she was an amazing person.
 A. At first, she was my best friend's "fun" aunt, until about three years ago, when she became better known as my boyfriend's mom.
 B. Cynthia was a supporting mother, a loving wife, a comforting friend and a giving person.
   1.If only there was something or someone that could have saved her life, her family of five sons and husband would still have her in their lives. Although she is no longer with us, her spirit lives forever in the hearts of her loved ones. She is someone that her family, relatives and innumerous amount of friends will never forget.
   2.I feel privileged to have known Cynthia and that I'm able to share her story with you. I know she would want me to tell this story and use it as an inspiration, and that is exactly what I am going to do.
III. After going through this experience, being in the hospital, talking to doctors and nurses, and doing further research, I have learned a lot about lung cancer.
IV. My name is Lisa Giametta, and today I will be speaking about what exactly lung cancer is, the causes of lung cancer, and how to prevent the disease.
V. As lung cancer is growing more rapidly in the world today, I feel we should all be more aware of the causes and prevention of the disease.

(Transition: I will begin by speaking about what lung cancer is.)

Body: I. Lung cancer is the uncontrolled growth of abnormal cells in one or both of the lungs.

    A. While normal lung tissue cells reproduce and develop into healthy lung tissue, these abnormal cells reproduce rapidly and never grow into normal lung tissue. Lumps of cancer cells, or tumors, then form and disrupt the lung, making it difficult to function properly.

    B. There are two major types of lung cancer.
        1. The more common type is non-small cell lung cancer, which grows and spreads slowly.
        2. The less common type is small cell lung cancer, which spreads quickly and is more likely to spread to other organs in the body.

    C. According to Dr. Glenn Birnbaum of the Health Scout Network, lung cancer is the most frequent cause of cancer death in the United States among both men and women, with an estimated 159,000 deaths in 1999.
        1. Despite aggressive approaches to therapy and new lung cancer medication, survival rates have changed little in the last decade.

(Transition: Now, we will move on to what causes lung cancer.)

Body: II. The major causes of lung cancer are known to medical practitioners.

    A. The American Cancer Society states that more than 87% of lung cancers are smoking related.
        1. This means that not all smokers develop lung cancer. Quitting smoking reduces an individual's risk significantly, although former smokers remain at greater risk of contracting lung cancer than people who never smoked.
        2. People who don't smoke, but who constantly breathe the smoke of others are also at high risk for lung cancer.
    B. Besides smoking, there are many other risk factors for this disease.
        1. According to www.cancer.org, Cigar and Pipe smoking are almost as likely to cause lung cancer as cigarette smoking.
        2. Working with asbestos is another risk factor. If those people who work with asbestos also smoke, their risk is greatly increased.
        3. Marijuana also has many cancer-causing substances. If it is inhaled deply and held in the lungs for a long time, it will be harmful to the body.
        4. Other risk factors include a diet low in fruits and vegetables, air pollution, radiation treatment to the lungs, exposure to coal, gasoline and diesel exhaust, and one's personal and family history.

(Transition: Next I will speak about the prevention of lung cancer.)

Body: III. Researchers believe that prevention offers the greatest promise at this
time for fighting lung cancer.
  A. Studies will determine the best way to help people quit smoking and
  ways to convince young people not to start smoking.
  B. Researchers continue to test ways to prevent lung cancer in people at
  High risk by using vitamins or medicines, although these have not yet
  been proven effective.
  C. Currently, however, oncologists treat cancer patients by applying
  chemotherapy and a cocktail of drugs to treat its many symptoms, but
  following the American Cancer Society's nutrition recommendations,
  such as eating at least 5 servings of fruits and vegetables each day, and
  staying smoke-free is clearly the best approach.

Conclusion:

  I. I hope that after sharing my story with you, and speaking about the causes
  and prevention of lung cancer, I have made you all more knowledgeable
  of the disease.

  II. As lung cancer is growing more rapidly in the world today, I feel we
  should all be more aware of what lung cancer is, its causes, and how it can be
  treated or prevented.

  III. On a positive note, I would like you to know that in remembrance of
  Cindy, the West Islip Lacrosse teams now wear arm bands engraved with
  C.G. during every game.
    A. Our High School also has a Cindy Galasso Memorial Scholarship Fund,
    which has already raised thousands of dollars that will contribute to
    academic scholarships at the schools.
  IV. Although Cindy Galasso is no longer with us physically, her memory
  lingers on in the collective minds of her family and the entire community she
  left behind.

Resources:
1. www.lungcancer.org, copyright 2005, last updated: 3/11/04
2. www.cancer.org, copyright 2005, last updated: 1/1/05
3. www.lungcancerissues.com, copyright 2001-2005, last updated: 04/05/05

Sample Informative Speech (4)

History of Captree Island
By Hannah Clock

Introduction:

Have you ever wondered what it would be like to have your own island paradise, for your friends and family only?

Or what about living without readily available electricity, gas, or decent water pressure?

On Captree Island, each of these seemingly opposite ideas becomes a beautiful reality.

Captree is a small island in the Great South Bay which has been used by many people of Long Island's South Shore since the late 1700's; it has a very rich and interesting history full of the bayman culture which has become almost non-existent today.

In this speech I will inform you about three distinct time periods that make up the history of the island: the late 1700's to the mid 1800's, the mid 1800's to the mid 1900's, and finally the post-World War Two era to the present.

This place has been in my life since birth, and it has been a part of my family's history since the 1930's.

(The island's history, however, begins far earlier than does my family's association with it, and the first to arrive were actually farmers from the mainland.)

Body I:

In the late 1700's to the mid 1800's, aside from possibly the Native Americans, salt hay farmers were the first to use the island, producing a lucrative business out of collecting and distributing the thick grass that then grew on the meadows.

Salt hay is no longer a part of the ecosystem on the island, but the farmers used to bring the grass back to the mainland on huge barges to feed their cattle, as well as the cattle of the many self-sustaining estates that were present on Long Island at the time.

According to my grandfather, Forrest Clock, in a personal interview on 4-24-10, it was these farmers who originally put up shelter and leased the land, due to arguments over who had rights to which area of land/salt hay.

People also originally had to put up houses because since it was before the time of motorized boats, you would have to have somewhere to wait for the fare wind to carry you back to the mainland.

These houses were probably originally simple lean-to's, made just to sleep in.

The demand for the salt hay began to die out around the mid 1800's because people started to find other sources for cattle feed that was just as cheap and easier to get.
The salt hay itself began to also die out due to being over-farmed.

(At this point in time, the island was just starting to be used for more commercial and recreational purposes, such as hunting, fishing, trapping, and clam digging.)

Body II.

Captree Island was popularized in the later 1800's and early to mid-1900's by very wealthy people of Long Island's North Shore, a.k.a. the Gold Coast, and New York City, as well as the local people from Long Island's South Shore.
During this time, the island was host to many businesses in the hunting and fishing industry.
Many people who settled here at this time were market gunners; these were men hunting specifically for game which they planned to sell at the market.
One very profitable business was made out of the local people working as guides for the wealthy who wanted to hunt and fish, as well as providing the bait and ammo for these expeditions.
One of the biggest businesses on the island came about in the late 1800's; it was a large, fancy gentlemen's fishing club called the Wa Wa Yanda.
As illustrated on a document dating back to the 1930's, the club was said to have been moved to Captree Island from Greenwood Lake, NY, in 1878, and was dubbed "The Favorite Fishing Spot for Famous Men".
It included a hotel, gymnasium, recreation hall, and 12 brick cottages.
The people involved in this club were wealthy men from Long Island and New York City, including many Tammany Hall politicians and even Teddy Roosevelt.
According to my father, Dean Clock, in a personal interview on 4-25-10, during America's prohibition in the 1920's and early 30's Captree Island - specifically the Wa Wa Yanda – was a huge rum running drop-off point. People would come by boat from the mainland to pick up the illegal alcohol and bring it back to speakeasies and other such underground drinking establishments on Long Island. This was actually such a huge drop-off point that the inlet running right in front of the houses, among other things, has been called Rumrunners Cove.

(This brings us to the 1930's, which was when my family came to own a house on the Island, and the following years, when it began to be used for more recreational rather than commercial purposes.)

Body III.

During the post WWII era America was doing very well and families had more leisure time as well as more money; along with this and the rise of motorized boats, it was easier for more people to stay at the Island more often and for longer periods of time.

At this point in time, the families of the hunters, fishermen, clam diggers and bait men began to come over to the island to enjoy it as well; it was no longer only a place for men.

It was because of this arrival of women and children that the houses began to become 'more homey,' not just simple shacks on the water.

Clamming was always a huge industry of the Great South Bay, but in the 1970's and 1980's that industry almost completely died out due to the brown tide, pollution, and over-clamming.

With the downfall of the clamming industry, Captree Island was no longer used for any commercial purposes, and became a place entirely devoted to the good times of the families which have since owned the houses.

In recent years, the Island still has no garbage pick-up, utilities, or emergency services; instead we use solar power, propane tanks which we have to bring back and forth from the mainland, and everything on the island has been built by the hands of those who've lived there.

Today, there are 15 houses on Captree, and since there is no insulation in the tiny houses, they are used only as summer homes.

We love our Island and of course the bay, and we do anything we can to maintain a healthy ecosystem as well stable houses.

For example, this year was the 13th Annual Shoreline Clean-up on the island, according to my Aunt Leslie Cane in an interview on 4-24-10, during which we go to all the small islands in the bay surrounding our own and pick up the debris which has accumulated on our shores throughout the colder months.

Although the atmosphere on the Island must be quite different today as compared to what it was in the past, the love that my family and I have for Captree as well as the bay is unconditional and undying. We are the last remnants of a culture specific to the Great South Bay.

Along with this position comes special knowledge of the bay and its resources, such as knowledge of the wind and tides, weather patterns of the water, where the sandbars and channels of the bay are, knots and rope-tying, and also simply a certain knowledge of the wildlife surrounding the island.

Conclusion:

Captree Island is undoubtedly my favorite place on earth.

I don't have to go anywhere else to know that, because no place else can hold this much significance in my heart, nor has held this much significance in my family's history.

This Island has been used by people from Long Island's South Shore since the late 1700's, and has played a large part in keeping the bayman culture of the area alive and well.

During each of the three time periods I discussed, the Island served a different purpose for those who lived there, yet some of the lessons learned there remained the same, while others were either added, or forgotten.

Having this beautiful Island paradise in my life and having the opportunity to interview my elders on the subject and to listen to all of their wonderful, fascinating stories, has for me brought to light one very important lesson: and that is to remember the important things in life, like love, family, friendship, and loyalty, and also to appreciate the little things – life's simple pleasures like mud fights and clam digging- because in the end, it's all just a memory.

Review Questions

1. **Identify and describe the different types of informative speeches.**
2. **Review the speech outlining process and adapt your speech to the preparation outline format presented in the chapter.**
3. **Identify and describe the different "materials of support" necessary in an informative speech.**
4. **Discuss the role of research in the process of writing an informative speech.**
5. **Write a 5-7 minute speech on the "importance of informative speeches in a democracy."**

Chapter Sixteen

The Persuasive Speech

What is Persuasion?

Persuasion is all around us and no one can escape participating in it or is immune from its consequences. The act of communication, which is the sharing or exchange of information through the joint creation of meaning between sender and receiver, assumes equal ability and willingness of participants to participate in this process. We are aware, however, that people differ in their ability to access information and the desire to propagate their ideas to a large number of people. What majority of the people do is go about their daily lives without the intent of effecting change in the lives of others either deliberately or surreptitiously.

But there are those whose business it is to propagate their individual or corporate ideas to others, to move ideas, to influence attitudes, values, opinion, and behaviors. This purpose is to create adherence of minds to promote their views of reality, issues, products, and business. Persuasion has been described as a common denominator in the world of politics, religion, business, and interpersonal relations. But what is this idea of persuasion and how does it work?

Persuasion is the conscious attempt to influence the attitudes, opinions and behaviors of others in order to achieve a desired goal. It is a form of influence exerted on self and others to come to a confluence of agreement about an idea, issue, event or person, all directed at a particular end. Persuasion is "a change process resulting mostly from shared symbolic thinking activity," (Ross, 1994). It has also been described as "process of communicating designed to modify judgments of others, and ... success at modifying the judgments of others in intended directions (Simons, 1986). Another definition posits that persuasion "is the co-creation of a state of identification or alignment between a source and a receiver that results from the use of symbols" (Larson, 1994). Or, according to Brembeck and Howell (1976), it is 'communication intended to influence choice." But a rather comprehensive definition is by Johnston (1994) which claims that "persuasion is a transactional process among two or more persons whereby the management of symbolic meaning reconstructs reality, resulting in voluntary change in beliefs, attitudes, and/or behaviors."

As a transactional process the persuadee and the persuader are constantly and simultaneously sharing information, each being influenced in the voluntary process of symbolically constructing and negotiating meaning, resulting in the modification of beliefs, attitudes and behaviors. Examining several definitions of persuasion, Benjamin (1997) identified a common thread among them, which has to do with four elements: **communication process, symbolism, deliberate, and influences**.

Persuasion is a dynamic, on-going communication process. It has identifiable senders and receivers, who encode and decode messages that are constantly subject to interference. The experiences of the participants influence the process to the extent that it may spur or hinder the outcome of the exercise.

The ability of humans to create and manipulate symbols characterizes the nature of persuasion. Such symbols as images, words, and nonverbal cues convey messages that are designed to influence and impress the receivers of such. Persuasion then becomes possible because of the agreements of meanings that are shared among the participants. There is a community of consciousness that both the persuadee and persuader must belong to in order for the management of meaning to reconstruct the different realities can be expected to take place.

Another common denominator of persuasion is intentionality. Persuasion is seen as a conscious effort to manipulate symbols (not people) to accomplish desired goals of adjusting people to ideas and ideas to people. As has been noted, the goals of persuasion usually include one or a combination of attitude change, attitude reinforcement and behavior modification. The expected outcome of persuasion is, therefore, influence and not coercion. Efforts at persuasion are directly at people who will voluntarily accept or reject the efforts. But as Benjamin (1997) puts it, the ultimate power {of persuasion} rests not with the source but the receiver, to attend or ignore, accept or reject, remember or forget, act or not act on persuasive efforts.

Persuasive speaking is a deliberate attempt to use the agency of the spoken word (speech) to bring about desired changes in the cognitive, affective, and behavioral dimensions of the listeners. In other words, persuasive public speeches aim to influence the thinking processes, emotional components, and the behaviors of the audience members. It may be to see an old issue from a new perspective, that is, to change existing views or mindset; or to maintain existing views or mindset; or it may be to engage in a specific action or not to take action at all. In all, the audience is at the receiving end of a persuasive effort, but persuasion is not automatic.

The arbiter of all persuasive messages is the receiver. The sender, therefore, has to be mindful of how well the receiver will evaluate his or her person, the message sent and the intentions for sending the message. Aristotle, the Greek philosopher, in the 4th century B.C., wrote extensively about the proofs a persuader or a rhetor must employ to bring about persuasion. Aristotle defined rhetoric as "the art of discovering, in any given case, the available means of persuasion." He wrote of two classes of means for achieving persuasion and these are **artistic and inartistic proof**. Inartistic proof is evidence that may be used to support a case but which the art of rhetoric did not create. These are physical evidence that can be collected for example at an accident scene or at a crime scene. The second class of proof is the artistic which is within the control of the rhetor or persuader and, of which the persuader can gain mastery to advance his or her cause. Artistic proof consists of three types, **ethos**-personal character, goodwill, and adherence to ethics of the speaker, **logos**—the logicality of the arguments and verbal evidence presented to persuade, and **pathos**—the appeal to the passions as well as the audience's perception of the emotional involvement of the speaker with the subject and the audience.

Knowledge of the Aristotelian artistic proof elements, aids the persuader to maximize the available means of persuasion on one hand, and on the other, it helps the receiver in determining to accept or reject persuasive efforts. Because the different manifestations of the elements of ethos, logos, and pathos influence the outcome of persuasive efforts, we shall examine them in detail here.

Speaking about Ethos.

The study of credibility or ethos focuses on the source of persuasion; it examines what the source can do to effect agreement or change in the potential targets of such information and not necessarily what the audience desires or supposedly needs. Simply put, credibility is the measure of speaker believability. It is the extent to which an audience is willing to accept and be persuaded by a source of information. According to Tubbs and Moss (2000), broadly "it refers to our willingness to believe what a person says and does." It is by and large the audience's judgment of a speaker. And "it is the attitude a listener holds toward a speaker," McCroskey (1993).

Credibility has two general dimensions which are **competence** and **character**.
Competence refers to the perceived expertise, how well informed, and the general intelligence of a speaker. Our world is replete with people who call themselves experts and are making a good living of "selling" their expertise because a whole lot of us believe in the wisdom of experts. "The Doctor Phil Show" is a popular draw of audiences of different backgrounds on American television perhaps because of the perceived expertise of the host of the show, a man who would unabashedly analyze human social problems and prescribe solutions to them that are fit for television and not real life! We are attracted to expertise just as honey attracts flies!

Character on the hand refers to the speaker's level of objectivity, reliability, motivation and likeability that is often referred to as **trustworthiness**. A likeable person is often trusted, especially when he or she appears to be well- informed and is perceived to have the interest of the receivers at heart. Motives of speakers are at the heart of the perception of trustworthiness. "Honesty is the first chapter in the book of wisdom," wrote Thomas Jefferson in 1786 in a book edited by Gordon Lee's titled: *Crusade Against Ignorance*. This underscores the relevance of trust as a form of proof in the enterprise of influence management. Who would you trust on the issue of stiffer penalty for a drug pusher, the Drug Czar or a reformed drug pusher who had served time for his offence? If you believe the drug Czar, it is probably because of his expertise and authority, but if you believe the reformed pusher, it is probably because of his sincere testimony borne out of real life experience. This example imitates the study pioneered by Herbert Kelman and Carl Hovland in 1953 to ascertain indicators of trustworthiness. All these variables, which can only be inferred, are weighted in the minds of the receivers who ultimately will judge a persuader to be credible or not.

The study of speaker credibility also has included a third dimension which is **dynamism**. A dynamic speaker is a person who is forceful, active, and is perceived to be highly interested and passionate about the subject of his/her speech. While it is advantageous to appeal to the passions of the receivers, the receivers, too, appreciate a passionate and animated speaker.

Source credibility, therefore, refers to the receiver's perception of the speaker's authoritativeness on a given topic, his or her character, and to a lesser degree, dynamism, Tubbs and Moss (2000). Some other scholars have attributed greater strength to dynamism in measuring the authoritativeness of a speaker. Based on the study of 153 students of the

University of New Mexico, Rosenfeld and Plax (1975), conclude that the most salient factor of a speaker's credibility could be the dynamism feature.

Larson (2009) describes credibility "as an elusive quality… It is sometimes related to physical appearance, in that attractive people tend to hold (other's) attention better than less attractive people... dynamic speakers seem to take a lot of psychic space—they have stage presence." So, speaker dynamism or charisma has more to do with nonverbal vocal and non-vocal dimensions of a speaker's performance on stage as a public speaker. The power and cadence of the projected voice, the physical body characteristics, the use of appropriate gestures, overall appearance and, of course, fluent delivery all combine to influence the perception of the elusive variable of source credibility often referred to as charisma.

What exact elements or dimension of source credibility influences the audience the most? Scholars have devoted time to explicitly calibrate a source's credibility by using sets of bi-polar adjectives relevant to the elements to form a rating's or semantic differential scale, an adaptation of Osgood's Semantic Differential Measurement to pinpoint a rater's aggregate attitude toward a speaker. Take a look at the following table.

Table 16.1/ Measurement of Perceived Speaker Extrinsic/Intrinsic Credibility

Speaker Name_____

1. Competent	_	_	_	_	_	_	Incompetent
2. Experienced	_	_	_	_	_	_	Inexperienced
3. Important	_	_	_	_	_	_	Unimportant
4. Honest	_	_	_	_	_	_	Dishonest
5. Open-minded	_	_	_	_	_	_	Closed-minded
6. Kind	_	_	_	_	_	_	Cruel
7. Active	_	_	_	_	_	_	Passive
8. Fast	_	_	_	_	_	_	Slow
9. Emotional	_	_	_	_	_	_	Calm

Source: Rosenfield, Laurence B.(1983). *Analyzing Human Communication (2nd ed.),* Kendal/Hunt Publishing Company.

The scale has been developed for measuring listeners' evaluation of any speaker.

Scales numbered 1, 2, and 3 measure **Authoritativeness**; 4, 5, and 6 measure **Character**; and 7, 8, and 9 measure **Dynamism**.
(The closer the rating to the left end of the scale, the higher the perceived credibility)

Some Principles about Source Credibility

Benjamin (1997) confirms that the research on source credibility is extensive and sometimes the results contradict; however, he documented the consensus of scholars on at least five principles of source credibility and these are:

1. **Highly credible sources will produce more persuasive effect than low credibility sources**.
   A sub-text to this principle is that people tend to avoid low credibility speakers rather than listen to them. Benjamin adds that in real –life situations, people are most likely to rate a source as neutral rather than as having low credibility.

> "Honesty is the first chapter in the book of wisdom."
>
> *Thomas Jefferson*

2. **Credibility is not something a source has; it is the receiver's perception of the source.**
   This speaks to the need of speakers to be sensitive and flexible when giving speeches, attempting to strike a balance between the audience's needs and their own ideas-all to influence the perceptions.

3. **Credibility is not a fixed entity**.
   The perceptions of a source's credibility shift depending on the **subject, time, situation and audience**. Credibility is indeed a dynamic phenomenon just as human perception is and, one might add, it is limited and possibly subject to error. In any case, when audiences hold a view of a speaker, either wrongly or otherwise, the consequences are real.

4. **Credibility is linked to external factors.**
   External factors that are most closely related to source credibility are power, **physical attractiveness, and similarity**. The power relationship between speaker and audience is better described as a situation whereby the speaker has authority over the audience. And research has confirmed that compliance is easier to achieve in situations where the persuader has authoritative power over the persuadee. In terms of perception of attractiveness, it is believed that the preponderance of avenues whereby attractive figures are used to promote ideas and products points to the fact that attractiveness persuades. Similarity, on the other hand, attractiveness creates a state of "identification," between audience and speaker and that which Aristotle called "common ground," as confirmed by investigation, may or may not induce compliance.

5. **Credibility is linked to internal factors**.
   Benjamin clearly states that there is "much stronger connection between credibility and internal factors than there is between credibility and external factors." The intrinsic factors

that influence credibility are **evidence, linguistic cues, and delivery factors.** Similar to what Aristotle referred to as artistic and inartistic cues; these are the factors that will enhance the reception and appeal of a speech or persuasive effort. Evidence is used as a material of support that will appeal to the listener's logic and passion. Linguistic cues have to do with the speaker's choice of words, use of metaphors, similes, and other parts of speech for dramatic and strategic effect in the speech. Delivery factors such as pronunciation, emphasis, fluency, and other kinesics and vocal dimensions of a presentation would influence the perceptions of the receivers most probably in positive ways.

Speaking about Logos

Aristotle was credited with systematizing the branch of philosophy called formal logic. His concept of logos was adapted from his writings on formal logic and its adaptation to verbal argumentation. Aristotle identified two forms of rhetorical reasoning which are **reasoning by enthymeme** and **by example**.

Reasoning by enthymeme in the art of rhetoric was an adaptation of syllogistic reasoning, the formal method for arriving at conclusions based on deduction (Benjamin, 1997). Syllogistic reasoning is a form of rationalization that starts with a major, general assertion or premise, followed by specific cases that support the major assertion and this is called the minor premise. The third element of a valid syllogism is a conclusion that will develop from the two stated premises. See the following examples:

> **Major premise**------------**Politicians are self-motivated people**
> **Minor premise**-------------**Obama is a politician**
> **Conclusion**----------------**Obama is a self-motivated person**

> **Major premise**------------**It usually snows in the Winter**
> **Minor premise**------------**January is a Winter month**
> **Conclusion**----------------**Snow is expected in January**

The major premise of an argument must be a valid statement from which the second premise can be deduced and a final conclusion reached. In many cases, a valid major general assertion or generalization can be provided from which an audience is expected to draw a specific conclusion. **This is abbreviated syllogistic reasoning and it is labeled reasoning by enthymeme.** This type of rhetorical reasoning invites the audience to participate in the logical-deductive reasoning of following the premises of a speaker and supplying specific conclusions in their mind, thus intuitively agreeing with the speaker. Note that the second premise is omitted because it would be apparent or self-evident within the context as in the following cases of:

> All politicians are self-motivated; therefore, Obama is a self-motivated person.
> It usually snows in winter; therefore, snow is expected in January.

Aristotelian Enthymemes are abbreviated Syllogisms

Reasoning by example is a form inductive reasoning, a process of thinking that proceeds from specific valid instances to general application or generalization. This is the argument or rationalization that is usually employed when speaking about persuasive speeches of policy to advance or advocate a change in policy. Examples are drawn from specific cases where such advocated policy had worked and it is expected that such results will be replicated in other similar cases. For example let us consider the argument in favor of legalizing marijuana in the United States. A student wrote the following:

Specific case 1. Many countries of Western Europe have relaxed marijuana laws.

These countries experience significantly less cases of drug-
related offences than the U.S.
These countries experience less crime rates than the United States
These countries have less cases of incarceration per capita than the U.S.

Specific case 2. Holland has liberal marijuana laws.

This country experiences significantly less cases of drug-
related offences than the U.S.
This country experiences less crime rate than the United States
This country has less cases of incarceration per capita than the U.S.

Specific case 3. If the United States should relax its marijuana laws,

She will experience significantly less cases of drug-related offences
She will experience less crime rate
She will experience less cases of incarceration per capita.

The inductive reasoning process asks the listener to take an "inductive leap" to conclude that what worked well in certain specific cases can work in other areas.
(Read more about inductive reasoning in the latter part of this chapter.)

Toulmin's Model of Reasoning

Reasoning and argumentations hinge on making claims and supporting such claims with verbal and physical evidence. Logic is the appeal to the reasoning faculty of humans, who expect arguments to proceed in some form of ordered progression. Stephen Toulmin's model of reasoning includes three elements: **claim, data, and warrant**. The three elements must complement in order for the argument to be believable. That is the claim must be supported by available data and the two must be connected by the warrant.

Claims are categorical statements about issues, events, persons, or things made by the persuader. They are assertions presented to the audience as the basis of a persuasive argument meant to be believed by the audience members. Often a statement of claim may be implied rather than stated categorically. Claims do have content and form—the content is the data or evidence that supports the logic of the assertion while form allows the evidence to be linked to the claim. The linking of evidence to claim is what Toulmin refers to as warrant in his model. A claim has persuasive force because of the content (the data) that supports it as well as the form that makes it possible to move from the data to the claim (Borchers, 2002).

A good example of a claim is the campaign slogan of presidential candidate Barrack Obama, who claimed: "Yes, we can! Can do what? How so? These are the natural questions that follow this claim and many of the town-hall meetings of the then candidate were to provide evidence and warrants that, indeed, 'Yes, we can.' This may be interpreted as: 'We can take our country back,' and 'We can elect a black man president.' 'We can raise the needed money to push the candidacy of a non-establishment candidate.' 'Yes, we can elect the first African American president.' Having been elected to the U.S. Senate by the State of Illinois and with initial evidence of early presidential primary wins, especially in predominantly White States in The U.S., and a positive showing in the nationwide Gallup polls that favored Barrack Obama for president, the sloganeering claim became supported by data and as such, the warrant became plausible.

Examples of unstated claims abound in modern day advertising where an advertiser's product is shown in apparent comparison to other competitive products in the same category in which visual cues are speaking to the superiority of one over the other without apparent statement to the fact. In public speaking situations, however, it has been found that when persuaders state their claims explicitly, audience members better understand the message, and when they understand the message, the audience members believe the persuader holds a more extreme position on the subject, which leads to more attitude change (Cruz, 1998).

Figure 16.1/ Toulmin's Model of Reasoning
(Creating sound arguments will include following the "reasoning map" below)

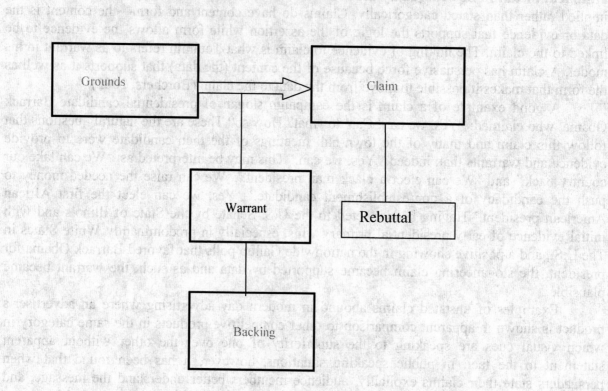

Source: Cindy L. Griffin, Cindy L. (2011) *Invitation to Public Speaking Handbook*. Boston, MA: Wadsworth.

Claim	What do you think or want to propose?
Grounds	Why do you think of this or want to propose it? (Basis of your Proposal)
Warrant	How do you know the grounds support the claim?
Backing	How do you know the warrant supports the grounds? (Extra evidence to support the basis of your proposal)
Rebuttal	What are the arguments that can be used against your claim?

Data is evidence used to prove a claim. Some of these are derived from cultural contexts such as beliefs and values of a people, which form the foundation of their arguments. Cultural beliefs and assumptions form the premises of persuasion. The average American believes that Democracy is the best form of government, and as an anchor, political practices that are at variance with democracy seem uncivilized. On that basis, the foundational principles of democracy are incontrovertible to the American, who would be easily persuaded of the inappropriateness of any activity that presumably is aimed at curtailing political freedom.

Another form of data is external **evidence**, external to the audience and persuader. Evidence is usually sourced from primary or secondary sources and is used to affirm the claim of an argument before an audience. If the audience's premises run counter the arguments of a speech, the speaker can use evidence to counter them. And if there is agreement between the audience's premises and those of the speech claim, evidence can be used to validate or reinforce them. The evidence types are the materials of support used in public speeches and these are **statistics, examples, and testimony**.

Warrant is the reasoning process, the rationale for moving between data and claim. There are two types of reasoning processes which are **Inductive** and **Deductive** reasoning.

Inductive Reasoning

Inductive reasoning cites from a single case, and moves to a general application. This means that, if some conditions are present in a particular situation or case, then to achieve the same status or result, it can be argued that the prevailing conditions can be recreated or located in other situations. And if that is the case, such prevailing conditions would support the claim that what happens in one situation or case can be applied to another with the same result. The reasoning is from particular cases to general cases, given prevailing or similar conditions. For example, one can argue that if democracy has been found to aid human and societal development in the United States, this model of human governance can be adapted to other nations for same probable results. Or, if previous specific experiences had shown that, for example, "alcohol consumption shortly before operating a vehicle is a major cause of accidents," then it can be argued that in other instances of drunk driving, the likelihood of accident is very high. One should be careful though, not to cite just an exception to the rule, but instances that can justify such a claim.

There are three types of inductive reasoning and these are **argument by example, argument by analogy, and argument by causal correlation.** As the name suggests, an example is a previous occurrence that seems to explain a present one. Or, it is a similar situation that explains another because of their corresponding explanation, situation, and consequence. For instance there are drunk driving fatalities to use as examples to support the claim that drunk driving kills. As with analogical reasoning, similar drunk driving situations can be compared and contrasted to argue a case. Causal correlation reasoning has to do with similar causes and consequences of events. How do you link drunkenness to accidents? First,

An argument is a statement or proposition that allows you to make a claim that is based in facts.

there must be evidence to support the state of drunkenness, two, there must be evidence of driving drunk and, three, all other possible causes of an accident must be ruled out to isolate drunkenness as the cause. What if taking prescriptions drugs can cause the same impairments as alcohol and thus lead to the same result—accident? That is why breathalyzers and other alcohol detection apparatuses are useful in determining the actual intoxicants in the blood stream that impair the judgment of drivers in the instance of drunk-driving arrest. The point is that you must be able to determine that the proof of cause is reliable and can be directly linked to its effect because it is easy to advance a false cause or what is referred to as **hasty generalization**.

Deductive Reasoning

This type of reasoning has been described as the analytical process used to move from generalities to structurally certain conclusions (Ziegelmueller & Kay, 1997). This is the reverse of inductive reasoning in that it moves from general conclusions to particular situations and, according to Griffin (2011) (you should) use deductive reasoning when there is a commonly accepted principle you can use to make a claim about a specific instance. For example, if it is found that level of education generally influence probable income of people, then, it can be assumed that a college graduate will earn higher income than a high school graduate or someone with a lower level or no education at all.

Scientific studies that favor quantification usually use deductive reasoning in justifying their claims or findings. Studies are conducted of representative samples and the findings are then generalized to a larger population than the one studied. What they are looking for are predictable patterns of cause and effect, such that predictions can be made of the cause of either a physical or a social phenomenon. When repeated studies confirm the cause and effect relationship, then a general conclusion can be reached about the occurrence of an event and its effects. In reality, though, we make a link between a sign and the occurrence of what the sign represents without conducting scientific studies. What we do is make a logical link between events and link one to the other. Generally we know that rain clouds will form when it is about to rain, so when we see rain clouds, we see the sign of rain and expect rain to fall. When it is night time we expect nocturnal animals to come out because that has been their predictable behavior. But not all rain clouds develop into rain and sometimes nocturnal animals are seen during the day. So, follow the logic of sound argument before making your claims or predictions by having enough evidence, examples and other support before "jumping into conclusions." The reason is that your audience will not buy your argument if it is not founded on sound argument and logic. See **Aristotle's syllogistic reasoning** for more explanation of this topic.

There are two types of deductive reasoning processes: **argument by causal generalization (see above) and argument by sign**. A sign is a special type of symbol that represents something else. In our example of rain clouds, this represents rain just as the sound of thunder does. A strange day it will be when under the blazing sun, without the sight of rain clouds, we suddenly hear the roar of thunder. This is the mental association we create through signs. What does it mean when a child holds her stomach, unable to stand or speak? This is a sign of sickness.

When you make arguments you can present signs as indication of causes and or effects of something. Griffin (2011) writes that signs have an important function in the reasoning process because they prompt us to infer what is likely to be. They help speakers establish relationships and draw conclusions for their audiences based on those relationships. Imagine the following: There are more vehicular accidents in one week than the whole of last year on the major highway that cuts across your town; there has been more rain in the month of February this year than any February on record; and, there has been unprecedented enrollment of students in community colleges across the United States in the last year than ever before. What do you think of these statements? Can you consider each of them as a sign of something unusual happening or are these just random events. These are signs of some things alright, but can we sufficiently make a deductive claim in each of these cases?

Is the increase in accidents on the major highway across your town an unusual occurrence compared to the past? The answer is yes. Is this a sufficient evidence to make a causal link that this is due to say: increase in drunk driving, exuberant teenage drivers, increase in older drivers who are impaired by failing senses, or increase in the driving population in your town that is witnessing unprecedented jump in new residents.

The case of burgeoning enrollment of students in community colleges can be a sign of the economy because people cannot find work, but choose to improve themselves in anticipation of a better job. Again, it could be because community colleges offer a cheaper alternative to four-year institutions or, perhaps, because they want to go to college near their home where they can benefit from free or subsidized room and board. All of these reasons can be classified under the umbrella of cost or the economy, so we can see the sign of increased enrollment as a sign of the economic situation the country is currently experiencing.

As we can see, signs are not perfect representations of the objects, events, and ideas they represent. They can point strongly to a case sometimes, but at other instances they may have a weak relationship. Your job as a critical thinker and speaker is to ensure that your use of signs meets the test of reasonable causal relationship. Again as Griffin (2011) suggests, signs are fallible and you should consider the following guidelines for their use:

Think about whether an alternative explanation is more credible.

Make sure a sign is not just an isolated instance.

If you can find instances in which a sign does not indicate a particular event, you do not have a solid argument.

The Argument against Legalizing Marijuana, Even for Medical Use.
By: <u>Ciccarello Rose</u>

It has been proven that smoking marijuana can diminish pain, nausea, vomiting and other symptoms caused by multiple sclerosis, cancer, and AIDS. Unfortunately, it has also been proven that marijuana does more harm than good. Although the initial reaction to marijuana may be helpful to small symptoms, it can also cause serious long term health problems. John Walters, Director of National Drug Control Policy states that "Smoked marijuana damages the brain, heart, lungs, and immune system. It impairs learning and interferes with memory, perception, and judgment. Smoked marijuana contains cancer-causing compounds and has been implicated in a high percentage of automobile crashes and workplace accidents" Marijuana can affect the immune system by impairing the ability of T-cells to fight off infections. According to the National Institutes of Health, studies show that someone who smokes five joints per week may be taking in as many cancer causing chemicals as someone who smokes a full pack of cigarettes every day.

The risks of medical marijuana are overwhelming. Studies done by the DEA prove that smoked marijuana has been shown to cause a variety of health problems, including cancer, increased heart rate, loss of motor skills, respiratory problems, and increased heart rate. For me, I wouldn't be willing to risk the chance of cancer just so I can relieve some minor symptoms for the moment. The problem with most people is that they are always looking for the easy way out. Of course it's easier to pretend there are no consequences from drug use, but the facts are out there.

Another huge problem with making marijuana a medical option is the potential legalization of the drug itself for social purposes. When Ethan Nadelman, Director of the Lindesmith Center (a project of the Open Society Institute dedicated to broadening the debate on drugs and drug policy), was asked by The New York Times if the medical marijuana issue will help lead toward marijuana legalization, Mr. Nadelman replied by saying, "I hope so." By making marijuana a medical option we would just be opening the door for the legalization of, not only marijuana, but of many other drugs.

Furthermore, marijuana has no medical value that can't be met more effectively by legal drugs. Because many people may argue the fact that there are such legal drugs, the DEA conducts research on the safety and efficacy of THC (the major psychoactive component of marijuana). As a result of this research, a synthetic THC drug, Marinol, has been available to the public since 1985. It was proven by The Food and Drug Administration that Marinol is safe, effective, and has healing benefits that can be used as treatment for nausea and vomiting associated with cancer chemotherapy, and as a treatment of weight loss in people with AIDS. However, it does not produce the detrimental health effects associated with smoking marijuana. Currently marijuana is a Schedule I substance under the Controlled Substances Act. Schedule I drugs are categorized as having a high potential for abuse, not currently accepted medical use in treatment in the United States, and a lack of accepted safety for use of the drug or other substance under medical supervision.

Marijuana is the most commonly abused illicit drug in the United States. Since smoking pot has already become increasingly acceptable in society, making it a medical option would only encourage more people to pick up a blunt and think it's okay. If it's okay for medical purposes, then it should be okay for social purposes too. "Many people who try marijuana stop their drug use right there–however, very few people who try 'harder' drugs do so without first trying marijuana. This is why marijuana is called a 'gateway drug,' not because it ensures that someone will go on to use other drugs, but because it increases the likelihood that they will. This statement made by Partnership for a Drug Free America is something that always stands out in my mind. The fact is that if you never decide to smoke your first blunt, you most likely won't start your drug use by shooting heroin. Of course, there are always exceptions.

It's extremely important that people understand the risks involved in smoking marijuana. Marijuana's damage to short-term memory occurs because THC alters the way in which information is processed by the hippocampus. This fact plays out in a 1990 the National Transportation Safety Board study of 182 fatal truck accidents. Through their research they found that there were just as many accidents caused by drivers using marijuana as caused by alcohol. On the other hand, marijuana also produces long term health risks. Someone who smokes marijuana regularly may have many of the same respiratory problems that tobacco smokers do, such as daily cough and phlegm production, more frequent chest illnesses, and a heightened risk of lung infections (U.S. Drug Enforcement Administration).

Obviously I am completely against the medical use of marijuana. After researching the topic I found much more evidence against its medical purposes than for. Too many people are ignorant of the effects that marijuana has on them. It is important that individuals realize these risks before they have gone too far. I strongly believe that if we make smoking marijuana acceptable for medical purposes, issues of drug abuse will significantly increase.

Table 16.2/Reasoning Types

Inductive	Deductive
Argument by example	**Argument by causal generalization**
Argument by analogy	**Argument by sign**
Argument by causal correlation	

Source: Borchers, Timothy A. (2002). *Persuasion in The Media Age*. Boston, MA: McGraw Hill).

Arguments and Support for Persuasive Presentations.

After identifying a topic for persuasive discourse, the speaker must then find or invent persuasive frameworks for presenting the arguments for their presentation. The two analytical frameworks a persuader can use are **stasis** and **stock issues**. The stasis framework is useful for fact or value speeches, whereas stock issues are used for policy topics, (Borchers, 2005). Stasis refers to the "trigger" points in an argument, the areas of contentions which the persuader can address to win over the audience. The three areas where opposing views usually clash are **definition, existence,** and **quality**. This is to argue that something is exactly what we describe and define it to be or not. Arguments arise when different people define the same thing or occurrence or idea differently.

There are different parts or components to an issue and the persuaders must come to an understanding of these different components and agree as to what they mean in order for the argument to be meaningful. The argument becomes what is included or excluded in framing an issue and once the framing is done, there is convergence of ideas and thoughts such that the premise or convergent point would become the proceeding point for argumentation. The next issue is that of existence of the current situation in view of the accepted definition. The question then is: does this current case fit into the established definition or does it meet the established criteria? Once there is a fit then a compelling case can be made that a case exists in terms of definition and it holds current because it fits into such definition, that is, there is a case. Now that the case is established, a persuader has to argue against the facts, that is, present an argument about the quality of the facts in an attempt to negate them. The O.J. Simpson murder trial in the U.S. is a case in point. The Los Angeles police department had collected evidence they believed implicated the accused in the murder of his wife, Nicole Brown and a companion, Ron Goldman. The case was all about the quality of the evidence collected and the complicity of the L.A. police department in tainting evidence and not that the evidence did not exist.

Borchers (2005) writes that **stock issues** are common arguments that are useful for contending that the audience should take a particular course of action. Applicable to persuasive speeches of policy (advocating action to change an existing policy), stock issues buttress arguments for proposing a new policy or course of action while identifying what defects are present in the old idea or policy and why it would be beneficial to change. These stock issues are **ill, blame, cure,** and **cost.**

The issue of ill is about what ails a system, what is not right with the current situation that needs examining and possibly fixing. As a public speaker you can present evidence of ill by statistics or by use of narratives. You can show evidence that teenage abuse of the drug ecstasy is on the rise by an alarming rate of 30% or that the U.S. deficit spending is on the rise, etc., or you can describe existing situation in clear, concrete, and concise language to make your case.

After identifying what ails the system, you can then identify who or what is to blame for it and why. Then you proceed to the cure which is the solution to the ill. Borchers (2005) identifies three forms of blame which are: structural, attitudinal, and philosophical. The structure of the current system, that is the way it's set up, cannot help the situation; the attitudinal component has to do with the mindset of people which will prevent their thinking about changing the situation and; the philosophical which opines that the situation should not be changed.

Cure is the plan or solution to the problem that ails the system. The cure to be acceptable must overcome the obstacles of the forms of blame. That is, argument for a structural change will be needed for the proposal to work; mindsets must be attacked and changed and; arguments must win over those who may not believe in the new idea or solution. For example, the United States Congress just passed the Obama healthcare plan. The plan met with vociferous obstacles across the country and the arguments of those opposed to the plan could be summarized as follows: 1. The system is too complex and cannot be easily changed; 2. The healthcare system works the way it is and it's in no need of fixing and; 3. America should not adopt socialized medicine as practiced in Canada.

Cost is always in consideration when proposing new ways of doing things or amending old ways of doing things. It is always better if your proposal would cost less than the current costs and better still if it will earn reasonable return on investment. The argument against the Obama-led healthcare reform was that it would be too expensive for the country and that it would bankrupt the nation. But the major counter argument was that it would cost less than the current national expense on healthcare and that, in the long run, it will start to save the country money.

Fallacies in Reasoning

Fallacies are errors in the logical presentation of arguments that often result in unsound arguments that often mislead the less critical listener.

Content Errors

There are six common content errors employed either knowingly or unknowingly in informative and persuasive presentations.

Faulty Generalizations

To generalize is to reach a conclusion about a group of people, things or objects by using the available information of a few or sample of those people, things, or objects. Thus a generalization is a form of conclusion that is based on limited information. The information drawn from the sample is considered to be applicable or generalizable to the larger group or population. Such conclusion may be valid if the information that it is drawn from is derived from a representative sample of the group of people, things or objects being generalized upon. However, it takes a critical, scientific random sampling study and evaluation of derived information, to be able to generalize without making the mistake of falsely assuming that the conditions and traits that are present in the sample are also present in the larger population.

We generalize all of the time. When we go about our daily lives and are presented with situations whereby we have to draw conclusion on issues, we cling to first impressions and on the basis of apparent information, we sometimes conclude or generalize without thinking that a cursory casual evaluation of available information does not constitute enough information to warrant applying such to all cases. Examine the following statements: "Chinese people are good in mathematics," "Italians are mobsters," "Tall African American males love to play the game of basketball." You can see the flaw in the reasoning that produced these stereotypical statements. Certainly some Chinese people you know may be good in math., but not all of the 1.3 billion Chinese are so disposed. Apparently very few Italians are mobsters and that does not warrant the generalization to all Italians. While many African Americans, males and females, love the game of basketball, how many tall African American males do you know that would lead you to conclude that all of them love the game of basketball?

The problem with faulty generalizations in speeches is the assumption that the speaker has done enough research and has enough evidence to make generalized claims about people, issues, things or objects that they speak about in the public arena. Benjamin (1997) writes that "faulty generalizations occur when persuaders jump to conclusions without carefully considering a sufficient number of cases or when they ignore counterexamples." For instance if a speaker argues that kids from poor communities do not have access to good schools and as a result do not go on to college, such speaker would be ignoring the fact that there are some good schools in poor neighborhoods and that, as a matter of fact, many of such students go on to college.

As you can see, some generalizations can be valid and others faulty. To deliberately make fallacious arguments based on faulty generalizations is unethical just as much as unwittingly presenting a spurious argument as valid to the audience.

Faulty Cause

Determining the cause of something is not as easy as it may appear. This is because there are usually many causes of events or actions of people. A common ground for persuasion is to determine the cause of something and to advocate cessation or continuance of such thing as the case may be. But if the persuader's premise or cause of argument is faulty, then the claim of causality will be false and thus misrepresent facts to the listeners. To claim that the cause of auto accidents is the evil desires of blood sucking vampires is to evade other plausible and verifiable causes such as driver behavior and conditions of the road. In the United States, a speaker could argue that the cause of the American recession of 2009 to early 2011, was a result of the excessive spending of the democratic government, not minding the global economy, the actions and policies of the past Republican administration, and many other plausible explanations for the economic down turn. Many gullible and cognitively simple listeners would take the arguments at face value without recognizing their inherent fallacies. It is unethical to knowingly or unknowingly present causes and consequences that are fallacious to the audience. The advice is for both speaker and audience to examine issues critically before subscribing to them as sound and believable.

Faulty Analogy

Analogy is comparison. A viable persuasive technique is to compare ideas, events, things and people. When persuaders make comparisons, they do so with the assumption of the equality of the nature and characteristics of what are being compared. In other words, comparison makes sense when things being considered share the same nature and characteristics, to the extent that a logical deduction can be made of the value of one to the other. But, when apples are not compared to apples and oranges to oranges, there is a risk of miss-representation of facts and logic. To assume that what operates or is present in one situation will be present or operate in another is to make an underlying assumption that the two are comparable in the first instance. As Seiler and Beal (2011) confirm, [t]he relationship in the analogy must be valid, and the conclusion should be based on the assumption that all other factors are equal.

Deductive reasoning is employed when one examines what operates in a single case and projects that to other similar cases, but if the test of similarity is not met then such inductive reasoning conclusions or comparisons will be in error. For instance, it is common to hear people say or write these days of the US war in Afghanistan that because the Soviet Union failed to win her war in that country, then the United States would suffer the same fate there. If we examine the realities of the Soviet Union's intervention and that of the United States in Afghanistan, we would see apparent differences in the opportunities and challenges. Therefore, it would be a faulty analogy to equate the two interventions and thus conclude that the latter would suffer the same fate as the earlier.

Another example is comparing the application of democratic principles in the United States to that of any other country. There are cultural, institutional, and structural differences in the two countries that would negate the logic in the comparison. People in Nigeria, in exasperation about the failings of their democratic institutions and principles, would often refer to the ideal of democratic principles as they operate in the United States by saying: If this were to be the U.S., so and so would not happen or would have been done one way or the other. The fallacy in the analogy as has been said is that there is enough dissimilarity in the two countries to negate the point of the comparison.

Appeal to Emotion

We know that humans are both logical and emotional beings, and we also know that speakers often combine logical and emotional appeals to persuade audiences. But speakers may misuse this appeal by eliciting emotions that would cause audience members to do things that might not be logical or ethical. Consider the abortion issue in the United States. Should a pro-life person bring a dead fetus to an anti-abortion rally to prove the point that a fetus is a baby? Will this "inflame the passions" or is it ethical?

The fact that we have the right to free speech, at least in the United States, does not give us the liberty to step on the rights of others and this thus imposes on us all the responsibility to use free speech within legal and ethical constraints. It is illegal to "incite the mob" and to verbally or physically threaten others. Again, it is unethical to appeal to the deep-seated, depraved emotions of human beings.

An examination of some newspapers published in Nigeria, West Africa, would show clearly the impact of culture on emotional appeals. Newspapers in this country freely publish nude photos of people, battered bodies of accident victims, with body parts strewn all over the road, and other images that may be considered "unfit" for general consumption in most Western countries. An ethical speaker should be mindful of the impact of emotional appeals on the audience and not violate their right to what is decent and truthful.

Appeal to Authority

Appeal to authority is invoking the power of an authority figure to convince listeners rather than through the use of the logical and verifiable arguments of the authority figure. It's an appeal to his/her power rather than his/her sense of logic and reason to convince listeners. Appealing to the audience to accept an idea just because an authority figure agrees with the idea is a clear misuse of the power of the authority. Such fallacy assumes that ideas acceptable to an authority figure should be acceptable to others. However, we should be mindful of the motivations and agenda of the authority figure, which may sway his or her inclinations, rather than just accept the ideas wholesale.

This shortcut to reasoning is often used in advertising and sales when celebrities are used to sell products that we know that the celebrities themselves may not necessarily be inclined to use. For example, Tiger Woods is used to sell Buick cars, but when he had the accident with his vehicle, which led to the revelation of his philandering, he was described as driving a Lexus utility vehicle. I have observed many parents use the authority claim to persuade their children rather than explain the logic of their reasoning, when they invoke the "because I say so" logic. The authority doesn't have to be a person; it could an institution or country. How many times have you heard people say: "At Harvard or Yale," or "In the United States of America"? These are examples of fallacious appeal to authority that may be used to persuade listeners who are not critical enough to challenge the premise of such argumentation.

Faulty Statistics

At a workshop I gave recently on Managerial Communication I asked what the participants understood the word 'statistic' to mean. Quite a number of them thought it was a synonym of the word 'fact'! The problem people have distinguishing numbers or statistics from facts is what makes them vulnerable to persuasive appeals that throw numbers at them. Smart people can make numbers lie for them and the unsuspecting receiver would have faith in the lie and construe it to be truth.

A statistic is a numerical representation of information; therefore the numbers are as good as the information they represent. Important considerations when dealing with numbers are the validity of the study, the source, and the method used to produce the data. Imagine a television commercial that claims that "90% of our clients agree that we are the best when it comes to customer relations." This statement should raise some questions in the mind of the critical consumer of information. These questions are: who conducted this study, how many customers were polled for this study, and what questions were asked of the respondents that led them to agree that "we are the best when it comes to customer relations"? Again, which other companies were compared to the company out of which "our clients agree that we are the best"?

Imagine that the company in question polled 200 clients that they had just given unprecedented rebates to, for agreeing to answer their customer relations questionnaire. Would you still find the report of the study to be valid and reliable? Unfortunately many unethical persuaders employ this tactic to convince unsuspecting people and this is because they have not taken seriously the old saying that "figures don't lie, but liars can figure," or they are not aware of the book titled *"Tainted Truth"* by Cynthia Crossen detailing the use of faulty statistics in advertising.

Process Errors

Here are the some common types of process of reasoning errors that are effective in confusing the listener, but to which we must pay great attention because they appear to be valid, but are erroneous.

Question Begging and Red Herring

This is often employed in an attempt to evade the issue being discussed. It is an attempt to circumvent the necessary process of reasoning in debating an issue by employing circular definition that questions a claim and then shifts attention to another, thus begging the issue. The examples given by Benjamin (1997) are appropriate here as he states that:

"the argument that claims [that] 'If guns are outlawed, only outlaws will have
guns' makes no reasonable point about the Fourth Amendment rights, about the
use of guns in sport, or in any other reasonable situation. Instead, it reasons in a
circular manner and appears to be making a legitimate point because it is
couched in "if… then" language which we associate with logic."

Question begging is similar to Red Herring which is an attempt to shift attention away from the real issue or concern of people.

Non Sequitor

"Eliminating Ben Laden will end terrorism" is an example of this type of fallacious reasoning because "it does not follow," as the Latin phrase states. As the world has come to realize, Al-Qaida is a loose and multi-cell organization that does not take command from a single authority. Though Ben Laden was a seminal figure in the terrorist movement, his absence will not necessarily end terrorism. We can argue, as a matter of fact, that eliminating the Al-Qaida leader will strengthen his movement. Another example of this type of faulty reasoning process is arguing that an individual who recycles paper, plastic and non-biodegradable products is just wasting his time because his effort is too little to make an impact on the planet. The fact that the effort's impact is minimal, does not justify the behavior to continue to pollute the earth.

Ad Hominem

This Latin phrase in English means "to the person." The arguments of persuaders, as we see in political debates, are not focused on issues but on the personalities and character of the people involved. To argue that your political opponents are unpatriotic for calling for a drawdown of troops from the battle field is to attach their allegiance to their country and not the logic in the reasoning behind their argument. Or to claim that people who defend abortion rights and the right of women to choose what to do with their body are "murderers" is to attack the person and it is an error in the reasoning process. You're to argue on the basis of issues advocated and the reasoning behind the claim and not attack the messenger's personality.

Slippery Slope

This is the argument that if one thing is done then many other things will follow.
It is the argument that attempts to prevent actions of others by claiming that if such action is allowed, many other similar actions calculated to overtake or overcome will follow. This is arguing that there is a pre-determined attempt to achieve a greater goal, but in small increases, and allowing the first increase, will lead to greater increases that are undesirable. The phrase: "If you give them an inch, they will take a mile," captures the fallacy of the slippery slope. A persuader who uses the slippery slope fallacy would claim that if you allow the government to wiretap suspected terrorists, it will lead to the government searching our homes without a warrant, jailing us without recourse to the law, and turning the country into a police state. Such an argument will inflame the passions of the audience, and take advantage of their fears which are elicited by such illogical reasoning.

Ad Populum

As the Latin phrase literally suggests, this is "to the people." This is an argument that is often advanced when the speaker lacks specific evidence to justify or support an argument, instead he or she would invoke the empty "majority" argument that "according to popular opinion," or "as most people agree," or "as we all believe," and "everyone is doing this." The critical listener must evaluate such assertions and question their validity. As has been proven time and again, the majority is not always right or wrong.

Post hoc

When relating one idea to the other, often assertions are made that preceding events cause the ones that follow. Because this is not necessarily the case, we classify this as an error or fallacy in reasoning. Post hoc reasoning is also called *post hoc, ergo propter hoc*, literally meaning ("after this, therefore because of this.") Mimicking the logical presentation of arguments, this fallacy presents arguments in the "if, then or after this, therefore," language that easily can lead listeners to assume the logic in the argument. For example consider the statement: "If you study hard, you will pass the test." This is suggesting that after studying hard, the result that follows is success on the test. But there are other variables that may influence one's success on the test; surely studying hard is one of them, but it must be studying the relevant material and with some level of understanding.

False Division or False Dilemma

Presenting listeners with "either or" argument, thus forcing them to make a choice between two, often extreme alternatives. It is possible that neither of the two alternatives is agreeable to the listeners thus putting them in dilemma of choice. When a politician presents the "you're either with us or against us" argument, the listeners may have the difficulty of not totally agreeing or disagreeing with the politician, but their choice is not included in the politicians alternatives.

Persuasion and Doublespeak

Persuasion is not value neutral; however, if done ethically, it will not injure others. Persuaders though are not often completely honest in informing their audience, because frequently we see the use of available tactics, knowledge of human psychology and the manipulation of symbols to not tell complete stories about products, ideas and events.

One key tactic used by persuaders is termed **Doublespeak**, which is the intentional use of words to miss-communicate with the receivers. The goal is to hide the true meaning of the message and to intentionally confound or cover up the truth about something. Oftentimes double speak is so cleverly delivered that the receivers may not detect its use, thereby falling prey to the linguistic manipulation of the persuader. And when used by credible, dynamic and articulate speakers, doublespeak can be outright dangerous in its effects on the unsuspecting, unsophisticated receiver. It is, indeed, linguistic perversion.

Examples of doublespeak can be found in government dispatches, press conferences and releases, and other documents. Corporations and politicians also liberally use doublespeak to minimize the effects of their language on their audience or to avoid making categorical statements about events, issues and policies. The use of words and phrases such as: "company downsizing," instead of "laying people off," "youthful exuberance," instead of "youthful antisocial behavior," "incontinent ordinance," instead of "misdirected bomb," "collateral damage," instead of civilian deaths," and "user fees" instead of "tax increases," are all examples of euphemisms that are designed to be evasive, ambiguous, and deceptive.

Luntz (1987) is deeply perturbed by the pervasiveness of doublespeak in our everyday lives, which he describes as language "designed to distort reality and to corrupt thought." This is particularly because doublespeak is insidious when it makes something inappropriate or negative seem to be appropriate or positive.

Larson (2010) advises that as receivers our job is to train ourselves to be responsible, patient, and critical processors of persuasive messages in order to "wisely and critically respond to the persuasion we encounter and to make wise choices and ethical decisions when we both process and craft persuasion."

Speaking about Pathos

As has been noted, humans are both emotional as well as logical beings; therefore, any attempt to persuade should invoke both the logical and emotional components of humans. Pathos is a word coined by Aristotle to capture the emotion of the speaker and those of the audience in the speaking situation. In this section we are going to examine the use of emotional proof in persuasion.

Emotions are things we feel; they are natural, biological and psychological components of our being. When we feel emotions, certain hormones are secreted into our blood streams which lead us to experience the feeling as negative or positive.

Many of the stimuli that impinge on our external senses are transformed into positive or negative experiences by our mind, thus leading to the feeling of different types of emotions. The speech act, therefore, as an external stimulus, can lead us to feel a complexity of emotions—some mild or intense, and some facilitative and others debilitative. It is common knowledge that most humans tend to avoid uncomfortable, negative emotions while they enjoy or seek comfortable, positive ones. Attacking negative emotions and promoting positive ones can be a platform for inducing persuasion. As a matter of fact, persuasive strategies include inducing negative emotions with the belief that an attempt will be made by the audience to seek comfortable emotional equilibrium, a state of mind which the persuader would in turn attempt to promote by supplying necessary inducements either through products or speech propositions. Emotions are, therefore, motivational and persuasive tools in the hands of persuaders because as Jaffe (2007) states, **emotions [are} feelings that change people and affect their judgment.**

To Aristotle, persuasive speakers must outline three conditions about the emotional status of the audience. One is to ask of the emotional state of the audience, two is to determine to whom the emotion is directed and, three is to ascertain why the audience feels that emotion. It is only when these three posers are answered that a speaker can bring about the emotional state that he or she wants to induce in the audience. Again, one might add that knowing the three-part emotional status of the audience will lead the speaker to know what can be done about which of the emotions that are at play.

According to Aristotle, the common emotions that are consequential to persuasion are **love** or **friendship, anger, mildness, fear, hatred, shame and shamelessness, pity, benevolence, indignation, confidence, envy, emulation, and contempt**. Evoking these emotions in the audience or identifying their presence can lead to the desired persuasive goals of the speaker. However, emotional appeals must be done ethically. Aristotle's ethos must be weighed against the need to exploit emotional appeals in persuasion. (Please read the chapter on ethics for ethical considerations in public speaking).

Human Needs as Framework for Persuasive Appeals

Just as human emotions provide the platform for persuasion, our basic needs and values also act as motivation for change, thus providing a framework for persuasion. Human needs are multiple and complex, as such, a good understanding of the complexity of such needs, emotions, and values will inform the persuader of how to cater to these qualities. Prague and Stuart (2000), underscore this understanding when they write that "[to] be human is to be rational, but it is more than that …Love sometimes overrules logic, reverence transcends reason, and emotion contradicts evidence." As public speakers we have to speak to the audience's values, needs, and emotions because these are the underlining drives that manifest in cognitive agreement or disagreement and behavior change that we seek.

One of the most referenced theories of human needs is that of Psychologist Abraham Maslow who developed what is now known as the **hierarchy of needs.**
Maslow believes that basically humans have inner drives that are natural and instinctive. These natural tendencies persist and tend to be the foundation of our different levels of motivation, hence the term hierarchy of needs. These human needs have degrees of potency such that some are primary, secondary, and tertiary. Maslow identified five levels of human needs.

The first level of human needs according to Maslow is physiological or survival needs of food, water, sleep, and sex. The second level of needs is safety needs which are the natural human instinct to want protection, security, stability, freedom from fear, need for order, and law. The third order of needs is belongingness needs which are affection, group membership, and need for love. Esteem needs are the next order of needs which are the desire for self-esteem, prestige, fame, glory, and recognition. The last order of needs is those of self-actualization, which is fulfillment of potential.

Maslow added two orders of needs to his original five, extending human propensities beyond overcoming deficiencies to such that transcend them, such as understanding the philosophy of life and appreciating beauty. Another principle of the hierarchy of needs that has been debated is the idea of the hierarchy itself, that a lower need must be met before moving up to a higher need. In other words, the potency of lower-level needs suggests that until that need is met, the other higher –level needs will not predominate; however, it has been found that some people would scale the stages of the needs. Think of many homeless people who have a great sense of pride and are content with their lives (esteem) but do not have shelter, security, and protection from the elements.

The fundamental lessons of Maslow's needs are their applicability to persuasion. Benjamin (1997) points out the fact that there are two principles of persuasion typically derived from Maslow which are that: 1. the idea of needs serve as ground for persuasion and, 2. that an unfulfilled need will be motivating.

Figure 16.2/Maslow's Hierarchy of Needs

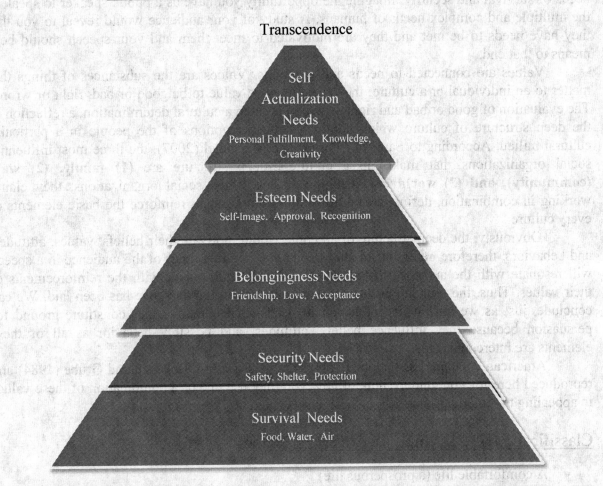

Source: Maslow, Abraham (1970), *Motivation and Personality* (2nd Ed.). New York: Harper & Row.

Adapting your speech to the audience's needs is a strategic way to motivate them in the direction of your desired persuasive goal. The arguments about human needs that you can present to your audience do not have to directly impact them, but it may do so vicariously as members of the human community. Take for example the damaging earthquake that hit Haiti in January of 2010. Before long, advertisements started appearing in newspapers, television and radio, asking for donations to help the people of Haiti who had been displaced from their homes, who had no food to eat, and, who were in desperate need. These appeals elicited immediate response from the American populace because they could indirectly feel the precarious situation the people of Haiti were in. Examine the appeal in the following paragraph:

> **The people of Haiti have suffered a great deal in the aftermath of the devastating earthquake of January, 2010. Thousands are dead and many more are buried in rubbled structures. But many survived. The adults, who are to help the children, are walking aimlessly in shock on the streets of Port Au Prince. The children are scattered all over the capital city without shelter, numbed, hungry, thirsty, and in physical and emotional pain. Just imagine that, in the spate of hours a people moved from hope to despair. These are America's neighbors and, without doubt, they need our help. Let us help them regain their dignity, their hope, and their humanity. Haiti needs donations—now!**

This is an appeal to the basic instincts of humans to survive the stripping of their basic needs of survival and security. Imagine the opportunity you have as a public speaker to speak to the multiple and complex needs of humans. A study of your audience would reveal to you that they have needs to be met and they are motivated to meet them and your speech should be a means to that end.

Values are connected to needs and emotions. Values are the substances of things that matter to an individual or a culture; they are things we value to be good or bad, right or wrong. The evaluation of good or bad and right or wrong is often a cultural determination, a reflection of the deep structure of culture which dominates the perceptions of the people in a particular cultural milieu. According to Samovar, Porter, and McDaniel (2007), the three most influential social organizations that make up a culture's deep structure are **(1) family, (2) state (community), and (3) worldview (religion)**. These three social organizations, they claim, working in combination, define, create, transmit, maintain, and reinforce the basic elements of every culture.

Obviously, the deep structure of a people would motivate their beliefs, values, attitudes, and behaviors; therefore, reference to and invoking cultural values of the audience in a speech will resonate with the audience to the extent that they will concur with the reinforcements of their values. Thus, the foundation for motivating change in the audience has been laid. We can conclude, just as we concluded about human needs, that human values constitute ground for persuasion because they influence beliefs, attitudes, and possibly behavior as all of these elements are interconnected.

American contemporary popular values are classified by Rokeach and Grube (1984) and reproduced here for you guide. Think of how you may use one or a combination of these values in appealing to Americans in your persuasive speeches.

Classification of Contemporary American Values

- A comfortable life (a prosperous life)
- An exciting life (a stimulating, active life)
- A sense of accomplishment (lasting contribution)
- A world at peace (free of war and conflict)
- A world of beauty (beauty of nature and the arts)
- Equality (brotherhood, equal opportunity for all)
- Family security (taking care of loved ones)
- Freedom (independence, free choice)
- Happiness (contentedness)
- Inner harmony (freedom from inner conflict)
- Mature love (sexual and spiritual intimacy)
- National security (protection from attack)
- Pleasure (an enjoyable, leisurely life)
- Salvation (saved, eternal life)
- Self-respect (self-esteem)
- Social recognition (respect, admiration)
- True friendship (close companionship)
- Wisdom (a mature understanding of life)

The Goals of Persuasive Speaking

When you engage your audience in persuasive speaking, there is the assumption that your message will not only be received by the audience, but that the message will have the desired effect on them. What are these effects or reasons why we engage others in persuasive speaking? If we revisit our definition of persuasion as "a deliberate act designed to influence beliefs, attitudes, values, and behavior," then we would understand that **the goals of persuasive speaking can be classified as two-fold: one is to achieve mental or cognitive shifts in the receivers, and the second is to achieve behavioral changes in the receivers.**

Persuasive speeches that focus on mental shifts include speeches to influence, in a particular direction, the beliefs, values, and attitudes of people. This category of persuasive speeches attempts a shift in the receivers' mental structures of beliefs, values and attitudes. The desired shifts in these mental structures could be to bolster or weaken them, to shift or change them. For instance if your audience is against a new piece of legislation to mandate recycling of plastics and other non-biodegradable products in your local town and your job is to persuade them to agree with the legislation, then you're set to weaken their argument against recycling by weakening their negative beliefs and values about recycling. You are also set to introduce new beliefs and values regarding pollution and the need to safeguard the environment for not only the immediate run, but on the long run for our children. You will then present arguments that will bolster their attitudes in favor of recycling. Your persuasive speech has targeted negative beliefs and values and has, in turn, promoted positive beliefs, values and attitudes toward the piece of legislation that mandates recycling.

You should note that beliefs, values, and attitudes are interconnected. A negative belief does not produce a positive value or attitude, and it will not result in positive behavior either. But a positive belief will lead to a positive value and attitude and, in many cases lead to a positive behavior.

Persuasive speeches that motivate action are categorized as different from the above because of the fact that speaking to influence mental structures is quite different from asking the audience to engage in an action. Asking the audience to tacitly agree with an idea or an argument might be a precursor to behavior change, but it is certainly less intrusive on the audience than when they are asked to change a behavior. Behavior change as the goal of persuasive speaking has been identified to be the most demanding task of a piece of communication. While some scholars argue that behaviors can be automatically triggered, most still agree that behavior change is predicated upon belief, value and attitude change. In other words, for you to get people to do something, especially as a goal of your persuasive speech, you have to evaluate their beliefs, values and attitudes and align them in the direction of that change before you can effect a behavior change in them.

According to Fotheringham (1966) there are four goals of persuasion which are adoption, discontinuance, continuance, and deterrence.

With the adoption goal, you're asking the audience to adopt an idea, a program, etc.

Example: **Adopt the use of birth control measures such as condoms to prevent unwanted pregnancies**

With continuance, you're urging the continuation of a positive attitude or behavior.

Example: **Continue the use of pregnancy control and disease protection when having intercourse.**

Discontinuance is advocating the cessation of an existing attitude or behavior.

Example: **Stop having intercourse without condoms.**

Deterrence is asking your audience members not to start engaging in an act.

Example: **Avoid sexual intercourse with multiple partners.**

Analysis of persuasive goals cannot be complete without a mention of the element in the Aristotelian proof which is **pathos**. Emotional proof is the appeal to the emotions of the audience members, as well as the speaker showing passion and interest in the topic and the audience—all these will strengthen the logical and ethical dimensions of persuasion.

The goals of persuasive speeches can be summarized as attempts to bolster, weaken, and change beliefs, values, and attitudes of people; it is also to influence action by encouraging the continuance and adoption of certain behaviors or; to discourage or desist from engaging in other behaviors. These can be achieved by motivating necessary changes in the cognitive, affective, and behavioral domains of target audience.

Types of Persuasive Speeches

There are three types of persuasive speeches namely persuasive speeches of facts, value, and policy. Facts suggest evidence; therefore, speeches about facts are set to argue, through evidence, the occurrence, existence, or truthfulness of something. Values are cultural, ethical, or moral valuation of things, events, or situations; therefore, this type of speech places value of moral or immoral, good or bad, and just or unjust on what people have to deal with in society. Policy speeches argue in favor or against issues, institutions and ideas. They may seek to stop or continue an action, to promote or to discontinue a policy action. The arguments of speeches of policy are derived from values established in a given society or on facts derived through evidence and study. When you argue that specific actions should be taken about an issue be it of value or of fact, you have entered the realm of persuasive speech of policy.

The thesis of a speech and the claim of an argument are also described as propositions which the speaker proposes to the audience (Sprague and Stuart, 2000). Now let us examine each of these propositions.

Proposition of Definition

Jaffe (2007) proposes a category of persuasive speeches as speeches of definition or classification. According to her, such claims of definition and classification are necessary when we must decide what kind of entity or phenomenon we have, in other words, when we must categorize it. When we define and categorize, we indicate exactly what the focus of attention should be in the speech and not the myriads of ways certain phenomena can be classified or defined. For example different people, depending on their motivation and experience, would define such words as *pornography, anti-Semitic, education, embryo*, and *murder* differently.

Defining ideas and issues differently will evoke different emotional reactions in people, thus influencing the enactment of different policies to deal with the different variations or classifications of such ideas and issues. This may be particularly relevant to persuasive forensic discourse in that legal issues of crime and punishment often vary depending on their different legal definitions. For example, when *is murder not a murder?* The answer lies in the different legal definitions of murder.

There are different classes or degrees of murder. What are the differences between felony murder, manslaughter, negligent homicide, and vehicular homicide?

MURDER, FIRST DEGREE

In order for someone to be found guilty of first degree murder, the government must prove that the person killed another person; the person killed the other person with malice aforethought; and the killing was premeditated.

To kill with malice aforethought means to kill either deliberately and intentionally or recklessly with extreme disregard for human life.

Premeditation means with planning or deliberation. The amount of time needed for premeditation of a killing depends on the person and the circumstances. It must be long enough, after forming the intent to kill, for the killer to have been fully conscious of the intent and to have considered the killing.

First-degree murder in California includes a killing that is "willful, deliberate, and premeditated," or, that is committed in the perpetration, or attempt to perpetrate, certain felonies, including burglary, and not including the petty offense of shoplifting. California Penal Code: S 189.

(Wikipedia, accessed 3/31/10)

Proposition of Fact

Proposition of fact depends on the assemblage of proven facts or evidence to argue a case and when we cannot directly verify a fact then we can use the logic of reasoning by analogy and generalization to arrive at a probable conclusion. We argue from available facts and make the most probable inferences to form a conclusion.

Examples:

1. Human activities are the major cause of global warming.
2. Increase in oil prices is not due to lack of production or supply.
3. Preventive medicine is less expensive than emergency medicine.

Proposition of Value

Proposition of Value is the normative judgment of issues, ideas, events, and things. This is the prescription of standards for evaluating which establishes criteria for judging in terms of good or bad, worthy or unworthy, ethical or unethical, wise or foolish, acceptable or unacceptable, etc. In this case the speaker establishes premises upon which some arguments can be built and concludes therefore as to the positive or negative evaluation of a case.

Examples:

1. The best soccer player of all time is Pele of Brazil.
2. Corporal punishment is wrong.
3. The best form of transportation is Bicycling.

Proposition of Policy

Proposition of policy is advocating a specific line of action to be taken by claiming that something should or should not be done and giving good reasons of fact and value to support the need for a change of action.

Examples:
1. College students, who are the leaders of tomorrow, must vote on Election Day.
2. The federal government should lower the drinking age from 21 to 18 years of age.
3. Abortion should be legal in the United States.

When advocating change in the audience through proposition of policy, the speaker should be aware of the level of opposition that may exist. You should realize that while some members of the audience may be in agreement with you, some others may advocate the direct opposite of your policy issue. Knowledge of how to deal with favorable, neutral, and unfavorable audience members is critical to your success in giving persuasive speeches.

You can use your knowledge of the **Likert Scale** for measuring attitudes of respondents to take a quick survey of your listeners prior to your speech. For example in your questionnaire you can state your proposition and draw the scale to elicit the audience's responses which can range from "strongly agree" to "neutral" and to "strongly disagree."

Please respond to the following statement using the scale below:

College students, who are the leaders of tomorrow, must vote on Election Day.

1. Strongly Agree
2. Agree
3. Neutral
4. Disagree
5. Strongly Disagree

Let us assume that the result of your survey is as follows:

1. Strongly Agree ==10%
2. Agree ==22%
3. Neutral ==40%
4. Disagree ==10%
5. Strongly Disagree ==18%

You have 32% of the audience already in your corner with 40% sitting on the fence on the issue, while 28% disagree with you. The question then is: where do you go from here?

To the audience members who already agree with you, you have to strengthen their agreement with you and move them further into the sphere of active involvement in the proposition; after all the best demonstration of agreement and interest is action. To those who are neutral you have to ascertain why they are neutral. Is this because of lack of interest, information, or are they simply unsure of where they stand on the issue? Whatever the reasons are, your job is to address them and move them along into the realm of agreement. And to those who are against your proposition, this is when you have to put all your skills as a persuasive speaker into full gear to advance your arguments to strategically weaken their counterarguments. This you would do with grace and professionalism that would endear you to them and not lead them to a wholesale rejection of your ideas.

Sprague and Stuart (2000) have precepts that would guide your approach at persuading these different kinds of audiences and their ideas are put into a table format here.

Table 16.3/How to Deal with Favorable, Neutral, and Unfavorable Audience

Favorable Audience	Neutral Audience	Unfavorable Audience
1. Make use of emotional appeals to intensify your listeners' support. 2. Get your audience to make a public commitment 3. Provide several specific alternatives for action 4. Present your arguments in abbreviated form so that audience members actively	1. Stress attention factors with an uninterested neutral audience. 2. With an uninformed neutral audience, emphasize material that clarifies and illuminates your position. 3. For an undecided neutral audience, establish your	1. Set realistic goals for a single speech. 2. Stress common ground. 3. Base your speech on sound logic and extensive evidence. 4. Pay particular attention to establishing a credible image.

participate in the reasoning process. 5. Prepare your audience to carry your message to others	credibility by presenting new arguments that blend logic and emotional appeals.	

Organizing Persuasive Speeches

As has been noted, audiences find it easier to listen to and follow organized and orderly presented ideas than disorganized thoughts and haphazardly presented arguments. It is also easier for the speaker to present a well-structured speech than a disorganized one. Because of the advantages it presents to both speaker and the audience, public speaking favors organization. The contents of persuasive speeches can be organized in many different ways depending on the type and the order that would best convey the speaker's message to the audience.

Problem-Solution Order

As a speaker if you claim that there is a problem or that the presence of something constitutes a problem, then you must be prepared to offer solution(s) to the problem. As a persuasive speaker, you're actually asking for something to be done to reduce or remove the cause of the problem in order to bring about a solution. First you have to provide adequate explanation of the problem, why it is a problem, and what can be done about it. As many problems are multifaceted and cannot be solved by a single solution, you must present two or three plausible solutions to the problem and recommend the best of the solutions to bring about the ultimate change you desire.

Problem-Cause-Solution Order

This type of order is a slight variation from the above because it includes an explanation of the cause of the problem. The three main points to be discussed in this order are the problem, cause(s) and solution in that order. The statement of the cause allows the audience to locate the roots of a problem and its different dimensions and prepares them for the logic in the solutions to be presented. Again, here you have to be able to link the cause to the problem without any confusion or doubt; this is because causal fallacy will undermine the solution that you may present to the problem. After all, if you're not clear of the causes of a problem, how then can you be sure of the solutions to it and how might you expect the audience to buy into such bogus solution?

Comparative Advantage Order

Comparative advantage suggests that when two things or ideas are compared, one has an advantage over the other. This is a concept used by economists to encourage specialization in production of goods and services that a particular company or country has the advantage over others in producing in terms of scale, expertise, and possible return on investment. As a speaker you're advocating that one solution is a better panacea to a problem than the other. To do this you have to lay out the merits and the demerits in each of the solutions proposed and to finally show by comparison that your suggested solution is the best line of action to take.

Direct Method

Oftentimes we have ideas that we believe are good and should be considered by others. It is not necessarily a problem, but a situation you believe would be advantageous to others for a number of reasons. For example you may wish to convince automobile owners of the three major reasons they should consider buying Ethanol. Because you directly state your ideas in the form of reasons, the name direct method is used to describe this type of speech presentation order. Another name for this is the **statement of reasons pattern**—a method that makes a claim and then states reasons that provide the rationale for the ideas (Jaffe, 2007).

Monroe's Motivated Sequence

A popular structure of persuasive speech presentation is the Monroe Motivated Sequence. Professor Alan Monroe of Purdue University developed this five-step speech structure in the 1930's. As its name suggests, people need motivation to act, especially because our actions are predicated on our needs and desires. Whenever we desire a need for change, we particularly want our course of action to be the right one—we want evidence that what we decide to do would work well. So, a speaker hoping to achieve behavioral change or action in the audience will need to motivate them to engage in such action because as stated earlier, behavior or action most time is intended and following the five stages in the motivated sequence will help the speaker along the process of inducing the audience to action. The motivated sequence is suitable for persuasive speeches of policy in that such usually advocate a change of policy position. The stages in the sequence are:

Gain Attention: This is a call to the speaker to focus the attention of the audience members to the speech right from the beginning to physically and psychologically induce them to pay their undivided attention to the speaker and the speech. This the speaker can attain by a combination of a number of tactics such as storytelling, rhetorical question, relevant quotation, shocking example or statistic.

Need: Identify and justify that a problem exists, that it's something the audience should care about because it affects their values, beliefs, and their state of well-being (motives). Hence, there is need to do something about the problem.

Satisfaction: This is the stage where the speaker explicitly enumerates how the problem is to be resolved, removed, altered, or eradicated; what it takes to accomplish this; and how long it will take. This is when the speaker presents an action plan that will affect the desires, values, and interests of the audience members and how such plan is to be implemented.

Visualization: This is the stage where the speaker "shows" how the plan would work and also pictures a scenario of what would happen if nothing is done. Examples are presented of where such remedies or interventions have worked and the benefits enjoyed by those who chose similar lines of action. This is when to narrate cases of where and when what you're advocating had been put in place with great success. By contrast, you will also enumerate the challenges faced by those who had chosen not to do anything about the problem

Action: Now the audience members will be told of the immediate action they have to take to make all that they have heard and have tacitly agreed to, to become a reality. As the speaker has convinced them of the right policy change, they should be ready to support it by doing something to make the desired change happen. Here the speaker reinforces his or her position and appeals for change through specific action.

Note that it is necessary to craft a good intro and conclusion to the Motivated Sequence order. In the following example, a student adapts the motivated sequence to his speech urging action on the part of his fellow classmates.

Topic:	**Now is the time for a Third Major Political Party in U.S. Politics.**
By:	**Mathew J. Leone**

Introduction

Attention:	"… One nation, under God…" This is a phrase taken from The Pledge of Allegiance; an allegiance for all those who are united together in preserving our rights in our country.
	However, we are no longer "one nation." A dividing line splits our country in half with the two sides being the Democratic Party and the Republican Party. It seems they fight back and forth on the correct line of action for the country, but are never willing to compromise to make things work. I believe our political system is broken and needs to be fixed.

Body

Need:	With the two Parties (Republicans and Democrats) there is no room for compromise. Each party has its own views and most of the time, their views conflict with each other. This is like a high school clique where you cannot do anything that your group doesn't like because if you do, you'll get kicked out. It is the same thing in American politics now. If a democrat were to side with the Republicans on an issue, he or she would gain the disfavor with the party. The consequence of this is that it has become a tug-of-war with us (the citizens) in the middle. When one party has more power, it strives to enact its own agenda and erase the other party's actions. With this happening, it is so much harder to get anything positive done in the country.

444

Satisfaction: As far as the compromise goes, I think there is need for more politicians who are willing to sit down and listen to everyone's stand on issues and then decide what the best short-term and long- term action will be. Although I do not agree with many of president Obama's policies, he is good at listening to everyone before choosing a course of action. Anyone can force his or her viewpoint on other people, but it takes a strong leader to listen and take advice from others. I fear that just compromising is not enough though. I would like to have never have been a two-party system. George Washington, our nation's first President was against the two-party system as well. However, it is far too late to abolish the system because the factions are already in place. The best thing to do is to find a medium- a third party that can quickly gain popularity and penetrate the system to bring balance. With a third party, there will hopefully be fewer clashes and more collaboration.

Visualization: There are more attacks on individuals in Congress than there are at issues. Imagine a session of Congress whereby they sat down and discussed the best course of action instead of trying to ruin each other's reputation. I think if a third party had more power, then we would see more compromise. It would be like the check-and-balance system we have in place between the legislative, executive, and the judicial branches of government. No single branch can gain too much power because it is divided amongst them. Likewise, the two-party system grants whoever has the more power at the time complete control making it a head-on heavy weight fight.

Conclusion

Action: I would like to see power distributed to a third party to balance the scales and make this less of a left vs. right or blue vs. red issue. I don't believe this can be done by one person, but with everyone's collective action I believe it can. The first step is to listen to both sides, do not reject what one party says just because it is coming from a Republican or Democrat. The compromise needs to begin within our own minds before it will ever reach the political level. Do not vote for a Democrat because you're one and not for a Republican because you're one. Really analyze who it is you want to represent you. We must force more options than just red or blue. There are so many colors and many choices; it seems to me like it's foolish to paint your world only one color. So, in the next election, go out and vote for what you agree with and not your political affiliation. This is the real third party- your collective non-partisan vote.

Persuasion: Some Theoretical Insights

According to West and Turner (2007) "**a theory is an abstract system of concepts and their relationships that help us to understand a phenomenon.**" The goal of theory is more than just aiding our understanding of phenomena; it extends to predicting the occurrence of social phenomena as well. We can further define a theory as **a statement of claim about the relationships of variables or concepts and the outcomes of such relationships on events, situations, and people**. The claim can be verified through measurement of perceived or real outcomes just as we measure the outcomes of our persuasive efforts on target audiences.

There are theories that lead to the understanding and evaluation of specific cases, while there are others that establish cause and effect and focus on predicting and generalizing findings. Craig (1999) identifies the communication field as a practical field and sees the enterprise of formulating theories in the field as a practical attempt to solve real life problems.

As we have noted, theories answer questions about the relationships of variables. For example, if you are to speak to a group of people about an issue that you're passionate about and your goal is to convince the listeners to accept your view on that issue, your questions become: How can I best organize my speech to influence my audience positively and how can I present my speech to my audience in the most effective way? The underlying assumption in this case is that an organized and well-presented speech would affect and influence an audience in the desired direction much more than a speech that is not organized and presented randomly. There are two claims here: 1. Organized speeches influence the receivers positively and 2. Well-presented speeches have a positive influence on the audience. If we can positively answer these questions, then the lessons gained from them will be applicable not only to specific experiences, but to the process of speech presentation and influence gaining in general.

There is no dearth of theories applicable to the practice of public communication, but the few that are explained here will, no doubt, inform you of some of the relationships among speech variables which have been established over time from study and practice. Your awareness and possible use of them will enhance your ability to speak more effectively, and have the desired effects on your listeners.

Theory of Balance
(Fritz Heider, 1958)

There are many theories classified under the umbrella of cognitive consistency or balance theories. These are theories that explain the tendency of people to want to have consistency or balance in their beliefs, values, attitudes, and behaviors. Not having a balance of all these variables would cause us to experience psychological imbalance, discomfort or stress. But experiencing balance is comforting and this is what Gass and Seiter (2011) describe as the inner peace of consistency.

Although you may know people who say certain things and do otherwise, or you yourself may act against your own conviction sometimes, these still do not invalidate the cognitive consistency tendencies in people. Within certain limitations, therefore, humans seek to maintain balance in their thoughts, attitudes, and action. People often have different levels and types of attitudes toward other people, things and ideas. That is, attitudes are not formed in isolation; they are oriented in particular directions with varying levels of potency.

The P-O-X theory, as Heider's balance theory is also called, states that in interpersonal relationships, a person (P) is oriented toward person (O) and an object (X) that is also connected to or belongs to the other person. For example, if as a mother you're vociferous about homosexuality as a sin and your son "comes out" about his being gay, you would no doubt experience great psychological discomfort. You're against homosexuality on one hand and on the other, the object of your affection, your son, is in this class of people whose sexual orientation you object to. This can be explained in a diagram.

Homosexuality

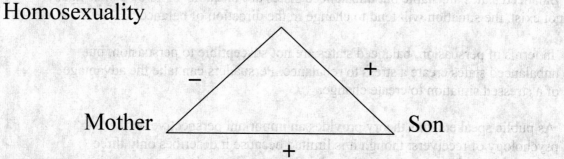

An incongruous state of attitude occurs when there is no harmony among them. In this case the son favors what the mother does not favor, and vice versa. For there to be harmony, something must change in this scenario. One, the mother could change her attitude toward homosexuality from negative to positive such that there then would occur three plus signs which is a state of balance. Or the son or mother could strain their relationship to the extent that they dislike each other, thus creating another balanced state in their attitudes because then the mother does not favor homosexuality and also does not favor her homosexual son. An old expression that captures these scenarios is appropriate here: The enemy of my enemy is my friend; the friend of my friend is also my friend.

Let us look at another example that will further illustrate the idea of attitudinal balance. Sunny and Susie love each other dearly and would like to become husband and wife someday if only they can reconcile their unfavorable attitudes to each other's religions. We can diagram these relationships these ways:

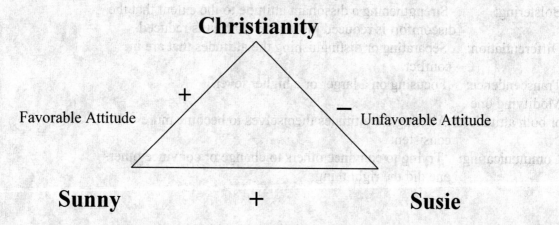

See the three major choices that Sunny and Susie have under the Cognitive Dissonance theory that follows.

To summarize, here are the tenets of the theory and their implication for persuasion.

✓ People prefer states of balance to states of imbalance or disharmony.

✓ According to the theory, balanced states consist of three positive relationships or two negative relationships and one positive relationship.

✓ Balanced states are stable but unbalanced states are unstable. Where balance does not exist, the situation will tend to change in the direction of balance.

✓ In terms of persuasion, balanced states are not susceptible to persuasion, but unbalanced states create a stress to rebalance. Persuaders can take the advantage of a stressed situation to create change.

✓ As public speakers, this theory provides an important perspective on the psychology of receivers; though it is limited because it describes only three relationships, whereas human beings develop complex webs of relationships.

We all experience imbalances or incompatibilities in the relationships of our beliefs, values, attitudes and behaviors. But the degree to which we experience them has to do with such factors as the importance attached to the value, belief, attitude, and behavior; and the importance of the issue under evaluation. We then attempt to reduce inconsistency by engaging in one or a combination of the processes that scholars have identified. But there is a caveat. Again, to quote Gass and Seiter (2011) people don't necessarily preserve or restore psychological consistency in logical ways. They do so in psycho-logical ways, that is, ways they find psychologically satisfying or comfortable but that may or may not be strictly logical...The rule of thumb is that a person tends to reduce dissonance in the most efficient way possible.

The possible routes for reducing inconsistency that scholars have identified serve as opportunities for persuasion. These according to Gass and Seiler (2011) include the following:

1. Denial: Not acknowledging that a dissonant situation occurs
2. Bolstering: Strengthening a dissonant attitude to the extent that the discomfort is reduced just as the conflict is reduced.
3. Differentiation: Separating or distinguishing the attitudes that are in conflict.
4. Transcendence: Focusing on a larger or a higher level.
5. Modifying one or both attitudes: Altering the attitudes themselves to become more consistent
6. Communicating: Trying to convince others to change or convince others one did the right thing.

Cognitive Dissonance Theory
(Leon Festinger, 1957)

Cognitive Dissonance theory is popularly referred to as "post decision theory." This is because of the claim by the theory that people experience a tension (dissonance) within themselves after they have made a decision. They engage in internal debate as to whether the decision they made was the right one or not. And because humans have been confirmed to prefer a state of harmony (consonance), that is, having a positive rationalization for their decisions rather than experience disharmony, they would strive to maintain consonance rather than dissonance. The experience of internal mental conflict as a result of decision making is uncomfortable and this will lead people to attempt to rationalize their behaviors in many different ways to resolve their conflict. These rationalization processes provide opportunity for persuasion.

Let's follow a scenario of decision making: Sunny is a devout Christian who believes in the Christian doctrine of not "being equally yoked with unbelievers." But he has a deep love for Susie who is not of the same faith. Susie equally loves Sunny and believes they should marry. Every time Sunny attends church service, he's reminded of the advice not to marry an unbeliever. Sunny has a dilemma. Should he give in to his desires and marry his sweetheart or should he leave her and find love within the church?

Obviously a decision has to be made here and a number of scenarios could play out in this case.

    a. He could marry his love and stay in the church, but face a constant reminder of his "wrong" choice of wife.

    b. He could marry Susie and leave the church.

    c. He could leave Susie and find love in the church.

Can you think of other reasonable choices for Sunny?

Whichever decision he makes, Sunny will experience "post-decision" dissonance. And to rationalize his decision he would give us insight into the tenets of CDT which are:

- ✓ Dissonance is the degree to which relationships among our cognitions about our attitudes, beliefs, feelings, environment, and actions are inconsistent with one another.

- ✓ Things are inconsistent when any two areas of our lives are not entirely compatible and this creates dissonance.

- ✓ We seek to reduce dissonance because it is unpleasant; therefore, it will motivate us to change our cognitions, attitudes, or behaviors.

- ✓ There are three ways to reduce dissonance: change the dissonant attitude; bolster or support one of the dissonant positions and; re-evaluate the relationship in which it occurs.

- ✓ As the magnitude of reward or punishment increases, dissonance will be decreased because there is strong motivation to make a choice and to rationalize that choice.

- ✓ The more opposing the choices, the greater the effort required to resolve them and the greater the dissonance.

✓ Research confirms that attitude and behavior change by the application of CDT are long lasting.

A persuasive message can target the dissonance in people and provide them with consonant information with which to bolster their position thereby resolving the dissonance. Or a speech might actually create dissonance in the audience, with the strategy of helping them to resolve such dissonance by providing a panacea to the problem.

Inoculation Theory
(William J. McGuire, 1964)

The word inoculation is used in the same sense as immunization, vaccination, and injection. Already I know you're thinking of a virus that needs prevention. And that is the sense of the inoculation theory: we can inoculate people against a viral infection if we introduce into them a weaker version of the virus that will (immunize) fight against the real thing if and when it comes. Just as doctors recommend inoculation against infectious diseases, persuaders inoculate receivers with a weak counterargument of their opponents' position, with the understanding that it will build their immunity against the stronger argument of such opponents.

The inoculation theory works in two ways: 1. The speaker can attempt to strengthen his or her arguments in favor of the desired or intended position or, 2. The speaker can present counterarguments that will weaken the argument against the desired position. In other words, a speaker can support his or her own arguments or undermine opposing arguments by presenting a rather weak reasoning that will help the audience to resist the opponent's argument against the intended position. McGuire calls these weak forms of counterarguments "refutational defense."

The following are the tenets of the theory:

✓ There are two things you can do to your persuasive position: 1. Present a supportive defense, 2. Present a refutational defense.

✓ Literally speaking, inoculation theory is injecting your audience with a weaker form of your opponent's argument (refutational defense).

✓ The injection of a weaker counter argument will lead your audience to build a defense or immunity against your opponent's counterarguments.

✓ The audience can build a stronger resistance to counter persuasion if told ahead of time of counterarguments. This is called forewarning.

Lessons of inoculation theory are twofold:

1. In order to help your audience build resistance against your opponent's ideas and favor yours, you should present two-sided arguments- supportive and refutational. According to Benjamin (1997), a persuader may utilize this two-sided approach by merely mentioning opposing arguments, by comparing opposing arguments to the

arguments that support the persuader's position, or by directly attacking opposing arguments.

2. Forewarning the receivers of an impending counterargument would help the receivers to generate counterarguments of their own.

Table 16.4/Hierarchy of Effectiveness for Message Sidedness

Type of Message	Effectiveness
Two-sided refutational message	Most effective (20% more effective than a one-sided message)
One-sided message	Second most effective (20% more effective than a two-sided non-refutational message)
Two-sided non-refutational message	Least effective

Source: Gass, H. Robert and Seiter, John S. (2011). *Persuasion: Social Influence and Compliance Gaining.* Boston, MA: Allyn & Bacon

Theory of Reasoned Action (TRA)

Martin Fishbein and Icek Ajzen (1980)

This theory takes the position that people are rational beings who employ rational thinking process in evaluating information available to them especially in persuasive situations. As the name suggests, behaviors or actions are reasoned or intended not directly from attitudes themselves. The theory identifies the relationships of beliefs to attitudes, which will motivate intention and then behavior.

Simply put, for me to engage in a particular behavior, say buy Chinese food, I must have intended to buy Chinese food. Let's back up for a moment. Prior to my intention to buy Chinese food, I must have evaluated other choices and created a positive attitude toward my choice of food at the given time; then, I must have believed that this would be a good choice and that other people (my significant others, i.e. colleagues, friends and family) who may see me engage in this behavior would be accepting of my choice because Chinese food is a popular choice of food for Americans. In some instances, though, I may not care much about what other people may think of my choices, whereas in other cases social approval may be important.

Here are the tenets of this theory:

✓ Behavioral intent is the best predictor of actual behavior and not attitudes themselves.

✓ Behavior intentions are the products of two assessments: (1) A person's attitude toward a behavior and its importance to him or her, and (2) the social component (normative influence) on an individual and its importance to the individual. (Peer pressure or authority influence).

- ✓ Attitude toward a behavior has two dimensions: Belief about the outcome of the behavior and one's evaluation of the outcome.

- ✓ The social component has two dimensions: the normative beliefs (what others think) and a person's motivation or willingness to comply.

- ✓ Behavior is a result of the combination of a person's attitudinal component and the social normative component.

- ✓ The different elements in the TRA can be assigned numerical values and statistically calculated.

Lessons from this theory will include the following:

1. To influence behavior it is necessary to evaluate not only a person's attitudes toward the desired behavior, but also the societal influence on the individual regarding that behavior.
2. Through survey, you can measure not only the attitudes and dispositions of the audience toward your topic of discourse; you can measure their desires to comply or intentions to engage in your recommended action.
3. In a persuasive speech, you may want to make references to the popularity of the behavior you're advocating among members of the social class that the group of audience belongs in addition to appealing to the common values of the audience members.
4. Monroe's motivated sequence of organizing persuasive speeches allows you to exploit the principles of this theory in your persuasive speech.

Elaboration Likelihood Model (ELM)
(Richard Petty and John Cacioppo, 1986)

In our context, to elaborate is to expand on, pay careful attention to and to evaluate a message critically. It also means to be careful and thorough in guiding our behavior.
The Elaboration Likelihood Model is one of the dual process models of persuasion whereby a consumer of information accesses information and decides what to do with that information using two paths of reasoning. The questions to ask to elaborate on this theory are: Is there a need to critically analyze the idea or issue before making a decision? Is the situation or decision peripheral or central to the life of the decision maker? If the decision is central, then it requires elaboration. But if it is peripheral, then it may not require elaboration.

The principles of the model are:

- ✓ There are two routes to persuasion or decision making.

- ✓ The two routes work together.

- ✓ The first is called the **Central Processing Route** which involves mental elaboration—thinking, reflecting, evaluating, elaborating on the message as a basis for decision making (Cognitive domain).

- ✓ The second is called the **Peripheral Processing Route** which focuses on information not directly related to the substance of the message such as the eloquence of the speaker, appearance, slogans, and catchy phrases as the basis for decision making (Affective domain).

- ✓ The two routes are two extremes on the elaboration continuum, from no elaboration to extreme elaboration.

- ✓ High level of involvement or motivation (how the topic of discussion or issue affects the receiver personally) is a condition for using the central route.

- ✓ Ability to process information will affect the choice of the central route of processing information and decision making.

- ✓ Some people enjoy seeking out information and processing them critically. These people are said to have the **Need for Cognition**.

- ✓ The type of processing affects the persistence of persuasion.

- ✓ Persuasion through the central route is found to be longer-lasting than the ones arrived at through the peripheral route.

- ✓ If receivers disagree with a message, the central route processing causes them to generate more counterarguments, but using the peripheral route causes fewer counterarguments.

The persuasive lessons from this model are as follows:

a. Do not assume that all your listeners use the same level and process of thinking.
b. Depending on the composition of your audience, appeal to both categories of listeners.
c. To make persuasion last, get people to think before making their decisions.

Fear Appeal: The Extended Parallel Process Model
(Kim Wittee, 1992, 1994)

We all feel emotions and fear is a strong emotion that may cause us to change our beliefs, values, attitudes, and behavior. The question is not if we should use fear in persuasive speeches, but how we should use it for maximum effect within ethical boundaries.

Researchers have confirmed that the higher the level of fear appeal, the higher the compliance gained from the recipients. That is, the relationship between fear intensity and persuasion is generally positive and linear (Gass and Seiter, 2011). Fear arouses the feeling of vulnerability in the receivers to the extent that they will be open to persuasion and for this to happen, certain conditions must be met. Here are the conditions:

According to Kim Witte (1992, 1994) the proponent of The Extended Parallel Process Model, when fear is aroused in a receiver, he or she is expected to do something about it.

- ✓ The receiver can engage in either **Danger Control** or **Fear Control.**

- ✓ Danger control is a rather effective way of dealing with fear appeal than fear control.

- ✓ The appeal to fear should be to trigger danger control (solution) in the receiver than fear control (fear of fear itself).

- ✓ To trigger danger control, the receiver must perceive the recommended action as effective and feasible. This is called **Perceived Efficacy.**

- ✓ Effectiveness means ability of the receiver to effectively respond to the danger. This is called **Response Efficacy**.

- ✓ The ability of the receiver to respond to the available response is called **Self Efficacy.**

- ✓ Fear appeals work when **high response efficacy** and **high self efficacy** are positively correlated.

- ✓ The **Perceived Vulnerability** of the receiver will make him or her more susceptible to persuasion.

- ✓ The more specific the recommendation the better the influence of fear appeals.

- ✓ The positioning of the recommended action immediately after the fear appeal, the greater the compliance.

The lessons of this model are clear and they are that:

1. Fear appeals work under certain conditions.
2. Fear appeals must trigger danger control attitude in the receiver; that is, a response to attack the problem and do something about it.
3. Fear appeals should not generate fear control attitudes in the mind of the receiver because this is an attempt to reduce the fear; that is, worrying about the problem rather than thinking of ways to solve it.
4. The higher the perception of vulnerability the higher the influence.
5. Fear appeal must be followed immediately with specific actions to resolve the fear.

6. All of these must be done with great ethical considerations.

In conclusion, Gass and Seiter (2011) advise that the trick is to use fear appeals that include workable, practical remedies, thereby triggering danger control which, in turn, leads to constructive responses.

Social Judgment-Involvement Theory
(Carolyn Sherif, Muzafer Sherif, & Roger Nebergall, 1965)

This theory examines the attitudes that we humans hold in our minds toward events, idea, persons or things. The attitudes represent our predispositions or perceptions, which serve as the filters we use to evaluate the events, ideas, people or things. Whenever we receive messages, i.e. persuasive messages, instantly, we categorize them as favorable, unfavorable or neutral to our held beliefs and attitudes. That is, we pass a social judgment on the messages received based on our degree of involvement with the message. So, we either accept (**latitude of acceptance**) or reject (**latitude of rejection**) the opinions or messages of persuaders based on our pre-established attitudinal criteria, or we may deem the message neutral and thus will fall in the category that the researchers have labeled the **non-commitment latitude**.

All these mean that when you receive a persuasive message, in your mind you place it somewhere along your attitude continuum, which ranges from the latitude of acceptance to latitude of rejection, with the area of non-commitment in the middle. An important element that influences the likelihood that a persuader will be able to influence the attitudes of a receiver is the receiver's degree of **ego involvement**. This is how important the issue is to the receiver, whether it is important or not, or central or not to the receiver's definition of self. The higher the receiver's ego involvement on an issue, the more likely he or she will hold on to predetermined attitudes about that issue. Here are the principles of the theory:

✓ We all have attitudinal dispositions that we carry around in our minds.

✓ We use these predispositions as filters for evaluating received messages.

✓ Attitudinal responses to received messages can be classified along a continuum, from latitude of acceptance, to non-commitment, to rejection.

✓ The discrepancy between held positions and advocated positions indicates the opportunity for persuasion.

✓ **Assimilation principle** suggests that positions will be perceived as closer to the receiver's anchor position than they actually are.

✓ **Contrast principle** suggests that positions will be perceived as been more different from the receiver's anchor position that they actually are.

✓ **Highly ego-involved receivers have narrow latitude of acceptance and non-commitment and wide latitude of rejection.** This means they will be less accepting of persuasive messages that challenge their ego and, as such, will readily reject such persuasive message. There is no considering the message and that is why they have narrow latitude of non-commitment.

✓ **Moderately ego-involved people have small latitude of rejection, moderate latitude of acceptance, and moderate latitude of non-commitment.** Because the ego-involvement is moderate, these people are willing to examine alternatives to their positions and, as such, are open to persuasion.

✓ **Low ego-involved receivers have wider latitude of acceptance, wider latitude of non-commitment, and narrow latitude of rejection.** These people will be easier to persuade because, as Benjamin (1997) puts it, the less the ego-involvement, the more the likelihood the person is to be willing to examine all sides of an argument. He added that people who have high ego involvement are less willing to look at a variety of sides on an issue.

The lessons of this theory to the persuader are that:

1. Finding the audience's anchor on an issue of persuasion is critical to understanding the job you have to do to bring about the desired change in them.
2. Once an audience's anchor is located, a reasonable persuasive goal can be set for your speech. It is clear that a one-shot effort such as a speech may not achieve the goal of changing the mind of a highly ego-involved person; this will take series of small persuasive efforts and shifts in established mindset over a period of time.

Table 16.5/The Latitudes of Attitudes in Persuasion

High Ego-Involvement	Moderate Ego-Involvement	Low Ego-involvement
Narrow Latitude of Acceptance	Moderate Latitude of Acceptance	Wide Latitude of Acceptance
Narrow Latitude of Non-commitment	Moderate Latitude of Non-commitment	Wide Latitude of Non-commitment
Wide Latitude of Rejection	Small Latitude of Rejection	Narrow Latitude of Rejection

Evaluating Persuasive Speeches

Assessment of performance is a useful exercise for ensuring expected outcomes and this guarantees necessary preparation prior to a performance and, in the case of public speaking, ensures adherence to guidelines for successful delivery during the performance. The use of evaluative scales in public speaking helps to assure that a speaker is competent in selecting a relevant topic, organizing its contents, citing necessary sources and materials of support, and delivers the speech effectively using appropriate body language according to established principles and experiential skills.

Public speaking assessment must be based on general communication and public speaking competencies that a speaker is expected to demonstrate in the process of giving a speech. From all you've learned about the principles of communication and public speaking, you should be able to identify with the competencies that the Speech Communication Association (SCA) has identified as the necessary evidence of competent public speaking. In "The Competent Speaker" speech evaluation form, the SCA itemizes eight public speaking competencies which are developed into a measurement scale to evaluate public speeches.

For each of the competencies, there are three performance ratings of "Unsatisfactory," "Satisfactory," and "Excellent." Each of these ratings can be weighted with or without numerical values depending on the context and purpose of the evaluation. If a value of (1) is assigned to the Unsatisfactory rating, (2) to the Satisfactory rating , and (3) to Excellent rating, the total obtainable score is therefore 24, while the least score would be eight. However, if some competencies are assigned greater weight for one reason or another, then the scores will vary accordingly. For instance, if competencies three, four and five are deemed more important than the other five, higher scores could be assigned to them, perhaps double that of each of the other competencies. Consequently, the total scores for the "more important" competencies would become 18 and that of the rest will be 15 points.

Sample Persuasive Speech (1)

Inadequacies of Advanced Placement Classes

By Sarah Heath

TEASER

"As a tenth grader in high school, Todd Rosenbaum took an Advanced Placement biology course. This course met just twice a week and offered no laboratories, but he crammed so successfully for the Advanced Placement exam, he earned a 5 (tops on AP's 5-point-scale). That score allowed the high school valedictorian to skip introductory biology at the University of Virginia, but Todd found himself woefully unprepared for an upper-level course." He told *Time Magazine*, November 1, 2004 that "pretty much as soon as I got in, I realized that there was no way I'd survive."

Even the gold standard calculus course is over-rated. On November 8, 2004 Professor Deborah Ball of the University of Michigan stated: "...have impoverished the high school curriculum by racing to AP calculus, and then you get this result: the students are not... competent."

So, while there is little Todd can do for his marred college transcript, we can campaign against the program that led him to have such a record—the so-called Advanced Placement Classes in our high schools. *Today, as we contemplate the inadequacies of the Advanced Placement program, we will, first, better understand the damaging grip AP has on our country, second, realize why these courses fail our nation's brightest children, and third, discuss ways to rid our nation of this Advanced MIS-placement!*

PROBLEM

What is the twofold nature of this academic disease called Advanced Placement? One, the program is growing too fast, and second, the courses don't prepare students for college!

The previously cited Time *Magazine* states: "The thirst to stand out in the brutal college-admissions game is driving a kind of AP mania all across the United States." In the first year of use, 1956, two-thousand exams were administered to one-thousand, two-hundred students." Last May, however, 1.9 million AP exams were taken by 1.1 million U.S. high school students. In fact, some experts think the AP plague is growing so fast and spreading so far it could eventually supplant that ACT and the SAT as America's most influential tests.

So, having examined AP's grip on the U.S., let us now consider how these courses hurt our students by NOT preparing them for college.

According to College Board, the creator of the Advanced Placement Program, these courses were designed so students can "demonstrate ...readiness for college." *The New York* Sun of January, 2005 found that students who took AP courses are "not performing any better in college than the kid who took the non-AP course." In response to this inadequacy, competitive colleges have intensified their terms for granting credit on the basis of AP scores. Harvard and

M.I.T. have recognized that an AP exam-oriented class taken by 10th and 11th graders is ...not the equivalent of a rigorous college course. On November 8, 2004, National Public Radio discovered that other top colleges-such as the universities of Maryland, Michigan, Arizona, and Chicago- are also genuinely concerned. Michigan University states: "...too many incoming freshmen aren't prepared for upper-level college courses, and they don't realize it until they're in over their heads."

CAUSE

So, why has the AP program failed so miserably? Let's discuss the contributing factors which are primarily the shallow subject material in AP's curriculum, the impractical expectations placed on AP teachers, and the academic pressure on ambitious high school students requiring heaps of AP credits.

CONTENT

First, the evidence of shallow subject material in AP courses directly contradicts College Board's promise. College Board states that "AP courses allow students to study subjects in greater depth and detail." Research, however, has proven that statement false. Advanced Placement Biology, Chemistry, and Physics courses were found to be too seeping in scope, lacking the depth of a good college course. 3 years ago, when the National Academy of Science conducted one of the few serious studies of the AP program, it was no surprise that the practice and understanding of laboratory work- a critical piece of college-level science- was given short shrift both in the AP teacher's manuals and on the exams. The study's authors further lamented that a "significant number of AP examination questions... appear to require only rote learning," rather than a deeper understanding of science. However, this problem is further complicated by our second cause: flaws in AP class instruction.

FLAWED AP CLASS PARTICIPATION

The aforementioned Time Magazine stated that: "...educators are worried that AP, which was created as a way to give bright high school seniors a taste of college, is turning into something it was never meant to be: a kind of alternative high school curriculum for ambitious students that teaches to the test, instead of encouraging the best young minds to think more creatively."

And, even if our nation's teachers are NOT to teach to the test, there is little recourse. The Washington Post of December 23, 2004 stated that AP risks being diluted by weak or uncertain teachers...yet AP has no mandated curriculum, and there is no required training for teachers of AP classes! Kent Peterman of the University of Pennsylvania stated in September 2003, "there is evidence that AP has been dropped into or even forced upon many high schools without sufficient faculty preparation."

PRESSURE

The last area of blame lies within the lofty expectations of counselors- both college admissions officers and high school guidance counselors. Experts agree that high school (counselors) could better serve students by putting less emphasis on getting to higher-level AP coursework, and accentuating more preparatory groundwork.

But, according to the previously cited NPR broadcast, "students and teachers know that a high grade in an AP course is a huge factor in college admissions." *The US News and World Report* of August 8, 2004, reported that grades in college prep classes were considered by admissions counselors to be THE criterion of most importance. Yet, the *Washington Post* of December 23, 2004, stated that the greatest predictor of future academic performance in college is not college-prep test scores- it is overall high school grades!

Having examined the three-fold drawbacks of shallow content, flawed AP class instruction, and the lofty expectations of counselors and admissions officers that plague the AP courses, the question then is: Just HOW will we solve our nation's Advanced MIS-placement dilemma?

SOLUTION

Solutions exist on two levels. First, replace AP with the International Baccalaureate Diploma program and second, accelerate able students to college.

For those depressed by Advanced Placement Course failures, let me introduce you to the International Baccalaureate or IB Diploma program. August 30, 2004 edition of the *Washington Post* recorded that "A leading indicator [of new emphasis on rigorous college preparation courses in high school] is the growing number…schools using International Baccalaureate program." *The Independent* of March 13, 2005 stated that the "International Baccalaureate is …considered the 'gold standard' in UK education." Also, the February 24, 2005 edition of The Independent claimed that "The IB is regarded very highly by the Ivy League and Liberal Arts colleges in the United States, and is also loved by most Universities in the UK…

So, what is the drastic difference between AP and IB? The March 2, 2005 *Roanoke Times and World News* states: "To earn the IB diploma, students are not only enrolled in grueling classes (including experimental science), but they must also participate in a special course called the Theory of Knowledge that contrasts learning styles, write a 4,000-word research essay, and also participate in creative sports, and community activities." Beyond these requirements, all IB school administrators and teachers must pass professional IB training and school inspections. And the student's work is graded by some of the world's leading professionals in science, mathematics and languages.

Andrew Roller, a senior at George Mason, loves the International Baccalaureate Diploma program. Andrew told the *Washington Post* of December 9, 2004, "The IB program… taught me how to manage my work better. I … learned to prioritize… and I have developed healthy work schedules … to prevent myself from procrastinating and burning out."

ACCELERATE

Finally, let's consider what acceleration might mean for a floundering group of America's youngest scholars. I propose that able students in high school dually enroll at local colleges. The September 2004 issue of *USA Today* states: ...to get college credit while still in High School, students could take one or more classes at a community college or state university." Virtually all States have some program that allows High School students to take such courses."

We'll take Virginia State for example. The Washington Post of September 16, 2005 notes: "in the next five years, [Virginia's]...community colleges hope to triple the number of students who are enrolled dually at a High School and local two-year college." So, while top schools such as Harvard, M.I.T., and the University of Michigan, must grapple with how to grant credit based on disheartening AP exam scores, High Schoolers with real college credit already have fair, predetermined academic standing.

CONCLUSION

Today we have contemplated the inadequacies of Advanced Placement by: examining the damaging grip these programs have on our country, looking at why these courses fail our children, and finally, deciding how we can solve this dilemma for our nation's brightest students-our nation's future doctors, scientists, engineers, and rhetoricians! So, while Todd Rosenbaum was forced to withdraw from his advanced biology course at the University, future generations will not be so quick to sign-up for overrated Advanced Placement Programs!

Sample Persuasive Editorial (2)

Obama for President

The Washington Post endorses the Senator from Illinois for President

<u>Culled from Washington Post of Friday, October 17, 2008; Page A24</u>

This is an editorial that appeared in the identified newspaper about the candidacy of now President Obama. If you examine the writing as a persuasive argument using Toulmin's <u>model,</u> <u>you'll find that it could as well have been presented as a speech.</u>

THE NOMINATING process this year produced two unusually talented and qualified presidential candidates. There are few public figures we have respected more over the years than Sen. John McCain. Yet it is without ambivalence that we endorse Sen. Barack Obama for president. The choice is made easy in part by Mr. McCain's disappointing campaign, above all his irresponsible selection of a running mate who is not ready to be president. It is made easy in larger part, though, because of our admiration for Mr. Obama and the impressive qualities he has shown during this long race. Yes, we have reservations and concerns, almost inevitably, given Mr. Obama's relatively brief experience in national politics. But we also have enormous hopes.

Mr. Obama is a man of supple intelligence, with a nuanced grasp of complex issues and evident skill at conciliation and consensus-building. At home, we believe, he would respond to the economic crisis with a healthy respect for markets tempered by justified dismay over rising inequality and an understanding of the need for focused regulation. Abroad, the best evidence suggests that he would seek to maintain U.S. leadership and engagement, continue the fight against terrorists, and wage vigorous diplomacy on behalf of U.S. values and interests. Mr. Obama has the potential to become a great president. Given the enormous problems he would confront from his first day in office, and the damage wrought over the past eight years, we would settle for very good.

The first question, in fact, might be why either man wants the job. Start with two ongoing wars, both far from being won; an unstable, nuclear-armed Pakistan; a resurgent Russia menacing its neighbors; a terrorist-supporting Iran racing toward nuclear status; a roiling Middle East; a rising China seeking its place in the world. Stir in the threat of nuclear or biological terrorism, the burdens of global poverty and disease, and accelerating climate change. Domestically, wages have stagnated while public education is failing a generation of urban, mostly minority children. Now add the possibility of the deepest economic trough since the Great Depression.

Not even his fiercest critics would blame President Bush for all of these problems, and we are far from being his fiercest critic. But for the past eight years, his administration, while pursuing some worthy policies (accountability in education, homeland security, the promotion of freedom abroad), has also championed some stunningly wrongheaded ones (fiscal recklessness, torture, utter disregard for the planet's ecological health) and has acted too often with incompetence, arrogance or both. A McCain presidency would not equal four more years, but outside of his inner circle, Mr. McCain would draw on many of the same policymakers who have brought us to our current state. We believe they have richly earned, and might even benefit from, some years in the political wilderness.

OF COURSE, Mr. Obama offers a great deal more than being not a Republican. There are two sets of issues that matter most in judging these candidacies. The first has to do with restoring and promoting prosperity and sharing its fruits more evenly in a globalizing era that has suppressed wages and heightened inequality. Here the choice is not a close call. Mr. McCain has little interest in economics and no apparent feel for the topic. His principal proposal, doubling down on the Bush tax cuts, would exacerbate the fiscal wreckage and the inequality simultaneously. Mr. Obama's economic plan contains its share of unaffordable promises, but it pushes more in the direction of fairness and fiscal health. Both men have pledged to tackle climate change.

Mr. Obama also understands that the most important single counter to inequality, and the best way to maintain American competitiveness, is improved education, another subject of only modest interest to Mr. McCain. Mr. Obama would focus attention on early education and on helping families so that another generation of poor children doesn't lose out. His budgets would be less likely to squeeze out important programs such as Head Start and Pell grants. Though he has been less definitive than we would like, he supports accountability measures for public schools and providing parents choices by means of charter schools.

A better health-care system also is crucial to bolstering U.S. competitiveness and relieving worker insecurity. Mr. McCain is right to advocate an end to the tax favoritism showed to employer plans. This system works against lower-income people, and Mr. Obama has disparaged the McCain proposal in deceptive ways. But Mr. McCain's health plan doesn't do enough to protect those who cannot afford health insurance. Mr. Obama hopes to steer the country toward universal coverage by charting a course between government mandates and individual choice, though we question whether his plan is affordable or does enough to contain costs.

The next president is apt to have the chance to nominate one or more Supreme Court justices. Given the court's current precarious balance, we think Obama appointees could have a positive impact on issues from detention policy and executive power to privacy protections and civil rights.

Overshadowing all of these policy choices may be the financial crisis and the recession it is likely to spawn. It is almost impossible to predict what policies will be called for by January, but certainly the country will want in its president a combination of nimbleness and steadfastness -- precisely the qualities Mr. Obama has displayed during the past few weeks. When he might have been scoring political points against the incumbent, he instead responsibly urged fellow Democrats in Congress to back Mr. Bush's financial rescue plan. He has surrounded himself with top-notch, experienced, centrist economic advisers -- perhaps the best warranty that, unlike some past presidents of modest experience, Mr. Obama will not ride into town determined to reinvent every policy wheel. Some have disparaged Mr. Obama as too cool, but his unflappability over the past few weeks -- indeed, over two years of campaigning -- strikes us as exactly what Americans might want in their president at a time of great uncertainty.

ON THE SECOND set of issues, having to do with keeping America safe in a dangerous world, it is a closer call. Mr. McCain has deep knowledge and a longstanding commitment to promoting U.S. leadership and values. But Mr. Obama, as anyone who reads his books can tell, also has a sophisticated understanding of the world and America's place in it. He, too, is committed to maintaining U.S. leadership and sticking up for democratic values, as his recent defense of tiny Georgia makes clear. We hope he would navigate between the amoral realism of some in his party and the counterproductive cocksureness of the current administration, especially in its first term. On most policies, such as the need to go after al-Qaeda, check Iran's nuclear ambitions and fight HIV/AIDS abroad, he differs little from Mr. Bush or Mr. McCain. But he promises defter diplomacy and greater commitment to allies. His team overstates the likelihood that either of those can produce dramatically better results, but both are certainly worth trying.

Mr. Obama's greatest deviation from current policy is also our biggest worry: his insistence on withdrawing U.S. combat troops from Iraq on a fixed timeline. Thanks to the surge that Mr. Obama opposed, it may be feasible to withdraw many troops during his first two years in office. But if it isn't -- and U.S. generals have warned that the hard-won gains of the past 18 months could be lost by a precipitous withdrawal -- we can only hope and assume that Mr. Obama would recognize the strategic importance of success in Iraq and adjust his plans.

We also can only hope that the alarming anti-trade rhetoric we have heard from Mr. Obama during the campaign would give way to the understanding of the benefits of trade reflected in his writings. A silver lining of the financial crisis may be the flexibility it gives Mr. Obama to override some of the interest groups and members of Congress in his own party who oppose open trade, as well as to pursue the entitlement reform that he surely understands is needed.

IT GIVES US no pleasure to oppose Mr. McCain. Over the years, he has been a force for principle and bipartisanship. He fought to recognize Vietnam, though some of his fellow ex-POWs vilified him for it. He stood up for humane immigration reform, though he knew Republican primary voters would punish him for it. He opposed torture and promoted campaign finance reform, a cause that Mr. Obama injured when he broke his promise to accept public financing in the general election campaign. Mr. McCain staked his career on finding a strategy for success in Iraq when just about everyone else in Washington was ready to give up. We think that he, too, might make a pretty good president.

But the stress of a campaign can reveal some essential truths, and the picture of Mr. McCain that emerged this year is far from reassuring. To pass his party's tax-cut litmus test, he jettisoned his commitment to balanced budgets. He hasn't come up with a coherent agenda, and at times he has seemed rash and impulsive. And we find no way to square his professed passion for America's national security with his choice of a running mate who, no matter what her other strengths, is not prepared to be commander in chief.

ANY PRESIDENTIAL vote is a gamble, and Mr. Obama's résumé is undoubtedly thin. We had hoped, throughout this long campaign, to see more evidence that Mr. Obama might stand up to Democratic orthodoxy and end, as he said in his announcement speech, "our chronic avoidance of tough decisions."

But Mr. Obama's temperament is unlike anything we've seen on the national stage in many years. He is deliberate but not indecisive; eloquent but a master of substance and detail; preternaturally confident but eager to hear opposing points of view. He has inspired millions of voters of diverse ages and races, no small thing in our often divided and cynical country. We think he is the right man for a perilous moment.

Can you identify the major persuasive arguments used in this editorial?

Sample Persuasive Theory Analysis (3)

"12 Angry Men:" A Persuasive Theoretical Analysis

By Karen Pollack

The classic 1957 film 12 Angry Men provides a fascinating look at how principles of persuasion can lead people to arrive at flawed conclusions. Rather than being set in a courtroom, this drama is set strictly within the confines of a jury room during deliberation of a capital murder case. The audience doesn't see or hear the presentation of the cases made by the prosecuting or defense attorneys, but it is made clear in the opening scenes that the collective mind of the jury is all but made up. Eleven men are prepared to send the defendant to the electric chair, thinking that they have seen a "slam-dunk" case made by the prosecution.

There is only one holdout, played by Henry Fonda, who feels that before sending a young man to his death, a discussion of the facts of the case must be made. As these facts are argued, the Fonda character convinces his fellow jurors, one by one, that they have been led not by pure reason, but by persuasive techniques that tapped into their own assumptions, prejudices and personal problems.

*In one memorable scene, the murder weapon is discussed, and brought into the jury room for examination. That weapon is a switch-blade (called a "switch-knife" in the film), with a distinctive handle and blade. Most of the jurors, using the **reasoning process of conditional syllogism,** conclude the following. If the murder weapon is unique enough to be "one of a kind" and the defendant owns such a weapon, then the defendant must be the murderer. Thus, most of the jurors assume that there couldn't possibly be more than one of these knives, and so the defendant must have committed the crime. The Fonda character demonstrates the flaw in the major premise of the syllogism, by pulling an identical knife out of his pocket. He explains how he bought it for $6.00 from a pawn shop not too far away from the murder scene, dramatically illustrating that any number of identical knives may be in circulation, and that it wasn't unique after all.*

***The fallacy of the undistributed middle**, revolving around the use of the murder weapon, comes under scrutiny in a later scene. In this case, the persuaders are the jurors themselves, and are convinced that what is true for one member of a group must be true for all members of that group. Many of the jurors, knowing that the defendant is a skilled knife-fighter, engage in "guilt by association". They conclude that because some of those who are handy with a switch blade have used them to commit murder, the defendant must have done so also. This time, the character played by Jack Klugman offers evidence that casts doubt on their belief. He explains that the typical use of a switch-knife is underhand, and not overhand, as was the case in the murder. He argues that the defendant's experience with a switch-knife, rather than supporting the prosecution's case, was actually exonerating evidence.*

In these scenes, and throughout the film, we see how the jurors make judgments, not based on the facts in evidence, but heavily colored by the attitudes they brought with them into the courtroom.

*When referring to the defend*ant, who is of Puerto Rican descent, their dialogue is peppered with remarks such as "You know how *those people* are", revealing their prejudice. It is clear that as they evaluated the facts, they already had a high degree of disfavor toward the defendant, and were predisposed to find him guilty. Attitude, one of the process premises of persuasion, was at work, and these jurors, having negative attitudes toward Puerto Ricans were made ready to bring in a guilty verdict because of it.

The testimony of eyewitnesses is examined in another pivotal scene in this film. We see how convincing this testimony is for the persuadees, and then we see how unreliable such evidence can be. The audience learns that a woman, who lives across the street from the murder scene, testified that she saw the murder actually being committed through the window of an empty elevated train that was passing by. Another witness is an elderly man, who claims to have seen the defendant flee the scene moments after hearing the words "I'm going to kill you!" and the body hitting the floor.

Most of the jurors accept the testimony of both witnesses, without questioning whether or not their accounts were truthful, accurate, or even possible. The eyewitnesses were powerful persuaders, but only the Fonda character wanted to be sure that the testimony was credible.
He performs a reenactment of the events as told by the elderly witness, and in doing so, showed that his testimony wasn't entirely truthful. Possible motives for the man's testimony were suggested, and we can see some of Packard's **"Eight Compelling Needs"** driving the witness towards distortion of the truth, such as his need for ego gratification and his need for a sense of power.

Further, the jurors realize that the elderly man may have been resolving **cognitive dissonance**, by shifting his memory of events away from the truth, and towards testimony that would allow him to feel important and listened to. He wasn't deliberately lying, but instead made himself believe his own version of the events. Rather than judge the witness harshly for his misleading testimony, several of the jurors then understood that the process of seeking consistency can occur beneath the level of consciousness.

The Henry Fonda character argues that it could not be possible for both of these witnesses to be accurately recounting the facts, because if the train was passing by at the time of the murder, as the woman testified, then the elderly man wouldn't have been able to hear a thing above the racket from the train.

As the film concludes, the Fonda character, whose name is finally revealed to be "Davis", has succeeded in forcing even the most hard-headed and bigoted juror, played brilliantly by Lee J. Cobb, to relent. By insisting that the jury use critical thinking skills, and analyze the facts alone, the tactics of persuasion used by the prosecution and the jurors themselves were stripped away. Instead of the "open and shut" case that they originally thought they saw, they now saw that the prosecution's evidence was "full of holes", leaving ample room for reasonable doubt and a verdict of Not Guilty. *12 Angry Men* is a compelling drama that shows how vulnerable we all are to make decisions while being influenced by the persuasive forces of others, and even ourselves.

Sample Special Occasion Speech (4)

REMARKS BY RT. HON. DIMEJI S. BANKOLE, CFR, SPEAKER, HOUSE OF REPRESENTATIVES, AS SPECIAL GUEST OF HONOUR AT THE MAIDEN NATIONAL ASSOCIATION OF NIGERIAN STUDENTS (NANS) LEADERSHIP LECTURE SERIES/DINNER, AT THE BALLROOM HALL, NICON LUXURY HOTEL, ABUJA, ON THURSDAY, 18TH DECEMBER, 2008.

Protocols.

It is my honor and pleasure to be invited to this unique event as Special Guest of Honor. I am particularly delighted to be given the opportunity to make these remarks. The fact that we are a part of this memorable Leadership Lecture/Dinner of the National Association of Nigerian Students goes to underscore our overall commitment towards the development of our youths for excellence and the attainment of the highest human ideals.

Permit me to observe that the subject of discourse at this Lecture is quite appropriate, against contemporary challenges of electoral reform in Nigeria. "Consolidating the Gains of the 2007 General Election and Democratic Process in Nigeria: The United States Example" is a theme that is also quite timely. Providing a forum for stakeholders to articulate the way forward for our future elections is perhaps the surest guarantee for the survival and sustenance of democracy in Nigeria. Against the backdrop of the recent elections in the United States of America (USA), this Lecture is also apt. In so many ways, the US elections provide lessons for many countries, particularly for us in Nigeria as we strive to consolidate our democracy. I am, therefore, delighted to have this opportunity to share insights and ideas with relevant stakeholders as well as deliver this brief remark.

Although democracy is not about elections, free and fair elections are the heart of democratic governance. Elections have been the critical decider of the disjointed sequence of democracy in Nigeria. Earlier democratic experiments in Nigeria failed largely because of failure to guarantee orderly succession and transition through credible and legitimate elections.

Elections matter because without orderly succession, democracies will not consolidate. They are important because they are the life-wire, indeed, the blood of democracy. We are sufficiently concerned about the quality of elections we have had in the past. This is because, democracies are worth very little if the people do not vote or votes do not count. It is for the importance of elections to democratic governance that the greater struggles for democracy have been waged in the name of the right to vote.

As we all know, the Committee on Electoral Reforms has undertaken a nation-wide tour of all geo-political zones of the country to sample and harness the input of the entire spectrum of Nigerians. At the end of their assignment, government would consider their recommendations towards ensuring a transparent, workable and credible electoral process for Nigeria.

In the Legislature, we recognize our critical role in this regard. For instance, our commitment towards a credible electoral process informed our 2006 amendment of the Electoral Act. But we do realize that a lot more still needs to be done. We would, therefore, utilize the valuable input from the Committee on Electoral Reforms to fashion out a new Electoral Act that would truly stand the test of time in Nigeria's quest for an enduring democratic culture. We also recognize that building electoral institutions is another way of complementing the realization of an acceptable electoral process. We are fully committed to providing appropriate legislative interventions that would strengthen and truly empower our electoral institutions and agencies.

Through collective wisdom, we must design processes that enhance the incentive and power of Nigerians to vote and protect their votes; processes and mechanisms that curtail the propensity of electoral officials and security operatives to undermine the integrity of the ballot box. There is nothing really mysterious about rigging elections. It is as a result of the failure of institutions. Our challenge is to build electoral institutions that can withstand the pressure of corruption and the inordinate quest for power.

There is no gainsaying the fact that America's democracy will continue to be of interest to Nigeria. This is essentially because the Nigerian people have modeled, in many respects, the American Presidential system of democracy. Beyond this, however, aspects of the US balloting method that continue to fascinate democrats the world-over would include the use of electronic voting system; voting by post; early voting procedure; and the opportunity for Americans resident in other countries to vote. We have also talked about open-secret ballot system as well as the manual on-the-spot counting methods. I enjoin this Lecture to appraise these and other components of balloting in order to come out with an acceptable method for Nigeria's use in future elections.

We must reach out to Nigerians in the Diaspora both in soliciting ideas to transform our electoral process and in providing opportunity for them to participate in every aspect of elections wherever they may reside in the world. This group is a highly skilled and mobilized group of Nigerians who must deliberately be brought into the mainstream of our democracy. I am confident that recommendations that would flow from this Lecture will be specific and effective in addressing the crisis of electoral legitimacy in our society.

Indeed, democracy anchored on a credible electoral process can help societies like Nigeria manage the distributional conflicts that arise from economic reform programs. The relationship between democracy and sustainable economic development depends on the stability and inclusiveness of the political process. In this wise, the legitimacy of the democratic process matters. The credibility of the electoral process will remain a key factor in assessing the stability of political governance.

Elections hold the key to entrench democracy in Nigeria; they hold the key to sustain the tempo of democratization in Africa. Nigeria's huge population and our strategic position in Africa guarantee the country's primacy as a democratic role model. We must find the will and resources to deliver free and fair elections. This challenge is for all Nigerians, and we in the House of Representatives look forward to the recommendations of this Lecture.

As I commend this initiative by the National Association of Nigerian Students (NANS), I thank you all for the attention.

Former Speaker, Rt. Hon. Dimeji S. Bankole, CFR.

Sample Persuasive/Special Occasion Speech (5)

Keynote speech at the International Congress of the Association of the Ogbomosho Sons and Daughters in North America, September 2, 2006. By Dr. *Daniel O. Awodiya*

The Chairman, Association of the Ogbomoso sons and daughters in North America, the executives, honorable members, invited guests, family members, associates, friends, ladies and gentlemen: Welcome to the annual convention of the Ogbomoso sons and daughters in North America. I thank the congress for extending the invitation to me, the second time, to be the keynote speaker of this august occasion. I consider your invitation a high honor and a privilege because, rarely does one have the second opportunity to create a first impression, but now I have the rare circumstance of recreating an impression I left with you exactly nine years and ten days ago. So, it is with great pleasure that I stand before you today to speak about issues we addressed about ten years ago, to offer an assessment of our performance thus far and, finally, to see what the future holds for us all.

I must first of all commend the organizers of this occasion for their hard work and perseverance, because without such, this event would not be a success that it is already. We must salute the leaders as well as the members for the longevity of this association. This is really exemplary, for many such socio-ethnic collectivities have be formed and many have unceremoniously disbanded due to internal squabbles brought about by myriads of reasons, prominent of which are egotism and egocentrism, highhandedness, frivolous nitpicking, vengefulness, obstinacy, ulterior agenda, and plain selfishness. I congratulate the entire members of this association for your selflessness, perseverance, determination, and steadfastness of purpose. I am, indeed, encouraged that there is hope for us and our people when I think of the association of Ogbomoso sons and daughters.
I salute each and every one of you for being here today.
Chairman, please indulge me to revisit my speech of about ten years ago before this congress at the Richard Conley Residence Hall of the Long Island University, in Brooklyn, New York.

African Americans

I reminded us of the common history of our presence in America- either as descendants of slaves or as freeborn Africans who relocated to the U.S. for economic and political emancipation. The experience of either set of Africans is fraught with repression and discrimination, hence the struggle for liberation and equalization as humans, at par with other ethnic groups in the United States. So, the primary fight of the African in America is in defense of his humanity.

The early Africans fought the agents and agencies that repressed and brutalized them-- they bounded together in the face of the divide and conquer rule of their captors and they developed a collective consciousness that recognized their 'Africaness,' their struggle, and their humanity. Today, despite media disparagement and negative stereotypes, numbers of African Americans have broken the shackles of oppression and have broken set boundaries to achieve success in this land. What remains to be taken down, however, is the ubiquitous fortress of racism, stereotypes, and discrimination.

The liberation of the African Americans was engineered by the intelligentsia and their visionary leaders. This handful of people described by W.E.B. Dubois as the "talented tenth" of the population, took the mantle of liberating their people upon themselves, determined to take them to the promise land. As a result of the struggles of the "talented tenth," and the quality followership of the rank and file, the African Americans have achieved phenomenal success in America and this they have done against all odds.

Consequent upon the African Americans finding a voice in America, they extended their clout to influencing, positively, the continent of their forebears. It was the incessant appeal, struggles, demonstrations, and political arm-twisting of the African Americans that led to the independence of many African nations, including the dismantling of apartheid in South Africa.

Africans in America

Chairman, ladies and gentlemen, let me remind the congress of what I said about the second set of Africans in America. These are the freeborn Africans in America. These are the Africans who willingly came to the U.S. for one reason or the other. I believe many of us in this auditorium belong to this second set. We worked hard or begged hard to secure money to purchase air tickets, then struggled day and night at Eleke (Carrington) crescent or Abuja, as the case may be, to obtain any type of visa to this great country. At first the reason for this transplantation was education, then it became economic, and then political.

Regardless of the reasons why Africans run away from Africa, we unwittingly paid handsomely to become partakers of a new form of slavery and oppression. Disillusioned by racism and its twin brother, discrimination, we quickly realize that we have transplanted ourselves into a sub-group, a sub-class, and a sub-citizen of a racially divided country. As time passes by, the Africans become disgruntled intercontinental interlopers, dissatisfied with life in America and worrisome of the conditions of life back home.

What a predicament! Stuck in America, many without functional education that would transform their plight into meaningful subsistence, perhaps entry into the middle class, they stay at the bottom of this society full of ignorance and illusion. Socially trapped into this neo-slavery and racism they paid handsomely to get into.

In this predicament, it is difficult to appreciate the depth of Black struggle in the United States because they are lost in the day-to-day struggle for subsistence. At best they are able to form mutually suspicious relationships with other Africans, African Americans in their social class. However, as role models to many of their ilk back home in Ghana and Nigeria, for example, claiming a sort of misplaced superiority, they misrepresent realities of life in America, hiding their sufferings and as rhetorical guise; talk ill of their home country and deride everybody and the government. Should I believe that the educated among us do not engage in such vulgarity?

Educated Africans

Well, now let us examine the plight of the educated among us. Those with college degrees and high-level skills in the Social Sciences, Medicine, Art, Engineering and the like; those with letters from Yale, Princeton, Howard, Wharton College, Harvard, Hofstra, Cornell, etc. I guess many of us in this auditorium belong to this category. Many of us trained in Africa and continued here in the United States. And many would vouch for the quality of training they received back home and that such training has put them in good stead in the U.S.

Many of us were prepared to function in the Western world rather than in Africa. Intellectually transformed into a stranger in his/her own land, the educated African aspires to go West, especially when the West is going to Africa in pursuit of the continent's immeasurable natural resources. African intellectuals continue to migrate West because they have been trained to espouse Western thought and appreciate its contraptions. No wonder we study Western Art, Literature, Medicine, Architecture, Political Science, etc., and are unable to create anything authentic to Africa.

So, many of us are educated, but not sophisticated enough to understand the real consequences of the type of education we have received. Real education brings about great awareness and such awareness, humbles the mind. Real education brings about communal success, not individual success! The real measure of our education is the general well-being of our people. Education is, therefore, a collective product that has collective liberating consequences.

So, many of us are educated but not really exposed. By being clannish and tribal, we create an intellectual and social fence around ourselves that we live in a cocoon of ignorance. By being arrogant charlatans, we mislead our people, who place so heavy premium on our education, thinking of us as wise, smart, and above all, deeply committed to their cause! Our people put faith in our capacity to shed obstacles of structure, culture, and frivolous traditions, to empower the Africa collective over its encumbrances of poverty, disease, ignorance, wars, and the like.

Instead of living up to these expectations, we corrupt our continent with contemptuous philosophies and selfish motives. We join others in disparaging our fatherland and abandon its people for the luxuries of Europe and America. Hence we collude with the West to rape the resources of the place and stash them away in faraway land. We refer to our people as "those people;" our lips drip with vitriolic commentaries that demonize all of our people.

Consequently, Africa's so called leaders act like mercenaries whose modus operandi is target, control, attack, and loot!

Ladies and gentlemen, this is a rather negative view of Africa's ruling class and intelligentsia, but the recurring leadership failures that we've all become accustomed to cannot be blamed on anyone else or another people. Africa's 'talented tenth" is to blame!

The 'talented tenth' who are supposed to put on the burden of liberating our people have in turn become a burden on the people. This small group of people who should have the vision of emancipating and structuring an enduring rule of performance for the people have become, for all intent and purposes, visionless and ruthless violators of the rule of law.

The Nigerian Example

In the Nigerian example, historically we blame our misfortunes on the colonizers- this is all too easy a crutch of the intellectuals and the ruling class. Yes, the British amalgamated the Northern and Southern protectorates of Nigeria and engineered the domination of the country by the Sultans and the Caliphate, but many events in the life of the country have superseded the machinations of Lord Laggard and the British Empire he represented.

Since then, we have witnessed the rise of internal colonization by different ethnic groups in the country. Again we have witnessed opportunistic military brass usurp power one regime after the other, plundering both our human and material resources, thus dashing the hopes of the people. Then we saw how opportunistic civilian lackeys trumpet the messianic prowess of dictators and vagabonds, in the consummate design to perpetuate illegal, corrupt, and bankrupt regimes. Many of us are more than willing to join this bandwagon of sycophants. Those who are to lead the country have compromised their ideals and have become apologists and orchestrate the hegemony of buffoons.

In the meantime, the Nigerian rulers of Northern extraction have perfected their political gerrymandering that has fundamentally rigged any democratic election in their favor (or so they thought). While the political elite of the South was busy sloganeering, the Northern elites had crafted more local governments for Kano than Lagos and instituted a revenue allocation scheme on the basis of the number of local governments that allowed more money to Kano than Lagos- a State with much more people. No, you cannot trust Nigerian leaders to conduct an unfettered census- "it is far too consequential an exercise to be conducted fairly." The Northern intellectual has allowed itself to acquiesce in the domination of its people, such that feudal lords reign supreme in the face of the people's illiteracy and abject poverty. The Southern leaders are all too busy scampering for opportunistic loot that they forget that they, too, have a birth right!

Ladies and gentlemen, I know you are very well aware of the problems with Nigeria, but let me employ the words of a great novelist and scholar to articulate it further. Chinua Achebe wrote in his book "The Trouble with Nigeria" that (and I quote) "the trouble with Nigeria is simply and squarely a failure of leadership." He identified the symptoms of failed leadership in Nigeria as indiscipline, tribalism, social injustice, and corruption. With these ailments present in the Nigerian polity, it is unmistaken then that the Nigerian experience is like 'taking two steps backwards for every one forward.'

Tribalism has led to the desire to favor clan over what is fair and just, to look forward to disintegration of the country, rather than its unification and emancipation. So, with favoritism comes corruption and indiscipline. The combination of these factors can only lead up to poverty and hopelessness.

Poverty is so pervasive in Nigeria that Chinua Achebe, in a recent interview, saw this monster as enabling the corrupt politicians and undermining our nascent democracy. He said: "it is difficult when the economic poverty of the people is so great that we cannot trust them to exercise control over who rules them- a situation in which they would accept a few naira from anybody in exchange for their votes." He further claimed that "the level of poverty is crucial in measuring the success of any kind of representation. And the most ruthless and cynical leaders know this. So they plunder the state and stash the money to use whenever there is an election."

Hope for the Future

Is the Nigerian situation hopeless? No, far from it!
We are not condemned to wallow in hopelessness. I am particularly encouraged by the efforts of the Organization of the Sons and Daughters of Ogbomoso, which has taken upon itself to institute and implement a progressive agenda to ensure that there is hope for their kinsmen and women. I am encouraged by the wisdom and virtue of this organization because you know what to do to emancipate our people and, am sure you have the skills to actualize your plans. Your virtue comes from doing what is right and for this I commend all of you. Oh, how I wish many other Nigerian Organizations would emulate the selfless efforts of the Ogbomoso Sons and Daughters in North America.

You, as part of the Ogbomoso 'talented tenth,' should not relent in doing the right thing because greater challenges await you and no one else will step to the plate but you. While you send resources, both material and financial to Ogbomoso, I want to encourage you to help the people realize that they can do for themselves by creating education programs and institutions that would instill self-awareness in them and foster political consciousness that would liberate them.

And what would such liberation engender? Electing the right persons to political offices, not selling their votes to the highest bidder, awareness of their power and control over their local government, determining how and for what local government monies are spent; holding political office holders to account; and more importantly, organizing and implementing programs that would serve the collective communities and not the narrow interests of the politicians and their cronies.

I hope that in the course of this convention, you would evaluate the performance of your Organization thus far. Having set laudable goals for yourselves, it is high time you started evaluating your accomplishments in order to improve on your achievements and redirect your energy to fulfilling promises yet to be realized. As at about ten years ago when I spoke before this congress, you itemized some of your program of action to include:

Portable water supply to Ogbomoso and environs
Stable electric power supply
Improvement of health of the people
Education (scholarship at the appropriate levels)
Better town planning/street naming/house numbering
Postal services in all local governments and adequate mail delivery
Help for the Baptist Hospital, Blind center, Leper settlement, Motherless home.

All these are laudable programs, desirable and much needed. With your dedication and steadfastness I am convinced that you have engaged all these squarely. But you should level your expectations with the reality of fulfillment. So, how much of these have you really accomplished and what are yet to be effected? For all that you have done so far, you deserve to be applauded for I know that your best is yet to come!

I had once said that what sets the Ogbomosos apart from the rest of the Nigerian Associations here in the U.S. is action, not just action, but the right action in the right direction. That is your virtue.

Let us stand tall for we are on the right track. Let us encourage our leaders to do right thing and let us commend our leaders when they do right. And let us not fail to do our best to contribute to what would make good leadership work.

By accepting to speak before you today, I hope I have participated in the process of making our people proud of us the 'talented tenth.' And by admonishing us, I have gently reminded us of our responsibilities to ourselves and to our fatherland.

So, Chairman, executive members, honorable members, invited guests, family members and friends, it is for our land that we strive, in the collective, we as a people, will reach our destiny and so let it be for the land we call home- Africa. Because of you, the Ogbomoso Sons and Daughters in America and your ilk, I am inclined to claim that there is hope for Africa.

Thank you.

Review Questions

1. Define persuasion and discuss how the speaker can persuade an audience.
2. Explain the relevance of the Aristotelian concepts of logos, ethos and pathos to persuasive speaking.
3. Identify and explain the elements of the Toulmin's model of argumentation.
4. Describe, compare, and contrast inductive and deductive types of reasoning.
5. Identify and describe the different content and process reasoning fallacies.
6. Identify and describe the different types of persuasive speeches and how they can be organized.
7. Write a 5-7-minute persuasive speech on why The United States should explore alternative, renewable forms of energy.

SECTION FIVE

Group Processes and Mass Communication

17. Small Group Processes and Communication

18. Mass Communication

Chapter Seventeen

Small Group Processes and Communication

For the individual, membership in different types of groups is inevitable in the world we live in today. Starting from the family unit, as a group, we discuss issues, propose solutions to them, and execute prescribed actions together with other family members. This is our first experience with functioning in a group and this is repeated in every sphere of life we may find ourselves. When you go to school you're asked to join with others to form groups for the purpose of learning particular issues, problems and to proffer solutions to them. You join the Boys Scouts or the Girls Brigades where, again, you're introduced to other forms of groups. Now to the world of work, most of the problems facing employers of labor, managers and employees are solved in the group setting. Certainly, there is no escaping the small group or participating in one. It is one thing to belong to a small group, but another to function effectively in one. Understanding the nature of small groups and how to effectively function in one is a worthwhile goal for all humans, more so for those who aspire to positions of responsibility and leadership in society.

There are many different definitions of the small group that we can find in literature, each emphasizing different characteristics that explain the functioning of this form of association of humans. Renz and Greg (2000) offer a definition that speaks to their expectations about the nature of small groups when they write that **a small group is a small number of humans, drawn together through interaction, whose interdependent relationships allow them to achieve a mutual goal.** The characteristics emphasized here are size of the group, interaction among members, interdependence of the members, and the group collectively having a mutual goal or sets of goals. Johnson and Johnson (2000) offer a slightly different definition of a small group when they describe it as **two or more individuals in face-to-face interaction, each aware of positive interdependence as they strive to achieve mutual goals, each aware of his or her membership in the group, and each aware of the others who belong to the group.** This definition identifies the following characteristics as important in capturing the nature of the small group and they are: face-to-face interaction, awareness of positive interdependence and membership in the group, and mutual goals. All these characteristics cannot be achieved without communication and, more importantly speaking.

Communication scholars differentiate dyadic or two-person communication from communication among three or more individuals. With the introduction of a third person to the dyadic communication situation, several changes are observable. Renz and Greg (2000) observe that communication among three or more individuals compared to that which takes place between a dyad, as less personal or intimate as it becomes more difficult to manage rules for turn-taking in the conversation and it is less likely that all could participate equally. These two communication contexts are significantly different and, as such, a small group is defined as a different level of communication from dyadic interaction. In terms of numbers, the minimum in a small group is three while the maximum number is not fixed. However, some scholars set a limit of fifteen while others say seventeen should be considered the cut off point for small group membership. There are no hard and fast rules about the ceiling number of members in the small group, but there are two rules of thumb that should guide our thinking in this regard. One is that **the smaller the number the better** because of ease of communication and intimacy among members. Second is that **it is better to have an odd number of members rather than an even number** and this is because it is possible for members to divide themselves into separate cliques of even numbers thus making it difficult for them to work together, especially that there is no extra member who may break the tie in case of voting on decisions of the group.

Members in a small group are not isolates, so they must exchange ideas and share feelings as well as opinions; their cooperative effort to achieve a common goal requires communication. It can be concluded that the galvanizing element of the group, its lifeline, and its essence is communication. Interdependence on the other hand, is a human attribute that requires individuals to work well with others, learn when and how to depend on others, and understand the responsibilities of individuals to each other and to the group as a whole. All of these can only be achieved through effective communication among the different elements that constitute the group or system.

When viewed as a system, a group is "greater than the sum of its parts." When parts of a system interact to create a product that could not have been produced by the individual member acting alone, this is described as a result of **synergy** (Salazar, 1995). The principle of wholeness confirms the importance of each member's unique relationship to the group. All of the parts of the system are so related that any change to a particular part affects the system as a whole; consequently, the attitudes and behaviors of any member of the group will impact those of the other members.

A system (group) exists within a supra system (larger environment) of which it is a sub part. The supra system exerts some normative and structural pressure on the system, but the interaction of the two depends on whether the sub part is closed or open. Closed systems would limit external influence, while an open system would encourage external input. It is considered advantageous for a system to seek information from outsiders to complement its members' ideas, while a system that does not seek information from without and does not welcome outside evaluation may deteriorate.

A system is never static, so a group is never static. A goal-directed group is constantly moving toward accomplishing its set goals and as the external environment is equally dynamic, both are constantly adapting to each other, especially changing to maintain homeostasis, which is internal equilibrium or stability. Different groups will achieve equilibrium differently by pursuing their goals through one or a combination of unique methodological routes and this tendency is called **equifinality.** Arriving at their desired goals, but through dissimilar routes reflects the uniqueness of group member interactions as they produce unique behavioral patterns. But what makes a small group effective and what are the observable characteristics of an effective group? Answering this question appropriately would depend on the purpose for which a group is established and how the members see themselves in relation to the group as a whole.

An examination of the characteristics of an effective group identified by Johnson and Johnson (2000), speaks to the centrality of communication in the effective functioning of the group. According to them, an effective group is more than the sum of its parts (Gestalt psychology); it is a group whose members commit themselves to the common purpose of maximizing their own and others' success. They itemized the **characteristics of an effective group** to include the following:

1. Positive interdependence that unites members together to achieve clear, operational goals.

2. Two-way communication.

3. Distributed leadership.

> *Knowing is not enough; we must apply. Willing is not enough; we must do.*
>
> Goethe

4. Power based on expertise.

5. A decision –making procedure appropriate to the situation

6. Challenge of members information and reasoning.

7. Constructive conflict resolution.

8. Accountability of each member to do fair share of work.

9. Promotion of member success.

10. Appropriate engagement in small group skills.

11. Evaluation of how group members work well together.

All of these characteristics center on effective communication and motivation, which usually result in effective performance. So, as a student of communication and public speaking, it is imperative that you learn about the nature of small groups in order to effectively function as participant in the many different types of small groups you will find yourself be it social, academic, or professional. And as Johnson and Johnson (2000) sum it, it is from using group skills that you will gain an understanding of what group dynamics is and how useful it can be.

How useful to you are group skills? One, you cannot escape working with others in different groups and as you climb the ladder of success, the more the need for you to work more in groups with others at the decision making levels of organizations and society. This is confirmed when it was reported that an estimate of about fifty percent of executives' time is spent in meetings (Cole, 1989). But such time spent in meetings is not always productive as reported by 75% of workers who confirmed in a study that the time spent in meetings could be more productive (Herring, 2006). Functioning effectively in the group setting is based on understanding the nature of the group and the behaviors of individuals in the group setting. More importantly, effective performance in the group setting requires turning such knowledge into manageable skills that will inform our future performance.

The most important skill you will gain from group performance is ability to communicate effectively in building consensus and motivating others to work with you to achieve desired team goals. One of the reported skills potential employers look for in their workers is teamwork and the ability to get along well with others; these are skills you will acquire working in different groups. As you can see, membership in different small groups is beneficial to the participant in personal and professional ways.

Why People Join Groups

© **Alexmax** | Dreamstime.com

People join groups for one or a combination of reasons; it may be because group membership enhances one's social status; it may look good on a resume or; it may provide an avenue to explore hobbies, interests, and desires and; it may help solve problems or generate ideas and enhance learning. The last reason appears to be the major reason why people join groups, but the others may be, indeed, more plausible.

Theoretical explanations of why people join groups include physical and psychological needs fulfillment as identified in Maslow's hierarchy of needs. Prominent of the reasons are the need for **social approval and satisfaction**. Schutz' interpersonal needs theory and Festinger's social comparison theory both explain other reasons why people may join groups.

Schutz's Interpersonal Needs Theory

Schutz (1958) in agreeing with the saying that "people need people," identifies three human needs that justify the assumption: **The need for inclusion, the need for control, and the need for affection.** As a human need, inclusion is being involved with others and being worthy of inclusion with others. We enjoy having others who are willing to acknowledge us by inviting us to join with them to work or play together. What is satisfying is the psychological recognition and valuing that comes with inclusion because it informs us of our identity and status in society. This is why we value being members of our families, local organizations, religious bodies, interest groups and work groups. Affection is desire for love- to love and to be loved. We have the emotions that motivate us to want to belong to others and for others to belong to us and to know that we are valued, respected, and more importantly desired. Control has to do with the ability to influence our surroundings and the world we live in by doing something to present the world to us the way we want it to be. But we cannot do it alone because there is so much to do and "one person does not make a forest." People need people in order to fulfill our desires and needs.

Schutz explains that human needs are bipolar. On one hand we need inclusion and, on the other hand we need to include others in our lives. The need for one to control others also yields to the need to be controlled by others and the need to show affection to others also includes the need to be shown affection. He further explains that these needs exist in degrees and, as such, they may be deficient at times, excessive at times, and exist at a normal level in other times. Individuals, therefore, will join groups that best satisfy their needs and in which there is the best matching of needs among the members. As with Maslow's hierarchy of needs, Schutz' needs are satisfied according to their prepotency and they follow the pattern of inclusion, followed by control, and finally affection.

Festinger's Social Comparison Theory

Festinger (1954) identifies that a basic need of humans is to evaluate their opinions and abilities. This they do in a social manner, using others as the measure of their own performance. According to Festinger, we affiliate with others whose opinions and abilities are fairly similar to ours in order to have a meaningful standard against which to measure ourselves. The search for "others like us" may pose problems for groups composed of diverse membership. If a group is too divergent from us, we avoid joining it or, better still, we seek out others who are similar to us within the group. In the diverse American workforce, for example, even if the workers interact with those "different" from themselves on tasks, they are likely to seek out others of their own ethnic group for social contact at work, which may be perceived negatively by their co-workers (Morrison, Ruderman, & Hugh-James, 1993). With increasing diversification of the American workforce, workers of different ethnic and social cultural backgrounds interact across these divides as a matter of necessity and compulsion. This is a sign that social segregation is fast becoming an outdated and out modeled phenomenon in the contemporary American reality.

In a group where membership is determined by **similarity**, a member who finds his opinions discrepant from those of others will strive to reduce the discrepancy in one of three ways (Rend and Greg, 2000):

1. The member may change his or her opinion if it is quite out of line with those of the other members.

2. The member may bring pressure to bear on other members if he or she finds her opinions close to others, but slightly off the mark.

3. A member may ignore some members of the group as he or she makes comparisons, narrowing the range of members he or she uses in evaluating herself.

There are other principles, other than similarity, that may influence why others join groups. Such principles include **proximity** (geographic closeness), **anxiety producing situations** (people who are anxious affiliate with others that are equally anxious), **changes in self-esteem** (people who have had their self-esteem lowered, lower their standard for choice of friends), and **complementary needs** (In this case opposites attract for the purpose of countering their personal characteristics).

Proximity plays a great role in determining which groups we join. In the classroom, however, where seats are arranged in rows and clusters, students who sit close to each other tend to affiliate more and being close to someone geographically also increases psychological closeness because opportunity for interaction and likeness increases. According to Tubbs & Moss (2000), when we are in close proximity to someone- living next door or working side by side over a period of time, we tend to minimize or even overlook that person's less desirable traits.

Different Types and Functions of Small Groups

A small group can be organized for a number of reasons and purposes; hence, groups defined are defined according to their set goals. There are four basic functions served by groups:

1. To create connections among people to counter isolation

2. To foster learning

3. To improve worker productivity, and

4. To facilitate democratic action in contemporary society.

Some of these functions may overlap such that a small group may be formed to serve two or more of these functions. According to Engleberg and Wynn (2007) each type of group can be recognized by observing its setting and its membership.

Primary Groups meet individual primary needs of belonging, affection and social approval. Membership consists of immediate family members and long term friends whose primary goal it is to provide each individual with support, sense of belonging and immediate identity. This becomes the foundational relationship upon which other relationships are built; hence, other group types are secondary in nature as they meet other human needs such as solving problems and making decisions and accomplishing tasks.

Social Groups as its name suggests provide opportunity for people to socialize and to provide the platform for members to share and enjoy each other's company. They provide an outlet for members to meet their need for emotional release and ego massaging. Such group members confirm one another and create an enabling climate in which to socially thrive.

Self -Help Groups come together to help solve specific problems that members may be facing. An example of this is Alcoholics Anonymous, whose focus is helping each other break the cycle of dependency on alcohol. This suggests that when people who share a common experience, in this case, a negative one, come together in self-help groups, it shows they need each other to lean on and to understand how they feel, and to jointly proffer a solution to that common experience and common situation they find themselves in.

Service Groups provide services that will bridge the gap between self- help and government help. "Service groups are dedicated to worthy causes that help other people both within and outside the group." Joining with others to perform civic duties is an example of service groups. Other examples include neighborhood associations, labor unions, Volunteer Fire Fighters, Parent-Teacher Associations and professional clubs.

Learning Groups exist to fuse members' efforts directed at understanding a particular subject, topic, or issue. This is common among students and company managers and staff. When a company changes its computer operating platform into another, there is need to form learning groups to learn and understand the new system. The goal is to jointly learn and gain working knowledge and mastery of the new system upon which their company operations and their jobs depend.

Work Groups are classes of people who jointly perform some duties or individuals in a particular line of work in a corporation or organization. Work group members are charged with particular functions that they perform on a permanent or periodic time frame. In the human organization, there are three general classes of work groups: management, supervisors and employees. Though their duties may differ, their performances are directed at achieving the overall objectives of the organization.

Public groups function in the public sphere and usually exist to serve a larger, more public purpose. The members come together in public and their deliberations are subject to public consumption and criticism. Such groups may be organized to gather information from the public, to deliberate on issues of public concern and, to make decisions on behalf of the larger public. Examples of public groups are panel discussions, forums, and symposia.

Group Leadership

Some groups appoint their leaders and some have leaders imposed on them. Sometimes there are self-appointed leaders who feel they have what it takes to lead a group. In some groups, leadership is informal- authority is granted to whoever emerges as the leader in the course of group role negotiation. However, it is believed to be impossible for a group to think of someone as a leader if that person does not have a positive influence on the members. It follows then that a group member must perform some tasks in the group to be considered the leader.

But what are leadership tasks and how does one acquire the skills to perform these tasks? A leader is a person who can influence others to be more effective in working to achieve mutual goals and maintain effective working relationships among members; whereas, leadership skills are the sum total of your ability to help the group achieve its goals and maintain an effective working relationship among members (Johnson & Johnson, 2000). Ability to help the group involves communicating and orienting group members to their functions and roles. The centrality of communication to the group function is emphasized when Hackman and Johnson (2003) define leadership as a process of using communication to influence the behaviors and attitudes of others to meet group goals. Clearly we can see that leadership over a group is by communication and persuasion and not by coercion.

Tubbs & Moss (2010) view leadership not as a quality, but as a series of functions that groups must have performed. The leader becomes the person who successfully performs a number of these functions. The effective performance of the series of functions that meet the goals and expectations of group members empowers the **emergent leader** to gain power or control over other members of the group. What is **power**? From the foregoing we can see that **power is the ability of one person to exert interpersonal influence over another or a group of individuals. This type of power exists in situations that require cooperative and not coercive effort to operate successfully.** There are different sources of power as there are different forms of power. These are enumerated and explained in the subsequent paragraphs.

Sources and Types of Power

Wilmot and Hocker (2005) state that group leaders may gain interpersonal influence that forms the basis for small group leadership by exercising three types of power: **distributive power, integrative power and designated power**. Distributive power occurs when a leader exerts influence over others; integrative power occurs when the leader depends on others to achieve agreed- upon collective goals, this is interdependent power; and designated power, as its name suggests, is holding power for others, especially in interpersonal relationships such that occur in a marriage or family.

To understand the general concept of power and how it may relate to the small group, let us look at how French and Raven (1981) classify the sources of power. The scholars identify five sources of power which dictate the type of influence the holders of such power would have on the other members of the group.

1. **Reward power:** **This is power derived from the ability of the power holder to give what the followers want and need.**

2. **Punishment power:** **Power derived from the ability of the holder of power to withhold from the followers what they want and need.**

3. **Referent power:** **Power based on other's admiration and respect for the power holder.**

4. **Expert power:** **This is power that is gained when others value someone else's specialized knowledge or expertise.**

5. **Legitimate power:** **This is power derived from status, position, or role.**

As is evident, there are different types of groups, and they are put together for various reasons. All of the members are capable of wielding any or a combination of these different types of power even if they are not appointed to wield legitimate power. Legitimate power is not enough to lead a group; the leader needs expert, referent and other types of power. So, all of the members influence one another, such that different types or integrations of some of these powers would be at play in the group process.

Leadership

Leadership can be defined from different perspectives; it may be looked at from situational, trait, functional, and styles perspectives. Communication scholars, however, take a communication approach to defining leadership and from this approach leadership is seen as "a process of using communication to influence the behaviors and attitudes of others to meet group goals" (Hackman and Johnson, 2003). Two types of communication competencies make up the approach and these are *task* and *relational*. Task competencies are described as communication skills necessary to perform tasks and to manage group goals; while relational competencies refer to communication skills necessary for managing interpersonal relationships and group climate (Barker, Wahlers, & Watson, 2001).

The two major leadership activities are identified as **Task and Consideration functions**. Task functions are described as activities that help the group achieve its goals (asking for suggestions, opinions, and information). Consideration functions are activities that improve the emotional climate or increase the satisfaction of individual members, for example, showing agreement, support or encouragement, and gatekeeping). Leaders are molded by the situations that exist in the group and the different situations require different sets of behaviors. To lead, therefore, is to exert some desired influence over other group members in order to achieve a common goal.

The different leadership styles employed by leaders would influence the performance of the different roles identified by Benne and Sheats. There are three generally identified leadership styles which are **autocratic, democratic, and laissez-faire**. Autocratic leaders are domineering as they dictate what goes on in the group, from the agenda to the decisions made. These types of leaders give orders and set policies that they expect other group members to accede to. Democratic leaders on the other hand encourage consultation, discussions, and consensus building in the small group. These leaders thrive on cooperation and majority rule, but laissez-faire leaders take a non-judgmental, hands-off approach to group leadership. In this case, the leader hardly contributes to group decision making and encourage a loose, free willing culture of "anything goes."

     The communication competency model of leadership developed by Barge and Hirokawa (1989) posits that leaders help their members achieve group goals through the application of competent communication skills. And as with competent communicators, a leader must have an array of communicative behaviors, have the ability to apply the right communicative behavior to the right situations, and have the skills to implement chose competencies. In other words, a leader must be flexible and knowledgeable enough to adapt to varying situations that a group may experience. Pearson et al (2011) summarize the communication competencies that leaders should possess and are presented here.

The Communication Competencies of Leaders

- **Effective leaders are able to clearly and appropriately communicate ideas to the group without dominating conversations.**
- **Effective leaders communicate a clear grasp of the task facing the group.**
- **Effective leaders are skilled at facilitating discussion.**
- **Effective leaders encourage open dialogue and do not force their own ideas on the group.**
- **Effective leaders place group needs over personal concerns.**
- **Effective leaders display respect for others during interaction.**
- **Effective leaders share in the success and failures of the group.**

On the other hand, there are communicative expectations of the group members for the effective running of the group. As group members, there are effective ways you can better participate in the group process that will enhance your performance and the overall outcome of the group process. These are the expected competencies of the individual group members. Pearson et al (2011) describe these as better ways to organize your comments during small-group discussions and are presented here.

Communication Networks in Groups

Frequently used communication networks in groups are the Wheel, Y, Circle, Chain, and All-channel networks. Please note that in the descriptions and explanations that follow, it is assumed that there are five members in the small group.

In the **Wheel network**, one person, usually the leader is the focus of comments from each and every other member of the group. As the central person in the network, he or she is free to communicate with other members of the group, but other members can only communicate with the leader and only the leader. In the **Chain network**, one person is the anchor and communicates with two members on his or her either sides. There is no communication link between the other two group members except through the central person. In the **Y network**, three of the five members can communicate with only one person. The **Circle network and All-channel networks** are decentralized and sometimes leaderless. In the Circle network, each person communicates with members on his or her either sides, while in the All-channel network, all communication lines are open and each member is able to communicate with all the other members.

The level of centralization of power and communication influences the performance of group members. The most centralized of the patterns produces the best organized and fastest performance, but the least centralized is disorganized and unstable and would be slowest in solving problems. In terms of creativity, cooperation, and complexity of issues to be resolved, it is found that the decentralized networks are more desirable. The All-Channel network, according to Tubbs & Moss (2000), seems desirable for a number of reasons. Although initially it tends to be more inefficient and time-consuming, it maximizes the opportunities for corrective feedback, which ultimately should result in greater accuracy.

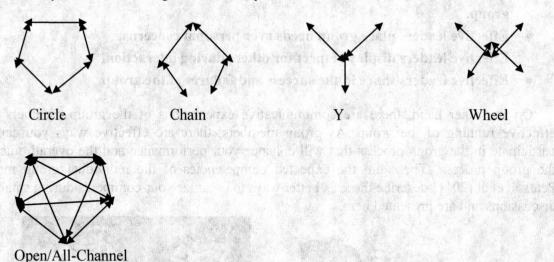

Circle   Chain   Y   Wheel

Open/All-Channel

Relevant Group Process Concepts and Member Behaviors

Goal: This is the purpose or end result for which individuals in the group collectively are set to accomplish.

Role: Expected behaviors of members of the group who occupy different positions

Task: An act or activity that group members engage in to accomplish the group
goals.

Role skills: Inherent characteristics of the group members that enable them to perform
their roles effectively.

Attempts have been made to classify the behaviors of group members which help to describe the **roles** they play within the group. The three interacting roles or behaviors engaged in by group members in the course of meeting their set objectives are **Task behaviors, Building and maintenance behaviors,** and **Self-centered behaviors.** These roles have been identified and classified by Benne and Sheats (1948) and described as follows:

- Task behaviors are behaviors directed toward accomplishing group objectives through the facilitation of problem solving.
- Group building and maintenance roles are those that help the interpersonal (relational) functioning of the group.
- Self-centered or individual behaviors are designed to satisfy individual selfish needs and do not advance the cause of the group.

The different behaviors under each of the broad categories are listed here.

Group Task Roles

Initiating-contributing
Information seeking
Opinion seeking
Information giving
Opinion giving
Elaborating
Coordinating
Orienting
Evaluating
Energizing
Assisting on procedure
Recording

Group-Building and maintenance Roles

Encouraging
Harmonizing
Compromising
Gatekeeping and Expediting
Setting standards for ideals
Observing
Following

Self-Centered Individual Roles

Aggressing
Blocking
Recognition seeking
Self- confessing
Dominating
Acting the playboy—social loafing
Help seeking
Special interest pleading

When performing these different roles in the group, members may experience different role conflicts such as ambiguity, conflict and role overload (McGrath, 1984).

Group Development Process

There are certain given features that groups possess and among these are that they have structures and change over time. Groups go through changes in their development from inception to dissolution, and these changes can be in the issues discussed, in the nature of membership, and in the changes that occur in the structure of the group itself. A group's growth and development is identified to be the result of both the needs of the individuals and the forces created within the group itself.

Do all groups go through the same stages in their development? Some theorists believe that the various phases occur even if the group meets only once (Tuckman, 1965; Fisher, 1970). However, Bennis & Shepard (1965) believe that the phases occur over the life history of a group that meets repeatedly, but Bales and Strodbeck (1951) and Schultz (1958) contend that all the group phases occur in each meeting and continue to reoccur throughout the group's life history.

The two theoretical perspectives of group development are **recurring-phase and sequential-stage theories**. Recurring-phase theories specify the issues that dominate group interaction that recur again and again, and sequential –stage theories specify the "typical" order of the phases of group development (Johnson and Johnson, 2000).

The most widely quoted and popular example of a sequential-stage theory of group development is that of Bruce W. Tuckman (1965; Tuckman & Jensen, 1977). Having reviewed several studies on group development, Tuckman identified a striking similarity among their findings especially that the ideas are apparently the same though described and identified differently. Tuckman identified five stages in the life cycle of a group and they are **forming, storming, norming, performing, and adjourning**. The important thing to note is that at each of these stages, groups focus on specific issues and this focus influences members' behaviors (Johnson & Johnson, 2000).

Table 17.1/Tuckman's Phases of Group Development

Forming	This stage begins prior to the first meeting of the group when members begin the process of identifying with the group to learn about other members, break the ice, and begin to establish a common base for group identification. This stage may be referred to as the "orientation," "inclusion," or "group formation" stage. This is the uncertainty stage when members are trying to figure out group goals, procedures and rules.
Storming	This stage represents a period when members start to exert themselves past the orientation stage and starts to resist the influence of the group and rebel against accomplishing group tasks. Now the members are distinguishing themselves from others, thus creating disagreement or conflict. This focuses the attention of the group on conflict resolution.
Norming	There is balance in the group at this stage because the group establishes consensus as to how to execute tasks and follow rules of procedure or norms. Cooperation and cohesion increase because members balance individuality and "groupness," group and individual goals, and understand the role of the leader.
Performing	This is the phase of maximum consensus and productivity. Members become adept at working together and become more flexible in their cooperative behaviors. Behaviors associated with the latter stage of this phase of group development include increased lateness, absenteeism, daydreaming, and general withdrawal.
Adjourning	This is the adjourning stage of the group. Activities end and the group submits its findings, resolutions, conclusions, and then the group ends.

Effective Group Problem Solving

Three main communication behaviors are helpful in effective problem solving: introducing relevant issues or ideas, amplifying or expanding on ideas, and documenting assertions. It is helpful if the group members maintain a goal orientation rather than getting sidetracked and, they should pursue issues systematically rather than haphazardly (Gouran et al., 1978). This underscores the relevance of clear objectives, organization, and established rules of performance to the successful execution of group projects.

Established structures allow the group to focus on relevant issues, pursue them systematically, and clearly document group processes and assertions. Regardless of the type of small group assignment, procedures for performance must be established that include leadership selection, individual and group responsibilities, schedule for task completion, and the criteria for accepting the outcomes of the whole enterprise.

Tubbs and Moss (2000), enumerate the likely recurring complaints by small group members as: 1. group objectives are not clearly stated, 2. group members do not come up with enough ideas, 3. the group does not carry through discussion of each issue until it is resolved, 4. members rarely help one another, 5. conflict between members become so intense that it is counterproductive, and 6. conclusions are not reached or agreed upon. These problems can be summarized under one or more of the following categories of problems that exist in group processes.

- ✓ **Groupthink:** This is a condition that occurs in the group as described by Janis (1972;1982) when members revere a group leader to the extent that the charisma of the leader does prevent group members from critically assessing the ideas suggested by the appointed leader or a charismatic member of the group. This may manifest in another form as Cline (1994) suggests that groupthink occurs in some groups when pressure to both reach the group goal and conform to group opinion are so great that individual members surrender their own beliefs, avoid conflict, and view the issues from the group's perspective. Believing that they have a unanimous decision, group members often stop their deliberations.

- ✓ **Illusion of anonymity/Invulnerability:** This occurs when group members think they can do as they please and become too optimistic they that they suggest somewhat risky, out-of –this-world solutions to problems because of the perception that there is no individual responsibility, so the group is to blame if anything should go wrong (Risky-shift phenomenon).

- ✓ **Social Loafing:** This situation occurs when some members of the group would rather depend on other members to do the work than for them to focus on the task at hand. These members engage in anti-social behaviors in the group by doing very little and spend time in a lazy, wasteful manner.

- ✓ **Domination:** This is the tendency for some members of the group to want to control the activities of the group and dominate the discussions and the decision making process. This creates tension in the group, especially with others who would also like to exert themselves and kick against the autocratic ways of the other members.

✓ **Lack of Individual Recognition:** This is the idea of being buried in the group without individual identity, especially when it comes to giving credit to the entire group equally, though the members did not contribute equally to the group process. This is the fear of some group members who take charge of the group work while others engage in social loafing. The expectation is that each should earn the credit each deserves, but often times this is not the case and it discourages people from wanting to work in groups.

✓ **Self-censorship:** This occurs when group members refrain from expressing opinions that may be contrary to popular opinion in the group. Such members may psychologically rationalize their "different opinion "as not necessary or of little importance to the group discussion.

✓ **Collective rationalization:** In defense of group collective position, the members may see themselves as "righteous," thus justifying their own position and negating the ideas and criticism that may run counter to group ideas and ideals.

✓ **Shared stereotypes:** Group members take "we and they" posture, thus stereotyping those of opposing groups. Because these stereotypes are usually negative, they inversely portray the in-group as inherently "good."

To resolve some of these challenges or to reduce their occurrence and impact on group success, a number of techniques must be used. For example, an **agenda** may be developed to guide group processes, a **brainstorming** session may prove useful, and, especially in the business setting, a **Nominal Group Technique** may be used.

The **standard agenda or reflective thinking procedure** for generating discussion in a problem-solving small group is credited to John Dewey, an American philosopher. This method offers a six-stage, step-by-step procedure for solving problems. Because of its wide acceptance and use, the reflective thinking method has become a standard for solving problems. The process of the standard agenda or reflective thinking is as follows:

1. **Define the problem:** As we have noted earlier in the book about the use of definitions, it is useful to know exactly what you are dealing with before you begin to deal with it. Definitions allow for clarification and the separation of core and peripheral issues relating to a problem. Without proper definition of the problem, the solution will be a misfit. Lucas (2009), states that the best way to define a problem is to state it as a question of policy. Also, as we have discussed earlier, persuasive speeches of policy are speeches that explore and question the importance, relevance, and practicality of courses of action to be taken to solve a problem. Again the quality and comprehensive nature of the questions asked will help in adequately addressing the problem at hand.

2. **Analyze the causes:** In analyzing the problem, what you're doing is diagnosing the problem- determining its scope in terms of people affected, geographic area covered, expense involved, and what the major causes are. Every possible cause should be found before categorizing them. Adequate research must be conducted to find valid causes and not spurious

ones. This means that the real causes must be identified rather than what may appear to be the causes. It is possible to confuse one with the other if critical analysis is not done.

3. Identify criteria: Before actually coming up with the solutions to the well-defined and analyzed problem, there must be a set standard that the proposed solutions must meet. For instance the criteria for the solutions may be that it must be a panacea for the extensive geographic region affected; the solution must be the most cost-effective; it must be the least labor intensive; it must be environment-friendly; it must be long-lasting and; it must take effect at a given date. The set criteria, if well taught out and comprehensive, would help the small group participants to spend enough time deliberating on the problem and its solutions, rather than to rush to judgment to produce ineffectual solutions.

4. Generate solutions: This is when the idea of **brainstorming** becomes most useful. Here the participants are asked to suggest at random any solution that comes to their minds without any restriction of immediate analysis and rationalization. This, the group members do by writing their ideas down on paper and then, all of the suggestions will be compiled into a master list that will guide the selection of the final solution to the problem being examined. Brainstorming allows the group members to participate equally in the process of solving a problem, making gatekeeping a necessity, just as it prevents a few member domination of the group.

5. Select a solution: Obviously not every solution generated will carry equal weight and that is why, at this time, each of the suggestions will be analyzed using the established criteria in the third stage of the reflective thinking process. After giving equal chance to all of the solutions, group members should strive at **consensus** to identify the most relevant, adequate, or best solutions to the problem. Because consensus asks for 100% agreement among the members, it further enhances their willingness to explore and analyze each solution more thoroughly, explaining and evaluating, before all the members are in agreement.

6. Implement solution: Implementation of the recommendations of a problem-solving group may be beyond the powers of the group, but it must make sure that the recommendations are implementable. This should have been taken care of in the criteria setting stage where one of the set expectations should be that the solution must be realistic.

Following a standard agenda gives structure to group performance and focuses members' attention to group goals. At the same time, it encourages complete examination of the possible solutions to a problem before finally selecting the best solutions.

The **Nominal Group Technique** (Delbecq et al., 1975) is used to generate ideas from brainstorming to discussion and evaluation of such ideas; it helps to identify problem areas, create solutions to such problems, and will lead to determining plans to be implemented to solve the problems. The use of these techniques will reduce if not totally eliminate some of the problems encountered by members working in the group.

The NGT process has six phases designed to eliminate some of the group problems already identified. These phases of the group problem solving process starts with the silent, independent generation of ideas that are written down on paper, followed by listing the ideas on a large newsprint for everyone to see, and then followed by the discussion and clarification of all the ideas without offering any critique. In the next step, the points are rated individually and then clarified. Finally, the ideas are ranked. By going through the process, everyone is involved in the group discussion and decision-making.

Barker, Wahlers & Watson (2001), confirm that when used effectively, this technique saves time, encourages everyone to participate, and increases the potential for agreement and consensus. See how the nominal group process is similar to the idea of John Dewey.

The Nominal Group Technique Process

1. Idea formation (This is when random thoughts and ideas are solicited from group members about the problem under discussion).
2. Idea documentation (Each suggested idea is written down for further consideration).
3. Idea ranking (Members examine each of the suggested ideas and put them into a rank Order, from the most important to the least important, using some agreed upon criteria).
4. Idea discussion and evaluation (Each idea is then discussed and judged for its relevance and fit to solving the identified problem).

Ways to Organize Your Comments during Small-Group Discussion

When you are participating in the small group, your job is to make sure you are relevant to the group as a whole. You must be willing to participate fully to arrive at the best solution possible for the charge that the group has. The following guidelines will help you to communicate more effectively in the small group setting (Pearson, et al., 2011) These are in addition to your being aware of your nonverbal gestures, including vocal characteristics when you're speaking (communicating) in the small group setting.

- **Relate your statements to preceding remarks**—briefly note the previous speaker's point that you want to address, state your point clearly and concisely, summarize how your point adds to the comments made by others.

- **Use conventional word arrangements**—after connecting your idea to the discussion or previous speaker, state your point and then provide one piece of supporting information or additional explanation. When done, ask if anyone needs you to clarify your point.

- **Speak concisely**—write down your ideas before speaking. Those who are wordy during group discussions often spend much of their time trying to figure what they want to say. Try not to talk for too long.

- **State one point at a time**—if you have ideas that vary in importance, provide some of the less important points to group members in written form for latter reflection. Have discussion time for the most important ideas.

Presenting Group Recommendations and Solutions

Although groups work in private, their recommendations are often presented to the public and these may take one of the many forms of public group presentations. These presentation forms are **panel, forum, symposium, debate**, and other forms of oral presentations. These are public speaking events and, as such, the speakers should prepare their contributions as if they were giving formal public speeches. That is, the presentations should follow the structure of a speech with an introduction, a couple of major points with supporting materials, and a conclusion. Attempt should be made to adapt the presentation to the nature of the audience; also, attention should be paid to the visual and auditory aspects of the delivery. It is always advantageous for the participants to prepare answers to all of the possible questions they anticipate from the audience and other participants. This will not only enhance their credibility, it will also focus the attention of all of the participants with minimal off- the-wall responses that may lead to protracted arguments and a waste of time.

Panel

This type of presentation occurs when experts publicly examine and discuss a topic among themselves for the purpose of sharing and learning new information. The presentation usually starts with brief opening statements from each of the panelists, followed by informal discussions among the participants who speak from their experiences. The goal of the panel is to react to the ideas of each of the participants and that of the audience. As a result, a semi-structured schedule is followed whereby a moderator, who usually directs the group though a problem-solving sequence, calls on each of the members to give a brief opening speech, followed by informal reactions from other participants and the audience. Often, speakers can be interrupted by other speakers and, in the end, there may be a summary of the discussions and a resolution to the problem discussed.

Forum

Forums are usually organized as information sessions that involve question and answer sessions. An expert or group of experts is questioned by a panel of people who may be journalists or other experts. The purpose is to encourage public discussion of issues and problems and to gather information with which to make decisions about issues and problems discussed. A leader may be appointed to lead the discussions and control the flow of the forum, making sure that as many speakers as possible voice their opinions and that everyone has the opportunity to ask questions as well as get adequate responses from the interaction.

Symposium

This mode of group presentation involves participants, usually three to five in number, who give short informative speeches on the same topic or related topics. The speeches are fully prepared, structured and formally presented manuscripts before an audience. The moderator, who controls the flow and structure of the symposium, introduces each of the speakers and, sometimes, summarizes each speech. After each of the presentations (usually 10-15 minutes), the speaker allows for the audience and participants to participate in a question and answer session. It should be noted that some of the views of the participants may be slanted or outright contradicting because of their different perspectives. This is a welcome idea because the idea of a symposium is to bring to the fore all of the different perspectives and ways of looking at similar events, issues and ideas.

Debate

A debate is an organized exchange of views through argumentation. Participants usually take opposing views of issues or ideas, or propositions and advocate their position publicly through persuasive arguments to convince the audience. Presidential debates follow this format when candidates state and contrast their ideas against that of their opponents in order to convince the electorate that their own position is, arguably, the more valid or reasonable. Usually there is a moderator who acts as the gatekeeper to allow for smooth flow of the debate and controls the time allotted to each speaker either for the main presentation or a rebuttal. In the example of the presidential debate in the United States of America, members of the audience are usually polled to find out their opinion as to who won the debate. Or as the debate progresses, the intensity of the applause after each candidate's remarks is measured to determine who has the loudest ovation. So, debates are verbal and nonverbal contests among participants and success in the exercise is measured in terms of the participants' oratorical appeal to logic and emotions of the audience.

Developing Communication Competencies through an Innovative Group Assignment.

Students of communication learn communication theories and principles in the classroom and undertake assignments that help to translate their knowledge into skills applicable to real life performance. In addition to learning the theoretical underpinnings of group processes, students learn how to organize, participate in, and monitor behaviors of group members.

Not all college students like working with others in the small group because of the perceptions they have of other members of the class who may be lazy, dominating, or just plainly non-cooperative in the class. The idea of working with these other students would raise such concerns, hence, the willingness to work alone. According to Blomberg (1998), students often resist group projects because they fear the following:

1. **My effort will carry a loafer and earn the grade for that person.**
2. **One person will take over and it will be her or his project.**
3. **Members of the group will be irresponsible and this will adversely affect my grade.**
4. **Too much out-of-class meeting will be required.**
5. **Everyone in the group earns the same grade.**
6. **The professor will be unaware of each member's individual effort.**

The group process assignment reported here is an innovative classroom experiential learning assignment designed to capture all of the different dimensions of group formation, execution, performance, and evaluation. Most importantly, the assignment is structured to eliminate all of the student concerns identified by Blomberg and many others garnered from several years of teaching group communication.

Assignment Goals

By participating in this assignment, the student will:

1. Learn to cooperate with others in a group setting.
2. Understand the nature of small-group communication and performance.
3. Learn to observe others' interpersonal behaviors and communication styles.
4. Listen effectively and purposefully.
5. Learn to coordinate listening, speaking, and writing skills.
6. Asses the performance of others using communication principles and theories as guide.
7. Learn about leadership and teamwork.
8. Discover strategies to eliminate challenges of working with others in the group setting.
9. Learn about relationship building and networking.
10. Learn about interpersonal persuasion.
11. Develop critical thinking skills.
12. Develop multi-tasking skills and
13. Learn about democratic citizenship.

These competencies are what employers of labor require of their potential employees and which will help the students in other areas of their professional and relational lives. When asked to rank, in their order of importance, the desirable competencies they hope their potential employees would have, employers ranked listening as the number one skill and written communication as number two. Ranked three is leadership, while informal oral communication is ranked number four and analytical thinking is ranked number five (Tubbs & Moss, 2000).

A ten-year study conducted by researchers at Carnegie Mellon University identified the most important skill that differentiated average job performers from outstanding job performers. Some of the most important skills relevant for job performance include interpersonal communication, relationship building, leadership, teamwork, networking, and persuasion (Kelley, 1998).

While it is not expected that a single classroom group assignment will lead to the critical development of all of the skills identified here, the project is a start in the series of process education methodologies that will empower students to become self-learners and growers.

Description of Assignment

The student is advised to join a group of **FIVE** members for the assignment. The choice of partners to work with is left to the student in order to demonstrate reasons why people join with some others to form a group (**Proximity, interpersonal attraction, complementary needs, similarity,** etc.). Once a group is formed, the assignment begins by the student documenting in his or her journal (This the student maintains throughout the project) how the group was formed using the necessary constructs to describe the process.

As observation, listening, and speaking are central to effective performance in the group setting, the student is advised to observe every detail of the behaviors (Verbal/nonverbal) of group members for documentation in the journal using appropriate terminologies as identified in literature. Then a leader is selected for the group followed by problem selection and discussion to provide **FIVE** solutions to the problem. To facilitate more discussion and to understand how members would defend their ideas or acquiesce to those of others, the group should rank the solutions in their order of importance.

As you can see the essence of this assignment is observation and listening. In the process of providing solutions to the group's identified problem, each member is monitoring, for documentation, the occurrence of task, maintenance, and selfish roles in the group. After the group completes its task, each member will present his or her individual journal to the class. The leader, in addition to the journal, will present the group's five solutions as well. This is an example of a panel presentation.

Group Responsibility

To facilitate group discussion, each group will choose a topic/problem of practical relevance to which it must proffer five solutions, better described as position statements. The group members will brainstorm, deliberate, and analyze the problem until the five solutions are determined. The discussion meetings will go on for two class periods to allow each member of the group to contribute meaningfully to group discussion, and to expose his or her tendencies when involved in group activities. The group members will see each other perform in the group and their observations are to be documented using the descriptors of group task, maintenance, and individual behaviors identified in literature. Consequently, the more important aspect of this assignment is the individual responsibility.

Individual Responsibility

Working within the group, every member will, in addition to participating in group discussions, keenly observe and keep a detailed journal of activities of the group, from group formation to leader selection, leader behaviors and member discussions to group termination. The journal must reflect group processes terminologies akin to all of these activities. This means that in addition to class lectures on group processes and activity descriptors, each student is compelled to read up on these concepts to not only understand them, but to also recognize them when they are being played out in the group.

The Journal

The individual member journal has two parts. The first is the documentation of how the member joined the unique group, that is, an explanation of how and why he or she joined with each member of the group using the already identified descriptors. Part one also contains leadership selection process and reasons for the choice; the choice of problem for discussion and why. In this part, the observant members will also document the group development process as it moves from forming to storming, norming, performing, and adjourning.

Part two of the journal contains record of the behaviors of group members as they each contribute to group discussions. This is a record of the task, maintenance, and individual behaviors of members during the entire discussion exercise.

Group Solution and Individual Journal Presentation

The group of five members will present its findings to the class in the form of a **panel**.
The leader introduces each member of the group and presents the group's charge and the five solutions it had developed to solve the problem. Members of the audience will ask questions about the solutions and each of the members will have an opportunity to defend the group's solutions.

After the solutions had been presented and discussed, it's time for each member to present his or her individual journal to the class. Here the audience is listening for details of recorded observations about the group process from five different perspectives, but a common denominator will be the use of relevant group process descriptors. The audience is quick to point to contradictions in observations, just as it is duly informed of those engaged in task or maintenance orientation among the members, and those who engaged in individual, antisocial behaviors.

After the presentation, the audience, including the professor will lead the discussion on group challenges of groupthink, illusion of anonymity, social loafing, domination, member truancy or tardiness, etc.

Student Assessment

By incorporating both group and individual performance requirements within the group activity, the traditional concern of group work, where one or a few of the active participants actually do most of the work is eliminated. Since everyone has to present a journal to the class, the members will seriously attend to group activities and pay great attention to the behaviors of other members in the group. In addition, this will greatly minimize such group problems as social loafing, lack of focus, domination and, perhaps, groupthink.

To have a good showing, each member would try to do his or her best by taking cogent notes and participating actively in the discussions. Periodically, though, the facilitator or professor visits with each group to assess its performance and direct it accordingly.

The total weight for this assignment is 15% of the total course grade. The group grade is divided into three parts. Five points are allotted to collective group performance, another five points for individual journal, and the final five points are allotted to individual journal presentation and performance in the panel presentation. This means that every member of the group is responsible for about 66% of his or her grade, but is dependent on the other members for only about 33% of the grade.

Small Group Project Appraisal

This group assignment has been used with great success in the small group component of the Introduction to Human Communication and Interpersonal Communication courses that I teach at Suffolk Community. Students have claimed that the assignment allows them to work in a group setting where they can freely express their constructive opinions and, at the same time, listen critically to the opinions of others. They particularly liked the fact that as they documented the behaviors of others in the group, others were equally observing and documenting their own behaviors as well. The students particularly expressed their approval of the strategy whereby each of the members of the group was responsible for his or her performance in the group, as well as having a collective duty to the group.

In the summer of 2000, when this small group assignment was evaluated, students were asked to freely comment on their group experience, especially on what they learned and how the group changed their perception of cooperative learning. Most of their comments were in favor of the group work and they are summarized as follows:

- The group assignment allowed us to interact on a personal level with some other members of the class. Prior to the group work, students maintained their territories and rarely exchanged words, except if they had assignments to complete together, such as interviews and papers. One of them commented that "I would have completed this course without really knowing anybody, but for this group assignment."
- The group assignment was a refreshing break from the lecture mode of teaching; putting the students in charge of their learning was advantageous.
- The students commented that they were less apprehensive of the public speaking element of this assignment because of the rapport they had built with the other group members who were referred to as "new friends."
- Some students particularly liked the idea of searching and reading up on the terminologies and descriptors with which to categorize and explain the behaviors of other group members.
- The real life experience of group dynamics (leadership selection, decision-making, orienting, gatekeeping, performance, etc.) showed the students the relevance of theory to practice, especially in the field of communication.
- The students expressed that they were better attuned to their personalities through the group experience. Some identified themselves as leaders, while others said they would never opt to be a leader.
- At first, many of the students had the idea (as already identified) that a few of them would have to do all the work while others would take the credit for their work. Or that the instructor would award the same grade to everyone in the group, regardless of the level of participation in the group task. But they were pleased that there was opportunity for individuals to excel according to their level of performance.
- The challenge to some of the students was the need to attend to complex, dynamic group processes all at the same time, but after they had actually participated in all of the activities, they appreciated the end result.
- Some of the groups found it difficult to organize themselves to perform their tasks effectively within given time and had to consult with the facilitator on different occasions. They appreciated the availability and willingness of the facilitator to attend to their questions and concerns.

Asked to identify the possible skills gained by participating in the collaborative learning group assignment, the participants identified twelve (12) competencies that are listed here: leadership, teamwork, responsibility, creativity, organization, listening, observation, problem-solving, diplomacy, writing, critical thinking, and public speaking.

GROUP ASSIGNMENT AS A COLLABORATIVE LEARNING METHODOLOGY
GROUP ASSIGNMENT PROCEDURES
(The moment you joined a group, your observation and journal entries begin).

1a. Freely identify with other four class members to form a group of FIVE.
 b. In your individual journal, please describe how this happened and why you joined with each and every member of this unique group. (Proximity, similarity, complementary needs, interpersonal attraction, etc.)

2a. Select a leader for your group.
 b. In your individual journal, describe the procedure for selecting the leader and describe why this particular person was selected as leader. Do you agree with the group choice? (Leadership and other qualities.)

3a. The group should select a problem to which it will suggest FIVE solutions.
 (See bottom of the page for problem choices.)
 b. Describe how and why your group selected this problem.

4a. On a sheet of paper (separate from your individual journals), the group should arrange the solutions in their order of importance and supply a paragraph to justify each of them.
 b. Describe the solutions evaluation process in your individual journal.
 c. Each person in the group will present his or her journal to the class.
 d. The group leader will present the solutions to the class, in addition to his or her individual journal.

NOTES

1. In writing your journal, please freely use the concepts relating to Group Task Orientation, Group Maintenance Orientation, and Individual Selfish Behaviors as contained in your textbook.

2. Your grade depends on: a. Quality of your observation as it is reflected in your journal; b. Quality of your writing in terms of language and accurate use of relevant concepts; and c. Quality of your journal presentation to the class.

3. Your journal should be typed (Double space/ 12 font size) and at least two, but not more than three pages long.

SAMPLE TOPICS:

1. TEENAGE PREGNANCY 2. POVERTY 3. ROAD RAGE
4. VIOLENCE IN SCHOOLS 5. TERRORISM 6. CHILD ABUSE 7. RACISM 8. DRUG ABUSE 9. SPOUSE ABUSE
10. VIOLENCE IN SPORTS

Sample Handout for In-class Small Group Assignment

An in-class small group assignment can be designed to incorporate some of the lessons learned about public speaking and problem solving. In the example below, **Professor Chris Holfester**, asks his students (COM 101 &COM 105) to work in groups to present a persuasive campaign about a significant problem in their college or in the community. This assignment can be replicated in different classroom settings, to offer students the opportunity to use their knowledge of the problem-solution structure of persuasive speeches to solve a communal or societal problem. See how the format follows the structure of speech presentation that was discussed in Chapters Ten and Eleven.

Small Group Persuasive Campaign Guidelines:

Goal: To identify a significant problem at the College or in the community and to offer a campaign to provide solutions to that problem.

I-Introduction
  A-Attention Getter
  B-Reveal Topic/Issue/Problem and why it is important
  C-Preview what each person will cover in the speech

II-Body-

  A-Explore the problem
    1.Break the problem up into sub-problems
    2.Discuss the history of the problem
    3.Discuss the effects of the problem
    4.Discuss the case studies of the problem

  B-Offer Solutions
    1-Solution #1 to the problem
      a-Explain the solution in detail
      b-Explain how the solution can be implemented
      c-Explain why the solution will work

    2-Solution #2 to the problem
      a-Explain the solution in detail
      b-Explain how the solution can be implemented
      c-Explain why the solution will work

    3-Solution #3 to the problem
      a-Explain the solution in detail
      b-Explain how the solution can be implemented
      c-Explain why the solution will work

III-Conclusion
  A-Review your main arguments
  B-End with a final appeal

Other Notes: 1-Each person must speak for 2-3 minutes; each person must cite 1-2 sources; the group must use power point demonstration and; you must hand in a completed paper that includes all of the presentations in order.

Guidelines for Classroom Small Group Projects

1. Explain the assignment and the framework for completing the group project, with clear instructions on group goals, tasks, individual responsibilities, expected outcomes, criteria for assessing outcomes, time frame for the project, etc. Provide a handout that explains all of these items and allow time in the beginning to entertain student questions to clarify issues and to ensure understanding of instructions/expectations.

2. Identify the learning objectives and performance criteria for the group project. For example, students will learn the process of group formation, leader selection, and group procedures by taking part in this project. Performance deals with the students' involvement in a group where they will experience the three processes identified.

3. Allow students to freely identify with a group of their choice (except if there is need to pre-select or group members according to certain variables and criteria). Freedom to identify with a group of choice helps in explaining why people join with certain other people to form a group (proximity, similarity, complementary needs, interpersonal attraction, etc.). Again, this helps alleviate some of the fears of joining groups and possibly hasten the group orientation process.

4. Allow time for leader(s) to emerge in the group and for natural stages of the group development to unravel.

5. Give the group and its leader(s) enough power to direct and make decisions about procedures for completing the project. This encourages creativity, insights, and uniqueness.

6. Develop with students a "Knowledge Map," that identifies relevant concepts with which they will describe group activities and processes.

7. Structure group activities such that every member at every meeting is required to observe, speak, evaluate, and document group processes and progress.

8. Design separate, but measurable individual assignments within the group project. This individual responsibility should connect with the overall objectives of the group. Individual assignments reduce social loafing and the tendency for one charismatic member to take over the group.

9. Individual members should keep a journal of procedures and individual responsibilities and report it in a panel presentation to the class. Knowing that they have to report their journals to the class, encourages members to work hard and participate effectively in their groups.

10. Plan periodic assessment of group members' performance within scheduled time frame. The purpose of this assessment is to identify student strengths, need for improvement, and insights for such improvements.

11. Anticipate group member absences and lateness.

12. Allow enough time for in-class group meetings and,

13. Finally, evaluate individual and group performance.

14. Evaluate the group holistically, giving each member a score for group participation, but assign greater weight to individual journal documentation and presentation and the ability to answer questions that follow.
15. Allow for the participants to answer questions from the rest of the class.

Review Questions

1. **Define small group and discuss the major reasons why people join them.**
2. **Describe the advantages and disadvantages of the different group communication Network patterns.**
3. **Critically examine Tuchman's stages of group development.**
4. **Identify and discuss the major problems of working in groups.**
5. **Discuss John Dewey's process for generating ideas and discussion in a problem-solving, small group.**
6. **Identify, describe, and explain group presentations forms of panel, forum, symposium, and debate.**

Chapter Eighteen
Mass Communication

In the introductory chapter of this book, we identified the different levels or types of communication to include intrapersonal, interpersonal, small group, public, organizational, and mass communication. We have explored different definitions of communication and have determined that it is a process of sharing meaning between two or more people for the purpose of creating understanding. The need to inform and create understanding at the mass level has led to the development of mass communication and the invention of mass media as vehicles for conveying designed messages to large, widely dispersed, and diverse audiences. Mass communication allows for the packaging of information about diverse groups of people for consumption by yet other diverse groups of people, thus reciprocally bridging the gap of ignorance and awareness across masses of people from diverse geographical and cultural regions of the world. Indeed, mass communication has become the vehicle for informing, educating, entertaining, mobilizing and creating communities of consciousness across a world that is fast becoming what Marshall McLuhan described as the "global village."

Mass communication is everywhere and its influence is pervasive in our world today. More people are being connected each day, thus expanding the frontiers of mass influence through mass media. The power and influence of mass media over society has necessitated that greater attention be paid to the nature of these means of mass communication, their different characteristics, influences, practices of their owners, the professions that they have engendered, and their uses and often misuse, to further the agendas of different classes of people in society.

The source of mass communicated messages is not a single person or a group of people as in the other forms of communication. Rather, the sources of mass communication messages are large organization or corporations, who have developed the business of news gathering, dissemination, and the production of entertainment for mass consumption. The face you see on television casting the news, or the field news reporter that you often encounter, are not the real sources of the messages you are exposed to via the mass media. These are professionals working with myriads of other professionals, many of whom are in the background, to produce information as a commodity that has been financed by corporations or joint ventures of many small communication business entities.

Defining Mass Communication

Communication between individuals, either from person-to-person, person-to-many persons, or from organizations to large audiences, always includes a number of elements. These are:

(1) the sender who encodes a message,
(2) the receiver who decodes the message,
(3) the message which is the content of the communication or the meaning that is being shared,
(4) the channel or means of conveying the message to its intended recipient, and
(5) effects, which is the result, impact, or consequence of the received message.

In mass communication, the senders are people who form themselves into a business, which engages in information and entertainment dissemination to targeted groups of people, otherwise referred to as the **mass audience**. The important difference about this form of communication is that it cannot reach the mass audience without the use of what we refer to as **media technologies** such as books, the internet, television, newspapers, magazines, radio, and the like. These devices are collectively called the **mass media of communication**. This means that without mass media technologies, mass communication will not be possible. The messages are packaged for delivery to mass audiences by **media outlets** which are businesses built around the technologies of mass communication that we have identified above.

Mass communication, therefore, may be defined as the sending of packaged information from a central position or series of locations, through the use of mass media technologies, for the consumption of different groups of people, who are widely scattered, oftentimes diverse, and somewhat anonymous to one another and the sender.

Turow (2003) captures this understanding when he defines mass communication as the **"industrialized production and multiple distribution of messages through technological devices."** He further clarifies that mass media outlets are different from mass communication media in that the outlets are media enterprises that send out messages via the media, while the mass media are the technological devices through which mass communication takes place. Radio, television, newspapers, etc. are technological devices used by media outlets such as NBC, ABC, FOX 5, etc. to disseminate their messages or contents. But how does this differ from the traditional definition of mass communication?

With increased **segmentation and fragmentation** of the audiences of mass communication, the use of the word "mass" in the definition of the practice is called into question. This is because there are myriads of media outlets reaching out to smaller audiences rather than the mass audiences of the past and, the increased knowledge that the outlets have of their audiences negates the hitherto anonymity of these audiences. Rather than use the idea of mass media, the increasing narrow targeting of audiences today, necessitates removing the "mass" concept from the idea of mass media. Also, because mass communication is **mediated** through media technologies, there is an attempt to use the term mediated communication in its stead. But Turow (2003) contends that **"what fundamentally separates mass communication from other forms of communication is not the size of the audience (it can be large or small) or the use of technology (mediated communication can be mass or interpersonal)."** He submits that **"what distinguishes mass communication is the industrialized – or mass production –process that is involved in creating the message material."** This argument makes sense when one considers the fact that **"it is the industrial process that creates the potential for reaching millions or even billions of diverse, anonymous people at about the same time."**

Mass communication occurs when the industrial process creates a message designed to be consumed by an audience that, Wright (1986), **describes as relatively large, heterogeneous, and anonymous to the source.** The mass communication experience is not face-to-face between the sender and receiver; therefore, it is a mediated experience with the mass media as intermediary. **We can identify some of the characteristics of mass communication, therefore, to include the anonymity of the communicators (senders and receivers), less sensory input and awareness of the receivers in the content production process, less control over the sources of the messages by the receivers, and little or no knowledge of the senders of the messages.**

The mass media technologies include books, magazines, radio, television, the internet, WebTV and other telemedia, billboards, film, video recording machines, etc. There are other technologies that can be adapted for mass and social communication purposes and these are the telephone, iPods, Blackberries, iPad, etc. All the technologies that have been developed are described as extensions of the capabilities of humans. Technologies evolve to extend the capacities of the human senses to the extent that communication technologies have enhanced our ability to communicate more rapidly and efficiently with one another. Through technology, we have been empowered to communicate at a scale and speed unprecedented and, to a large number of people more than we had ever imagined.

Through mass media, it has become possible to reach small or mass of people for various reasons, from informing and creating awareness and education, to persuasion and entertainment. By packaging information for all these stated reasons and others, media conglomerates package culturally embedded messages that communicate a sense of identity, social expectations, worldview, and perceptions of events and peoples. In other words, mass media messages are not culturally neutral and, as such, influence and orient us in predetermined ways. The pervasiveness of these messages depends on the characteristics of the media conduits used in disseminating them. Not only do the media and their messages influence in consequential ways, they do so sometimes deliberately to achieve desired goals of political, economic and social control. Technological development is not new, although we refer to this modern era as that of exploding telecommunication and computer technologies. There are segments of time in the history of humans on the planet earth that we can correlate with certain technological developments. As the inventions of the means of communication progress, so do the capacities of these technological devices to capture our imagination in their abilities to extend the human senses. Let us now examine the evolution of communication technologies in our world.

The Evolution of the Media of Mass Communication

The Spoken Word or Tribal Era

The spoken word is considered the first communication innovation in human history because it endows us with the ability to speak and symbolize meanings that we would share with others. Without the spoken words, the primitive man was sentenced to a life of grunting, sighing, mating, killing, and brute existence. With spoken words, humans became truly social by exchanging meanings and ideas via a symbolic system that allows for direct and vicarious experiences to be narrated, evaluated, and used to inform future actions or choices. Larson (2010) writes that "the spoken words permitted humans to become social animals and to work together for the common good. It allowed one generation to pass down the history and knowledge of the tribes in myths, ballads, or legends, and thus progress could occur."

The spoken word era is also referred to as the tribal epoch. This was an age of face-to-face interaction which allowed for giving and receiving direct feedback in the process of sharing oral information. The dominant sense extended during this epoch was that of hearing. Marshall McLuhan (1962), who coined these terms, identified the tribal epoch as the starting point in the four epochs in human media history. According to the media ecologist, oral cultures were knotted together by stories and rituals that passed along the history and traditions of a culture, as well as by oral transmission of information and entertainment…Reliance on the spoken word for information and recreation fostered cohesive communities and made hearing a dominant sense, McLuhan (1969).

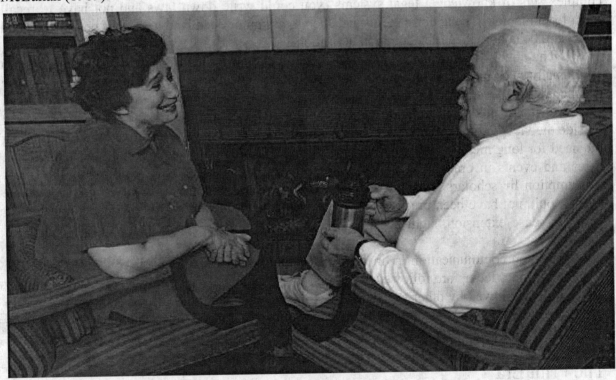

Figure .1/ Media Epochs in Human History

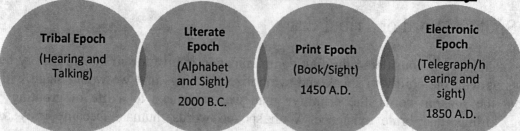

This figure is an adaptation from the writings of Marshall McLuhan (1964) *Understanding Media: The extensions of man.* New York: Signet Books. And the depiction by Julia T. Woods (2011) *Communication mosaics: An introduction to the field of communication.* (6th ed.) Boston: Wadsworth.

The Written Word or Literate Era

The era of the spoken word gave way to the era of the phonetic alphabets which allowed direct use of speech sound symbols to represent meanings that people shared. This was advancement over the pictorial alphabets of ancient Egyptian and Chinese languages. People became literate because they could read and write, though this was a privilege enjoyed by the rich and powerful in society. Larson (2011) comments that with the advent of phonetic alphabets, people could collect knowledge and store it for long periods of time – far longer and more reliable than history in the old spoken words. Adding, he states that the written word allowed societies to develop complex sets of knowledge, legal systems (you could write down laws and not have to recall them from memory), behavior patterns and such to assign or deed land and other possessions and to declare behaviors illegal by common definition.

The ability of humans to document communication through the written word has led to various advances in many other spheres of the human endeavor. The advantages of the literate era include the possibility of accurate and precise recall of documented information, individual access to mass, public information, which they could read in the privacy of their homes and outside the view of others. Such written documents could be read over and over, thus eliminating the need for long memorization and the possibility of forgetting lines, especially very important dates and events in oral history. Also, it was possible to mass produce information for mass consumption by scholars and priests alike. The holy books of the different religions we have today would not have been preserved were it not for the innovation of the phonetic alphabet. In terms of sense extension, sight became the dominant sense as opposed to hearing in the oral tradition.

Written communication is linear in nature and as McLuhan had discovered in phonetic alphabet writing, letters are followed by letters, words precede and follow words, and sentences are naturally followed by other sentences. This linear sequencing of writing had an influence on the thinking of the people. McLuhan observed that this sequencing cultivated linear thinking and gave rise to linear logic and mathematics.

The Print Era

The printed word came with the invention of the movable type and the printing press by Johannes Guttenberg in the late 1400s. The consequent development was increased literacy of the mass of people in this era due to mass production of books at reduced costs. Just as social media nowadays have made it possible to bypass traditional means of mass communication, thus resulting in the creation of social movements that have shaken down hitherto established organizations and governments, the printing press made possible an event described as the industrial revolution of the 1800s. In affirming this, McLuhan (1962), attests that the industrial revolution was prompted by the medium of mass production (of information), the printing press which according to Woods (2010) cultivated homogeneity of perspectives and values because the same message could be delivered to many people. The fact that books could be read individually, also led to the isolation of individuals in society. This meant that widely dispersed and diverse people were exposed to common contents of books, thus creating a society of consciousness even among atomized, fragmented classes of people. This has had tremendous impact on the information, education, and persuasion of large numbers of people. Perhaps, the advent of the mass printing medium of communication can be identified as the precursor to the economic rule of large numbers and the growth of capitalism.

The Electronic Era

The electronic era challenged the dominance of the print medium of mass communication by introducing an era of multisensory mass communication. Not only were people exposed to the print medium that extended the sense of sight, they were also exposed to the new medium that extended their sense of hearing. A combination of the senses of sight and sound and touch, revolutionized mass communication such that communities of people were able to hear, read, see, and touch images far beyond their geographic location, thus leading to the development of and reconnection of increasingly isolated people. The electronic media had, therefore, rekindled the oral tradition and had made hearing and touch the senses people depended on (McLuhan, 1969).

The electronic word which came into being after the advent of the telegraph in 1844, eventually led to the introduction of radio in 1922 and the telephone came in 1876 with the transducing of words into electronic impulses that could travel long distances via wire lines. Television made its epochal appearance in 1926. It must be noted that these different electronic media took time to develop and the dates that are identified to mark their entry into the world are significant times in their development and not when they were actually invented.

Later additions to the electronic assemblage are satellite and cable transmissions, which have increased the speed, coverage, and the possibility of capturing images and sounds for telecommunication. The electronic media made possible the mass connection of people and communities to streams of electronic images, sounds and events that would have otherwise escaped them. The speed of access and the contents of the media as well as the interconnectivity have transformed society into what Marshall McLuhan termed a **global village** (McLuhan & Fiore, 1967). Just as tribal communities are connected and close-knit, the electronic media have created a worldwide community connected by fast-paced information sharing and a wired globe sphere that transcends space and time.

The electronic era has been transformed by the invention of the computer which allows people to engage in all of the previous media all at once through electronic and digital processing of both the print and video images. The revolution that this brings is the availability of such multimedia information to individuals in their cocooned environments where they are connected virtually as isolates, but not interpersonally.

The Interactive Word Era

With the advent of personal computers and the development of nanotechnologies, it has been possible to present the microchip in tiniest of technologies that can be hand held and personalized for individual use to share combined digitized print and video contents with multiple people simultaneously. The interactive nature of the new media has led to the reawakening of the sense of community and resurgence of the oral culture. As articulated by Larson (2011), with the newly emerging interactive media, we are becoming more and more both producers and consumers of messages. This is unlike in the electronic era, which made individuals mass consumers of contents produced by others, thus making the mass audience dependent consumers.

Virtual reality technology is a new dimension to the new interactive media era. Images are now 'pixelized' and digitized so that once real events are captured, they can be replicated in the virtual domain to simulate "real" human interaction. Remote sensing and operations are now possible such that surgical operations, wars, flights can be operated virtually without actually involving real people.

On the following pages, communication scholars Akinfeleye, Ibraheem, and Daramola discuss the social and political impact of the Internet and social media in contemporary society.

The Internet, Social Media and the New Geography of Power

By:

Ralph Akinfeleye, Ismail Ibraheem, & Yomi Daramola
Department of Mass Communication
University of Lagos, Lagos, Nigeria

New information and communication technologies, especially the internet are now a major driving force of societal transformations between and across different countries. Significant progress has been recorded in the development of information and communication technologies in the last decade. The internet is probably the most important of all. The internet exhibits some unique features, in that it can be used in diverse ways. It allows individuals to voice their opinions and concerns, and it provides excellent platforms for the exchange of opinions.

With regards to the Internet, Kofman and Youngs (2003) suggest that technology and social change are two of the central dimensions of diverse processes of globalization. The role of the Internet in the penetration of geographical boundaries of states was particularly stressed:

> ...as societies and individuals and entities within the state operate via the Internet, whether through e-banking or business, e-mail and chatroom activity, or political activism, the more they are caught in it, identified by and through the networks they are involved in and the information they contain about them. This situation where boundaries can easily collapse and this goes much further than just the idea that the internet crosses geographical and political divides and separations between public

(institutional) and private (personal) social spaces and places (Kofman and Youngs, 2003:9).

This development brings about a technologically-induced interdependence and interconnections across different levels of the society with direct and indirect influence on the "fabric of society itself and challenging established patterns of conceptualizing, analyzing and understanding it" (Kofman and Youngs, 2003: 9) The ability of the Internet to bypass the state to get to society makes the case for the Internet's influence (cyberspace) in overriding geographical space an important one.

The influence of the Internet is generally attributed to the powerful influences traditional mass media are thought to exert in societies and their use for identity formation. McQuail (2000) stresses that the media are considered to have immense power of influence; hence, they are used as vehicles for development and modernization. Most governments also use the mass media for promotion of national identities or the "Self" against the "Other" (Lerner, 1958). However, with increasing global interconnectedness, new media such as the Internet are penetrating geographical boundaries of states, thereby challenging the state's exclusive control of its territory.

In this regard, Hirst and Thompson (1999) suggest that new communication and information technologies have reduced the state's exclusiveness of control of its territory, reducing its capacities for cultural control and promotion of national identities. In this way, the new media exert more powerful influence on states than traditional mass media such as radio, television and the print media.

The increasing influence of the Internet and other factors which Appadurai (2001) describes as objects of flow has created situations of "disjuncture" or tensions which are challenging conceptions of concepts such as state, territoriality, deterritorialisation and sovereignty in contemporary times. This development has a significant impact on the authority and sovereignty of states to successfully control developments within their geographically defined boundaries, hence the concern among some states in particular to control the use of the Internet through legislation.

While discussing the ways the Internet is shaping the working of contemporary societies, Lull (2001) also stresses that

> …The Internet has evolved to become less a technological form and more a communication medium, which opens up limitless cultural possibilities. Rather than just reinforcing traditional structures of political-economic-cultural authority, information technology, the Internet, and mass media make those structures all the more porous (2001:3).

The potential for societal transformation due to Internet penetration is huge in Africa. Africa is considered one of the fastest developing continents in terms of telecommunications and internet connectivity. Over the last couple of years, the continent witnessed incredible growth, especially since the laying of undersea fiber optic cables. At the end of 2011, Africa had 139 million internet users (Fripp, 2012). In 2000 it was a mere 4.5 million. That's 2988.4% growth! Out of these 139 million,

37.7 million have Facebook accounts. With 11.4% internet penetration, well behind the 30.2% world average, Nigeria has the most users at 44 million. Egypt has 20.1 million and Morocco 13.2 million. South Africa is the fourth most connected with 6.8 million internet users. Zimbabwe had a modest 1.4 million. Although South Africa ranked fourth, it is second when it comes to Facebook with 4.8 million users, while Nigeria has 4.3 million users (Fripp, 2012).

The Internet revolution has many adjuncts. There are currently 610 million mobile phone subscribers with 24 million new connections in 2011. The estimated number at the end of 2012 is about 735 million subscribers. South Africans are leading the tweeting revolution with 5 million tweets over the last quarter of 2011. Second is Kenya with 2.4 million tweets and Nigeria, third, with 1.6 million tweets in the first quarter of the same year. Data indicate 57% of tweets in Africa are sent from mobile devices and, that young adults ages 20 -29 sent out 60% of the tweets in Africa. Twitter in Africa is widely used for social conversation, especially for communicating with friends (81%) and 22% use it to search for employment opportunities (Fripp, 2012).

In the United States, Leggatt (2012), citing statistics from Digitas, indicates that 82% of US adults use social media, and 88% of those are registered voters. Furthermore, almost two-thirds (61%) expect candidates to have presence on social media sites such as Twitter and Facebook. Such is the power and reach of social media that Digitas expects that, just as John F. Kennedy (JFK) was considered the first television president, 2012's winner could sway their victory via social media (Leggart, 2012). "In at least the last two election cycles, digital media has taken a profound a role in determining our next president as TV did in earlier generations," said Jordan Bitterman, SVP and Social Marketing Practice Director,

Digitas. "But the results of this new research show that the extraordinary power of social networks to connect us and build relationships may have even greater impact on who wins in 2012. Of significance is the findings cited by (Leggart, 2012) that majority (86%) of social media users own a mobile device as do 88%of social media users who are registered voters and, that 38% report that social media will have the same influence on their vote as would traditional media such as television and radio.

With increasing availability and use of the Internet and other telephonic devices across the world, the burgeoning cyberspace becomes potentate over geographical boundary power of traditional societies. The new world "information and technological order" is no longer about directional flow of information, but the consequences of individual empowerment through the use of ubiquitous digital technology, which has unprecedented social organizing capabilities and important political consequences in a borderless cyberspace.

The Growing Powers of Social Media and the Blurring of Traditional Boundaries

The internet has enabled cyber social organizing through what are now popularly referred to as social media. The growth of social media has forced a rethinking of the boundaries of the power of the media and that of political power. The embrace of the social media by an increasing number of people in society is challenging established notions of power and blurring traditional boundaries of relationship between different power centers. A number of anecdotal evidence highlights the role of social media as game changers in electoral contests.

The first known case of the role of social media in swinging electoral contest is that of Barack Obama in the 2008 Presidential election in the US. Obama's case is often cited of the way social media could be used to swing an election. Obama's widely successful campaign in the US used Facebook and Twitter, as well as apps on iPhones to get people to vote. Writing just after Obama's election, Mathew Fraser and Soumitra Dutta (authors of "*Throwing Sheep in the Boardroom: How Online Social Networking Will Change Your Life*) note that: The statistics are telling. Obama had more than 2 million American supporters on Facebook while McCain had just over 600,000. On…Twitter, Obama could count on more than 112,000 supporters 'tweeting' to get him elected. McCain, for his part, had only 4,600 followers on Twitter (Arthur, 2010).

Social media also played a prominent, if tenuous, role in the 2010 parliamentary election in the United Kingdom. A study carried out by Echo research, cited in Arthur (2010), stressed that the Internet played a significant role in the 2010 parliamentary and found that almost half of the population has gone online for information about the parties and candidates. "Online shows the greatest increase as a source of information about the elections, ahead of all other sources, particularly for men," says Sandra Macleod, its group chief executive (Arthur, 2010).

Paul Mason, BBC Newsnight economic editor, put forward his thoughts on Twitter's effect on the parliamentary election. He suggests that Twitter gives potentially perfect realtime feedback to any political event (through realtime searching); it can amplify the impact of an event; it can spread suppressed information and humorous rejections of the official line; it is resistant to propagandists; it helps journalists engage in "collaborative competition." His conclusion: it "has the potential to partially or completely neutralise the ability of the corporate media to transmit the dominant ideology (Arthur, 2010).

In Nigeria, social media were also considered to have played significant roles in the 2011 national elections. Mvunganyi (2011) notes that a vibrant and tech savvy youth population influenced the electoral process in Nigeria. Harwood (2011) puts the perceived success of the elections to the increasing use of social media in Nigeria. The elections marked the first time that new forms of connectivity—social media, mobile phones, and digital cameras—have given Nigerians opportunities to act as citizen observers, documenting and reporting on the electoral process. Led by civil society organizations like 'Enough is Enough' (EIE) and 'ReclaimNaija,' citizen observers reported a huge body of electoral observations via smart phone applications (SMS) and digital cameras, previously unavailable, and distributed widely on Facebook, YouTube, and Twitter (Hardwood, 2011; Campbell, 2011).

The impact has been threefold—contributing documentation to Nigeria's electoral record, empowering Nigeria's connected youth to participate in the democratic process, and building capacity around technologies that are increasingly becoming indispensable tools for securing democracy globally. Beyond outreach and voter education, Nigeria's civil society groups created the necessary technological platforms to channel these new streams of information. ReclaimNaija.net set up an election incident reporting system built on the Ushahidi platform that allows Nigerians to text in incidents, which are then plotted on an interactive map. Between the April 9 national assembly elections and the April 16 presidential elections (as well as the aborted April 2 election), citizen observers

submitted 6000 incident reports (Harwood, 2011).

"Enough is Enough" built a mobile phone application, Revoda, which interfaces with a similar electoral mapping platform. Revoda standardizes reports, makes it easier to code and quantify data, and improves accountability by requiring users to register the application. EIE reports that users have downloaded Revoda 7000 times and submitted over 500 reports. Informed by its citizen observers' findings, "Enough is Enough" released its own statement on the election, commending both voters and Independent National Electoral Committee (INEC) but warning that improvements need to be made to address the myriad of irregularities (Campbell, Harwood, 2011).

Conclusion

The first political campaign in history to correctly exploit the power of social media to spread a candidate's message, gain support and get the public engaged was the 2008 campaign for the American presidency by the then Senator Barack Obama. The Obama campaign reached 5 million supporters on fifteen different social networks over the course of the campaign season. By November 2008, Obama had approximately (some sources say as many as 3.2 million) Facebook supporters, 115,000 Twitter followers, and 50 million viewers of his YouTube channel.

Learning from the successful use of the social media platform by Obama and the desire to connect with the technologically savvy Nigerian youth, President Goodluck Jonathan embraced it before he commenced campaigns for his party's ticket (Igbindu, 2011).

Twenty days after President Goodluck Jonathan joined Facebook in 2010, he was able to attract over 100,000 fans. Before the elections in April 2011, he had more than 500,000 fans on the social networking site. His current Facebook fan base number places him second only to that of United States' President Barack Obama among other world presidents on Facebook (Igbindu, 2011). Due to the intense use of social media in the 2011 elections Campbell (2011) suggests that Nigeria now holds the continent's record for most tracked reports of social media use during an election, with nearly half a million examples cataloged by the proprietary software at the Social Media Tracking Centre in Nigeria. On the day of the presidential election alone, the Centre collected over 130,000 tweets and public Facebook posts. Campbell (2011) concludes that though Nigeria is sub-Saharan Africa's most populous country, for technologies so new, this is an accomplishment, and it underscores Nigeria's leadership in the use of social media on the continent.

The impact of social networking on political power is universal. The nature of the technology and its different applications have revolutionized elections and opened new horizons in campaigning for political office, conducting elections, and monitoring their results. No longer is the power to conduct and declare election results vested only in the controlling power of the government, but now, it has been dispersed to all and sundry willing to exploit the dimensionalities of the new social media.

Bibliography

Appadurai, A. (2000). *Globalization*. London: Duke University Press.

Arthur, C. (2010). The First British General Election in the Social Media Age: What Difference has it Made? *The Guardian*, Monday 3, May, 2010, London: Guardian News and Media Limited.

Asuni, J. B. & Farris, J. (2011). *Tracking social media: The social media tracking centre and the 2011* Nigerian election. Abuja: Shehu Musa Yar'Adua Foundation.

Campbell, J. (2011). *Technology, social media and Nigeria's election*s. Council on Foreign Relations. www.cfr.org

Fripp, C. (2012). In http://www.itnewsafrica.com/2012/02/africa%2%80%99s-internet-usage-by-numbers-1093356_50971166. Accessed on February 4th, 2012.

Harwood, A. (2011). *Nigeria's first Facebook election*. In www.movements.org/blog.

Hirst, P. & Thompson, G. (1999). Globalisation in Question. In *The international economy and possibilities of governance* (2nd ed.). Cambridge: Cambridge Polity Press.

Igbindu, C. (2011). *Social media and the 2011 elections*. http://businessdayonline.com/NG/index.php/media-business/20773-social-media-and-the-2011-elections. Accessed February 4th, 2012.

Kofman, E. & Youngs, G. (20030. Globalization: Theory and practice (2nd ed.).London: Continuum.

Leggatt, H. (2011). Social Media to Play Pivotal Role in 2012 Presidential Elections. *In Bizreport: Social Marketing*, November 01, 2011. www.bizreport.com. Accessed February 4th, 2012.

Lerner, D. (19580. *The passing of traditional society*. New York: Free Press.

Lull, J. (2001). *Culture in the communication age*. London: Rutledge.

McQuail, D. (2000). *Mass communication theory: An introduction* (4th ed.). New York: Sage.

Mvunganji, J. (2011). Social Media to Play Big Role in Nigeria's Election. *In Voice of America News* @ www.voanews.com. Accessed February 4th, 2012.

The Mass Communication Process

In examining the process of mass communication, we find the same elements that are involved in the process of communication. The differences that might occur result from the number of people involved in the process, whether the communicators are individuals, groups, or organizations, and whether they are communicating face-to-face, or that the communication is mediated by some technologies that allow for the mass distribution and reception of messages in the process.

The elements in the process of mass communication can be identified as the source, message, channel, receiver, feedback, noise and effects.

The Mass Communication Source

The source of mass communicated messages is usually not an individual working alone, but an organization of professionals each specializing in an aspect of the production process that results in the content that the receivers are exposed to on television, newspapers, magazines, and the like. Usually referred to as media organizations, these complex orchestra of people create verbal or nonverbal images that are encoded for transmission or distribution through different mass media for their audiences to consume. The organizations include news wires, advertising agencies, publicity agencies, corporate entities, individual families, government information agencies, and many more.

In the case of a newspaper organization, the product is the collective message packaged in a particular print medium such a magazine or evening tabloid, or a widely circulated newspaper. Note that the contents are the news stories, features, headlines, pictures and captions, cartoons, advertisements, obituaries, sports reports, editorials, and letters to the editor. The mass medium is the newsprint or the physical newspaper itself and the outlets are the newsstands, distributor locations, and bookstores and the like where these papers can be bought. As many newspapers, if not all, have websites nowadays, the source or medium also includes the websites, where the newspaper versions are accessible to the readers.

The mass communication source is usually an organization, a part of a conglomerate.

The Mass Communication Message

As in the example of a news organization we have used, the contents or message designed for audience consumption by the source are the news stories, features, headlines, pictures and captions, cartoons, advertisements, obituaries, sports reports, editorials, news releases, letters to the editor and the like. As you might have guessed, many of these contents of the newspapers are not directly sourced by the newspaper organizations, but by different groups or businesses interested in reaching the diverse audiences of the newspapers. The advertisement sources are usually producers who use the newspaper as a mass medium for reaching their potential customers. The news releases are often sourced by public relations agencies and company publicity people who use the platform of the mass medium to deliver their messages to the intended mass audiences. As we can now appreciate, it is not enough to own or establish a medium of mass communication, what is more important is the content that must be delivered through the media to the targeted audiences. The message or content of mass communication is referred to as the **software** of this type of communication while the media are considered the **hardware**.

The messages or contents of a newspaper can be delivered in print via the printing press onto newsprints, or as electronic impulses from computers to earth-bound transmitters, to satellites in geo-synchronous orbit, to other interconnected computers throughout the world and, finally delivered to individual desktops and laptop computers for reading and viewership. In some cases, many contents of the print and electronic media are produced in satellite locations but assembled electronically at a central production center for final packaging and mass dissemination.

The business of producing the contents of mass communication is a complex one. Many professionals are involved and these will include writers—fiction, feature, news, editorial, and script writers, reporters and copy editors; computer operators, stage managers, engineers, Video/TV /Movie camera technicians, directors, producers, actors, stage designers, analog and digital movie editors; creative designers, public relations and advertising experts, newscasters, presenters, and many more. Many businesses are interconnected in the process of producing and disseminating mass communication messages to their intended audiences, and this is why these businesses are collectively referred to as the **mass communication industry**—a group of organizations whose businesses are interconnected to the extent that what happens in one sector, affects all of the interconnected others.

The Mass Communication Channels

The channels of mass communication are the means (technologies) through which messages are sent to the mass audience. As we have identified earlier, the technologies of mass communication otherwise referred to as the **mass media include books, magazines, radio, television, the internet, WebTV and other telemedia, billboards, film/movies, video recording machines, special events, etc.** The technologies for disseminating mass messages are identified as mass media and the corporations that own them such as The Vanguard News Corporation, Channels Television, Silverbird Productions, and Newswatch Communications are all **media outlets**. While WebTV is a medium, The CNN Corporation is a media outlet that uses among other media, the Web for disseminating international news.

The characteristics of the different media of mass communication will be examined later in this chapter.

Pixstar

Anchor people on a TV set

Pixstar

Satellite Dish on a building, facing the South horizon

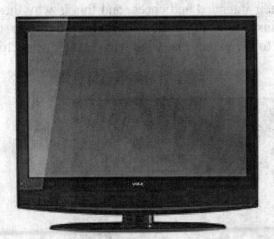

Typical HD TV

Radio Announcer at Work

Marshall McLuhan:
"The medium is the message."

The proponent of media ecology studies, Marshall McLuhan, is best known for his ideas about the impact of the medium of communication on the audience. Not discounting the effects of the content, McLuhan placed greater emphasis on the influence of the technology of communication on the total habits of the generation that produced it. Think of how television or the internet have changed the entire behavior and thinking of the people of this generation. The real or substantive message, therefore, is the impact the technology has on both the message and how it is received. Further, McLuhan claimed that "the medium is the massage," that is, the nature of the medium used in communicating messages, massages our perceptions and alters our consciousness. Again, McLuhan concluded that the dominant means of communication of an age had become the real message or mass communication. This is the idea that "the medium is the mass age."

Mass Communication Audience

Everyone in modern society is an audience of some sort of mass communicated messages. The ubiquitous nature of mass media makes their message reach unavoidable, even to the most unsuspecting of people. Those who are not literate can partake in radio messages that transcend the barriers of language illiteracy. Because television captures the senses of sight, sound, and touch, it, too, transcends many traditional communication barriers. While internet use has become second nature to most people of the industrialized nations, the culture is also catching on in the developing world.

The mass media are effective in drawing the attention of large numbers of people to the same events to the extent that the common sharing of such realities has produced in the audience the **currencies for social interaction** among people who have participated in the community of consciousness produced by the media.

As we have defined the word 'mass,' the audiences of mass media are described as large and diverse and widely scattered. We must equally add that they are not monolithic. As a matter of fact, the variation in the compositions of these different aggregates of people has led to what scholars have called the de-massification of the mass audience. Because of special interest programming on television, and specialized magazines that cater to the different categories of audiences,

Media behavior Statistics
- ✓ *39 million Americans saw Barack Obama's Jan. 20, 2009 inauguration on television. (Nielson, 2009).*
- ✓ *America's top choice of national news is T.V. (70%), Internet (40%), and Newspapers (35%) (Pew Research Center, 2008).*
- ✓ *Among 18-29 year-olds, internet is more popular as a news source than among older people. However for these younger people, T.V. and newspapers are reportedly equal as their primary source of news (59%) Pew Research Center, 2008).*

more and more audiences are being fragmented and segmented for narrow focus rather than mass focus.

Audiences can be segmented according to their **demographics**, that is, according to their age, income, race, gender, location, interests, and other sociological variables that they may possess in relation to others. It has become more fashionable and cost-effective to segment the audiences for narrow casting because of the direct targeting that is possible, matching specific contents with the desired audience for maximum effect. On the other hand, audiences may be categorized according to their shared values, opinions, beliefs, and other **psychological** variables that identify an individual's uniqueness among the group. Aggregating these psychological variables allows media practitioners to target audiences of like minds, interests, values, and worldview to specific audiences for mass and efficient effect.

At the individual level, we must recognize that each audience member is not necessarily willing to accept and view in like manner the messages received from the mass media. Every message directed at a receiver is usually filtered according to the three basic principles of perception (See chapter 2). These processes are selective exposure, attention, and retention. The sum of this is that we are more likely to expose ourselves to media contents that will agree with or confirm our attitudes, value and opinions. This will take place against the backdrop of discriminating against those stimuli or media contents that do not conform to and confirm our mindsets and expectations. These processes take place in all our communication encounters, be it interpersonal or mass. The filtering process takes place when we are listening to music, news, watching television programs, movies or reading a newspaper.

The audience of mass communication is not passive but active in the process of consuming mass mediated messages. Thus, they may seek opinions from various sources and leaders, just as the opinion leaders themselves seek the opinions of those they consider higher sources of credible information.

Delayed Feedback in Mass Communication

Feedback is an element of communication that occurs in all the forms of communication that we have identified. We have defined feedback as **the return to you of the behavior that you had generated or a reaction that your message generates in the receiver**. We may distinguish between immediate and delayed feedback depending on how quickly such can be received by the sender. In face-to-face interpersonal communication encounters, one can easily hear or see a reaction to one's message. Therefore, the feedback in that situation is instantaneous and can be deciphered right away and considered in the deconstruction of a new message possibly designed to address the feedback which may also be positive or negative.

In mass communication, the senders are often not directly known to the receivers and, the audience members are not directly known, either, to the sender(s). Though the media practitioners or senders may have access to sociographical and psychographical information about their audiences, they do not necessarily know them personally. Again, the nature of the media of mass communication, which are technologies for wide dissemination of messages, does not allow for direct and immediate contact between the senders and receivers. This reality makes the feedback in the mass communication context a delayed phenomenon. That is, the reaction to mass communication messages is not immediate and direct or instantaneous. If you want to react to a new story in your local newspaper about an event that you are involved in, your option, apart from going directly to the newspaper facility, is to write a letter or send an e-mail as a rejoinder to the published article. This may take weeks to materialize. Sometimes, the editors may even disregard the letter or e-mail depending on what merit is accorded the issue at hand. Or you're watching a television show and you are offended by some of the contents and you want to show your discontent, but this you cannot achieve immediately because of the nature of the practice of mass communication. Therefore, we can conclude that mass communication messages receive delayed feedback.

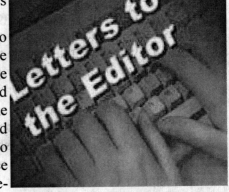

New interactive technologies that are now adapted to disseminate information to masses of people are challenging the traditional views of mass communication, especially the phenomenon of delayed feedback. Nowadays, the immediacy and ease with which messages are disseminated is matched with the immediacy and ease with which responses can be sent and received. Viewers can phone in to live television programs to register a complaint or commendation; some shows have audience responses built into them and; comment boxes are attached to e-newspapers such that readers can register their immediate feedback. Electronic media responses are easier and faster because of the nature of electronic transmissions, but more traditional mass media may still fall within the frame of delayed feedback.

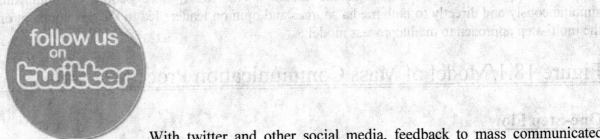

With twitter and other social media, feedback to mass communicated messages can be instantaneous.

Mass Media Processes

Scholars have conceptualized and represented the relationship between the sender and the receivers of mass communication messages by model depictions. The approaches of how the media work include what have been described as the one-step, two-step, and multi-step flow of information models. These different approaches have changed over the years because of the different research findings that have informed the thinking of scholars in the field.

In the one-step flow of information model, the source/sender or media outlets send messages directly to the audience/receivers who use the messages for one or a combination of the reasons of information, education, and entertainment. The obvious missing element in this configuration is the feedback that the audience gives to the source. In the mass communication process, the feedback is traditionally thought of to be delayed. This is because the audience may not directly know the source(s), and the nature of the media technologies for delivering messages to the mass media is such that it does not allow for immediate feedback. Once in a while newspaper readers may write letters to the editor in reaction to some news or items read in the medium, but the media practitioners may choose not to publish the rejoinder or the publication may take weeks if not months depending on the frequency of the publication. But during the period of delayed feedback, the audience members do not usually brood over the issue or information received from the media, they usually discuss it with others, especially those that they consider competent to answer their queries. This was the idea that led to the concept of opinion leadership in the flow of messages between senders and receivers in mass communication.

The two-step flow model recognizes the idea of an **opinion leader** who acts as bridge between the source and the receivers. This was borne out of the research by Lazarfield et al (1944) that found that people were more likely to pay attention to and discuss issues with people whom they think are knowledgeable and are respected than the media sources. This finding was based on the study of the 1940 presidential election in the US. Lazarfield and his co-researchers studied the reactions of people to the elections and found the presence of opinion leaders in every community and that they responded to some media messages while other people responded to the opinion leaders. Subsequent studies found that in some cases, people interacted directly with the media sources as they at the same interacted with influential individuals called opinion leaders. Zeuschner (1997) **states that opinion leaders may be influential people in business, politics, religion, civic, or community groups; they may also be employees of the media organizations.** The intricate link between opinion leaders and the media is established when as Zeuschner further states "one thing is probable: If they are opinion leaders, they are probably communicating their opinions through the media." The reality that people communicate simultaneously and directly to both media sources and opinion leaders led to the development of the multi-step approach to media process model.

Figure 18.1/Model of Mass Communication Processes

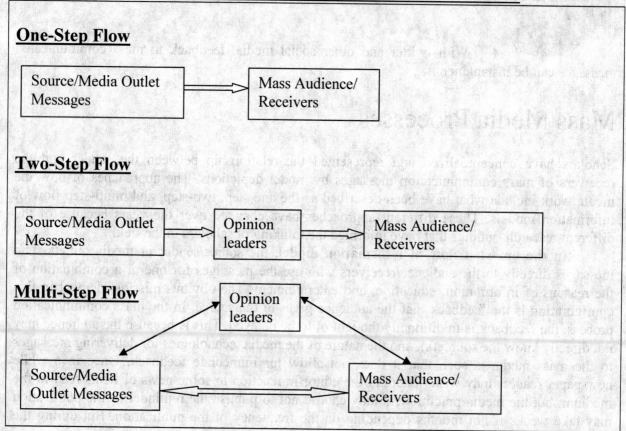

The multi-step or three–part approach examines the interactions among receivers, between receivers and the opinion leaders, and between the receivers and the media sources. Since this approach to the communication process, many influences on the media and their audiences have been identified and it is confirmed that there are many intervening elements in the process beyond the three elements that have been identified. Thus, the use of the idea of **n-step flow** to depict the multilayer of information sharing that takes place in the process of mass communication. This takes us into a leap forward to the seventies to the HUB model of communication developed by the scholars whose names symbolize the model -- Hiebert, Ungurait, and Bohn (1974).

Figure 18.2/An Adapted HUB Model

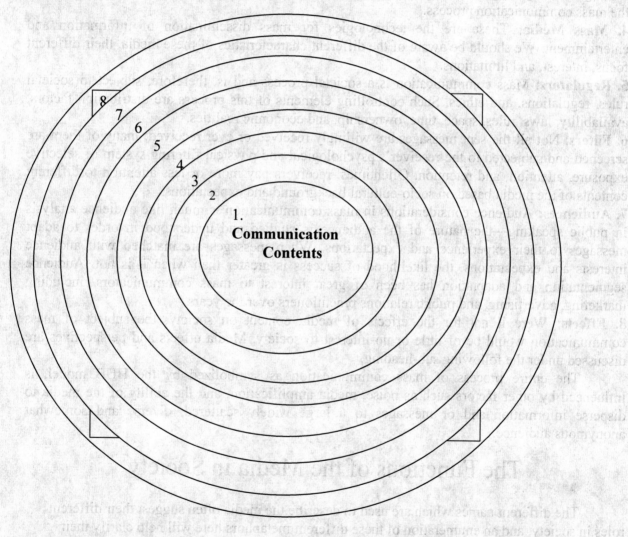

The partially visible rectangle is an addition to the original HUB model. It represents many barely visible factors that operate in the process of mass communication from circle 1-8 in the model above, but that are important influencing elements in the outcome of the communicative experience.

The HUB model of mass communication captures most of the elements involved in the rather complex process of sending information or messages from the source to the receivers. The core of the concentric circles can be compared to the position in a pool of water where a stone is dropped. The following circles are the ripples that follow. Each of these circles is given a number which represents each of the different elements that operate in the process identified as follows:

1. **Encoding:** The core of the concentric circles where the process of organizing information into a sendable form occurs. This is where the encoding process takes place.

2. **Codes:** To encode, we have to use language or some nonverbal symbolic system in order to be able to share commonly understood messages. These are derived from particular cultural experiences, orientations, such as educational backgrounds of the senders and the receivers.

3. **Gatekeeper:** These are different levels of people who allow or prevent different types of messages from getting across to their final destinations. They regulate the flow of information in the mass communication process.

4. **Mass Media**: These are the technologies for mass dissemination of information and entertainment. We should be aware of the different characteristics of these media, their different focus, interest, and limitations.

5. **Regulators**: Mass communication is a societal process and is, therefore, subject to societal rules, regulations, and ethics. Such controlling elements of this process are distribution factors, availability, laws, rules, space, time, ownership, and economic realities.

6. **Filters**: Not all the sent messages are willingly received or ever received; many of them are screened and subjected to the receiver's psychological and physical filtering system of selective exposure, attention, and retention. Oftentimes, receivers pay more or less attention to different contents of the media based on socio-cultural background and expectations.

7. **Audiences:** Audience considerations in mass communication is much like audience analysis in public speaking—the nature of the audience is studied and understood in order to adapt messages to their experience and expectations. When messages are matched with audience interests and expectations, the likelihood of success is greater than when it is not. Audience segmentation and adaptation has been of great interest to mass communicators, including marketing, advertising, and public relations practitioners over the years.

8. **Effects:** Were it not for the effects of media content on society, the subject of mass communication would be of little or no interest to society. Media effects and perspectives are discussed under the following sub-heading.

The entire process of mass communication as symbolized by the HUB model, is influenced by other factors such as noise, media amplification, and the ability of the media to disperse information and or messages to a large widely scattered, diverse and somewhat anonymous audience.

The Functions of the Media in Society

The different names which are used to describe the media often suggest their different roles in society, and an enumeration of these different metaphors here will help clarify their different functions and identify their direct or indirect influence on society. Denis McQuail (1987) identifies **the different metaphors for describing media functions** as follows:

1. A window on experience, which extends our vision, enables us to see what is going on for ourselves, without interference or bias.

2. An interpreter, which explains and makes sense of otherwise fragmentary or puzzling events.
3. A platform or carrier for information and opinion.
4. A interactive link which relates senders to receivers by way of different kinds of feedback.
5. A signpost, which actively points the way, gives guidance or instruction.
6. A filter, selecting out parts of experience for special attention and closing off other aspects of experience, whether deliberately and systematically or not.
7. A mirror, which reflects back an image of society to itself---usually with some Distortion-- by accentuating what people want to see of their own society or sometimes what they want to punish or suppress.
8. A screen or barrier, which conceals truth in the service of propagandist purpose or escapism.

Media practitioners and their advocates argue that the media reflect society because they position themselves as advocate and representative of society whose duty it is to present a systematized, integrated, and coherent view of an otherwise disorganized world. However, they accept the responsibility imposed by ethical considerations and expectations in the media business.

McQuail (1987), after reviewing the different functions of the media in society espoused by different scholars, concludes that "nearly everywhere, the media are expected to advance national interests and promote certain key values and behavior patterns, but especially so in times of crisis." However, in developing countries and many social countries, he observes further that a mobilizing role is formally allotted to the media.

In summarizing the major functions of the media in society, McQuail (1987) identifies the following inclusive functions:

1. **Information.**
   --*providing information about events and conditions in society and the world*
   --*indicating relations of power*
   --*facilitating innovation, adaptation, and progress.*
2. **Correlation.**
   --*explaining, interpreting and commenting on the meaning of events and information*
   --*providing support for established authority and norms*
   --*socializing*
   --*coordinating separate activities*
   --*consensus building*
   --*setting orders of priority and signaling relative status.*
3. **Continuity.**
   --*expressing the dominant culture and recognizing subcultures (co-cultures) and new cultural developments*
   --*forging and maintaining commonality of values.*
4. **Entertainment.**
   --*providing amusement, diversion, the means of relaxation*
   --*reducing social tension.*

5. Mobilization.
  --*campaigning for societal objectives in the sphere of politics, war, economic development, work and sometimes religion.*

Media Characteristics

The nature of the technologies of communication influences their users in peculiar ways. Such nature influences content design, distribution and consumption. Some media are mobile and their messages fleeting while others can be stored permanently and made available for future reference. Some media extend two to three senses while others extend just one. Some are widely available while others are restrictive in their use because of language barriers. In terms of access and expense, some of these media are cheap but some are rather expensive to the extent that those who have access to them and can afford them are viewed as privileged and of higher status in society. Ownership of certain media, therefore, can be viewed as a status symbol. In all, the nature of each medium of mass communication allows for its use in peculiar ways such that the physical characteristics of the media and how they are put to use by the practitioners affect the audience in unique and different ways.

Sensory extension and attraction:

  The media can be classified according to the sense(s) they extend and capture. A medium may show an event and feed the viewers with the sound of the event as well. Television and film can do these while radio and books can only extend the sense of hearing and sight respectively. According to Uyo (1987), normally, the more sense organs a medium engages, the more the receiver is arrested by the medium. This suggests that the more senses an audience member uses in receiving and deciphering media messages, the more impactful these messages will be on them. Consequently, to capture the attention of the audience, it is important to place messages in the media that capture more senses of the audience members. This definitely has consequences for public relations and advertising media decisions.

Fidelity:

  Fidelity is the efficiency, effectiveness, and reliability of a medium to reproduce an event as it really occurred. Since events take place in time and space, a medium that can reproduce events in time and space would be considered to possess greater fidelity. The dimensions of message fidelity include the accuracy of verbal symbols, pictures, color sound, and motion (Blake and Haroldsen, 1975). While television and film have the technical characteristics to reproduce these elements, radio and books and other print media do not.

Impersonality:

  Some media reproduce human encounters at the personal level, that is, such depictions are interpersonal in nature and exude warmth, affection, and tenderness. The opposite of this is coldness—not personal but rather impersonal. Media that are high in fidelity can be considered to be low in impersonality and high in warmth and tenderness. Reading the newspaper report of a thrilling soccer game can be a rather cold and impersonal experience, but watching the same event on television can be a scintillating personal and involved experience.

Velocity, Simultaneity, and timeliness:

Velocity is the speed at which something travels and both television and radio and film can be considered the fastest, while books and newspapers are delivered according to the speed of the available transportation mode. In this digital age, however, books, newspapers, and magazines can be delivered electronically just as radio and television. These media can all now be delivered at the speed of light, which is 186,000 miles per second.

Simultaneity has to do with the ability of the media to present events or news to the audience as they are occurring, while timeliness is the ability of the practitioners of the media to decide that an event is current and present it to the audience in a timely fashion. That is, a medium may have the capacity to deliver messages instantaneously, but if the practitioners, who would make the decision to place a story or event in the medium, do not, then, the technical capacity of the medium is subject to the administrative decisions of the practitioners. Naturally though, a medium that is swift (technical capacity), and can cover an event at the same time that it is happening (simultaneity), is best placed to be timely, (Uyo, 1987: 27).

Permanency:

The contents of radio, television, and film, as they are aired are not permanent, instead they are fleeting. If one is listening to a radio program and is distracted and loses the trend of the program, it is rather difficult to recall and recount the event as it has been told. In this age of digital storage, however, it is possible to store electronic images and data—be it radio or television—in real time and to have access to it at a delayed time. This undermines the idea that these electronic data are not permanent such as that of any of the print media. Traditionally, newspapers, magazines and the like are considered to contain permanent messages because they can be retrieved and read over and over. But so can television programs, especially with the invention of **TIVO**! This device allows one to record electronic images and sound in real time for retrieval at other times. Video and audio recordings are available on VCDs and DVDs, so that now we can consider all media contents permanent. It is even possible to rewind live audio and video images on digital radio and television!

Portability:

When something is described as portable, we mean it can be carried about and made available almost anywhere and everywhere. Again, we used to think of radio and books and other print media as portable because they could be carried to remote places one goes. These days, however, all media are portable! Both sound and video are combined in digital form on the internet which is available on **Android** phones and the like. Video can be watched on portable devices such as iPads and smart phones. So, not only print media and radio are portable, so also are television and film.

Costliness:

This is the amount of human and material cost necessary to acquire, produce, and present messages through the different media to their respective audiences. To many in the United States, television is a rather inexpensive medium because it is readily available and the cost is relatively inexpensive. But to many in the developing countries, the cost of a television set may equal the monthly income of many and, even, in some cases, their annual GDP.

Consider this: In the United States, Hollywood, the movie Avatar cost in excess of $500 million to produce—just one movie! But in Nollywood, the cost of a movie is about $7,500! Media cost should be viewed from the perspective of capital and recurring expenditure. While a TV set may last five years and more, newspapers and magazines are periodicals whose real cost can be summed monthly or annually. But a television set cannot deliver programs without subscription to content providers such as cable and satellite provider companies. With the cost of hardware and programming, television can be considered the most expensive medium. Film could have won the title of most expensive medium, both in terms of production and the audience's expenditure to access it, but movies are also packaged as DVDs and are available for viewing on home videos and theatres.

The image of the hero of the animated movie: AVATAR.

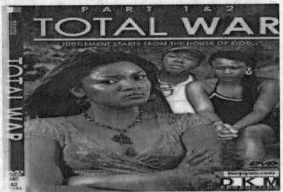

Omotola Ekehinde stars in Nigerian movie: TOTAL WAR

Universality and Access:

This has to do with the overall availability, access, cost, and the sensory attraction of the different mass media. As we have demonstrated that television attracts more senses and that radio is more readily available and portable and cheap, we can agree that radio is the more common of the mass media. Radio is not only available in terms of transistor radios that are relatively inexpensive, radio can transmit its messages in common languages that allows it to transcend the barriers of illiteracy and, perhaps, the formal training needed to understand the contents of many print media. So, the pervasiveness of radio and its ability to reach indigenous people as well as urban dwellers—literate or illiterate, make it the most common medium of all.

Channel Capacity:

Uyo (1987) describes the channel capacity of a medium as the upper limit of its ability to carry information, plus the ability of the sensory organs that perceive the information to cope with the amount of information (being) sent. In terms of volume of information contained in a medium, newspapers, books and other print media do have higher capacity than radio and television. The restricted time nature of the electronic media makes them of less capacity than the print media. Media that do extend more than one sense also have higher channel capacity such that the senses are not overloaded as is the case with radio which extends only the hearing sense.

Credibility:

This is the expertness and trustworthiness of a channel as perceived by the receivers, (Blake and Haroldsen, 1975). This is a question of how much trust the audience places on a medium of communication or how believable they perceive the contents to be. In other words, this leads us to ask the question whether radio is more believable than radio or television or newspapers. But the paraphernalia of communication are inanimate and cannot be imputed with credibility. This has to be the measure of the performance of the practitioners of the media, that is, the factors such as accuracy, fairness, objectivity, balance, and overall quality of the contents of the media are the standard of measure of the credibility of the media. We cannot, as matter of finality, claim that one medium is more credible than another at any particular time. This depends on the practice of the practitioners at any given point of study.

Mass Media Writing

Writing for the media is a varied specialization as the media vary. The different characteristics of the different mass media impose a unique form on their contents. The form of radio writing is different from that of television because they extend different senses. Radio writers write for the ears while television writers write for both ears and the eyes.

Writing for Television/Film

Writing for television or film is unique because it complements pictures and moving images that are seen and heard by the viewers. Writings meant for the electronic media must be performed or translated into action, one way or another. This type of writing should be descriptive, direct, logical, and detailed. Descriptive in the sense that it should capture all of the actions expected from the actors, such as a crooked posture, smile, unkempt appearance and melancholic behavior. It should be direct and to the point rather than long winded and confusing. Every expected action must be captured in great detail, leaving out very few to the imagination and improvisation of the actors. Because human actions follow a sequence, a kind of time arrow, then the writing should be logical and portray action in natural, logical pattern that is easy to follow.

The common element in electronic media writing is the script. Whether written and developed in detail or loosely organized around a concept or an actor, a script is the foundation of most of the programs that you would see in film or television or that you would hear on radio. For example, Rosenthal (1990) writes that using a script is usually the most logical and helpful way to make a film... The script is like an architect's plan… that makes the task of film-making a hundred times easier. A script is many things whether it is for radio, film, or television. Although he was writing about documentary films, the description and enumeration of the functions of the script by Rosenthal (1990) is instructional as it is applicable across the different electronic media. He claims the following:

1. The script is an organized and structural tool, a reference and a guide that helps everyone involved in the production. The script communicates the idea of the film to everyone concerned with production and it tries to do this clearly, simply, and imaginatively.
2. The script is particularly vital to the sponsors, telling them in detail what the film is about and whether what has been loosely discussed in conference has been translated into acceptable film ideas.
3. The script is also essential to both the cameraman and the director. It should convey to the cameraman a great deal about the mood, action, and problems of the camera work. It should

also help the director define the approach and the progress of the film, its inherent logic, and its continuity.

4. The script is also an essential item for the rest of the production team because, apart from conveying the story, it also helps the crew answer a series of questions:
   a. What is the appropriate budget?
   b. How many locations are needed and how many days shooting?
   c. What lighting will be required?
   d. Will there be any special effects?
   e. Will archive materials be needed?
   f. Are special cameras or lenses called for because of particular scenes?

5. The script will also guide the editor, showing the proposed structure of the film and the way the sequences will fit together. The editor usually works off the editing script—different from the original script.

The script is a plan just like the architect's drawing which is subject to change. The script, therefore, is a guide or a working document that can be altered as situations dictate, especially in the course of production.

Writing for Radio

In an online commentary, Avinash (2012) writes that radio is a medium where the "theatre of mind" can be created by using sound only; it has an imaginative potential for the listener to add his/her own visual interpretation. This statement captures the essence of radio writing—that which extends the sense of sight and hearing, though the sight is imaginary.

The power of good radio writing lies in the ability of the writer to capture the immediacy—emotional atmosphere of the events being portrayed and the psychological nature of the audience. In this type of writing, use of short, action-oriented sentences is advised; use of direct, to-the-point descriptors preferable and; writing the way people speak is customary. Sound as the essential means of communication in radio, should be manipulated to mimic the ebb and flow of everyday conversation that people can relate to.

Time is of essence in radio writing. Regardless of the type of program—commentary, feature, news, drama, docudrama—all that has to be said must be crammed into the given time slot and the more effectively and judiciously time is used the better. This calls for brevity of words, characters, plots, etc in the programming. Again, time dimension also includes timeliness of the contents. Psychologically, audiences respond to breaking news and current events than those that are dated and stale.

Radio messages are fleeting or transient. Once a message passes, it's gone, except if it is repeated. And when this is the case, the hearer may not be present to catch the repetition. This adds another dimension to radio writing—it must be simple. It should not require much thinking to process because if it does, while the thinking is going on to catch the meaning of a particular message, others are rolling by. Avinash (2012) further comments that "emphasis is on simple writing, but simple language does not mean a language devoid of embellishment, ornamentation or an extension of meaning. In addition to the words being simple, they must be familiar and concrete, proper, precise, direct, and used in brief sentences. With the right mode of delivery, the audience is sustained and kept interested in the program. Concluding, Avinash declares that "the words used must be such that they can show, point out, announce, declare, with rich effect, without visual aids."

Newspaper Writing

Writing for the eyes is quite different from writing for the ears and the eyes as in the electronic media. The nature of newspapers and magazines makes these print media messages more permanent and portable. A news story, feature, editorial opinion, can be read once or twice, or as many times is wished by the reader. A print edition can be kept for a long time and be revisited. Consequently, the readers spend more time thinking about what they are exposed to in the print media and this influences writing for these types of media. Newspaper or print writing is generally more detailed than electronic media writing; it can be more intellectual and more rigorous. And it usually is illustrated with visual elements such as graphs, photographs, and charts.

Visual elements in print writing perform the roles of stories and drama in electronic media writing. These elements draw people's attention to the contents, and they help in sustaining interest and getting stories read and programs watched and/or listened to. Research evidence confirms that 98 percent of readers are first drawn to a photograph on a newspaper page. Newspaper writing, especially news writing, hinges on elaborating on the Lasswellian formula of who says what, to whom and with what effect.

Generally, news writing is mindful of six elements described as the **FIVE Ws and H**. That is **Who? What? Where? When? Why? How?** A good news story, feature article, editorial opinions, and other genres of writing in print dwell on some or all of these elements. Sometimes the Who is the lead focus of the writing, especially if the person involved is a political figure, economic potentate, or a celebrity of sort. The 'what' may be prominent if the event or occurrence is unique, an oddity, or an event that will affect a large number of people. For example, a media practitioner once wrote that **"when a dog bites a man, that is no news; but when a man bites a dog, that is great news!"** At times where an event occurs may be of greater importance than who was involved in it. For example, if a thief breaks into a church to steal the offerings of the day, the location –a sacred place of worship that condemns such antisocial and criminal behavior is not expected to fall victim to such occurrence. When an event occurs could be the most important element in the news because there are certain expectations associated with different times in different

> When a dog bites a man that is not news, but when a man bites a dog that is news.
> *Charles Anderson Dana*
> *American journalist, 1819-1897*

societies. Imagine a news story that breaks in this manner: **"Today, in broad daylight, hoodlums paraded themselves naked in front of thousands of onlookers … What a sight it is to see hoodlums naked in broad daylight! Isn't it for their antisocial and criminal behavior that they are called hoodlums?"** This is a cultural treatment of time that is reflected in all forms of writing. Again, the 'how' of an event may feature more prominently than any other of the elements because the writer perceives how the event took place as more news worthy than the other attendant elements. Imagine this:

After having been in the public eye for most of his life, President Crimson at the end of his speech to the Assembly today, rendered these stunning words: " I will cease to be your president from this moment on."

As may be noted, some of the elements in news writing can be combined in the introductory paragraph of a news item. It does not follow that only one of the items should be featured in the lead sentence. News is read by people and, therefore, must appeal to them. Oftentimes they want more information than featured in the lead sentence and that is why news also includes background stories or information, which would clarify some of the issues readers may ponder in their minds having read the introductory paragraph.

Writing the News

Journalism schools teach a working or practical theory of news writing that takes into consideration the nature of news, the media for presenting them, and the behaviors of the consumers of news. News readers have many different media to choose from and generally don't have the time to read all of the contents of most of the newspapers, magazines, and watch news on television. The readers skim and the watchers do so intermittently. News writers have to adapt to these consumption patterns of their readers. What has been found to work is the mantra of giving 'short and swift' information to people who are on the go and, when they have the time in the case of the print media, they can read the details and, in the case of viewers they can capture the recap of the news. The media practitioners working theory of news writing is called **the inverted pyramid style.**

The inverted pyramid is a style of journalistic writing that features the most important elements in a news story or a piece of writing first and subsequently presents other parts of the story that may be considered less important. The lead (lede) paragraph should contain sufficient overview information about the entire story. Everything else that follows is connected one way or the other to the summary sentence in the lead of the story. This is a smart method of media writing because it considers audience behavior as has been noted and allows for management of newspaper space and radio or television time. When newspapers have less space for a long story or have to edit severely, the summarized lead paragraph would be sufficient for a good mention of the news item without necessarily occupying much space. In the case of radio or television, time is of essence, therefore, when the important items in the news have been mentioned, the rest can be cut off should the time segment be running out. All these are done without losing the essence or gem of the story. The inverted pyramid is a style of writing that saves time and space while allowing for the reader, viewer, or listener to be informed. (Note that there are different types of lead paragraphs and different types of news stories featured in print writing).

A reporter may focus on a particular angle of a story, but the readers may be interested in another. The background information included to further develop the story may satisfy the **expected news angle** of the reader. This brings us to the definition of news, what determines it, and what other factors influence news reporting.

What is News?

News is the communication of selected information on current events which is presented by print, broadcast, Internet, or word of mouth to a third-party or mass audience (Wikipedia). There are two categories of news: hard and soft news. Rich (1994) describes **"Hard news" to include stories of a timely nature about events or conflicts that just happened or are about to happen, such as crimes, fires, meetings, protest rallies, speeches and testimonies in court case.** She underscores the hard approach is basically an account of what happened, why it happened and how readers will be affected. In contrast, she opines **"soft news" to be characterized as news that entertains or informs, with an emphasis on human interest and novelty and less immediacy than hard news...Soft news can also be feature stories that focus on people, places or issues that affect readers' lives.**

The Elements of News

Journalists, as any other professionals, are influenced by their training. To understand why certain events are prominently reported and others untouched, we should look at how a journalist's training defines how he or she views and relates to news. Let us examine the elements of news and peek into the journalist's mindset.

The elements of news are the characteristics that qualify an occurrence as news to the journalist; these are sometimes referred to as the determinants, nature, or conditions that define news.

Impact:

News is any occurrence that impacts the way of life of a people in a significant way; it is any event that affects a large number of people, making the scale of that occurrence a determinant of that which is newsworthy. The impact could be who is involved in the event or how the person or thing would affect the livelihood, lifestyle, and the existence of the community or the group of people, a country, or the world.

When the Twin Towers in New York were attacked by terrorists who flew two hijacked passenger airplanes into them on September 11, 2001, the impact was global. Not only was this an attack on American home soil, but an attack on the business capital of the world with reverberating financial losses to many countries of the world that invested money in the American /global economy. Again, the impact stemmed from the large number of people that died (about 3000) in that singular event, and the reaction that followed. Because of "9/11" the US government invaded Iraq and is still in Afghanistan, fighting a decade-long war that has cost the American taxpayers in upward of two trillion dollars.

Local events that have tremendous impact on the local socio-economic and political life are newsworthy. The death of a local monarch, a scientific discovery at the local university, and the success of a local sports team--- all are newsworthy events because of their impact on the immediate society and beyond.

Proximity:

This is the geographic closeness of an event. This relates to impact as well, because an event's effect is most felt closest to home. Any event that occurs in New York city, is directly felt by New Yorkers and, perhaps, by extension felt by other people outside of New York city and then the nation. News reporters consider events that are close home prime news because of the direct impact on the locals who, by nature, are drawn to events that directly affect their lives and that of their neighbors. People can relate to tragedies in faraway places because of shared humanity, but they are most drawn to tragedies in their immediate environment because they threaten their survival.

Timeliness:

News is considered a fresh, immediate occurrence and not something that is dated or stale. Reporters are drawn to current events and breaking news as opposed to something that has passed and has less news value. This is because of the psychological disposition of people to be drawn to such and not be bored with something whose impact has dissipated as a result of the passage of time. This element is what would not compel you to feverishly seek to read yesterday's newspaper, or view yesterday's news broadcast, again. In journalism, timeliness of reporting is key; it is the driving force of media competition. Often, such timeliness is announced by "breaking news" to which viewers and listeners are drawn automatically. Not to be outdone, newspaper houses create evening papers to fill the news void in between their daily editions. In the news business, time is money and it is survival. It is considered timely to report anniversaries, and cycles of events to remind people of such occurrences.

The internet has created a news-on-the-go culture in the world today, such that the linear time orientation of news reporting has been broken by the digital media where people can asynchronously access news 24/7.

Prominence:

Reporters are drawn to reporting events about celebrities, politicians, captains of industry, and people that are unique in society. These people attract attention because of their unusual accomplishments, gifts, and lifestyle. Because people have the tendency to compare themselves to others and to admire those whose lives are considered extraordinary, they are drawn to news and stories about important people in their society and, indeed, in other societies. Tabloid magazines thrive because of this psychological disposition and that is why there seems to be an insatiable appetite for gossip, intrigue, and personal interest stories about prominent people in human society. For example, Americans know much about the life of Justin Bieber and Mariah Carey than Benjamin S. Carson Sr., M.D., and director of pediatric neurosurgery at the Johns Hopkins Children's Center in Baltimore.

Human Interest:

Just like the element of prominence, people focus on the lives of other people who have problems, unusual achievements and /or experiences. These are stories that massage the ego or stir the pathos of people. People vicariously experience the pains, joys, and ups and downs of others whose experiences have become examples or models for others. Stories about births, marriages, celebrations, deaths, and obituaries are of human interest, so are stories about incredible poverty, reverent love, disturbing subservience, and inhumane cruelty. Why are they important? Because they happen to the likes of us humans, and more importantly, it could happen to us and ours.

Conflict:

Life is full of opposing forces and such divergence results in conflict—a struggle caused by different expectations and outcomes, conflicted orientations, and expressed desire for insufficient resources. Such conflicts between people and the government, people and organizations, political parties, classes of people, etc., attract attention and are considered newsworthy. Reports about protests, ethnic squabbles, and allocation of resources are examples of stories about conflict.

Relevance:

Impact and relevance are somewhat connected. How relevant is an occurrence to the audience of a particular story is a question that should be uppermost in the minds of the reporter. This asks a fundamental question about news writing: What is the purpose of this story to my readers? In other words, the question is: What impact would this story have on my audience? Will it inform, educate, persuade, dissuade, improve their lives, or help them in any manner? Relevance has to do with the usefulness of a news story to its audience. These will include information, entertainment or emotional release, practical guide to better living, etc. How relevant is a story on the "Melting Ice Caps of The Kilimanjaro" to the lives of Africans and the rest of the world? This is not only a special interest story of concern to scientists, but a story that should start us thinking of global warming and the shifting world climates. The impact is huge, thus making the story extremely relevant to all of our lives. Journalists refer to relevance of their stories as the **"Nut Graph,"** that is, the point of the story or the question why he or she is writing the story, and the query of how it will impact them.

Oddity:

An odd occurrence is unusual and people are drawn to the unusual. The Guinness book of records is noted for documenting the unusual in the world to the extent that it has become one of the most popular books and most visited museum in London. People are interested in learning about the tallest man on earth, the longest snake, the smallest person, the most married person, and the person with the largest head! Events that are out-of-the-ordinary, bizarre, and very rare are newsworthy. Remember the quotation: 'When a dog bites a man that is not news, but when a man bites a dog, that is news.

Elements of Good Writing

The chapter on verbal language dealt with language, its challenges, and how we can communicate more effectively through the use of words. The precepts for effective language use include using accurate and clear language, as well as engaging metaphors and immediate tone to capture the emotional context of our communication. Good communication hinges on effective use of verbal on non-verbal messages, and effective writing thrives on the use **of appropriate**

and precise words to describe events, situations, and experience. Nothing beats clarity of thought and ideas that are articulated with precise words.

Effective writing captures or establishes a **prevailing mood and atmosphere** surrounding the object or subject of writing. This is often referred to as pacing in journalistic writing. With pacing are also **transitions**—the twists and turns of a story portrayed through the use of conjunctions and use of linguistic signposts and connectives which make a story seamless even as it moves from plot to plot, atmosphere to atmosphere, and from one main point to another.

Effective writing engages the reader by **extending more than one sensory organ**. As imaginatively as possible, a good writer should be able to create imagery through ingenious allusions and illusions, thus creating a multi-sensory connection with the narrative experience. Furthermore, good writing creates a parallel reference in the mind of the reader by comparing like and unlike terms, **drawing analogies** that concretize the narrative experience for the reader. Usually this is achieved by describing events, objects, and situations as being like or familiar to the readers.

Objectivity and Fairness

Good journalistic writing, especially news reports need to be unbiased, fair, and balanced. There is the assumption by the general public that journalists are disinterested purveyors of news and not agents of a particular ideology or agenda in society. That they are important gatekeepers who determine what people pay attention to and who eventually mould their perceptions. The claim of journalists to be the watchdogs of government and its agencies as the fourth estate of the realm may not be a credible claim if they do their job with fear and favor. It is for this reason that progressive nations seek freedom of the press laws to guarantee unfettered reporting of the affairs of the State to guarantee that "the other side" is given a voice and that of the other elements of society are not muffled. Parks (2012) succinctly articulates the essence of objectivity and fairness in the practice of journalism when he states that "the public needs unbiased information in order for democracy to succeed."

As it is with every right, there is a corresponding responsibility. Freedom of the press imposes a duty or responsibility on journalists in the practice of their profession. The men and women of the press should demonstrate honesty in their role as observers of society; they should seek to balance their reporting with diverse opinions and should endeavor to use neutral language in their reporting and; they should seek to promote the public good rather than be adversarial. Journalists should champion the cause of the poor, the environment, good governance, and judicial propriety. The journalist's call is indeed a noble one in society.

HOW TO WRITE A NEWS LEAD (LEDE)

1. Condense story into one or two words. Put those words as close to the beginning of the first sentence as possible without destroying the flow of the lead sentence.
2. Keep leads short — 20 to 30 words for the first sentence, or fewer.
3. The news lead should tell the reader what the story is about and be interesting enough to draw the reader into the rest of the story. Remember that the readers won't know what the story is about until you tell them.
4. Find the action in the story. Put the action in the lead.
5. Always double-check names and numbers. Check spelling, style and grammar. Put every thing in order.
6. Attribute opinions. Stick with the facts.
7. Details, description. Report first, and then write. Learn all, tell 10 percent.
8. Decide which of the news values best applies to the lead of the story. Write a lead that emphasizes that news value.
9. Write in the active voice. 10. Don't lead with a name, time or place unless that is the most interesting/important thing in the story.

WHAT NOT TO DO IN LEADS

1. Don't make the lead too complicated. Don't load it down with too many names, figures or details. Keep the lead sentence short -- never more than 35 words.
2. Don't begin with the time, day or date, or place. Better to focus on the action, the who or what.
3. Don't begin with an empty, say-nothing expression or a generality that fails to distinguish this news from other news: *There were... In a report released today... According to...*
4. Don't begin with a question if the question is answered in the story. Question leads are cliché leads.
5. Don't begin with a direct quote if it is a full sentence. Don't start with a quote unless it is an exceptional quote.

Source: Bill Parks, Professor of News Writing- Ohlone College.
http://www.ohlone.edu/people/bparks/docs/basicnewswriting.pdf

Sample News Story

Pastor Adeboye at 70

By Laolu Akande 02/03/2012

Pastor Adeboye "has made big plans to save your soul, "writes *Newsweek*, a prominent US-based international newsmagazine in 2008, when he was named one of the world's *Top 50 Global Elites.* **At 70, a milestone age that he attains today March 2, there is no suggestion that he is about to relent on that effort. To say Adeboye is a true man of God is well known and stated already. But he is also one man of God, who deliberately and constantly elevates the God, more than the man.**

In the interest of full disclosure, let me state from the onset that I am a Parish Pastor of one of the thousands of parishes of the Redeemed Christian Church of God around the world. But I write here in my personal capacity to pay tribute to the General Overseer of the church who has touched and continues to touch millions of lives including mine.

Let us briefly highlight some exemplary virtues that his life represents, starting with his legendary humility. My very first experience of seeing Pastor Adeboye was at the University of Ibadan in the mid-90s, when he came to minister at the Chapel of The Resurrection. As he proceeded into the chapel alongside other ministers and aides, I was asking, where is the man? His *Danshiki* successfully concealed the influence and accomplishments already well noted in his life and ministry then.

Daddy G.O., as many of us fondly refer to him, keeps in his office, an old photo of himself when he was new and very fresh in church leadership. At that time no one knew him as such, those were the leaner times. Then Adeboye, (as he refers to himself in public speeches), was only a hopeful promise packaged in a controversial order from the late redoubtable founder of RCCG, Pa. Josiah Akindayomi. The photo is left there to remind him regularly, the story goes, of his humble background, helping him to remain as humble as possible.

In 2004, here in New York, the church held its annual North American Convention and some of us were involved in the several areas of planning. I still remember how Adeboye needed to get a new shoe and gave clear instructions that the shoe must not exceed $30! If any of the aides around planned to outwit him and get a "better" shoe, he gave the clincher-he has to see the receipt! This is one of the reasons I am personally convinced that Adeboye is not using a private jet today because of the luxury it

connotes. It was purely a decision based on need and easier access for a global evangelical itinerant like him and his wife, Pastor Folu Adeboye, a woman of virtue in her own standing.

What about Pastor Adeboye's integrity? There is no point to represent that he is perfect. But he is a tireless pursuer of it. I will give two quick illustrations.

After the Redeemers University for the Nations, RUN was established, Pastor Adeboye brought in a world-class academic and administrator, Prof Oyewale Tomori, one of the best products of the University of Ibadan Virology department and College of Medicine. As soon as Tomori took charge, Adeboye heaved a sigh of relief and yielded the control and management of the place to Tomori, the governing bodies and Council.

Those who think access or relationship to RCCG pastors and leaders could influence the way the university would operate soon found out that the G.O. himself was acting in tandem with university regulations, limiting his role to that of the Visitor. Some church ministers, leaders and their relations lost their jobs in the school because they were found wanting and not up to the task. Those who think the G.O. will intervene to stretch university policies and apply double standards found out he will not meddle.

Influential leaders who kept approaching the school for all kinds of favours against regulations and who kept dropping the G.O's name to influence decisions, soon discovered that the university management was truly free to manage the school. The story is told of how a relative of a very senior pastor was fired for dereliction of duty. And when a confidential secretary/typist was asked to type out a letter of dismissal, the secretary was shaking and reluctant seeing the name of the notable person involved. She then was warned to either type promptly or else two letters of dismissal would be due! That dismissal stood.

I was also personally present in the US where the General Overseer personally took responsibility for the failure of a church project to which many members had contributed funds and resources- over a billion in naira. The project failed because of the arrant mismanagement of some officials put in charge.

Before the G.O. spoke, someone who knew I am a journalist sent me a package of documented details on the mismanagement perpetuated by some of the officials involved and I was worried at the extent of carelessness and wrangling by those charged with implementing the project. But when the G.O. stood up to take responsibility and apologised to the people, even offering to personally repay all those who had contributed, I relinquished my investigation and my fears were dissuaded. Of course the people involved were also relieved of their roles in the project.

Finally I want to highlight, Pastor Adeboye's willingness to aggressively promote people under him. Then, Engineer James Fadele, the former top designer of Ford Motors in Michigan, USA, and a well-known business owner relinquished his career and sold his business to take up the leadership of the church here in the US and Canada. Fadele, himself an inspiring leader tells of how Adeboye encouraged him to start a church in the basement of his home then in Michigan in the mid-90s.

Daddy G.O. corroborated the story in one of his many interactions with pastors and ministers here, that he had been asking RCCG members in the US to "start something." But many did not want to take the plunge, but Fadele did. Pastor Adeboye, then personally joined Pastor Fadele to make posters and paste them around when they started the first house fellowship of the church in the USA. Today there are over 500 RCCG parishes in the US and Canada. Besides, the church also owns a massive camp in Dallas, Texas, its North American headquarters, where another Redemption Camp is now being developed.

One is not unaware of some critical views regarding Pastor Adeboye, but a birthday tribute is no right place or time to address them. Those issues would not escape public review and dissecting, since *Daddy G.O.* is clearly today a national and global religious elder-statesman. But what people will ultimately discover after all the intellectual scrutiny, I suspect, is Adeboye's truly humble heart, a profoundly gracious disposition, and a depth of wisdom

There is however a humble but urgent request: Let Pastor Adeboye raise his voice, -a powerful and influential voice for that matter-more often on national issues like he did last year when he warned that the elections must not be rigged!

•Akande, is a New York-based reporter.

Becoming Media Literate

Traditional definition of literacy has to do with the ability to read or write. To be literate in another sense means to be critically aware of something or not to have just a cursory look at something that has deep and consequential influences on people and society at large. Specifically, Turow, (2003) writes that literacy is "the ability to effectively comprehend and use messages that are expressed in written or printed symbols, such as letters." Literacy can also be extended to the ability to effectively and critically evaluate oral messages and technologically mediated messages. Literacy, again, should be extended to the ability to effectively, actively, and adequately respond to media messages.

We have confirmed that the media are an integral part of society and do affect society in tremendous ways. The reasons to become mediate literate include understanding the power of the media to expose masses of people to contents that may influence them in particular ways, and to orient the masses to a common mindset or consciousness. It should also be understood that the rich and powerful in society not only control the media and influence their contents, they also enjoy the economy of scale and of mass consumption that the media foster. Students of communication and the media should be aware of the important roles the media play in society, especially the overwhelming influence and control they exert on the social relations, economic and political realities. People in modern, media society should become media savvy. That is, the consumers as well as the professionals in the mass communication industry should become critical evaluators of how the contents of the media are designed, the purposes for which they are procured, and the impacts that they have on their consumers. It is relevant here to define exactly what media literacy is.

Media literacy has been defined as the ability to apply critical thinking skills to the mass media, thereby becoming a more aware and responsible citizen—parent, voter, worker—in our media-driven society. It is also the ability to access, analyze, evaluate, and communicate messages in a variety of forms (Turow, 2003). Let us analyze this definition by explaining some of the concepts employed in it. The word critical is a Greek derivative of *kritikos* which stands for "able to perceive, detect, judge, or analyze." Critical thinking is the process of understanding the world and phenomena from different and complex perspectives, not from a rather simplistic and thoughtless dimension. It is having thoughtful and creative insights and applying such to good judgment in regard to a subject, an idea, or an occurrence. With a critical mindset, the consumer of mass communicated messages selectively assesses which contents are deemed important and relevant, and upon access, he or she analyzes and evaluates such contents, that is, separates facts from fiction, opinion from evidence, and really understands the purpose for which the contents were constructed and presented. Finally, the consumer is able to understand the sender's message from the sender's perspective and, then, pass his or her judgment on the message, thus responding to it with a degree of literacy.

Media literacy presupposes a two-dimensional ethical responsibility—that of both the source and the receiver of mass communication. Because media messages have political, class, and ideological orientations, the responsibility for critical performance lies with both the producer and consumer of such messages. There is 100% responsibility on both sides and this is referred to as the 200% responsibility of the effects of persuasive messages through the media in society. Becoming media literate takes motivation and knowledge acquisition and, this will take the following articulated processes.

There are foundational principles that scholars have identified to aid media literacy (Masterman (1985); Aufterheide (1992); Kubey (1997); Hobbes, Worsnop). These different ideas are summarized by Turow (2003) as follows as media principles:

Media Principle 1. **Media materials are constructed.**

When media practitioners present their ideas via the media, they are presenting ideas that have been formulated and produced within their cultural, ideological, and philosophical biases. The contents are constructed and, therefore, are not real in the pure sense. Actually nothing can be considered to be pure in the real sense. Even a raw footage of a documentary film is constructed in a biased way because the producer chooses to show certain images at the expense of others. What about the news? The media present to their viewers what they (the media) identify as news. Not only that, of all the happenings in the world, the media do choose to pay attention to some based on their "informed perspectives" at the expense of other events that may be considered important by other media practitioners. So, the media contents that you are exposed to are human constructions that reflect a culture, a philosophy, and an ideology.

Media Principle 2. **Media materials are created and distributed within a commercial environment.**

As a cultural production that follows cultural software or scripts, media contents are created to meet certain needs in society to the extent they provide a good return on the investments if the consumers identify with and use such contents. Media organizations are business organizations that are concerned with return on investment and efficient use of resources. A media producer is, therefore, primarily driven to produce contents that have mass appeal even if they appeal to the base instincts of man! The need to sell advertising at the highest rate to pay for programs trumps any other, but ethical considerations.

Media Principle 3. **Media materials are created and distributed within a political environment**.

The political philosophy that governs the environment in which media contents are produced and consumed influences the nature of the contents and the patterns of their consumption. Political environment suggests prevailing ideologies that produce the rules, regulations, and laws that govern the process of mass communication. As we learn in subsequent pages, there are different ideological orientations that govern the practice of mass communication in the different geo-political regions of the world. These orientations include the authoritarian press policy, libertarian, social responsibility, communist, etc.

Media Principle 4. **Mass media present their ideas within the primary genres of entertainment, news, information, education, and advertising**.

Different media present contents in different formats that we can easily recognize. A political speech on radio is different from such on television and, even the internet. What government media in Iran or North Korea consider as entertainment would be viewed as "sergeant drills" in the United States or United Kingdom. News from the national television authority of Nigeria is viewed differently from news from 'Channels Television,' a privately-owned medium in Nigeria. In all, the media present the world to the consumers in capsules identified differently as news, entertainment, advertising, information, or education.

Media Principle 5. **People are active recipients of media messages**.

Media consumers are not considered blank slates who readily and willingly accept 'hook line and sinker' what the media present to them. Every consumer of media contents operates according to the psychological principles of selective exposure, attention, and retention. No one can be forced to consume any media content. Even if choices are not available, ultimately, the decision to listen or not, or to view or not, rests with the consumer. Beyond this, people bring their different biases, be it ideological, economic or sociological to the process of media content consumption. They may react positively or negatively or be indifferent to some media contents. Though people are active consumers of media contents, we must recognize that media influence is ultimately irresistible in society because, invariably what we choose to react positively or otherwise to, is what the media choose to expose us to. The media, therefore, have the power not to dictate how we think, but what we think about and that is a tremendous power, indeed. This is the phenomenon that media scholars refer to as the **agenda setting function of the media**.

Media Principle 6. **Media representations play a role in the way society understands its reality.**

We now live in a media-saturated world in which there is a blurring of what media present as real and society's sense of reality. Media presentations are the constructed realities that ultimately help to reflect or affect society. Much of the cultural teachings of today's societies are received via the media and, as such, media as agents of socialization present society with visions of itself and how to react to such visions.

The foregoing six media principles can form the basis for media literacy skills such that any literate media consumer can be thought of as having the skills to be aware of, understand, detect, and partake of media messages as an educated consumer. To summarize, let us look at the six attributes (Turow, 2003) of a media literate person.

Attributes of a Media Literate Person

A media literate person is :

- Knowledgeable about the influences that guide media organizations
- Up-to-date on political issues relating to the media
- Sensitive to ways of seeing media content as a means of learning about culture
- Knowledgeable about scholarship regarding media effects
- Sensitive to the ethical dimensions of media activities
- Able to enjoy media materials in a sophisticated manner

In identifying the guidelines for engaging the mass media, Wood (2011) writes that consumers should develop media literacy and respond actively to the media. In developing media literacy, Wood identifies the following precepts: realistically assess media's influence, become aware of patterns in the media, actively interrogate media messages, expose yourself to a range of media sources, and focus on your motivations for engaging the media.

In assessing media's influence one should be mindful of the two extreme views of the media's influence on society. One position is that mass communication determines individual attitudes and social perspectives, while the second perspective is that mass communication does not affect us at all. This is the **affect/reflect** idea discussed in the previous pages and to which we must assume that the reality of the matter is somewhere in the middle of the two extreme positions.

The media contents are packaged in predetermined patterns, knowledge of which would make an observer a critically minded one. Stories follow certain patterns and so do the news, information and other genres in the media. The news follows the inverted pyramid style with the lead sentence capturing the most important or a combination of the Who, What, When, Where, Why, and How? (The 5Ws & H Pattern). Movies have major and supporting characters and the lead actors usually triumph as a hero or villain. On the other hand, most entertainment pieces almost always include conflict, love, and sex.

To actively interrogate media messages, especially news, Woods states that it is important to ask the following questions:

- Why is the story getting so much attention?
- Whose interests are served, and whose are muted?

- What are the sources of statistics and other forms of evidence?
- Are the sources current?
- Do the sources have any interest in taking a specific position?
- What's the hook for the story, and what alternative hooks might have been used?
- Are stories balanced so that a range of viewpoints are given voice?
- How are different people and viewpoints framed by gatekeepers such as reporters, photographers, and experts?

In exposing oneself to multiple media sources, the term "mindful exposures' is key (Potter, 2009).This means that one should actively participate in the mass communication as a listener, reader, or viewer. The opposite is to sit there and absorb, without any reflection, the contents one is exposed to. This would be referred to as 'mindless exposure and consumption.' It is always advantageous to be exposed to multiple sources as well as varied opinions in order to discern the tilts in perspectives and to form one's opinions from the different perspectives rather than to accept without critical reasoning the opinions of and images presented from one media outlet.

The reasons for consuming media contents are varied and one should make a conscious effort to match one's situation—emotional, physical, and the like with the content exposed to. Some contents build up while others tear down and some increase awareness and others dumb down the intellectual experience. The point is that you should know when to watch a movie about 'breaking-up' and when to watch a comic relief or news.

When we participate actively in the mass communication process, especially as consumers, we influence and improve the practice. It is acceptable to protest obscenity in the media, or indecent publications; it is equally appropriate to identify stereotypes and abuse of all kinds. Rush Limbaugh, a syndicated radio talk show host in the U.S. found out that calling someone names unjustifiably is unethical and can result in huge financial loss. After Rush, a conservative commentator called a female, Ms. Sandra Fluke, of prestigious Georgetown University, a whore, after she testified in Congress about the rights of women to contraception, the inflammation resulted not only in massive and immediate condemnation of the commentator, but also in advertisers pulling out of the show with huge financial consequences to the show and its employees.

Georgetown University law student and activist Sandra Fluke (c.) speaks to co-hosts
Joy Behar (l.) and Sherri Shephered during an appearance o the daytime talk show, 'The View.'
Fluke talked about conservative radio host Rush Limbaugh, who insulted her on his radio program.
LouRocco/ABC/AP.

Table 18.1/Stages in the Development of Media Literacy

Adapted from: Wood, Julia T. (2011). *Communication Mosaics*: An introduction to the field of communication (6th Ed.). Boston, MA: Wadsworth Cengage Learning.

6 Months	3 Years	4 Years	7-8 Years	Throughout Life
Children pay attention to television.	Children engage in exploratory viewing.	Children search for preferred viewing.	Children make clear distinctions between ads and programs.	People who commit to media literacy learn to recognize puffery, hooks, and other devices for directing their attention and behavior.
	Children establish preferred patterns of viewing.	Children develop a viewing agenda.		
	Children do not distinguish between programs and ads.	Children's attention is held by a story line.	Children become skeptical of ads for products with which they are familiar; they are less skeptical of ads for products they haven't tried or don't own.	People who commit to media literacy learn to use media in sophisticated ways to meet their needs and to compensate for media bias and techniques.
		Children begin to distinguish between ads and programs.		
		Children do not realize that ads seek profit.		

Ownership and Press Theories

The societies in which mass media outlets operate dictate the frameworks—legal, ethical, socio-cultural, that guide their performance. Scholars have examined the different socio-political conditions in which different forms of mass communication take place and have classified such into six categories generally referred to as the normative theories of the press. Note that the term 'press' is used generically to refer to mass communication operations which include radio, television, newspapers and other newer forms of mass communication delivery systems such as the internet. The word normative refers to prescribed standards under which something ought to operate and to which an action and its actor must subscribe. There are guidelines to which the media ought to adhere as institutions of the societies in which they operate. This marks the link between the practice of mass communication and societal values, expectations, and performance.

The classification of the different media practices under the different political terrains in which they operate is an obvious artificial construct, but caution must be applied in order not to sweepingly brush all forms of media operations, even under a particular theory of the press, with the same monolithic stroke. Generally, though, we can, for obvious political ideologies, assume the commonness of expectation and performance of different media organizations in the six ideological zones of the world, which correspondingly produce the different normative theories of the press. The traditions, as they are often referred, are not static, especially in the face of the political restructuring that has taken place in many parts of the world in recent times. For example the Soviet Union is now defunct, and shifts in political and economic ideologies are sweeping the Arab world, South America, Africa and, even China.

Authoritarian Media Paradigm/Theory

Under the authoritarian media development paradigm, the State, religious organizations and other powers in society had the power to control the production and distribution of the means of mass education and communication. The available means of mass communication in the era before the movable-type printing press were books and manuscripts. In those early years the media were subject to the control of the State and/or ruler and any attempt to be independent would be deemed as subversion and may end up in the charge of treasonable felony. The ultimate control comes from the top and trickles down to agents of the State and /or the ruler, who determines what is good for the State and otherwise.

The authoritarian model of the media was the original form of relationship between the press, State, and the people. Historically, this is described as consistent with classical Greek, Roman and Chinese as well as medieval European and Middle Eastern concepts of the proper relationship between the government and the governed peoples. Usually, the media are privately owned, but the practitioners are subject to State licensure and control. The function of the press is to collect and disseminate information that is in the interest of the State. Adversarial press practice is an act in opposition to the State and the authority and ruler, as determined by agents of State or ruler. Such an act is usually met with censorship or proscription.

The authoritarian model is present, though with varying degrees of State controls, in Africa, parts of Europe, Central Asia Latin America, and the Middle East. The other different media development practices are off-shoots of this initial authoritarian model of the press.

The Communist Model

This used to be in operation in the old Soviet Union, but now only exists in Cuba and North Korea. An extension of the Authoritarian model, the communist media philosophy is that of total control by the communist party that in turn dominates the politics of the people under its sphere. The media practitioners—reporters, editors, managers, publishers, etc., are employed by the party of power. The higher echelons of the communist party are not to be criticized by these practitioners and they are precluded from ever criticizing the communist ideology.

Sanctions against practitioners who violate the rule of communist media engagement are discipline by the party and loss of employment. Also, an irate practitioner can cause a media outlet to be censored and possibly shut down. The communist media theory assures that the media and their practitioners are an extension of the State and cannot deviate from the party prescribed guidelines for their operation.

Development Media Theory

The media in many of the developing nations of the world are seen as agents of development—collaborating with the government to foster political, social, cultural, and economic emancipation of the people. This is yet another variation to the authoritarian paradigm of the press. The media in this case may be publicly owned, as it is usually the case, but could also be privately owned. A prime example is media ownership experience in Nigeria where the government owns and controls the NTA (Nigerian Television Authority) which is a national agency that acts almost like a government parastatal and a mouthpiece of the government and the political party in power in the country. At one-time the government owned a prime national newspaper called the *Daily Times,* and the network radio under the aegis of the Nigerian Broadcasting Service. In addition, States and Regions in the country also owned radio, television, and newspapers. Now, there is private ownership of radio, television, newspapers, and magazines in the country.

The media market in Nigeria is exploding with a number of private individuals and organizations clamoring to set up media outlets. Even with preponderant private media ownership, often, there is government pressure on journalists' freedom to report news without fair and favor. This occurs usually when there is criticism of the government or the ruling party in the media. Also, individuals who are highly placed in government may influence the police to censor and censure practicing journalists both in print and electronic media.

This theory can be considered a hybrid because it is partly authoritarian and partly democratic; equally, it is partly privately and publicly owned. There is freedom of the press to some degree, but there is always the threat of censorship.

Sometimes, however, the media play a revolutionary role in society and in many of the developing nations, the media have fanned embers of discontent among the citizenry to the extent of championing a revolution, a revolt against totalitarianism and oppression and the establishment of emergent democratic governments.

The Libertarian Paradigm/Theory

Reflective of the practice in many Western European countries, United States and Canada, the libertarian orientation of the press presupposes that citizens should be free to have access to, report on, and consume media contents that they desire. The underlying assumption here is that the individual is sufficiently well-informed and have the ability to determine in the **free market of information** to make appropriate decisions through responsible choices. Rather than vest the ultimate power in society of the government and its agents, the libertarian philosophy sees the citizens as the ultimate potentates in society. Another prime assumption of this paradigm is that the media, often called the fourth estate of the realm, are empowered to pursue and report the truth which is supposedly not subject to economic, political, and social structural encumbrances. Beyond Western Europe and North America, other areas we could find media operating under this philosophy will include Australia, parts of Middle East and Eastern and Southern Asian countries.

The Western Model

This is the model that operates in the democracies of North America, Western Europe and Japan. Essential distinguishing elements of this model of the press are that press freedom is guaranteed in the constitution and the media are privately owned and, enjoy a great deal of freedom from government control.

The constitutional guarantee of freedom of the press encompasses the belief that they are charged with the responsibility of protecting individual liberties and freedoms, and are to act as watchdog of government activities in order to protect the citizenry from oppression, misinformation, and misrule. The practice of the free press of the Western world is advantageous to media practitioners in other countries as well because it serves as the ideal to which many practitioners in these countries aspire. In the face of global communication access, contents of the free press permeate boundaries of oppression and totalitarianism, to inform people whose governments choose to suppress, and who have no recourse against the government short of an outright revolution as occurred during the Arab Spring of 2010 to 2011. Again, advantageous to the rest of the world as well as the West are the surveillance and news production activities of the international press agencies such as United Press International (UPI), Associated Press (AP), Agence-France -Presse (AFP), and the British, Reuters.

The Western model has been criticized as being over commercialized, sensational, and geared toward entertainment. Of consequence, also, is the power of concentrated ownership on the content, orientations, and responsibility of the press. There are certainly anti-trust issues when newspapers, magazines, television stations, and publishing houses are owned by a few oligopolies.

Social Responsibility Theory

Another off-shoot of the libertarian paradigm, this idea assumes limited governmental control of the media, but a reliance on self-regulation of media practices by the owners and the practitioners who are guided by their professional ethics and expected social responsibility, as well as an obligatory act of fairness in the pursuit of social needs and interests. The social responsibility philosophy assumes that the owners and practitioners of the media, under the directive of their ethical standards would act in the public interest. This philosophy operates to some extent in the United Kingdom and United States and Canada.

The Democratic-participant Media Theory

As a response to the over commercialization of the media, and the dominance of the major media by private, business monopolies, rose the alternative view of democratic-participant, that is, 'media for all and by all' philosophy. According to McQuail (1994, p.131), "the theory supports the right to relevant local information, the right to answer back and the right to use the new means of communication for interaction and social action in small-scale settings of community, interest group or subculture." Further expatiating, he comments that "both theory and technology have challenged the necessity for and desirability of uniform, centralized, high-cost, commercialized professionalized or state-controlled media. In their place should be encouraged multiple, small-scale, local, and non-institutional, committed media which link senders to receivers and also favor horizontal patterns of interaction."

With this criticism of the dominant media practice, it is understood why many alternative, albeit, local media have sprung up in many countries of the world, from developing nations to the democracies of the West. Such responses have manifested in community radio, community newspapers, community cable systems, free-access media, community utility media channels, and media designed to serve ethnic minorities including women and children as well as rural people. The outcome is an indictment of the centralized and professionalized media which engage in top-to-down communication and which pays minimal attention to the genuine concerns of the local and fragments of society.

'Social responsibility' has been criticized as been tethered to the dictates of the market while 'free press' has been dominated by the forces of capitalism; on the other hand, bureaucracy and legalism have undermined responsible ethical performance. The 'mass society' has been hijacked as a mining field of commercial and political opportunities and thus, it has alienated and disenfranchised many. To label this model 'democratic and participatory' is to acquiesce that the so-called free and socially responsible press, as long as they are centrally manipulated, cannot attempt to democratize, by means of participation, the means of communication between the senders and receivers in society.

No Press Is Totally Free!

There is no place in the world where the media are given unfettered reign; there is always one form of control or restraint on the practice of information gathering, production, and dissemination. From the authoritarian to the libertarian media theories, there are controls such as **censorship** and **outright banning** of the press. There are **legal controls** in terms of laws for **registration or licensure** of media business and **laws** that protect the citizenry against unscrupulous practice and illegal communication, which are actionable and punishable by law. **Ethical responsibilities** are imposed on media practitioners to be fair to all and not to present incomplete, biased information and not to have hidden agendas. Economic sanction is primarily loss of revenue or income. If a practitioner, who is an employee, promotes **ethical practice** above the desires of the publishers, the conflict will leave only one person looking for a job and it will not be the media owner. In many countries of the world, political office holders and highly influential and even not-so influential people, often seek to influence the contents of the media that pertains to them. Good image is what everyone is supposedly seeking and some resort to **bribing** media practitioners to curry their favor through financial inducements. Then there are organizations whose ideas are not represented as they expect by the media. The result is to withhold patronage in advertising and other revenues to the media house. Most media organizations are businesses that are concerned with their **bottom-line**. And if customers or potential customers threaten to withdraw their **advertising money**, a media house is pressured to tow the line.

Governments and controlling powers in society can censor the press by arresting journalists and trying them for sedition or, even, treason. **Repression** is a form of media control that threatens the individual freedom of practitioners, or that may cause a practitioner to fear for his or her life. And if all fails, the government and people who wish to control the media may choose to be secretive and preclude news practitioners and others from having access to pertinent information. **Official media** are also available to represent an alternate view which may be falsehood to counter the views of the 'free' press.

The press and the general media are accorded degrees of freedom in society. The extent to which the press is free is the degree to which the society views and protects individual liberties, rights, and the duty to keep a vigilant eye on those who are empowered to run the affairs of State. The normative theories are, therefore, relative to the social expectations and temperament of those who have the power to establish the type of governance philosophy they desire. But, for the most part, it is ultimately the people who drive the type of political, albeit press philosophy that their country adopts.

Mass Communication Theories

Theories attempt to explain and predict phenomena. The predictive and explanatory powers of theories differ and we must accept that social theorizing is fraught with normative issues that may make alternative explanations seemingly valid. The reality that media are an integral part of society and are subject to values and ideological frameworks of the societies in which they exist as embedded elements, makes theorizing about them multifaceted. The theories applicable to the study of mass communication include four types of theories identified by McQuail (1987) as social scientific, normative, practical or working, and commonsense (direct from experience) theories. Throughout this section, especially in explaining the functions and practices of the media, references will be made to these different types of theories.

The Uses, Gratification, and Effects of Mass Media

Mass communication and mass media have become an integral part of society to the extent that we hardly can do without them. Those that were born in the age of mass media saturation in society cannot imagine life without radio, television, newspapers, and the like, especially the internet. The mass media of communication in many cases have become social partners that many cannot live without. Indeed, we all put the mass media to various uses and studies have confirmed that individuals adapt their use of mass media to their own particular needs (Katz, et al, 1974).

How the mass audience or individuals in society use, seek gratification from, and are affected by media messages has been a preoccupation of researchers over the years. The focus is due to the usefulness of such knowledge to media practitioners, advertisers, and governments who may find the information derived useful in social planning, media message sourcing and dissemination, advertising and marketing, as well as political behavior of voting in democratic elections.

Turow (2003) identifies four broad categories of how people use the media and they are **enjoyment, companionship, surveillance, and interpretation.** To this list we should add the use of mass media for *persuasive purpose.*

Persuasion: Individuals may choose to encourage media coverage of personal, social, and professional events in order to garner visibility and to create an air of credibility for oneself and one's ideas and ventures. Corporate entities as well as individuals advertise products, commemorate events such as births, deaths, awards, and others for self, idea, or product promotion. Through the different mass media technologies, we are able to reach large numbers of people at the same time, and to present contents to them that are designed to influence their attitudes, values, and behavior. The opportunity to buy space and time in the media for personal or corporate use presents a unique opportunity to those who have access to these media to shape a media community's social reality to their advantage. In this case, the media have become agents for deliberate social change, for ill or for good in society.

Enjoyment: The human senses crave that which is pleasing and enjoyable and the media bring direct and precarious experiences to our senses that sedate us to a state of psychological escape we humans desire periodically, away from the drudgery of life and the mundane. Put in Turow's (2003) words, "the desire for enjoyment, or personal pleasure, is a basic human urge." People enjoy watching television programs, either individually or with others; they spend considerable amount of money purchasing home videos and going to the movies; they read books that captivate and transport them to places of surreal experiences. Enjoying media contents also comes with an important by-product which is termed **Social currency**. One's knowledge of what's going on in the media world and using it as the basis (contents of discussion) for interacting with others makes these contents the currency of your social exchange with others. If one is not exposed to the same media content and is unable to socially connect with others on the basis of that information, there is a sense of disconnect from current social reality. If you're not in the know, you'll feel like an outsider. The fact is that the media contents that a community listens to, watches, and reads, create a community of consciousness to which these members belong. And the commonality among the community is the knowledge of and ability to discuss such common experiences—using common media parlance, discussing media events, and commenting on the actions of media characters. The reality is that the contents of many office social interactions are stories of new books read, movies watched, and sitcoms or sporting events watched on television.

Companionship: Societies are becoming increasingly modernized and, with such advancement, comes increased opportunities that afford people to live independent of others. Traditional communal practices are being replaced with "modern" individualistic living that lends itself to being isolated and disconnected. Mass media have become the void fillers in the lives of many people; they become the other voice, the hand person, or the other set of eyes in the home. Sometimes the media contents comfort the lonely, they babysit for the working parents and, they massage the ego of the social hermit. Many social isolates feel connected to society by watching sporting events on television, watching the evening news, or praying with a televangelist. Often, consumers of mass media contents feel a sense of personal connections with celebrities they see on television, in the movies or read about in the magazines.

The term **parasocial interaction** has been used to describe the psychological relationship that develops between celebrities and their media user admirers. This relationship between media users and the celebrities they admire in the media can become psychologically exaggerated to the extent that it may lead to antisocial behavior on the part of the media consumers. Many celebrities have resorted to having bodyguards and having limited their public appearances because of the excessive, untoward bonding gestures of their admirers. In all, the media have become a useful friend and companion to many that are sick in the hospitals, to lonely nursing home residents, and teacher to school kids and an important babysitter in the home.

Surveillance: The word surveillance is similar to close watch, inspection, and examination. **We have the need to become aware of and examine what is going on around us and, we put the media to use to fulfill the desire to learn about what is going on in the world of other humans and in the world that we all live in.** Every morning when we wake up, we instinctively want to know what has happened in our immediate and distant worlds overnight while we were asleep. Surveillance of the environment can be done both consciously and unconsciously and it may be limited to our immediate environment or extended to cover faraway places. The news channels on radio and television and the newspapers thrive because of the need we humans have to scan our world, to be in the know, and not to live in ignorance.

Interpretation: This is using the media to find out why things are happening –who or what is the cause—and what to do about them (Turow, 2003). For many people it is not enough just to know what is happening and that is why they must go beyond that to understand why things are the way they are and who can be identified to be involved with them and the reasons behind them. Reading straight news in the papers or watching them on television may not give us the background information needed on an event and as a remedy, we read news commentaries, feature stories and editorials concerning the event. Specialized magazines, whether on television or in print, enjoy patronage because of their analysis and interpretation focus.

Having exposed ourselves to various interpretations in the media, we may choose to agree or disagree or we may value a source more than the other for their interpretation of events and issues. This introduces the issue of **source credibility** to the study of mass communication. The degree to which a source is believable and to which we agree with its motives will influence how reliably we view the source. To summarize the conclusion of Grossberg, et al, the credibility people assign to the positions that mass media take depends on the extent to which the individuals agree with the values they find in that content. Many media outlets allow for the representations of alternate or contrasting views in the content interpretation in order to cater to people with differing ideologies who may not subscribe to a particular outlet because of his or her ideology. For example, FOX News channel in the United States is identified as a conservative outlet that caters to the Republicans, whereas MSNBC is considered a liberal channel that espouses the ideals of the Democratic Party. In Nigeria, the NTA is considered government–oriented and conservative, while Channels, Galaxy, and other privately owned TV outlets can be considered to be more liberal.

The Spiral of Silence

This theory acknowledges the influence of the media on public opinions held in society. Confirming that the media do not adequately explain news events to the public, but present a limited view of reality and that the most potent of the media in this case is television, Noelle-Neumann (1984, 1993) explains that this limiting influence of the media stems from three major characteristics: **ubiquity, cumulativeness,** and **consonance**. Ubiquity suggests that the media have overwhelming presence in society and that it is not easy to escape their reach and influence. Cumulativeness suggests that the media messages are repeated over time across several media to the extent that they have a joint influence in building up common frames of references for the people. Consonance suggests agreement or similarities of beliefs, attitudes, and values held by the media. The media arrive at consonance when they confirm their own thoughts and opinions, making it look as if they came from the public. According West and Turner (2007), the characteristics of ubiquity, cumulativeness, and consonance, allow for majority opinions to be heard, while those in the minority who wish to avoid isolation—from the majority—will remain silent.

The essence of the spiral of silence theory is that people who perceive or believe they hold a minority opinion on a public issue will choose to remain in the background where their communication will be unheard or constrained; and those who perceive or believe that they hold majority opinion will be more encouraged to speak. The spiral idea comes from the nature of the media to focus on and orchestrate majority opinions at the expense of minority opinions, thereby perpetuating the dominance of perceived majority views and diminishing the importance of perceived minority opinions. By so doing, those who hold majority opinions will continue to espouse their ideas and the media will continue to give them prominence, at the expense of those who hold minority opinions, who will be less willingly to risk isolation by voicing that opinion. Consequently, the majority opinion holders **ascend** into prominence and dominance, while the minority opinion holders *descend* into a spiral of silence and irrelevance.

Is it possible that people can be wrong in judging popular or unpopular public opinion? The answer is yes because individual gauging of public opinion is a perceptual assessment and we know that perception is subject to error. There can be a misreading of public temperature on issues to the extent that members of the public would believe that they are in the minority. Noelle-Neumann (1993) uses the term **pluralistic ignorance** to describe this possible mistaken observation or distorted and inaccurate public opinion. This occurs because "people mix their own direct perceptions and the perceptions filtered through the eyes of the media into an indivisible whole that seems to derive from their own thoughts and experience."

Again, the media may also have a misreading of the popularity of perceptions regarding issues in society. We must not discount that media practitioners may have agendas they are pushing, thereby giving prominent treatment to certain opinions over others in society.

Like any theory, we can certainly take a critical look at the tenets of the idea of the spiral of silence and develop new thinking regarding them and possibly increase new understanding of how the media influence or affect society.

The major assumptions of the spiral of silence theory that we should examine are as follows:

- **Society threatens deviant individuals with isolation and fear of isolation is pervasive.**
- **The fear of isolation causes individuals to try to assess the climate of public opinions at all times.**
- **Public behavior is affected by public opinion assessment.**

Are the media all about glitz and glamour?

Do the Media Affect or Reflect Society?

The media are a part of society, and a rather significant part because of their nature and the roles they play in society. The media are a potent agent of socialization and their ability to reach mass, diverse, and widely dispersed audiences simultaneously makes them a great influence on the thinking and perceptions of these audiences. If influence starts at the level of exposure to certain influencing contents, then the mass media score high on the scale of exposing mass amounts of people to same cultural productions such as news, fictional movies, characters, and other mass media contents and representations.

At the heart of the study of media influence in society is the dichotomous **media affect/reflect perspectives**. The question is whether the media, in performing their functions of educating, informing, and entertaining society, do create contents/messages which affect society in measurable ways by projecting what is referred to as **media reality** to the mass audiences they reach, or that in performing their duties, the media only **reflect what already exists** in society. The opinion of Turow (2003) is telling when he states that "when mass media encourage huge numbers of people who are dispersed and unrelated to share the same materials, they are focusing people's attention on what it is culturally important to think about and to talk and argue with others about." The flip side of this statement is that what the media choose not to focus attention on does not become primed in the minds of the mass audience, rather the power of the media to choose or limit directs and frames the socio-cultural and political orientation of society.

Media Are 'All Powerful'

George Gerbner, a Hungarian-born, American media effects scholar at the Annenberg School of Communication, University of Pennsylvania, describes the influence of television in particular on the American society and posits that in significant ways, the media create shared ways of selecting and viewing events, by delivering to them "technologically produced and mediated message systems," thereby creating a common or uniform way of viewing and understanding the world. The media, by selecting dominant cultural images as relevant and important, are tacitly propagating the ideals of the dominant power in society. This process, Gerbner (1973) calls the **'cultivation of dominant image patterns'** in society. That is, the media tend to offer uniform and relatively consensual versions of social reality and their audiences are **'acculturated'** accordingly (McQuail, 1987). Gerbner claims that the media are a dominant force and thus have powerful effect over society—that is they are considered **framers of society**.

The **all-powerful media theory** has been challenged and alternative theories have emerged about the influence of the mass media on society. While some scholars have argued that the media do have limited effects on society, there is agreement that the media, though they may not tell us how to think, they indeed direct our attention to what to think about. Again, according to Joseph Turow (2003), the mass media present the ideas of the culture in three broad and related ways:

1. The mass media direct people's attention toward codes of acceptable behavior within the society and how to talk about them.
2. The mass media tell people what and who counts in their world and why.
3. The mass media help people to understand themselves and their connections with, or disconnections from, others.

As the word suggests, the media mediate; they are not just conduits for conveying contents, but as organizations they are part of society with an agenda, which they set and perform with discernible consequences.

Cultivation Theory

The nature of the mass media to focus on dominant image patterns in society and to offer predictable, mainstream ideas and images, is the foundation of the Cultivation Theory (Gerbner and Gross, 1972). That is, the media, in practice, "cultivate" predictable, dominant image patterns of society. According to McQuail (1987, p. 99), the media tend to offer uniform and relatively consensual versions of social reality and their audiences are "acculturated" accordingly. Gerbner (1998) predicts that because of the systemic nature of their message and consistencies over time, the media, especially TV, have powerful effects on people and, as such "mould" society. This is because the media create shared ways of selecting and viewing events, by packaging and delivering to the audience technologically mediated message systems.

Underlying media cultivation theory is the idea that patterned images (with the exclusion of other images) that audiences are repeatedly exposed to would influence their perceptions in particular ways. And according to West and Turner (2000), cultivation analysis focuses on the role of television in our lives and the long-term effects of exposure to TV on our perceptions of the world.

Cultivation analysis is, therefore, a theory that predicts and explains the long-term formation and shaping of perceptions, understanding, and beliefs about the world as a result of consumption of media messages. Gerbner (1999, p. ix) surmises that mass communication, especially TV cultivate certain beliefs about reality that are held in common by mass communication consumers. He further observes that "most of what we know or think we know, we have never personally experienced." And we know these things because of the stories we see and hear from the media. The media in this case are not only transmission means, but performs the rituals of presenting and representing shared beliefs and values.

There are real consequences of cultivation analysis on different classes of consumers of media messages. A distinction is made between heavy media users, that is, those who consume more television and other media messages than others, and light media users who consume less media contents. Such difference is found in the idea described as **mainstreaming,** which, according to West and Turner (2000, p. 413) "is the tendency for heavy viewers to perceive a similar culturally dominant reality to that pictured on the media, although this differs from actual reality." That is, collectively heavy media users perceive a common, uniform reality that differs from what is really is taking place in the real world.

Thus, a distinction between media and 'real' reality is made. For example, heavy media users who are exposed to crime reports in the media, tend to believe that there is more crime and violence out there than it really is. This is an interesting idea because it shows us that those who spend more time cultivating the ideas that the media cultivate may actually be subjecting themselves to an exaggerated reality or underrepresented reality. If you are a heavy media consumer and you are subjected to media over-reporting of inner city activities, you'll then tend to have some misperceptions of reality. One, you'll think that there are more people living in the inner cities than other areas; two, you would believe that those in the inner cities are more prone to violence as it is often reported in the mainstream media and; three, you would tend to assume that the world around you is more violent and dangerous than it really is. This is a part representation of the "**mean world index**" in cultivation studies.

There is a **cultivation differential,** between heavy and light users of the media, especially television. This is a term used to describe the differences, often represented in numerical value, between the study responses of these two classes of media consumers. And when one's lived reality mirrors that depicted in the media, this is described as **resonance**, that is, there is correlation between media reality and an individual's lived reality. A viewer of the Maury Povich Show would certainly be exposed to the use of DNA tests to prove paternity and infidelity of lovers. To think that this is a common practice in society is to believe a media reality. And to really believe and carry out DNA tests to prove the paternity of one's kids, regardless of suspicion of infidelity and, to think it normal to do this because this is what happens in reality in the world in which one lives, is an example of resonance, which Gerbner (1998: p.182) describes as a '**double dose**' of messages that 'resonate' and amplify cultivation.

Media Ecology---Marshall McLuhan

Marshall McLuhan, a one-time University of Toronto English professor, wrote *Understanding the Media: The Extensions of Man* (1964), a book which examined the relationships of media and culture and posits that media and technology should be examined from the context of their impact on society, especially how people process and share meaning through them, thus influencing the **symbolic landscape.** "The symbolic environment is the socially constructed, sensory world of meanings," (Griffin, 2012: p. 321). The nature of the medium of communication, in the view of McLuhan (1964) exerts greater impact on how people receive, process, and share symbolic meanings in society, much more than their contents. This thinking gave birth to the perspective of viewing the media/technology of communication as significant variables that alter the social, symbolic environment and the overall nature of society. This is the media ecology theory of Marshall McLuhan and its thesis is that "changes in technology alter the symbolic environment –the socially constructed, sensory world of meaning that in turn shapes our perceptions, experience, attitudes, and behavior" (Griffin: p. 321).

Students of communication, practitioners and many in society are familiar with the phrase: "The medium is the message." This is a shift in thinking that places greater premium on the media of communication, not as mere conduits for delivering messages, but as significant influences on the message. No longer are we to view the message and the medium separately— they are inextricably interwoven and the medium may play a more significant role in influencing the meaning socially constructed from the message/medium.

The relationship between content and medium can be likened to the contents of an egg—yolk and albumen, which co-exist inside a shell. Visual and auditory images—the yolk and the albumen—cannot be successfully delivered without the shell. This is a metaphor for how television works, whereby the nature of the medium influences the content such that without the medium, there will be no content! (See chapter 2). And as Griffin (2012: 321) elaborates, "we focus on the content and overlook the medium—even though content doesn't exist outside of the way it's mediated... Whether a TV show is about killer whales, current events, crime scene investigation, or discovering the next American pop star, the message is always television... It is the distinct experience of TV that alters the symbolic environment."

Media ecology, which is the "study of different personal and social environments, created by the use of different communication technologies," focuses on social and cultural change brought about by the different media environments (Griffin: p. 322). There are several such environments, and a multitude of other factors that may influence them. McLuhan advises that we focus on our everyday experience of technology—how it shapes us because we partake of it serially, and how it becomes a part or an extension of us.

Different media extend different senses and they build different consumption habits and patterns which may make certain stimuli preferred over the others. The nature of the medium, whether it extends one, two, or three senses, alters the degree of using that sense or senses in human sensory perception. The dominant sense a medium extends becomes the dominant sensory perception of its users. And in human history, different technologies have induced adaptation to the different senses they extended and the symbolic environments they created. This thesis led McLuhan to identify the different epochs in human history as eras of different, dominant communication technologies (See the evolution of mass communication).

Neil Postman (founder of the Media Ecology Program at New York University), a follower of McLuhan though agrees with the points of McLuhan on media ecology, and takes it further to include ethical analysis and implications of media created symbolic environments, questioning if a specific media environment is beneficial or destructive. This is his philosophical bent as he proclaims that "I don't see any point in studying the media unless one does so within a moral or ethical context," (Postman, 2000).

Introducing a new technology into society can be a double-edged sword—it can enhance and it can destroy. Therefore, Postman sees a need to strike a bargain between good and bad—a Faustian bargain which is a deal with the media devil. On one hand we cannot eradicate them and, on the other, we have to deal with the evil they portend. The debate about the good and bad of the media will continue in society.

Hot and Cool Media

The nature of the technologies of communication serves as the basis for McLuhan's (1964) dual classification of the media as **Hot** and **Cool.** These are descriptors borrowed from jazz music, a genre that dominated the music scene of the 60s and 70s in North America. Audience participation in the improvisation akin to some jazz renditions prompted McLuhan to label media that allow for and encourage audience participation and involvement as cool media. Cool media have low definition that demands active involvement from a viewer, listener, or reader," (West and Turner, 2007. P.470). Cool media are described as having low definition because not much information is provided through the medium, but much participation is required of the audience. Essentially, cool media stimulate high sensory involvement and imagination in the audience in the process of jointly creating social meaning. Visual or auditory codes are scant from which the receiver must decode and encode meaning. Because television stimulates participatory imagination in the audience who provides the mental closure to create whole and patterned meaning from the fragmented information it supplies, it is considered a cool medium.

Hot media are the opposite of cool media—they stimulate less imagination and require less participation of the audience in the process of deducing meaning from their codes. That is, they provide "high definition communication that demands little involvement from the audience," (West & Turner p.469). How would McLuhan classify the new Apple Ipad2 and T. Mobile's Smart phone?

Agenda-Setting Theory

Maxwell McCombs and Donald Shaw (1972) developed the agenda-setting theory of the media. In the debate about whether the media mould or reflect society, and whether they have limited effects on their audience, or are all powerful, the agenda-setting theory is on the all-powerful and mould side. The theory sets to establish that there is a relationship between media agenda and the public's agenda and what the public considers as important.

Agenda-setting of the media is identifying, by practice and pattern, what the media focus greater attention to in their contents. That is, what the newspapers, TV, radio, etc. consider salient and are favored in terms of length of stories, time allotted them, and their placement. **Agenda–setting also occurs among the audience members, otherwise referred to as public agenda. This is what stories, issues, ideas and events the public considers to be important,** especially when it comes to politics and governance.

The media agenda-setting hypothesis states that "the mass media have the ability to transfer the salience of issues on their news agenda to the public agenda," (Griffin, 2012, p.378). After experiencing that an issue of seemingly low importance, the 1972 break-in into the National Headquarters of the Democratic National Committee, was given repeated mention in the *Washington Post* and subsequently developed into the gigantic story labeled The Watergate Scandal and the eventual resignation of President Nixon in the Spring of 1974, Maxwell McCombs and Donald Shaw (1994: 4) posit that "the mass media have the ability to transfer the salience items on their news agenda to the public agenda."

The agenda-setting function of the media does not presuppose that the media have a deliberate ideology of influencing their audience in predetermined ways, but the authors of the theory confirm, however, that there is a patronizing relationship between the media and their audience, because the audience tend to judge as important what the media judge as important McCombs and Shaw (1974:28). This suggests that the media set the agenda for public discourse, as such, directing what we talk and think about. This is a portrait of a dominant media with greater influence on the audience and this runs counter to the presumption that with active audience, discriminating members, the media have limited effects on the audience (Lippmann, 1922).

Certainly telling people what to think may be a stretch, but in the words of Cohen (1963, p. 13), the press may not be successful much of the time in telling people what to think, but it is stunningly successful in telling its readers what to think about. And when it comes to media framing issues, they may, indeed, be influencing what we think about and how we think about it. **Framing is presenting a particular perceived reality or mindset as more important than others in interpreting events and issues to the public.** For instance, the media have lately been focusing much attention on the issue of same-sex marriage either in the context of marriage or participation in the military. The media framing has always been overwhelmingly in favor of, rather than being a neutral, uninterested, observer.

Can it be generalized that all audience members behave in the same manner when it comes to taking news and discussion lead from the media? No, some are more critically minded than others. As a matter of fact, McComb and Bell (1996) affirm that "people are not automatons waiting to be programmed by the news media." People are not equally influenced by the media. Those who are more susceptible to media influence are those who rely on the media to shape their thinking and are judged to **need media orientation**. Also referred to as **curiosity index, "this is a measure of the extent to which individuals' need for orientation motivate them to let the media shape their views,"** (Griffin, 2012, p. 380). The need for orientation depends on two factors: relevance and uncertainty. Relevance has to do with how the news or story connects with an individual. How much one knows about the issue about which one has to make decisions is termed **uncertainty**. According to the authors of the agenda-setting theory, the combination of uncertainty and curiosity equal **media susceptibility**.

But who sets the agenda for the media? Certainly media agenda are not miraculously set—they are set by some individuals. Some select practitioners of mass media do set the agenda for the media. The handful of practitioners such as editors, managing editors are the 'gatekeepers' or those who have the power to determine media content coverage. The news editors of the various media houses often meet to determine what to focus their attention on and these become the driving force of their agenda-setting function.

Scholars and practitioners in the media professions also acknowledge the influence of the executive and legislative arms of the government as agenda setters. Congress, politicians, and other officers at the state, town, and municipal levels influence media agenda. There is also the influence of the information subsidizers in society. These are public relations and media publicity agents who represent corporations by formulating press releases and video news releases (VNRs) of proprietary information, which the media often pass on as news and stories to the unsuspecting readers and viewers. Because they cost the media houses nothing to produce, as the cost is usually borne by corporate public relations, advocacy, and publicity budgets, and not the media houses directly, the term: **information subsidy** describes such corporate contents in the mass media.

Application of Mass Media to Advertising and Public Relations

The advent of mass communication gave birth to the new profession of press agentry and has enhanced the old professions of marketing, sales, and advertising. With mass media, it has now become possible to reach large numbers of people with the same message over periods of time. This has led to advertisers, propagandists, political operatives, and other entities wishing to reach these masses of people the opportunity to do so, especially for the purpose of informing, persuading, and entertaining them, all with the underlying motives of selling wares, influencing attitudes and opinions, and securing votes.

Two major professions that have spun out of the media technology-enabled mass communication are public relations and advertising. The lifeline of the media industry is the financial support of advertisers and media campaigners. These industries have a symbiotic relationship with media conglomerates and outlets because, while the media provide space and time to expose contents to the mass audience, the advertisers and PR professionals pay for the space and time to expose their persuasion messages to the mass audience, thus providing the funds for running the media industry. To understand how this works, Turow (2003: p.555) writes that "to get advertiser's money, mass media practitioners often choose to target audiences and to focus on topics that they believe will attract sponsors. As a result, how and why ad people decide to spend their money can affect which magazines survive, which kinds of music radio stations play, and which audiences and topics the creators of new cable networks decide to pursue."

Public Relations

Public relations is a practice or profession that means different things to many people. This is because the practice practically touches on every profession, practice, and calling that one can imagine. So, it is viewed from many different perspectives that, sometimes, making it fit a particular mold is difficult, if not impossible. Hence, because of the scope of the functions performed by public relations practitioners, people see it as something practically anyone can do, even without much training!

Any enterprise that involves and connects people, one way or another, has an element of public relations embedded in it. Call it relating to people to effect a mutual understanding regarding a desired change, or you look at it from the perspective of a corporation or organization reaching out to win customers and to maintain some level of satisfaction among them --this is people relations at the mass or public level. Therefore, it entails some elements of the practice of public relations and many feel that they are 'people persons,' thus claiming expertise in the field. The practice has not been fully understood by many, especially those who need it the most. Even those who practice it do not have a unifying definition for their practice.

PR, as it is sometimes referred, is thought of as 'spin,' that is, manipulating people and information to the advantage of somebody or something or event not deserving of it. It is seen as an unscrupulous practice that is economical with the truth and that is done at the disadvantage of the general public who is suckered into the PR spin. Nothing could be further from the truth about professional PR practice.

Defining Public Relations

Public Relations is a theory-based communication and business practice that relies on scientific, artistic, and practical methodologies of engineering consent, or adapting one entity to another in a symbol-based, symbiotic free market place of ideas and strategies, where responsible performance is paramount. We would come to a better understanding of the profession and practice of public relations after examining the different definitions offered by PR organizations, scholars and practitioners alike.

Edward Bernays, considered by many the father of modern public relations, offered to describe the functions of his PR consulting firm in 1923 as "*information given to the public, persuasion directed at the public to modify attitudes, and actions, and efforts to integrate attitudes and actions of an institution with its publics and of publics with those of that institution,*" (Bernays, 1961). This quotation confirms PR as a public function, a service of providing information to the public for the purpose of modifying mindsets and arriving at desired behavior. Also it is the service of scanning the environment, especially attitudes and predispositions of the public to the management, who must manage it for mutual satisfaction of both the public and the management. The PR practitioner is not only a unifier of perspectives through communication, but also an interpreter of trends both within and outside of the organization. Though the ideas expressed by Bernays are relevant even today, but it is one of many definitions and explanations of the profession of PR by its practitioners.

Media scholar, Joseph Turow, captures the essence of PR when he defines it as "the art or science of establishing and promoting a favorable relationship with the public through various methods and/or activities," (p: 538). The methods of public relations can be based in science or the arts, and the purpose is to maintain a favorable relationship with the public

Concerned about the myriads of definitions pervading the field of public relations, practitioners and scholars under the aegis of the Foundation for Public Relations Research Education, in 1975, orchestrated a search for a unified definition of the profession. 472 different definitions were analyzed by seventy-five participants, who came up with a somewhat universal definition of public relations as: ..."*a distinctive management function which helps to establish and maintain mutual lines of communications, understanding, acceptance, and cooperation between an organization and its publics; involves the management of problems or issues; helps management to keep informed on and responsive to public opinions; defines and emphasizes the responsibility of management to serve the public interest; helps management keep abreast of and effectively utilize change, serving as an early warning system to help anticipate trends; and uses research and sound and ethical communication techniques as its principal tools*," (Harlow, 1976, p.36). The first statement of this definition confirms PR as a management function—it starts with management who sets policies and approves programs of action as well as their funding. Good PR, therefore, starts at the management of an organization. Public relations involves, again, managed two-way communications that is responsive to both parties involved. Clearly we can glean from this definition the understanding that PR is not a reactionary action, but a strategized effort based on forecasting and anticipating trends through environmental scanning. PR actions are informed by theory and research and it is guided by ethical standards. Public relations is, therefore, based on responsible performance.

Lucien Matrat (1990, p.8), the creator of the profession's international code of ethics, opines that "*public relations, in the sense that we use the term, forms part of the strategy of management. Its function is two-fold: to respond to the expectations of those whose behavior judgments and opinions can influence the operation and development of an enterprise, and in turn to motivate them.... Establishing public relations policies means, first and foremost, harmonizing the interests of an enterprise with the interests of those on whom its growth depends. The next step is putting these policies into practice. This means developing a communication policy which can establish and maintain a relationship of mutual confidence with a firm's multiple publics.*" This definition brings to light the fact that PR is not practiced in a vacuum of policies, strategies and programs, but in an environment of careful planning based in research and measurable outcomes.

John Marston (1963), a communication professor, suggests a definition of public relations based on the functions of the practice. Each of the letters in the formula stands for a specific function, if well-articulated and executed would serve to encompass the practice. The functions include what is described as the **RACE** formula. R stands for research, A for action, C for communication, and E for evaluation. To integrate these functions with the management function of PR, the formula has been extended to include five parts by Professor Sheila Clough

Crifasi, and it is described as the ROSIE strategy where R still stands for research, O stands for objectives, S for strategies, I for implementation and E for evaluation.

The RACE formula is a mnemonic device that is useful to practitioners to conceptualize their PR ideas and programs. Any PR activity must be predated by research because it is only when one knows what obtains out there, be it positive or negative, that a program of action can be developed to resolve or promote it. Research is fundamental and so is Action. Once a problem is identified, the action plan to attach it is next. A good plan must be as exhaustive as the problem is exhaustive. Action by itself is incomplete; it must be communicated to the desired publics for consumption and prescribed outcomes. This is where message and media strategies are developed to match the direction and scope and aim of the campaign. In order to effectively identify the contributions of PR efforts to the management bottom line or return on investment, measurement of the effectiveness of PR programs is essential and that is why E stands for evaluation. You should note that evaluation starts at the onset of a PR program---from research, to action and to communication. At every step and stage of the PR program, evaluation of efforts and alternatives are considered.

The ROSIE formula introduces Objectives, Strategies, and Implementation into the RACE formula. This is in acknowledgment of management practice whereby objectives are clearly stated in measurable terms and strategies delineated before careful implementation. This ensures focus, measurement, accountability, and effectiveness of PR programs and their contribution to the bottom line of the organization.

The founder of *Public Relations News*, Dennis Grisworld, captures the managerial essence of public relations in his often quoted definition which is: *"the management function which evaluates public attitudes, identifies the policies and procedures of an individual or an organization with the public interest, and plans and executes a program of action to earn public understanding and acceptance."*

The different definitions of public relations suggest that it is a concerted two-way communication between an organization or an entity and its various publics. The organization must understand the worlds of their publics and so should the publics made aware of organizational goals, policies, and actions. The PR practitioner becomes the interpreter of the public to the management of an organization and the different publics to the organization.

Seitel (1998, p. 8) confirms that "public relations practitioners are interpreters. On one hand, they must interpret the philosophies, policies, programs, and practices of their management to the public; on the other hand, they must convey the attitudes of the public to their management." As it has been noted, the active and responsive practitioner must be proactive in gaining understanding, acceptance, and induce action of the publics in regard of management programs. Often, the job of the practitioners starts with educating the management about the functions of PR and they achieve this by understanding the functions of management and the place of strategic public relations in it.

The PR Practitioner as an Interpreter is Sandwiched between the Organization and the Larger Society

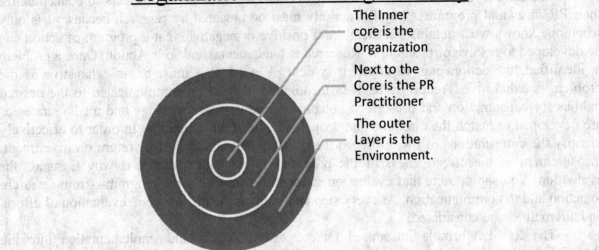

The Inner core is the Organization

Next to the Core is the PR Practitioner

The outer Layer is the Environment.

The concentric circles illustrate the position of the PR practitioner as an interpreter of both the organization and the general public to each other. This is why the practitioner is sandwiched between the organization and the larger society in which the organization and its different publics exist. It is worth noting that the context of both the practitioner and the organization is the same larger society---so, ultimately, the larger good of society is the goal of public relations.

According to Newsom et al (1996) the functions and role of public relations practice can be understood by identifying the practice's ten basic principles. The principles they identified are paraphrased as follows:

1. Public relations deals with reality and not false fronts…Meaning PR deals with facts and not fiction.
2. Public relations is a service-oriented profession in which public interest, not personal reward should be the primary consideration.
3. Public relations practitioners must have the guts to say no to a client or to refuse a deceptive program.
4. Because the public relations practitioner reaches many publics through the mass media, which are the public channels of communication, the integrity of these channels must be preserved.
5. Because PR practitioners are in the middle between an organization and its publics, they must be effective communicators—conveying information back and forth until understanding is reached. This is an ombudsman/woman position.
6. To expedite two-way communication and to be responsible communicators, public relations practitioners must use scientific public opinion research extensively.
7. To understand what their publics are saying and to reach them effectively, public relations practitioners must employ social sciences—psychology, sociology, social psychology, public opinion, communication study and semantics. (This confirms that intuition is not enough as the foundation for PR programs).
8. Because a lot of people do PR research, the PR person must adapt the work of other, related disciplines, including learning theory and other psychological theories, political science,

economics, history. The PR field requires multidisciplinary applications.
9. Public relations practitioners are obliged to explain problems to the public before these problems become crises. (PR practitioners should alert and advise, so people won't be taken by surprise).
10. A public relations practitioner should be measured by only one standard: ethical performance. (A PR practitioner is only as good as the reputation he or she deserves.)

The Publics of Public Relations

A public is an aggregate of people (sometimes one person) who, individually or collectively, exert attitudinal or behavioral influence on the mission of an organization. The action or inaction of the members of a given public of an organization may cause the organization to succeed or fail. Therefore, it is important to identify the different publics with which an organization does business, and to communicate effectively to satisfy their different needs.

Publics include an organization's neighbors, customers, employees, competitors and government regulators… Publics and organizations have consequences for each other (Newsom, et al, 1996). So, whatever an organization does has consequences beyond the organization, and what the different publics do affect the organization one way or the other. Imagine all of the different publics of a College or University. There are internal and external publics. The internal publics either work or are students of the University. Such publics include professors, administrators, students, counselors, custodial workers, etc. The external publics of a university include the department of education, potential students and their parents, the alumni association, different accreditation agencies, media, etc. If the student population has a negative view of the university, and the opinion abates, soon the enrollment numbers will start to drop and the university may find it challenging to recruit students who are the life blood of any educational institution.

A multinational corporation has many local and international publics some of which are proponents, others opponents; some primary and others marginal. The following is a list of 20 different publics of a multinational corporation (Seitel, 1998):

Publics of a Multinational Corporation

Customers; federal, state, local legislators; regulatory authorities; academic community; labor unions; board of directors; clerical employees; employee families; managers/supervisors; press; stockholders; investment community; competitors; suppliers; special interest groups; community neighbors; international community; banks and insurers; trade associations; dealers/distributors.

The PR practitioner within a multinational corporations such the one with the identified publics above, should be a professional communicator who plans, executes, and evaluates programs of action designed to effectively manage the potentials of the different publics of the corporation to the advantage of both.

PR and Related Activities

The activities of PR that the practitioner engages in directly or indirectly are the following: press agentry, promotion, publicity, public affairs, research, graphics, advertising, marketing, financial relations, corporate relations, crisis management, and consumer relations. The tools of public relations include: the news or press release, newsletter, journal, handbill, brochure (traditional or electronic), annual report, fact sheets, speeches, meetings/personal contact, feature articles, the internet, Video/Audio News Release (VNR/ANR), billboards, lobbying, and Press conference.

The Education of a Professional PR practitioner

To effectively perform the duties of a seasoned practitioner, the education needs touch on three important areas.

The first is knowledge of the theory and practice of public relations. This will include understanding what PR is, its focus and characteristics. Of advantage is the knowledge of the evolution of the practice, the way it used to be practiced, and the evolution that has taken place to propel the profession into the digital era. Once this is acquired, the practitioner needs to be grounded in communication theories, principles, and practice.

The second level of educational preparation will include such courses as theory and practice of communication, writing for mass media, editing, graphics of communication, media analysis, research, media law and ethics, and advertising. Beyond communication theory courses, there should be familiarity with business and managerial courses, which would place the practitioners at the managerial level, at par with their counterparts from other departments who are business or management majors.

The third area of necessary expertise, therefore, includes a myriad of subjects that the practitioner must have working knowledge of, even if some of the work are contracted out to experts. As a manager, the PR executive should be familiar with subject areas such as: business administration, economics, political science, government organizations, public administration, management science, personnel management, humanities, social services, languages, statistics, organization structure and behavior.

Advertising

"Advertising is the activity of explicitly paying for media space or time in order to direct favorable attention to certain goods and services," (Turow, 2003). Production in the advertising industry involves several layers of professional working together with the goal of creative persuasive messages for placement directly to the target audiences.

The professionals who work in a typical advertising agency operate in the following different departments: creative service, which include writers, art directors, print production, TV and radio production; account services, which consists of account executives; marketing services, which include media planning, research, and sales promotion; administration, which include personnel, office management, clerical staff, and accounting. The overall business of the advertising agency is to produce and place in the various media, targeted persuasive messages or campaigns directed at segmented audiences. An advertising campaign involves series of advertisements and other tactics orchestrated under a unified theme, to promote certain products and services in targeted media over a period of time.

Review Questions

1. Define mass communication and discuss how it is different from the other forms of communication.

2. Identify and discuss the different media eras in human history.

3. Explain the elements in the process of mass communication.

4. Explain your understanding of Marshall McLuhan's statement that "the medium is the message."

5. What is news and what are the elements of news?

6. How are radio and TV writing different?

7. Describe and explain your understanding of the Agenda Setting Theory of the media.

8. How have the mass media enabled the business of public relations and advertising?

9. How is the Uses and Gratification Theory of mass media useful to the process of advertising and public relations?

10. Describe and explain the impact of social media on human communication.

11. How has the internet revolutionized power and elections in contemporary society?

APPENDIX A.

Preparation Outline Evaluation Form

Speaker Name_____ Topic_____

	Competency	Rating Unsatisfactory-0	Satisfactory-1	Excellent-2
1	Demonstrates knowledge of good outlining form by using proper heading, symbolization, capitalization, and indentation to identify the hierarchy of ideas and their order of importance			
2	Labels and states clearly the title, the purpose statements and central idea statement (in a complete sentence)			
3	Labels the introduction and includes essential components of this section as well as citing of sources of information (when and where applicable).			
4	Labels the body and includes essential components of this section as well as citing of sources of information (when and where applicable)			
5	Labels the conclusion and includes essential components of this section as well as citing of sources of information (where and when applicable)			
6	Chooses an appropriate organizational pattern to strategically sequence main points.			
7	States main points in full sentences to ensure that the ideas being developed are exact and specific.			
8	Includes and labels sub-points (sub-sub-points, etc) that act as explanations and expansions and other additional and relevant materials			
9	Uses and labels transitions to ensure the smooth and logical progression of ideas.			
10	Includes a bibliography listing of a minimum of three credible sources (academic caliber).			

Summative Scores of Outline Competence:_____

This outline evaluation form is in use at Suffolk Community College for grading preparation outline competencies of students in Introduction to Human Communication and Public Speaking courses.

The preparation outline evaluation form identifies all the different elements of a good speech, such that if the speaker organizes, develops, formats, and cites relevant sources as required, the speech exercise would be a phenomenal success. This is expected should the speaker combine this high level of preparation with good presentation skill in performing the speech.

The following form (Appendix B.): SUNY General Education Learning Outcomes for Introduction to Human Communication at Suffolk County Community College, the largest community college in the State of New York, identifies other necessary requirements of a well written and performed speech. Note in the outline, the nonverbal performance requirements in presenting an informative and, indeed, any form of speech.

The columns represent the competencies expected of a student in researching, outlining, developing and presenting an informative speech. These competencies are matched with the general education learning outcomes (row) expected of students who take Introduction to Human Communication at Suffolk Community College. Please note that credits obtained at community colleges are transferrable to four –year colleges and universities in the United States. In other words, the competencies measured here are university learning outcomes.

APPENDIX B.

SUNY General Learning Outcomes for COM 101

The Learning outcomes to the right should be matched with the competencies outlined below by placing an X in the corresponding box	Research a topic, develop an argument, and organize supporting materials	Develop proficiency in oral discourse	Evaluate an oral presentation according to established criteria
Purpose: gives an informative speech on a topic appropriate for audience and occasion			
Introduction: provides a clear and well-defined introduction (acquired audience's attention/created rapport, previewed thesis and main points, and purpose made clear)			
Uses clear and effective transition statements among main ideas.			
Organization is evident, making the speech easy to follow and understand.			
Uses appropriate sources and citation (material should be relevant, current, and interesting			
Provides a clear and effective conclusion (reviewed main points/thesis, left audience with a lasting impression).			
Demonstrates vocal variety (pitch, volume, rate changes).			

Delivers speech extemporaneously, in a conversational tone.			
Demonstrates clear articulation, pronunciation, and appropriate grammar			
Demonstrate effective use of kinesics			

APPENDIX C.

STORY WITH A POINT—EVALUATION FORM

Introduction
Attention--1 2 3 4 5

Credibility--1 2 3 4 5

Preview of Rationale/Premise/Point-------------------------1 2 3 4 5

Connective/Transition--1 2 3 4 5

Body
Scene Development--1 2 3 4 5

Character Development---1 2 3 4 5

Coherence---1 2 3 4 5

Style / Appropriateness of Content----------------------------1 2 3 4 5

Major Premise/Rationale or Point

Fidelity (Does the story ring true/is it realistic?)----------- --5   10   15   20

Conclusion
Summarization--1 2 3 4 5

Connection with opening--1 2 3 4 5

Memorable Exit---1 2 3 4 5

Delivery
Clarity of Voice--1 2 3 4 5

Pronunciation--1 2 3 4 5

Rate-- 1 2 3 4 5

Extemporaneousness/Eye Contact-----------------------------1 2 3 4 5
Allocation of Time--1 2 3 4 5

Total Score_____/100

APPENDIX D.

"THE COMPETENT SPEAKER SPEECH EVALUATION FORM"

SPEAKER'S NAME: _____ ASSIGNMENT: _____

EVALUATOR'S NAME: _____ DATE: _____/_____/_____

EIGHT PUBLIC SPEAKING COMPETENCIES   SPEAKER PERFORMANCE RATINGS

	Unsatisfactory	Satisfactory	Excellent
Competency One: CHOOSES AND NARROWS A TOPIC * Assign Scoring Ranges: **APPROPRIATELY FOR THE AUDIENCE AND OCCASION** Comments:			
Competency Two: COMMUNICATES THE THESIS/SPECIFIC PURPOSE IN A MANNER APPROPRIATE FOR AUDIENCE AND OCCASION Comments:			
Competency Three: PROVIDES APPROPRIATE SUPPORTING MATERIAL BASED ON THE AUDIENCE AND OCCASION Comments:			
Competency Four: USES AN ORGANIZATIONAL PATTERN APPROPRIATE TO TOPIC, AUDIENCE, OCCASION, & PURPOSE Comments:			
Competency Five: USES LANGUAGE THAT IS APPROPRIATE TO THE AUDIENCE, OCCASION, & PURPOSE Comments:			
Competency Six: USES VOCAL VARIETY IN RATE, PITCH, & INTENSITY TO HEIGHTEN AND MAINTAIN INTEREST Comments:			
Competency Seven: USES PRONUNCIATION, GRAMMAR, & ARTICULATION APPROPRIATE TO THE DESIGNATED AUDIENCE Comment:			
Competency Eight: USES PHYSICAL BEHAVIORS THAT SUPPORT THE VERBAL MESSAGE Comments:			

General Comments: **Summative scores of Competencies:** _____

"The Competent Speaker" Speech Evaluation Form was developed by the Speech Communication Association (SCA) in 1993.

APPENDIX E.

INFORMATIVE SPEECH OUTLINE

I-Introduction:
  A-Attention-Getter

  B- Relevance/Thesis

  C- Credibility Statement

  D- Preview

(Transition)

II-Body:
  A-Main Point 1
      1-Sub-point a
      2-Sub-point b
      3-Sub-point c

(Transition)

  B-Main Point 2
      1-Sub-point a
      2-Sub-point b
      3-Sub-point c

(Transition)

  C-Main-point 3
      1-Sub-point a
      2-Sub-point b
      3-Sub-point c

III-Conclusion:
  A-Summary of Main Points

  B-Re-state Thesis

  C-Reconnect with the Opening

  D-Final Appeal

APPENDIX F.

INFORMATIVE SPEECH EVALUATION SHEET

Name:_____

Speech Topic_____Time_____

Introduction:

Attention Getter --1   2   3   4   5
Purpose & Topic Statement--------------------------------1   2   3   4   5
Relevance/Thesis--- 1   2   3   4   5
Credibility Statement-- 1   2   3   4   5
Preview of Main Points---------------------------------------1   2   3   4   5
Transition to the body---------------------------------------1   2   3   4   5

Body:

Organization --- 1   2   3   4   5
Research--- 1   2   3   4   5
Connectives--- 1   2   3   4   5
Balance-- 1   2   3   4   5
Use of Language-- 1   2   3   4   5

Conclusion:

Transition from Body--1   2   3   4   5
Summary of Main Points/Thesis--------------------------1   2   3   4   5
Connection with Opening----------------------------------1   2   3   4   5
Exit Appeal-- 1   2   3   4   5
Use of Time-- 1   2   3   4   5

Delivery:

Vocal Variety: Pitch, Volume, Rate----------------------1   2   3   4   5
Articulation, Pronunciation, & Grammar-----------------1   2   3   4   5
Extemporaneous Delivery---------------------------------- 1   2   3   4   5
Effective use of Kinesics---------------------------------- 1   2   3   4   5
Appearance-- 1   2   3   4   5

OVERALL GRADE_____

Comments:

APPENDIX G.

The National Communication Association Credo for Ethical Communication

The question of right and wrong arises whenever people communicate. Ethical communication is fundamental to responsible thinking, decision making, and the development of relationships and communities within and across contexts, cultures, channels, and media. Moreover, ethical communication enhances human worth and dignity by fostering truthfulness, fairness, responsibility, personal integrity, and respect for self and others. We believe that unethical communication threatens the well-being of individuals and the society in which we live. Therefore we, the members of the National Communication Association, endorse and are committed to practicing the following principles of ethical communication:

We advocate truthfulness, accuracy, honesty, and reason as essential to the integrity of communication.

We endorse freedom of expression, diversity of perspective, and tolerance of dissent to achieve the informed and responsible decision making fundamental to a civil society.

We strive to understand and respect other communicators before evaluating and responding to their messages.

We promote access to communication resources and opportunities as necessary to fulfill human potential and contribute to the well-being of families, communities, and society.

We promote communication climates of caring and mutual understanding that respect the unique needs and characteristics of individual communicators.

We condemn communication that degrades individuals and humanity through distortion, intimidation, coercion, and violence, and through the expression of intolerance and hatred.

We are committed to the courageous expression of personal conviction in the pursuit of fairness and justice.

We advocate sharing information, opinions, and feelings when facing significant choices while also respecting privacy and confidentiality.

We accept responsibility for the short- and long- term consequences of our own communication and expect the same of others.

CODE OF ETHICS FOR NIGERIAN JOURNALISTS

PREAMBLE

Journalism entails a high degree of public trust. To earn and maintain this trust, it is morally imperative for every journalist and every news medium to observe the highest professional and ethical standards. In the exercise of these duties, a journalist should always have a healthy regard for the public interest.

Truth is the cornerstone of journalism and every journalist should strive diligently to ascertain the truth of every event.

Conscious of the responsibilities and duties of journalists as purveyors of information, we, Nigerian journalists, give to ourselves this Code of Ethics. It is the duty of every journalist to observe its provisions.

1. EDITORIAL INDEPENDENCE
Decisions concerning the content of news should be the responsibility of a professional journalist.

2. ACCURACY AND FAIRNESS
i. The Public has a right to know. Factual accurate, balanced and fair reporting is the ultimate objective of good journalism and the basis of earning public trust and confidence.

ii. A journalist should refrain from publishing inaccurate and misleading information. Where such information has been inadvertently published, prompt correction should be made. A journalist must hold the right of reply as a cardinal rule of practice.

iii. In the course of his duties, a journalist should strive to separate facts from conjecture and comment.

3. PRIVACY
As a general rule, a journalist should respect the privacy of individuals and their families unless the issue is of public interest.

A. Information on the private life of an individual or his family should only be published if it impinges on public interest.

B. Publishing of such information about an individual as mentioned above should be deemed justifiable only if it is directly at:

 i. Exposing crime or serious misdemeanour;

ii. Exposing anti-social conduct;

iii. Protecting public health, morality and safety;

iv. Preventing the public from being misled by some statement or action of the individual concerned.

4. PRIVILEGE/NON DISCLOSURE
 i. A journalist should observe the universally accepted principle of

confidentiality and should not disclose the source of information obtained in confidence.

ii. A journalist should not breach an agreement with a source of information obtained as "off the record" or as "back ground information"

5. DECENCY

i. A journalist should dress and comport himself in a manner that conforms to public taste.

ii. A journalist should refrain from using offensive, abusive, or vulgar language.

iii. A journalist should not present lurid details, either in words or picture, of violence, sexual acts, abhorrent or horrid scenes.

iv. In cases involved in personal grief or shock, enquiries should be carried out and approaches made with sympathy and discretion.

v. Unless it is in the furtherance of the public's right to know, a journalist should generally avoid identifying relatives or friends of persons convicted or accused of crime.

6. DISCRIMINATION

A journalist should refrain from making pejorative reference to a person's ethnic group, religion, sex, or to any physical or mental illness or handicap.

7. REWARD AND GRATIFICATION

i. A journalist should neither solicit nor accept bribe, gratification or patronage to suppress or publish information.

ii. To determine payment for publication of news is inimical to the notion of news as fair, accurate, unbiased and factual report of an event.

8. VIOLENCE

A journalist should not present or report acts of violence, armed robberies, terrorist activities or vulgar display of wealth in a manner that glorifies such act in the eyes of the public.

9. CHILDREN AND MINORS

A journalist should not identify, either by name or picture, or interview children under the age of 16 who are involved in cases concerning sexual offences, crimes and rituals or witchcraft either as victims, witnesses or defendants.

10. ACCESS TO INFORMATION

A journalist should strive to employ open and honest means in the gathering of information.

Exceptional methods may be employed only when the public interest is at stake.

11. PUBLIC INTEREST

A journalist should strive to enhance national unity and public good.

12. SOCIAL RESPONSIBILITY

A journalist should promote universal principles of human rights, democracy, justice, equity, peace and international understanding.

13. PLAGIARISM

A journalist should not copy, wholesale, or in part, other people's work without attribution and/or consent.

14. COPYRIGHT

i. Where a journalist reproduces a work, be it in print, broadcast, art work or design, proper acknowledgement should be accorded to the author.

ii. A journalist should abide by all rules of copyright, established by national and international laws and conventions.

15. PRESS FREEDOM AND RESPONSIBILITY

A journalist should strive at all times to enhance press freedom and responsibility.

APPENDIX I.

Different Communication, Journalism, and Related Programs in US Colleges and Universities

COMMUNICATION, JOURNALISM, AND RELATED PROGRAMS

Communication and Media Studies

Communication Studies/Speech Communication and Rhetoric
      Communication/Media Studies
      Communication and Media Studies, Other

Advertising, Public Relations, and Organizational Communication

      Advertising
            Business Marketing and Marketing Management
            Marketing Research
            International Business Marketing
      Public Relations/Image Management
      Business/Organizational Communication
            Agricultural Communications
            Family and Consumer Sciences/Human Sciences Communications
      Political Communication
      Health Communication
      Advertising, Public Relations, and Organizational Communication, Other

Journalism

      Journalism
      Broadcast Journalism
      Journalism, Other

MEDIATED AND TELECOMMUNICATION PROGRAMS

Computer and Information Sciences and Support Services

      Radio and Television
            Film/Video and Photographic Arts
            Radio and Television Broadcast Technology
            Recording Arts Technology
      Digital Communication and Media

Communication, Journalism, and Related Fields, Other

      Communication, Journalism, and Related Fields, Other

2000 U.S. Department of Education Classification of Instruction Programs, as reported in Pathways to communication careers in the 21st century. NCA (2000, p. 2).

Areas of Concentration/Emphasis in the Communication Discipline

Applied Communication:
The study of processes used to analyze communication needs of organizations and social interaction, including the design of training to improve communication between supervisors and employees.

Communication and Aging:
The study of the impact of aging on all aspects of communication, including intergenerational relationships and communication, age stereotypes and communication, health issues of aging and communication, and life span and communication.

Communication and Disabilities:
The study and integration of disability issues into communication contexts.

Communication and the Future:
The study of any aspects of communication and the future , including novel methodologies, new theoretical perspectives, the interaction of communication and technology and uses of technology, communication networks, emergent communication networks, communication and strategic change, pedagogy, and ethics.

Communication Education:
 The study of communication in the classroom and other pedagogical contexts.

Communication Theory:
The study of the principles that account for the impact of communication in human social interaction.

Critical and Cultural Studies:
The study of communication and culture, particularly how communication relates to cultural and social practices in a variety of contexts.

Electronic Media:
The study of radio, television, media technology, and web design with streaming audio and video.

Environmental Communication:
 The study of the production, reception, contexts, or processes of human communication regarding environmental issues.

Family Communication:
The study of communication unique to family systems.

Feminist Communication: The study of aspects of communication that address intersections of power and challenge existing theoretical paradigms that have excluded the voices of marginalized groups, particularly women.

GLBTQ Communication:
The study of gay, lesbian, bisexual, transgender, and queer issues from a communication perspective, including issues from the past or present, on a local or global scale, and across various disciplines.

Gender Communication:
The study of gender and sex differences and similarities in communication and the unique characteristics of male-female communication.

Health Communication:
The study of communication as it relates to health professionals and health education, including the study of provider-client interaction, as well as the diffusion of health information through public health campaigns.

International and Intercultural Communication:
The study of communication among individuals of different cultural backgrounds, including the study of similarities and differences across cultures.

Interpersonal Communication:
The study of communication behaviors in dyads (pairs) and their impact on personal relationships.

Language and Social Interaction:
The study of the structure of verbal and nonverbal behaviors occurring in social interactions.

Legal Communication:
The study of the role of communication as it relates to the legal system.

Mass Communication and Media Literacy:
The study of the uses, processes, and effects of mediate communication.

Mediation and Dispute Resolution:
The study of understanding, management, and resolution of conflict within intrapersonal, interpersonal, and intergroup situations.

New Media and Technology:
The study of the impact on all aspects of human communication from the interpersonal to the organizational and global arising from both the scale and speed of new media development and the use of new media. This includes social networking, blogging, virtual communities, gaming, cell phone usage, text messaging, virtual teams or groups, instructional technology, open source, politics, and information accessibility and literacy.

Organizational Communication:
The study of processes used to analyze communication needs of organizations and social interaction, including the design of training to improve communication between supervisors and employees.

Performance Studies:
The study of the components, such as performers(s), text, audience, and context within the communication discipline.

Political Communication:
The study of the role communication plays in political systems.

Public Address:
The study of speakers and speeches, including the historical and social contexts of platforms, campaigns, and movements.

Public Relations:

The study of the management of communication between an organization and its audiences.

Rhetorical Criticism:

The study of principles that account for the impact of human communication between speaker and the audience.

Risk and Crisis Communication:

The study of how government agencies and organizations assess and manage risk and crisis situations, and how they communicate the nature of a crisis to stakeholders and members of the public.

Semiotics:

The use of verbal and nonverbal symbols and signs in human communication.

Small Group Communication:

The study of communication systems among three or more individuals who interact around a common purpose and who influence one another.

Spiritual Communication:

The study of spirituality expressed through myriad experiences, practices, and belief systems in all communication contexts

Visual Communication:

The study of visual data such as architecture, photography, visual art, advertising, film, and television as it relates to communication.

2000 U.S. Department of Education Classification of Instruction Programs, as reported in Pathways to communication careers in the 21st century. NCA (2000, p. 19).

Index of Subjects and Key Terms

Chapter 7.

Chapter 8.

Chapter 9.

Chapter 10.

Chapter 11.

Chapter 16.

Chapter 17.

Chapter 18.

Bibliography

Adler and Proctor (2007) *Looking out /looking in* (12th ed.). Belmont, CA: Wadsworth

Adler Ronald B. & Rodman, George (2003). *Understanding human communication* (8th ed.). New York, NY: Oxford University.

Adler B. Ronald & Rodman, George (2000). *Understanding human communication* (8th ed.). Fort Worth, TX: Harcourt Brace.

Adler, Ronald B. & Towne, Neil. (1999*). Looking out/ looking in* (9th ed.). Forth Worth: Harcourt Brace.

Alesandrini, K. L. (1983). Strategies that influence memory for advertising Communication. In R.J. Harris (Eds,) *Information processing research in advertising.*

Altman, I. & Taylor, D.A. (1973). *Social penetration: The development of interpersonal relationships.* New York: Holt, Rinehart, and Winston.

Anderson, Kenneth E. (1984). Communication ethics: The nonparticipant's role. *Southern Speech Communication Journal*, 49: 220.

Andrews, P.H. (1996). *Group conformity.* In Engleberg & Wynn. *Working in Groups* (4th ed.) Boston, MA: Houghton Mifflin, 2007.

Au, K.H. (1993). *Literacy instruction in multicultural settings.* New York: Harcourt Brace.

Aufterheide, Patricia (1992). "Media Literacy: A Report of the National Leadership Conference on Media Literacy." Washington, D.C.: Aspen Institute.

Avinash, Chandra. http://nuvvo.com/users/chandra_avinash Accessed March 20, 2012.

Awodiya, Daniel O. (2005). *Effective employee-management communication.* New York: AdPlus Press.

Axtell, R. (1991). *Gestures: The do's and taboos of body language around the world.* New York: John Wiley.

Ayres, Joe & Tim Hopf (1993). *Coping with speech anxiety.* Norwood, NJ: Ablex.

Bales, R. & Strodbeck, F. (1951). Phases in group problem solving. *Journal of Abnormal and Social Psychology.* 46, 485-495.

Barker, Larry L., Wahlers Kathy J. & Watson, Kittie, W. (2001) *Groups in process: an introduction to small group communication.* (6th ed.). Boston, MA: Allyn and Bacon.

Barlund, D. C. (1970). A transactional model of communication. In J. Akin, A. Golberg, G. Myers & J. Stewart (Eds.) *Language behavior: A book of readings in communication.* The Hague: Mouton.

Barneys, Edward (1961). *Crystallizing public opinion.* New York: Liveright.

Bates, D.G. & Plog, F. (1990) *Cultural anthropology* (3rd ed.). New York: McGraw-Hill.

Baxter, L. (19820. Strategies for ending relationships: Two studies. *Western Journal of Speech Communication,* 46, 223-241.

Beebe, Steven A., Beebe, Susan J. & Diana K. Ivy (2001). *Communication-principles of a life time.* Boston, MA: Allyn and Bacon.

Behnke, R.R., Sawyer, C.R., & P.E. King (1987). The Communication of Public Speaking Anxiety, *Communication Education* 36: 138 – 41.

Benjamin, James (1997). *Principles, element, and types of persuasion.* Orlando, Florida: Harcourt Brace and Company.

Benne, Barge, J.K. & Hirokawa, R.Y. (1989). Toward a communication competency model of group leadership. *Small Group Behavior.* 20, 167-189.

Benne, K.D., & Sheats, P. (1948). Functional roles of group members. *Journal of Social Issues.* 4, 41-49.

Bennis, W. G. & Shepard, H. A. (1956). A theory of group development. *Human Relations.* 9, 418-457.

Bennis, W. G., & Shepard, H.A. (1956). Functional roles of group members. *Journal of Social Issues.* 4, 41-49.

Bell, S. (2004). End PowerPoint dependency now! *America Libraries*, 35(6), 56-59.

Berger, C.R. and Calabrese, R. J. (1975). Some explanations in initial interactions and beyond: Toward a development theory of interpersonal communication. *Human Communication Research.* 1, 98-112.

Berger, C. R. (1986). Response- uncertain outcome values in predicted relationships: Uncertainty reduction theory then and now. *Human Communication Research* 13, 34 –38.

Berko, Roy M., Wolvin, Andrew D. & Darlyn R. Wolvin (2001) *Communicating,* (8th ed.). Boston, MA: Houghton Mifflin.

Berlo, David, K. (1960). *The Process of communication: An introduction to theory and practice.* New York, NY: Rinehart and Winston.

Birdwhistell, Ray L. *Kinesics in context* (1970). Philadelphia, PA: University of Pennsylvania Press.

Blake, Reed, H. & Haroldsen, Edwin, O. (1975). *A taxonomy of concepts in communication.* New York: Hastings House.

Borchers, Timothy A. (2002). *Persuasion in the media age.* Boston, MA: McGraw Hill).

Borchers, Timothy A. (2005). *Persuasion in the media age.* (2nd ed.) Boston, MA: McGraw- Hill.

Borhis, J. & M. Allen (1992).Meta analysis of the relationship between communication apprehension and cognitive performance, *Communication Education,* 41: 68-76.

Bower, B. (1992). Truth aches: People who view themselves poorly may seek the "truth" and find despair. *Science News*, 110 -111.

Bradac J.J., M. R. Hemphill, & T.H. Tardy. Language style on trial: The effects of 'powerful' and 'powerless' speech upon judgments of victims and villains, *Western Journal of Speech Communication* 45 (1981), 327-341.

Brownell, Judi. (2002). *Listening: Attitudes, Principles, and Skills*, (2nd ed.). Boston: Allyn and Bacon.

Burgoon, J. Walther, J. & Baesler, E. 1992 "Interpretations, Evaluations, and Consequences of Interpersonal Touch." Human Communication Research 19: 237- 263.

Burgoon, J. K., & Bacue, A. E. (2003) Nonverbal communication skills. In J.O. Greene & B. R. Bureleson (Eds). *Handbook of communication and social Interaction* (pp. 179-220). Mahwah, NJ: Erlbaum.

Burgoon J.K., T. Birk, & M. Pfau. (1990). Nonverbal behaviors, persuasion, and credibility, *Human Communication Research* 17: 140-169.

Burgoon, J.K., Buller, D.B., & Woodall, W.G. (1989). *Nonverbal communication: The Unspoken Dialogue.* New York: Harper and Row.

Burke, Kenneth (1941). *The philosophy of literary form: Studies in symbolic action,* pp. 110-111. (3rd ed.). 1973 Reprint, Berkeley: University of California Press.

Burke, K. (1966). *Language as symbolic action*: *Essays on life, literature, and method*. Berkeley: University of California Press.

Burke, K. (1970). *A grammar of motives*. Berkeley: University of California Press.

Burke, K. (1970). *A rhetoric of motives*. Berkeley: University of California Press.

Butler, Samuel (1989). *Homer, Iliad,* Trans. Book iii. New York: Longman Green.

Bush, G. (2003, March 20). George Bush's address on the start of the war. *The Guardian*. Retrieved from http://www. guardian.co.uk/Iraq/Story/0,2763,918031,00.html

Calloway-Thomas, Carolyn, Cooper, Pamela J., & Blake, Cecil (1999). *Intercultural communication: Roots and routes.* Boston, MA: Allyn and bacon.

Canli, T., Desmond, J.E, Zhao, Z. & Gabrieli, J.D.E (2002). Sex differences in neural basis of emotional memories. *Proceeding of the National Academy of Sciences*, 10, 10789-10794.

Carmeli, A., Yitzhak-Halevy, M., & Weisberg, J. (2009). The relationship between emotional intelligence and psychological wellbeing. *Journal of Managerial Psychology*, 24, 66-78.

Casteel, 1992. *A cross-cultural study of touch avoidance*, West Virginia University Master's Thesis.

Chaiken, Shelly. (August 25, 1978). Communicator physical attractiveness and persuasion. *Journal of Personality and Social Psychology* 37. pp1387-1397.

Cohen, Bernard, C. (1963). *The press and foreign policy*. Princeton, NJ: Princeton University Press.

Coopman, Stephanie J. & James Lull (2011). *Public speaking: The evolving art*. Boston, MA: Wadsworth.

Cole, D. (1989, May) Meetings that make sense. *Psychology Today*, 23, 14.

Cole, J.G. & McCroskey, J.C. (2000). Temperament and socio-communicative orientation. *Communication Research Report*, 17, 105-114.

College of the Air (2001). The Communication Process DVD. New York: Insight Media.

Collins M. A. & L. A. Zebrowitz (1995). The Contributions of appearance to occupational outcomes in civilian and military settings, *Journal of Applied Social Psychology* 71: 129-63.

Cooley, Charles (1912). *Human nature and the social order*. New York: Scribner's

Craig, Robert T. (1999). Communication theory as a field. *Communication Theory*, Vol. 9, p. 120.

Craik, K. (1943) *The nature of explanation*. Cambridge: Cambridge University Press.

Crifasi, Sheila, Clough. Cited in Seitel, Frank (1998) *The practice of public relations*, 8th ed. New Jersey: Prentice Hall.

Crook, Tim. *Radio Drama: Theory and practice*. http://www.irdp.co.uk/scripts.htm Accessed March 20, 2012.

Crossen, Cynthia (1994). *Tainted truth.* New York, NY: Simon and Schuster.

Crusco, A. H. & C. G. Wetzel. (1984). The Midas Touch: Effects of Interpersonal Touch on Restaurant Tipping, *Personality and Social Psychology Bulletin.* 10: 512-517.

Cruz Michael G, (1998) Explicit and Implicit conclusions in persuasive messages. In M. Allen & W. Preiss (Eds.), *Persuasion: Advances through meta-analysis* (pp 217- 230), Cresskill, NH: Hampton Press.

Dance, F.E.X. & C.E. Larson (1972). *Speech Communication: Concepts and Behavior*. New York, NY: Holt, Rinehart & Winston.

DeAngelis, T. (1992). Illness linked with repressive style of coping. *APA Monitor*, 23(12), 14-15.

Deep, Sam & Sussman, Lyle (1998). *Yes, you can!* Reading, MA: Addison-Wesley.

Delbecq, A.L, Van de Ven, A.H. & Gustafson, D.H. (1975) *Group techniques for program planning: a guide to nominal groups and delphi processes.* ILL: Scott Foresman.

DeVito, Joseph (2006).*The essential elements of public speaking*, 2nd ed. Boston: Allyn and Bacon.

Dewey, J. (1910). *How we think*. Lexington, M.A: Heath.

Devereaux-Ferguson, Sherry (2008). *Public speaking: Building competency in stages*. New York: Oxford Press

DeVito (2003). *Messages: Building interpersonal communication skills (5th ed.).*Boston, MA: Allyn and Bacon.

Dictionary.com

Duck, Steve & McMahon, David T. (2012) *The basics of communication: A relational perspective*. Thousand Oaks, California: Sage

Duck, S.W. & Miell, D.E. (1991). Charting the development of personal relationships." In R. Gimour & S. W. Duck (eds.) *Studying interpersonal interaction* (pp. 133-144). New York: Gilford.

Duck, S. W. (1987). How to lose friends without influencing people. In M.E. Roloff & G.R. Miller (Eds.). *International processes: New directions in communication research*. Beverly Hills, California: Sage.

Einhorn, L.J. (1981). An inner view of the job interview: an investigation of successful communicative behaviors. *Communication Education*, 30, 217-228.

Ekman, P & Friesen W. V. (1969). The repertoire of nonverbal behavior: Categories, Origins, Usage, and Coding. *Semiotica*, 1, 49-98.

Ellis A. (1977). *A New guide to rational living*. North Hollywood, CA: Wishire Books.

Engleberg, Isa N. & Wynn, Dianna R. (2011) *Think communication*. Boston, MA: Allyn and Bacon.

Engleberg & Wynn (2007) *Working in groups (*4th ed.). Boston, MA: Houghton Mifflin.

Epstein, Steven L. & Barr, Linda (2007). *Research navigator.com: Resources for college research assignments.* Boston, A: Allyn and Bacon.

Epstein, Steven L. & Yarberry, Wendy (2009). *Fundamentals of public speaking*. Boston: McGraw-Hill learning Solutions.

Festinger, L. (1954). Theory of social comparison processes. *Human Relations*. 7, 117-140.

Fisher, B. Hilda (1975). *Improving voice and articulation* (2nd ed.). Boston: Houghton Mifflin.

Fisher, B. A. (1970) Decision emergence: Phases in group decision making. *Speech Monographs*. 37, 53-66.

Floyd, K. (2002) Human affection exchange v: Attributes of the highly affectionate. *Communication Quarterly*, 50, 135-152.

French, J.R.P. & Rowen, B. (1981). The bases of social power. In Cartwright & Zander

(Eds.), *Group dynamics: Research and theory* (3rd ed.). New York: McGraw- Hill.

Gamble, Teri Kwal & Michael W. Gamble (2010). *Communication works* (10th ed.) New York, NY: McGraw-Hill.

Gamble, Teri Kwal & Michael W. Gamble (1998). *Public speaking in the age of diversity* (2nd ed.) Needham Heights: MA: Allyn and Bacon.

Gass, H. Robert & Seiter, John S. (2011). *Persuasion: social influence and compliance gaining. Boston*, MA: Allyn & Bacon.

Gas, Robert H. & John S. Seiter (1999). *Persuasion, social influence, and compliance gaining.* Boston, Massachusetts. Allyn and Bacon.

Gardner, H. (1983). *Frames of the mind: The theory of multiple intelligences.* New York: Basic books.

Genzer, D. (1987-1988) *The disorientation manual: A guide for American students studying at the University of St. Andrews, Scotland.* St Andrews, Scotland: University of St. Andrews.

Gerbner, G., & Gross, L. (1972). Living with television: The violence profile. *Journal of Communication*, 26, 173-199.

Gerbner, G. (1998). Cultivation analysis: An overview. *Mass Communication and Society*, 3/4, 175 -191.

George, G., (1999). What do we know? In J. Shanahan & M. Morgan (Eds.), *Television and its viewers: Cultivation theory and research* (pp. ix – xiii). Cambridge: Cambridge University Press.

Gibbs, Jack R. (1961). Defensive communication. *Journal of Communication, 11: 3 pp.141-148.*

Goffman, E. (1959). *The presentation of self in everyday life.* Garden City, NY: Doubleday.

Goffman E. (1971). *Relations in public.* New York: Basic Books.

Goleman, D. (1995). *Emotional intelligence: Why it can matter more than I.Q. New York: Bantam.*

Goleman, D. (2006). *Social intelligence: The new science of human relationships. New York: Bantam.*

Goldsmith, D.J. & Fulfs, P.A. (1999).You just don't have the evidence: An analysis of claims and evidence in Deborah Tannen's "You Just Don't Understand." In Roloff, M.E. (Ed.) *Communication Yearbook* 22 (pp. 1-49). Thousand Oaks, CA: Sage.

Gouran, D.S., Cadance B. & David, R.H. (1978). Behavioral correlates of quality in decision making discussions. *Communication Monographs.* 45, 51-63.

Gray, G. W. (1946). The precepts of kagmenmi [sic] and ptah-hotep. *Quarterly Journal of Speech,* 31, 446-454.

Griffin, Cindy L. (2011). *Invitation to public speaking handbook.* Boston, MA: Wadsworth.

Griffin, Em. (2012). *A first look at communication theory* (8th ed.). New York, McGraw-Hill.

Griswold, Denis (   ) *Public relations news.* New York.

Grossberg, L, Wartella, E., & Whitney, D. C. (   ). Media making (Eds.) Thousand Oaks, California: Sage Publications.

Hackman, M.Z. & Johnson, C.E. (2003). *Leadership: A communication perspective* (4th ed.). Prospect heights, IL: Waveland Press.

Hale J. & J. B. Stiff (1990). Nonverbal primacy in veracity judgments, *Communication Reports* 3:75-83.

Hale, R. Garlick, Stiff, J. B. J &. Rogan, R. G. (1990). Effect of cue incongruence and social normative influences on individual judgments of honesty and deceit, *Southern Speech Communication Journal* 55: 206-229.

Hall, E.T. (1966). *The hidden dimension*. Garden City, NJ: Doubleday.

Harlow, Rex, F. (1976). Building a Public Relations Definition, *Public Relations Review*: 2, no. 4 Winter.

Harper, M.S. & Welsh, D.P. (2007).Keeping Quiet: Self-silencing and its association with relational and individual functioning among adolescent romantic couples. *Western Journal of Speech Communications*, 55, 159-179.

Haviland, W. A. Prins H.E.L.Walrath, D. & McBride B. (2005). *Cultural anthropology: The human challenge* (11th ed.). Belmont, CA: Wadsworth.

Heisel, A.D., McCroskey, J.C. & Richmond, V.P. (1999). Testing theoretical relationships and non-relationships of genetically-based predictors: Getting started with communibiology. *Communication Research Reports,* 16, 1-9.

Heider, Fritz. (1958). *The psychology of interpersonal relations*. Hillsdale, NJ: Lawrence Erlbaum Associates.

Hendrick, Clyde, Hendrich Susan S. (1986) A theory and method of love. *Journal of Personality and Social Psychology* 50, 392-402.

Herring, H. B. (2006, June 18). Endless meetings: The black hole of the workday. *The New York Times*, 2.

Hobbes, Rene "The seven great debates in the media literacy movement. http://interact.uoregon.edu/MediaLit/FA/mlhobbs/hbindex.html

Hofstede, G. and Hoftede, G. J. (2004).*Cultures and organizations: Software of the mind* (2nd ed.). Boston: McGraw-Hill.

Hofstede, G. (1991). *Cultures and organizations: Software of the mind*. London: McGraw-Hill.

Hollingsworth, H. L. (1935). *The psychology of audiences*. New York: American Book Company.

Hussein, S. (2003, April). Strike at them, fight them. *The Guardian*. Retrieved from http://www.guardian.co.uk/Iraq/Story/0,2763,927647,00.html.

Hybels, Sandra & Richard L. Weaver II (2009). *Communicating effectively* (9th ed.) New York: McGraw Hill.

Hybels, Sandra & Richard L. Weaver II (2007). *Communicating effectively* (8th ed.) New York: McGraw Hill.

Infante, D.A. (1987) Aggressiveness. In McCroskey, J.C. & Daly, J.A. (Eds.) *Personality & interpersonal communication*. Newbury Park, CA: Sage.

Jaffe, Clella. (2007) *Public speaking: Concepts and skills for a diverse society*. (6th ed.) Boston, MA: Cengage/Wadsworth.

Jaffe, Clella. (2004) *Public speaking: Concepts and skills for a diverse society* (5th ed.). Belmont, CA: Wadsworth/Thompson Learning

Jefferson, Thomas. Edited by Gordon C. Lee (1967). *Crusade against ignorance*. New York: Teacher's College, Columbia University.

Johannesen, Richard L. (2002). *Ethics in human communication* (5th ed.). Prospect Heights, Illinois: Waveland.

Johnson, David &. Johnson, Frank P. (2000) *Joining together: Group theory and group skills.* (7th ed.). Boston, MA: Allyn and Bacon.

Johnston, Deidre D. (1994). *The art and science of persuasion.* Dubuque, IA: Brown and Benchmark.

Johnson-Laird, P.N. (1983). *Mental models: towards a cognitive science of language, inference and consciousness.* Cambridge, UK: Cambridge University Press.

Karlins, M., & H. Abelson (1970). *Persuasion: How opinions and attitudes are changed (2nd ed.).* New York: Springer.

Katz, E, Blumler, Jay, & Gurvitch, Michael (1974). *Uses of mass communication by individuals.* Beverly-Hills, California: Sage Publications.

Kleinke, C.R. 1977.Compliance to requests made by gazing and touching experiments in field settings, *Journal of Experimental Social Psychology* 13: 218-223.

Klopf, Donald W. & McCroskey, James C. 2007. *Intercultural communication encounter.* Boston: Pearson.

Knapp, Mark L. & Vangelisti, Anita L. (2005). *Interpersonal communication and human relations* (4th ed.) Boston: Allyn and Bacon.

Knapp, M.L. & Vangelisti, A.L. (2006). *Interpersonal communication and human relations* (6th ed.).Boston: Allyn and Bacon.

Kubey, Robert (1997). *Media literacy in an information age* (ed.). New Brunswick, N.J.: Transaction Publishers.

Kunkel, A.W. & Burleson, B.R. (1999). Assessing explanation for sex differences in emotional support: A test of the different cultures and skills specialization accounts. *Human Communication Research*, 25, 307-340.

Larson, Charles U. (2010). *Persuasion: Reception and responsibility* (12th ed.).Boston: M.A. Wadsworth.

Larson, Charles U. (2001).*Persuasion: Reception and responsibility* (9th ed.). Belmont: Wadsworth/Thompson Learning.

Larson, Charles (1994). *Persuasion: Reception and responsibility.* Belmont, CA: Wadsworth Publishing Company.

Lasswell, H.D. (1948). The structure and function of communication in society. In L. Bryson (Eds.). *The communication of ideas.* New York: Harper and Row.

Lazarfield, P., Berelson, B & Gaudet, H (1944). *The people's choice.* New York: Duell, Sloan and Pierce.

Leary, M., Nezlek, J.B., & Downs, D. et al (1994). Self –presentation in everyday interactions: Effects of target familiarity and gender composition. *Journal of Personality and Social Psychology.* 67, 664 -673.

Leathers, D. (1986). *Successful nonverbal communication: Principles and applications.* New York, NY: Macmillan.

Ledbetter, A. M., Griffin, E. & Sparks, G.G. (2007). Forecasting friends for ever: A longitudinal investigation of sustained closeness between best friends. *Personal Relationships*, 14, 343-350.

Lee, J.A. (1973) *The colors of love.* Done Mills, Ontario: New Press.

Lippmann, Walter (1922). *Public opinion.* New York: MacMillan.

Lucient, Matrat (1990) The Strategy of Confidence. International Public Relations Review. 13(2) 8-12.

Luft, Joseph (1984). *Group processes: An introduction to group dynamics*, (3rd ed.). New York: McGraw-Hill.

Luo, S. & Klohnen, E. (2005). Assortive mating and marital quality in newlyweds: A couple-centered approach. *Journal of Personality and Social Psychology,* 88, 304 -326.

Lewi Kelley, R. E. (1998). *How to be a star at work*. New York: Times books.

Lewin, K. (1947). Group decision and social change. In T.M. Newcomb & E.L. Hartley (Eds.), *Readings in social psychology* (pp. 330-34). New York: Henry Holt.

Likert, R. (1932). A technique for the measuring of attitudes (special issue). *Archives of Psychology*, 42, 853-863.

Little, Charles E. ed., Vol. 2 (1951). *The instituto oratoria*. Nashville, TN: George Peabody College for Teachers.

Lucas, Stephen E. (2009) *The art of public speaking* (10th ed.). New York, NY: McGraw- Hill.

Lucas, Stephen E. (2007) *The art of public speaking* (9th ed.). New York, NY: McGraw- Hill.

Luntz, W. Doublespeak. (1987). *From "revenue enhancement" to "terminal living": How government, business, advertisers and others use language to deceive you.* New York: Harper and Row.

McCombs, Maxwell & Shaw, Donald (1974). "A progress Report on Agenda-Setting Research," *A paper presented to the Association for Education in Journalism and Mass communication, Theory and Methodology Division*, San Diego, CA. April 18-27, 1974.

McCombs, Maxwell & Shaw, Donald (1994).News Influence on Our Pictures of the World." *In Media effects: Advances in theory and research*, Jennings, Bryant and Zillman, Dolf (eds.), Hillsdale, NJ: Lawrence Earlbaum.

McCombs, Maxwell & Bell, Tamara (1996). "The Agenda –Setting Role of Mass Communication," In *An integrated approach to communication theory and research*, Michael Salwen and Donald Stacks (eds.). Hillsdale, NJ: Lawrence Erlbaum.

Mark V. Redmond, *Communication: Theories and applications.* Boston: Houghton Mifflin, 2000.

Martin, Judith N. & Nakayama, Thomas K. (2011). *Experiencing intercultural communication: an introduction* (4th ed.) New York: McGraw Hill.

Marston, John, E. (1963) *The nature of public relations*. New York: McGraw-Hill.

Maslow, Abraham (1970), *Motivation and personality* (2nd ed.). New York: Harper & Row.Masterman, Len (1985). *Teaching the media*. London: Comedia.

McCroskey, J.C. & Richmond, V. P. (1996) *Prospect of human communication: An interpersonal perspective*. Prospect heights, Il: Waveland Press.

McGrath, J. E. (1984) *Groups: Interaction and performance*. Englewood Cliff, N.J.: Prentice-Hall.

McGuire, William J. (1964). Inducing resistance to persuasion: some contemporary Approaches. In L. Berkowitz (Eds.). *Advances in experimental social psychology,* Volume 1, pp 191-229. New York: Academic Press.

McCroskey, J.C. Heisel, A.D., & Richmond, V.P. (2001). Eysench's big three and communication traits: Three correlational studies." *Communication Monographs*, 68, 360-366.

McLuhan, Marshall (1962). *The Gutenberg Galaxy*. Toronto, Canada: University of Toronto Press.

McLuhan, M. (1964). *Understanding media: The extensions of man*. New York: McGraw-Hill.

McLuhan, M. & Fiore, Q. (1967). *The medium is the message*. New York: Random House.

McQuail, Denis (1987). *Mass communication theory: An introduction (*2nd ed.)Beverly-Hills, California: Sage Publications.

Mehrabian, Albert (1972). *Nonverbal communication*. Chicago: Adline.

Menzel, K.E. & Carrell, L. J. (1994). The Relationship between preparation and performance in public speaking. *Communication Education*, 43:17-26.

Merten, J. (2005). Culture, gender and the recognition of the basic emotions. *Psychologia: An international journal of psychology in the Orient*, 48, 306-315.

Metcalfe, Sheldon (2000). *Building a speech*. Orlando: Harcourt Inc.

Miller, George A. (2009). "WordNet - about us." WordNet. Princeton University. "http://wordnet.princeton.edu"

Morreale, Sherwyn P., Spitzberg, Brian H. & Barge, J. Kevin (2007). *Human communication: Motivation, knowledge, and skills*. (2nd ed.).Belmont, CA: Thompson Wadsworth.

Morris, Charles G. (1976). *Psychology: An introduction*. Englewood Cliffs, NJ: Prentice-Hall.

Nanda, S. & Warms, R.L. (1998). *Cultural anthropology* (6th ed.). CA: Wadsworth.

National Communication Association Credo for Ethical Communication, http://www.natcom.org/aboutNCA/Policies?Platform.html

Newsom, Doug, Turk, Judy Vanslyke, & Kruckeberg, Dean (1996). *This is pr: The realities of public relations* (6th ed.). Belmont, CA: Wadsworth.

Nielson. (2009). http://content.usaoday.com/communities/theoval/post/2009/01/61713320/1

Nigerian Guild of Editors. (2008). http://www.nigerianguildofeditors.com/index.

Osgood, C.E., Tannenbaum P.H., & Succi, G. J. (1957). *The Measurement of meaning*. Urbana, IL: University of Illinois Press.

Pearson, C. Judy, Nelson. Paul E. & Harter, Lynn (2011) *Human communication* (4th ed.). New York: McGraw-Hill.

Pearson, Judy C., Paul E. Nelson, Scott Titsworth, & Lynn Harter (2011). *Human communication* (4th ed.). New York, NY: McGraw Hill.

Pearson, C. Judy & Paul E. Nelson (2000) *An Introduction to human communication: understanding and sharing* (8th ed.). Boston: McGraw-Hill.

Petronio, S. (2007). Translational research endeavors and the practices of communication privacy management. *Journal of Applied Communication Research*, 35, 218-222.

Piaget, Jean. (1962) *The Language and thought of the child*. (3rd ed.) Atlantic Highlands, NJ: Humanities.

Plutchick, Robert (1962). *The Emotions: Facts, Theories, and a New Model*. New York: Random House.

Plutchick, Robert (1980) *Emotion: A psycho evolutionary synthesis*. New York: Harper and Row.

Potter, W. J. (2009). Media literacy. In W.F. Eadie (Ed.), *21st century communications: A reference handbook* (pp. 558-567). Thousand Oaks, CA: Sage.

Postman, Neil. (2000). The "humanism of media ecology." *Keynote address, inaugural media ecology conference*, Fordham University, New York, June 2000. Available at http://www.media-ecology.html.

Renz, M. A. & Greg, J. B. (2000). *Effective small group communication.* Boston, MA: Allyn and Bacon.

Pew Research Center (2008, December). Http://people-press.org/report/479/internet-overtakes-newspapers-as-news-source.

Rubin, D. L. (1993). Listenability in oral-based discourse and considerateness. In Wolvin and Coakley, Perspectives, 261-268.

Rochman, G.M. & Diamond, G.M. (2008). From unresolved anger to sadness: Identifying physiological correlates. *Journal of Counseling Psychology*, 55, 96-105.

Ross, Raymond S. (1994). *Understanding persuasion.* Englewood Cliffs, N.J.: Prentice-Hall.

Rollie, S.S. & Duck, S.W. (2006) Stage theories of marital breakdown. In J.H. Harvey & M.A. Fine (Eds.), Handbook of divorce and dissolution of romantic relationships (pp. 176-193). Mahwah, NJ: Lawrence Erlbaum.

Rosenthal, L. B. & Gilbert, J. R. (1989). The measurement of cohesion and its relationship to dimensions of self-disclosure in classroom settings. *Small Group Behavior*, 20, 291-301.

Rosenthal, Alan (1990). *Writing, directing, and producing documentary films.* Soutnern Illinois University Press. http://www.ohlone.edu/people/bparks/docs/basicnewswriting.pdf

Rosenthal R. and Jacobson, L. (1968). *Pygmalion in the classroom.* New York: Holt, Rineheart and Winston.

Rosenfeld, Lawrence B, & Timothy Plax (1975). The relationship of listener personality to perceptions of three dimensions of credibility," *Central States Speech Journal*, 26. P. 278.

Rothwell, J. Dan. 2000. *In the company of others—An introduction to communication.* Mountain View: Mayfield.

Salazar, A.J. (1995). Understanding the synergistic effects of communication in small groups: Making the most out of group member abilities. *Small group Research.* 26, 169-199.

Samovar, Larry A., Porter, Richard E., & McDaniel Edwin R. (2010). *Communication between cultures* (7th ed.). Boston, MA: Wadsworth/Cengage Learning.

Samovar, Larry A., Porter, Richard E. & McDaniel, Edwin R. (2007). *Communication between cultures.* (6th ed.).Belmont, CA: Wadsworth.

Schramm, W.L. (1954). *The process and effects of mass communication.* Urbana: University of Illinois Press.

Schutz, W. C. (1958). *FIRO: A three-dimensional theory of interpersonal behavior.* New York: Rinehart.

Schutz, W. C. (1966). *The interpersonal underworld.* Palo Alto, CA: Science and Behavior Books.

Schutz, W. C. (1996). *The interpersonal world: FIRO: A three-dimensional theory of interpersonal behavior* (reprint ed.) Palo Alto, CA: Science & Behavior Books.

Seligman, M. E. P. (1993). *What you can change and what you can't.* New York: Knopf.

Semali, Ladislau (2000). *Literacy in multimedia America.* New York: Falmer Press.

Sternberg, Robert J. (1998). *The triangle of love: Intimacy, passion, commitment.* New York: Basic Books.

Swann, W.B. (2005). The self and identity negotiation. *Interaction Studies*, 6, 69 -83. Phoenix, Arizona.

Seiler, William J. & Beall, Melissa L. (2011) *Communication: Making connections.* (8th ed.) Boston, MA: Allyn and Bacon.

Seiler, William J. & Beall, Melissa L. (2007) *Communication: Making connections.* (7th ed.) Boston, MA: Allyn and Bacon.

Seitel, Frank (1998) *The practice of public relations*, 8th ed. New Jersey: Prentice Hall.

Shannon, C., & Weaver, W. (1949) *The mathematical theory of communication.* Urbana: University of Illinois Press.

Sheldon Metcalfe (2000). *Building a speech* (4th ed.). Fort Worth, TX: Harcourt College.

Sherif, C., Sherif, M. & Nebergall, Roger (1965) *Attitude and attitude change: The social judgment-involvement approach.* Philadelphia, PA: W.B. Saunders.

Spicer, Christopher & Ronald Basset (1976).The effects of organization learning from an informative message. *Southern Speech Communication*, 41 Journal: 290-299.

Sieberg, Evelyn & Larson, Carl (1971). *Dimensions of interpersonal response.* Paper presented at the annual conference of International Communication Association,

Sillars, A.L & Wilmot, W.W. (1994). "Communication strategies in conflict and mediation," *In communicating strategically: Strategies in interpersonal communication* (Eds.) Wiemann, J. and Daly, J.A. Hillsdale, NJ: Erlbaum.

Sillars, A. L. (1986). *Procedures for coding interpersonal conflict.* Department of communication Studies.

Simons, Herbert W. (1986). *Persuasion: Understanding practice and analysis.* New York: Random House.

Smith L, Heaven, P.C & Ciarrochi (2008).Trait emotional intelligence, conflict communication patterns, and relationship satisfaction. *Personality and Individual Differences*, 44, 1314-1325.

Sprague Jo & Douglas Stuart (2000). *The speaker's handbook* (5th ed.). Troy, MO: Harcourt Brace.

Sprague, Rosmond, trans. George Kennedy. (1972). *Gorgias, encomiums on helen, in older sophists*, p.52. Columbia, SC: University of South Carolina Press.

Tannen, Deborah. (1990), *You just don't understand: Women and men in conversation.* New York: Harper Collins.

Taylor, D. A. & Altman, I. (1987). Communication in interpersonal relations: Social penetration theory. In M.E. Roloff & G.R. Miller (Eds.), *Interpersonal process: New directions in communication research* (pp. 257-277). Beverly Hills, CA: Sage.

Thibaut, J. W. and Kelly, H. H. (1986). *The social psychology of groups (2nd ed.).* New Brunswick, NJ: Transaction Books.

Thourlby, W. (1978). *You are what you wear.* New York: New American Library.

Turow, Joseph (2003). *Mass media today: An introduction to mass communication* (2nd ed.). Boston: Houghton-Mifflin.

Trenholm, Sarah, (2005). *Thinking through communication: An introduction to the study of communication*, 4th ed. Boston: Allyn and Bacon.

Trenholm, Sarah & Jensen, Arthur (2008*). Interpersonal communication* (6th ed.). New York: Oxford.

Triandis, H. C.(2000). "Culture and conflict." International Journal of Psychology 35,146.

Tubbs, S. L. & Moss, S. (2000). *Human communication* (8th ed.). Boston: MA: McGraw-Hill.

Tuckman, B. W. (1965). Developmental sequences in small groups. *Psychological Bulletin*. 63, 384-389.

Tubbs, S. L. & Moss, S. (2000). *Human communication* (8th ed.). Boston: MA: McGraw-Hill.

Uyo, Adidi, O. (1987). *Mass communication : Classifications and characteristics*. New York: Civiletis International.

Verderber, Rudolph F. & Verderber, Kathleen S. (2008) (12th ed.). *Communicate!* Belmont: Thompson/Wadsworth.

Verderber, Rudolph F. & Verderber, Kathleen S. (2005). *Communicate!* (11th ed.). Belmont, California: Thompson/Wadsworth.

Verderber, Kathleen S., Verderber, Rudolph F. & Sellnow, Deanna D. (2010). *Communicate!* (13th ed.). Ohio: Wadsworth- Cengage Learning.

Walker, Michael A. & Harris, George, L. (1995). *Negotiation: Six steps to success*. Upper Saddle River, NJ: Bantam Books.

Wallace C. Fotheringham (1966) *Perspectives on persuasion*. Boston, MA: Allyn & Bacon.

Watzlawick, P., Beavin, J. H., & Kackson, D. D. (1967). *Pragmatics of human communication: A study of interactional patterns, pathologies, and paradoxes*. New York: Norton.

Watzlawick, P. (1987). *The language of change: Elements of therapeutic communication*. New York: Basic Books.

Weaver, Richard M. (1963). Language is sermonic. *Dimensions of Rhetorical Scholarship (*Eds*.)*. Roger E. Nebergall. Norman, OK: University of Oklahoma Press.

Wells, W. & B. Siegel (1961). Stereotyped somatypes, *Psychology Reports* 8: 77- 78.

West, Richard & Turner, Lynn H. (2007). *Introducing communication theory: Analysis and application*. (3rd ed.) Boston: McGraw Hill.

Whorf, B. L. (1956). Science and linguistics. In J.B. Carroll (Eds.), *Language, thought and reality* (pp. 207-219). Cambridge, MA: MIT Press.

Wilmot, W. W. (1987). *Dyadic communication* (3rd ed.) New York: Random House.

Wilmot, W.W. & Hocker, J.L. (2010) *Interpersonal Conflict* (8th ed.). New York: McGraw-Hill.

Wilmot, W.W., & Hocker, J.L. (2007). *Interpersonal conflict* (7th ed.) New York: McGraw Hill.

Willis, F.N., & H.K. Hamm. 1980. The Use of interpersonal touch in securing compliance, *Journal of Nonverbal Behavior* 5: 49-55.

Wood, Julia T. (2008). *Communication mosaics-An introduction to the field of communication*, 5th ed. CA: Thompson.

Woods, Julia T. (2007). *Gendered lives: Communication, gender, and culture*. (7th ed.) Belmont, Ca: Wadsworth.

Woods, Julia T. (2007). *Interpersonal communication* (5th ed.) Belmont: CA: Thompson Wardsworth.

Woods, Julia (2011). *Communication mosaics: An introduction to the field of communication* (6th ed.).Boston: Wadsworth.

Worsnop, Chris M. "20 important reasons to study the media. http://interact.uoregon.edu/MediaLit/FA/articles/worsnop/cwindex.html Accessed February 28, 2012.

Wigley, C.J. (1998). Verbal aggressiveness. In J.C. McCroskey, J. A. Daly, M.M. Martin, & M.J. Beatty (Eds). *Personality and communication: Trait perspectives*. New York: Hampton.

Wilmot, W. W. (1987). *Dyadic communication* (3rd ed.) New York: Random House.

Wright, Charles, R. (1986). *Mass communication:-- A sociological perspective* (3rd ed.). New York: Random House.

Yum, J.O. (1998). The impact of Confucianism on interpersonal relationships and communication patterns in East Asia. *Communication Monographs*, 1998, 21, 374-388.

Zayas-Baya, Elena (1977). Instructional media in the total language picture. *International Journal of Instructional Media*, 5. pp145-150.

Zeuschner, Raymond (1997). *Interpersonal communication* (2nd ed.) Boston: Allyn and Bacon.